VIET-NAM:
POLITICS
AND
PUBLIC
ADMINISTRATION

VIET-NAM

**POLITICS
AND
PUBLIC
ADMINISTRATION**

by Nghiem Dang

EAST-WEST CENTER PRESS   HONOLULU

PREFACE

AT A TIME when headlines the world around are devoted to events in Viet-Nam, it is especially appropriate that a major contribution to understanding Vietnamese public administration and development be made. The conflict in Viet-Nam is military and ideological. It also involves competition in governmental effectiveness among different parts of this troubled country. In the long run, the capacity of the administrative machinery to reach wisely chosen development goals will be as important in determining the future course of the country as the armed men so evident at present.

Viet-Nam's struggle for independence, freedom, and leadership has involved elements of development administration that are found in many of the less developed countries. Still, these elements have been present in combinations that have proved to be especially troublesome. Viet-Nam's administrative fabric has been woven from four foreign strands—Chinese, Indian, French, and American—as well as indigenous strands. Its communication and transportation system has kept one region relatively isolated from another. Important ethnic differences mute the call to national unity. The country has lost, or failed to develop, its sense of mission. Subversion abounds. In such a situation, the planned use of public administration to promote national development is presented with serious, even insurmountable obstacles. In some ways, therefore, the selection of Viet-Nam for an intensive case study of development administration presents problems more serious than encountered elsewhere because of the complications that have beset the country over the last decade or two.

The present study is the first comprehensive work on Vietnamese public administration available in English. But its role in the literature derives essentially from its other attributes. It breaks new ground in utilizing an ecological approach and in subordinating the more historical and legal interpretations. The use of recent theoretical concepts in describing and analyzing Vietnamese public administration provides a pattern that could well be emulated in other studies. Throughout, the author's concern has been on the development of the Vietnamese nation and relating administration to the effectuation of rapid social change. All told, this volume is in a new mold, one that is most promising for the study of development administration.

The author has been a prominent public official in what is now North Viet-Nam and a scholar and educational administrator at the National Institute of Administration. For twelve years the Institute has benefited from his thoughtful leadership. He thus brings the experience of both the practitioner and the scholar to his subject.

Within the last decade he has traveled throughout Asia, Europe, and the United States, observing recent innovations in public administration and, in turn, contributing his insights. He was a member of the first development administration group of senior scholars at the East-West Center in 1962–1963. It was composed of colleagues from the United States, Thailand, the Philippines, and Viet-Nam. The bulk of the manuscript for the present volume was completed while he was in residence at the Center. The present study is a fitting tribute to the group's creativity.

Edward W. Weidner
Vice Chancellor
East-West Center
University of Hawaii
July 9, 1965

ACKNOWLEDGMENTS

I WISH to present here my most sincere gratitude for my moral obligation to all the authors to whom I have made reference. I extend particular thanks to Dr. Edward Weidner, Vice Chancellor, Institute of Advanced Projects, East-West Center, who not only inspired me to undertake this study by offering the intellectual and material facilities of the Institute, but has also sacrificed his time to read my manuscript carefully and to offer constructive criticism on the presentation of the ideas. I am also indebted to Dr. Henry Bush, visiting professor at the National Institute of Administration, who carefully read the manuscript and made many suggestions as to both matter and form. I wish to thank also my colleagues of the Development Administration Group of the Institute of Advanced Projects for the academic year 1962–1963, Dr. Fred W. Riggs of Indiana University, Dr. Raul P. de Guzman of the University of the Philippines, and Dr. Amara Raksasataya of Thammasat University, whose apposite observations in the course of many seminars held at the Institute enabled me to approach certain fundamental problems in the light of comparative method. I am also under obligation to the members of the Michigan State University Viet-Nam Advisory Group, who, in Saigon between May 20, 1955, and June 30, 1962, fanned the flame of research in discussions, often informal, on public administration in Viet-Nam; particularly to Dr. John Dorsey, Jr., now at Vanderbilt University, who has continued to maintain a scientific correspondence with me regarding our respective research. I must offer my deep thanks to Mr. George I. Burkett, instructor of French at the University of Hawaii, who, in the course of the writing, has given me his devoted assistance in expressing my ideas in English. He translated into English my first manuscripts, which were roughly prepared in French; we then worked together over the English manuscripts, he often introducing the pertinent remarks of an acute observer who is not a specialist and who judges objectively the ideas presented, while I contributed to the best of my ability by extracting new ideas from our discussion or by simply providing the proper technical vocabulary.

The physical work of assembling the materials, the typing, and the final presentation were performed by the many services of the Institute of Advanced Projects, especially Research Translations, whom

I beg to accept my gratitude. Lastly, it would be unjust not to mention my wife, who made the sacrifice of being separated from her children in Saigon in order to bring me the comfort of her presence and to relieve me completely of all material concern for the entire period of the composition of the present work.

Nghiem Dang

Honolulu
August 1, 1964

CONTENTS

MAPS AND CHARTS

Maps

Charts

INTRODUCTION

TO THE PRESENT TIME no systematic and scientific study has ever been made of public administration in Viet-Nam with regard to the behavior of the administrators and of the people. Works written in French emphasize sometimes the legal aspect, sometimes the historical or cultural aspect of public administration. Studies in English are the results either of the short visits of United Nations experts and professors from American universities or are monographs on certain specialized aspects of Vietnamese administrative life. Works in Vietnamese follow more or less the same tradition as those in French, although they may have been inspired by Chinese sources that reflect the wisdom of the ancients concerning the human being in society.

In order to explain fully public administration in Viet-Nam, it is necessary to point out first the fundamental features of the philosophy behind this administration. Most misunderstandings, both on the part of the visitors studying it and on the part of the administrators being interviewed, are derived, it seems to me, from different interpretations of the idea of public administration. The idea of public administration, as conceived by the Vietnamese, is much broader than the usual conception. In Viet-Nam, administration includes both the immediate and the eventual goals of the public authorities, and also the means of achieving them. Traditionally, the government has not been formally a democracy governed by representatives elected by the people, for the very good reason that under the monarchy the emperor held all the power and under the colonial regime the administrators were similarly all-powerful. Thus a long tradition was created which gave the administrators the heavy responsibility of deciding on details of administrative action within the very broad outlines of policy established by the emperor or by the governor-general who received his powers from the French Republic. This essential point is often missed by authorities writing on Vietnamese government.

The fact that the government has been given considerable freedom of action stems from the fundamental idea that there exists a natural order of things, called *tao,* which makes men live at peace with each other, and that there is no point in disturbing this natural order with unseasonable interventions. Hence, the administrator of the period of the emperors acted on the whole under the pressure of events, guided by experience acquired in the course of a long administrative career or in a careful study of the writings of the

ancients. It is understandable that there was no long-range administrative planning, with the exception of measures taken at decisive
moments in history (e.g., the marches to the South and colonization)
or against great national catastrophes (e.g., a break in the dikes or
widespread famine).

In other terms, the imperial government remained essentially
pragmatic. In this tradition, too, the colonial administration introduced only such reforms as were absolutely necessary to the
establishment of a colonial policy: such engineering works as roads,
bridges, canals, and ports; the levying of taxes, the creation of a
budget, and so on. Even in these reforms this administration made
every effort to incorporate in its system the traditional pattern of
distribution in the program of the assessment of taxes and the
allocation of lands, insofar as this program could contribute to the
general colonial policy.

Differences in the Western and Vietnamese conceptions of
public administration exist not only in regard to the methods of
developing a general policy, but also in regard to the means used to
carry out that policy. French public administration traditionally uses
important material means: *privilège d'action d'office* (i.e., the
administration may take steps of its own in the event the individual
does not obey the injunctions of the government); public expenditure for public works; requisition and expropriation, and so on.
Likewise, public administration is conceived as a series of services
prescribed by law and rendered to the people. On the other hand,
Vietnamese tradition places much less emphasis on the specific
lawful means used by the administrators; it depends much more on
the power of persuasion, on setting an example, and particularly on
the integrity of the administrators. Of course, with the advent of the
colonial regime this tradition was not entirely observed; although
they had wished to maintain the imperial philosophy of public
administration for economic reasons, the French created more and
more services: postal and telegraph systems, a food distribution
office, etc. Subsequently, under the pressure of circumstances, the
national government not only continued to operate these services but
was obliged to create new ones: a refugee bureau, a ministry of
foreign affairs, a commissariat of civic action, an information
service, and so on. What influence has the introduction of these new
services had on the traditional Vietnamese concept of administration? In the urban centers? In the rural areas?

It is not necessary to be a prophet to know that the Republic of
Viet-Nam will have to create still more agencies in order to satisfy its
needs. Communication with the rest of the world makes this new
country painfully aware of the present limitations of its resources. If
these new aspirations cannot be realized immediately, will this lack
further modify the people's idea of public administration?

The answer to these questions will shed new light on the study of a great many administrative problems existing today in Viet-Nam.

The administrative organization, for example, must be able to absorb any change in the philosophy of public administration. Obviously, the monarchy was essentially a centralized administration, but this centralization did not result in too complicated an organization of the administrative machinery since the need for administrative measures in such an agrarian society were not too great. In the colonial period, the centralization necessary to the unity of the colonial policy brought about the creation of agencies only at the central level, and did not require the addition of services of execution. How can the traditional aspiration to centralization that inspired both the emperors and the colonial government be reconciled with the idea of reducing the administrative machine to its simplest possible form and at the same time extending more services to the people?

Vietnamese tradition offers a very ingenious means: to make the commune the basis of public administration, both in the application of the set general policy and in the management of affairs that are essentially local. All decisions of whatever importance were made at the commune level by the headman, who was highly respected by the people, and the carrying out of these decisions was assured of their own free will by the villagers: this was the principle of communal autonomy. The colonial government found this system very convenient, all the more so since it corresponded vaguely to Napoleon's territorial administration. However, a vast difference lay in the fact that, in France, provincially located offices of the central government existed alongside the communal administration, which was autonomous, whereas the Vietnamese commune was the only administrative division responsible for both the central administration at village level and the communal administration proper. This major concept, *the commune as the sole agent of the execution of administrative decisions* made either by the central government or by the local authorities, has not been sufficiently brought out in the past.

In any case, it should be pointed out that, even before World War II, the specialized public services had become more and more complex and were beginning to involve first the provincial level and then the district level (e.g., land registry, public health, education, agriculture, forestry, etc.). District administrators had to come more often into the villages, either to consult with the communal authorities or to inspect the work of those authorities, which was getting more and more complicated. The breakdown of the idea of regarding the commune as the only agent of execution was beginning.

Since Viet-Nam became independent, with the rapid development of transportation and communication, the administrators representing central power have been drawn more and more into communal affairs (public security, civic action, assimilation of refugees, agrarian reform, rural development, etc.). To what extent can government expenditures be kept to a minimum, with the increasing profusion of public services? To what extent, in the village itself, will services operated by the agents of the central government be accepted willingly by the rural population?

The changes in the philosophy of administration are reflected in personnel management. The basic idea of the old regime with regard to personnel was that the civil servants who represented the imperial government must be recruited among an elite which combined the principles of culture and virtue. This criterion of culture and virtue eliminated the possibility of government by a privileged class of nobles whose titles would be handed down solely on the basis of birth. The French, upon their arrival in Indo-China, were impressed by this essentially democratic system of recruiting government personnel, based exclusively on severe examinations given at three-year intervals. Naturally, the colonial government quickly adopted this tradition, which had been established in France only after several successive revolutions, beginning with that of 1789.

Although the system of examinations was retained, the spirit of the examination was changed, because of the new prerogatives ascribed to the civil servants of the colonial government. In carrying out his duties, the "native" administrator was instructed to behave exactly as his predecessors had behaved under the imperial regime. However, a tendency towards specialization developed, and the system of administration by men was gradually replaced by one of administration by regulation and laws. A certain friction resulted: while the people, particularly those of rural regions (which constitute most of the population), were not yet adjusted to the principles of administration by laws, and continued to respect the administrator as a patriarchal father who could be approached for help and advice, the administrator himself could no longer regard himself as more than a passive cogwheel in the governmental machine, which was becoming more and more complicated with the constant addition of specialized services.

Furthermore, the administrator, particularly the province chief and the district chief, saw himself more and more frequently confronted with technicians who felt they had the right to question certain of his decisions. Thus the attitude of the administrator changed little by little. Instead of acting as the proxy of the Son of Heaven (the emperor), and fulfilling his duties with a certain sacerdotal spirit, he came to regard himself as a simple executive agent of the will of the colonial government which was expressed only through colonial laws and rules.

Since the civil servants were recruited more and more among persons who had had a Western education, and were therefore more often from the cities, the idea of values changed gradually. The concept of the apostle-like mandarin was supplanted by the idea of a salaried worker. The civil servant was acutely aware of the value of his remuneration in comparison to that of the munificent compensation of the colonial administrators, as well as to that of the substantial profits of men in private companies. This was the beginning of the problem of corruption, which is completely different from the question of the supporting of the administrators of the imperial government by contributions from the people, in the form of work, money, or supplies.

This breach between the new attitude of the civil servant who withdraws more and more behind the passivity of legal texts and rules and the traditional behavior of the people who persist in seeing in him the proxy of the Son of Heaven explains, on one hand, the relative effectiveness of the colonial administrative machine in that it tended to exploit the country to the profit of the colonial power and, on the other hand, the complete failure of that same machine in promoting the well-being of the population.

The Vietnamese government has inherited a serious problem in this domain. It is obliged, in the first place, to fill the positions left vacant by the French administrators in many central agencies and in the provinces by promoting civil servants who served before in the capacity of assistants. These people must be trained quickly to accept their new roles as leaders in the administration and in the public services. Moreover, new civil servants must be recruited, and their training must allow for the social dualism that is the result of the opposition of a more or less Westernized urban culture and a rural culture which has remained more or less traditionalist, in spite of efforts of the Communists to undermine it.

This massive introduction of new civil servants has of course caused certain conflicts within the administration itself: between the workers of long service proud of their experience and the young probationers imbued with new ideas, as well as between executives too preoccupied with the problems of security and technicians who have such occupational prejudices that they can often see only one side of a complicated administrative problem. These conflicts are a source of great concern to the government, which is trying to reconcile the training of specialists demanded by the division of labor due to the complexity of modern problems with the training of generalists capable of understanding quickly the fundamental problems of the moment, and of finding adequate solutions rapidly.

Another serious problem which faces the government today is that of financial administration. France left behind a fairly good tradition of budgetary administration. Careful financial accounts have long been required from the administrative authorities in order to provide the French government with an effective means of keeping a check on the activities of the colonial authorities thousands of miles away from France. The decree of December 12, 1912, which codified the financial regulations, provided for the intervention in the preparation of the budget of organizations elected by limited suffrage, but this intervention was of a purely consultative nature. As a matter of fact, the power of making the budget rested with the head of each territory (the governor-general for all Indo-China, the governor or resident superior for the region, the province chief for the province), with a certain amount of supervision from the upper echelons in each case.

The execution of the budget was entirely up to the same authorities. A self-auditing system was brought in from France, introducing the practice of separating the administrators who authorized expenditures (*ordonnateurs*) from the disbursing officers (*comptables*), and requiring the approval of a special examiner (called the comptroller of obligated expenditures) for the budget of the Indo-Chinese Union and for those of certain member countries. The procedure for drawing up contracts for public works was also fixed in scrupulous detail. It is natural that these procedures, first of all, ran counter to the habits of the people, who were accustomed to the lack of precision of an economic system based vaguely on a market economy. These complicated procedures profited only the European contractors who were used to this system; the Vietnamese contractors, not being well organized, could not compete with them, and were reduced to the role of subcontractors. This explains why, after independence, the Vietnamese government was obliged to admit foreign contractors in awarding contracts for important public works or for the large-scale purchase of equipment. How could the extreme nationalism of the first hours of independence be reconciled, in the minds of the people and in business circles, with this concession in favor of foreign firms?

The conflict between the underdeveloped rural economy and the demands of modern technology also explains the fact that, in an effort to provide the people with the essential public services consistent with the recent developments of technology, the government was obliged to create several public enterprises. How did the people interpret this intervention of the government in new areas of activity?

Special mention should be made of the tax system. As has been stressed already, the emperors had found the village council very convenient as an agent of execution of the orders of the central authority. The fiscal administration was equally the responsibility of the commune: the various taxes were divided among the communes; the imperial government recognized only the commune as the collective taxpayer; in other words, the collective responsibility of the commune was called into play, and when the total amount of the taxes collected in the commune fell short of the commune's obligations, it was necessary to collect from the solvent members of the commune the amount lacking because of the insolvent members. This was especially true for the head tax and the real estate tax, which were two major sources of revenue for the emperors. It was equally true of the salt tax and of other excise taxes.

With the arrival of the French, the fiscal system became complicated. The imperial system of taxation was kept, with certain changes, but the principles of the former fiscal administration based on communal responsibility were retained in full. New taxes were soon added: customs duties, registration taxes, and subsequently income taxes and other indirect taxes (in particular on the opium, salt, alcohol, and tobacco monopolies). With these new taxes came new principles of fiscal administration which involved the direct use of tax agents. However, the communal responsibility was retained in order to obtain a more effective collaboration on the part of the communal authorities in keeping down fraud in the matter of indirect taxes.

The problems of financial administration became even more complex after independence because of two facts: (a) Viet-Nam received substantial aid from the United States and to a lesser extent from other countries (France, the Nations of the Colombo Plan, and the United Nations). Accounting problems were greatly increased because of the many different accounting systems called into play that the commission responsible for administering this aid must know thoroughly. (b) Insecurity in the villages made the collection of taxes so difficult that indirect taxes necessarily have been substituted more and more for direct taxes, since the revenue from the latter decreases regularly in proportion as the general situation gets more critical.

How does the man in the street regard all these complications in the fiscal administration? Does the government get willing cooperation from the taxpayers? To what extent can the system of communal responsibility be counted on in the new fiscal administration?

The problems of the recruiting and training of administrative workers, as well as those of finance administration, are examples of problems which occur in the decision-making process. Under the imperial government, in which the philosophy of administration tended towards extreme simplicity, the decision-making process was not complicated. Most decisions were made at the commune level and the representatives of the government knew well the circumstances of every villager. The procedure was the same whether it concerned imperial orders transmitted by the provincial and district authorities or less important decisions made by the latter: all these decisions were carried out by the village, and their execution followed the same pattern as for purely local matters. The cases in which decisions had to be made by provincial authorities were rare. They concerned particularly the appointment by provincial authorities of the canton chiefs and village chiefs, the execution of imperial decrees concerning military recruiting, taxes, and the maintenance of order and public security.

Although the colonial government maintained approximately the same general administrative structure for so-called "native" affairs, it was not so with the numerous specialized services that it was obliged to create under the pressure of local circumstances or in carrying out a program for colonial expansion. In these cases, an entire new procedure had to be imported from France—a procedure with a centuries-old tradition of increasingly precise laws that subjected administrative decisions to increasingly complicated formalities. The financial regulation passed December 30, 1912, is a typical example of procedure imported into the colonies by the colonial administrators. Little by little, two distinct spheres of administrative action were created: a native sphere in which a good deal of simplicity in the form of the decisions predominated in spite of a certain formalism introduced from time to time by the colonial government, and a Western sphere in which the most complicated procedures were imported, more or less altered, from France. Thus, a real administrative dualism was created which has had important consequences in the current administrative organization.

When Viet-Nam gained its independence in 1954, it goes without saying that the central government had a tendency to adopt various laws and regulations of the colonial government so long as they were not contradictory to the new status of independence. Indeed, in a reaction against the tendencies of the colonial government, which were considered autocratic and arbitrary, the Vietnamese administrators themselves leaned over too far in the direction of formalism and added a new element to the procedure in order to conform to a certain democratic ideal: the practice of consulting organizations or interested persons in a given administrative decision. From this developed a multitude of administrative commissions (e.g., interdepartmental meetings and meetings of several agencies or of several provinces) that provided the new civil servants with the opportunity to exchange information, but also slowed down the handling of current administrative affairs.

Formalism and the use of commissions seem to be the two main characteristics of the decision-making process. These characteristics should be studied in the light of two considerations: (a) How do the officials of the various administrative organizations interpret this formalism and the frequent use of commissions? (b) Is it to the advantage of the people that these administrative decisions be made with so much precaution? In other words, what are the reactions of the urban and rural population to the slowing down of administrative decisions as a result of these procedures?

All of these problems lead to a fundamental question of public administration: how can the performance of the administration be kept subject to check? In countries of long-standing democracy, there is always the very strict control by public opinion over the various activities of the administration, either indirectly (press, pressure groups) or directly (elected chambers). Punishment for irregular conduct is usually administered by the courts. In imperial Viet-Nam, only at the village level was there a council of elders watching over the activities of the agents who were appointed to administer the village and whose responsibility was the direct concern of this council. Only very serious breaches of duty on the part of the village agents were dealt with by the mandarin district chiefs or province chiefs. At the upper administrative levels, aside from the normal supervision of one rank over the next lower, there was no organized control on the part of the people. It is true that there was an unofficial but rather effective device: members of the literate class (*gioi si phu*) administered the punishment of boycotting those of their colleagues who failed to observe the class code of honor. From time to time, too, imperial censors went around the country to hear complaints of the people with regard to malpractice on the part of the administrators; although legally this constituted a form of checking through official channels, in point of fact it constituted an unofficial control by public opinion. As a last resort, there was the possibility of presenting a petition to the emperor, but the mechanics of this device were so cumbersome that the people scarcely preferred it to open rebellion with all the risks implied by this dangerous solution.

Under the French, this device of informal checks was replaced by a much more systematic and formal device. An a priori check was established by the introduction of the system of prior approval by the comptroller of obligated expenditures and final approval by the superior at the higher echelon. A certain number of decisions of the authorities at the lower levels had to be submitted for approval to the immediate superiors before they could be put into effect: drawing up contracts for public works or for purchasing certain quantities of equipment, the appointment of certain categories of civil servants, and so on. Other items of a financial nature, such as purchase orders and payment orders, had to receive the formal stamp of approval of the comptroller of obligated expenditures before they could be acted upon.

This pre-audit system was reinforced by a post-audit system. Inspectors of political and administrative affairs went through the provinces, inspected various offices and bureaus, disclosed errors and cases of malpractice, and reported them to the governors of the regions. Organizations at the regional and central levels also exercised a certain supervision by means of the reports of province chiefs and district chiefs. Mention should be made also of the check on disbursing officers made by the Cour des Comptes (Audit Office) in France.

A semblance of control was even established in behalf of the people. Alongside each administrative organization, at each level, elected councils were set up whose duties included giving advice on the management accounts of the administrators: the Superior Council of Economic and Financial Interests at the Governor-General's level; the Colonial Council or Assembly of People's Representatives at the level of the region chiefs. Considering the very broad powers of the colonial administrators, however, it must be understood that this control was much more for form than for effect.

With the arrival of independence, the government of Viet-Nam retained the previous system insofar as it was compatible with the status of an independent nation. The pre-audit system of checks was continued almost wholly, with the exception of fixing the minimum expenditure requiring formal approval to conform with the present cost of living. The same is true of the post-audit checks. But to what extent does this system of checks remain effective? How, in point of fact, are infractions of the regulations adequately punished? What social changes explain the fact that the regulations for control have become virtually out of date? These questions must be investigated with the methods of the social sciences in order that the political authority responsible for the final decisions in these matters be better informed.

The present work has required an extensive documentation, compiled over a period of many years, both in Viet-Nam and in the foreign countries I have been fortunate enough to visit. Aside from general works on public administration, particularly on comparative administration and on development administration, this documentation is derived from three different sources:

(1) The official documents published by the government, of which the National Institute of Administration receives copies regularly. These documents include laws, minutes of the National Assembly, decrees, orders, and even correspondence between executive departments, largely nonconfidential.

(2) Sociological, judicial, economic, and administrative studies undertaken during the period of French domination. These studies were made by French administrators during the early days of the conquest as a basis for administrative action, or by authors who had a special interest in Viet-Nam (e.g., philosophers, historians, and geographers). A certain number of Vietnamese have also made a contribution in French, e.g., scholars of the Ecole française d'Extrême-Orient (French Far-Eastern School), and of the Institut

indochinois pour l'étude de l'Homme (Indo-Chinese Institute for the Study of Mankind), and some works have been written directly in Vietnamese.

(3) Studies on these same aspects of administrative life, written since the country became independent. These are studies made either in French (on history, geography, or international relations between France and Viet-Nam); in English (by experts of the United Nations, for technical assistance in public administration; by experts from organizations deriving from AID, for American aid to Viet-Nam; and—a particularly important contribution— by research scholars of Michigan State University in Viet-Nam); or in Vietnamese (articles in *Nghien Cuu Hanh Chanh*, the journal of the Vietnamese Society for Administrative Research; in *Que Huong*, a review published by a group of intellectuals; and in *Hanh Chanh Khao Luan*, a publication of the Department of the Interior).

I have also had the inestimable advantage of being able to gather freely expressed information from many new sources since the overthrow of the Ngo Dinh Diem government by the military Revolution of November 1, 1963. The work has been brought up to date regarding the measures taken by the Revolutionary Government, insofar as these measures shed light on the problem of public administration in Viet-Nam. I have made no effort to analyze the Revolution in general or the consequences it may have, except for matters directly concerning public administration. The November 1 Revolution has offered an excellent opportunity to test the endurance of the fundamental principles of this administration, of which the political upheaval will alter only the superficial details.

In spite of this abundant documentation, the reader who expects to consult the present work as a complete manual of public administration in Viet-Nam will be disappointed. I have had neither the time nor the space to cover in detail all aspects of the many administrative problems of a country which has recently become independent, and which must make rapid strides on all fronts— political, economic, cultural, and social. At the risk of being accused of superficiality, instead of undertaking a critical analysis of each institution, both from the point of view of administrative technique and from that of administrative development, I have limited the scope of the work to a precise presentation of the problems to be solved. References will be made to more comprehensive works on public administration by qualified authors, and their arguments for or against each institution. Naturally, these arguments are often developed in the special context of a given civilization, usually a highly industrialized civilization, in which scholars have the means and the training necessary to push analysis of a problem to the limit. I will attempt to adapt these arguments to the contingency required by the study of these same problems or of similar but not identical problems in underdeveloped countries by references to other types of writings on these subjects, classed as cultural change, social change, and development. I will also strive to clarify points of view by placing them more particularly in the context of the Vietnamese civilization, which has been influenced both by the Chinese and by the French. Here also the work will be original only to the extent that specialized sources may not treat the subject fully enough, or that I disagree fundamentally with the authors quoted.

In consequence, the present work may appear insufficiently thorough in certain areas. The reader is asked to complement these areas by reading the sources cited. I offer as an excuse only the fact of having come into a world too old, in which everything has been said, where it is difficult to find unexplored territory in which to clear a path. The only contribution I hope to make is simply to present Vietnamese public administration in its true light and to set down certain matters for future researchers.

PART I

SOCIAL SETTING
AND ADMINISTRATIVE
DUALISM

"PUBLIC ADMINISTRATION" is translated into Vietnamese as hanh chanh, *which means, literally, "policy execution." This definition seems at first glance to agree with the opinion which restricts administration to putting into motion the means for realizing certain goals of the community, the setting of which goals falls within the domain of politics.*

In the Vietnamese society, however, this dichotomy between politics and administration is less marked than the Western student might expect; a detailed analysis of the ways of approaching the problems of administration in Viet-Nam and in the West shows appreciable difference in defining the scope of public administration. In this study it will be necessary to borrow from the West the methods of studying the approaches to these problems, since the science of public administration as such was unknown to the Vietnamese until quite recently.

It is superfluous to recall here in detail the principal tendencies in the Western study of public administration: the legalistic tendency of certain European schools,[1] the political orientation of American writers previous to World War II (e.g., Woodrow Wilson), the combination of political and managerial orientation (L. D. White), the emphasis on human relations (M. Marx), and socio-psychological analysis (Simon, Smithburg, and Thompson).[2] In more recent years, students of comparative administration have emphasized the importance of examining administration, not in general, but in each specific social environment; in other words, they investigate administration from an ecological point of view.[3] But, even with these later refinements, problems of administration are always considered primarily as having to do with the search for the means of achieving objec-

tives already determined in other spheres. On the other hand, the problems of substantive administration are not objects of concern for theoreticians of public administration who are primarily interested in discoursing on strategy or expedience from an ethical point of view, or on administrative processes from a purely analytical point of view.

SUBSTANTIVE ADMINISTRATION
VERSUS PROCEDURAL ADMINISTRATION

Nevertheless, the ecology of public administration is already opening new horizons. The comparison of different administrative systems points up the dissimilarities existing even among the fundamental institutions. Thus, in a so-called totalitarian regime, several governmental functions are seen as concentrated in the hands of a single agency, the dictator, while in so-called democratic regimes, the policy-making function and the policy-implementing function are entrusted to different agencies. Certain authors therefore have thought they have found the key to the problem by using a structural-functional approach, which prepares the terrain for some theories of development.[4] The principal object of this approach lies, nevertheless, in the analysis of the means of implementing the policies, and yet the dissimilarities still remain to be explained. In effect, to consider those functions universally recognized as administrative, it is difficult to explain why the personnel administration system of Viet-Nam differs from that of the United States of America, or why the public finances of Viet-Nam resemble only very vaguely the public finances of England, even if these administrative systems are placed in the more general framework of the culture of each country. But these differences can be made clear quite easily if the institutions are related to the ultimate goals which they serve. Personnel administration is more easily understood when the kind of government programs to which this personnel is assigned is known; similarly, fiscal administration will necessarily be understood in the general context of the program of economic development. In other words, the explanation of these dissimilarities can be found, not only in the study of procedural administration, but also and particularly in the analysis of substantive administration.[5] Thus, when a country considers that the role of the government should be reduced to a strict minimum, it is quite natural to consider administration as the means of putting into effect a policy whose definition is the responsibility of the people who know their rights and intend to maintain them integrally as far as possible. A normal consequence of this conception is that the laws not only present the principle of a determined expressed policy, for example, the struggle against tendencies toward an exaggerated concentration of finances in the hands of the trusts, but also regulate in detail the measures designed to put these principles into effect, i.e., measures which in other countries would be considered administrative.

Elsewhere, on the other hand, policy may not be defined in detail as laws passed by a legislative assembly; it may consist of a series of moral norms, which are generally accepted but whose exact expression can be given, according to custom, only by an elite. In this case, the administration can no longer be conceived as a simple purveyor of means; it becomes identical with the administrator, and the administrator himself, by the simple fact of his existence, acting through the practice of virtue, gives the example of good conduct, and, as a natural consequence, good administration ensues.

PHILOSOPHY OF PUBLIC ADMINISTRATION

In order to see clearly the public administration problems of a country, the student must become imbued with the philosophy of that administration and with the commonly accepted idea of the role of public administration in that country. Of course, it is not possible for any one student to go into all the details of substantive administration, such as the matter of public security, public health, education, and of labor. However, in each field, a law generally can be found which formulates the policy, and which also regulates certain details; thus there are presidential decrees, departmental orders, decisions, instructions, and circulars prescribing more and more detailed measures. There are also daily practices, composed of the actions and reactions of the administration as well as those of the public itself, which give the execution of governmental decisions a special character. From the entirety of these measures of substantive administration emerges a philosophy of public administration peculiar to each country.[6] If this philosophy is considered also from the point of view of putting into effect a policy concerning a given matter of substantive administration, the integration of substantive administration and procedural administration has been achieved.

It is from the point of view of this integration of substantive administration and procedural administration that the present study of public administration in Viet-Nam will be undertaken. In order to place public administration in Viet-Nam in its social context, a historical survey, outlining the characteristic traits of its philosophy, seems necessary. The general outline of a certain process of administrative development can also be observed from such a summary.

CHAPTER I

THE FORMATION OF AN ADMINISTRATIVE TRADITION

> Society does not naturally have as a pendulum either resting in a stable position of economic relations, or after having had this position disturbed, in some circumventive way moving towards its restoration.[1]

AT THE THRESHOLD of history, Viet-Nam fell completely under Chinese domination. This was the period in which Tan Thi Hoang De (Ts'in Che Houang Ti) joined under his command the multitudes of small Chinese states known as Chien Quoc, or Warring States (221 B.C.). The army of Ts'in was able, however, to overcome only the southern provinces of what is now China, located on the border of the country of Thuc which later was to become Viet-Nam. Still later, under the emperors of the Han Dynasty, China annexed Viet-Nam and made it the province of Giao Chi.

The Chinese domination was to last ten centuries, until A.D. 939. At that time, taking advantage of the dissensions which weakened the authority of the last of the Chinese Duong (T'ang) emperors, the Vietnamese people gained their independence, and retained it for more than nine centuries. This period of independence was marked particularly by the strengthening of the authority of the kings of Viet-Nam, and by a slow but sure advance which extended the southern frontier from the Hoanh Son Mountains (approximately the 18th parallel) as far as Ca Mau Point (8th parallel).

Toward the end of this advance to the South, the Vietnamese met the French, who were looking for a route to China. In the one-sided struggle against the French which followed, the emperors of Dainam, as the territory of Viet-Nam was then called, lost successively the provinces of the South (1862–1874) and those of the North (1874–1884), and finally were obliged to accept the French protectorate of the rest of their territory. The French created the General Government of Indo-China to govern Viet-Nam, as well as two other states (Laos and Cambodia) over which France extended its authority.

It was not until the end of World War II that an independent Vietnamese state was able to take its place in the fraternity of nations, and to settle independently its own administrative problems, although these problems were not clearly defined until after the Geneva Agreements (July 20, 1954).

The present-day problems of public administration are affected by three fundamental facts, which correspond approximately to the historical divisions indicated above: (1) the great influence of Chinese culture—the result of ten centuries of occupation—and the formation of the traditional administrative philosophy; (2) the advance towards the South, the resulting contacts with countries which had undergone a strong Indian influence, and the affirmation of the traditional administrative philosophy; and (3) the French conquest and the dualism of the colonial administration, of which certain elements remain in the present-day administrative system.

The Chinese Domination

The long period of Chinese domination, from the first century B.C. to the ninth century A.D., was to exert a profound influence on the culture and the minds of the Vietnamese people, an influence which was all the stronger because of an intermixing of the races that amounted to an almost complete metamorphosis of the basic Vietnamese. This domination corresponded to the Chinese Han Dynasty (206 B.C.–A.D. 221); the Three Kingdoms (A.D. 221–265); the Ts'in Dynasty, whose rule was to continue only in Southern China (266–420); the Six Dynasties Period (420–589); the Souei Dynasty (589–617); and the T'ang Dynasty (618–907). In the course of this period, the Vietnamese, while almost completely assimilating Chinese culture, nevertheless succeeded in developing a common feeling strong enough to provide a firm united effort when the moment came to revolt against their weakened masters. It was during this period of Chinese domination that the most important features of Chinese public administration were introduced gradually into Viet-Nam, to be finally adopted by the Vietnamese as their own.

CENTRALIZATION VERSUS FEUDALISM

Before the arrival of the Chinese, the population of Au Lac (North Viet-Nam) formed a feudal society, of which the Muong and Thai peoples in North Viet-Nam still retain certain traditions today. These little communities had been governed by hereditary chiefs (*lac hau*) who had religious, civil, and military powers together. The hereditary chiefs paid tribute to King Hung Vuong and, later, to King An Duong Vuong. The economy was essentially agrarian, but the methods used were primitive: fields were tilled with a hoe and not with a plough. Archaeological studies seem to indicate that this culture was fundamentally Indonesian, with later influence of the Thai (a people originally from Central Asia, who spread over that part of southeastern Asia which includes today Laos, Thailand, and perhaps Burma and Cambodia).[2]

It is into this Thai-Indonesian background that the Hans

introduced the first elements of Chinese civilization. This Siniciza-
tion was brought about first by means of an independent conqueror,
the Chinese General Trieu Da (Tchao T'o), who proclaimed himself
king of Viet-Nam (208 B.C.), and whose capital was Phien Ngu (P'an
You, now Canton). Curiously enough, Trieu Da seems to have been
inclined to adopt the customs of the country, and seems not to have
forced the population to copy the Chinese way of life. He apparently
conserved the local administrative organization, with the addition of
two Chinese delegates, one in Giao Chi (Kiao Tche) and the other at
Cuu Chan (Kieou Tchen); these delegates were particularly responsible for setting the quota and collecting taxes in kind.[3] Here we
observe already a certain administrative dualism, since a single
territory was governed simultaneously by the feudal regime of the *lac
hau* lords, and by the royal regime of Trieu Da which was more or
less inspired by the methods of centralization of the Emperor Ts'in
Che Houang Ti. The loose ties which Trieu Da hoped to maintain
with China proper, however, brought about a reaction on the part of
the Hans when they succeeded in establishing their power in the
mother country. After the conquest of Viet-Nam, the Hans at once
undertook to give it an administrative organization modeled on the
Chinese system; this system was to remain with only a few
alterations throughout the entire period of Chinese domination.

The territory which is now North Viet-Nam became part of the
Chinese province of Giao Chi (Kiao Tche). This province included
nine commanderies occupying the present Chinese provinces of
Kouang Tong (commanderies of Nam Hai, or Nan Hai; and of Hop
Pho, or Ho P'ou), Kouang Si (commanderies of Thuong Ngo, or
Ts'ang Wou; and of Uat Lam, or Yu Lin), and Hai Nan (commander-
ies of Chau Nhai, or Tchou Yai; and of Dam Nhi, or Tan Eul) and
also North Viet-Nam and Central Viet-Nam as far south as the Col
des Nuages, i.e., the 18th parallel (commanderies of Giao Chi, or
Kiao Tche; of Cuu Chan, or Kieou Tchen; and of Nhat Nam, or Je
Nan).[4]

The power passed into the hands of the delegate of the Chinese
Emperor, the *thu su*, governor of Giao Chi Bo (which in 203 became
Giao Chau—a *bo* was a colonial province and a *chau* was a province
of the mother country itself), who was assisted by a small staff and
by nine commandery chiefs (*thai thu*). Naturally, this administration was centralized in the upper echelons, in a reaction against
the loose ties with China proper which had existed during the brief
period of the semi-independent dynasty of Trieu Da. However, the
massive introduction of Chinese customs and ideas was accomplished by peaceful means. Although the *thu su* and the *thai thu* had
been chosen from among the Chinese mandarins, the former feudal-
ism subsisted at the beginning: among the *lac tuong*, or feudal
chiefs, only one revolted and was killed; the others submitted and

collaborated with the Chinese governors. Later, when Vuong Mang (Wang Mang) usurped the Chinese throne (A.D. 9–23), a large current of Chinese refugees came to Viet-Nam and brought a new wave of Chinese culture, techniques, the written language, and especially the rites (*li*). It should be emphasized that "Confucian concepts of the forms appropriate to social actions played an important role in the process of Sinification." [5] A certain number of the governors devoted themselves completely to their task of indoctrinating the Vietnamese people: among these were Tich Quang (Si Kouang), commander of Giao Chi from A.D. 1 to 25, who caused Chinese characters and rites to be taught, and Nham Dien (Jen Yen), commander of Cuu Chan (A.D. 29–33), who introduced the plough and the use of marriage ceremonies.

This successful diffusion of Chinese culture deluded the Chinese governors into thinking they could become more authoritarian, particularly since the new requirements of the administration had brought into existence a new class of native employees who were as devoted to the Chinese cause as they. One of the Chinese governors, To Dinh (Sou Ting), demonstrated such brutality and such disregard for the native population that a general revolt nearly put an end to this first wave of assimilation. This was the revolt of the Trung sisters (A.D. 39–43), and was the last feudal opposition to the tendency towards centralization. The Emperor Quang Vu (Kouang Wou) of the Han Dynasty sent a great general, Ma Vien (Ma Yuan), who quickly and easily became master of the situation. Although short-lived, the revolt had a lasting effect: after the military victory the emperors of the Han Dynasty undertook seriously the task of assimilation.[6] Since the former aristocracy had perished in the course of the revolt, Ma Vien created a new class of local mandarins whose devotion to the Chinese authorities was complete. Some good administrators succeeded in disseminating even more widely the elements of Chinese culture. Special attention should be drawn to Si Nhiep (She Sie, 187–226) who stimulated education and the improvement of technological methods.

SINICIZATION OF THE BUREAUCRACY
AND DEVELOPMENT OF NATIONAL FEELING

It must be said, however, that well before Si Nhiep, the assimilation of Chinese culture had already become so profound, at least among the upper classes, that a certain number of natives of Giao Chau had been admitted as mandarin administrators in other Chinese provinces. One of them, Ly Tien, had even been named governor of Giao Chi in 187. This first concession to national feeling after the assimilation of Chinese culture constituted the strength of the Vietnamese people by giving them institutions which drew them together.

In the year 264, the province of Giao Chau was divided into two territories: Koung Tcheou in the North, and Giao Chau proper, which included the low commanderies of Hop Pho, Giao Chi, and Cuu Chan. It was from Giao Chau proper, the most remote Chinese colony, that Viet-Nam was to be born. As soon as the control of the central Chinese government was relaxed—particularly during the troubled period of the great barbarian invasions—new excesses were committed. In particular, under the Luong (Leang) Dynasty, the tyranny of Governor Tieu Tu (Siao Tse) was the cause of the revolt of Ly Bon (542), who, after an easy victory, proclaimed himself king. At his death, his kingdom was divided between his kinsman Ly Phat Tu and General Trieu Quang Phuc. It was reunited by Ly Phat Tu (A.D. 571), who was later obliged to surrender to the Tuy (Souei) emperors, then masters of China (601).[7]

Under the Tuy (Souei) emperors (589–617) and the Duong (T'ang) emperors (618–907), new administrative reorganization tended to strengthen Chinese authority in the country. Viet-Nam was officially named Annam Do Ho Phu (the expression *"do ho phu"* was used in the names of the other Chinese provinces) and subdivided into *chau*, then into *huyen* (subdistricts). The mandarins were chosen by an examination based on Confucian classics, under the same conditions as the administrators of the provinces of China proper. In short, the assimilation of Chinese customs was nearly complete. It was apparently under the T'angs that Buddhist influence was the strongest in Viet-Nam, although this religion was introduced into Viet-Nam as early as the first century.[8]

However, Chinese domination was so oppressive that from time to time it provoked revolts on the part of the nationals (Mai Thuc Loan, A.D. 722; Phung Hung, 791) and even foreign invasions (Nam Chieu, or Nan Tchao, 846 and 862). The Chinese General Cao Bien (Kao P'ien) succeeded in driving out the Nam Chieu and in keeping the country at peace for a short time, during which some reforms were made in the Chinese administration leading to greater centralization. With the decadence of the T'ang emperors, the Chinese governors no longer had the support of the central government, which had been divided into seven kingdoms. The progressive accession of Vietnamese to high public positions, which had begun as early as the second century A.D., permitted the inhabitants of Annam Do Ho Phu to propose successfully to the weakened Emperor T'ang a Vietnamese candidate for the position of *tiet do su*, or governor, Khuc Thua Du (906); his successors were his son Khuc Hao and his grandson Khuc Thua My. The latter attempted a new form of national administration, but was obliged to yield his authority to the Chinese (923). After a brief period in which Chinese superiority was re-established, it was finally completely overthrown by the founder of the first national dynasty (Ngo Quyen, 939).

Independence and the March to the South

Once they had become independent, though they still had to struggle against their hereditary enemies of the North, the Vietnamese undertook to carry the culture of these very enemies, which was now their own, into the territories of the South, in the course of their expansion during the nine centuries of independence (939–1862).

THE ORGANIZATION OF THE INDEPENDENT STATE

During the period of independence, the successive royal dynasties strengthened the central authority and established a more and more solid territorial organization.[9]

The first king, Ngo Quyen, spent the six years of his reign (939–944) putting down the revolts of the former mandarins who had become feudal lords as a result of the decadence of the last of the Chinese governors. Later, Dinh Tien Hoang (968–979) brought all of the feudal lords (*su quan*) into submission and unified the country, establishing severe punishments for any who might try to disturb the public order.

The real centralization of the monarchy began as early as the Ly Dynasty (1009–1225); the first king, Ly Thai To, divided the country into 24 provinces, or *lo*, commanded by princes of the blood or by military leaders. These provinces, which were later to be governed by civil mandarins, were subdivided into *phu* (districts), which in turn were divided into *huyen* (subdistricts), also administered by mandarins. It is to be noted that by way of reaction against the feudal tendencies, centralization was pushed further down to the village (*xa*) level, where the tasks of administration were similarly entrusted to low-ranking mandarins (*xa quan*). The choice of mandarins was at first made upon presentation by Buddhist bonzes, so great was the influence of the Buddhist religion during the first years of the dynasty. Later, the mandarins were chosen by examinations given periodically, in which compositions were written on three religions (*tam giao*): Buddhism, Taoism, and Confucianism. In order to make sure of their loyalty, a solemn oath was administered every year at Dong Co. Also, in order to keep them constantly aware of the need to study, the king compelled the mandarins themselves to take the examinations from time to time.[10]

The transfer of power from the Ly Dynasty to the Tran Dynasty, which ruled from 1225 to 1400, was effected without disturbance by means of the marriage of Tran Canh to the last Ly queen. In an effort to insure good government, the practice was instigated of transferring the powers during the lifetime of each monarch, who then became *thai thuong hoang*, an expression which implies retirement, although this "retired king" still exercised a fairly strong tutelage over the reigning king. The periodical examinations continued to supply the bureaucracy with mandarin scholars, but the subject matter of the examinations eventually concerned only Confucian books, since the Buddhist and Taoist religions gradually were excluded (1304). In order to make certain of good and loyal mandarins, there was a high degree of mobility in the system of promotions and assignments: thus, a mandarin could be a *ngu su,* a censor of a very high rank; then be degraded and sent to the provinces as *tri chau,* a much lower rank; and then be promoted once more to the high rank of *tham tri,* at court. Such was the case of Nguyen Trung Ngan.[11] This mandarinal bureaucracy continued to fill the administrative structure even at the village level.

NATIONAL UNITY AND NEO-CONFUCIANISM

After a brief period of Chinese invasions under the Ming emperors (1414–1428), the Vietnamese Le Dynasty (1428–1788) laid the foundations of a monarchy inspired by the Neo-Confucian doctrine of Chu Hy (Chu Hsi), imported by the Mings. Although the return of the Chinese was for only a short period, the influence on the Vietnamese people was far more lasting than Chinese influence had been in the past: as Ts'in Che Houang Ti had done with the Confucianist writings in the third century B.C., the Chinese generals confiscated all the works of Vietnamese scholars that might appeal to a Vietnamese national feeling, particularly the historical treatise of Le Van Huu entitled *Dai Viet Su Ky* (first published in 1272) and the biographies of great men who might serve as models for future generations. In their schools, the Vietnamese were obliged to use the Chinese books the Ming generals had brought.

It was a Confucian philosophy restored by Chu Hy that the future mandarins of the Le kings found in these writings. The Le Dynasty marked incontestably the triumph of the scholars; the names of the laureates of the periodical examinations were engraved on steles set in the temple dedicated to Confucius. The same laureates constituted the king's court and performed the functions of administrators in the provinces. Curiously, it was during this period of Neo-Confucianism, supposedly very conservative, that two unprecedented administrative institutions were introduced: (1) The institution of the hereditary *chua,* or princes, who really ruled in place of the king from the beginning of the seventeenth century on: they belonged to the Trinh family north of the 18th parallel, and to the Nguyen family in the south; during almost two centuries the two sections existed separately, although Vietnamese national feeling was not disturbed because of the fiction that these princes were merely serving the Le kings.[12] (2) Communal decentralization, which consisted of gradually replacing the *xa quan* (village mandarins) by the *xa truong* (village authorities) chosen by the inhabitants of the villages themselves. This was about the time of the reign of Long Duc (1732–1735).[13]

With the reunification of the country by Gia Long, the first emperor of the Nguyen Dynasty (1802–1945), the Vietnamese administrative system became more original. As suited the scion of the Nguyen *chua,* Gia Long kept in force several institutions peculiar to the South that had been originally instigated as reactions against the desires of the Trinh *chuas* to incorporate the South in the name of the Le kings.[14] But Gia Long also wanted to deal tactfully with the North, where the memory of the Le kings was still strong. The country was divided into three regions, of which the center was placed under the direct authority of the court, and the North and the South under the authority of imperial delegates, called *tong tran.* Each region contained a certain number of *tran,* or provinces, which were made up of *phu* (districts), which in turn were divided into *huyen* (subdistricts). These various administrative posts were entrusted to mandarins, at first selected among the early collaborators, and later recruited by means of the three-year examinations, which were based on the teachings of the Confucian classics. Within the *huyen* (subdistricts) the *xa* (villages) maintained their local autonomy.

THE MARCH TOWARD THE SOUTH

The administrative organization which existed under the Nguyens cannot be explained without taking into consideration another important historical event: the Vietnamese expansion toward the south.

At the end of the ninth century, when the Vietnamese were beginning to regain their independence, the southern border of the country stopped at about the 18th parallel (the Hoanh Son Mountains). The countries to the south of this border had been for a long time subjected to the influence of India.

The first contact between the Vietnamese and peoples of the South was with the Chams. At the time when the Chinese were extending their domination over the territory of Giao Chi, the Chams had controlled Lam Ap, a rather large territory, later called Champa, that extended from the present province of Quang Nam to the present province of Binh Thuan. The Chams were already more or less Indianized, but whereas the Chinese influence had been first introduced to the Vietnamese by force and by political means, the Indian influence was imposed slowly by the conquest of hearts and souls. In effect, the cult of Hinduism has always been limited to the upper classes; the common people retained the essential part of their own characteristics.[15]

The social hierarchy was of Hindu origin, since it included four castes: the *Brahmans,* or men of the pen; the *Kshatriyas,* or men of the sword; the *Vaisyas,* or men of business; and the *Sudras,* or men of the soil. Although ancient Cham custom traced descent in the female line, the succession to the Champa throne nonetheless followed the paternal line, as in India. The characteristics of the prince, taken from the inscription of Mi-Son, resemble curiously the prescriptions of the Hindu *Arthaśāstra*. The authority of the Cham king was also absolute; the public official did not receive any pay, but the people were expected to provide for him by *corvées* and tributes set according to the lands they occupied.[16] The country was divided into provinces corresponding to the coastal plains: Amaravati (Quang Nam), Vijaya (Binh Dinh), Kauthara (Nha Trang), and Panduranga (Phan Rang).

In 298, the Chams advanced to the North, into the territory of K'iu-Soo (now Thua Thien), and even farther north (to the present-day province of Quang Binh), to the Annam Gate (Hoanh Son) in 340. The Chinese governors generally succeeded in confining the Chams to their own territory. In 446, one Chinese governor, Dan Hoa Chi (T'an Ho Tche), succeeded in maintaining the peace for a century. Later, another Chinese general, Luu Phuong (Lieou Fang), having suppressed the revolt of Ly Phat Tu in Viet-Nam, continued his march toward the South and defeated the Chams at Tra Kieu (605). However, the Cham kings, who had resided for a long time in Panduranga (Phan Rang), decided in 875 to transfer their capital to the North, to the city of Champapura in Quang Nam. This attempt at northern expansion was halted by a contrary movement on the part of the Vietnamese, once they had gained their independence. The Vietnamese king, Le Hoan, destroyed the northern Cham capital (982), which obliged the Cham kings to establish their capital in the South, in Vijaya (in the north part of the present-day province of Binh Dinh). At the beginning of the Ly Dynasty, the Chams once more made raids into the Vietnamese *chaus* of Hoan (now Nghe An) and Dien (now Ha Tinh), which obliged Ly Thai Tong to seize the capital, Vijaya (1044), and to transfer a part of its population into colonies situated in the very center of North Viet-Nam (present province of Hung Hoa). Later, the Chams again became aggressive, and as a result Ly Thanh Tong burned the capital of Vijaya with its 2,500 dwellings (1069); the captive Cham king gained his freedom only in exchange for three districts: Bo Chanh, Dia Ly, and Ma Linh (present province of Quang Binh). These districts were immediately organized into Vietnamese provinces, and the Vietnamese were invited to settle there, as the country had been abandoned by the Chams.

It should be noted that Champa had to defend itself not only against its enemies from the North, the Vietnamese, but also from those from the South, the Cambodians. In the eleventh century, the kingdom of Cambodia, Tchen La, which might be called the heir of

**VIET-NAM AND SURROUNDING REGIONS SHOWING
DATES OF VIETNAMESE EXPANSION TO THE SOUTH**

Founan,[17] was already at the height of its power. Under the reign of Suryavarman II (1113–1145), the Cambodians tried unsuccessfully to attack Viet-Nam, either directly or by crossing the Cham territory. The Cambodians fell back on the Chams, whose capital, Vijaya, they occupied until 1149. After a brief period of restoration, Champa became for a time a Khmer province (1203–1220), then once more gained its independence, and remained almost at peace with its neighbors on both sides. It was then that the Chams narrowly escaped the Mongol invasion; Koublai Khan was organizing a long and difficult expedition against them (1283–1285) in conjunction with an expedition directed by Prince Togan (Thoat Hoan) against Viet-Nam. Having failed in their invasion of Viet-Nam, the Mongols were obliged at the same time to abandon their expedition against the Chams. During the reign of Tran Nhan Tong, the marriage of a Vietnamese princess with the Cham King Che Man (1306) gained for Viet-Nam the territory of two *chaus,* O and Ri (present provinces of Quang Tri and Thua Thien). Later, Champa even placed itself under Vietnamese protection and was able to repel a Siamese invasion (1311). However, the Chams still tried several times to reconquer territories ceded to Viet-Nam. One of these attempts was that of Che Bong Nga, whose flag was twice carried as far north as Hanoi (1371 and 1380).

Although these Cham victories were short-lived, the Vietnamese leaders were very bitter over them. As soon as the Ho kings had won the power from the Tran kings, they moved quickly to avenge their compatriots, with an expedition against the Chams that won for them the territories of Chiem Dong, in what is now Quang Nam, and Co Luy, in the present province of Quang Ngai (1400). Once more Vietnamese colonists were established in these territories, but this time the Chams sought vengeance by seeking the support of the Ming emperors in China. Under the pretext of aiding Champa, the Mings invaded Viet-Nam and occupied it for fourteen years (1414–1428). Later, with the assurance of the protection of the Mings, the Chams once more invaded the province of Hoa Chau with a powerful army (1470). King Le Thanh Tong organized a punitive expedition against them, and, after seizing the capital of Vijaya and annexing the province of Quang Nam, Le Thanh Tong divided the remaining Cham territory into three principalities: Chiem Thanh, Hoa Anh, and Nam Phan (1471).

If, at this point, we can speak of a territorial spread effect [18] of this Vietnamese form of Chinese culture, resulting from the activities of the Vietnamese, it must also be said that the victory of Le Thanh Tong marked a purely Vietnamese conquest that extended the sphere of action of Vietnamese culture in defiance of the very will of the Chinese themselves. It was probably after the eviction of the Chams from Vijaya (1471) that the Chams, who were essentially Buddhists and who did not begin to come into contact with the Moslem Indians until the eleventh century, were converted en masse to Islam. This conversion could be explained as a backwash effect [19] produced by the extension of the Vietnamese conquests, since the Chams hoped to find refuge in a more dynamic religion than Hinduism or Buddhism.[20]

However, the Vietnamese expansion to the South continued, with the seizing of Phu Yen by Nguyen Hoang in 1611, the seizing of Khanh Hoa in 1653, and the capture of Binh Thuan in 1697. These events occurred under the Nguyen princes during the long period when the country was divided between the princes of the Trinh family who ruled the northern part and the Nguyen family who ruled the southern part—both families claiming to serve the cause of the Le kings (1600 to 1788).[21]

At the southern limits of the former Cham kingdom, the Vietnamese were to meet the Khmers. The land in this region was covered with forests, and the first Vietnamese to arrive cleared lands which the Khmers had left uncultivated (the present-day provinces of Bien Hoa and Baria).[22] The first armed invasion of Khmer territory by the Vietnamese princes of Cochinchina did not occur until 1658, at which time the Cambodians appealed to the lords of the South to settle their own dissensions. Meanwhile, when the Chinese took refuge in Viet-Nam after the fall of the Ming Dynasty in 1655, they were sent to these same territories in the South, where, in the name of the princes of Viet-Nam, they colonized the present-day provinces of My Tho and Bien Hoa. In 1690, at the death of the Cambodian viceroy in his seat at Saigon, the territory fell under the direct control of Prince Nguyen of Cochinchina. Almost at the same time, other Ming Chinese took refuge on the western coast of what is now South Viet-Nam, and created there some prosperous colonies, which demanded the protection of Prince Nguyen (1708). After certain dissensions in the ruling family of Cambodia, the Nguyen princes were once more called to intervene, and received by way of compensation territories which were to join Baria and Bien Hoa in the East with Ha Tien in the West. The present-day boundaries of the territory of South Viet-Nam were established at the beginning of the nineteenth century, during the reigns of Gia Long and Minh Mang, except for slight modifications made under Thieu Tri and Tu Duc.

The French Influence

The Vietnamese expansion toward the South and West stopped, for all practical purposes, with the intervention of the French. The French had become interested in the Far East after the loss of their Indian Empire. The Opium War with the China of the Tsings (1839–1842) brought about the beginning of this period of intervention in Viet-Nam, which the French were to use as a naval base of operations and a transit point for trade with China.

CONTACT WITH THE WEST

The persecution of Catholic missionaries served as a pretext for an armed aggression (the bombardment of Tourane in 1856; the siege of Saigon in 1859; the assault on Ky Hoa in 1861; the capture of Bien Hoa, Baria, and Vinh Long in 1862), leading to the Treaty of June 5, 1862. This treaty constituted a first assault on the territorial integrity of Viet-Nam, with the ceding of three provinces of Eastern Cochinchina (South Viet-Nam), as well as an indemnity of four million francs. When the population resisted, abetted by systematic patriotic propaganda provided by the provinces of the West, the French annexed the latter as well (1867–1868). After a respite, brought on by the revolution in France in 1870, the French Republic set out once more on the road to territorial expansion and conquered Tonkin (North Viet-Nam) under the pretext that the Emperor Tu Duc was persecuting missionaries and was preventing European traders from using the Red River to establish commerce with China. The Vietnamese put up strong resistance, but spears and arrows could not hold out against cannons and rifles. Three times, in 1874, 1883, and 1884, the Dainam Court was obliged to sign treaties recognizing French sovereignty in the six provinces of Cochinchina (South Viet-Nam) and a French protectorate of the rest of the country (North Viet-Nam and Central Viet-Nam).

With the French domination, the administrative dualism that had existed in the early period of Chinese domination reappeared to a marked degree. In fact, although the Chinese had easily succeeded in imposing their civilization and their administrative system on the simpler autochthonous peoples, the same was not true in the case of the French, who encountered a people with a thousand-year-old civilization, and a relatively adequate administrative system. Out of this meeting of two civilizations, one devoted to moral and human values, the other rather to intellectual and material values, certain compromises occurred which led to a highly original organization in the administrative domain.

The opinion of the first Frenchmen who came to Viet-Nam, whether they were missionaries, soldiers, merchants, or diplomats, was that every effort should be made to maintain the framework of the Vietnamese administrative organization. Thus, as early as 1864, Francis Garnier, a naval lieutenant, wrote: "The communal organization remains at the base of Annamite society; this base constitutes such a social force that in spite of the war, in spite of the efforts made by the Annamite authorities in the French provinces, emigration outside of French territory occurs only in the most restricted sense. Here we find a powerful machine of which we must protect the least cogwheel with care." [23] With regard to the mandarinate, which constituted the basic structure of the Vietnamese administrative system, fervent admirers, such as Luro and Captain Aubaret, were found among the first French colonists. Luro, for example, wrote of the mandarin Phan Thanh Giang, in his book *Le Pays d'Annam:* "A faithful observer of the doctrine of Confucius, he often made respectful observations to the Emperor Minh Mang. . . . This doctor, whose concern for the interests of the Crown often compromised him, after having been several times punished for his candor, was finally stripped of his rank and of his titles. But Phan Thanh Giang submitted to this punishment with rare nobility." [24]

ASSIMILATION VERSUS ASSOCIATION

At the beginning of the French conquest, the mandarin scholars refused their co-operation, and the first admiral-governors were obliged to create a core of French inspectors to replace the defaulting mandarins. These inspectors later became career administrators; they were seconded by the less estimable elements of the population, who were ready to serve any master. These parvenus often abused their official power in order to take advantage of the people in the name of the French authorities.[25]

When the French extended their authority over Tonkin and Annam in 1884, they had already had a certain amount of experience with direct administration in Cochinchina. Although Cochinchina was a colony, and Tonkin and Annam were protectorates, the nationalist resistance in the two latter territories caused the French to become involved in native affairs there as well, by setting up a rather strict political control over the administration of the mandarins. This move later brought about the famous controversy between the policy of association, which advocated the restoring of Vietnamese values side by side with Western values, and the policy of assimilation, which attempted to install in Viet-Nam institutions similar to those of France.[26]

The policy of association did not succeed in Cochinchina in the first days of the conquest, for the good reason that the mandarins refused to co-operate. In Tonkin, the French were at first inclined to apply this policy under the administrations of Paul Bert (1887) and of De Lanessan (1891–1894). In an effort to gain the sympathy of the scholars, Paul Bert had created a commission of forty notables, who retained their functions under the government of De Lanessan.[27] However, the scholars remained very retiring and, furthermore, the French administrators regarded with considerable suspicion these consultative bodies which were much more of a hindrance than a help in their colonial activities. Hence, it is not surprising that after the administration of Paul Bert, the policy of assimilation prevailed.

This policy of assimilation was first established in Cochinchina. In 1880, the French set up a Colonial Council, composed of six Frenchmen elected by universal suffrage by their compatriots, six Vietnamese elected by the delegates of the elders of the communes, two delegates of the Chambre de Commerce (Trade Council), and two members appointed by the governor. In the provinces, provincial councils were created whose members were appointed. This constituted, therefore, an assimilation, but a purely superficial one.

In Tonkin and in Annam, although the legal framework of the protectorate precluded the possibility of a direct administration, actually the same policy of assimilation was practiced. The authority of the Council of Ministers of the King of Viet-Nam (the *Co Mat*) was in the hands of the French resident superior. Behind each minister (cabinet member) was a French councilor who held the real authority. In Tonkin, the functions of the *kinh luoc*, the imperial delegate, were suppressed and fell to the French resident superior (1897). Although the treaties had not made provision for the installation of representatives of the French government at the provincial level, French residents were appointed to the capital of each province to supervise the work of the Vietnamese province chiefs, and to assure directly the carrying out of such policies as interested the so-called French administration.

The policy of assimilation became necessary also to assure a certain uniformity in the financial domain. In view of the administrative philosophy of the emperor and also of an economy based essentially on agriculture and on a very limited commerce, the financial needs of the empire were not very great, and the emperors were able to manage with a rather summary fiscal program. On the other hand, because of military expenses as well as the expenses of exploiting the colonies, the French were obliged to increase public expenditures considerably, and to become more and more involved in the administration of public finances.

A third reason for the policy of assimilation was the formation of the General Government of Indochina. As the French had already extended their protectorate over Cambodia (1863), they considered it necessary to assure a certain co-ordination in the various administrative and military activities by the creation of an Indochinese Union (1887) placed under the administration of a governor-general in whom was vested the authority of the French Republic. Later, the French added Laos to this Indochinese Union, after the French protectorate of this country had been recognized (1893–1895).

CENTRALIZATION OF THE COLONIAL GOVERNMENT

The proconsulate of Paul Doumer (1897–1902) marked a decisive point in the administrative history of Viet-Nam. Paul Doumer provided the Indochinese Union with a solid administrative

structure. The power was centralized in the hands of the governor-
general, who had great power in financial matters, such as customs
duties and the government monopolies of opium, salt, and alcohol,
and in administrative matters through the general technical services
to assure directly certain important functions, such as postal service,
public works, education, and the management of the treasury. In
addition to these important developments, beginning with the administration of Paul Doumer, the French colonial government began to
develop strongly rapacious and presumptive characteristics, in the
sense that economic expansion was advanced with no other aim than
the profit of French enterprises.[28]

From this point on, the French colonial policy never ceased to
fluctuate, but developed in the general direction of strengthening the
authority of the mother country. Nevertheless, the reforms of Paul
Doumer and of his successors provoked a certain reaction among the
Vietnamese people. The armed resistance led by Phan Dinh Phung
during the reign of Ham Nghi (1884–1888) was replaced by a more
subtle resistance in the form of efforts leading to the modernization
of institutions similar to that of Thailand, and particularly to that of
Japan, and inspired by Chinese reformers such as Kang Yeou Wei
and Liang K'i Tch'ao. Exiles formed the Viet-Nam Quang Phuc Hoi
(Association for the Restoration of Viet-Nam), which stirred up
revolts in the interior (1912, 1913, and 1924). Other revolutionaries
in the country itself created a reform movement (Dong Kinh Nghia
Thuc), which sought to raise the cultural level of the masses, and to
suppress customs which were judged too archaic. Governor Paul
Beau, at first continuing Paul Doumer's work of centralization but
altering the government methods to aim at moral conquest rather
than military, created an Office of Public Instruction which included
an embryo university to respond to the aspirations of the population
(1907). Albert Sarraut created many schools and hospitals, and in
an effort towards decentralization brought the Vietnamese to participate, in the capacity of consultants, in certain administrative activities, particularly at the regional level. The so-called University
of Hanoi dates from the administration of Sarraut (1917). A.
Varenne (1925) opened to the Vietnamese certain posts which had
been previously reserved for the French.

All efforts made by the French authorities seemed insufficient,
and only strengthened Vietnamese national feeling, which was
hostile to half measures. Thus, in 1930, a revolution of nationalist
tendency broke out under the leadership of Nguyen Thai Hoc.
Although this revolution was quickly and violently repressed, it had a
deep effect on the state of mind of the population. It might be said
that a true nationalism, in the modern sense of the term, was born at
this period. By reaction, the French government increased its efforts
towards centralization. The General Government of Indochina was

placed in the hands of career administrators in order to carry out more faithfully the government policies.[29] Although an apparent relaxation of the protectorate occurred with the return of Bao Dai to the throne (1932), French intervention in so-called native affairs was greater than ever, particularly since the colonial governors knew they could count on the Vietnamese administrators who had been trained in the French schools, and who were supposedly devoted to the French cause. The creation of the Grand Conseil des Intérêts Economiques et Financiers (Grand Council of Economic and Financial Interests) appeared to be a step in the direction of decentralization since it gave decision-making powers to the Council in certain areas, particularly in fiscal matters, but it actually amounted to the creation of a supra-national power, in the sense that the Council thus relieved the Emperor of Annam of a part of his own prerogatives. In other words, as the powers of the Grand Council increased, so did the interference of French authorities in the administration of Vietnamese affairs, for the good reason that this Council deliberated and gave opinions which had been submitted to it by the French governor-general.[30]

Many new services were created, at the federal level as well as at the regional level: Inspector of Labor, Director of Economic Affairs, Office of Internal Revenue, etc. Although a certain number of administrative positions were, in principle, open to Vietnamese, by and large, Vietnamese were not allowed to occupy these positions, under such pretexts as that of reducing employment as a result of the economic crisis (1929–1932) or as a result of preparations for war (on the eve of World War II).[31]

DEVELOPMENT OF NATIONALISM

This strengthening of French authority in the administrative domain was accompanied by a more or less open resistance in the political domain on the part of the Vietnamese. The nationalist movement, no longer limited to a small number of intellectuals, gained much favor among the working classes who had been reduced to the rankest poverty by a slump in rice. This opened the way for the Communist movement (Dong Duong Cong San Dang). This political development was thus quite advanced when World War II provided it with an unparalleled opportunity to reach full maturity.

At the beginning of World War II, the French succeeded in maintaining their authority over the entire territory of Indochina. Even after the fall of France, in June, 1940, the Vichy government, by means of arrangements with the Asiatic powers and particularly with Japan, continued to administer the Indochinese colony until 1942. By this time, after several skirmishes with Japanese troops in Lang Son, the French were obliged to accept the presence of Japanese troops in the principal strategic points of the country.

Although, to all appearances, a relative peace was maintained over the entire territory of Viet-Nam, in a world at war, this was a period rich in political developments. As a matter of fact, the Japanese sought to win over the population by painting a bright picture of an independent Viet-Nam in the framework of Greater East Asia, while Admiral J. Decoux was trying by means of excuses and bargaining to maintain the French position, until the cessation of hostilities in 1945.[32]

It was then that the Communist Party, to rally the bourgeoisie which was still mistrustful of communism, created the Vietnam Doc Lap Dong Minh Hoi (League for the Independence of Viet-Nam)—commonly shortened to Viet-Minh—which allegedly combined into a single front all classes and all nationalist parties for a simultaneous struggle against French colonialism and Japanese imperialism. On the other hand, the nationalist parties, with the aid of the Chinese Kuomintang, joined to form the Vietnam Cach Menh Dong Minh Hoi (League of Vietnamese Revolutionary Parties). This league even received for a while the co-operation of the Viet-Minh, but the latter group quickly became aware of the instability of this coalition, and established itself independently in the upper region of North Viet-Nam, and toward the end of October, 1944, with the support of the Allies, gave the signal for guerrilla warfare.[33] The victory of the Allies precipitated the fall of the colonial government, but brought about also a very troubled period from 1945 to 1949, during which the French sought to re-establish their authority by negotiating alternately with the Communist leaders of the Viet-Minh, and with the so-called Nationalist Government of Bao Dai.

SOCIAL CHANGES RESULTING FROM FRENCH COLONIZATION

During the entire period of French domination, a firm and constant effort was made to assure the French position and to protect French interests. French policy in Viet-Nam was often dictated by requirements completely foreign to the aspirations of the Vietnamese people. The opinion of a Dutch administrator who observed the same phenomenon in Indonesia was as follows:

As the system progressed, this direction from above and from without penetrated everywhere; every year saw some new Western initiative, some further extension of Western influence, some additional adaptation of native customs and institutions to Western standards. In practically every phase of life this trend appeared, introducing new conceptions, erasing traditions, letting light and air into dark and stuffy chambers, but nearly always hurting somebody in his interests or feelings.[34]

With the arrival of the French, the most remarkable change was of an economic nature: by investing in Vietnamese industries and in large agricultural ventures, the French introduced the idea of capitalist enterprise. Similarly, from the exchanges of goods and services that took place between the mother country and the colony there resulted an international movement of merchandise and of capital involving modern techniques of foreign trade. In order to accommodate this capitalistic economy, the French improved or constructed roads, bridges, navigable waterways, and seaports. A certain number of institutions were created to insure the normal operation of this economy: banking institutions, professional commissions, commercial companies, etc. These modern activities progressed side by side with traditional activities such as agriculture, cattle raising, and crafts; these fields received so little modernization that it might be said that they were still, on the eve of World War II, just as they had been in the time of the emperors. The following estimate of Paul Bernard gives us a rather clear idea of the structure of Vietnamese economy at the eve of the war: 74 per cent of the total production was from the primary sector (agriculture, fishing, crafts, exploitation of natural resources); 13 per cent from the secondary sector (manufacturing); 13 per cent from the third sector (public and private services).[35]

These economic changes brought about certain changes of a social nature. The more the capital was concentrated, the greater was the inequality of the distribution of wealth, as is shown in the following summary:

INCOME OF THE WORKING POPULATION

Class of Workers	Annual Income Per Capita (in Indochinese piasters)	Number of Workers in Group	Total Income of Group (in millions of piasters)
European civilians	5,000	13,400	66
Europeans in armed forces	600	10,500	6
Rich Indochinese	6,000	9,000	55
Average Indochinese	168	920,000	153
Poor Indochinese	49	9,600,000	470
Total		10,552,900	750

This unequal distribution of wealth corresponds to the unequal distribution of the population between the country and the cities. The mass of farmers, which represents the great majority of the poor Indochinese, remained in the country, content with an almost rudimentary life. Some were simple farm workers; others were farmers who paid all the expenses of the rice fields (hiring cattle, equipment, planting, etc.) in addition to the rent of the farm, of which the total often amounted to 70 per cent of the value from the harvest. The number of landowners was comparatively large (1,874,-880); that of the large landholders was smaller (6,530, or 2.5 per cent), although the large landholdings occupied almost 45 per cent of the total area. With the exception of the large landholders who lived in the cities, all of this population still lived in the traditional manner as large families and village groups. Here the traditional method of administration found the setting of its choice.

The other categories of the population, including the Europeans, lived in the large cities and formed the urban population. Here the rich landholders could afford to live a life of ease and to give their children an expensive education; the contractors and merchants maintained frequent contacts with Europeans, which gave them the mentality of businessmen; and the civil servants began to grow familiar with the modern techniques of commerce and industry. Little by little the urban population was divided into a capitalist class, a middle class, and a working class, and adopted, from contact with the Europeans, the attitudes consistent with these classes. Thus, the serene scholar tended to be replaced by the busy entrepreneur, the benevolent master by the implacable boss, the faithful subject by the salaried worker all too aware of his rights, family solidarity by impassive city life, and the courtesy which governed human relations by the impartial law of competition. At any rate, it was from this urban population that the future political and administrative leaders of the country were to be recruited. The modernization of administration was also felt in this urban sector long before it began to affect the rest of the country.

Administrative Dualism and Political Development

Of course, the social change which has just been outlined is not the exclusive work of public administration. The colonial policy of assimilation played an important role, and the resistance of Vietnamese tradition against this assimilation also contributed greatly to the formation of the new society. But the compromise between these tendencies is indeed brought about by public administration, which is the resultant of administrative dualisms, more or less accentuated according to the periods, but still persisting throughout the course of the history of Viet-Nam. From the historic example of Viet-Nam, the idea of administrative dualism can be defined in the following manner: There is administrative dualism as soon as two different systems of administration having different administrative philosophies exist in a given national territory. The administrative system includes certain institutions which perform fundamental functions: policy implementing, programming, staffing, budgeting, reporting, and so on. With respect to institutions, the administrative system includes essentially the central government, the local administrative organizations, personnel, finances, and control of administrative activities.

THE CIRCULAR CUMULATIVE CAUSATION OF SINICIZATION AND POLITICAL DEVELOPMENT

Thus, for example, at the beginning of the period of Chinese domination, two different administrative systems existed side by side.[36] The Vietnamese system was of an agrarian type, but feudalized: the central authority of the king was weak, and the feudal lords had been bound to the king only by the ties of vassalage; the functions of authority exercised by these lords were hereditary, and public finances were raised by a system of tributes; the central authority had only a very loose control. The other system was that of the Chinese Han emperors, which was strongly centralized and in which the functions of authority were exercised by mandarins chosen essentially according to loyalty and merit, taxes were paid partly in money and partly in kind, and control was exercised both by reports made by inferior authorities to their superiors and by frequent inspections made by *missi dominici*. In short, it was an agrarian administrative system of a bureaucratic type.

The ten centuries of Chinese domination are characterized by a progressive assimilation by the Vietnamese of all aspects of culture, particularly that of public administration. The first stage in this long assimilation was the coexistence of the centralized Chinese government and the native feudal administration, which resulted in a remarkable absorption of Chinese concepts by the Vietnamese. The Chinese mandarins at first took command in the higher echelons (*thu su* and *thai thu*); in order to curry favor with them, the Vietnamese, or feudal mandarins of lower rank, had to study Chinese writing and to adopt, to all appearances at least, Chinese customs. This absorption of Chinese culture permitted them to compete with certain Chinese mandarins of lower rank, and the latter became more and more uncompromising in requiring the Vietnamese to conform to their way of working. Feudal lords and feudal practices were gradually eliminated. Chinese customs became more entrenched in the administrative machine. Thus Chinese colonization had a cumulative spread effect in the development of the administrative system.

Nevertheless, this very Chinese culture gave the Vietnamese a certain idea of national consciousness and of solidarity in the face of foreign invaders. The more the Chinese strengthened their authority, the greater became the tendency of the Vietnamese to unite. In this way, Chinese colonization had a cumulative backwash effect, which led to the revolt of the Trung sisters (A.D. 39–43). Then, once more, under the strong drive of Ma Vien and his successors, a very strong centralization developed, with the formation of a new class of native mandarins devoted to the Chinese cause replacing the nobles wiped out during the war of independence. The spread effect became more intense. But the revolt of Ly Bon and of his successors (542–602) constituted a new and more durable expression of backwash effect, although in public life the Vietnamese were already behaving more or less as Chinese.[37]

The third stage seems to have been more decisive, with a nearly complete adoption of the colony as one of the original Chinese provinces (Annam Do Ho Phu). Administrative customs and practices became even more deep-rooted from that moment on. The Buddhist ceremonial helped make more venerable the agent of the Son of Heaven in the colony; and, with him, the entire Chinese administrative, religious, and cultural apparatus was imported to Viet-Nam indiscriminately. This is especially true with regard to the upper classes of the population, which formed the bureaucracy. But it is also true to a certain extent with regard to the lower classes, and even to the peasants themselves. Although they persisted in retaining their own customs—the turban in preference to the skull cap, *nuoc mam* (a fish sauce) in preference to soy sauce, betel nuts and lacquered teeth in preference to unornamented teeth—the people still applied the essential principles of a Confucian morality, among which the idea of *trung quan* (loyalty to the emperor) was more easily expressed toward the person of the national leader.[38] Thus, when the country gained its independence in 939, Chinese culture, euphemistically called Confucian culture, had made an indelible impression on the minds of the Vietnamese, while at the same time a nationalistic feeling inspired by the same sources had become stronger than ever.

Three instances, among others, illustrate how deeply rooted Confucian philosophy is in the Vietnamese mind:

1) Although the country was completely independent of the Chinese emperors from 939 on, with a very brief interruption (1414–1428) under the Ming Dynasty, the various kings from the Ngo Dynasty to the Le Dynasty, and even the emperors of the Nguyen dynasties always sought and obtained a nominal investiture from the emperors of China. It was not until 1885, when France formally obtained from China her withdrawal of all claims to the allegiance of Viet-Nam, that the last silver seal conferred upon the emperor of Annam by China was melted.[39]

2) The program of studies and examinations leading to the selection of mandarins consisted principally of commentaries on classical works, so that in 1823, after nine centuries of independence, when the Emperor Minh Mang made an investigation of the historical studies required of the candidates, the mandarins in charge reported to him that the studies were limited to the authors of the Chinese Han, T'ang, and Tsong dynasties. Minh Mang gave

instructions that the program of studies should henceforth include also the authors of the Nguyen (Yuan), Minh (Ming), and Thanh (Tsing) dynasties.[40]

3) During the First Republic of Viet-Nam, Confucian studies were more than ever the order of the day. The birthday of Confucius was considered a legal holiday; although the ceremony was celebrated by a private group, the Hoi Khong Hoc Vietnam (Association for Confucian Studies), at least one member of the cabinet of the president of the Republic presided over the ceremony, at which he read a message from the president, which always contained reference to certain teachings of the Master.[41] After the November 1 Revolution, the revolutionary government abolished the legal holiday on the birthday of Confucius, a measure which met with some objection, including a formal protest made by the Association for Confucian Studies.[42]

VIETNAMIZATION VERSUS INDIANIZATION

During the period of independence, a mitigated administrative dualism appeared in the newly conquered Champa provinces. The centralized mandarinal system of the Vietnamese, based on Confucian models, was superimposed on the authoritarian system of the Chams, which was based on caste and inspired by India. The embryo public finance system of the Vietnamese differed from the Cham system of payment in kind.

Unlike the Chinese, who imposed their culture progressively on the Vietnamese as soon as they had a firm footing in the newly conquered territory, the Vietnamese themselves preferred more radical methods: either the transplanting into Vietnamese provinces of autochthonous peoples far from their native lands, or else a systematic emigration of Vietnamese—either volunteers or deportees —into the conquered provinces. Thus, the assimilation of culture was brought about more rapidly, although these methods led to reactions which were often bloody and costly for the two peoples concerned. But this assimilation must be further explained by the fact that, during nearly two centuries when the country was divided (the seventeenth and eighteenth centuries), the Nguyen princes consolidated their power in order to resist the Trinh princes. The conviction of both sides that they were still serving the Le kings contributed strongly to the continuation of cultural unity and national feeling in spite of the division, and it is this conviction much more than the everyday life of the Vietnamese that made the strength of the Vietnamese administrative system when confronted with systems of the conquered countries.[43] The spread effect of this system was so much stronger than the backwash effect of the reactions of the Chams that it might be better to speak of substitution of culture rather than of assimilation. After a short period of transition, largely of a military nature, the administrative system rapidly adopted a Vietnamese form, except in the lowest echelons. Thus was born the problem of Cham and Khmer minorities in South Viet-Nam. This substitution of the Vietnamese administrative system for the autochthonous systems is explained not only by the extreme national feeling of the Vietnamese, but also by the innate characteristics of the peoples of the South.

The Chams were at first Hindus and Buddhists. In principle, the ultimate goal of Buddhism is to attain Nirvana; this fact implies belief in peace, brotherhood, nonviolence, and in the essentially transitory nature of worldly things. Buddhism does not preclude other beliefs, not even the most varied political ideas. Therefore, it should not be expected that any reaction on the part of the Chams stemmed from the Buddhist religion.[44] Furthermore, after regaining independence, the Vietnamese kings continued to broaden their protection of the Mahayana Buddhist religion. The fact that the two peoples shared the same religion contributed greatly to the assimilation of Vietnamese culture by the Chams. On the other hand, the Cham political organization inspired by the Hindus resembled the Vietnamese system in many respects. It is true that the two principal ideals taught in the *Dharmashastra* (Sacred Law) are the organization of social life through a well-defined and well-regulated caste system based on the role played by the castes (*varnas*) in the communal sacrifices, and the organization of the life of the individual into four stages (*ashramas*): the student, the householder, the mentor, and the ascetic. This idea of the stages of life is completely foreign to the Confucian philosophy. Similarly, the division of society into castes does not exist in Viet-Nam, although the distribution of the population into four classes (the *si*, or scholars; the *nong*, or farmers; the *cong*, or workers; and the *thuong*, or merchants) is in a way analogous to the division of Indian society into castes. But the *Arthaśāstra*, or treatise on material gain, contains many formulas for the struggle for power and the methods used to gain and keep control over the land and its people; it lays down policies aimed at welding the smaller states into a more or less unified pattern under the control, direct or indirect, of a single authority; this supposes the elaboration of a complex bureaucracy in the executive function.[45] These formulas find close parallels in the doctrine of Neo-Confucianism. It should be noted that, although the Chams were converted to Islamism rather late, their conversion did not halt the Vietnamization which had begun immediately after the conquest of the Cham territory.

In summary, in their march towards the South, the Vietnamese brought with them the broad principles of administration which they had inherited from the Chinese; as the dominating authority, they imposed these principles all the more easily since they were not contradictory to those of the native populations. They met a certain resistance on the part of the Chams, who many times succeeded in reconquering territories they had been obliged to yield by force, but because of the similarity of principles of government, this did not constitute a very strong backwash effect. Thus, after the period of expansion, the Vietnamese administrative system prevailed entirely.

THE VAIN ATTEMPT OF FRENCH ASSIMILATION

The idea of a centralized government seems to have been common to both the French and the Vietnamese systems. However, communal autonomy in the Vietnamese system, although it was never clearly defined, seems greater than the powers accorded to the French commune. Although both systems seem to involve a bureaucracy recruited according to merit, the Vietnamese examinations were based on studies of Chinese humanities, while the French examinations placed the emphasis on law. Vietnamese public finance was still based on a very limited market economy; French public finance involved a well-developed commerce based on a stable currency. The control exercised by the imperial censors concerned all aspects of the attitude of public servants, whereas the hierarchical control and inspections of the French system concerned only specific matters, and sanctions were very carefully defined. Thus, with the arrival of the French, there was a formal administrative dualism, since the French authorities maintained the agrarian and bureaucratic Vietnamese system side by side with the industrial French system, which was based essentially on a free-market economy.

Nevertheless, throughout the history of French colonization, we observe a continued strengthening of the French influence in the administrative organization of Viet-Nam, even in the realm of indigenous administration. This strengthening was accelerated each time an outbreak of nationalist resistance occurred, so that the influence of French policies and methods became deeply rooted in the administrative life of the country (spread effect). Meanwhile, each advance made in the centralization tendency was accompanied by a similar advance in the nationalist movement. Ironically, this movement reflected the French philosophy of the eighteenth century (e.g., Montesquieu and Rousseau), which inspired the Vietnamese revolutionaries, at first indirectly through translations by Chinese authors, but later directly, when the new generation, trained in French schools, found themselves able to understand the French sources themselves (backwash effect).

By a process of circular cumulative causation, the dominating administrative system, i.e., the one which holds the power, either by force or by other means, tends to absorb little by little the traditional system. Nevertheless, the more pronounced this absorption becomes, the more national feeling crystallizes and grows, and by an unexpected backwash effect, the resulting new system serves to support effectively a national political regime. This is what occurred on a large scale during the period of Vietnamese independence, from the tenth to the nineteenth century. The special case of the absorption of Champa by Viet-Nam is the result of the weakness of the backwash effect, which is to be explained by the dominant religion of the Cham people, and the similarity of certain political institutions of the two peoples. The domination of the French was not sufficiently long to bring about a complete integration of the two systems; however, the backwash effect was sufficiently strong to explain the rapid recovery of the administrative apparatus by the government of Viet-Nam, as soon as the French were obliged to renounce all claims to political hegemony in Viet-Nam, by the Geneva Agreements, July 20, 1954.

CHAPTER 2

TOWARD A PHILOSOPHY OF PUBLIC ADMINISTRATION IN VIET-NAM

> Ceux qui vivent, ce sont seux qui luttent;
> ce sont
> Ceux dont un dessein ferme emplit l'âme
> et le front,
> Ceux qui d'un haut destin gravissent
> l'âpre cime,
> Ceux qui marchent pensifs, épris d'un
> but sublime.[1]

BEFORE ANALYZING the influence on current public administration in Viet-Nam of traditional ideas brought about by the singular combination of Confucian concepts of a humanistic inspiration and French theories which tend towards legalism and rationalism, it is important first to trace briefly other factors contributing to the formation of the present administrative philosophy.

The Problems of Substantive Administration

These problems can be grouped under three headings: political development, economic progress, and social balance.

THE NEED FOR POLITICAL DEVELOPMENT

From a political point of view, the adjustment from the position of a colony to that of an independent state has brought about many changes in the administrative system.

Developing a National Spirit. In effect, the upper part of the administrative structure collapsed the day that France recognized the complete independence of Viet-Nam. After having tried vainly to negotiate with the government of the Democratic Republic of Viet-Nam (preliminary agreement of March 6, 1946, *modus vivendi* of September 14, 1946, and the events of December 19, 1946, in Hanoi), the French were obliged to turn to a national government rather hastily contrived under the aegis of the former Emperor of Annam, Bao Dai. The Elysée Agreement of March 8, 1949, set forth the principles of an independent Vietnamese state, with membership in the French Union.[2] As a matter of fact, by the intermediary of federal agencies (Exchange Control Office, Treasury Office, Foreign Trade Office, Immigration Office, etc.) and under the pretext of guarantee-

43

ing the peace of the country by military force, the French still, to all intents and purposes, retained the power, although a certain freedom was left to the Central Government of Viet-Nam in decisions of lesser importance. Moreover, this Central Government was weakened also by the presence of three regional governors, appointed by the Central Government on the basis of political considerations, who retained in effect all the administrative functions: appointment of public servants, settling of the regional budgets, and the maintenance of a check on budgets in the lower echelons. This ambiguous situation did not end until after the Geneva Agreements, which granted complete independence to Viet-Nam, with a provisional partition of the country into two zones, one of which—the zone south of the 17th parallel—was placed under the authority of the Government of Free Viet-Nam.

The president of the government, Ngo Dinh Diem, who was appointed by Bao Dai in 1954, realized at once that the chances for survival of his government would be quite limited if he could not count heavily on the rapid development of a national spirit.[3] In truth, it has been shown that, by way of reaction against colonialism, a real patriotism was already felt, at least by the more advanced of the Vietnamese people. But this nationalism had been expressed only verbally during the so-called Independence of Bao Dai. After the Geneva Agreements it was a question of putting this nationalism to the test. The immediate and principal difficulty of a political nature was the overcoming of the politico-religious sects of Hoa Hao and Cao Dai and the politico-commercial sect of Binh Xuyen, all three of which had established large areas of influence during the period of collaboration with the French. The purge of these sects was effected on a double front: on the territorial front by regrouping under the national government the provinces formerly controlled by the sects, and on the political front by eliminating from public office the agents of the sects. In the same effort towards political unity, the regional governments were abolished and were replaced by an Inspection Service (Dai Bieu Chinh Phu) which was to serve as eyes and ears for the Central Government.

Stabilizing the Position of the Government. Less urgent, but essential for reasons of political support, was the problem of stabilizing the position of the government. Ngo Dinh Diem had been placed in power in the name of a certain legal fiction: Bao Dai, as titular chief of state, delegated to him full powers in order to bring about the independence of Viet-Nam. No constitutional act, no popular vote had named Bao Dai the chief of state. On October 26, 1955, a referendum deposed Bao Dai and entrusted to Ngo Dinh Diem the responsibility for setting up a republic. The Constitution of the First Republic was promulgated October 26, 1956, providing for the elements of a new government: the Chief Executive, the National Assembly, the Constitutional Court, and the National Economic Council.[4] The task of putting these institutions into operation (taking the census, finding office space for personnel for each new institution, etc.) required the mobilization of great financial resources and of large numbers of administrative personnel. The administrative work of setting up elections for the posts of president of the Republic and members of the National Assembly was to be accompanied by an educational program for the people, who for the first time were facing universal suffrage on a national scale—a task all the more difficult since it is easy to induce the uneducated to support a dictatorial regime.

Another aspect of the securing of political support included lengthy negotiations with French authorities for the transfer of powers. In the eyes of the people, the most conclusive evidence of national sovereignty would be the departure of French administrators from civil service posts and of French soldiers from the garrisons. The Ngo Dinh Diem government bent itself to this urgent task, which, at the same time, demanded that new men be placed in the various echelons of command, civil and military, even at subordinate levels. Moreover, new cadres had to be formed to replace promptly the former cadres of Vietnamese public servants who were often promoted suddenly, without any training for their new positions.[5] Also, the increased work in the field of international relations that accompanied the cessation of bilateral relations with France required the developing of a special class of public servants capable of dealing with international problems, either to represent Viet-Nam abroad or to meet in Viet-Nam with foreign diplomats: e.g., representatives of the International Control Commission (supervising the application of the Geneva Agreements) and working groups setting up programs of foreign aid to Viet-Nam, especially members of the United States Operations Mission, responsible for administering the United States aid program to Viet-Nam.

Developing Communication with the People for the Simultaneous Struggle against Three Enemies: Communism, Underdevelopment, and Disunity. The problems of finding new men for public offices were further complicated by the lack of communication with the people either directly or through political groups. At the very beginning of the period of independence, the government had to find a way to communicate directly through the public servants. In order to ask the administrators to increase their contacts, their number had to be substantially increased, and they needed competent assistants.

This fuller contact with the people was first necessary in the pursuit of another political objective—the struggle against communism. This struggle was and is carried on in many forms, of which open battle between military units is only one. Propaganda and counterpropaganda constitute a second form of the struggle, which must be maintained at all administrative levels. Defense against subversive activities is a third; subversive activities are often so subtle that the individual must be constantly on the alert, even within intimate groups. The stakes were so vital that the government had to put into operation as quickly as possible every available means of defense, including the mobilization of urban and rural masses, both men and women, the old as well as the young. Although this struggle was carried on by many semiprivate organizations, it was still necessary to have more or less specialized civil servants who could devote themselves entirely to this work. New outbreaks of communism made this need so urgent that on October 15, 1961, the government declared a state of emergency, which was officially prolonged in 1962 for one year and in 1963 for two more years.[6]

The Revolution of November 1, 1963. In order to combat disunity, it is particularly necessary to have a well-developed communications system. In the early days of independence, elements contributing to disunity were the different groups which had been defeated by the forces of Ngo Dinh Diem, the many refugees from the North, and a feeling of separatism that had existed at the time of the French domination. As the Ngo Dinh Diem government gradually evolved in the direction of dictatorship, a new element of disunity appeared: groups which, dissatisfied with the state of affairs, opposed the policy of indiscriminate repression, the disastrous economic policy, and the exaggerated family spirit displayed by Ngo Dinh Diem and his brothers.[7] This dissatisfaction reached its climax during the Buddhist affairs, in the course of which stringent measures of persecution were taken towards the Buddhist priests and their followers.[8] Since the majority of Vietnamese are Buddhists, this persecution was an indication of deliberate disunity. As a result, the Revolution of November 1, 1963, put an end to the First Republic and set up the Second Republic, for which the constitution is still being prepared.[9]

In the first days of the November 1 Revolution, the Military Revolutionary Council, composed of generals and other high-ranking officers, proclaimed the principles of anticommunism and of alliance with the free world. The Council promised to serve only the higher interests of the nation, and not to instigate any dictatorial regime, making it understood that a democracy was to be established and national discipline strengthened.

As a demonstration of the desire of the new government for unity, the chairman of the Military Revolutionary Council participated in the ceremonies re-establishing the religious sects of Cao Dai and Hoa Hao and the unification of various Buddhist groups.[10]

The problem of the administrative cadres in putting into effect the principles of the new government was not so acute as in the early days of the First Republic, since the civil servants and the military personnel had had a certain amount of training. On the other hand, the Revolutionary Council and the Provisional Government faced the difficult task of eliminating from the civil service, without allowing the excesses of the spoils system, those persons who had compromised the national interest under the former government.

AWARENESS OF THE STATE
OF ECONOMIC UNDERDEVELOPMENT

The afore-mentioned major political events would have sufficed to constitute the catalyzing element necessary to overcome the obstacles of this decisive stage on the road to economic progress. The slogans devised by the government of the First Republic, urging the population to make effectual contributions to economic recovery, openly recognized the underdeveloped condition of the country: a condition that constituted in the eyes of the public authorities a formidable enemy, comparable to communism and to the spirit of disunity. How can this state of economic underdevelopment be characterized more scientifically? Is it the traditional stage of economy, or is the country, in spite of this state of underdevelopment, simply fulfilling certain "preconditions for the 'take-off,'" to borrow Rostow's terminology? [11]

The Economic Situation. Certainly, the Vietnamese economy is no longer in the traditional stage, despite the fact that 85.1 per cent of its people live from agriculture.[12] In the field of agriculture a great deal is being done to increase the area of cultivated land, to modernize techniques, and to increase the commercial flow of produce. A recent government publication reports that agricultural development has increased the area planted in rice by 15 per cent and that in rubber by 32 per cent; owing to an effective agricultural credit system, loans totaling more than three and a half billion piasters were extended to one and a quarter million farm families for small investments and for harvests. These results were obtained through a series of programs: selected planting, chemical fertilizers, treatment of crops against insects, and a great water-control project. The country already possesses, in addition to this water-control project, a sizeable social overhead capital: highways and bridges, seaports, river ports, airports, urban centers equipped with electricity and water, and technical schools and universities.[13] According to an evaluation made March 31, 1960, of the different types of economic activities of the working people of Saigon, in a total of 33,760 business firms studied, 191,030 workers were employed, of which 59,260 were technical or administrative personnel, 76,260 were skilled workers, and 55,510 were unskilled workers.[14] These proportions seem to be normal, even when compared with statistics taken in the United States at the beginning of the century; unskilled or nearly unskilled workers in the United States in 1910 made up 36.1 per cent of the working force, and in 1935, 36.2 per cent.[15]

These figures regarding a limited part of the economic situation —the labor force in Saigon—agree with estimates made by economists in terms of aggregates. One economist, with the usual reservations as to the value of statistics in underdeveloped countries, observes that from 1956 to 1960 the gross national product increased by 24 per cent, a much greater increase than that of the population (15 per cent). This increase in the national product represents a higher standard of living, in which the rate of consumption per capita was increased by about 0.5 per cent per year.[16]

Although statistics concerning the increase in the gross national product are not up to date, it is certain that the economic situation has grown worse since 1960. In a press conference held soon after the November 1 Revolution, the Secretary of State for Economy, deploring the disordered psychology of the consumer, the spirit of speculation, and the bitter profit seeking of the merchants, emphasized the importance of measures planned to strengthen the economy by means of regular food supplies, price stabilization, the promotion of investments and of exportation, and the restricting of the consumption of luxury items.[17] A comparison of the schedule of

ASSETS AND LIABILITIES OF THE NATIONAL BANK,
WITH CURRENT PRICE INDEXES *

	Dec. 1960	Dec. 1961	Dec. 1962
Total Assets	19,836	19,225	21,578
Gold and foreign exchange	7,577	6,137	5,360
Consolidated debt of government	10,681	10,681	10,681
Advances to Banks	150	521	275
Fixed assets	137	130	170
Other assets (including advances to the counterpart fund)	1,291	1,756	5,092
Total Liabilities	19,836	19,225	21,578
Notes in circulation	12,158	12,887	14,107
Deposits	4,382	2,940	2,808
Miscellaneous creditors	2,181	2,024	3,461
Provisions and reserves	781	939	1,110
Other liabilities	334	435	12
Price Index (1959: 100)			
consumer price	99	106	109
wholesale price	105	117	121

* All figures are given in millions of piasters.

assets and liabilities of the National Bank with the current price indexes shows a definite tendency toward inflation:[18]

The Will to Develop Economically. Although it is difficult to conclude from these figures that Viet-Nam is about to enter the phase Rostow calls "preconditions for the take-off," there are certain favorable factors of a psychological nature, in particular the will to achieve a certain economic progress, either for reasons of national prestige, or for a general well-being or individual profit. This will to progress economically has been expressed on various occasions, both in messages of the public authorities and by the press. Moreover, the average city-dweller and the better-informed men from the rural areas seem more than ever to appreciate the idea of economic development. Indeed, this determination to advance economically was preceded by an almost radical transformation in the spirit of the Vietnamese people, upon contact with the free world, whose horizons were opened to them by their political independence.[19]

This will to have an economic revolution, keeping pace with the political revolution, incurred consequences of an administrative nature. A long and tedious plan for economic development had to be made; this involved, first, a five-year plan from 1957 to 1961, then a second five-year plan. The adoption of these long-term plans required a series of administrative measures; the creation of planning services, the mobilization of internal and external resources to finance the plan, a procedure for the allocation of resources, etc. Various administrative activities had to fit, more or less, the plan adopted. Numerous economic public services must be created to correct possible maladjustments. Specialized administrators, of a sort far removed from the dilatory bureaucrat of tradition, must be mobilized. It has become clear, either as a result of the sometimes unpleasant lessons of experience or because of contact with international experts from more advanced countries, that new techniques are needed: in the planning itself, the setting up of the budget, etc.

Although the Revolutionary Government has not yet declared itself either against or in favor of the 1962–1967 five-year plan, it can be assumed that some form of development plan is necessary, and that the same administrative requirements must be fulfilled.[20]

CHANGES IN SOCIAL VALUES

These political and economic problems seem to be the ones whose solution is the most urgent. But the government still must establish another long-range policy of a social nature. According to certain authors, after the French colonial period, which lasted nearly a century and which was followed by profound changes during World War II and the struggle for independence, the basic foundations of Vietnamese society were shaken.[21]

Materialism versus Humanism.   In the eyes of the postwar generation, the Confucian order, tempered by the Buddhist philosophy of
self-denial, has become outmoded. The truth is that changes began to
occur as soon as contact with the French went beyond the purely
military stage of cultural transplantation by force. In the urban
center a middle class gradually grew up, composed of minor public
officials, employees, small merchants, and middlemen. Some members of this class succeeded with surprising rapidity during the war
in acquiring a certain amount of wealth as a result of relations with
the expeditionary forces and the French authorities. The shock was
great, particularly when the spending power of the people dwindled
before the rapidly rising cost of living. The change in values, which
had begun to appear before the war, increased rapidly. The people
realized that the Confucian superior man, no longer having the
material means to persuade the common mortal to follow him, now
had only limited prestige. Consequently, in the cities and in the ports,
any means for achieving material gain became acceptable: black
marketing, bribery, gambling, smuggling. Certain vices, tolerated by
the occupation authorities, even received semiofficial sanction: two
examples of this were the gambling firm of Cho Lon and the great
Vuon Lai prostitution establishment. The time had come to put an
end to these vices; it was all the more urgent because they threatened
to spread to the country.

The Introduction of Class Distinctions.   Certain merchants who had
speculated became large landholders, so strong was the ancient belief
in the perennial value of land, while many of the former large
landholders were taking refuge in the cities.[22] On the other hand, the
propaganda of the Viet-Minh, which had little success in the cities,
spread especially into the outlying regions, where the people were
almost completely isolated. Here the Viet-Minh promoted, on the
surface if not profoundly, ideas of class struggle in which the farmer
was opposed to the landowner. The former scale of values was no
longer respected; the idea of the relativity of human fortunes was
beginning to bother the farmers, whose Buddhist ideals of self-denial
were also beginning to be criticized. It was on this mass of rural
inhabitants, still undecided as to the route to take, that the glowing
picture of city life was to have great influence. Fleeing the insecurity
of the villages, a massive exodus of people from the farms suddenly
filled the cities, particularly Saigon.

   The balance between city and rural population was further
jeopardized by the arrival of approximately 830,000 refugees from
North Viet-Nam. These had to be relocated. A great number of these
came from rural areas; new lands had to be provided for them. The
lands left uncultivated during the war were rather extensive; swamp
lands needed to be reclaimed. There was also a serious need for

relieving the congestion in certain overpopulated provinces in Central Viet-Nam, the administration of which had long been under the influence of the Viet-Minh. Finally, certain nomadic peoples from the mountain areas needed to stabilize their way of life by settling on arable land where they might be defended against unforeseen attacks.[23]

The Ideal of the Welfare State. These social problems, however far-reaching, have a certain topical quality. Other problems, perhaps seeming less urgent but still demanding the immediate attention of the government in the first days of independence, were those of public health and education. The sanitary situation was far from satisfactory; medicine had been lacking during the war; there was the risk of displaced people carrying contagious diseases; and during the war nutrition had fallen far short of adequacy. To these factors were added the lack of sanitary installations, of medical personnel, etc. As for education, although illiteracy was not excessive, the government had set the year 1961 as the target date for a campaign against illiteracy. Primary and secondary education, particularly, was to be developed but consideration was to be given also to professional schools and universities. In short, the youth of Viet-Nam received the special attention of the government.[24]

These three factors—political, economic, and social—have had a strong influence on the philosophy of administration in Viet-Nam. To what extent did they alter the traditional philosophy? According to certain authors, in times of crisis an appeal to tradition seems a normal attitude on the part of governments. But, at the same time that the traditionalist ideology can have a retarding influence on development, the traditional norms may also have a positive influence on a people seeking to become modernized.[25] We shall first outline the principal characteristics of the traditional philosophy of this administration and then examine the main features of modern public administration in Viet-Nam.

The Traditional Philosophy of Public Administration

The word "philosophy" is used here, not to denote that science that seeks the basic truths of the universe, but to refer simply to the fundamental principles that govern human actions and that permit administrative institutions to survive. To borrow Marshall Dimock's skillful explanation, it is a combination of ethics and action, simultaneous studies of both ends and means, and concentration on the basic elements of administration.[26] The word "strategy" has often been used by both economists and students of political science to indicate the essence of administrative action. Henceforth the expression "philosophy of administration" will be used in this sense.

THE CONFUCIAN PHILOSOPHY OF ADMINISTRATION

From the historical perspective of Chapter 1, it may be presumed that the traditional philosophy of public administration in Viet-Nam, which is deep-rooted in the Vietnamese mind after ten centuries of Chinese domination and which has not been entirely replaced by the veneer of nearly a century of French domination, must continue to govern Vietnamese society, in spite of the vicissitudes this society has experienced since World War II.

Conformity to the Natural Order. By the time Confucian philosophy was introduced into Viet-Nam, it was already the product of a combination of various doctrines that had flourished during the period of the Warring States: the *yin-yang,* or negative-positive, school of which the general principles of change followed the various combinations of *am (yin)* and *duong (yang);* the *dao (tao)* school, whose founder Lao Tu (Lao-tzu) disclaimed the need for formulating laws since in order to be in harmony with Nature it was sufficient to follow *tao;* the legalist school, which stood in opposition to the *tao* school and which sought to strengthen imperial authority by establishing well-defined rules; and the *Mo* school, whose founder Mac Tu (Mo Ti) was the first to emphasize the problem of the public interest. Although the original idea of Confucius was simply that, since men live in society, human relations should be studied objectively with a view to improving that society, commentaries, in particular that of Dong Trong Thu (Tung Chung-shu), took into consideration other trends of thought, and the Confucian doctrine was considerably modified by the time the Han mandarins introduced it into Viet-Nam.[27] Although Vietnamese culture, as it developed during the nine centuries of independence, is not just a carbon copy of Chinese culture, in the following discussion of the traditional ideas retained by the Vietnamese, no attempt will be made to distinguish Vietnamese and Chinese contributions to the over-all formation of the traditional administrative philosophy of Viet-Nam.[28]

In this philosophy, primary attention should be given to the general idea of natural order, *tao,* which in Chinese thought governs all phenomena, those of Nature as well as those of men. *Tao* is the result of the harmonious meeting of the female and male principles, called *yin* and *yang.* This harmony, however, is unstable, as is the behavior of men. Social order requires a perfect synchronization between the natural course of events and men's actions.[29] If men conform to the natural order, events will follow their course normally, and there will be peace. If they transgress this natural law, such catastrophes as floods, drought, or epidemics will serve to indicate that certain attitudes or ways of living should be changed.

Many kings, in the course of Vietnamese history, have shown

themselves repentant, accusing themselves of having disturbed the natural order, and of thereby causing their people to suffer countless calamities. Under Ly Than Tong, for example, in the year 1129, an edict was proclaimed containing the following passage:

> We have little virtue; we have transgressed the order of Heaven, and upset the natural course of events; last year the spring was blighted by a long rain; this year there is a long drought. . . . Let the mandarins examine my past acts in order to discover any errors or faults, so that they may be remedied.

Similar events occurred under other kings, such as Le Nhan Ton (1449) and Thieu Tri (1844).[30] The theory of social and celestial harmony resulted in a certain stability in the existing social organization; it served also as a basis for the worship of the celestial authorities, and in this way the various official or private social activities of peoples dedicated to Confucianism came to be impregnated with a religious quality, in spite of the fact that Confucianism itself is not a religion.[31]

Government by Moral Prestige. This natural order primarily concerns the man himself. He must constantly improve himself, *tu than* (*hsiu shen*), in order to achieve for himself the ideal of the superior man, or *quan tu* (*chun tzu*). It is by striving to perfect himself that a man can be a good father to his family, or *te gia* (*ch'i chia*); and if he is able to conduct properly the affairs of his own family, he will succeed as a statesman in administering his principality or kingdom, or *tri quoc* (*chih kuo*). At the third or higher level, that of the Son of Heaven himself, or *thien tu* (*t'ien-tzu*), self-perfection and the good administration of his kingdom will help him to bring peace to the entire world—*binh thien ha* (*p'ing-t'ien-hsia*).[32] Thus, it is evident that the Son of Heaven must be extremely circumspect in his least act or deed; to this end, an etiquette was set down in great detail, governing his acts of communion with the celestial authorities (e.g., the ceremony of *Nam Giao*), his relationships with the high mandarins and his immediate collaborators, as well as his personal behavior and his relationships with his family and his subjects.[33]

It should be observed that this rigid conformity is required, not only by the normal course of events, as has been pointed out in the preceding paragraphs, but also by the voice of the people. Mencius, a disciple of Confucius, explains the various revolutions which occurred during the periods of Xuan Thu (Spring and Autumn) and of Chien Quoc (Warring States) by attributing to the people the sacred right to rebel. In Viet-Nam, a more refined doctrine taught by Le Van Huu as early as the thirteenth century, specified that Heaven creates men and gives them a king to guide them and not to satisfy his—the king's—own personal desires. Leading men into harmony with the natural order means assuring them of security and peace.[34] The same idea is expressed in a slightly different way in a saying attributed to Khuong Thoung, the minister of Vo Vuong: *Thien ha gia phi nhat nhan chi thien ha, nai thien ha nhan chi thien ha* ("The country does not belong to a single man, but to all men of the country").[35]

The Personal Nature of the Administrative Organization, Taking the Commune as the Basic Unit. In any event, the long list of types of relationship between the sovereign and his people is sufficient to show the essentially personal nature of the political and administrative organization, observed at all levels throughout the administrative hierarchy. The state stood as a large family; the Emperor represented the patriarch, the mandarians represented the other adult men, and the people represented the rest of the family— women, minors, and incompetents. Just as children were expected to carry filial devotion to the point of sacrificing their own flesh to cure their fathers, so were subjects expected to be devoted to their sovereign. Confucian doctrine included a great pyramid in which the individual family, composed of a father, a mother, and children, was included in the greater family headed by the grandfather, and so on for five generations, all of whom were part of a great clan of descendants of a single ancestor; several clans made up a village, which, grouped with other villages in the same region, made up a district, which, with other districts became a province, which was part of the empire. At each echelon, relationships were more or less comparable to those between parents and children. Although the Vietnamese administrative system interrupted this chain, stopping at the communal level and not insisting so much on the family, the quasi-personal nature of the relationships between the administrator and the people still persisted in popular tradition, and also in legislative depositions, as can be seen in the code of Hong Duc, and particularly in that of Gia Long.[36]

It cannot be overemphasized that the basic unit of the administrative organization was the commune. Here relations of a personal nature were materialized in the daily life, with the village notables at times taking part in agriculture, crafts, and family activities of the inhabitants of the commune. These inhabitants were often grouped inside a bamboo enclosure, or lived in hamlets united by rapid and easy means of communication. Religion and administration were often brought together in these contacts, which made the relations more intimate; various religious (*hoi hieu hy*), literary (*tu van*), and professional (*phuong*) associations, in which the people worked in mutual appreciation, also strengthened the ties. It is easy to understand how all community projects were administered by the assembly of notables, and how all instructions emanating from the central power through the district chief were executed with the active participation of the inhabitants of the commune. It is also easy to see how the imperial administration was able to place in the commune the double responsibility of the maintenance of order and the execution of the orders coming from the central government.[37]

But this comparison of the administrative organization with that of the family must not be carried to the point of supposing that administrative positions were hereditary, as was family property. Far from it. To clarify this point, let us consider the idea of the mandate. The emperor, the Son of Heaven, received his mandate from the Celestial Emperor; in turn, the high mandarins were the mandataries of the emperor, and so on down the line of mandarin hierarchy. As mandataries of the Son of Heaven, the mandarins were similarly obliged to dedicate themselves to virtue, to behave as honest men, and to serve as examples in the eyes of the people. It can be easily understood that this administration by example required a minimum of organization, but that the choice of administrators was of the utmost importance.[38]

The Importance of Proper Conduct and Ritual. Administration by example demanded scrupulous care in the selection of mandarins, who were the mandataries of the Son of Heaven. They could not be chosen automatically from the hereditary nobility, since it could not be taken for granted that every nobleman is a superior man. Neither could they be selected arbitrarily by the emperor from his court; although the idea of a mandate implies a certain confidence on the part of the mandator, the question of the talent and virtue of the individual had to take precedence over the will of the emperor. Hence, the selection of mandarins was made by means of examinations based on the teachings of the classics. These classics analyzed in detail the three basic elements of social ethics, *tam cuong* (*san-kang*), corresponding to three of the five fundamental relationships, and also analyzed the five basic virtues, *ngu thuong* (*wu-ch'ang*), of the individual. These three elements of social ethics concern the relationships between the ruler and his subjects, *quan than* (*chun-ch'en*); those between father and son, *phu tu* (*fu-tzu*); and those between husband and wife, *phu phu* (*fu-fu*). The five basic virtues are: *nhan* (*jen*), or human-heartedness; *nghia* (*yi*), or righteousness; *le* (*li*), or proper conduct according to ritual; *tri* (*chih*), or wisdom; and *tin* (*hsin*), or good faith. These virtues make the superior man, *quan tu* (*chun-tzu*), as opposed to the common man, *tieu nhan* (*hsiao-jen*). The superior man is thus the generous man, who sets a sense of dignity above his own interests; he is constant in that he must refrain from hating that which he has loved and from harming those to whom he has previously been kind. Similarly, he must fulfill all explicit and implicit promises arising from his acts and attitudes. He must never allow himself to be led by resentment or grudge.

These details of the behavior of the superior man formed the subject matter of the dissertations in the mandarinal examinations.[39]

Furthermore, the elements of social ethics and the virtues were represented in precise rituals. These rituals derive from the idea that in Nature, as in society, each thing and each man has a certain role, designated by a specific name. It is only with the proper name that a man is able to communicate adequately: this is the doctrine of the rectification of names, *danh chinh ngon thuan* (*ming chang yen shun*). The materialization of the appropriate functions were effected by specific rituals, whether they concerned the relationships between the emperor and his subjects (*trieu*), those between the mandarins and the people (*quan*), those between the notables of the commune and the villagers (*huong am tuu*), occasioned by religious ceremonies (*te*), or purely private relationships, such as marriage (*hon*), burial (*tang*), etc.[40]

It was necessary to be a scholar in order to study these complicated rituals. These scholars analyzed the ancient texts profoundly—in the long run it was they who discovered that Confucianism and legalism each has its own sphere of application: Confucianism is concerned with the social organization, moral and spiritual culture, and studies; legalism can be restricted to the principles and techniques of government.[41]

The Reconciliation of Humanism with Legalism. Although Confucian thought, which was essentially pragmatic, insisted on the human aspect in public relations between the officials and the people, certain scholars, even during the life of the Master, advocated that, particularly in troubled times, emperors and kings should make strict decrees providing severe punishment for those who tried to disturb public order. This legalist school, of which Han Phi Tu (Han Fei Tzu) was the principal leader, had a far-reaching influence. Its theories were based on the principle that man is by nature wicked and that severe rules must be set down in order to curb his conduct. This was contrary to the theories of Mencius, who believed in the basic goodness of man. In its original form, this Legalist school to aid in the unification of the Universal Empire of Ts'in Che Houang Ti, went as far as to recommend the abolition of all social traditions (e.g., family solidarity, ancestor worship). This would weaken and isolate the individual, who would then be defenseless before a mammoth state. This meant a change of concept: the emperor, instead of being the sovereign of men, or *nhan quan* (*jen chun*), became their master, *nhan chu* (*jen chu*). This School was responsible for the great administrative centralization which occurred in China under Ts'in Che Houang Ti, and which his successors applied subsequently in Viet-Nam, then a Chinese colony. When the Han emperors came to power they set about gradually restoring Confucian principles, and retained of this legalist doctrine only the great idea of centralization, with certain legal consequences. The first domain of legality includes all human actions which affect public order. These actions occur in the five fundamental relationships already mentioned. Infractions of certain rules in these domains were severely punished by law. The second domain of legality included public finances and taxation; here also infractions of rules set down by the public authorities brought on corporal or pecuniary punishment. A third domain of legality involved military service and *corvées*. Countless imperial decrees prescribed punishment for those who disturbed the public order.[42] Little by little there developed two categories of mandarins: the *khoc lai* (*k'u-li*), or oppressive officials, who leaned towards the legalistic school and who were faithful to the doctrine of centralization; and the *thuan lai* (*hsun-li*), or principled officials, associates of the local elite, who sought to develop local cultures insofar as they were not contrary to the teachings of Confucius.[43]

The alliance between the legalist and humanist schools was brought about under the Hans in the following manner: it was understood that, except for those things forbidden and punishable by law, the people—and the administrators—were, practically speaking, free to do as they wished as long as they conformed to the natural order. Still, it is not rare for administrators to intervene in the family or social life of the people, either to settle a problem in a friendly way or to recommend a course of action. The history of Viet-Nam has seen many great administrators who have made particular achievements in the promotion of the well-being of the people; for example, Nguyen Cong Tru, whose name is linked with the conquest and colonization of the maritime provinces along the Gulf of Tonkin; and Dao Duy Tu, who helped the Nguyen lords establish solidly the Nguyen Dynasty in South Viet-Nam. The lower the rank of an administrator in the hierarchy (province chief, district chief, village chief, etc.), the more often he was called upon to intervene in the private life of the people. It must not be forgotten, however, that the Confucian principle of the natural order was reinforced by taoist thought, and that, according to the latter, in order to achieve communion with *Tao*, that ultimate reality in which opposites harmonize, it is necessary to avoid any vain or unreasonable activity and to let things run their natural course.[44] This intervention of the administrator must then be regarded more as advising or teaching than as deciding matters for the individual. It is very important to understand thoroughly this traditional philosophy of administration: within the sphere of action not expressly forbidden by law, the administrator did not act directly, but satisfied himself with teaching by example. From this, all the logic of the system becomes apparent: not being bound to positive action, the administrator was not disposed to do any planning, either long-range or short-range.

Furthermore, the fact of "acting" through counsel implies intermittent intervention, essentially empirical. The administrator was obliged to take positive action only in important political events (struggles against foreign enemies—in particular China—many incidents of which are found in the history of Viet-Nam), expansion toward the South under the pressures of an increasing population, or widespread calamities (flood, drought, or epidemics). Even then, empiricism prevailed over rationalism, although not infrequently great administrators necessarily had recourse to some planning, particularly in agricultural development and territorial expansion. Naturally, in the course of administrative routine, the mandarin was also obliged to take some positive measures: the levying of taxes, the raising of troops, the assignment of *corvées*, etc.; but these duties were so minimal and so regular that there was no need for any strict or detailed planning. Considered in this more general context of humanist philosophy, this sort of government can hardly be called pseudomorphic.[45]

The Confusion of Policy Making with Policy Implementing.   It must also be understood that there was scarcely any distinction between general policy and public administration. Since the supreme powers were concentrated in the monarch it was he who determined the general outlines of governmental policy. Being himself the illustrious mandatary of Heaven, he did not have to consult the will of the people beforehand through elected representatives. Similarly, the mandarins at each echelon, being his mandataries, performed their duties according to what they believed to be in keeping with the natural order, and, of course, in keeping with the directives of the emperor. In order to do this, the mandarins consulted quite informally the principal persons in the locality: retired former mandarins; scholars of a high reputation who did not enter the mandarinal competitions, or who, having been accepted, preferred not to become mandarins; and important landowners (designated by their degree of wealth: *thien ho, van ho, ba ho,* etc.). This gentry formed a kind of unofficial council for the mandarins in their search for conformity to the natural order of things in the framework of the locality. Thus, it would be difficult to draw a line between the domain of politics and the domain of administration. This was naturally true for a nation still in the farming-economy stage, as Viet-Nam was during the first Chinese domination; it was also true of Viet-Nam during the entire period of independence, when royal power was being consolidated and centralization was so far advanced that Viet-Nam, like China, could be called a "hydraulic state" since it had "large-scale works of irrigation and flood control." [46] Besides, a purely agricultural economy did not pose many problems in the way of administrative policy: aside from the maintenance of general order and flood control, there were few or no traffic problems, no problem of crowded or unsanitary slums, no problems of road repairs or public lighting. The principle of minimizing the intervention of public officials tended to exclude also economic intervention, with the exception of agrarian reforms linked to the traditional conception of the emperor's eminent domain, under which an individual was authorized to exploit certain land against the payment of a fee, which later came to be regarded as a property tax. The same principle also excluded all social intervention, although from time to time the emperors advised the people to set up public granaries against eventual famine, or decided to intensify the teaching of the classics among the various layers of the population. In short, the idea of public administration as a series of positive services rendered to the people according to a set program seems to have been almost unknown under the imperial regime.

THE FRENCH CONCEPT OF ADMINISTRATION

It has already been pointed out that, in the first days of their occupation, the French felt a certain admiration for the Vietnamese administrative system, and, on the advice of intelligent public servants, such as E. Luro and J. Sylvestre, the colonial authorities decided from the beginning to intervene as little as possible in the native administration. However, faced with the attitude of noncollaboration on the part of many of the mandarins, and also under the pressure of modern needs, France was obliged to create institutions modeled after those of Europe and bearing only a vague resemblance to native Vietnamese institutions.

Administrative Centralization and Weberian Bureaucracy. First, the agencies indispensable to the setting up of the colonial policy were organized in the French manner: the General Government and the so-called general bureaus, such as the Finance Office, the Personnel Office, the Public Works Bureau, and so on, and at the regional level, a governor or a resident superior, assisted by local agencies. French influence was also reflected in a semblance of consultation with the people concerning serious decisions affecting the colony: the creation of a Grand Council of Economic and Financial Interests, composed of elected French members and a certain number of appointed Indochinese members, which was to give its advice on the budget of Indochina and other important federal matters; and the creation at the regional level of a Colonial Council (in Cochinchina) and of a French Council of Economic and Financial Interests alongside a Chamber of People's Representatives (in Tonkin and in Annam).[47] In actual practice, these assemblies served for consultation only, since final decisions always fell to the governor-general, or in some instances, to the president of the French Republic. Thus, the general organization lines of the administrative offices, as well as those of personnel and finance administration, were borrowed directly from the Napoleonic tradition of centralization. Gradually, as the economy of the country developed, as new activities were introduced, regulations brought greater government intervention in the economic life of the country, especially when it was a question of preserving the interests of the colonists. The General Government on occasion even engaged in certain remunerative activities designed to increase the budget (monopolies on alcohol, salt, opium, matches, etc.); thus the idea of government enterprise was introduced into Indochinese administration.

A corps of French administrators was created to direct the general bureaus and various regional administrative offices. Although some French administrators demonstrated a certain selflessness and loftiness of purpose, it is certain that they could not have been expected to consider their functions as sacred duty, particularly since they came from a country governed by a market economy. It was to be expected that they would take into consideration the high salary and the other material advantages which accompanied their positions.[48] On the other hand, because of the legalistic nature of their training, they tended to show the characteristics of bureaucracy as defined by Weber: their functions as public servants were clearly established both by their position and by the organic service orders; the general organization followed the principle of the hierarchy; the operations were executed according to a previously defined procedure, impersonally, without hatred and without passion; the assignments of public servants were made with respect to the accepted qualifications of their status. All these trends led to a sort of efficiency, which only an industrial civilization could appreciate.[49] These French administrators were seconded by native personnel whose numbers and responsibilities increased gradually as the improvement of public instruction enabled intelligent persons to earn the higher degrees that made them eligible for these positions. Naturally, the native assistants of the French administrators, restricted to a secondary role, did not dream of aspiring to serve as examples of conduct for their compatriots, as the mandarins had done.

Expansion of Colonial Legality. Both the French and the Vietnamese were obliged to obey the law, for the rule of law is a great principle which governs all French administration. A Conseil de Contentieux (Administrative Claims Council) was responsible for seeing to the proper application of laws and regulations by the administrators, and decisions of this council could be appealed to the French Conseil d'Etat (Council of State).

Nevertheless, the French have defined colonial law in a rather specialized sense. Although French laws govern automatically all

French people residing in the colonies—as well as others who have acquired French citizenship—in the private affairs of the colonists this is not the case. A specially formulated law was promulgated by the Senatus Consultum of May 3, 1854, making certain French laws applicable to the colony; other regulations having the force of laws, pronounced by the president of the Republic in his position as colonial legislator, were promulgated by the governor-general of Indochina. As for the natives of the countries of the protectorate, the laws emanated from the emperor of Annam, but had to be promulgated by the governor-general in order to have the force of law.[50]

This legalistic tendency had advantages, but also shortcomings. It contributed greatly to the clarification of certain ideas concerning public administration that had been rather vague in the time of the emperors: (1) the concepts of centralization and decentralization, concentration and delegation of powers—which are well known to French administrators, and which shed new light on the imperial administrative organization; (2) the ideas of the *fonction publique* (civil service system), in which the duties and prerogatives of the public servants were clearly specified by law, and even more finely determined by a jurisprudence set down by administrative courts; (3) the idea of *personnalité morale*, that a corporation or society or even a government body might have separate legal status as a person; and (4) the entire legal concept of public works—the eminent domain of the government, its position as a contractor and a builder, and its responsibility for these works.

These ideas were introduced little by little to regulate the relationships between the government and the people. This legalistic tendency has often been criticized for its excessive proliferation of forms, procedures, and endless legal mysteries, which often bind the honest administrator hand and foot and, at the same time, shield or even encourage the negligence or the breaches of trust of the corrupt official. It must be said that these criticisms are justified in certain spheres of administration, in which French laws were automatically applicable in the colony without any special formalities. But even in the so-called colonial domain of administration, where the share of *compétence liée* (i.e., strict adherence to the rule of law) was reduced to a minimum and the administrator had considerable discretionary power, that very fact often effectively paved the way for misuse of authority.[51]

Reduction of the Scope of Native Administration. The above-mentioned phenomenon can be explained by the fact that, although the jurisdiction of French administration was constantly increasing, still a very large sphere of action was left for what the French authorities called "native administration." In all fields that belonged to the traditional administration (police, justice, taxes, and *corvées*), the

French attempted to maintain, insofar as was possible, the former administrative framework. It has already been shown that this framework consisted essentially of an *administration by men,* resting on the principle of common sense and equity. This meant that, except in certain specific instances, the laws and regulations concerning native matters were very indefinite and left a great freedom of action to the native administrator. To the extent that the French administrator supervised the decisions of the native administrator, it can be said that the discretionary powers of the latter were almost unlimited.[52]

However, the behavior itself of the native administrators altered somewhat upon contact with the French administrators. More and more frequently educated in law schools, the native administrators tended to respect the laws and regulations so scrupulously that administrative action was often forestalled by the faulty wording of a document or by the expiration of a time limit. On the other hand, trained in the economic ideals of the capitalist doctrine, they also tended to follow the advice of the *homo oeconomicus,* interested more in the lucrative aspect of public service than in the idealistic aspect. With this modification of the conception of the *fonction publique,* discretionary powers became an evil. Although saving face, which in the administrative hierarchy was represented by priorities or doing the honors in official ceremonies, continued to govern human relationships at the village or canton level, some people were disposed to buy communal public offices, in order to obtain these prerogatives, rather than to acquire the true esteem of the people by simply acting as honest leaders. This also contributed to the misuse of discretionary powers.[53]

Under the pretext of establishing stricter control, the French administrator intervened more and more directly in the affairs of the so-called native administrator. The vacillations between the policies of association and assimilation mentioned earlier can be explained by the contradiction between the principle of the superiority of law that he was to obey and that of the administration by men which was to prevail in the native sphere. However, a rather unexpected consequence resulted from this vacillation, for the greater good of independent Viet-Nam: the stage was being progressively set for the introduction of the principle of legality even at the lowest levels of the administrative hierarchy. Indeed, in order to apply the principle of the priority of the law, it was important to develop an effective communication system, with a satisfactory system of control, which would permit the free flow of information between the upper and lower echelons. Although means of communication and transportation, such as roads, waterways, postal service, telegraph, and even the telephone were not specified, the principle came to be more and more accepted that one of the most important objectives of the administration was to develop to the maximum at least the communication between the administrators at intermediate levels and those responsible for the general policy.

The Increasing Size of the Colonial Budget. Every step of the development of the material means of administration was attended by a parallel development in public finance. It became important to find more sources of financing for colonial activities; at the same time, because of the size of the budget, a stricter system of control was needed to insure careful use of the always limited financial resources. Although it was out of the question to grant the native population the right to vote on taxes and the budget, nevertheless the French government devised a form of consultation with the people in these matters, at the province, regional, and national levels, by the creation of province councils, assemblies of people's representatives, and the Grand Council of Economic and Financial Interests. Once a semblance of the principle of consent to taxes was established, the French maintained their sovereignty over budgetary matters by requiring the formal approval of each budget by the immediately superior authority.[54]

This required the instituting of detailed accounting rules covering the preparation and execution of the budgets. All that was necessary was to apply the rules used in France where the same suspicion existed between the representatives of the people and the government. Indeed, just as the financial powers of the president of the French Republic in his relationships with the Legislative Assembly were limited by rules covering the unity, comprehensiveness, and integrity of the annual budget and specifying the appropriations, so these same rules might contribute to the limitation of the powers of the colonial governors in their relationships with the French authorities, who intended to see that the expenditures of the colonies should serve well their imperial objectives.

In short, the French superimposed a legalist philosophy, which entailed a sometimes antiquated formalism and was conceived along the lines of a market economy in which competition automatically brings about a certain balance, upon an essentially Confucian background, which was based on the principle of striving to make human relationships conform as much as possible to the natural balance of the universe by following rather strict rituals. The result was a real administrative dualism, with a Westernized sector, including the capital, the urban centers, and the French holdings, set in juxtaposition to a traditional sector in which communication and commerce were considerably restricted.

This dualism, well-defined at the beginning, tended to become more and more indistinct as the Vietnamese, through education, imitation, and a slow assimilation of culture, discovered that it was to their interest to adopt the dominating system, with its superior force and other economic powers. This assimilation was cut short by events resulting from World War II and the subsequent independence of Viet-Nam.

Outlining a Modern Philosophy of Administration

How does the data that we have summed up in the beginning of this chapter modify the traditional philosophy of public administration previously defined?

The Principle of Legality.   The first principle that should be emphasized is the principle of legality. This was a French contribution, but one that was in no way contradictory to the Sino-Vietnamese conception of public administration. This principle has been proclaimed many times by the authorities of the Republic of Viet-Nam. Immediately after the referendum that deposed Bao Dai and established the Republic (October 25, 1955), a temporary Constitutional Act (October 26, 1955) specified that all existing laws and regulations were to remain in force insofar as they were not contrary to the new republican regime. During the First Republic, official messages affirmed the principle of the protection of the law, understood in a special way: according to this official doctrine, the laws and regulations of the nation must harmonize the contradictions between individual liberty and centralization. In other words, the citizen must be free within the limits of legality; his possessions, his liberty, and his life must be protected by the law. It has been pointed out that in underdeveloped countries these principles often are not applied integrally, particularly at the commune level, because the villagers are not prepared for it. But the government was determined to insure the complete application of the principle of legality defined above by means of the strategic hamlets, i.e., the smallest territorial administrative units.[55]

Behind this legality, there still exists the human person, whose full development, both as an individual and as a member of society, must be respected. According to the preamble of the Constitution of the First Republic, personalism constituted the official doctrine of the state: "Confident in the transcendent values of the human person, whose free, harmonious and complete development on the individual as well as on the communal plane must be the object of all state activity. . . ."

The preceding statement to a certain extent expresses in modern technical terms the old Vietnamese thought with its preponderance of Confucianism. It is not surprising that on each anniversary of Confucius, an official message emphasized the similarity between this personalist doctrine and Confucian thought. On September 28, 1962, the message contained the following: "I ask our compatriots to recall the Confucian principle that man is contiguous with the path of virtue. Human-heartedness must thus govern man in his integrity, the human person itself, composed of the individual in his higher spiritual aspirations and in his relations with his fellow men." [56]

What constitutes the value of man, what places him at the summit of the hierarchy of living beings, is, precisely, his soul. The cultivation of the soul implies freedom of action, freedom of thought, religious freedom, and freedom of association.[57] But this is not a purely organic liberty that permits the individual to do whatever he wishes; it is, rather, a functional liberty that should permit the human person to develop fully, with a view to realizing his social goals. Thus it was to be expected that the president of the First Republic would demand discipline, moral strictness, and the sacrifice of certain leisure and comforts so that society could develop, since only with the full development of society will the human person be able to realize his own supreme goals.

Still, as one author has justly said, "Personalism risks degenerating into a doctrinal justification of political coercion and oppression." [58] Indeed, in its last years, the Ngo Dinh Diem government did become a veritable dictatorship, so much so that even its policy of severe repression could not prevent outbursts of dissatisfaction.[59] Although the personalist republic was overthrown, the new republican government proclaimed the principle of legality in the Provisional Constitution Act of November 4, 1963, which officially maintains in force all laws and regulations effective before the revolution, except those that are contrary to the spirit of the revolution.[60] The question now arises whether all—or only some—of the applications of the doctrine of personalism are to be considered contrary to the spirit of the revolution. This spirit of revolution seems to be reflected in the following slogans from the revolutionary government's program of action: [61] "Liberty and Democracy"; "Justice and Happiness"; and "Independence and Unification."

Humanistic Bureaucracy. It is curious that the principle of legality was somewhat reinforced by the doctrine of personalism, insofar as the basic concepts of this doctrine were expressed in laws, such as agrarian reform laws, laws relating to the improvement of women's rights, and moral improvement laws. This legislation seemed to interfere more in the private life of the individual, and lent itself to increased administrative action.

However, the principle of legality seems to have been tempered by the appeal of the Ngo Dinh Diem government to the virtue and morality which are the basis of personalism. A major example of this is the fact that the Constitution of the First Republic invested the president with the role of national leader—thus placing him above parties and powers—and conferred upon him a moral power over the nation.[62] This power is comparable to that of the chief of state in the old Confucian concept, with the difference that here the president is elected by the people and is not a mandatary of Heaven. When the Constitution was promulgated, the press greeted this provision as a good omen for the administration, since Ngo Dinh Diem himself set the example of a simple and temperate life designed to encourage the proper conduct of public servants and to curb the misappropriation of public funds.[63] Although Ngo Dinh Diem later gave instructions that actions that might be interpreted as leaning toward a personality cult should be ruled out of administrative life, in reality a personality cult *was* created, leading to a veritable autocracy.[64]

Nevertheless, the influence of the old Confucian tradition was still strong, and an interministerial committee was established to develop a broad program of studies (*phong trao hoc tap*) for public officials, emphasizing the three basic virtues of the superior man of Confucian tradition: *nhan* (*jen*), or human-heartedness; *tri* (*chih*), or wisdom; and *dung* (*yung*), or courage; or more specifically, the four virtues of the ideal public servant: *thanh* (*ch'ing*), or simplicity; *can* (*ch'in*), or industriousness; *liem* (*lian*), or honesty; and *chinh* (*cheng*), or rectitude.[65] It should be noted that, in spite of repeated appeals to his patriotism, the civil servant understood that these appeals were not based on loyalty in the Confucian sense of fidelity to the person of the chief of state, nor on filial piety—which served as a basis for this fidelity—according to which the son-father relationship was analogous to that between mandarin and sovereign. He seemed to discriminate naturally between those virtues which were capable of being reconciled with the exigencies of modern life and those which definitely belonged to the past.[66]

The enumeration of these virtues is sufficient to show how much importance the public authorities, as well as the people themselves, attached to the morals of public officials. This is a far cry from a purely legalistic system in which the public servant is simply one cog among many in a great machine, with no other responsibility than to perform conscientiously the duties assigned to him by laws and regulations. This cult of virtue, taken in a broad sense, does not seem to be a simple backward step toward the old tradition. A comparative study of governments would show that, even in advanced countries, an important trend of thought favors the selection of administrators from among men of good character who are motivated by certain ideals of independence and honesty and are able to communicate their ideas and enthusiasm to the men around them. Needless to say, this cult of virtue does not go so far as to become a personality cult.[67]

In short, a legal framework alone is not sufficient to regulate all administrative activity; the government depends on a complete change in the soul of the public servant himself. Not only must he demonstrate a remarkable spirit of self-sacrifice; his behavior must serve as an example to the people as well. Without resorting either to the language of personalism or to that of Confucianism, the Revolutionary Government also urges civil servants to follow these precepts and to continue the programs of study in a spirit of self-improvement.[68]

Development Administration and the Integration of Policy Making and Policy Implementing.   If so great a sacrifice is demanded on the part of the public servant, it is because the government must wage a determined warfare against three major enemies: communism, disunity, and underdevelopment, or as they were called in the official slogans of the First Republic: *Giac Cong San, Giac Chia Re, Giac Cham Tien.* Public servants are asked to work actively and without delay in promoting this governmental policy and to enter into the spirit of development administration, so that one wonders if the new administrative philosophy is not taking a firm position on the side of nonseparation of politics and administration.[69] Although favored by the old tradition, this new administrative philosophy seems to constitute a radical change. French administrative tradition, well established since the time of Napoleon, demanded that the administration be entirely separated from politics; there is an old French saying that testifies to the strength of French administration: "Governments change but the administration remains the same." In the colonial government, this principle permitted the exclusion of the native public servants from participation in political activities; this simply meant exclusion from all attempts at resistance against colonial authority. Moreover, this principle of separation of politics and administration seems to find theoretical justification in the well-established French tradition of the separation of powers: the authority for establishing laws, i.e., for setting down the general principles of action for the country, was vested in the legislature, while the power of executing the laws, of applying them at a given time and under given circumstances, was vested in the executive body. In more current terminology, this principle is derived from the idea of separation of functions: the political function consists of "determining, defining and declaring the will of the community," and the administrative function consists of "applying this will, once it has been made clear by the political procedure." [70] More recently it has been further affirmed that the principle of separation of politics and administration must always be considered an "ideal goal," since the most successful administration seems to be the one which is maintained almost entirely separate from politics.[71]

This gives us cause to wonder why the administrative system of the First Republic seemed to run counter to such well-established theories and practices. This attitude of the government cannot be explained as a simple reaction against colonial tradition, nor can it be explained on a purely theoretical level by pointing out that many people do not share the opinions of the authors quoted. Since the government is becoming the super-holding company in the economic life of the nation, a new theory of the division of powers will be needed—the division between policy veto, on one side, and policy planning and execution, on the other.[72] According to another author, as soon as there is any discretionary power, there is politics; the lowest ranking public servant is involved in politics if he has any discretionary power.[73] Other writers point out that the higher public officials play an essentially political role, since they must maintain good relations with a widely varied public, from the legislative representative to the simplest citizen.[74]

In many older democratic nations, the principle of the separation of politics and administration seems also to be unknown: thus, the British parliamentary system includes the Crown, the cabinet, and the civil service, and all three share both policy-making and administrative functions.[75] Even in France, the saying *"Le gouvernement change, l'administration reste"* concerns only holders of political and administrative posts in the strictest sense, but not the functions of policy making and policy implementation, which are shared by the legislative and executive branches.[76]

The question of theory aside, the administrative policy of Viet-Nam can be justified on traditional as well as practical grounds. The First Republic appealed to the great Confucian principles in the conduct of public affairs. In accordance with Confucian doctrine all public powers are centered in the ruler, who receives his mandate from Heaven; the mandarins, as his mandataries, are to a less extent similarly endowed with these powers. Administrators, therefore, participate in politics to the extent that they are obliged to make decisions, within the very general framework of directives drawn up by the government.

The word "politics" can be construed in two ways. On the one hand, it can refer to the struggle for power. In this sense it is dangerous to link politics with administration, since it means introducing an essentially unstable element into a system which requires continuity. Public officials are changed when the politics of the government changes (the spoils system), and influential politicians primarily interested in the profit or power obtained from political office, seek to interfere with the administration. On the other hand, the word "politics" can mean simply the direction a nation gives to governmental activities. In this sense, the administration cannot be separated from politics, since its purpose is to uphold the policies of the government. When the government of Viet-Nam asks its administrators to enter into "politics," it seems to be understood in this latter sense.[77]

Another reason might be that, in spite of the rule of law, a country resolutely dedicated to economic development lacks, in several respects, basic legislation concerning the new activities of the state; administrators at the various levels often must make important decisions on economic or administrative matters, subject to approval by the chief executive.[78] Article 3 of the Constitution of the First Republic appointed the chief of state the "leader of the nation." In this role, he could authorize his subordinates to make decisions concerning policies of development. It should be noted further that the problem of decentralization is somewhat different from that of participation in policy formation. Without prejudice to the present government of Viet-Nam, we believe that an administrative system can include policy in its sphere of activity and at the same time progress toward centralization, as long as the public servants participate in the formulating of policy as well as in its execution.

Finally, there seems to be a general rule in newer countries that the administrative system develops rapidly when the political institutions are not yet too well established. It is therefore important that the public servants be imbued with the broad political principles of the moment and possess that national conscience which was lacking among the collaborators of the colonial administration.[79]

Since the November 1 Revolution, the Revolutionary Government has also been granted legislative functions, with the exception of budgetary and fiscal powers; these remain the province of the Military Revolutionary Council. The question may well be asked whether the integration of policy-making functions with policy implementation is not strengthened by this measure, as it is by the tendency to promote more and more active participation of the people in administrative activities.

Citizen Participation in Administrative Activities and Emphasis on Local Government. One form of popular participation in administration, by far the most general, is community development (*phat trien cong dong*), which was related by the theoreticians of the First Republic to the personalist doctrine: personalism (*nhan vi*), community (*cong dong*), and common progress (*dong tien*). It is perhaps more scientific to explain the idea of community development by the notion of small groups. The citizen of the small community is expected to realize fully and on his own initiative the obvious interests of the community: the construction of small dikes to protect the rice paddies from flooding, the digging of small drainage canals, the building of a primary school or kindergarten, and so on. Aware of the usefulness of these projects, he willingly contributes physical if not financial assistance to their completion, the more readily since in an agricultural economy there exist many periods of forced or concealed idleness. Of course, his interest in the realization of these works will be all the greater if he knows that the government is in a position to help him substantially in the technical planning of the projects, in the use of machines, in financing a part of the works, and in appealing for co-operation to the inhabitants of neighboring regions.[80]

Participation of citizens is the most active at the lowest levels of the administrative hierarchy: the basic organizations called "new life hamlets" (*ap dan sinh*)—formerly called "strategic hamlets" (*ap chien luoc*)—which are subdivided into "family groups" (*lien gia*) in the country [81] or into "new life wards" (*khom dan sinh*) and family groups in the urban centers. In these various organizations, the citizens, women as well as men, participate in defense, education, mutual aid, and relief. The "new life hamlet" is not a mere unit of defense against subversive activities; it is the new form, adapted to the development of modern technology, of the traditional village in which the sense of public interest was advanced to a very high degree, in which the inhabitants knew that they must count particularly on themselves, and in which they formulated their own rules of conduct, even to the point of counteracting those laws of the kingdom which became too interfering. The emphasis at present is on the active participation of the people, especially in the lower echelons of the rural administration, in order to eliminate all complaint regarding the concentration of administrative efforts only on the cities.[82]

Since the young people make up the group with the greatest energy and altruism, they are often called upon to collaborate in the work of community development and in many other tasks, in particular, the education of the illiterate and the defense of the towns and villages against aggressive or subversive activities of Communist guerrillas. Not only do the young men take part in administrative activities, but young women also play an active role in the defense of the village. In certain cases, the young people of the First Republic were even trained so they could operate various administrative agencies at the village level in case of the absence of the village authorities.

In the upper echelon, participation of the citizens is through the provincial councils. Despite the fact that a decree provided for the election of councilors by the people, owing to the state of emergency the province councils of the First Republic were appointed by the secretary of state for the interior; after 1962 they played a certain role in the provincial administration through deliberation on the budget and through advice given in various important administrative matters, such as the acquisition of real estate and the allocation of contracts for public works.[83] The Revolutionary Government has recently promulgated a series of decrees providing for elections to "citizens' councils in all cities, provinces, and villages." [84] It has also organized a Civil Defense Service, in which all citizens between the ages of 20 and 45 must participate.[85]

The National Assembly also constituted participation of the people in the administration inasmuch as the Assembly voted on the budget and on various resolutions of an administrative nature.[86] The many arbitration committees in economic and social domains, in which both sides are equally represented, are another form of participation of citizens in administrative activities. Examples are committees for the settling of disputes resulting from the operations of agrarian reform and committees for smoothing out difficulties created by the application of labor laws. Shortly after the November 1 Revolution, the Military Revolutionary Council created a Council of Notables, recruited from persons well known in intellectual, commercial, industrial, and agricultural circles, to give advice on important matters regarding public life. This Council was subsequently dissolved, to be replaced by an elected Constituent Assembly.[87] A more recent example of citizen participation is the establishment of the Press Council, composed exclusively of editors of newspapers and reviews, elected by a general assembly of press representatives. This council is organized for the defense of the freedom of the press, as well as for the maintaining of journalistic discipline in times of national crisis.[88]

The Revolutionary Government affirms categorically that "to raise the standard of the political parties of the nation, in order to realize a truly democratic and popularly elected regime, the Government advocates the encouragement of open political activities." [89]

This formal participation in the making of decisions as well as in the execution of projects is complemented by a certain informal participation, by the fact that the citizens in various functions are members of professional or social groups and thus contribute to the forming of recommendations for the councils. These recommendations the administrators take into consideration, not by formal obedience to a majority vote, but in the more subtle form of decisions made after consultation with the interested parties. It might be said that this is a tendency to render institutions more democratic, if we break away from the narrowness of the common concept of democracy.[90] As a matter of fact, the word "democratic" in its original sense refers to a government in which the citizen must be at once the object, the instrument, and the author of the politics of the nation—"government of the people, by the people, for the people." In other words, the participation of the citizens is an instrument of democratic government; the achievement of independence returns the government to the people, and the goals to which the government is dedicated are the well-being of the population and the economic and social development of the country. Whether interest groups are spontaneous or co-ordinated or whether they are organized for the purpose of public control or for population regimentation, the very fact of their existence shows the extent to which citizens participate in administrative activities.[91]

The Importance of Technique. In order for the public servant to participate effectively in the general policy of the nation, or for him to encourage citizens to participate in administrative activities, it is not sufficient that he be inspired with respect for the law and anxious to cultivate his own virtues. In the current Vietnamese administrative philosophy, much importance is also attached to technical methods. In order to achieve the goals set by the government, the public servant must know the various techniques of his specialty, and must constantly adapt this knowledge to the demands of economic and social development. If administration is an art from the humanistic point of view, from the technical point of view it is a science. There was a real surge of interest in the science of public administration in Viet-Nam when the first American experts came to speak of the principal elements in the breakdown of administrative action, in the famous POSDCORB (see page 85), of Gulick analyzing "scientific management" and the efficiency of the public bureaus. There was a time when the principal ministries were provided with experts, or consultants for the reorganization of public offices and the establishing of new procedures.[92] Other American experts assisted in the linear programing experiments of the Budget Office.[93] It was even proposed that an electronic computer be acquired to evaluate the data assembled by the IBM machines with which certain offices were equipped. (A Vietnamese delegate to the Conference of the International Institute of Administrative Sciences in Wiesbaden in July, 1959, emphasized the fact that, in new countries where such equipment is still nonexistent, it is easier to import new techniques with ultramodern equipment than it is in older countries where the major problem is to know what to do with old equipment that has become obsolescent but could still be used for a long time.) [94]

  This passion for adopting modern techniques continues, and has opened new horizons for administrative science. The authorities soon realized that administrative science, dependent as it is on the study of man's behavior, demands that pure technique be reconciled with the needs of human relations. A great quantity of practical literature has been written to serve as the basis for discussion of these questions in study sessions for various officials. The National Institute of Administration has championed this idea of human relations in many articles written for the benefit of public servants in office and published in the magazine *Tien Thu* (Progress). Thanks to the advance in the studies of administrative science, the West has joined the East in attaching importance to the personality of the administrator and to human relations. It seems proper here to apply the distinction between technics and techniques, so well stated by another author: "Part of the technology is hedged about by sanctions, and is therefore included in the social order (animals for food, for instance, may be killed only in a ritually prescribed manner). Other parts of a given technology may be almost wholly free of entangling sanctions. The former are group *techniques;* the latter are group *technics.*" [95] The problems of procedure, accounting, and material organization lend themselves much more easily and quickly to the application of modern technics, while the techniques of personnel administration and of decision making encounter a certain resistance due to tradition.[96] Moreover, in this tendency toward modern techniques, the rationalization of tradition denudes it of all sacred characteristics, so that it is also ready for eventual changes, if they seem desirable.[97]

In this chapter, it has been shown that the essential features of the philosophy of administration are the priority of law, the development of human personality on the part of the public official, the integration of politics and administration, a more and more effective participation of the people in administrative activities, and the improvement of administrative techniques. The main goal of this philosophy is to bring about a harmonious but rapid economic and social development. We shall see how these various principles can be reconciled in practice by studying the following problems: (1) the administrative structure (Part II), (2) the material means of administrative action (Part III), and (3) the administrative action proper (Part IV).

PART II

ADMINISTRATIVE STRUCTURE: RATIONALITY VERSUS EMPIRICISM

WHEN AN administrative philosophy is formed, either sub-consciously, after long practice, or through the conscious will of political leaders, it materializes into certain forms of action, such as the regulation of activities of individuals in certain situations; the performance of certain services of a diffuse nature (e.g., the assurance of public security), or of a concrete nature (e.g., public education); the providing of certain material advantages (e.g., aid to flood victims); or, as has already been shown in Part I, simply the example set by a virtuous leader. These activities can be regarded as reciprocal relations between persons occupying positions in the government and the entire body of persons composing society. The relations that develop between the interested parties within the central government or in a village administration constitute the structure of these political entities. But the central government and the village administration do not exist only in order to exist; they fill certain specific roles with regard to the population; they perform certain functions. Each structure-function complex forms an institution.

Thus, the central government is an administrative institution. The relationships between the prime minister and his ministers and those between the prime minister and the director of the Cabinet at the Office of the Prime Minister are examples of the kind of relationships that make up the structure of the central government. The central government is intended to represent the state in domestic situations as well as abroad, to assure public security and tranquillity, and to provide for the well-being of the people; these specific activities are called the functions of the state.

75

The government of Viet-Nam is already a large organization, considering its relations with its 14,400,000 inhabitants. Indeed, from the earliest historical times, administrative units of the field organization of the national government, as well as territorial administrations distinct from the national government, have existed in practice. Without prejudice to legal conceptions of the organization of these territorial units, they are referred to as "local administrations." These administrations also perform certain functions that are either the territorial counterpart of functions of the state, such as security or financial functions, or functions peculiar to the local unit, such as the maintenance of civil records. In order to perform these functions, particular relationships between the various officials have developed within these administrations. These relationships make up the structure of local administrations. The local administration, a structure-function complex, constitutes an administrative institution additional to the national government.[1]

The preceding definitions may imply that each structure has a corresponding function or functions, and that each function has a specific corresponding structure. Sociologists find that this is not always the case. According to them, traditional society is characterized by "diffuseness," i.e., the functions are not always clearly defined, and are often assured by a nondifferentiated structure. Thus, a given structure—the traditional central government represented by the king and the court—performs several functions: political functions (making important decisions), administrative functions (the appointment of officials), social functions (the creation of social classes), and economic functions (the administration of crown property). In developed countries, these various functions are performed by different structures; in other words, specificity is characteristic of developed societies. With regard to organization, another characteristic feature of traditional societies is particularism; i.e., the organization takes into consideration specific individuals, at a specific moment, as opposed to being concerned with the needs that a given function is intended to satisfy in an objective manner (universalism). The diffuseness-particularism complex, in the course of development, gives way little by little to the specificity-universalism complex; but in the transition phase, a mixture of these various characteristic traits can often be observed. One author refers to a society in this transition phase as a "prismatic society."[2]

The influences behind the changes are discernible more in the concrete domain of administrative structures than in the abstract regions of human relations. It would be possible, for instance, to reconstruct the process by which exogenous structures have been transmitted and to detect the degree of facilitation afforded by endogenous cultural factors to the adoption of modern organizational patterns.[3] Perhaps there is reason to ask simply if the new pattern of organization constitutes a humanistic conception of organization as opposed to a mechanistic one, which is championed by certain theoreticians of administration.[4] From a more practical point of view, the problem arises of determining the extent to which the administrative organization has developed in adapting itself to the changing functions of the state, and of determining whether there is an appropriate structure to satisfy the requirements of the new administrative philosophy.

CHAPTER 3

THE CENTRAL GOVERNMENT

> We should learn to think of organization
> in terms of its human, social and contrib-
> utory effects; if we succeed in doing this,
> organization theory and practice can be-
> come a powerful force for good.[1]

ANY EXAMINATION of the structure of the central government of
Viet-Nam must take into consideration certain political factors
underlying the constitutional regime. Following the Geneva Agreements of 1954, a relatively stable political organization was created
with the personalistic First Republic of Ngo Dinh Diem. This regime
was overthrown in the Revolution of November 1, 1963, and the First
Republic was replaced by the Revolutionary Government. Except for
certain modifications required by the revolutionary spirit, the structure of the central government has been generally unchanged, up to
the present at least, as can be seen from the organization charts I to V
at the end of this chapter.

These charts designate two echelons in the organization of the
central government: the chief executive (formerly the president of
the Republic, now the prime minister), and the Cabinet Council and
the ministries.

The Executive Power

The Constitution of the First Republic reflected, with minor
alterations, the traditional theory of the separation of powers: the
legislative power was entrusted to the National Assembly, members
of which were to be elected by universal suffrage for four years
(Articles 49 and 51); the executive power was vested in the
president of the Republic, assisted by a vice-president, each elected
by universal suffrage, for a term limited to four years (Articles 30
and 32); the judicial power was entrusted to a corps of independent
magistrates, appointed by the president of the Republic but responsible to a Superior Council of Magistrates (Article 73).[2]

In the Revolutionary Government, provision has not yet been
made in detail for all of these institutions. According to Article 3 of
the Provisional Constitution Act of November 4, 1963, as modified by
the Constitution Act of February 7, 1964, the Military Revolutionary
Council holds provisionally all legislative and executive powers.
These powers, with the exception of the powers concerning budge-

tary and fiscal matters and public security, are further delegated to the Revolutionary Government,[3] of which the prime minister is the head. Since the November 1 Revolution, no change has been made regarding the judicial powers.

Only the organization of the executive power, which constitutes the highest level of the administrative hierarchy, will be examined here.

THE PRE-EMINENCE OF THE EXECUTIVE POWER

The power of the executive branch was relatively greater than that of the other two, since the provisions of the Constitution favored preserving the continuity of the state, as represented by the president of the Republic. For instance, the president could proclaim a state of emergency, with all of the attendant consequences, particularly the curtailment of the exercise of legislative and judicial powers (Article 44). Also, the Constitution gave the National Assembly only a limited time in which to vote on appropriations, at the end of which time the president could promulgate a provisional budget. The stipulations of this provisional budget, which had been implemented before the National Assembly voted a budget, were permanent; and it was the responsibility of the National Assembly to solve any problems resulting from other modifications of the provisional budget (Article 43). Since there is no separation of legislative and executive powers, the Revolutionary Government occupies a similarly pre-eminent position in the directing of public affairs.

The Constitution of October 26, 1956. Article 3 of the Constitution of October 26, 1956, stipulates that the president of the Republic performs the double function of chief executive and national leader. Not stipulated was a third—which should have been mentioned first —that of chief of state. It was the president who represented the state officially in its relationship with foreign countries, accrediting foreign ambassadors and designating ambassadors to foreign countries (Article 35); he conferred decorations and exercised all forms of executive clemency; he was supreme commander of the armed forces (Article 37). The powers that he assumed at times of national emergency, by virtue of Article 44, must be considered as powers of the chief of state.[4] Mention should also be made of the provisions of Article 41, granting the president of the Republic the right to make *décrets-lois;* these had the force of law and might modify the provisions of certain existing laws in case of national emergency, as well as during the interval between sessions of the National Assembly. The National Assembly had to ratify these *décrets-lois* in the next succeeding session; precedent favored the ratification *in toto* of a given *décret-loi,* since after it had become law the National Assembly could make modifications in its provisions.[5] The president might also sign *décrets-lois* with the explicit authorization of the National Assembly (Article 42) under two conditions: the authority had to be delegated under emergency conditions of war, internal disturbance, or financial and economic crises; also it had to be delegated by a law setting a fixed period of effectiveness and the precise objectives of the *décrets-lois*.[6]

The executive function included the promulgation and the execution of laws passed by the National Assembly (subject to presidential veto); the giving of general instructions for the proper functioning of the national services; the setting of rules for the proper organization and operation of public offices; and the appointing of all civil and military employees, except when the Constitution stipulated otherwise. With regard to the promulgation of laws, the veto power consisted of returning to the National Assembly a law which it had already passed but which contained certain provisions with which the president did not agree.[7] A three-quarters majority vote by the National Assembly was required to overrule the president's veto. According to Articles 57, 58, and 59, a law was considered to be tacitly promulgated if within thirty days the president failed to either sign it or return it for new deliberation. Tradition, stemming from the French school, gave the chief executive the power to make executive orders. The classic conception of this added power stems from the idea that the executive order, or measure taken by the president, although as broadly applied as a law, is subordinate to the law; a new conception has developed little by little in that jurists have recognized that there is a domain proper to these executive orders, and that the executive orders can be made even in the absence of law.[8] It appears that the First Republic set out definitely in this direction, if we judge from the enormous volume of executive orders issued by President Ngo Dinh Diem, especially since under these legislative powers in the intervals between sessions of the National Assembly the President often issued *décrets-lois*.[9]

According to the Constitution of the First Republic, certain executive orders might derive from the second function of the president, that of national leader. French judicial doctrine is certainly not the source of this tradition, since it is silent on this particular aspect of presidential power: such a question could not arise in a parliamentary regime, because the president has only representative functions and nominal power; even when the Constitution expressly provides that "the Government determines and conducts the politics of the Nation" (Article 20, Constitution of the Fifth French Republic of 1958), the commentaries concerning the role of the president of the Republic as the national leader are not generous.[10] To find an explanation for this new function of national leader, it is perhaps necessary to go back to older sources. Obviously, in an administrative philosophy based on the Confucian ideas of *nhan* (human-heartedness) and *nghia* (righteousness), it is difficult to deny the chief of state—whatever his title may be and regardless of the means by which he was brought to power—the role of leader of the people. Confucius and his disciples always cite as examples the emperors Nghieu (Yao) and Thuan (Chouen), who were much less "rulers" than "leaders," wisely guiding their people into the paths of virtue and happiness.[11] The long historical tradition of the country demands that the saviors of the nation must take the helm in order to lead the country into the path of progress. This Confucian conception of the leader makes an interesting comparison with the conception of the chief of state set down by the early theoreticians of the Chinese Nationalist Party during the period of the Kuomintang tutelage.[12] It is also interesting to compare this concept of national leader with the same concept drawn from American literature concerning the president of the United States. According to this literature, the president as leader should combine in his personal traits such qualities as intelligence, energy, and the ability to "lubricate human relationships." [13]

This similarity to the American conception of the role of the president is easily understood because the Constitution of 1956 institutes a presidential regime, a type which students of political science attribute historically to America.[14] Still, the essential difference rests in the fact that in this case the personality of the charismatic leader was so strong that as a result of the legal pre-eminence of the chief executive, the regime degenerated into autocracy and dictatorship [15] and was ended by the November 1 Revolution; this was in accordance with Confucian tradition, which admitted the right of insurrection whenever the emperor, by evil actions, had lost the mandate of Heaven.[16]

Organization of the Revolutionary Government.   The Revolution of November 1, 1963, abolished the Constitution of October 26, 1956. The Provisional Constitution Act of November 4, 1963, accords all legislative and executive powers to the Military Revolutionary Council. The Council itself has an administrative committee composed of a chairman, three vice-chairmen, a certain number of councilors and a secretary-general.

The Provisional Constitution Act further stipulates that the chairman of the Council will exercise the prerogatives of the chief of state, and the first chairman of the Council, Major General Duong Van Minh, did exercise these prerogatives until the purge of the Council on January 30, 1964. After the purge, he was not re-elected chairman of the Council, but an amendment to the Provisional Constitution Act dated February 7, 1964, provides that the functions of the chief of state may be delegated to a person other than the chairman of the Council; by virtue of this amendment, these functions were subsequently delegated to Major General Duong. Through long tradition, it is possible that the chief of state might command such prestige that, even if he did not hold the legal authority, he nonetheless would remain a symbol to the nation and exercise considerable moral authority.

The Military Revolutionary Council first created a provisional government, distinct from the Council, headed by a prime minister (*thu tuong*) appointed by the Council and assisted by ministers of his choice, subject to the consent of the Council. With the exception of budgetary and fiscal powers and authority in matters of security, all legislative and executive powers were delegated by the Council to the Provisional Government. It is not even specified that the prime minister is responsible to the Military Revolutionary Council. Following the purge of January 30, the new chairman of the Council, Major General Nguyen Khanh himself, assumed the functions of prime minister, and his Cabinet constitutes the Revolutionary Government. The executive power thus seems to have passed from the chief of state, who has no more than a representative function, to the prime minister, who is also chairman of the Military Revolutionary Council.[17]

There has been frequent criticism of the Revolutionary Government from the press, because the powers (e.g., those of the chairman of the Council and of the chief of state) are not strictly delineated, and because the occupying of several posts by one man is detrimental to the system of checks and balances.[18]

THE OFFICE OF THE PRIME MINISTER

The Military Revolutionary Council has not yet published any regulations concerning the organization of the Secretariat of the Council. On the other hand, the Revolutionary Government seems to be retaining the former organization of the Office of the Presidency, with such modifications as are demanded by the current situation.

The Staff of the Prime Minister.   In addition to the Cabinet, which assists the prime minister in important political administrative decisions, the prime minister has at his disposition a Cabinet at the Office of the Prime Minister, a Secretariat-General, and a number of services attached directly to the Office of the Prime Minister.

The Cabinet at the Presidency was, in principle, responsible for centralizing all the documentation concerning political affairs submitted for the decision of the president, transmitting to the departments and to the provinces orders coming from the president, keeping minutes of the meetings of the Cabinet Council, and for the organizing of the president's honorific functions, his private affairs, and his personal security. To assist the director of the Cabinet at the Presidency in these many functions, eleven chiefs of service have been provided. The organization of the Cabinet at the Presidency does not require any lengthy commentary, but it should be pointed out that the simultaneous creation of a Public Relations Service and of a Press Service indicated, first, the apparent concern for the development of a maximum of communication between the Presidency and the public, especially the foreign public, and, second, the intention that the Mailbox Service be a link with the old tradition which demanded that the supreme power have available a direct means of information concerning the wishes of the population.[19] Since these agencies had been established principally for propaganda purposes, the prime minister of the Revolutionary Government discontinued the Mailbox Service and the Public Relations Service, as well as the Service for Chinese Affairs and the Service for Political and Social Studies. All the other services of the former Cabinet at the Presidency, however, have been retained in the Office of the Prime Minister.

The Secretariat-General at the Prime Minister's Office is essentially an agency of study and centralization and is concerned with affairs, other than political, submitted by the ministries for the decision of the prime minister. It insures the unity of legislation and of executive orders proposed by the various ministries. It publishes *Cong-Bao Viet-Nam Cong-Hoa* (The Official Gazette of the Republic of Viet-Nam), in which are recorded the texts of legislation and executive orders and of decisions made by the ministers, particularly those concerning personnel, such as appointments, promotions, and retirement.[20] The Secretariat-General represents, to a certain extent, the permanent administrative part of the government. As a matter of fact, there is considerable stability in these functions, owing to the fact that the positions of secretary-general and his assistant have been filled by the same persons since the country acquired independence. The value of such stability can be easily understood, considering the instability of the departments during the early years of the First Republic.

The Cabinet at the Office of the Prime Minister and the Secretariat-General are the formal agencies intended to assist the prime minister directly. In addition to this formal organization, during the First Republic there was a group of advisors, the most important of which was the political advisor. His role, not unusually prominent at the beginning of the regime, became more and more important through his presiding over many ceremonies and, particularly, through his leadership of the movements of republican youth and of strategic hamlets. He gave talks of an academic nature covering the major policies of the government, before groups of young people or before public servants at meetings of the Government Officials' League, e.g., the talks given before the high officials of the Ministry of the Interior.[21] Only the very close personal relationship between the political advisor and the president of the Republic (his brother) can explain the progressive increase in the number and importance of the functions of the former, to the point that he exercised an unofficial authority that sometimes rivaled the official authority of the president himself.

The economic advisor and the financial advisor performed duties limited to their regular functions as advisors, but nevertheless they played an important role in certain phases of administrative life. Thus, in practice, the financial advisor made decisions on various details of the proposed budget to be presented to the National Assembly each year; he also served provisionally as governor of the National Bank. The economic advisor, who was a distinguished economist, often took part in technical negotiations with international financial organizations, or with representatives of the United States for technical and economic aid to Viet-Nam; he was also elected vice president of the National Economic Council. The functions of the military advisor were not clearly defined, since this post was created only on December 8, 1962.

In addition to these national advisors there were foreign advisors. Mention should be made particularly of the Michigan State University Group, which functioned from May 20, 1955, to June 30, 1962. There were also French advisors, especially on problems concerning Chinese immigrants.

It is interesting to note that the presence of advisors around the president in a presidential regime is very common. In the White House office, for example, approximately four hundred persons perform the functions of keeping the president of the United States informed on matters concerning the politics of the country, helping him to co-ordinate the various activities in liaison with the legislative and judicial branches of the government, advising him on affairs of a personal nature, and preparing the numerous communications that issue from the office of the president.[22] Analogies can also be found during the time of the emperors, when there were high officials who played no well-defined role in the administrative hierarchy, and who were either counselors to the king, called *tam cong* (*thai su, thai pho,* or *thai bao*) or *tam thieu* (*thieu su, thieu pho,* or *thieu bao*), or advisors to the king (*gian nghi dai phu*).[23]

Nevertheless, after the November 1 Revolution, the posts of advisors were discontinued; after the purge of January 31, 1964, however, the former chairman of the Military Revolutionary Committee was appointed to the post of high military advisor.

Agencies Attached to the Office of the Prime Minister.   One innovation in the Ngo Dinh Diem government was the organization of agencies directly dependent on the Presidency. These agencies existed only in a rudimentary state at the time of the provisional government just preceding the republican regime. It is curious to note that, at the time of the establishment of these agencies, the famous administrative formula of Gulick was not yet sufficiently known in intellectual and political circles in Viet-Nam.[24] Nevertheless, the agencies directly attached to the Presidency can be grouped according to this formula, POSDCORB, in the following manner.

> Directorate-General of Planning (P)
> Directorate-General of Civil Service (O and S)
> National-Institute of Administration (S)
> Directorate-General of Budget and Foreign Aid (B)
> Office of the Inspector General of Administration and Finance (R)
> Office of the Secretary of State at the Presidency, for the functions of directing (D) and co-ordinating (CO).

No doubt, certain experts working in the Executive Office of the Presidency at the time played a certain role in this organization, which ran counter to the more or less solidly established traditions, which demand that the president exercise only the functions of co-ordination, and that the entire active administration should fall to the secretaries of state.[25]

Planning. The planning function existed only in a sporadic form at the time of the emperors, because of the essentially pragmatic administrative philosophy, which has been previously discussed. Under the Bao Dai government, a Ministry of Planning and Reconstruction was created in 1951; it was transferred, as the Directorate-General of Planning, to the Ministry of Finance in 1953. However, this office was never able to set up a plan of economic and social development, in spite of the fact that it succeeded the Federal Commissariat of Planning, established in 1947 by the French authorities, which drew up a Five-Year Plan of Social and Economic Development for Indochina, in 1948. It was not until the Directorate-General of Planning was attached to the Presidency August 16, 1955, and given the authority accompanying this attachment, that it was able to set up, with the assistance of United Nations experts, a first Five-Year Plan (1957–1961), which was not published, and subsequently a second Five-Year Plan (1962–1966), which was published after some discussion in the Economic Council and in the National Assembly.[26] Program planning and factors planning are also included, to a certain extent, in the Second Plan, but, in general, at the planning stage these details are not taken up very thoroughly.[27] It is curious to note that the Directorate-General of Planning was entrusted, shortly after its attachment to the Presidency, with functions quite different from those of a purely staff agency: in particular, advisory and reporting functions with regard to certain government enterprises and the keeping of minutes in the Commission on Overseas Training.

The only justification for its being concerned with government enterprises is that these enterprises were set up in order to fill the gap left by private enterprises in certain sectors considered essential to the economy of the country, and included in the Plan of Development: the cement factory at Ha Tien, the paper mill, the glass factory, and the exploitation of mineral water. The Commission on Overseas Training is intended to put into effect a rational program for the choice of candidates and the utilization of funds available for advanced study abroad; the reason for entrusting these programs to the Directorate-General of planning was that they are often part of more general programs of foreign technical aid (United Nations Special Funds, United Nations Technical Assistance, the Colombo Plan, French Technical Assistance, German Aid, etc.), which were included in the general Plan of Development. It is quite possible that, by a curious particularistic note in a universalistic composition, the personality of the director, a technician of considerable worth, may also have been considered in relegating these responsibilities to his office. In the Revolutionary Government, the Directorate-General of Planning has been retained in the Office of the Prime Minister.

Staffing. Where the staffing function was concerned, the traditional organization of the Imperial Court always provided for a specialized ministry: the Ministry of the Interior (*Bo Lai*). Under the Bao Dai government, the civil service was sometimes assigned to a ministry, but sometimes reduced to a directorate-general attached to the Ministry of the Interior or to the Secretariat of State at the Office of the Prime Minister. In this case, the new French conception of the civil service also played a certain role. The government of the Fourth French Republic conceived, as a matter of fact, a Directorate of Civil Service attached to the office of the Prime Minister, and responsible for the formulation of a civil service policy, in order to remedy the inconsistencies inevitable in a system in which each ministry had complete authority in problems concerning its agents.[28] When the experts, inspired by the United States Commission on Organization of the Executive Branch of the Government (Concluding Report 1949),[29] suggested the creation of this agency in the executive branch, the terrain had already been prepared for attaching this office to the Presidency (November 14, 1955). Moreover, a philosophy of administration based partly on the scrupulous choice of administrators also implies that the chief executive must have in his hands supreme control of personnel administration. The same philosophy also explains the fact that the director-general of civil service was a collaborator of the President, not only in matters concerning civil service regulations, but also in the choice of administrators, which requires the consideration of many tenuous factors. Here also the problems of policy making and those of routine administration were interrelated because of the personality of the director.[30] The Directorate-General of Civil Service has been retained as an agency attached directly to the Office of the Prime Minister.

Organizing. The same reasons justified attaching to the Presidency the National Institute of Administration, an agency responsible for the formation of administrators prior to appointment.[31] At one time, as a result of the activity of many consultants at the National Institute of Administration, the question even arose as to whether or not to entrust to the Institute, in addition to its training and research programs, the organization and methods function. The Michigan State University Viet-Nam Advisory Group attached to the Institute produced a large number of reports on the organization of certain departments and services, such as the Department of National Economy, the Department of National Education, the Department of Finance, and the Commissariat-General for Refugees.[32] Although these reports were written by experts, some of whom had had long practical administrative experience, in most cases their value was largely academic, because they brought out theoretical and technical problems, and lacked factual knowledge of the Vietnamese context.[33]

In truth, many of the President's decisions concerning governmental organization were prepared for him by agencies that normally assisted him in the execution of his authority. Indeed, the Directorate-General of Civil Service performed this function because of the close relationship between personnel organization and personnel management. This relationship is shown by the formal approval given by this directorate at the time of the examination of proposed orders and regulations concerning the organization or reorganization of departments and services. The Directorate-General of Budget and Foreign Aid, by reason of the periodical examination of budget proposals presented by the departments and by other agencies and because its prior approval was required for the signing of organizational orders, also occasionally exercised a certain authority in the domain of organization of services. In the Revolutionary Government, the Directorate-General of Budget and Foreign Aid has been transferred to the Ministry of Finance, and a new Organization and Methods Service is being created as one of its agencies.

Budgeting. The budgetary function tends, in effect, to extend beyond the framework of budgetary technique, since the country must answer many needs for which the financial resources are inadequate, and since the executive power is striving to give an energetic forward motion to government operations through strict control of the budget. It is easily understood that, in spite of the very ancient tradition according to which the budgetary function was entrusted to the Ministry of Finance (*Bo Ho* under the emperors; *Bo Tai Chinh* under the Bao Dai government), this particular function was removed from the Department of Finance during the First

Republic and was by stages assigned to a directorate attached to the Presidency. First, the nucleus of the Directorate of the Budget was transferred from the Ministry of Finance to the Presidency on November 14, 1955. To this nucleus was added the Directorate of Foreign Aid, which, because of the circumstances (the personality of the Director, and the principal object of the aid at any given moment), has been attached successively to the Ministry of Public Works (December 14, 1950), to the Ministry of Finance (August 13, 1952), to the Ministry of Planning and Reconstruction (January 21, 1955), once more to the Ministry of Finance (August 16, 1955), and was finally made a part of the Directorate-General of Budget (April 24, 1957). On this last date, a third directorate, the Directorate of Obligated Expenditures, was transferred from the Ministry of Finance and added to the combined directorates of Budget and Foreign Aid. This structure allowed the president to watch over the budget-making process through its various phases to the final execution.[34]

Because of the complexity of the affairs to be handled by the Directorate-General of Budget and Foreign Aid and because of the high degree of confidence which had to be given its director, only an interim director was appointed, an engineer who had gained his experience in the Directorate of Foreign Aid. To aid him in technical budget matters, an assistant director had been chosen from among eminently qualified officials, and this assistant was promoted to the post of director on the resignation of the first in 1962.

After the November 1 Revolution, the budgetary functions were returned to the Ministry of Finance, but at that time the prime minister himself was also filling the post of minister of finance, assisted by the secretary of state for finance. When the present Cabinet was constituted, however, the secretary of state for finance was placed under the vice prime minister for economy and finance. This is the first time since the independency of the nation that the budgetary function has not been assigned directly to the chief executive.

Reporting. Another administrative agency attached directly to the Presidency and included in the POSDCORB formula performed a rather controversial function: reporting. This function can be understood in two ways: as keeping the people informed of administrative activities, particularly in the name of the chief executive, and as keeping the chief executive informed on developments at all levels of the administrative hierarchy.[35] With respect to the first of these two responsibilities, at one time the Directorate-General of Information, the function of which was to keep the public informed on various governmental activities, was attached directly to the Presidency. This provision had been made for reasons of personality, however, and shortly afterwards the Directorate was transferred from the Presidency to the Department of Civic Action. The Cabinet at the

Presidency nevertheless maintains a Press Service, responsible for relations with the press, particularly for communicating presidential messages to the public.

Concerning the responsibility for keeping the president informed of governmental activities, mention should be made of the Corps of Inspectors of Administration and Finance on one hand, and of the Corps of Government Delegates on the other. This latter body had five members: a delegate each for North Central Viet-Nam, South Central Viet-Nam, the Mountain Regions, Southeast Viet-Nam, and Southwest Viet-Nam. In principle, these delegates were the eyes and ears of the president, maintaining a check on the activities of the offices of the central government as well as those of the provincial offices, and reporting to the president the results of their inspections. These reports contained firsthand information, gathered on the spot, to be compared with information contained in the official reports that constituted the official source of intragovernmental communication. The functions of the inspector general, who was chief of the Corps of Inspectors of Administration and Finance, required a great deal of diplomacy, experience, perspicacity, and complete devotion to the task.[36] This institution proceeded from a very old tradition. Good monarchs always had at hand a corps of censors who had broad powers of investigation and who could even criticize the Crown.[37] It is easily understood that the Office of the Inspector General ranked first in seniority among offices attached to the Presidency, having been assigned there February 12, 1954. It should be pointed out that during the First Republic the deputies themselves asked that the duties of the Corps of Inspectors be made even more extensive.[38]

After the November 1 Revolution, the duties of the governmental delegates were assigned to the commanders of the military zones.[39] Furthermore, the Corps of Inspectors of Administration and Finance was enlarged by the addition of inspectors from the former departments of the Interior and Finance. Decree No. 21/TTP of December 2, 1963, vested in this Corps of Inspectors very broad powers of investigation in the public services, the autonomous agencies, and the offices of mixed economy: it can recommend any reform measures it considers necessary. The Corps of Inspectors makes its reports both to the Military Revolutionary Council and to the Revolutionary Government.[40] Recently, the General Office for People's Suggestions and Complaints was set up to "soothe the sufferings and grievances the rural masses have endured; [the agency has] real power and competency to settle the people's problems right on the spot."[41]

Other Functions. In addition to the above agencies, which perform administrative functions, there are others attached to the Presidency which perform specific functions.

After November 14, 1955, there were added to the Presidency a great number of offices whose attachment cannot be justified by purely technical administrative considerations. These were in chronological order of attachment: the Commissariat-General of Civic Action (November 18, 1955), the Directorate-General of the Civil Guard (November 19, 1955), the Office of the Inspector General of Rural Militia (July 10, 1956), the Commissariat-General of Agricultural Development (April 23, 1957), the Directorate-General of Social Action (August 23, 1957), the Permanent Secretariat of Defense (March 28, 1958), the Directorate-General of Reconstruction and City Planning (October 7, 1958), the Atomic Energy Office (October 11, 1958), the Directorate-General of Radio Broadcasting (December 5, 1958), the Pasteur Institute of Viet-Nam (December 29, 1958), the Commissariat-General for Agricultural Co-operatives and Credit (February 27, 1959), the Directorate-General of Information (October 19, 1960), and the Directorate-General of Youth Activities (October 19, 1960). This tendency to increase the number of services attached to the Presidency came to an end after May 28, 1961, on which date a decree was promulgated which entirely reorganized the central government and transferred back to departments a great number of these services. A careful examination of the reasons behind the structural fluctuations of this period will reveal in each case: either justification on theoretical grounds, as in the case of the Director-General of Information which has been mentioned; or a practical reason, such as the importance attached to a given problem at a given moment, as for example the problems of refugees, agricultural development, or scientific research; or simply a consideration of the personality of the high official in question.[42]

Other transfers of agencies to the ministries following the November 1 Revolution left only the following attached to the Office of the Prime Minister: the Inspectorate General of Administrative and Financial Affairs, the Directorate-General of Planning, the Directorate-General of Civil Service, and the National Institute of Administration.[43]

However, two new agencies were created by the Revolutionary Government: the Commissariat-General for New Rural Life, and the Commissariat-General of Administration. The first is the former Commissariat-General of Agricultural Development and Agricultural Affairs (which was attached to the former Department of Rural Development), to which had been added the former Secretariat-General for Strategic Hamlets (formerly attached to the Department of the Interior). The Commissariat-General of Administration was intended to include all those services of the former Department of the Interior which would not be included in the newly created Ministry of Security. These two commissariats-general had a brief existence. The first was made a directorate-general after certain of its services had been transferred to the Ministry of Rural Affairs, and the second was abolished after its services had been returned to the Ministry of the Interior.

Subsequently, the General Office for People's Suggestions and Complaints,[44] and the Special Commissariat for Open Arms [45] (to call the Viet Cong to rally to the national cause) were created and attached to the Office of the Prime Minister. At the same time, the Commissariat-General for Youth and Sports [46] and the Directorate-General of Political Rural Cadres [47] were created and placed under the Office of the Vice Prime Minister for Pacification.

Directing and Co-ordinating. Two important administrative functions are entrusted to the Secretary of State at the Office of the Prime Minister: directing and co-ordinating. If directing is understood in Gulick's terms as "the continuous task of making decisions and embodying them in specific and general orders and instructions," it is difficult to conceive that this function might be entrusted to another person than the prime minister himself, within the confines of his office. But because of the great number of his duties, a part of this function concerning routine administrative matters has been delegated to the Secretary of State at the Office of the Prime Minister, whose major function is co-ordinating.

Although the other functions are clearly defined in the organizational orders of the various directorates, the same is not true of the co-ordination function, which is concerned essentially with the handling of unforeseen problems as they occur, since in this case the agencies responsible could not confine themselves to following precedent. In the government of the First Republic, the co-ordination function included liaison with the National Assembly (or the individual deputies) and with other assemblies and councils, in particular the National Economic Council, the Cabinet, etc. It is for this reason that the Secretary of State at the Presidency appeared before the National Assembly to answer questions concerning the transfers of public officials by rotation between the central government and the provincial governments, or those concerning the census or the mobilization of the army reserves.[48] The assignment of the co-ordination function to the Secretary of State at the Presidency also involved the personality of the man in question and the state of his personal relations with the president, fluctuations in general politics, and the state of the president's relations with the other departments and services attached to the Presidency.

This seems to apply also to the present Secretary of State at the Office of the Prime Minister. In the Provisional Government, a Council of Notables was created for the purpose of giving advice to the government on all public matters regarding which the government saw fit to consult it or on such matters as the Notables themselves considered important. The Secretary of State at the Office of the Prime Minister performed the delicate function of liaison between this Council or its individual members and the government.[49] Following the dissolution of the Council of Notables by the Military Revolutionary Council, the Secretary of State has continued to serve as liaison agent with the political parties, although he does not seem to have to concern himself with military matters.

General Observations on Agencies Attached to the Office of the Prime Minister. From a broader point of view, it might be said that the proliferation of structures within the Presidency until 1961 was evidence of a tendency toward a greater concentration, since, in principle, agencies that were dependent on the Presidency received their instructions directly from agents of the president himself; whereas the reform of 1961 showed an attempt at deconcentration and rationalization. It should be pointed out that, although the transfer of services was carried out, the personnel responsible for the operation of those services were not affected. Most of the director-generals were chosen at the beginning of the government of President Ngo Dinh Diem, in 1954 and 1955, and remained at their posts until the November 1 Revolution. The director-general of social action, although appointed Secretary of State for Finance, preformed the functions of both posts. With the exception of the director of the Atomic Energy Office, all the director-generals were career civil servants. If it happened that a director-general was a technician of great merit or of international renown, his assistant would necessarily be a high administrative official of long experience. The great stability in the staff of the president might cause the casual observer to believe that the administrative system of the First Republic was an extremely conservative one, although certain critics reproached it for attempting too intensive reforms in too short a time. Indeed, this reproach may have been justified, considering the almost revolutionary programs put into effect by the government: the struggle against political and religious sects, the integration of political refugees, agrarian reform, community development, *agrovilles*, and, finally, the program of strategic hamlets.[50]

The Cabinet and the Ministries

Although the Cabinet at the Office of the Prime Minister, the Secretariat-General, and the offices attached to the Office of the Prime Minister are the immediate collaborators of the prime minister, these agencies are not considered on an equal level with the ministries, whose heads, with the Secretary of State at the Office of the Prime Minister, form the Cabinet (*Hoi Dong Noi Cac*).

THE CABINET AND THE INTERMINISTERIAL COMMITTEES

Decree No. 1/TTP of the President of the Provisional Government, dated November 4, 1963, provides as follows for the composition of the Cabinet: the prime minister (who also held the posts of minister of national economy and minister of finance), the minister of national defense, the minister of security, the minister of foreign affairs, the minister of justice, the minister of national education, the minister of rural affairs, the minister of information, the minister of public works and communication, the minister of public health, the minister of youth and sports, the minister of labor, the secretary of state at the Office of the Prime Minister, the secretary of state for finance, and the secretary of state for economy.[51]

In a reorganization of the ministries on February 8, 1964, the prime minister ceased to exercise the functions of minister of finance and minister of national economy (the secretaries of state for finance and economy were replaced by the ministers of finance and national economy), the Ministry of Security became the Ministry of the Interior, the Ministry of Youth and Sports was replaced by the Ministry of Social Welfare, and one minister without portfolio was appointed. Interministerial co-ordination was entrusted to three vice prime ministers: one for pacification, one for economy and finance, and a third for cultural and social affairs. These vice prime ministers are also members of the Cabinet. A regulation, dated February 17, 1964, defines the respective relationships between the ministers, the vice prime ministers, and the prime minister.[52]

The present organization of the Cabinet follows the general structure of the Cabinet of the First Republic, and thus carries on a certain tradition in the governmental framework.

The Cabinet during the First Republic had no power of its own —unlike the Cabinet of the Bao Dai government, which took the title of Council of Ministers when it was presided over by the chief of state, and whose advice had to be considered when the chief of state made executive orders concerning public administration. Similarly, there was no question of the collective responsibility of the Cabinet of the First Republic.[53] Only its individual members (secretaries of state, or *bo truong*) were responsible to the president. Indeed, it was not rare that changes of titles or of functions were made according to the needs of the moment, at the discretion of the president. These precedents can also serve to determine the responsibility and the powers of the ministers in the Revolutionary Government.

Problems of Liaison. In the government of the First Republic, the distribution of functions among the secretaries of state seemed to depend on rational grounds. According to Decree No. 123/TTD, dated May 28, 1961, the various governmental activities were grouped essentially into four major functions: security, economic development, social development, and the administrative function as such. For each of these functions, there was a corresponding secretary of state responsible for liaison, who was not himself a "superminister," but who provided liaison between his peers, sharing the same broad function, in the name and the service of the president of the Republic.

Thus, the secretary of state at the Presidency was responsible for the administrative function, and in order to discharge this responsibility, he co-ordinated the activities of the various agencies attached directly to the Presidency. Except for his own cabinet, he had no department, but the director of the Cabinet at the Presidency and the secretary-general at the Presidency were, in point of fact, his collaborators for liaison with the other departments.

The secretary of state co-ordinator for security activities maintained liaison with the Department of National Defense and the Department of the Interior. Although the departments of Justice and of Foreign Affairs were not included in the list of departments that require liaison, these departments might also fall into the category of public security, if their functions were considered from the point of view of legal sanctions or of foreign relations.

The group of departments which performed economic functions collaborated with the secretary of state co-ordinator for economic development, who was the vice president of the Republic himself. In this group were the Department of National Economy (commerce and industry), the Department of Finance (which included also the National Bank of Viet-Nam and the National Office of Foreign Exchange), the Department of Rural Development, and the Department of Public Works.

A fourth secretary of state performed the liaison function in the social sector, grouping the Department of Civic Action, the Department of Education, the Department of Health, and the Department of Labor. To this sector were attached the various cultural institutions, such as the National Scientific Research Center, the Institute of Historical Studies, and so on.

In point of fact, it was rather difficult to reconcile the role of co-ordinator with equality of rank, particularly in view of the fact that except for the secretary of state at the Presidency, who had powerful means at his disposal through the directorates of Budget and of Civil Service, the only powers the secretaries of state co-ordinators had were powers of persuasion. In the case of the secretary of state co-ordinator for economic development, these powers were somewhat enhanced by the prestige of the function of the vice president of the Republic, by that of the president of the National Economic Council, and also by a long administrative and political career. The secretary of state co-ordinator for cultural and social affairs was obliged to establish his own authority, although he had been for a short time vice president of the National Assembly, and had certain other functions, such as that of the president of the Scientific Research Council. The secretary of state at the Presidency was also acting secretary of state co-ordinator for security activities, and was in a good position to perform these additional functions because of the prestige attached to his principal function.

In the first days after the November 1 Revolution, the Provisional Government abolished these positions of co-ordination, although the general structure of the former departments was kept, with alterations which will be presented in detail later in a study of the organization of two typical ministries. However, after the January 30 purge, as has been shown, three vice prime ministers were named: the vice prime minister for pacification, who provides liaison between the ministries of Information, National Defense, Interior, Rural Affairs, and Public Works and Communication; the vice prime minister for economy and finance, who co-ordinates the activities of the ministries of Finance and National Economy, and the vice prime minister for cultural and social affairs, who acts as co-ordinator for the ministries of National Education, Public Health, and Labor, and the Department of Social Welfare.

This new organization allows the vice prime ministers a higher rank than that of the ministers; indeed, the prime minister and the vice prime ministers often meet without the other members of the Cabinet, to decide on general policies to be followed.

Interministerial Meetings. During the First Republic, because of the great number of matters brought to the attention of the President in sessions of the Cabinet, the practice was established of having the decisions to be made in the Cabinet prepared by an interdepartmental committee presided over by the vice president of the Republic. The director-generals, and, on occasion, even the chiefs of the services concerned, participated in this interdepartmental committee, called Hoi Dong Lien Bo (Interministerial Council). This committee and this practice are not used by the Revolutionary Government.

To complete an outline of the formal organization of the Presidency, it is necessary to mention other commissions and committees whose objects were limited but which were so important that the President of the Republic or his delegates presided over them: [54] the National Committee for Foreign Aid,[55] the National Committee for Agrarian Reform,[56] the Supreme Council on Money and Credit,[57] and the Committee for Strategic Hamlets.

The following new National Committees have been created by the Revolutionary Government: (1) the Central Pacification Committee, which replaces the former Committee for Strategic Hamlets, and whose object is to establish the general direction for government action in the villages. This committee is headed by the prime minister and includes the interested ministers (national defense, interior, information, rural affairs, and public works and communication), as well as high officials such as the chairman of the joint chiefs of staff, the commissioner-general of the intelligence services, and the commissioner-general for youth and sports.[58] (2) The Special Committee on Economy and Finance, replacing the Supreme Council on Money and Credit.[59] (3) The Central Joint Psychological Warfare Committee.[60] (4) The Consultative Council for Social Action.[61]

In general, these councils and committees have no power to make decisions; rather, they give advice. Only the ministers have decision-making authority of their own. Normally, each ministry was created by an act that set down its functions, and a second act that defined the organization of the department, i.e., provided the necessary directorates, services, and bureaus within the department. It may be instructive to study the process of the evolution of a very old ministry, the Ministry of the Interior, and that of the formation of a very new one, the Ministry of Rural Affairs.

THE MINISTRY OF THE INTERIOR

Of the various ministries, there is one which has always existed, because it provides the most essential function of the state: the Ministry of the Interior (*Bo Noi Vu*), which is responsible for public security. In the time of the emperors, it was called *Bo Lai,* which indicates the importance attached to the recruiting of mandarins (*lai*), who were responsible for domestic administration. Created under its present title by Ordinance No. 1, dated June 2, 1948, this Ministry has continued to function in spite of the vicissitudes which the government has undergone. Decree No. 26/NV of July 8, 1952, defines the functions of this Ministry as follows:

(1) To maintain order and public security in the national territory by centralizing the information concerning this matter, studying, putting into effect various measures regarding public order in the cities and in the country, control of police and security forces, preparation of legal texts or executive orders concerning public security, and maintaining a check on the movements of foreigners.

(2) To set up control of political organizations and various other associations within the country, including organizations of foreigners, non-profit organizations, and religious organizations.

(3) To organize elections at the various administrative levels (national, provincial and communal), and to make sure the elections are properly administered.

(4) To supervise the activities of the various territorial divisions which are not part of the central government.

The Central Organization. Because of the great number of these essentially administrative functions, the Ministry of the Interior was organized with the aim of fulfilling them as effectively as possible. This concern for effectiveness is shown by the many changes the Ministry has undergone since its creation. It would be tedious to give the details of all these changes, but an idea of their extent can be given by citing the dates of the other decrees providing for the successive modifications of this Department: July 27, 1952; October 10, 1952; May 20, 1955; February 1, 1956; June 8, 1957; March 8, 1958; August 26, 1958; December 1, 1958; June 1, 1959; and September 8, 1959. A number of reform measures took into account the suggestions presented by consultants in response to presidential instructions, such as the elimination of regional delegates and the transfer of part of their functions to the Department of the Interior.[62] Other measures were put into effect under the pressure of circumstances, such as the assignment in 1957 of one man to the offices of Secretary of State at the Presidency and Secretary of State for the Interior, which led to the creation of two undersecretary positions (*tham ly*)—one for security and one for administration—until eventually the undersecretary for administration was appointed secretary of state.

After the November 1 Revolution, the Department of the Interior became the Ministry of Security (with the loss of several services), but was later called the Ministry of the Interior (with the recovery of these services). The organization of this ministry is prescribed by the ministerial *Arrêté* of March 18, 1964. The minister of the interior is aided by a director of cabinet (*dong ly van phong*), who assists him in political affairs, and a secretary-general (*tong thu ky*), who aids him in administrative matters.[63] The division of political and administrative functions between the cabinet director and the secretary-general is not very clear; indeed, administrative affairs which are not truly routine are also examined by the cabinet director from a political point of view before being submitted to the minister.

Under the supervision of these two officials, the various services (*so*) of the ministry are organized into nine distinct units, directed by chiefs of service (*chanh su vu*): the Service of Political Affairs, the Service of Control (for control of associations, meetings, firearms, etc.), the Service of Militia (*Nghia Quan*), the Service of Immigration, the Service of Administration, the Service of Research, the Service of Administrative Personnel, the Service of Budget and Accounting, and the Directorate of Telecommunications (created August 17, 1960).

Particular note should be taken of the important part played by the Service of Administration, through which passes all correspondence with the provinces; with all the complex problems of keeping check on the local administrations, this service alone performs the function of the traditional role of the Ministry of the Interior under the emperors. The importance of the Service of Administration during the First Republic can be judged by the many debates in the National Assembly every time the subject of the budget of the Department of the Interior was brought before it.[64]

All the afore-mentioned services assist the minister through the two directors indicated, by means of the study of various records, by examining proposed measures, instructions, letters, etc. These services are what students of public administration call "overhead units," although they are very numerous, since they assist the minister in the administration of the provinces and of two directorate-generals that might be called "line agencies." [65]

Besides the supervision of regional administrations, the Ministry of the Interior performs a double function of security, entrusted to two separate agencies: the Directorate-General of National Police (*Nha Tong Giam Doc Canh Sat Quoc Gia*), and the Directorate-General of Rehabilitation Centers (*Nha Tong Quan Doc Cac Trung Tam Cai Huan*).

The Directorate-General of National Police. The Directorate-General of National Police existed even before the creation of the Ministry of the Interior as such, since the public security function is of prime importance in any organized state. It was one of the best organized services at the time of French domination, and yet it underwent several successive changes before reaching its present form under Decree No. 146, of June 27, 1962. At first, it merely supervised the activities of three regional directorates (South Viet-Nam, Central Viet-Nam, and the Central Viet-Nam Highlands). On September 10, 1958, the South Viet-Nam Regional Directorate was eliminated and its functions were attached directly to the Directorate-General. Subsequently, the Central Viet-Nam directorate was divided in two: the North Central Viet-Nam Directorate and the South Central Viet-Nam Directorate (May 29, 1961), but the two new directors met every month with the directors of the Central Viet-Nam Highlands Police Service, with the director of the North Central Viet-Nam Police Service presiding, in order to co-ordinate activities and exchange information to be reported to the superior authorities. The results of these groupings seem rather curious: South Viet-Nam, which includes most of the population, has no other director than the director-general himself, while Central Viet-Nam, with barely 35 per cent of the population of the country, has three regional directors. Aside from this territorial division of responsibilities, there is also a functional division, both in the directorate-general and in the various regional directorates: the Special Police Service (*Canh Sat Dac Biet*), the Judicial Police Service (*Canh Sat Tu Phap*), the Traffic Bureau (*Canh Sat Trat Tu Luu Thong*), the Administrative Police Service (*Canh Sat Hanh Chinh*), the Emergency Combat Police Service (*Canh Sat Chien Dau*), the Scientific Police Service (*Canh Sat Khoa Hoc*), the Service for Foreign Visitors (*So Di Tru Ngoai Kieu*), and the Education and Training Service (*Huan Luyen Va Tu Nghiep Chuyen Mon*).[66]

The Directorate-General of Rehabilitation Centers. Unlike the Directorate-General of Police, which functions both in the central government and at all administrative levels, the Directorate-General of Rehabilitation Centers, which was transferred from the Department of Justice on October 10, 1958, is essentially an agency of supervision and study. Its role is to study programs and methods of rehabilitation, to appoint and train personnel for the penal services, and to supervise the penal institutions (called rehabilitation centers because of the educational goal which has been added to the corrective goals of these institutions, and which motivated the transfer of this directorate from the Department of Justice, to which it had been traditionally attached). Another reason for the change lies in the fact that in the rehabilitation centers there are not only persons who have been judged by a court decision but also persons detained under remand, who have committed crimes or political offenses, or offenses against the public security. For this latter group, a double problem of rehabilitation and political control arises, and this can be dealt with only by agents of the public security services.[67]

To sum up the organization of the Ministry of the Interior, which is a traditional ministry:

1) The command function is fulfilled by the minister, aided by a director of cabinet and a secretary-general.

2) The study and co-ordination functions are fulfilled by the principal services of the ministry.

3) The purely administrative function (personnel and accounting) is assured by a certain number of other services which are placed strictly on the same administrative level as the former.

4) The execution of certain important responsibilities of the Ministry is assured by the directorates-general which have services in the Interior or which control certain services in the Interior.

It is easy to observe here the various types of specialization referred to by Gulick in his theory of formal organization: [68]

1) The grouping of activities having a common purpose: Directorate-General of National Police.

2) The grouping of activities employing common processes: Service of Budget and Accounting.

3) The grouping of activities serving a particular clientele group: the Administrative Service, Service of Control, and Service of Immigration.

4) The grouping of activities performed in a particular area: territorial divisions of the Directorate-General of Rehabilitation Centers.

THE MINISTRY OF RURAL AFFAIRS

The same can be said of the newly formed ministries, with the difference that, because of the newness of the agency, the share of initiative in the setting up of the agency is greater. The Ministry of Rural Affairs can be taken as an example, having been created May

28, 1961, at the time of the reorganization of the Cabinet Council of the First Republic, based on suggestions in a report made five years earlier.[69] It was provided that this department, as the ministry was then called, would group under its authority services attached to the former Department of Agriculture, the former Department of Land Property and Agrarian Reform, the special Commissariat for Co-operatives and Agricultural Credit, the Commissariat-General for Agricultural Development, and the Rural Reconstruction Service (formerly attached to the Directorate-General of Reconstruction).

The reasons for this broad reorganization were clearly indicated in the Department's report on government progress during seven years:

> Establishment and improvement of social and economic conditions is one of the many purposes of the government. . . . In so doing, efforts have been shifted principally in improving rural conditions and development of agriculture [because] it affects the interests of large majorities of population. . . .
> With a view to increasing the efficiency of the executive and proper delegation of authority, integration of these organizations into one department helps facilitate program layout and preparation and should permit full utilization of existing common facilities.[70]

The organization of this Department required a great deal of time and work, particularly because of the personalities of the heads of certain commissariats and directorates. The problem was further complicated by the fact that the new department was to combine under a single authority two powerful agencies previously attached to the Presidency, whose heads were accustomed to direct relationships with the president himself. The solution adopted consisted of a compromise: only the administrative services of the former departments were regrouped, while the technical services became so-called attached agencies; in addition, the agencies previously attached to the Presidency retained a relative autonomy, and were called special agencies. The decree of October 28, 1961, officially set down a rather complicated theoretical organization, according to which the agencies of the Department were grouped in three categories: the central agencies (*co quan trung uong*), the attached agencies (*co quan ngoai thuoc*), and the special agencies (*co quan dac biet*).[71]

The Central Agencies. The so-called central agencies constitute the staff of the minister. They are composed of the Cabinet Directorate for Affairs of Government; the Secretariat-General, which includes the Administrative and Financial Directorate and the Technical and Planning Directorate; and the Inspectorate of Rural Affairs for on-the-spot supervision of the various field agencies of the ministry.

The principal difficulty in the organization of these so-called central services lay in the fact that each former department had its own administrative services, its secretaries-general, and its directors. The fusion of the administrative services posed many problems: choice of office locations; transfer of activities; transfer of services, particularly of accounting; and, above all, reclassifying public officials who occupied posts of authority in the former departments.

It should be noted that three central organizations are responsible for co-ordinating the activities of the attached and special agencies—first, by the centralizing of planning and statistics and studying economic measures intended to promote agricultural production, in particular problems of foreign exchange and the mobilization of resources (Technical and Planning Directorate); second, by on-the-spot inspections, both at the central level and at the territorial level, of all services dependent on the Ministry (Rural Affairs Supervision Office); and third, by centralizing the overhead units (Directorate for Administration and Finance).

The Attached Agencies. The attached agencies are the technical services belonging to the two former departments of Agriculture and of Agrarian Reform, in the following order: (1) the Directorate-General of Land Administration (which retained the same internal organization it had in the department of Agrarian Reform), (2) the Directorate of Forestry (which retained the same internal structure as when it belonged to the Department of Agriculture), (3) the Directorate of Animal Husbandry (which retained the same internal structure as when it belonged to the Department of Agriculture), (4) the Directorate of Rural Engineering and Hydrology, which includes certain services formerly a part of the Department of Public Works (the Agricultural Hydraulics Service) and of the former Department of Agriculture (the Service of Agricultural Works), (5) the Directorate of Research, formerly the Directorate of Research and Documentation for Agriculture and Forestry under the former Department of Agriculture; and (6) the Botanical Garden in Saigon.

Four more attached agencies were added to the Ministry by the Revolutionary Government: the Directorate of Agricultural Affairs, the Directorate of Agricultural Development, and the Directorate of Machine Agricultural Development, all of which were transferred from the Commissariat-General for Agricultural Development; and the Directorate of Fisheries, transferred from the former Department of National Economy.

The Special Agencies. Under the First Republic, the special agencies were the Commissariat-General for Agricultural Development and the Commissariat-General of Co-operatives and Agricultural Credit.

The Commissariat-General for Agricultural Development included the following directorates: the Directorate of Administrative and Financial Affairs, the Directorate of Agricultural Affairs (formerly the Directorate of Agriculture), the Directorate of Agricultural Development, the Directorate of Machine Agricultural Development, and the Directorate of Resettlement and Transfer.

It should be noted that this Commissariat was organized on new principles, replacing the Commissariat for Refugees, which had also been created under the pressure of circumstances. It is thus easy to understand the great number of commentaries that experts have written about its organization.[72]

In 1961, a new function was added to this Commissariat that seems completely foreign to its purposes: the execution of social works in the Central Viet-Nam Highlands.[73] This decision can be explained by the personality of the new commissioner, who was a delegate of the former commissioner in the Central Viet-Nam Highlands, and also by the fact that it was felt that under his direction more active care would be given to the material life of the ethnic minorities in this region.

In the reorganization of the government that followed the November 1 Revolution, social development was considered a more important aspect of this Commissariat-General than its original function of agricultural development. The Directorate of Agricultural Affairs was transferred to the Ministry of Rural Affairs, and the remainder of the Commissariat was integrated with the Interministerial Committee for Strategic Hamlets, formerly attached to the Department of the Interior. The new agency was then named the Commissariat-General of New Rural Life (*Phu Tong Uy Tan Sinh Nong Thon*), and was attached directly to the Office of the Prime Minister. There it later became the Directorate of New Rural Life, after all the services of an agricultural nature had been returned to the Ministry of Rural Affairs.[74]

The Commissariat-General for Co-operatives and Agricultural Credit retained its previous status as an agency attached directly to the Presidency, i.e., the commissioner-general retained his own cabinet director, his secretary-general, and his inspectors. The secretary-general has under his authority the following directorates: the Directorate of Administrative Affairs, the Directorate of Planning and Training, and the Directorate of Co-operatives.

Two autonomous agencies are still attached to this Commissariat: the National Office of Agricultural Credit, and the Study and Training Center for Co-operatives.

Chart III indicates whether the goals of this reform of agricultural administration have been attained. One goal, obviously, was a greater cohesion in agrarian and agricultural policy, as all of these problems now receive a stronger co-ordination. Another was certainly economy, since certain offices were eliminated (one cabinet director and one secretary-general instead of two of each), others were combined (directorates of research and training, and the directorates of agriculture and of agricultural extension). However, the chart shows that the new organization, although apparently more rational, attempts to maintain the key positions of the former organizations, no doubt in order to prejudice as little as possible the interests of the holders of these positions. Moreover, the Commissariat-General of Co-operatives and Agricultural Credit retains integrally its former organization; thus, since it was formerly an agency attached to the Presidency, this Commissariat has a cabinet director and a secretariat-general, like the ministries from which it differs in name only. This means that in a single ministry there are now two cabinet directors and two secretaries-general enjoying the same prerogatives, while the jurisdiction of one extends over the entire ministry and that of the other remains limited to its specialized agency.

GENERAL REMARKS
ON THE ORGANIZATION OF THE MINISTRIES

The study of the organization of two typical ministries gives the reader an idea of the general structure of the ministries. The agencies which make up each ministry include generally a cabinet directorate; a secretariat-general, which supervises the administrative directorates or services and sometimes the technical directorates or services; and a certain number of directorates-general, whose functions are clearly differentiated, so that certain of them become offices, i.e., agencies which have civil status and financial autonomy. The study of the functioning of these agencies brings new light to the role played by the minister and his assistants in the central government.[75]

The Minister. The minister is the direct collaborator of the prime minister in the domain assigned to him. Thus, he is chosen by the prime minister, with the consent of the Military Revolutionary Council. In the course of the ministerial reorganization of February 7, 1964, all but four of the ministers were changed. Beyond the facts that a certain number of the present ministers are military officers, and that many of them belong to the Dai Viet party which was opposed to the Ngo Dinh Diem regime, it is too early to attempt any generalizations regarding the present Cabinet. However, some information concerning the secretaries of state of the First Republic may be useful for purposes of comparison.

The government formed by virtue of the Constitution of October 26, 1956,[76] already seemed to break with the tradition established during the preceding period, in which the selection of a Cabinet was made only after exhaustive negotiations with representatives from interest groups (groups concerned with foreign policy, regionalism, the spirit of religious and political sects). The thirteen secretaries of state were chosen according to their competence, and, to a certain extent, according to their provinces of origin. Most of them were already career public administrators, but five were political figures and one was a technician who had just returned from study abroad; all but one had university degrees; in order to balance power among different parts of the country, seven were from the South, four from the North, and two from Central Viet-Nam.[77] The reorganizations subsequent to the promulgation of the Constitution of October 26, 1956, followed approximately the same tendencies. If the Cabinet Council as it stood after the last departmental reorganization (May 28, 1961) is compared with the first Cabinet (October 29, 1955), it can be seen that the number of executive departments had been reduced from 13 to 12; two secretaries of state (Foreign Affairs and Labor) had remained at their posts since the beginning; a number of departments had changed secretaries only once, but five had changed secretaries twice (Interior, Land Property and Agrarian Reform, National Economy, Finance, and Agriculture), the Department of Health three times, and the Department of Public Works four times. Thus a relative stability existed in the appointment of secretaries of state, although naturally less than in that of the director-generals of the Executive Office of the President. The great difference between a secretary of state and a director-general was that the first participated officially in the general policy, as a member of the Cabinet Council, and in the special policy concerning a specific activity of the government, as the head of the department responsible for that activity. Sometimes a secretary of state was given several additional functions, as was the case with the last secretary of state at the Presidency, who also performed the functions of both secretary of state co-ordinator for public security and assistant secretary of state for national defense. This must be considered quite unusual, and is explained by the fact that the matter concerns departments in which political responsibility was greater than in others, and in which the president wished to exercise personal control. Moreover, the personalities of the president and of the secretaries of states counted for a great deal in their reciprocal relationships, so that the study of relationships between the chief executive and the heads of the executive departments is a question of fact much more than of law. To say that this is an example of concentration of power is not quite exact, as in many matters there existed no regulations subordinating the decision of the secretary of state to the formal approval of the president. If the secretaries of state referred much more often to the decision of the chief of state than in other similar regimes, it was simply a practice that was becoming customary. At any rate, this relative stability in the functions of the secretaries of states should be considered a positive factor for progress, in the domain of the formation of a general policy at the present time, in the region of Southeast Asia, where political instability is a common matter.[78] The secretaries of state who were heads of departments could also inspire their collaborators with this spirit of progress which must permeate the various levels of execution of the policy of the government.[79]

Since the secretary of state was appointed by the president of the Republic, he could be relieved of his functions at any moment by the authority that had appointed him. Under the former monarchy, it occurred occasionally that the mandarins who occupied the highest functions of the Court were downgraded several levels, for reason of high politics, or simply for the emperor's good pleasure. During the Bao Dai regime, the ministerial instability left the minister with the sword of Damocles hanging over him, which dampened any initiative and discouraged any long-range policy. Although no regulation prevented the president of the Republic from frequently changing the members of the Cabinet Council, the new tradition of stability is responsible for the progress realized in certain domains of substantive administration, as has been pointed out.[80] The responsibility of the secretary of state before the president remained intact, however, in spite of the changes (Amendment No. 1/62 HP, of July 8, 1962) brought about in the provisions of Article 47 of the Constitution.[81] According to these changes, the secretary of state could appear either before the commissions, or before the plenary meetings of the National Assembly, to give precise explanations on particular points of general politics, when such explanations had been requested in writing on behalf of the Assembly. These provisions should be considered as providing for a more rational communication with the Assembly, and through the Assembly, with the people. This is not a matter of responsibility of the secretary of state before the Assembly, as in a parliamentary regime.

Since the November 1 Revolution, one minister (Information) has been changed three times. In the ministerial reorganization of February 8, all ministers were changed but four (National Economy, Justice, Public Health, and Public Works and Communication). Since this reorganization, only one minister has been changed (Interior). These changes are too recent, however, to be interpreted as a new tendency.

The Director of Cabinet. In principle, the director of the cabinet assists the minister in so-called affairs of government. As a member of the Cabinet Council, the minister may, as a matter of fact, have to deal with questions of general politics sometimes completely foreign to the functions of his own ministry. A given minister might be responsible for negotiating with certain representatives of the opposition; another may have to meet with foreign representatives to change the current flow of technical assistance. Under certain political pressure, it is occasionally necessary to change the director of a service, but it is important for the minister to convince the person in question himself, beforehand, of the desired change. It is in these delicate missions that the director of cabinet renders a real service to the minister through his skill and *savoir-faire*. Examining these principal activities may lead the reader to believe that the minister places in his cabinet men of his choice. Actually, a glance at the qualification of cabinet directors of the First Republic will reveal that they were often career civil servants, tested administrators, or technicians of recognized ability; but in the lines of centralization, the appointment had to have the approval of the president, even though the appointment was a departmental decision. Sometimes, because of complications of a personal nature, the position of director of cabinet was left vacant, as was the case in the Department of Foreign Affairs, or his functions were added to those of a high official in the department, as was the case in the Department of Labor. At the present time, the minister seems to have the power to appoint anyone he chooses to this position.

The Secretary-General. In the regulations for various departments, the tendency is to make the secretary-general the highest administrative official of the department. In principle, it is he who, in good Anglo-French tradition, is to represent the administration that remains, when the government changes. In order to provide him with a certain legal guarantee of stability, the appointment of the secretary-general must be made official by a decree of the prime minister (formerly of the president of the Republic), while that of the director of cabinet is made simply by a ministerial order.

Although it is not an absolutely fixed rule, the secretary-general usually fulfills first the administrative functions of the ministry: budget, personnel, equipment, transportation, sometimes even planning. In certain technical ministries, sometimes the secretary-general also supervises some directorates of a technical nature (ministries of Public Works and Communication, National Economy, and Finance). Other ministries have such clearly defined technical functions that the administrative services are reduced to their most simple forms, and do not require any co-ordination by a secretary-general (ministries of Justice, National Defense, and Health).

In fact, the secretaries-general are often chosen from among public servants who have had long experience in the ministry. Experience with routine procedures can contribute greatly to the smooth operation of services, whereas, on the other hand, the spirit of initiative is developed only with a certain training in matters of public administration. Since the November 1 Revolution, there have been a certain number of changes in the positions of secretary-general.

The Commissaries-General and the Director-Generals. While the secretary-general often performs the function of so-called procedural administration, the director-general is an agent of substantive administration. In other words, it is here that the idea of staff and line comes into the organization. While the director of cabinet and the secretary-general, with their assistants, constitute the staff of the minister, the director-generals are the first in the hierarchy of line functions. And as each ministry accomplishes at the maximum a few functions, it is easy to see that there exist in the government only a limited number of directorates-general, equal to all these functions together. At the present time, there are 33 directorates-general (see Chart IV), among which seven belong to the Office of the Prime Minister. Because of the special importance attached to certain functions, the holder of this position takes the title of Commissioner-General, Governor of the National Bank, Recteur of the Institute, or Inspector General. Certain of these have the power to make regulations (for example, the commissioner-general of co-operatives); others have powers of decision clearly defined by the regulations (for example, the director-general for taxes, and the director-general for customs duties).

Most of the director-generals are chosen from among career civil servants, but, contrary to the principle of seniority, they can be chosen from the cadres, and may not have yet attained the heights of the hierarchy. Certain director-generals do not belong to the cadres. Others are general or superior officers (Police and Rehabilitation Centers). The position of director-general also enjoys considerable stability; among the 31 directorates-general which existed at the time, only four changes of post occurred in the last two years of the First Republic. Thus, although by right the appointment of director-generals belonged to the president of the Republic, in point of fact, this stability is convincing proof that the presidential decisions were not arbitrary in this matter. As might be expected, because of the great importance of these functions, all the director-generals were changed following the Revolution of November 1, 1963.

Directorates and Services. In principle, a directorate is placed either within a secretariat-general, or within a directorate-general. Normally, those that are part of secretariats-general perform administrative functions of a procedural nature, while those in directorates-general fulfill functions of substantive administration. This is not necessarily always the case; certain important directorates-general are provided with an administrative directorate, while certain substantive subfunctions whose importance is not great enough to warrant creating a directorate-general, are entrusted simply to attached directorates to aid a secretariat-general, or can even depend directly on the minister, as is the case at present in the Ministry of Rural Affairs.

In the line organization hierarchy, below the directorates, are the services, in which are grouped several bureaus, which are the smallest units in the formal organization. In point of fact, certain bureaus are divided into sections, which simply represent organizations set up to answer a need for a more precise division of the work. In regard to services and bureaus, there is no question of political choice in the assignment of public servants responsible for their administration. There exist already in administrative practice certain norms which will be examined with the personnel management problem.

Although the creation of new directorates, services, and bureaus, which is treated in the act defining the organization of the ministry, must be carefully examined by the Directorate-General of Civil Service and the Directorate-General of Budget and Foreign Aid, still it may occur that, foreseeing needs in the near future, certain departments may be provided with some services or bureaus which do not function yet in fact, or which have only a bureau chief with personnel limited to two or three. This can be explained also by a certain demonstration effect: the minister (formerly the secretary of state) may wish to give a more modern appearance to the organization of his department; [82] or by a certain particularistic spirit the minister may wish to favor one of his collaborators and give him a certain authority by the device of a relatively important position in the hierarchy of the organization; on occasion, it might simply be a question of an exaggerated concern for a theoretical organization, in which Parkinson's law often finds its application. [83] In truth, such situations are not numerous; organization plans that would tend to increase inordinately the number of services and bureaus would meet strong objection on the part of the Directorate-General of Budget and Foreign Aid. On the other hand, through excessive concern for economy, it sometimes occurs that the Directorate-General of Budget and Foreign Aid proposes rather strange groupings in order to reduce the number of services and bureaus in each organization of the department. Sometimes, the two directorates responsible for looking out for efficiency and economy in problems of organization, i.e., the Directorate of Budget and Foreign Aid and the Directorate of Civil Service, present divergent opinions. It is here that the need is felt for the intervention of either the director of the cabinet or the secretary-general of the interested department, or even of the directors or chiefs of the services themselves in negotiation with these agencies, to arrive at occasionally happy compromises. At any rate, in case of disagreement, the prime minister must intervene to give the final solution. Since the November 1 Revolution, the reorganization movement has so far affected only the higher executive positions, and has not yet reached the level of the directorates and services.

Financially Autonomous Agencies. The most lengthy negotiations concern the establishing of new autonomous agencies whose budgets are distinct from the national budget. The suspicion of the Directorate-General of Budget and Foreign Aid in these cases is natural, since the financial administration of these services is more or less beyond the control of that Directorate-General. As a matter of fact, as long as these services succeed in administering their finances correctly, the Directorate-General of Budget and Foreign Aid exerts only a vague control over them, and intervenes actively only when the service in question requests a budgetary subsidy. Even the National Assembly of the First Republic regarded this practice as a means for certain services to escape its control, and frequently requested the reintegration into the national budget of the proposed budgets for agencies when there was no major reason for detaching them from the government.[84]

Among these agencies enjoying financial autonomy, the most important are placed under the authority of the director-generals, while others are simply entrusted to directors. These directors are often appointed either by the prime minister or occasionally by the minister concerned, but they are all supervised by an administrative council, presided over by the minister concerned, and of which the rule is that a representative of the Directorate-General of Budget and Foreign Aid must be a member, along with representatives of the ministries more or less concerned. Representatives of private interests are sometimes admitted to the administrative council. The council sets the budget of the agency, and votes its administrative account; it also determines the general lines of activity of the agency.[85] In reality, the director of the agency has rather extensive powers, since the meetings of the administrative council are rather infrequent, and sometimes because of the fact that certain members of the administrative council prove not too interested in the administrative problems of a service which is not in their fields.

The reasons which officially justify the designation of autonomous agencies are many, but are centered on the ideal of efficiency. They include (1) the rapid and expeditious execution of certain economic and social objectives (The Pasteur Institute, the Thu Duc Orphanage, the Industrial Development Center, and the Crafts Development Center), (2) the commercial nature of operations performed by the agency (the Viet Nam National Bank, the Commercial Credit, the Agricultural Credit, etc.), and (3) the industrial nature of the operations (the An Hoa Industrial Center, the Water Supply Office, the Viet-Nam National Railways, and the Dan Him electrification program).

But the final decision for setting up an autonomous agency belongs always to the prime minister.[86]

FIELD OFFICES OF THE CENTRAL AGENCIES

In some cases, a ministry has only a single province service which represents it in the provinces; thus the Ministry of Public Works and Communication has in each province a Provincial Service of Public Works, which provides the services of several directorates-general or directorates of the central administration (Roads and Bridges, Agricultural Hydrology, Airports).[87]

Often, each directorate-general of a ministry has its own provincial service; thus in the Ministry of Rural Affairs, the Directorate-General of Land Administration is represented in the provinces by a provincial service; the Office of Agricultural Credit is represented by provincial offices of agricultural credit; and the Directorate of Agriculture by a provincial agricultural service. In the case of several provincial services which belong to the same ministry, there is sometimes a problem of co-ordination; certain ministries have tried to solve this problem by consolidating in one office all the provincial services of the same ministry, but without notable success, because of the technical nature of the functions of the various services, occasionally also because of the personality of the chiefs of service, and in some instances because of the feeling of loyalty that has developed between counterpart units. The Department of Civic Action, for example, even after the directorates-general of Civic Action, Information, and Youth were regrouped under it, made an unsuccessful attempt to consolidate the provincial services formerly dependent on the three directorates-general. The problem of co-ordination will be examined in the light of powers and responsibilities of province chiefs.

Conclusion

The analysis of facts concerning the problems of organization in the central government permits the verification of the statements which have been made with regard to the present administrative philosophy in Viet-Nam.

The profusion of organic texts, in the Office of the Prime Minister as well as in the line organization echelons, is adequate indication of the tendency toward legality in the administration. Personal consideration is nevertheless a concession to a humanistic tendency. The various agencies which can develop points of contact with the people are multiplied in order to promote greater co-operation on the part of the population. Moreover, the setting up of new agencies, certain of which constitute a pure concession to the demonstration effect, is a revealing indication of the tendency to adopt new techniques.

Certain authors, analyzing the phenomena of development, see rather a progressive differentiation of functions: the fusion in a single structure of responsibility for the execution of different functions, which characterizes traditional society, is replaced by a refraction which makes each function correspond to a special structure. Thus the traditional six ministries which constituted the emperor's court for ten centuries (*Bo Lai,* the Ministry of the Interior; *Bo Ho,* the Ministry of Finance; *Bo Le,* the Ministry of Rituals; *Bo Hinh,* the Ministry of Justice; *Bo Cong,* the Ministry of Public Works; and *Bo Binh,* the Ministry of the Army) were replaced by thirteen new ministries, after the fluctuations of the colonial period, during which some directorates of the Government-General duplicated the imperial ministries. Some ministries, in becoming more specialized, have taken up certain functions of the former ministries: those of the old Ministry of the Interior are performed by the new Ministry of the Interior and by the Directorate-General of Civil Service; the functions of the former Ministry of Rituals have been entrusted to the Ministry of National Education; etc. Other ministries perform functions which existed only in an embryonic stage under the imperial regime; the functions of the Ministry of National Economy and of the Ministry of Rural Affairs existed sporadically in the former ministries of Interior, Finance, and Public Works. Still other ministries, such as the Ministry of Labor, have been created to face entirely new problems. Thus, in the present organization, the administrative function that consists of putting into force the various means of realizing the objectives set by the agencies which perform political functions is more and more clearly defined as one descends in the administrative hierarchy. Within the administrative function, the subfunctions are more precisely set down, and are entrusted to more specialized agencies.

Nevertheless, certain critics consider this tendency formalistic because it sometimes presents officially, in legal texts, situations quite differently from what they are in reality. In truth, it can be seen from the various facts cited, that in spite of the concern for setting up official organizations by regulations which defined the functions of various government services, there existed a tendency toward centralization, since the final decision was often referred to the President of the Republic himself. Moreover, in problems of organization, the personal factor was often taken into account. This is an application of the idea of particularism as opposed to universalism. Other authors might see here a certain imperfect integration in the process of development, since the formal organization which expresses the will of the power represents only an ideal toward which the various activities move, but which they have not yet reached.[88]

However, upon reading the behavioral descriptions of Simon, one finds, strangely enough, the same subjacent ideas behind the most spectacular reforms of organizations, even in the most advanced countries.[89] Although it may be a little premature, before examining the administration in action in Chapter 7, it might still be permissible to conclude here and now that the distinction between the formal and the informal exists to a rather high degree in the organization of the central government of Viet-Nam, but that this phenomenon is not solely characteristic of the transitional stage of Vietnamese society. It is possible, since the central government is composed of an elite which is more or less Westernized and consequently more susceptible to the adoption of new ideas of organization which come from democratic countries, the behavior of these men does not differ greatly from that of men from an industrialized country.[90] It will be possible to find other tests for the theory of development in the study of territorial administrations.

CHART I

ORGANIZATION OF THE EXECUTIVE BRANCH
OF THE CENTRAL GOVERNMENT OF THE FIRST REPUBLIC

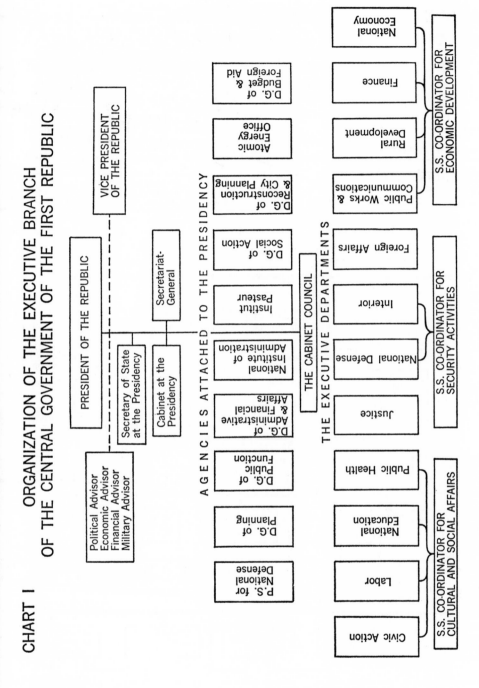

CHART II
THE GOVERNMENT OF THE REPUBLIC OF VIET-NAM

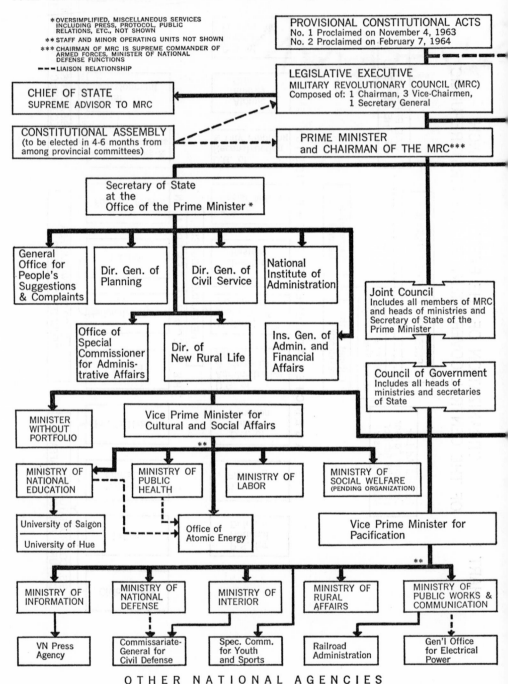

* OVERSIMPLIFIED, MISCELLANEOUS SERVICES
INCLUDING PRESS, PROTOCOL, PUBLIC
RELATIONS, ETC., NOT SHOWN

** STAFF AND MINOR OPERATING UNITS NOT SHOWN

*** CHAIRMAN OF MRC IS SUPREME COMMANDER OF
ARMED FORCES, MINISTER OF NATIONAL
DEFENSE FUNCTIONS

--- LIAISON RELATIONSHIP

PROVISIONAL CONSTITUTIONAL ACTS
No. 1 Proclaimed on November 4, 1963
No. 2 Proclaimed on February 7, 1964

LEGISLATIVE EXECUTIVE
MILITARY REVOLUTIONARY COUNCIL (MRC)
Composed of: 1 Chairman, 3 Vice-Chairmen,
1 Secretary General

CHIEF OF STATE
SUPREME ADVISOR TO MRC

CONSTITUTIONAL ASSEMBLY
(to be elected in 4-6 months from
among provincial committees)

PRIME MINISTER
and CHAIRMAN OF THE MRC***

Secretary of State
at the
Office of the Prime Minister *

General
Office for
People's
Suggestions
& Complaints

Dir. Gen. of
Planning

Dir. Gen. of
Civil Service

National
Institute of
Administration

Joint Council
Includes all members of MRC
and heads of ministries and
Secretary of State of the
Prime Minister

Office of
Special
Commissioner
for Adminis-
trative Affairs

Dir. of
New Rural Life

Ins. Gen. of
Admin. and
Financial
Affairs

Council of Government
Includes all heads of
ministries and secretaries
of State

MINISTER
WITHOUT
PORTFOLIO

Vice Prime Minister for
Cultural and Social Affairs
**

MINISTRY OF
NATIONAL
EDUCATION

MINISTRY OF
PUBLIC
HEALTH

MINISTRY OF
LABOR

MINISTRY OF
SOCIAL WELFARE
(PENDING ORGANIZATION)

University of Saigon

University of Hue

Office of
Atomic Energy

Vice Prime Minister for
Pacification
**

MINISTRY OF
INFORMATION

MINISTRY OF
NATIONAL
DEFENSE

MINISTRY OF
INTERIOR

MINISTRY OF
RURAL
AFFAIRS

MINISTRY OF
PUBLIC WORKS &
COMMUNICATION

VN Press
Agency

Commissariate-
General for
Civil Defense

Spec. Comm.
for Youth
and Sports

Railroad
Administration

Gen'l Office
for Electrical
Power

OTHER NATIONAL AGENCIES

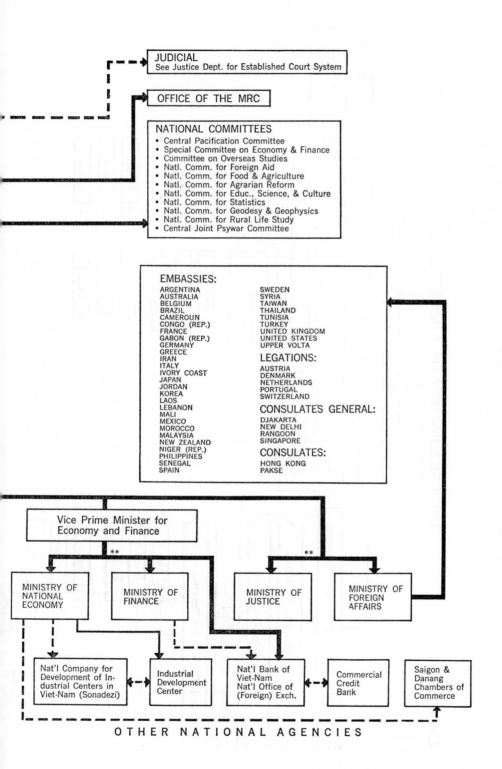

JUDICIAL
See Justice Dept. for Established Court System

OFFICE OF THE MRC

NATIONAL COMMITTEES
- Central Pacification Committee
- Special Committee on Economy & Finance
- Committee on Overseas Studies
- Natl. Comm. for Foreign Aid
- Natl. Comm. for Food & Agriculture
- Natl. Comm. for Agrarian Reform
- Natl. Comm. for Educ., Science, & Culture
- Natl. Comm. for Statistics
- Natl. Comm. for Geodesy & Geophysics
- Natl. Comm. for Rural Life Study
- Central Joint Psywar Committee

EMBASSIES:
ARGENTINA
AUSTRALIA
BELGIUM
BRAZIL
CAMEROUN
CONGO (REP.)
FRANCE
GABON (REP.)
GERMANY
GREECE
IRAN
ITALY
IVORY COAST
JAPAN
JORDAN
KOREA
LAOS
LEBANON
MALI
MEXICO
MOROCCO
MALAYSIA
NEW ZEALAND
NIGER (REP.)
PHILIPPINES
SENEGAL
SPAIN

SWEDEN
SYRIA
TAIWAN
THAILAND
TUNISIA
TURKEY
UNITED KINGDOM
UNITED STATES
UPPER VOLTA

LEGATIONS:
AUSTRIA
DENMARK
NETHERLANDS
PORTUGAL
SWITZERLAND

CONSULATES GENERAL:
DJAKARTA
NEW DELHI
RANGOON
SINGAPORE

CONSULATES:
HONG KONG
PAKSE

Vice Prime Minister for
Economy and Finance

**

**

MINISTRY OF
NATIONAL
ECONOMY

MINISTRY OF
FINANCE

MINISTRY OF
JUSTICE

MINISTRY OF
FOREIGN
AFFAIRS

Nat'l Company for
Development of In-
dustrial Centers in
Viet-Nam (Sonadezi)

Industrial
Development
Center

Nat'l Bank of
Viet-Nam
Nat'l Office of
(Foreign) Exch.

Commercial
Credit
Bank

Saigon &
Danang
Chambers of
Commerce

OTHER NATIONAL AGENCIES

CHART III

THE ORGANIZATION OF A MINISTRY

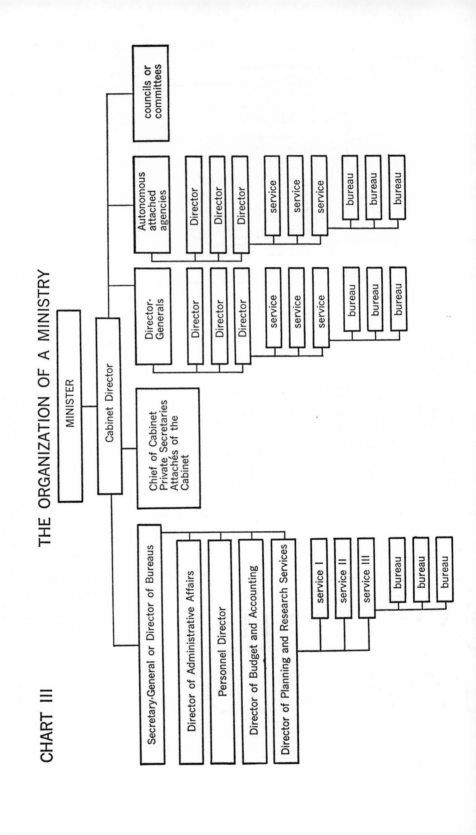

CHART IV DIRECTORATES-GENERAL

OFFICE OF THE PRIME MINISTER (7)

    Directorate-General of Planning
    Directorate-General of Civil Service
    National Institute of Administration
    Inspectorate-General of Administrative and Financial Affairs
    General Office for People's Suggestions and Complaints
    Office of the Special Commissioner for Administrative Affairs
    Directorate of New Rural Life

OFFICE OF THE VICE PRIME MINISTER FOR PACIFICATION (2)

    Special Commissariat for Youth and Sports
    Directorate-General for Political and Rural Cadres

MINISTRY OF NATIONAL DEFENSE (2)

    Directorate-General for Administration, Budget, and Accounting
    Permanent Secretariat-General for National Defense

MINISTRY OF THE INTERIOR (3)

    Directorate-General of National Police
    General Administration of Rehabilitation Centers
    Commissariat-General for Civil Defense

MINISTRY OF FOREIGN AFFAIRS (1)

    Mission in Charge of Relations with the International Commission for Control in Viet-Nam

MINISTRY OF JUSTICE (NONE)

MINISTRY OF NATIONAL EDUCATION (1)

    Directorate-General of Secondary, Primary, and Popular Education

MINISTRY OF INFORMATION (1)

    Directorate-General of Information

MINISTRY OF NATIONAL ECONOMY (2)

    Directorate-General of Commerce
    Directorate-General of Mining, Industry, and Handicraft

MINISTRY OF FINANCE (6)

    Directorate-General of the Treasury
    Directorate-General of Customs
    Directorate-General of Taxation
    Directorate-General of Budget and Foreign Aid
    National Bank of Viet-Nam
    National Office of Foreign Exchange

MINISTRY OF RURAL AFFAIRS (2)

    Directorate-General of Land Administration
    Commissariat-General for Co-operatives and Agricultural Credit

MINISTRY OF LABOR (1)

    Inspectorate-General of Labor

MINISTRY OF PUBLIC HEALTH (1)

    Directorate-General of Health and Hospitals

MINISTRY OF PUBLIC WORKS AND COMMUNICATION (5)

    Directorate-General of Public Works
    Directorate-General of Transport
    Directorate-General of Ports
    Directorate-General of Telecommunications
    Directorate-General of Reconstruction and City Planning

CHART V
SHOWING THE REGROUPING OF TWO EXECUTIVE
TO FORM THE DEPARTMENT OF RURAL DEVELOPMENT

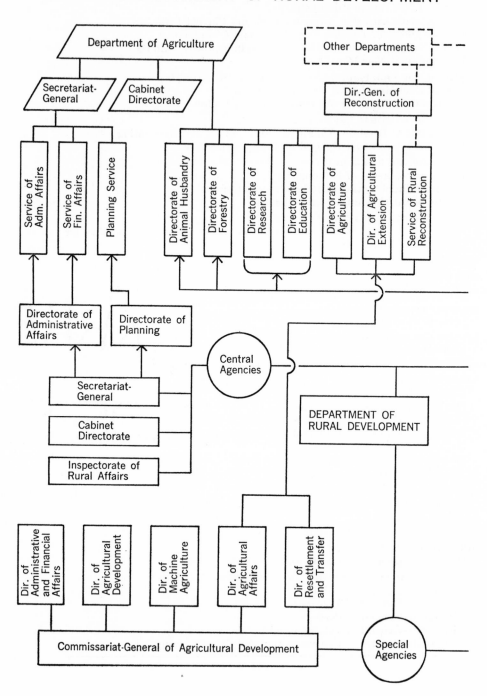

DEPARTMENTS AND TWO COMMISSARIATS-GENERAL
(NOW MINISTRY OF RURAL AFFAIRS)

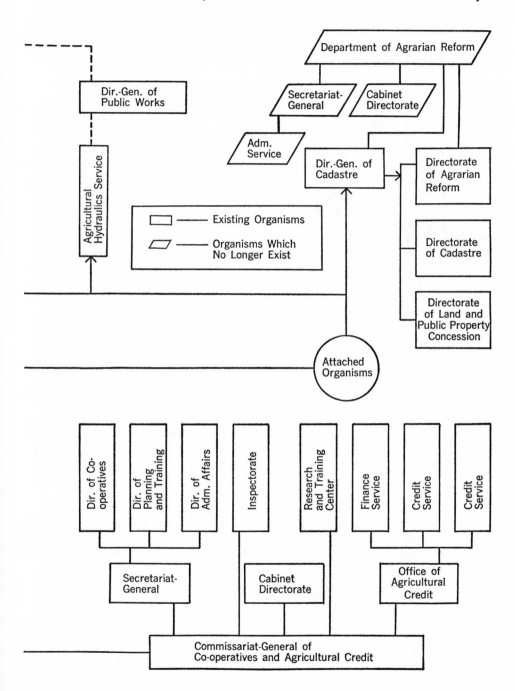

CHAPTER 4

FIELD ORGANIZATION
AND LOCAL GOVERNMENT

Phep vua thua le lang.[1]

HISTORIANS, sociologists, jurists, and political scientists, in speaking of village administration, all seem to agree on the reliability of the old Vietnamese proverb: *Phep vua thua le lang* ("Imperial orders give way to village customs").[2] It could be supposed, then, that at this administrative level the traditional factor will predominate, and that the theoretician of social science can rejoice in finding here an ideal terrain for studying the factors of resistance to change.

However, since World War II, the geographic disposition of administrative areas has itself changed so much that it is rather difficult to compare the traditional administrative structure described by Nguyen Huu Khang in 1944 with that described by J. D. Donoghue in 1962.[3] The circumstances of war, Communist propaganda, economic changes, and the development of communications have often been cited as causes of these changes. From the point of view of public administration, it is important to analyze this process of change to determine whether it follows the slow and rather vague process of any social change, or whether it has been provoked by a central government desirous of applying expeditiously its administrative philosophy.

The lowest local Vietnamese administrative unit is the commune, which is further subdivided into hamlets. The administrative divisions, in the order of decreasing size, are: the province, the district, the canton, and the commune.

The Province: Centralization and Deconcentration

An examination of the organization of the provincial administration will show whether the proverb quoted at the beginning of the chapter applies only to the village, or to the higher administrative units as well.

CHARACTERISTICS OF THE PROVINCE

At present, the Republic of Viet-Nam is divided into 42 provinces, subdivided into 237 districts.[4] An early systematic study of local administration showed 38 provinces, subdivided into 209 districts.[5] At the time of the first important reorganization of local administration the number of provinces was 35: South Viet-Nam, 22; Central Viet-Nam, 9; the Highlands, 4.[6]

In the light of Vietnamese expansion to the South, the creation of many provinces dates from the conquest of new territories; in point of fact, the provinces of Central Viet-Nam, with the exception of Quang Tin which was created only recently, still retain the boundaries of the period of southern expansion. On the other hand, South Viet-Nam, at the time when the territory was ceded to the French, included only 6 provinces (*tran*); in a territorial reorganization, the French soon divided South Viet-Nam into 24 provinces, or *so tham bien* (1867); this number was reduced to 22 toward the end of World War II (1944), but has since been increased to 25; however, the boundaries are not the same as those of 1867.[7] The Highlands, which formerly had only 4 provinces, now has 7, of which 4 have Vietnamized names, and the others still retain their old names.

This brief historical note simply shows that provinces and their subdivisions, the districts, are only territorial subdivisions of the state, without any natural autonomous existence. The fixing of boundaries is motivated by complex reasons—sometimes the rationalization of territorial organization, at other times certain administrative practices found in organizational matters in general.[8] Among environmental factors, the following may be cited: military needs (the boundaries of a province are sometimes modified to agree with those of a military sector, as in the case of the creation of the province of Chuong Thien, December 24, 1961); the demands of security (the province of Phu Bon was created September 1, 1962, to encompass an important strategic junction; also the case of Phuoc Thanh in 1959); and the demands of communications (the two provinces of My Tho and Go Cong were regrouped into the single province of Dinh Tuong, and the two provinces of Cho Lon and Tan An into the single province of Long An, October 22, 1956).

Since the creation or regroupment of provinces is not necessarily determined by natural boundaries, the question might arise as to whether or not the government systematically considers only administrative factors, such as the area of the territories or their population. The map of administrative divisions (page 122) shows that Southwest Viet-Nam and Southeast Viet-Nam, the two smallest regions, have, respectively, the highest and next highest number of provinces; that Central Viet-Nam follows; and that the Highlands, the largest region, have the lowest number of provinces. This is confirmed by statistics concerning the areas of the provinces: the Highlands include two provinces of more than 1,000,000 hectares (approximately 4,000 square miles) and one of more than 500,000 (approximately 2,000 square miles); in Central Viet-Nam there are one province of more than 1,000,000 hectares and three of more than 500,000; in Southwest Viet-Nam, there are two provinces of more

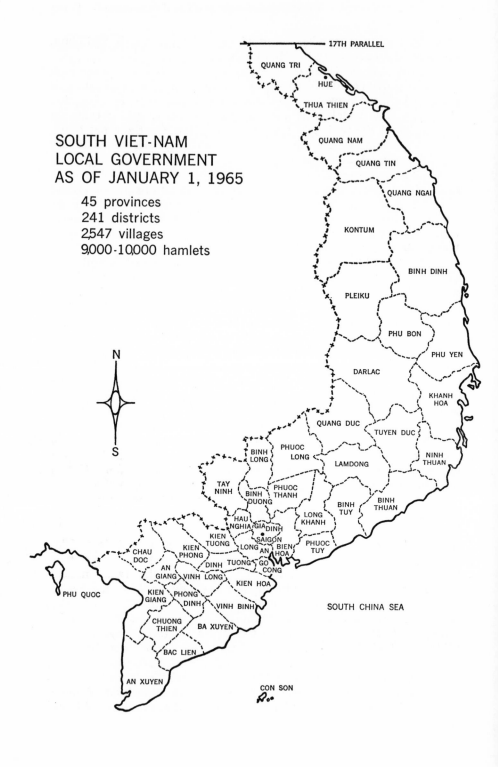

SOUTH VIET-NAM
LOCAL GOVERNMENT
AS OF JANUARY 1, 1965

45 provinces
241 districts
2,547 villages
9,000-10,000 hamlets

17TH PARALLEL

QUANG TRI

HUE

THUA THIEN

QUANG NAM

QUANG TIN

QUANG NGAI

KONTUM

BINH DINH

PLEIKU

PHU BON

PHU YEN

DARLAC

KHANH HOA

N

S

QUANG DUC

TUYEN DUC

BINH LONG

PHUOC LONG

NINH THUAN

TAY NINH

BINH DUONG

PHUOC THANH

LAMDONG

BINH TUY

BINH THUAN

HAU NGHIA

GIA DINH

LONG KHANH

KIEN TUONG

SAIGON

CHAU DOC

KIEN PHONG

LONG AN

BIEN HOA

PHUOC TUY

AN GIANG

DINH TUONG

GO CONG

VINH LONG

KIEN HOA

PHU QUOC

KIEN GIANG

PHONG DINH

VINH BINH

SOUTH CHINA SEA

CHUONG THIEN

BA XUYEN

BAC LIEN

AN XUYEN

CON SON

than 500,000 hectares; in Southeast Viet-Nam, there are no provinces of more than 500,000, in spite of the fact that the average area of a province is approximately 420,000 hectares. With the exception of the island province of Con Son (6,374 hectares), the smallest province is Gia Dinh, which has an area of 70,587 hectares.[9]

Regarding population, the following table can still be used, in spite of the fact that recent changes have modified certain figures: [10]

PROVINCES: POPULATION CHARACTERISTICS
OCTOBER 30, 1959 *

Region	Number of Provinces	Mean	Population Median	Range
Highlands[a]	6	89,851	66,134	27,000–183,067
Southeast Viet-Nam	10	188,879	103,088	34,083–643,877
Central Lowlands	9	457,130	341,345	123,623–939,761
Southwest Viet-Nam	12[a]	473,166	503,827	54,333–801,477
Viet-Nam	37	330,253	271,944	27,000–939,761

* Approximate date.
[a] The prison island province of Con Son was excluded.
Source: Records of the National Institute of Statistics, Republic of Viet-Nam

From the foregoing, it is evident that the factors of area and of population are of little importance in setting boundaries of the provinces.

The same is true of the districts. The population of districts varies from 1,278 to more than 190,000, with an average of 58,102: [11]

DISTRICTS: POPULATION CHARACTERISTICS
OCTOBER 30, 1959 *

Region	Number of Districts	District Population		
		Mean	Median	Range
Highlands	18	29,950	23,750	7,753–109,097
Southeast Viet-Nam	38	49,705	39,333	1,278–190,085
Central Lowlands	72	55,984	44,375	3,437–183,526
Southwest Viet-Nam	81	70,098	78,571	8,091–171,535
Viet-Nam	209	58,102	50,000	1,278–190,085

Approximate date.
Source: Records of the National Institute of Statistics, Republic of Viet-Nam.

CENTRALIZATION VERSUS DECENTRALIZATION

Consequently, the existence of the provinces as administrative units can be explained only by the idea of administrative centralization with delegation of the power of decision, and not by the idea of a decentralization which gives real autonomy to these territorial divisions. A centralized power needs representatives inspired with a high sense of duty and a keen sense of responsibility with regard to that central power; these representatives must be capable of making on-the-spot decisions along the lines of general policy fixed by that power. The boundaries of the provinces are designed to satisfy as well as possible this demand for centralization. The interests of the nation at large must take precedence over the local interests; the local population can always make itself heard, and indicate its wishes, demanding that measures be taken in the local interest, but only providing these measures do not hinder the putting into effect of the national policy.[12]

There were several symptomatic indications of the centralization movement in the First Republic: for example, the elimination of cadres of local personnel (Instructions No. 34, TTP/VP, dated December 28, 1955) and the strengthening of the powers of the province chiefs, who are representatives of the central power (Ordinance of October 24, 1956). These measures kept pace with the various reorganizations of the Executive Office of the President, in which the major administrative functions were concentrated, and of the various executive departments, whose control extended over their various territorial branches. This tendency toward centralization was all the more marked since it indicated a clear reaction against the hesitations of an interdepartmental committee instituted for the purpose of studying measures resulting from the elimination of the functions of the regional governors,[13] and also a reaction against the equally inconsistent recommendations of the experts of the Michigan State University Viet-Nam Advisory Group.[14] This group proposed an increase in the size of the provinces, with a resulting decrease in number. It also proposed the election of province councils (with power to approve any economic or social program, to adopt resolutions concerning any administrative program, and to give consent to the appointment of province chiefs); at the same time it proposed the elimination of provincial budgets.

The reasons that motivated the maintaining of provinces as subdivisions of the state are numerous: the fear of rebellion in territories having too great an autonomy or too large a population; the need for a certain unity in the application of the general policy against the three current enemies; and the lack of maturity on the part of the local populations for acting on affairs which have a rather general application.[15] From a historical point of view, the tradition of centralization has been strongly established since the period of Chinese domination, through the period of independence under the emperors, to the French domination (see Chapter 2). From a comparative point of view, it is generally agreed that in all developing nations there is a general tendency toward centralization for the improvement of local government. A sociological explanation of the problem has been attempted, which could be applied to the case of Viet-Nam: poverty, stagnation, and lack of initiative contribute to an ineffective and inefficient local administration, and, reciprocally, bad local administration reinforces poverty and stagnation in a vicious circle of backwash effect.[16]

Nevertheless, the advantages of decentralization were still well known, as shown in the old adage already quoted: *Phep vua thua le lang.* This served for a long time as a guiding principle for the imperial administration, and was also retained by the colonial administration. There was only the question of knowing to what extent and at what echelon of the territorial administrative hierarchy the principle of decentralization should be applied. In the old regime, centralization consisted of the appointment of province chiefs by the imperial authority; with a philosophy of administration through example, the weight of centralization was not too heavy, and it harmonized easily with communal autonomy. Under the colonial regime, administrative services began to increase in number; but, because of administrative dualism, communal autonomy could persist even with centralization at the province level. Today, with the multiplication of administrative services brought about by the need for defense and for economic development, the advantages of decentralization at the province level have been frequently stressed by eminent administrators,[17] and by experts from the United Nations or from American universities.[18] Consequently, the Revolutionary Government has outlined certain measures to be taken toward decentralization. The decree of May 31, 1964, provides for the election by universal suffrage of provincial councils which would have the power to make certain decisions, particularly in financial matters; however, decentralization has not yet advanced so far as to provide for the execution of these decisions by local authorities. At present, there exists at the base of the administrative organization of the province a provincial charter, a single ordinance defined by the central government. The province chief continues to be a representative of the central government, as is the district chief. The province chief also comes under the control of the military commander of the tactical zone, who is ex officio the governmental delegate.

Centralization is clearly evident, for example, in the process of creating a new province. The first official step in the creation of the province of Chuong Thien was Decree No. 244/NV, dated December 24, 1961, proposed by the secretary of state for the interior, naming the new province and its capital, setting its boundaries, specifying the names of the districts, cantons, and villages formerly belonging to three different provinces (Phong Dinh, Kien Giang, and Ba

Xuyen), and stipulating certain temporary financial measures. The same procedure was followed by the Revolutionary Government in Decree No. 36/TTP, dated December 20, 1963, which re-establishes the province of Go Cong. These decrees were issued in application of Ordinance No. 59a, dated October 24, 1956, concerning the administrative reorganization of Viet-Nam; from this it must be inferred that Ordinance No. 59a constitutes today a general charter of territorial organization.[19]

Ordinance No. 59a recognizes laconically that the provinces have legal status, a domain, and a budget—the three traditional attributes of the autonomy of an administrative unit, at least according to French legal doctrine, which inspired the authors of the ordinance. The ordinance also provides for the appointment of the province chief by the central government, and stipulates certain of his powers as an agent of the central government. Apart from these expressed dispositions in defining the powers of the provincial authorities, great latitude was left for historical precedents, laws and regulations in effect at that date (insofar as they were not contrary to the principles of republican reform), and to custom. With this general charter, there is no need to make too precise an enumeration of the restrictions which the population would place on the exercise of authority, as in the administration of autonomous states, nor to circumscribe too carefully the prerogatives and responsibilities of these authorities, for fear of conflict with the powers of the central government.[20]

Certain controversial points were settled by new acts or by recent precedents. The first of these points concerned the provincial elective assembly. Since the colonial period, there has been a well-established tradition that all administrative units which have legal status must have an assembly of representatives of the population, in order to exercise the rights provided for this legal status. The existence of provincial councils created by the decrees of June 22, 1953, October 15, 1953, and June 2, 1954, which followed this tradition, did not run counter to republican principles. However, the provincial councils had not functioned, to all practical purposes, since 1956. The controversy was resolved by Decree No. 237/NV, dated December 8, 1961, which re-established the provincial councils with some democratic features. The Revolutionary Government replaced this decree by Decree No. 203b/NV, dated May 31, 1964.

The second controversial point concerned what authority had the power to create a province or a district. Comparative study tends to give this power to the legislative body.[21] However, historical precedents are in favor of the chief executive. In the days when power was concentrated in the hands of the monarchs, territorial changes of administrative units seem to have been rather frequent.[22] In the colonial period, it was the responsibility of the governor-general to set the boundaries of the provinces, after having consulted with the local assemblies.[23] Consequently, since the independence of the Republic of Viet-Nam, all changes of province and district boundaries are the work of the executive power, within the general stipulations of Ordinance No. 59a.

THE PROVINCE CHIEF

Based on a thousand-year-old tradition, Ordinance No. 59a clearly stipulates that the province chief will be appointed by the president of the Republic; in the Revolutionary Government this power falls to the prime minister. At the beginning of a regime, more than at any other time, the central authority needs men who will execute faithfully the new policy and will interpret it to the people with confidence, also with competence. Thus, the greatest discretionary powers are left to the prime minister in the choice of province chiefs. As a matter of fact, certain of these men were chosen from among career civil servants, called *doc phu su* in the South and *doc su* or *giam su* in the Center, particularly at the beginning of the regime; subsequently, because of the insecurity which reigns in the country, and because of the need for the concentration, simultaneously, of civil and military powers in the hands of province chiefs, they are most often chosen from among military men of the rank of major or lieutenant colonel.[24] In the beginning, the regions of origin of the candidates were also taken into consideration to a certain extent, inasmuch as the province chiefs of Central Viet-Nam were as often as possible natives of Central Viet-Nam, etc., but in recent years, particularly with the appointment of military men as province chiefs, this consideration has become secondary. In principle, the choice of military men for this post is also supposed to preclude considerations of political affiliations, but, at the same time, considerable attention is paid to experience in making these choices: most of the province chiefs were appointed only after they had spent several years as district chiefs, and had shown outstanding ability in these positions. In fact, it was not rare that men were given military rank *ad hoc* in order to be appointed province chiefs.

The Revolutionary Government has replaced some of these province chiefs with other career military officers. It can be presumed that the choice of military officers is becoming unavoidable in view of the fact that since the November 1 Revolution and the purge of January 30, military men are playing a progressively greater role in the political leadership of the nation. This can be explained largely by the pre-eminence of the problems of security in the provinces and the need for officers to lead the troops sent to restore that security.

It is difficult to determine precisely whether the position of province chief has lost some of its former prestige, but it must be admitted that because of the difficulty of the task, this position is not particularly sought after in academic circles, as used to be the case. Formerly, the *tong doc* or *tuan phu* (province chief) held all the prestige of a scholar who has achieved the highest academic degrees (*dai khoa*), of the superior man (*quan tu*) whose conduct was impeccable in the highest Confucian tradition, or of the "father and mother of the people," to whom the citizen knew he could appeal in the event of any injustice or misfortune, whether it came from Nature or from Man.[25] Although, as a rule, the mandarin province chiefs were recruited from among the provincial mandarins (*bo chanh, an sat, doc hoc*), all of whom held high academic degrees (*tien si*), it was still not unusual that a mandarin district chief (*tri phu*, or *tri huyen*) with lower scholastic degrees might attain the position of province chief if he showed exceptional capability.[26] With French colonization, the French province chief, most often trained at the National French Overseas School, had behind him all the unassailable authority of the colonial government, and was sometimes appreciated for his vitality and his activity. In some regions of the country, with the support of the French resident, the Vietnamese province chief, promoted after long years of experience as district chief or as assistant to the French province chief, continued to be obeyed, although the fitness of the personality of certain of these was questioned, both in intellectual circles and among the people. This very criticism is a definite indication that the position has always been highly esteemed in Vietnamese circles.[27]

The fact is that the role of the province chief has always been of prime importance. He was the mandatary of the Son of Heaven; in governing the province he performed, in the name of the Emperor, all functions, both as leader and as governor. During the Nguyen Dynasty, the *tong doc* often performed nominally the added functions of the *binh bo thuong thu* (minister of the army) so as to have effective command over the military units stationed in his territory and also to indicate the importance of the public security function.[28] It should be noted that, although the functions of the province chief were not set down in detail, the objectives were clear; thus, a high mandarin province chief was congratulated when he succeeded in reconciling the material and the moral situations of the people, in presenting honest and competent men for administrative posts, in allowing remission of taxes where justified, and in protecting the population from theft and pillage.[29]

As for the period of French colonization, thanks to the analytical and judicial spirit of men of law and of authors who have written on the period, it is possible to distinguish the following functions, which in many respects resemble those of the prefect in France: [30]

(1) Political: as the representative of the central power, the province chief was responsible for directing all public services; in his reports, he passed judgment on all public officials with regard to

loyalty and professional ability. (2) Administrative: he was responsible for the execution of laws and regulations; he supervised and co-ordinated the activities of the provincial services, proposed measures concerning the development of the province, guided the communal administrations, and presided over the province council. (3) Financial: he was *ordonnateur secondaire* of the national budget; he established the provincial budget, of which he was the *ordonnateur principal;* [31] he administered the provincial domain; he approved the register of direct taxes; he made proposals to the superior authorities concerning additional percentages of the direct taxes to be levied for the province and for the villages; and he approved the communal budgets. (4) Military: since he was responsible for public security, he could requisition the army, and had at his disposal the province police force.[32]

The same tradition governs the functions of province chiefs today, insofar as it is not contrary to the principles of the Republic or to the stipulations of Ordinance No. 59a and the instructions for its application.[33]

From the political point of view, it cannot be overemphasized that the province chief is the representative of the central government in the province, and that as such he corresponds directly with the prime minister, the ministers, and the directors of the central agencies. He receives directives directly from the prime minister: the ministers may send him instructions only when they have signed them personally, and have addressed copies to the prime minister. The province chief has under his supervision many public servants working in field offices of the ministries other than the Interior. If their work does not seem satisfactory, he can recommend to the ministers that they be transferred out of his province. Decree No. 59a also provides that he may recommend his own candidates for the post of district chief. Lastly, as representative of the central power, he presides over all official ceremonies—a symbolic but important function, since it represents political unity to the people, and reminds them of the existence of the central authority. These functions, which are derived from the formal organization of the province, have not been altered by the Revolutionary Government, but many of the unofficial functions have been changed. One of these which required a certain finesse and a good deal of *savoir-faire* was his relationship with the political parties, in particular with the National Revolutionary Movement (Phong Trao Cach Mang Quoc Gia), with the members of the National Assembly, and with the clergy—especially the Catholic clergy, which is very well organized, and the Buddhist clergy, whose following includes the majority of the population. The November 1 Revolution ended the National Revolutionary Movement and re-established religious freedom, but in spite of the fact that an official statement of the prime minister has made it clear that military and administrative personnel must not engage in political activities during the performance of their duties, the relationship of the province chief with the leaders of the freely constituted political parties still remains a delicate matter.

From an administrative point of view, the province chief is co-ordinator of all provincial services, both the overhead services which constitute his office, and the technical services dependent on the executive departments.[34] He automatically represents those executive departments which do not have any provincial services. Special mention should be made of the public security function, which at the present time demands most of the attention of the province chief; in this respect, he is called to co-operate with the military authorities. The activities of the province chief in security matters, as in all other matters, reach far into the heart of the population, through the district chiefs, who, in particular, help him in cantonal and communal administration. Here again it is interesting to note the informal aspects of the administrative activities of the province chief during the First Republic. He often received oral directives in the course of personal visits from the president himself; since the secretaries of state could also send him instructions, he sometimes found himself in a difficult position, although officially and incontestably he was directly under the authority of the president. In particular, the province chief found in the Department of the Interior a natural support, and felt particularly obliged to make reports to the secretary of state for the interior, although officially the latter was on a level with the other secretaries of state in his relationships with the province chief. In general, the delicate nature of the relations with the ministers arises particularly from the feeling that the central authorities do not fully understand local problems. In the case of the minister of the interior, traditionally there is expected to be a greater understanding, through the more frequent and more direct contact with the province chief.[35]

The same can be said of the relations of the province chief with the government delegates. At one time, the province chiefs were under the direct authority of the regional governors (one each for the South, the Center, the North, and the Highlands). After the elimination of the regional governors (Ordinance No. 17, of December 24, 1955), they were to a certain extent replaced by four government delegates (*dai bieu chinh phu*). Each of these delegates exercised within his region the functions of inspector and of assistant to the chief executive, seeing to the execution of laws and regulations and of instructions coming from the central government. Although they did not have the power to make regulations or decisions, they could give the province chief instructions in the name of the president. Because of their authority and because of the confidence placed in them by the president, they often succeeded in settling possible conflicts between the province chiefs and other authorities, particularly military authorities.[36] At the present time, the functions of the government delegates are automatically performed by the military commander of the tactical zone.[37] The province chiefs have received instructions to address all correspondence to the central government through the military commanders of their tactical zones. It is possible that in the future these commanders may gradually acquire a certain power of veto or inspection, similar to that exercised during the Bao Dai regime by the regional governors. A general evaluation of the principal functions of the province chief suggests that in spite of the announced policy of decentralization, in practice the tradition of centralization is still very strong.

THE PROVINCE CHIEF AND THE PROVINCIAL BUDGET

From the financial point of view, the province chief continues to perform the same functions as the province chief in the colonial regime, except with regard to certain limits of the total or particular expenditures, above which the approval of the higher authority is required; these have been increased to correspond to the increased cost of living, and also with a view to deconcentration. Thus, the province chief can approve expenditures chargeable to the provincial budget, not exceeding 60,000 piasters (VN $). He can approve the communal budget provided that the total amount is less than VN $500,000. In his capacity as *ordonnateur secondaire* of the national budget, he can also approve expenditures of less than VN $60,000 for appropriations delegated to him by the heads of the executive departments.

The financial powers of the province chief seem rather broad, since, in point of fact, he has at his disposal three kinds of budgets, which correspond to three sources of funds for works which he considers indispensable: (1) the national budget, insofar as funds are delegated directly to him, or as they are placed at the disposal of provincial chiefs of technical services by delegation from the head of the ministry concerned; (2) the provincial budget, reservations being made for the powers of resolution of the Province Council, and the approval of the prime minister through the minister of finance and the director of the budget; and (3) the communal budget, which he approves or transmits for the approval of the director of the budget, but the execution of which he can strongly influence through the district chiefs.[38]

The provincial budget is often the subject of controversy. The imperial regime had only a summary system of accounting, and made scarcely any distinction between the different kinds of budgets. The idea of a provincial budget, which puts an effective tool into the hands of the province chief, originated with French colonization; as a matter of fact, the French authorities considered the province as the counterpart of the French department, which is also provided with a budget. The setting up of this institution was nonetheless quite difficult, because of insufficient revenues, particularly in the North and in the Center. It was not until 1931 that every province had a budget. It is easy to understand that after World War II, the reestablishment of these budgets created considerable difficulty. The normal sources of funds for the provincial budgets are: (1) income from provincial lands, forests, etc.; (2) percentages added to the direct taxes of the state (property taxes and license fees); (3) taxes paid in lieu of *corvées* (based on the ownership of certain work aids such as rowboats, vehicles, and draft animals); and (4) various other taxes, such as vehicle inspection and registration taxes, head taxes for residents born outside of the province, taxes on amusements and the patronage of bars and restaurants, and parking fees for commercial vehicles and junks.

These sources were inadequate to cover all the expenses of the province, however, and, in order to provide more funds for their budgets, the province chiefs had recourse to two principal expedients: levying local taxes, which the central government considered illegal (particularly the taxing of local production, and the security tax), or asking the treasury to advance money before taxes had been collected.[39] As has been mentioned, in 1957 certain experts recommended that these budgets be eliminated. In reality, the provincial budget is intended to provide for absolutely indispensable services; the government limited itself to asking the province chiefs to cease the two taxes mentioned. After 1958, the government granted rather generous subsidies from the national budget in order to permit the provincial budgets to survive; these subsidies are still granted by the Revolutionary Government.[40]

The study of the provincial budget shows that the tendency toward centralization is here somewhat mitigated, since the province chief has certain powers of decision in financial matters. But, to the extent that the provincial budget is not itself sufficient and requires additional funds from the national budget, this power is nominal. Moreover, the province chief is only the agent of execution of the provincial budget, as the setting up of that budget is the prerogative of the provincial council.

THE PROVINCIAL COUNCIL

One example of decentralization in the Revolutionary Government is the decision that a council elected by the local population may make local administrative decisions, especially in budgetary matters.

The idea of formal representation of local interests proceeds from the Western democratic concept, and was not introduced into

Viet-Nam until the period of French administration. However, there existed around the province chief in the time of the emperors an unofficial council represented by scholars, former mandarins, merchants, or farmers of some repute. They did not meet formally in council, but had frequent contacts with the provincial and district mandarins, and they expressed indeed the opinions of the more advanced part of the population.[41]

This system of consultation was completely different from the French system of councils-general of the departments, whose members are elected by the inhabitants of the department, and whose responsibilities and prerogatives, as well as the relationships with the prefect, the agent of the central power, are clearly defined by an old law dated August 10, 1871 (modified subsequently several times).[42] In the same spirit, the French instituted provincial councils (in 1889 in South Viet-Nam, and in 1913 in the other parts of Viet-Nam), with members who were elected by a limited ballot, but whose powers were purely advisory.[43]

The Republic of Viet-Nam faced the problem of choosing an adequate formula for the representation of the population in the administration of local interests. The colonial solution was to be thrown out as not sufficiently democratic because of the limitations on the right to vote and because of the purely advisory powers of the council. In France, the Constitution of 1946 even tried to confer on the council-general all the administrative powers, by making the president of the council-general (and no longer the prefect) the executive agent of the department. This disposition was not continued by the Constitution of 1958: once more the prefect, a representative of the central government, is the agent of execution of the decisions of the General Council.[44]

Following are certain observations concerning the state legislatures of the United States which might be useful—though the state is not the equivalent of a province. The states have all powers that are not given to the federal government or specifically denied them, but, in exercising these powers, a state legislature is closely controlled by constitutional limitations (procedure, power of taxation, etc.). In fact, the average state legislature has fewer able and high-minded men among its members, and is surrounded by temptations relatively greater and guarded by less watchful and less interested public opinion, than its federal counterpart, the Congress. Here are some specific recommendations from a group of experts for improving legislative performance: removal of the restrictions upon the length of regular sessions; increase of the salaries of legislators so that competent persons can serve without sacrifice; establishment of legislative councils or interim committees with adequate clerical and research facilities.[45]

This comparative study will permit the examination in a new light of the formation and the operation of the provincial council, defined by Decree No. 203/NV, of May 31, 1964.[46]

With reference to the makeup of the council, Decree No. 237/NV, dated December 8, 1961, provided for the election of councilors by universal suffrage and by direct secret ballot, with the district as the electoral unit. Because of the state of national emergency, however, this election was temporarily replaced by the appointment of councilors by the secretary of state for the interior, who received proposals from the province chief.[47] The new decree does not provide for any transitional measures, and the elections will undoubtedly be held in the near future.

Every year the provincial council will elect its own chairman and its own executive committee (*van phong*), without consulting the province chief, whereas during the colonial period, it was the province chief himself who presided over the council. Nevertheless, the province chief may be asked to take part in several phases of the work of the provincial council. He may attend all meetings of the council, and may present his ideas, or he may send a representative. The chairman of the provincial council sets the agenda and communicates it to the province chief, who may call special sessions of the council on his own initiative or at the request of more than one-half of the members. Decisions voted by the council become effective, depending on the matter treated, 15 days after the report on the proceedings has been sent to the office of the province chief, except in cases specifically indicated in the laws and regulations when the province chief is required to submit decisions to a given minister for his approval. The act defining the organization of the provincial council even provides for the eventuality of a disagreement between the province chief and the council: the chairman of the council and the province chief have the right, in this case, to refer the matter to the prime minister or to the minister concerned for a decision.

From a theoretical point of view, the nature of the relationships of the province chief with the council varies with the prerogatives of the council. Thus, the council has the power to make decisions concerning the following matters: the setting up of the provincial budget and administrative account; the determining of the amounts of provincial taxes and percentages added to national taxes; the administration of lands and other property belonging to the province, and accepting gifts and legacies; the making of contracts for supplying goods and/or services to the province (after calling for bids and judging them); and the organization of markets and fairs.

With respect to these decisions, in those cases mentioned above in which the law requires the approval of a given minister, or provides for arbitration, the province chief can only add his opinion. On the other hand, in the following administrative matters the council has only advisory power: provincial programs involving the public interest, provincial bond issues, the granting of franchises for public utilities, and the making of changes in the boundaries of the territorial divisions within the province.

The council may also express its wishes concerning cultural, political, and security matters involving the interest of the province.[48] The decree defining the organization of the provincial council expressly mentions two instances in which the province chief cannot intervene: (1) in case of a conflict between the province chief and the council, in which the president of the provincial council refers the matter directly to the prime minister or to the minister concerned; and (2) in the case of desires or advice on problems concerning the interest of the province which the council judges see fit to present directly to the prime minister.

In brief, the system seems to provide for a subtle apportionment of powers in order to avoid conflict of authority between the elected council and the representative of the central government at the province level, whereas in the colonial regime, the preponderance of power was clearly on the side of the representative of the central government. In short, centralization is tempered by a certain delegation of power in favor of the province chief, the representative of the central government, and by the affirmation of the principle of decentralization in favor of the elected local assemblies.

The creation of the provincial council is too recent to allow any evaluation of its performance. The reduction of appropriations for ceremonies proposed by the province chief of Darlac during a session of the provincial council on the provincial budget of 1963 (under the First Republic) can be cited as an example.[49] Only the experience of a number of years will permit the observer to determine which of these two powers will control the other in practice. At any rate, judging by the old French administrative adage, "Deliberation is the work of several; action is the work of a single man," it appears that the powers of the provincial council will not have any far-reaching effect in the near future. Nevertheless, the afore-mentioned recommendations for the state legislatures of United States, concerning the length of the sessions, research and reference bureaus for assisting the legislators, and the means for attracting conscientious men who are really devoted to the public interest, can henceforth be applied to the provincial councils.

THE RELATIONSHIPS OF THE PROVINCE CHIEF
WITH HIS COLLABORATORS

Mention has already been made of the members of political parties and of the National Assembly, and of their intervention in provincial affairs. They could speak for the general interest of the country as well as for purely local interests. The same can still be said of the press, which is concentrated in Saigon or in Hue, but which may sometimes present to the public certain needs of a local population. However, the province chief particularly enters into contact with the population, either directly, in the many visits that he makes in the interior of the province, or indirectly, through the official representatives of the people in the provincial council, or through his own collaborators. The province chief can make inspection tours alone or accompanied by several chiefs of the provincial services, and is often accompanied by the interested district chiefs. He may also accompany the prime minister, a minister, or the military commander of a tactical zone on visits of their own.[50] The discussion that follows concerns only the institutionalized relationship of the province chief with his staff.

The Deputy Province Chiefs. Because of the great number of matters requiring his attention, the province chief needs numerous assistants.[51] His immediate collaborators are appointed by the prime minister on the proposal of the minister for the interior: the deputy province chief for security, and the deputy province chief for administration. All the deputy province chiefs for security at present are career army officers or officers of the *dia phuong quan* (civil guard). The deputy province chiefs for administration are very often chosen from among career civil servants in administration (from the cadres of the *doc phu su* or the *doc su*), and at present a great many of the latter are graduates of the National Institute of Administration.

The deputy province chief for security, who is assisted by the Service of Security and of Military Affairs, is responsible for coordination with the military authorities of the sector (group provinces), or with those stationed in the province. The chief of the provincial technical service of the *canh sat* (national police) and the chief of the provincial technical service of *dia phuong quan* (civil guard) have frequent contacts with him. However, because of the great importance attached by the central government to security matters, they are also in constant contact with the province chief himself, whose duty is to consolidate the information received from the public services and from his own secret agents. During the First Republic, in several provinces the deputy province chief for security also performed the functions of the chief of the provincial service for youth; his role was to assist the youth groups, which are organized in territorial units: at the provincial level, the provincial committee played the role of co-ordination with respect to the district committees, and the district committees performed the same function with respect to the village committees. In view of the fact that the political aspects of the youth movements have been eliminated by the Revolutionary Government, it seems safe to predict that the assistant province chief for security will no longer automatically be chief of the provincial service for youth. However, he may well be responsible for co-ordinating activities involved in the new civil defense system, and in this capacity he may still have close ties with the youth movements.[52]

The deputy province chief for administration officially directs a larger number of collaborators. In the first place, all provincial services, with the exception of the Service of Security and Military Affairs, are placed under his direct authority: the Administrative Service (responsible for correspondence with the central government and with the districts, the appointment of cantonal and communal authorities, construction permits, registration of arms, etc.); the Economic and Social Service (responsible for problems of price control, food supply, relief, social security, etc.); and the Financial Service (responsible for authorized expenditures coming from the national budget, expenditures and receipts of the provincial budget, maintaining a check on the communal budgets, etc.). In addition, he is responsible for co-ordination with the other provincial technical services dependent on the ministries: services of taxation, customs, treasury, education, public works, public health, and so on.

Thus, officially, the provincial services are divided into two categories: (1) the provincial overhead services, which second the deputy province chiefs and do not correspond to any ministry; and (2) the provincial technical services which are dependent on the ministries, but which nonetheless fall under the authority of the province chief, who establishes co-ordination through his two assistants.

As for the provincial overhead services, it seems that no difficulty would exist in their relations with the province chief, who considers them as staff services or auxiliary services, depending on each case. At one time there was a rather exaggerated tendency to create numerous provincial services and bureaus; thus in Vinh Long, there existed in 1960 a secretariat, a service of administrative affairs, a correspondence bureau, a political affairs bureau, a bureau of military affairs, a service of economic and social affairs, and a service of budget and accounting. With a view toward uniformity and economy, an *arrêté* of the secretary of state for the interior dated March 25, 1961, limited the number of provincial overhead services to five: the cabinet, the service of security and military affairs, the administrative service proper, the economic and social affairs service, and the financial service.[53] Here can be seen the effect of centralization and the tendency to regulate from the central government details of provincial activity, but this measure can be better understood by referring to the extraordinary number of services, often created solely in consideration of certain persons. This profusion of jobs did not even have the merit of giving satisfaction to the local populations, since the functions were often performed by nonlocal officials appointed by the central government to serve in the provinces. Practically speaking, it is up to the chiefs of service to establish informal relations with the assistant province chiefs, as well as with the province chief himself. At the present time, conflicts arising from the "empire-builder" spirit of the overhead organizations may exist in their relationships with the district chiefs, but because of the strong personalities of many military province chiefs, in most cases these conflicts have been solved by the province chief himself.[54]

Provincial Technical Services. The measure taken by the secretary of state for the interior in the organization of the provincial overhead services is still significant because of the preponderant influence of this department (now the Ministry of the Interior) over provincial administration. The other ministries have little power over provincial administration, but their action on their provincial technical services is more direct. To continue the comparison of two ministries from the preceding chapters, the following shows their respective provincial agencies:

Ministry of the Interior: civil guard service, (*tinh doan bao an*), provincial criminal investigation service (*ty cong an*), provincial police service (*ty canh sat*), and re-education center (*trung tam cai huan*).

Ministry of Rural Affairs: provincial service of agricultural affairs (*ty nong vu*), which is the result of the regrouping of three former services: the agricultural service (*ty canh nong*), the agricultural extension service (*ty khuyen nong*), and the veterinary service (*ty thu y*); the provincial forestry service (*ty lam vu*); the resettlement center (*dia diem dinh dien*); the service for co-operatives and agricultural credit (*ty nong tin va hop tac xa*); and the cadastre and agrarian reform service (*ty dien dia*).

All these provincial services are directly responsible to their immediate superiors in the ministry, director-generals, directors, etc. The ministries can influence indirectly the action of the province chiefs, by making restrictions on their provincial services. However, general instructions sent by the ministries to their provincial services must be addressed to the province chief; and the same is true for similar correspondence from the chief of the provincial service to the department concerned. On the other hand, as *ordonnateur secondaire* of the national budget and *ordonnateur principal* of the provincial budget, the province chief has, practically speaking, a broad financial control over all provincial services, which must constantly refer to him for funds. Indeed, the procedure provided may give rise to delays in making decisions that could prejudice the proper functioning of the service concerned. Some services have complained of the excessive meddling of the province chief, even in the technical details of the operations of the service (this is particularly true of the internal revenue service and of the service of public works). Others have complained that they have not as much support as they could wish from the province chief because their activities are not closely concerned with public security (in particular the public health service and the services of public instruction).[55]

In reality, the province chief has a twofold problem in regard to his relationship with the provincial technical services: the delegation to the province chief by the Minister of powers regarding provincial technical services, and the co-ordination of the various provincial activities.

With regard to the headquarter-field relations, the various factors which control the extent of the delegation of powers are numerous: factors of responsibility (of the minister or of the director-general, which make them hesitate to delegate their authority to the provincial services), administrative factors (the age of the service concerned, and the stability of the general policy and methods, competence of the field personnel, and pressure for speed and economy), functional factors (does the function require national uniformity or diversity among provinces?), or external factors (bringing the citizen into the administrative process, collaborating with other national or local agencies).[56] But the major factor still remains the political factor: it is important that all provincial services receive impetus from the qualified representative of the central government, the province chief. Thus, whenever there is any delegation of powers, i.e., whenever an on-the-spot decision can be made, this delegation is not made in favor of the provincial technical service chiefs, but remains on the side of the province chief, in his position as delegate of the central government.

This delegation of authority is all the more necessary since the government recognizes the principle of dual supervision, by virtue of which the administrator (the province chief) is responsible for co-ordination, while the functional authority (the minister and the director-generals) retains technical control.[57] In other words, the ministry sends instructions of a technical nature to the provincial services, but whenever the instructions have political or administrative implications, they must be addressed through the province chief, who may interpret their provisions to the best interests of the province. Co-ordination in this case means avoiding duplication of effort, easing interfunctional maladjustments, and securing voluntary co-operation and synthesis.

The importance attached to the administrative aspect of decisions made at the province level corresponds, moreover, both to the old mandarinal tradition, in which the principal collaborators of the province chief (*bo chanh*, or *thua ti*, and *an sat*, or *hien ti*) were always supposed to act in the name of that chief, and to the Franco-

Vietnamese tradition, which inherited a double centralizing tendency both Napoleonic and colonial. It should be noted that, during the colonial period, the increase in the number of provincial technical services in no way compromised the principle of centralization of the powers in the hands of the province chief. In spite of the even greater number of provincial services existing today, this tradition still holds.

This clearly hierarchical organization was intended to allow the province chief to exercise a rather strict control and, in particular, an effective co-ordination of activities in the provincial framework at a time when it was essential that national feeling become deeply rooted among the people. It is interesting to compare this organization to that, often criticized by authorities, of state and other local governments in the United States. During the nineteenth century, the state governor had little power over the administration, because he shared the executive powers with numerous other elected officials. He did not appoint them and could not dismiss them. If they were his political enemies, they would not accept his leadership. Since 1917, the universal recommendation of reorganizers has been to integrate the executive structure and to centralize its administration under the governor; the most important weapon in the governor's arsenal is his control over the budget; there would be little danger of creating dictators, because the legislature could more effectively supervise an integrated administration than one with the responsibility diffused.[58] This comparison emphasizes particularly the informal aspect of co-ordination of the various provincial services, which has been pointed out earlier.

THE DISTRICT CHIEF

Directly under the province chief in the line organization is his exact replica at a lower administrative level, the district chief. He exercises, in the name of the province chief, as the latter exercises in the name of the chief of state, the functions of directing and co-ordinating all administrative activities of the district.[59] He constitutes the lowest territorial echelon of the state administration in that he is appointed by the central government without consideration of any ties he might have with the district before his appointment, in that he is responsible to the province chief (who is a representative of the central government), and in that he can be given instructions or recalled at any time by the central government.

Although he is at the lowest territorial echelon of the state organization, and even for that very reason, the district chief is the representative of the central power who has continual contact with the population, indirectly, through the cantonal or communal authorities chosen from or elected by the local population, and directly, through his many inspection tours in the country or through the matters brought directly to him for his decision. This has been the case from the time when the district, called the *huyen* (Chinese *hsien*), was used as the principal tool for colonial domination by the Chinese,[60] through the centuries of independence and the years of French domination,[61] down to the present time.[62]

At present, most of the district chiefs are career military officers, although a small number of them are still career civil servants—the older *doc su*, or the more recent trainees of the National Institute of Administration, or sometimes *tham su*, a rank lower than that of *doc su*.[63] To the extent that the functions of the district chief are filled by career military officers or by career civil servants, the right of the province chief to propose candidates for these positions, recognized by Article 15 of Ordinance No. 57a, is in fact restricted. This provision seems to be a compromise between experts who recommend that the province chief be given the right to make appointments to various positions in the province [64] and the regulations of the civil service that provide that all appointments follow specific rules and that the power of appointment be centralized in the hands of the prime minister (for the ranks of *doc su*) or the ministers. The right of the province chief to propose candidates is also comparable to ancient tradition, since aside from the three-year examinations, the emperors often issued edicts requiring province chiefs and high-ranking mandarins to recommend to him men of high reputation (*hien nang*) for appointment as district chiefs.[65] On the other hand, it would clash with the centralizing tradition, strongly established since the period of French domination, in which the appointment of district chiefs was to be made at the discretion of the chiefs of local administration (the governor of Cochinchina or the resident superior).

Since the November 1 Revolution, it has become the general rule to appoint military officers to the posts of district chief. The minister of the interior makes these appointments, frequently upon the recommendation of the province chief, but, in view of the fact that the appointees are military officers, the recommendation of the commanders of the tactical zones are also taken into consideration. In order to prepare these officers for their administrative functions, the National Institute of Administration offers intensive in-service training courses for them.

In addition, the district chief is always assisted by a deputy district chief, who is chosen from the regular cadres of the civil service and is preferably a graduate of the National Institute of Administration. The principal function of the deputy district chief is to relieve the district chief of much of the purely administrative duties so that he can give more attention to matters of security and pacification. The district chief also has a staff provided by the central government, which is composed of clerks and day workers and varies from five to fifteen persons. Often there is a tacit agreement between the province chief and the district chief that the latter may take members of the district self-defense corps to serve as assistant clerks and help with the large amount of paper work confronting the district chief. The number of technical workers is very limited, however, and the district chief would have to channel any requests for provincial technical services through the province chief.

Like the province chief, the district chief performs essentially two functions: (1) As chief executive in the district, he is responsible for the execution in the district of the laws and regulations, as well as instructions sent to him by the province chief; he is responsible for maintaining order and security in the district; he coordinates the activities of the various official agencies (*chi*) which function in his territory; he is the official agent of all public services which do not have representatives in the district, particularly the internal revenue service and the judicial police service; he reports to the province chief any irregularities which he observes in political, administrative, economic, or financial affairs. (2) As the delegated tutelary authority over local communities, he exercises constant supervision over their operations, both by inspection tours and by the convocation of local authorities to the district seat; he is particularly their advisor in matters of communal works, and in setting up and putting into effect the communal budget.[66]

The customary official conception is that the district chief has no power of his own, and that the functions just mentioned are exercised solely in the name of the province chief. If this were really the case, the district chief would be only a simple agent of transmission, but on close examination it can be seen that the district chief exerts considerable influence on the administrative and economic development of all communities within the district, and of the district as a whole.

As a matter of fact, because of his double function of chief executive and tutelary authority over local communities, the district chief is responsible for solving all problems of public security. He is the direct chief of the village self-defense forces, and the civil guard (*dia phuong quan*) is also at his disposition. The chief of the district branch of the national police (*chi canh sat*) makes reports to him concerning the various political activities of the district. Other information regarding security may come from the communal authorities themselves. Since public security today means the struggle against communism, the district chief may develop anti-Communist action in the villages, by suggesting the introduction into the village customary, or book of laws (*huong uoc*), of a new principle concerning anti-communism. Another possible means is the issuing of identification cards to the inhabitants as a means to discover infiltration; closely related to the issuance of identity cards is the taking of a census. Finally, the district chief has the recourse of exercising his official authority as officer of the judicial police.

His second task concerns the economic development of the district. He receives first the general instructions from the province chief, but particularly he must enlist the assistance of many committees: *uy ban nong vu* (committee on agricultural affairs), *hiep hoi nong dan* (association of agricultural people), *uy ban xa hoi* (social affairs committee), *uy ban phat trien cong dong* (community development committee), and *uy ban chong nan mu chu* (committee on illiteracy).[67] The members of these committees, recruited from among the notable citizens of the district, can exercise considerable influence and pressure, so that their decisions will be put into effect. In technical matters, the district chief can also call on the services of the ministries represented in the province or in the district (although in the district these may be limited to three: *chi thong tin* (information service), *tram y te* (infirmary), and *chi dien dia* (land administration service).

The district chief is responsible for presenting to the people the policies of the government and for communicating to the central government the wishes of the population. In this matter he often takes instructions from the province chief, and, during the First Republic, he was often approached by the deputies representing the region, members of officially recognized political parties, members of the youth organizations and of other organizations of the province, representatives of religions, and so on. In principle, all measures taken must be formally reported to, or authorized by, the province chief, although in practice a really active district chief may judge it unnecessary to encumber the provincial report with details of his action. This explains why certain authors have remarked the wide discrepancy between the limited formal powers of the district chief and the broad practical authority that he may exercise.[68] This also justifies the old saying: *"Te tuong bai huyen quan."* [69]

In order to finance economic development and other activities, the district chief may approach the communal authorities to procure from the communal budgets funds necessary for the execution of works for the common interest of several villages. He may also request funds from the provincial budget if the expenses can be financed from the mutual funds of the villages (*quy bo tro*). This points up the necessity for making sure of incoming revenues. One of the major duties of the district chief has always been supervising the collection of taxes; his agents collect the indirect taxes and transmit them to the treasury; they also prepare the lists of license fees to be submitted for the approval of the superior authorities. They prepare the rolls for property taxes; even when the villages are responsible for the collection of taxes, the district chief must still supervise this collection closely. Because of the importance of the financial respon-sibilities of the district chief, certain observers have even proposed the replacing of the provincial budget by district budgets in order to permit the district chiefs to handle certain funds directly. This proposal might cause considerable reorganization of existing admin-istrative structure.

THE CANTON CHIEF

In principle, the functions of the canton chief should not figure in this outline of the national administrative hierarchy; the canton chief has never been considered an agent of the central government, as he is always a member of the local population, and has no status as a civil servant. Neither do his functions constitute an intermediate echelon between the district chief and the communal authorities, for the good reason that the district chief has regular direct contacts with these authorities. Consequently, the elimination of this function has often been proposed, even in the National Assembly.[70]

In many provinces, the canton no longer exists,[71] or exists in name only, since the canton chief has become a collaborator in the office of the district chief.[72] At one time, particularly under French domination, there were regular provisions for the functions of canton chief: these appointments gave satisfaction to the landowners or influential citizens who thus had access to a part of public authority without having to take the difficult tests of the mandarinal examina-tions. The administration thus enlisted influential local men who were entirely devoted to its cause. The functions of the canton chief were, particularly, to aid the district chief in the supervision of the village police, in the collection of taxes, and in the settling of differences between villagers or villages. These functions may well become important again, since administrative tutelage will be strengthened, in view of the full recognition of communal autonomy. Consequently, in spite of the unofficial elimination of these functions in several provinces, Ordinance No. 57a, of October 24, 1956, still provides in principle for the canton in the local administrative organization, allowing for the possibility that political needs may require the eventual re-establishment of this unit.[73] The only relation-ships between the province chief and the canton chief stem from the fact that the province chief has the power of appointing canton chiefs on the proposal of the district chiefs, after consultation with communal authorities, and that the province chief has disciplinary power (reward and censure) with respect to his agents.[74]

THE MUNICIPALITIES

Comparable in many respects to the provinces are the munici-palities, which are urban agglomerations that constitute administrative entities entirely distinct from the province, although their territory is often included in the territory of the provinces (the case of the municipalities of Hue, Da Nang, and Dalat). There are four of these municipalities, including the prefecture of Saigon, the capital of Viet-Nam.[75]

At the head of the municipality is a mayor (a prefect in the case of Saigon), appointed by the central government, except that at the present time the functions of the mayor of Hue are performed by the province chief of Thua Thien. The prefecture of Saigon is divided into districts (*quan*), each administered by a district chief appointed by the government; these are subdivided into wards (*phuong*), and then into groups of families (*lien gia*). The district chief is responsible for the execution of laws and regulations in the district, particularly with respect to hygiene, economy, the census, and elections, but he has no power to make regulations. He is authorized to certify legal documents and to date them officially and to issue permits for meetings. He is the vital statistics official, and is also an officer of the judiciary police. The ward chief has duties regarding the census and liaison between the population and the higher administrative authorities, and has recently been authorized to certify documents. The *lien gia* chief is principally responsible for taking the census of his group of families. The municipality of Dalat is subdivided into quarters (*khu pho*); that of Hue into *quan, phuong,* and *van* (coastal wards); and that of Da Nang into *xa* (villages). Thus it can be seen that there are differences in the internal organization of the different municipalities.

During the First Republic, similar differences existed in the representative part of the administration of these municipalities. Aside from the prefect of Saigon, there was a prefectural council, elected by the population by universal suffrage, but which had only advisory powers. In Hue, the members of the municipal council were chosen from among the members of the district council, who were elected. At Da Nang and at Dalat, the municipal councils had been elected since 1955.[76]

Since the November 1 Revolution, however, these differences regarding the representation of the people in the administration of municipal affairs have been eliminated. According to Decree No. 203/NV, dated May 31, 1964, the members of the prefectural council (in Saigon) and of the municipal councils (in the other cities) are elected by direct secret universal suffrage, and have the power to make decisions in matters of budget, taxes, municipal lands, and city planning.

The tutelary power of the ministers can be exercised only in cases specifically indicated in the laws and regulations, which means, in principle, that the decisions of these councils can be executed in the same way as those of the provincial council.

Village Administration

The importance attached to the role of the district chief, the lowest territorial representative of the central government, shows the tendency of the current administrative organization toward centralization tempered by the delegation of powers. How can this tendency toward centralization at the upper local territorial echelons be reconciled with the traditional autonomy of the villages expressed in the old Vietnamese sayings? The answer can be found by examining this village autonomy in its historical and geographical context.

THE XA, THE HISTORICAL BASIC ADMINISTRATIVE UNIT

Realizing that it was impossible to extend the official administrative network beyond the district (*huyen*), the Chinese governors as early as the Han Dynasty had adopted a system in which the inhabitants assisted in the control of communal affairs. This system was easy to impose, since it corresponded more or less to the old Vietnamese feudal system. At that time, there existed the *ho* (household), of which a certain number—approximately 200 to 500 —formed a *huyen* (district), which was part of a *quan* (prefecture), itself part of a *chau* (province). Thus, Giao Chau was composed of 7 *quan*, 53 *huyen* (of which 14 formed the Giao Chi Quan), and 25,600 *ho*. Under the T'ang emperors, Annam Do Ho Phu included 8 *huyen*, 14,230 *ho*, and 99,652 *khau* (mouths, i.e., inhabitants).[77] This organization seems not to have been a mere reflection of that of the Chinese territory. The Hans had, as a matter of fact, adopted the territorial divisions of the Chous: "Five households constitute a *lin* (Vietnamese *lan*), five *lin* a *li* (*ly*), four *li* a *tsan* (*toan*), five *tsan* a *p'i* (*bi*), five *p'i* a *hsien* (*huyen*), and five *hsien* a *sui* (*toai*).[78] The intermediate echelons *lin*, *li*, *tsan*, and *p'i* do not seem to have been introduced into Viet-Nam, but the *huyen* is certainly the equivalent of the Chinese *hsien*, although the *hsien* included 2,500 *ho*, while the *huyen* included approximately 500 *ho*. The T'ang emperors modified this territorial organization: 100 *hu* (Vietnamese *ho*) constituted a *li* (*ly*), and five *li* a *hsiang* (*huong*), and it is probable that the *hsiang* was dependent on the *hsien* (*huyen*). This local system combined in the same hands the duties of census taking, tax collection, and police supervision.[79] It should be noted that this system was independent of a territorial group called the *she* (commune, Vietnamese *xa*). This institution, which had already existed in the provinces of Southern China before the T'ang Dynasty, was constituted of 25 (later 100) adjacent households grouped so that the inhabitants could extend mutual assistance in farm work or in the event of death or sickness. In some regions, as in Annam Do Ho Phu, the *she* appears to have replaced the *li*.[80]

The Sung emperors instituted an important reform in local

administration, the brilliant invention of Wan An Shih: 10 house-holds were to be organized into a *bao* (Chinese *pao*), with a *bao truong* (*pao chang*) at its head; 50 households were to constitute a *dai bao* (*ta pao*), and one person was elected to be *dai bao truong;* 10 *dai bao* were to constitute a *do bao* (*tu pao*), for which a person respected by the inhabitants was appointed *do bao truong* (*tu pao chang*).[81]

Although Viet-Nam became independent from China just before the Sung dynasty, the territorial organization seems to a certain extent to reflect this reform.[82] Under the province chiefs, or *an phu su*, there existed in fact the *dai tu xa*, and then the *tieu tu xa*, who supervised three or four communes (*xa*). The difference was that the communes, designated as *xa* from the very first years of the independence were administered by mandarins, *xa quan* or *chanh su giam*.[83] The *xa* system was the only one applied in Viet-Nam during the period of independence, while in China the *xa* system coexisted with two others: the *pao chia* (Vietnamese *bao giap*) system for police control, and later the *li chia* (*ly giap*) system for tax collection.

Under the Mings, the number of households constituting a *she* was increased to 100, and its function of rural control was increased; the Mings joined to this system of rural control the system of tax collection, or *li chia* (*ly giap*), which also included 100 households. This linking of the *xa* system and the *ly giap* system was also imposed in Viet-Nam during the brief domination of the Ming emperors. The *ly giap* system functioned in the following manner:

> In compiling the *hoang sach* (Chinese *huang ts'e*) for tax collec-tion, 110 households constituted a *ly*, from which the ten with the greatest area of taxable land and the largest number of *dinh* (*ting*), or tax-paying adult males, were selected to serve as *truong* (*chang*), and the remaining were to be organized into ten *giap* (*chia*). This unit of 110 households was known as the *phuong* (*fang*) in the city, *huong* (*hsiang*) in areas near the city, and *ly* (*li*) in the country. The *ly truong* (*li chang*), *huong truong* (*hsiang chang*), or *phuong truong* (*fang chang*) was responsible for col-lecting taxes from the *giap truong* (*chia chang*), who collected them from the households.[84]

Le Thai To, after having driven out the Mings, reinstated the *xa quan* (the communal mandarins), responsible for the administration of the *xa*, which was identified with the *ly*. The number of mandarins was increased in larger villages to two or three under the Le kings. These mandarins were chosen from the *nho sinh*, or students of the *quoc tu giam* (National School), or even from the *sinh do*, holders of the *tu tai* (bachelor's degree); they were required to take periodic examinations (*khao khoa*) to verify their knowledge and their performance.[85]

It is interesting to note the variations of terms used in different provinces since the Le Dynasty to designate the various subdivisions of the village, or *xa:*

Province	
Thua Thien Phu	*xa, thon, ap* (p. 128 *)
Binh Dinh	*xa, thon* (p. 134)
Nghe An	*xa, thon, phuong, toc, giap* (p. 139)
Thanh Hoa	*xa, thon, trang, phuong, so* (p. 152)
Quang Nam	*xa, thon, phuong, chau, ap* (p. 156)
Binh Thuan	*xa, thon, ly, sach* (p. 160)
Gia Dinh	*xa, thon, phuong, ap* (p. 166)
An Giang	*xa, thon, phuong, pho* (p. 176)

* Page references are from Nguyen Sieu, *Phuong Dinh Dia Du Chi.* (Saigon: Qu Do, 1960).

With the exception of the terms *giap* and *toc,* which were used only in Nghe An, the above terms had a definitely geographical quality, as opposed to the Chinese terms (*chia* and *hu*), which had a family character.[86] Still, some of the terminology introduced by the Ming Dynasty was often used in the daily language, for example, *ly truong* instead of *xa truong.* This confusion of terminology should not lead the student into error; although the family remained an important social institution, it was not considered a basic administrative unit. On the other hand, the commune (*xa*), which in the Chinese organization was simply an administrative subdivision, became the basic administrative unit in Viet-Nam.[87]

THE TRADITIONAL ADMINISTRATIVE ORGANIZATION OF THE XA

Since it did not adopt the family as the basic unit, the Vietnamese monarchy was obliged to find another effective means of reaching the population for purposes of maintaining public order and of obtaining the taxes necessary for the operation of the state. This goal was reached in two ways: (1) by developing to the maximum a local leadership dependent on certain moral values; and (2) by assuring effective communication between the local leader and the representative of the central authority, namely, the *tri huyen,* or district chief.

With an eye to developing local leadership, the inhabitants of the village were encouraged to meet in order to determine the moral and spiritual foundations of the community; these were inscribed in the village customary, or *huong uoc* (Chinese *hsiang yueh*), a tradition going back at least as far as the eleventh century.[88] The customary often recalled Confucian principles: respect for elders, for scholars, for mandarins (either active or retired), and for retired cantonal and communal authorities. Due respect was evidenced by priorities given them in places of honor at village festivals or periodic meetings (*huong am*). These meetings were held in the communal house or *dinh* (*t'ing*). The tradition gradually grew that the men tried to achieve the highest places of honor in the *dinh*.[89] The men who occupied these places exercised in the commune, by the tacit agreement of all the inhabitants, an incontestable authority composed of an ingenious mixture of authority of confidence and authority of identification.[90] It should be noted that, in order to arouse the interest of the inhabitants and to encourage them to participate actively in communal life, the greatest latitude was left to the villagers in the composition of the customary.[91] In this way, certain customaries had greater respect for age (*trong thien tuoc*); others merely presented the order of precedence of the ranks of the mandarinate (*trong hoan*); others specified that academic degrees should take precedence (*trong khoa*). Organization took on a definitely oligarchic character, tempered by the fact that the members of the ruling class were recruited, not by co-optation, but by mandarinal recruiting procedures, literary examinations, or privilege of age. The functions of the elders, i.e., the persons who occupied the highest places of honor and who formed the village council (*hoi dong ky muc,* or *hoi dong hao muc*), were twofold: to take various measures concerning the material aspects of communal life and to maintain a high moral level among the population. This moral level was encouraged by the periodic celebration of ceremonies dedicated to the tutelary genius of the village, during which the customary was often read to the population for indoctrination purposes. Sometimes judgments were pronounced in the course of these meetings, in punishment of those who had violated the village customary. The various measures taken by the council might concern organizational security, the construction of a pagoda, the digging of a canal, the preparation of dikes, or other works of communal or intercommunal interest; they might also concern the application of instructions from the imperial authority, through the district chief.[92]

How was co-ordination between the representative of imperial authority and the village elders achieved? It was out of the question to place these elders under the authority of the district chief, since, in the first place, they were not appointed by the emperors, but had acquired their position by customary right, and, in the second place, the elders were sometimes the superiors of the district chief, either in mandarinal rank (a province chief may be an elder in his village) or in academic degrees. For a long time, the emperors appointed the *xa quan* (communal mandarins) to direct communal affairs, but after the fifteenth century it was the custom to have the village itself appoint the commune chief (*xa truong*), who was to serve as co-ordinator between the village and the representative of imperial authority, the district chief. In principle the commune chief was to report to the council of elders the instructions he had received from the district chief and to ask them to take measures necessary for the execution of these instructions. The district chief did not himself prescribe the material means for executing these instructions, but merely indicated the results required of the village. Thus, if the village was to provide a contingent of recruits for the army, it was up to the village to decide the manner in which the young men would be selected; or, if the village was to pay a certain sum in taxes, the council of elders divided this sum to be paid among the inhabitants, according to village custom.[93] It is in this sense that the saying *phep vua thua le lang,* should be taken. Village custom did not really block imperial orders; however, the imperial order was expected to stipulate only the ends desired; it was the prerogative of the village to find the means for realizing these ends. And it was precisely in recognizing this autonomy of the village that the state was able to impose on the village a collective responsibility for the execution of orders coming from the central government.

THE PROGRESSIVE INTRODUCTION OF REFORMS IN
COMMUNAL ORGANIZATION

The organization just described was perfectly suitable for an agricultural economy. However, as the means of communication increased, as the needs of the state became more engrossing, paving the way for the possibility of unscrupulous elders and abuses of power, state control was to become gradually stronger. Furthermore, the colonial authorities could not accept too great a communal autonomy, all the more since in France the commune itself was also subject to administrative tutelage.

In truth, all these reforms were not brought on exclusively by the colonial authorities. In the time of the emperors, particularly during difficult periods, a certain effort had been made to exercise tight control over the communal authorities. The general lines of reform introduced in three aspects of communal administration follow (without precise distinction as to the authorities who originated them): [94] (1) the choice of the elders, or the elite group; (2) the appointment of the village representative for co-ordination with the central government; and (3) the procedure regulating various administrative operations at the village level.

The methods of selecting the elite group were influenced either by a general order or by suggested modifications of the customary. In general, the modifications concerned the election or at least the co-optation of the elders, instead of automatic elevation to the rank of elder on the fulfillment of certain conditions of age, academic degrees, or mandarinal rank. These elections or co-optations were subject to the approval of the province chief, whereas previously the acquisition of the rank of elder by right had not required any approval. The number of elders was more and more restricted, and the specific function of each varied according to the title conferred upon him. A certain automatic advancement was assured among elders who were classed by order of precedence according to their functions. On the whole, this tendency consisted of eliminating the natural leaders and replacing them by men who were supposed to be more devoted to the cause of the central government. In other words, the authority of confidence and of identification was replaced little by little by the authority of sanction and of legitimacy. The oligarchy was replaced by a halfhearted democracy.[95]

With the gradual elimination of natural local leaders, the necessary reforms tended to increase the authority of the commune chief, who represented the village before the central administration. The commune chief, although a subordinate under the emperors, became himself an elder and participated with full rights in the meetings of the council of elders with a voice in the proceedings. Like the commune chief, each of the elders had an executive function in a specialized field: *chanh luc bo,* or registry officer; *huong quan,* or tax officer; *huong hao,* or police officer; and so on. Of course, since the conferral of all titles on the elders was subject to the approval of the province chief, the administration of communal affairs was expected to be more in conformity with the administration of the central authority.[96]

More and more uniform procedures were introduced: the election of elders, the keeping of registry lists, methods of approving communal decisions, and methods of drawing up contracts. It is interesting to note, particularly, the appearance of budgetary procedure: the communal budget was subject to approval, as were all expenditures exceeding a certain amount. Although this procedure definitely brought a certain lucidity into the administration of communal affairs, it also permitted the provincial authorities to intervene more and more in this administration, even to the point of obliging the villages to contribute to a common district or province fund, in the administration of which they had absolutely no voice.[97]

BASIC FACTORS IN COMMUNAL ORGANIZATION

From the very first days of independence, the Republic of Viet-Nam was faced with the crucial problem of communal organization, in view of the great importance of this basic unit in the administrative life of the country. Several problems occurred which had to be solved simultaneously.

The colonial administration succeeded to some extent in formally replacing the authority of confidence and of identification of the former elders with the authority of sanction and of legitimacy of the new ones. As long as the central authority—the colonial governors—was strong, the people were obliged to accept the orders of the new authorities or face punishment. However, as soon as the central authority weakened, the authority of confidence and of identification once more prevailed. At first, the elders adopted a passive boycott, and decided not to participate in any way in the official administration of the village, although actually they continued to make unofficial decisions. Later, because of the action of militant political parties, nationalist or Communist, secret cells were organized, which inspired the villagers to make various demands or protests against the raising of troops or the levying of taxes. Although the term of authority of the Viet-Minh government was brief in South Viet-Nam, this government brought about a radical reform, at least on paper: village affairs were to be directed by an assembly elected by the inhabitants (*hoi dong nhan dan xa*), which was to choose from among its members an administrative committee (*uy ban hanh chanh xa*).[98] In point of fact, the members of the administrative committee were members of the party who had forced an entrance. This organization was discarded as soon as the nationalist government took control of all the territory of South Viet-Nam. Clandestinely, the Viet-Minh continued to spread vicious and destructive propaganda against governmental activity; having lost official authority, they clung to an authority of sanction, using fear to enforce their demands.[99] The problem remained then of re-establishing an authority which could combine the fourfold qualifications of the old traditional oligarchy and, at the same time, carry some democratic guarantees provided by the Constitution.

The second factor in the problem of communal organization is geopolitical. The traditional organization was quite suitable to a small area, with the houses concentrated in an agglomeration or a small number of agglomerations, surrounded by a bamboo fence, as was the case in North Viet-Nam and in Central Viet-Nam. Under these circumstances, the district could supervise a large number of villages: thus the *huyen* of Yen Mo, in North Viet-Nam, administered 72 villages; the *huyen* of Son Lang, in North Viet-Nam, 75; and the *huyen* of Nga Son, in Central Viet-Nam, 112.[100] At present, it is the province which administers an average of 70 villages—the average number of villages controlled is slightly larger in Central Viet-Nam (109) than in South Viet-Nam (40 in Southeast Viet-Nam and 71 in Southwest Viet-Nam). The reasons for this are, first, that the number of provinces has been increased, as has the number of districts, and, second, that the villages have often been consolidated into larger villages (*lien xa*). Taking 58,000 as the average population of a district, and 4,700 as the average population of a village, we see that the district controls an average of only approximately 12 villages (58,000 ÷ 4,700).[101] There were many reasons in favor of the consolidation of villages, including the concentration of material means for emergency works, and the suppression of the particularist and separatist spirit harmful to the conceptions of those works.[102] In any case, the consequence of this consolidation is that the central government can supervise the villages more closely; on the other hand, the communal administration, which has become more important, has also become more bureaucratic. The personal contacts characteristic of the relationships between the old communal authorities and the people are becoming more and more difficult to maintain, and are partly replaced by more formal relationships and more red tape. Furthermore, because of consolidation, piecing together, and regrouping, several villages have lost their former natural limits, while at a lower level, the hamlets, or *ap,* continue to be natural groupings.[103] An informal administration is developing in which the *ap* corresponds approximately in dimensions to the former village. In fact, 50 per cent of the hamlets have fewer than 500 inhabitants; out of 16,398 hamlets (grouped into 2,574 villages in 1959), only 77 have populations of more than 5,000.[104]

A third factor must also be considered in the present communal organization: in order to promote national development, the central government has been obliged to adopt many programs whose execution requires the active participation of the population. More and more the *xa* has thus had to develop an adequate administrative apparatus in order to be able to participate in these programs, whether they concern community development, the struggle against the four fundamental vices, or the struggle against illiteracy. The communal authorities are obliged to have more frequent contacts, not only with the intermediary representatives of the central authority, the district chief, but also with the technical civil servants, particularly those in the services of agriculture, agricultural credit, agrarian reform, public works, public health, etc.[105] At the same time, the old tradition of communal autonomy, which has survived all political vicissitudes, must be respected if the local authorities are to be expected to encourage the active and effective participation of the people in government programs. Some effort was made during the First Republic to codify the communal customaries in order to establish a formal basis for communal autonomy, and, since the Revolutionary Government places great emphasis on the improvement of local government, this work will probably be further promoted.

These three factors explain the provisional organization of the communal administration, the construction of *agrovilles,* and, particularly, the rapid development of strategic hamlets.

THE COMMUNE SINCE INDEPENDENCE

In order to provide the villages with a temporary administrative framework after the abolition of the *uy ban hanh chanh,* the provisional government of 1946 set up communal councils of between 6 and 8 members appointed by the province chief. In 1953, an ordinance provided for the election by universal suffrage of the members of these councils (numbering between 3 and 12, depending on the population), and establishing the functions of the president (*chu tich*), the vice president-treasurer (*pho chu tich*), the secretary-general (*tong thu ky*), and, where necessary, councilors of education, public records, public health, finance and taxes, and economy.

Ordinance 57a in 1956 continued to recognize the status of the *xa,* but provided no stipulations concerning its organization. This organization was thus provisional, and based on memoranda (*thong tu*) of the secretary of state for the interior, dated June 28, 1956, and November 16, 1956. The communal administration was reduced to its simplest expression, since it was constituted by a village council (*hoi dong xa*) made up of three persons, the representative of the commune (*dai dien xa*), the police councilor (*uy vien canh sat*), and the finance councilor (*uy vien tai chinh*), all appointed by the province chief upon the recommendation of the district chief. In some cases there was a fourth member, the youth councilor (*uy vien thanh nien*), who, unlike the other three, was formally elected by the young people of the village. The larger villages were by exception provided two additional councilors.[106]

This solution did not exclude the former elders from village administration. On the contrary, some instructions prescribed that the district chief take into consideration many factors: age, education, place of birth, loyalty to the republican regime, prestige, etc., and there was nothing to prevent the appointment of a former elder to a new communal council. To increase the efficiency of the agents, many in-service training courses were offered at the province level, with materials provided by the National Institute of Administration.[107] In this connection, mention should be made of the village clerk, who was not a member of the council, but whose role was nevertheless important, because of the full-time nature of his work.[108]

The communal council participated in almost all aspects of the communal life: the execution of laws and regulations, tax collection, vital statistics, health, justice, public works, and, particularly, the maintenance of public security.[109] The council had at its disposition a communal budget, but, because of the limited resources of this budget (additional percentages of the direct taxes, the rental of public properties, and bid market taxes) and the lack of experience in budgetary techniques on the part of the communal authorities, the budget often did not fill the role of a management tool at the village level.[110] Another means of action available to the communal council was the mobilization of the population by means of many associations and committees organized within the commune, with the participation of elders and ordinary inhabitants: *hiep hoi nong dan* (the farmers' association to eliminate middlemen in buying equipment), *hop tac xa nong dan* (farmers' co-operative for selling rice), *uy ban xa hoi* (social welfare committee to assist widows, orphans, and the poor), *uy ban nong vu* (agricultural affairs committee to settle disputes between landlords and tenants), *uy ban phat trien cong dong* (community development committee, now affiliated with the *uy ban kien thiet nong thon* [rural development committee] to promote activities of common interest), and *hoi phu huynh hoc sinh* (association of parents of students). These organizations all have an administrative character in the sense that the members of the communal council always participate actively in their proceedings and that the organizations themselves often receive instructions from the same organizations at higher area levels.

In addition to these organizations, mention should be made of political and religious groups created by the Ngo Dinh Diem government but disbanded after the November 1 Revolution: Phong Trao Cach Mang Quoc Gia (The National Revolutionary Movement), Thanh Nien Cong Hoa (The Republican Youth), Thanh Nu Cong Hoa (Young Women of the Republic), and Lien Doan Cong Chuc Cach Mang Quoc Gia (Government Employees League). The various groups also collaborated occasionally with the communal council for activities involving their objectives.[111] In some provinces, there have been instituted unofficial organizations of the elite, composed of former elders or influential men for assisting the council, i.e., the *uy ban dan quan chinh* (a tripartite commission representing the people, the army, and the administration).[112]

The village customary is established for each village, according to its needs, by the communal authorities, the hamlet chiefs, and the leaders of the various groups in the village, but it must conform to the broad outline of the general policy, understood in the sense of legal democracy, community development, and social justice. In general, the customary sets a scale of new social values, according the highest rank to those who have borne arms against communism, and their families; next to the leaders elected by the population for the administration of communal affairs; then to the producers who combat underdevelopment.[113]

The provisional communal administration was often the subject of criticism: the opinion was expressed in the National Assembly that the communal council was not representative of the population; [114] other criticisms were that the function filled by the council was of a rather negative character in that it was concerned solely with control and regulation, that the village appeared as a level of execution for the central government rather than the autonomous organization of a local community,[115] that local governmental authorities were not in an enviable position,[116] that the breakdown in the communications network due to overload and poor reception facilities had been detrimental to the development process,[117] and that the "myriad of political, semi-military administrative organizations has confused the village officials and inhabitants instead of increasing the efficiency of village government." [118]

After seven years of experience with a provisional administration, Decree No. 45/NV, dated May 3, 1963, defined the general outlines of the communal administrative organization. The commune continued to be the basic administrative unit, but included an official subdivision, the *ap,* or hamlet. The administration of the commune rested in the hands of the *hoi dong xa,* or communal council (Article 4 of Decree No. 45/NV), which included: the *dai dien xa* (representative of the commune), the *hoi vien kinh te va tai chanh* (economic and financial councilor), the *hoi vien canh sat* (police councilor), the *hoi vien thanh nien* (youth councilor), and the *hoi vien ho tich va y te cong dong* (councilor for the registry and for public health).

The administrative work of the council was the responsibility of the *thu ky xa* (communal clerk), although in communes of more than 5,000 inhabitants, a maximum of three additional clerks could be employed to assist the council.

The communal council was elected by secret ballot by the members of the administrative councils of the *ap* (hamlets), and by the leaders of the groups recognized by the customaries of the hamlets. This amounted to election by indirect suffrage, since the electors were themselves elected by direct universal suffrage. The only exception was the youth councilor, who was elected by the leaders of the youth groups. All these elections were closely supervised by the district chief, to avoid irregularities, and had to be approved by the province chief. It should be noted that no special conditions of eligibility were prescribed, except the general current ones: majority, no criminal convictions in court, residence in the commune for at least a year, and so on.

The communal council made resolutions concerning the administration of the commune: budget, communal taxes, acquisition of property, public works, and the boundaries of the hamlets. Certain of these resolutions could be put into effect only upon the approval of the secretary of state for the interior, after the agreement of the departments concerned (budgets greater than VN $500,000, public works involving more than VN $50,000, etc.), and others upon the approval of the province chief.

With the exception of the methods of electing the members of the council, Decree No. 45/NV made official many of the former practices of communal administration. The question of communal administration was again considered by the Revolutionary Government, and Decree No. 203 d/NV of May 31, 1964, provides that the new communal council (*hoi dong nhan dan xa*) will have between 5 and 11 members; each hamlet is a constituency for the election of one member to the communal council, although each hamlet may itself be divided into many constituencies, depending on its size, and upon the local situation and needs. According to the same decree, however, in addition to the council, the commune will have an administrative committee (*uy ban hanh chanh xa*) appointed by the province chief and composed of a chairman (who will also be the communal clerk), a vice-chairman, and from one to four commissioners: for police and security, finance and economy, information, and youth and civil defense.[119]

The communal council makes important decisions, and the administrative committee appointed by the province chief executes these decisions, as well as those of the provincial authorities. Moreover, provision is made for more financial autonomy for the commune: decisions involving expenditures of less than VN $30,000 no longer need the approval of the province chief.

Although it is too soon to evaluate these new measures, it should be noted that this decree shows real concern for all measures which might help the rural population. Similarly, intensive training courses have been organized by the National Institute of Administration in collaboration with the Ministry of the Interior, for future members of the communal administrative councils and, particularly, for training instructors for the cadres of pacification. These latter cadres are recruited from areas recently liberated from the Viet-Minh, to help in the setting up of communal administrations in these areas.[120]

During the First Republic, two programs were initiated to provide adequate leadership and communication to rally the rural population: the villages were encouraged to become urbanized and to adopt municipal administrative institutions (the *agroville* program), and a basic unit was selected small enough to develop the personal contacts common in earlier days, in order to develop from these relationships the natural leaders (the strategic hamlet program). In these two programs, the Revolutionary Government has made only the changes required by the new revolutionary spirit.

AGROVILLES

Agrovilles (*khu tru mat*) seem to be an answer to the first of these objectives. On July 7, 1959, when the president of the Republic presented the idea of setting up centers which would represent a happy compromise between teeming city life and placid rural existence, an intensive campaign developed among provincial administrators to show the population the double objective in view: to create a framework for social and economic development of the rural area and, at the same time, to strengthen internal security.

The *agrovilles* were to be set up near the principal routes of communication, in order to permit the easy circulation of men and materials. At the same time, these *agrovilles* would shelter behind their fences the houses of the inhabitants, protecting them against unforeseen attacks from the Communists; also, urban facilities would be provided for the inhabitants—electricity, water, educational facilities, etc. The construction and displacement operations were to be effected partly by subsidies from the national budget, and partly by methods of community development by the villagers themselves.[121]

In spite of intensive efforts, only 23 *khu* were set up in 11 provinces, grouping more than 32,000 inhabitants over an area greater than 6,000 *mau* (one *mau* = 1.32 acres).[122] The delays were due to the fact that, in spite of large subsidies provided by the government, the tasks were beyond the means of community development; they were extensive and sometimes required the use of agricultural workers even during the harvest season, and, in addition, intensive counterpropaganda was directed by the Viet-Minh in order to delay the works, which threatened to isolate them for all practical purposes. The criticism has often been made that the *agroville* program is bringing back the old *corvée* system because of overzealous province and district chiefs, and that the people have been suddenly uprooted from their homes and placed in unfamiliar surroundings where they are ill at ease and far from their fields.[123] These factors explain why the *agroville* program was to all intents and purposes suspended during the last years of the First Republic, and why there has been to date no mention of it in the programs of the Revolutionary Government.

Theoretically, the proposition is still practicable, particularly if it is set in the framework of national development. It is, after all, a matter of using the phenomenon of urbanization with the goal of improving the process of national development.

Using Robert Redfield's terminology, a characteristic of many underdeveloped countries is the relatively high degree of prevalence of a folk-like society which is usually opposed to rapid change and unable to adapt itself quickly enough to the pressures exerted on it by the increasing integration of underdeveloped countries into the world economy. But the cities, even in underdeveloped countries, are modeled, at least in some significant aspects, after the urban centers of the West. They exhibit a spirit different from that of the countryside. They are the main force and the chief locus for the introduction of new ideas and new ways of doing things.[124]

The development of communications, education, experimental demonstrations, and the exchange of products and services is indeed more easily achieved in the urban centers than in the country where the population is scattered. These facts alone are sufficient to make the spirit of the urban population more receptive to new ideas and techniques. Since the *agrovilles* are to be close enough to each other to constitute a rather tight network, it is possible to hope that from these agglomerations an induced development of purely agricultural regions will occur. In other words, these agglomerations are to serve as transition points between such large cities as Saigon, Hue, Da Nang, and Dalat—where a marked difference exists between the workers, the middle class, the bourgeois, and the group of entrepreneurs and the country, in which the unit of production is reduced to the family and where the large landholders are set in contrast to the small farmers or sharecroppers. In more scientific terms, the *agroville* is intended to develop a sort of orthogenetic transformation which implies a minimum of cultural change and which constitutes an adaptation of the native to new techniques, rather than a heterogenetic transformation, such as occurred in Saigon, where hybrid institutions appeared, either because of the necessity of adapting to new conditions of life or else by a demonstration effect-cause by foreign contacts.

Consequently, the psychological factor of the problem of social change should be emphasized here. Usually it takes time for people to decide to change their way of life. The more radical the change appears, the longer a time will be required for psychological adaptation. If this program is to be resumed in the future, careful psychological preparation will have to precede all other positive measures, and this will require scrupulously detailed planning. It is also in consideration of this psychological factor that a second solution of the problem of communal organization has been considered: to make the *ap*, or hamlet, the basic unit of local administration.

STRATEGIC HAMLETS

In 1963, according to official statistics, more than 10,000,000 of the 14,400,000 inhabitants of South Viet-Nam, or approximately 70 per cent, were living in the nearly 9,000 strategic hamlets (out of a total of 11,864 hamlets) and in the urban centers (the urban population was 1,541,000 as of October 7, 1963).[125] After the November 1 Revolution, verification of these statistics showed that only 10 per cent of the hamlets are really defensible, the others having few or no means of defense.[126] Until the reform of May 3, 1963, the organization of the hamlet was rather summary, since it was composed of a number of five-family groups, a self-defense corps, and a hamlet chief.[127] The five-family system groups households in units of five, according to their proximity to each other; although, in principle, the five-family system was set up as a mutual assistance institution, in practice it has come to be recognized as part of the security, propaganda, and information organization of the village. The hamlet self-defense corps consisted of all men between 18 and 45, and served as night watch and for periodic patrols. The hamlet chief, who was chosen by the people and who performed general administration, was head of the five-family group and leader of the self-defense corps. He thus became the natural leader, and acquired easily the authority of identification and of legitimacy.[128]

Decree No. 45/NV has given a legal form to the administration of the hamlet for the first time. It provides the hamlet, which has no civil status, with an administrative council, which includes: the *truong ban* (hamlet chief), the *uy vien chanh tri* (political councilor), the *uy vien thanh nien* (youth councilor), the *uy vien an ninh* (security councilor), and the *uy vien kint te va tai chanh* (economic and financial councilor).

In the smaller hamlets, the number of councilors may be reduced to three, the president performing also the function of the political councilor, and the youth councilor performing the function of security councilor. The councilors were elected by direct secret universal suffrage, except the youth councilor, who was elected by all the members of the Republican Youth Group. All these elections were subject to the approval of the province chief. In Decree No. 203 d/NV, of May 31, 1964, the Revolutionary Government has reduced the number of popularly elected members of the hamlet administrative council to two: the hamlet chief and the assistant hamlet chief. The other members are to be appointed by the district chief in order to provide technical specialists in various fields. The administrative council of the hamlet has a twofold function: (1) executing laws, regulations, and the instructions of the superior authorities, and (2) executing the communal customary.[129]

The hamlets were at first designated as "strategic" because the government of the First Republic hoped to bring about through these hamlets a fourfold change: a military change, by setting up a continuous front line at the level of the individual hamlet as well as of a group of interdependent hamlets co-ordinating their efforts along a common scheme; a political change, by implementing democracy in rural areas through the election of the hamlet administrative council and the establishment of the customary as the law of the hamlet; an economic change, by developing the provincial technical services, which, by means of sound advice to the rural population on technical matters, can help to increase productivity; and a social change, by setting up a new scale of social values, inscribed in the village customary. The official philosophy of the strategic hamlet was based on a series of tripartite concepts leading toward personalism, and expressed in the form of equations, thus:

> *tam tuc* + *tam giac* = *tam nhan* = *nhan vi;*
> where *tam tuc* = three aspects of self-reliance
> *tam giac* = three aspects of consciousness
> *tam nhan* = three aspects of personalism
> *nhan vi* = personalism.

The three aspects of self-reliance concern ideology, organization, and technique.

Misled by colonialist propaganda, the people have wandered away from the path of virtue; it is important that they return to this path by an effort of personal reflection within the concrete framework of the hamlet, where the people will realize more fully the idea of public interest and will be ready to defend the ideal that they have found by their own efforts at reflection. This is the first aspect of self-reliance (*tu tuc tu tuong*). Guided by this ideological self-reliance, the people will be able to organize their public and private lives also on the bases of self-reliance. They will become imbued with the idea that the organization must be adapted to practical means available to them, and that thus they must not count on external aid. They will realize that the initiative of organizing their hamlets is their own responsibility (*tu tuc ve to chuc*) and that they must not expect instructions from superior authorities. In technological matters, it should be recalled that imported technology may be based on means beyond the reach of the population, while technology developed according to the very needs of the population is more adequate to the material means available at the time (*tu tuc ve ky thuat*).

In order to create a spirit of self-reliance within the framework of the strategic hamlet, the people must be conscious of the three factors of success: health (*suc khoe*), morals (*dao duc*), and spirit (*y thuc*). To be aware of health leads to preserving one's body from all sickness, in order to strengthen effectively the working mass. To be aware of morals means considering one's conduct in Confucian terms; physical strength without morals is only brute strength; on the other hand, the proper conduct of men influences the conduct of other men reciprocally, and is the basis of the solidarity so necessary to life in common. The third awareness stimulates one to continually take the initiative in finding new means, new techniques, new activities; the enlightened man is never at a loss in any situation.

Thus, moved by a spirit of self-reliance and conscious of his physical, moral, and spiritual strength as an integral part of society, the man of the strategic hamlet will be able to put into effect easily the doctrine of personalism, developed in three different ways: in depth, in breadth, and in height. Personalism in depth concerns the individual; it implies a sense of responsibility toward oneself, the duty of cultivating oneself in order to develop one's own talents. Personalism in breadth urges the individual to act for the good of society, both the small family society and the larger state society; in order to do this, he will respect the rights of others and the public interest, and will struggle for right and for liberty, in order to permit the community to develop. Personalism in height means communion with God; in order to achieve this, the individual must strive toward purity in his feelings and in his actions.[130]

It is rather difficult to grasp this philosophy of the strategic hamlet, which attempted to cover up a thousand-year-old tradition with some complicated modern formulae. This philosophy did not succeed in concealing the many abuses which occurred in the application of a sound idea. In many localities, the contributions in money and in kind that were demanded of the people were exorbitant in comparison with their means, and amounted in reality to uncompensated forced labor for long periods of time. The transfers of households from the country to the strategic hamlets inhibited the regular activities of the farmers, who were accustomed to living near their fields. The matter of security was considered so much more important than economic considerations that the economy of the hamlets was seriously threatened, particularly in view of the fact that the government representatives sent to assist in the setting up of the hamlets sometimes did irreparable harm through excess of zeal: young people were mobilized for long periods during harvest time; excessive contributions were demanded of the people during "slack" periods; and interminable meetings were held by these agents in the safe hamlets, while visits to the less secure ones were rare.

The statistics concerning the number of strategic hamlets have been questioned, as certain reports from the province chiefs have proved inaccurate. Consequently, while continuing to regard the hamlet as the basic unit of territorial administration, the Revolutionary Government, to put an end to such abuses, has outlined certain measures: the restriction of payments required of the people in setting up the hamlets; the judicious scheduling of the community work programs so as not to interfere with the work in the fields; the developing of a spirit of voluntary co-operation; the reinforcing of the cadres sent to aid in the setting up of the hamlets; and further emphasis on the social and economic development of the hamlets.

This new attitude behind the development of the hamlets is symbolized by a change in the official name: the former "strategic" hamlet (*ap chien luoc*) is now called the "new life" hamlet (*ap tan sinh*).[131] An indication of the importance attributed by the Revolutionary Government to this program is the fact that it has been entrusted to the newly formed Directorate of New Rural Life (*Nha Tan Sinh Nong Thon*), which has been attached directly to the Office of the Prime Minister.

Conclusion

With the adoption of the "new life" hamlets, the center of interest of local administration moved from the *xa* (commune),[132] since the administration of the *xa* had by the force of circumstances become bureaucratized, to a lower level constituted by a natural unit: the hamlet. It is to be supposed that the hamlet will achieve the ideal of autonomy that previous regimes allowed to the villages. With the spirit of self-reliance, the hamlet will become accustomed to administering its own affairs and to counting only on its own means, both for works of purely local interest and for the execution of instructions that the representatives of the central government may hand down in the field of public security or in that of economic and social development. Daily contacts and the participation in work and festivals develop the sense of identification necessary to community life. The leaders of the hamlets already had the authority of identification; with the support of the central government, which endows them with the authority of legitimacy and the authority of sanction, it is hoped that they will be able to acquire the authority of confidence.

The new communal organization thus revives the old tradition of communal autonomy, which goes hand in hand with a systematic centralization accompanied by a delegation of powers at all higher administrative echelons, from the district through the province to the central government. This old organization was the strength of the great Chinese empire for thousands of years; it made a powerful contribution to the strengthening of royal authority in Viet-Nam and aided in the expansion of Viet-Nam toward the south. However, although the main idea of this new organization coincides with the broad guiding principles of ancient administrative tradition, every citizen is still faced with the necessity of building this organization on new foundations. Once the Chinese had recognized the principle of communal autonomy, they superimposed the principle of patriarchal authority, and made the families responsible for the proper functioning of the commune, through the *pao chia* system. When this same principle was recognized in Viet-Nam, the administration of the commune was entrusted to a natural oligarchy. Thus, the principle of communal autonomy lent itself easily to adjustments, even in the earliest times. Nothing is to prevent the new regime, granted that this principle is well founded, from adjusting it in the light of recent political developments. The system of co-optation in an oligarchic regime might well be replaced by the democratic system of election. As a matter of fact, a formal elective system was begun during the First Republic, with the election of the delegate of youth to the communal council, and soon the election of the administrative council of the hamlet will be initiated. At the hamlet level, since the inhabitants know the candidates personally, they can vote with full knowledge of the case; if there is any electoral platform, the voter can easily see where the true public interest lies.

The propensity to think in terms of public interest may, moreover, be used as a criterion of development. The expression "public interest" is a controversial one, as will be seen in the study of the dynamics of administration.[133] We can define this term as a feeling for the interest of a specific community. Beginning with the level of the hamlet, it is possible to conceive the interest of the hamlet as distinct from the interest of the individuals who compose it. This interest may be the security of its inhabitants, the neatness of the roads leading from one house to another, or the primary education of the children. In the rather narrow framework of the hamlet, with the close relationships which develop daily, the idea of public interest may emerge, perhaps implicitly, perhaps openly, but in general quite easily. Because of the propensity to think in terms of the public interest, within the narrow framework of the hamlet it seems possible to expect the active participation of all the inhabitants, through the process of community development, in the carrying out of works in the public interest, either in matters of security, of public instruction, or in smaller agricultural projects. The problem would be solved simply by finding an elite capable of promoting these community works. But here the people can be expected to know each other well enough to be able to themselves choose the men to direct these matters. In this way, the hamlet constitutes what sociologists call "folk society" or *"gemeinschaft."* [134]

In the progressively higher levels of the administrative hierarchy, the idea of public interest may become more and more abstract, to the point of being beyond the feelings of men of the hamlet, who live isolated by the difficulty of communication with the rest of the country. In the village, which includes both a larger area and a larger population, it is more difficult to mobilize the cooperation of all the inhabitants for activities of community development, and it has become necessary to set up a financial system which is a far cry from the simple division of responsibilities possible in a small society; it is similarly difficult to agree on the choice of persons to direct the works of common interest. Thus the village represents the transition from the *gemeinschaft* stage to the *gesellschaft* stage. [135] However, with the progress of civic education and with the development of means of communication, local autonomy in the form of a comprehensive local government system still appears possible at this level. [136]

At the district level, the principal issues concerning public interest have already begun to take less well-defined forms, although there certainly exist intercommunity activities easily recognizable as being in the public interest. The choice of persons called to direct the district would become more difficult if it were left to the inhabitants themselves; it is possible that in certain districts, the local elite might not prove equal to district problems, or that capable men might consider that their place is not within the restrictions of a district. Moreover, the problems of intercommunity interest require the mobilization of funds often beyond the means of the district. These facts explain why the district has never been more than an intermediate echelon in the administrative organization, although the role of the district chief has uncontestably always been very important.

The province seems to have available the necessary conditions for forming a distinct administrative unit: at this echelon, the necessary means can be found to aid the villages in intercommunity works, the undertaking is sufficiently important to attract an educated elite conscious of the public welfare, the personnel is sufficiently numerous to permit a judicious division of the labor, and communications can be developed to encourage the exchange of opinions and the propensity to think in terms of the public interest. Moreover, the province is large enough for the many issues of provincial public interest to become merged with those of national public interest, such as the setting up of the democratic ideal, the important water distribution projects, public education, and, particularly, public security. Politically speaking, these considerations explain the division of power at the province level between the province chief appointed by the central government and the provincial council composed of representatives of the local interest. Administratively speaking, the solution of the problem of co-ordination between the provincial services seems to rest in the fact that the province chief, who is the local executive power, also represents the central executive power. This is a typical example of the integrated administrative system.[137]

The preceding analysis, based on the propensity to think in terms of the public interest, leads to conclusions similar to another analysis based on the idea of clientele. In this conception, there is a distinction made between the internal clientele (local population) and the external clientele (people living outside any particular local area, such as the central government). The degree of local autonomy is measured by the degree of compatibility between the interests of these two clienteles. It may occur, for example, that "the external clientele considers that their demands on local government can only be met through relatively strong central control, while local clienteles, considering the satisfaction of their wants to depend in large measure on aid from the national government, are unwilling to abandon the benefits of dependency in exchange for the advantages (and accompanying costs) of self-rule." [138]

Under these circumstances, it is conceivable that a certain degree of centralization should result, both from the concept of economic and social progress through a rational system of planning from the top to the bottom of the administrative ladder and from the concept of assistance brought to the local communities to allow them to achieve an optimum of real autonomy.

PART III

THE TOOLS OF ADMINISTRATIVE ACTION: EFFICIENCY AND ECONOMY

IN ORDER *to understand the structural-functional analysis of administration, a certain effort of abstraction is necessary: as has been indicated, the relationships between the various central and local authorities are based only on abstract entities called the central government, the cabinet, the province, the commune, the services, and the agencies. Actually, these entities are materialized in daily life by human beings who make decisions, perform certain acts, move about, make speeches, sign correspondence, prepare statements, draw up reports, and so forth. The study of the status of these persons and of their behavior falls under the heading of personnel administration. On the other hand, all these acts result in the consumption of services or of tangible goods; administrative action is reflected directly in the market of goods and services, in which the administration is represented both as an enormous producer of goods and services and as a consumer of other goods and services which contribute to the production of the first. These exchanges of goods and services are materialized in a market economy by a flow of money between the government and all the citizens. The operations involved in this monetary circulation through the public sector constitute public finance.*

The functions of the state just described, which seem so familiar to persons accustomed to a market economy, did not appear quite so simple at the beginning of the administrative history of Viet-Nam. It has been shown in Chapter 1 that in the early days, with a feudal agrarian regime, administration amounted merely to providing the population with a certain security; the lord received prestations, which were not considered as payment for services rendered, but rather as con-

tributions expressing a certain bond of vassalage. Similarly, the security of the fief against attacks from the other fiefs was assured by the authority of the king, to whom the lords offered a tribute. When the Han emperors extended their domination over Viet-Nam, they merely substituted Chinese prefects (thu su) for the king, and, at the beginning, the bond of vassalage remained unchanged. But the Han emperors had already inherited from the Ts'in emperors a centralized empire, in which the provinces were headed by administrators appointed by the emperor after nomination by active high public officials. Thus, little by little the mandarinal bureaucracy emerged; it began in the upper echelons (the immediate collaborators of the prefect and of the governor of the province) and gradually became prevalent in the lower echelons. After regaining their independence, the Vietnamese used the same bureaucratic system, although history reveals vain attempts from time to time to re-establish the feudal regime. Upon their arrival in Viet-Nam, the French, who had already a well-developed bureaucratic system, based more or less on merit, contented themselves with setting up their own system alongside the native one. As a result of this administrative dualism, a certain number of French rules were gradually adopted into the Vietnamese bureaucratic system. This is the source of the modern Vietnamese bureaucracy, although it differs in spirit from the colonial administration.

The French also introduced some precision in financial affairs. The use of money had already existed under the emperors, but commerce among regions was quite limited, since poor communication did not permit the setting up of a really flexible market economy. Consequently, the existence of money did not imply any uniformity of prices in different parts of the kingdom. Thus, it can be seen why the kings, after having quickly passed beyond the stage of tribute in financing the activities of the state, were obliged to have recourse to both taxes and the old prestations of service. The prestations of service constituted a transitional form between the personnel function and the finance function. The French instituted a modern fiscal system—first at the federal level, beginning with so-called indirect taxes; later at the lower levels, through successive reforms of the system of direct national and local taxes, in which, however, traditional ways of collecting taxes were maintained. Another important innovation was the establishment of periodic budgets, at the federal level (in French

Indochina), at the national level (in the protectorates of Tonkin and Annam, and in the colony of Cochinchina, as well as the protectorates of Laos and Cambodia), and at the province level. Accounting regulations were even introduced for the administration of communal finances. An even more remarkable novelty was the tendency of public finance to develop to the point of requiring the lion's share of the national income. This tendency —appearing first at the time of the depression of 1932, in the course of which the amounts of the public budgets decreased more slowly than the national income—became progressively stronger with World War II and during the long struggle for independence in the postwar period, mainly after the partition of the country by the Geneva Agreements.

Thus, with the development of these institutions, at the time of Vietnamese independence (July 20, 1954) the function of personnel administration was clearly distinct from the function of finance administration, although the two functions necessarily complement each other in administrative action.

In the analysis of these functions, which consist of the mobilization of the means of administration (personnel and finance), the ideas of efficiency and economy have been examined thoroughly in the various studies of Western countries. Personnel and financial studies have also been made in the scientific management movement, which is a product of highly industrialized countries. Certain authorities have justly criticized these movements as being too mechanistic, but the norms of efficiency and economy and those of the scientific management movement continue to regulate the thought of many authorities who see in administration only a co-operative rational action.[1] Others contest, in these ideas, the value of universal dogmas, seeking to analyze the problems of personnel and of finance according to the context of social organization and economy. Thus it is that a society organized on a sala *model or an economy patterned after the bazaar canteen model may possess personnel or finance systems in which the ideas of efficiency and economy play only a secondary role.[2] The examination of Vietnamese institutions will provide an opportunity for seeing to what extent the afore-mentioned ideas are applicable in the domains of personnel and public finance.*

PERSONNEL
AND PERSONNEL ADMINISTRATION

Dao chi di chanh, te chi di hinh
Dan mien nhi vo si
Dao chi di duc, te chi di le
Huu si tha cach.[1]

IN ANALYZING the problems created by administrative personnel, its behavior, the results obtained through its activities, and the reactions of the social environment provoked by these activities, it is customary to use the term "bureaucracy." This term is used here in an objective sense, as opposed to the common derogatory sense which implies slowness, waste, and formalism. Sociologists after Weber have characterized bureaucracy by the legally defined hierarchic organization, the rationalism in the division of labor, the formalization of activities in a written form, the special abilities and education required by the administration, and, finally, recruiting by means of competitive examinations.[2] Students of public administration have emphasized the important role bureaucracy has played in implementing social change, recommending policy, framing legislation, influencing legislative bodies and weighing competing interests; on the other hand, they have criticized bureaucracy for unresponsiveness, the will to power, and the usurpation of policy determination.[3] In general, writers on the history of Asia never fail to profess a profound admiration for the Chinese bureaucracy which made for the perenniality of that immense empire: "The mandarins remained for thousands of years the best officialdom in the world, an iron armature of great moral value which preserved intact for countless generations the most delicate culture the world has ever known"— although this bureaucracy might be reproached with "having preserved and never having created."[4] The same might be said of the Vietnamese mandarins, considered by tradition as "the father and mother of the people,"[5] but whose behavior began to change with French colonization.[6] Personnel administration problems, at least in the context of Asian culture, are especially related to ethics. In this matter, Asians are not alone in their preoccupation with the moral aspect of bureaucracy; it is also considered of prime importance, for example, by the British.[7]

Because of the administrative philosophy prevalent in Viet-Nam, the principal problems concerning personnel administration will be regarded particularly from the ethical point of view, although a complete analysis must examine successively the following points: (1) the civil service system, its history and current situation; (2) the cadre system, which is currently in force; (3) the problem of the recruiting of civil servants; and (4) the problem of morale building for bureaucracy.

The Civil Service System

To the casual observer, the present civil service system might appear to have been directly influenced by that of France after World War II. A thorough study, however, would show that, on the contrary, this system constitutes a modernization of the oldest traditions of the Vietnamese regime as it was before French colonization.

CIVIL SERVICE UNDER THE KINGS AND THE EMPERORS

The most complete document concerning the former system of civil service in Viet-Nam is the third part of a voluminous work by Phan Huy Chu, entitled *Lich Trieu Hien Chuong Loai Chi* (Rules Established by the Various Dynasties, Classified According to Subjects).[8] The third part of this work is entitled *Quan Chuc Chi* (Concerning the Mandarins), and treats the classification, titles, pay, and recruiting of mandarins.

The hierarchy of the Vietnamese mandarinate was patterned after that of China, although it included positions that did not exist in the Chinese mandarinate.[9] At the top of this hierarchy were the very high mandarins called *tam cong* or *tam thieu;* these titles were sometimes honorary and sometimes official. The highest effective function was that of the *te tuong* (although this title varied under different rulers), who was the equivalent of a prime minister, and whose collaborators were the ministers, or *thuong thu,* who formed the Cabinet of Six (*Luc Bo*). The ministers were aided by a battery of mandarins of the interior, or *kinh quan* (*thi lang, hoc si, vien ngoai lang,* and *lang trung*). The civil hierarchy was separated from the military hierarchy (*vo quan*), which was dependent, however, on the *te tuong,* and which included the *tiet che,* or commanders-in-chief, the *do doc,* and the *do chi huy su.*

The mandarins of the field organization, or *ngoai nhiem,* performed the functions of province governors, either *tong quan, tran thu,* or *doc phu.* All the civil collaborators of this latter group formed a distinct hierarchy: *tuyen phu su, an phu so, tri phu, tri huyen, tri chau,* and *xa quan.* The military officials were placed under the command of the *tong binh* or *quan linh,* who were themselves under the authority of the governor.[10]

The different positions were clearly distinguished in this functional hierarchy, often by a description of the work to be accomplished. Thus, the minister of the interior was to discover valuable men to be appointed to the public positions; on the basis of the behavior of each mandarin and his knowledge, as well as his capabilities, the minister might assign him to functions in the central government or in the field organization; as for the functions of field organization, a post was not to be left vacant for more than three months, and so on. The governor of a province was responsible for public security in the province; he was to prevent theft, looting, and other criminal actions; he was to be particularly careful in investigations concerning crimes and misdemeanors as well as in those concerning disagreements between the inhabitants.[11] In accordance with the doctrine of the rectification of names, these positions were scrupulously respected. As soon as a mandarin was given an assignment, the people, as well as his superiors and colleagues, expected that he perform the assignment in all conscience.

In spite of these generalities, it is somewhat difficult to find a term of comparison between the rather dissimilar functions, both in the court and in the field. The kings imitated the Chinese rules of precedence, grouping the various positions in a common hierarchy composed of nine ranks, each rank including two classes. For example, the highest-ranking mandarins, such as the *tam cong,* were grouped in the first class of the first rank, or *chanh nhat pham;* the ministers, or *thuong thu,* belonged to the first class of the second rank, or *chanh nhi pham;* among the mandarins of the field organization, the *tri phu* were in the second class of the fifth rank, or *tong ngu pham,* as were the *vien ngoai* among the court mandarins. (See Chart VI, page 173.) This constituted, then, an employee classification, in which a mandarin of a given rank could alternately occupy several different functional positions. The following statement, made concerning the former Chinese bureaucracy, can be applied perfectly to this type of classification: "When the policy or goal is diffuse and the official duties are of a multifunctional character, men of general ability seem better equipped to handle the situation, men whose efficiency cannot be measured by the order-result criterion that applies to the specialist." [12]

There was no privilege attached, however, to the individual himself: if a mandarin was removed, for disciplinary reasons, from a given position and placed in an inferior position, he was automatically reclassified according to his new position. The purpose of the classification in rank seems to have been to find a common denominator for precedence at the court and for setting salaries.[13]

The ranking system of the mandarinate should not be confused with the system of titles of the nobility, or *tuoc cap.* These classes, in descending order, included the *vuong,* or prince; the *cong,* or duke; the *hau,* or marquis; the *ba,* or count; and the *nam,* or baron.[14] These titles were conferred on princes of the blood or on mandarins who had rendered extraordinary service; they served as symbols of respect

CHART VI OUTLINE OF THE HIERARCHY OF THE FORMER MANDARINATE*

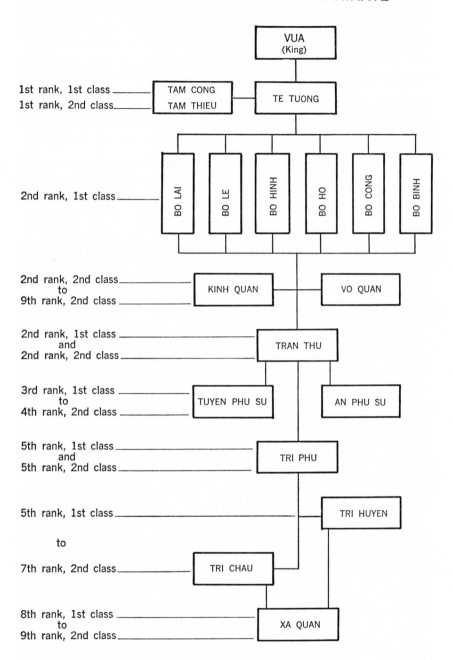

VUA (King)

1st rank, 1st class —— TAM CONG
1st rank, 2nd class —— TAM THIEU —— TE TUONG

2nd rank, 1st class —— BO LAI | BO LE | BO HINH | BO HO | BO CONG | BO BINH

2nd rank, 2nd class
to
9th rank, 2nd class —— KINH QUAN —— VO QUAN

2nd rank, 1st class
and
2nd rank, 2nd class —— TRAN THU

3rd rank, 1st class
to
4th rank, 2nd class —— TUYEN PHU SU —— AN PHU SU

5th rank, 1st class
and
5th rank, 2nd class —— TRI PHU

5th rank, 1st class —— TRI HUYEN

to

7th rank, 2nd class —— TRI CHAU

8th rank, 1st class
to
9th rank, 2nd class —— XA QUAN

* Details varied from one reign or dynasty to another

conferred on these persons, but included no prerogatives in the administrative hierarchy.

THE FRANCO-VIETNAMESE SYSTEM

The afore-mentioned mandarinal classification system dates from the Ly Dynasty (1009–1225), and shows that the Vietnamese people were long accustomed to a hierarchical administration. Consequently, when the French settled in Indochina, they had no difficulty in transplanting their own bureaucratic regime, which operated alongside the Vietnamese regime in the territories of the protectorate (Annam and Tonkin).

The coexistence of these two regimes helps us to understand the multiplicity of categories of cadres during the colonial period: [15]

(1) The colonial cadres, including the civil servants working in the colony but holding the same titles they would have held in France, such as the cadre of treasurers or that of comptrollers; also French civil servants recruited especially for the colonies, as, for example, the cadres of administrators in the civil service, and those of judges.

(2) The local European cadres, including French civil servants recruited especially for Indochina, such as the cadres of public works engineers, land administration engineers, etc.

(3) The "lateral" cadres—the highest rank attainable for the Vietnamese—which included Indochinese civil servants who had the same qualifications as civil servants of the local European cadres.

(4) The general Indochinese cadres, which included Indochinese civil servants employed in the general services, who might serve in any country of the Indochinese Union (Tonkin, Annam, and Cochinchina—which make up the present state of Viet-Nam—and Cambodia and Laos).

(5) The local Indochinese cadres, especially appointed for each country of the Indochinese Union, in which, for example, a civil servant from Tonkin would not normally serve in Annam.[16]

This diversity in the categories of cadres corresponded to the double necessity of distinguishing the races of origin of the civil servants and the territories in which the civil servants worked. The principal interest in this distinction lay in the many advantages bestowed on the French civil servant under the pretext of expatriation, and in the variations in the wage scale according to the standard of living of each territory. Each of the afore-mentioned categories included several cadres itself, distinguished according to such factors as the functions which the individual was expected to perform, the level of technical ability demanded at the time of admission into the cadre, the diplomas or degree of formal education required of the candidate, and so on.

Following are some subdivisions of the Indochinese cadres:

A superior cadre of agents of the general services, who were administrative civil servants and who could be assigned to any administrative position in the services of the former federal government of Indochina. At the time of recruiting, the candidate was expected to have a baccalaureate degree of secondary education.

A superior cadre of technical public works agents, who had received slightly less technical instruction than engineers, and who were expected to perform technical functions in the different public works services.

A secondary cadre of clerks of the federal government open to persons holding the diploma of *études primaires supérieures* (an abbreviated secondary school program). These workers might be placed in the various clerical services of administrative agencies.[17]

Another example might be chosen from the Indochinese "lateral" cadres (later called "local" cadres), from which have come most of the public servants occupying high administrative positions at the present time. Among these can be mentioned (1) The cadre of Indochinese *rédacteurs*—writers, who drew up bills, laws, legal documents, official letters, etc. They were chosen from among persons holding the law degree (*licence en droit*), and were to assist the French administrators in office work, and in directing the smaller administrative units. (2) The cadre of Indochinese agricultural engineers; candidates were required to hold a diploma of agricultural engineering. Members of this cadre were assigned to positions requiring technical knowledge in agriculture, and so on.[18]

The mandarins and their assistants in Tonkin and in Annam were not included among the local cadres, but formed special cadres of so-called native administration, regulated by special statutes.[19]

THE PRESENT CIVIL SERVICE SYSTEM IN VIET-NAM

Even before the independence of Viet-Nam was completely recognized, the government codified an outline of rules concerning the civil service in a single document called the Statute of Civil Service (Ordinance No. 9, dated July 14, 1950). This ordinance was inspired by the movement of codification of the acts regulating the civil service in France, set down in the law dated October 19, 1946, which established a general statute for civil servants (replaced later by Ordinance No. 59–244, dated February 4, 1959).[20] The civil servant is designated, as in the French statute, in the following manner:

. . . every individual who, having been appointed to permanent employment in a public civil administration in Viet-Nam, is titularized thereafter in a cadre whose organization has been established by a decree of the chief of state (now the president) or an *arrête* promulgated by an administrative official who has received a delegation of power to that effect.[21]

This definition points up a fundamental characteristic of Vietnamese personnel administration: the statutory position of the civil servant. Civil servants are not bound to the administration by a contract the terms of which are agreed upon by both parties, but by a statute which can be modified by the administration at any time. Thus, at the beginning of his career, a *pho giam su*, or office administrator, may belong to a different cadre from that of the *pho doc su*, or field administrator; the government may combine these two cadres—a real possibility at the time the first draft of this book was written, and a fact at present—in which case the civil servants concerned would be considered to have no right to complain. Thus, at any moment, the government may also modify the scale of salaries, the system of leaves of absence, the retirement system, etc. This statutory position of the civil servant is a long tradition inherited from France during the colonial period and is a strong argument against the thesis that the Vietnamese system is an employee classification system. The Statute of Civil Service regulates the career of the civil servant from beginning to end; the employment of those who are not career civil servants is governed by a regulation which in many points has the force of a statute, and which, moreover, evokes the application of the statute itself in the absence of dispositions specifying otherwise.

It will not be possible to present here in detail the general Statute of Civil Service.[22] Consideration will be given to only the following three main points of this statute, under which French judicial clarity is superimposed on the profoundly humanistic Vietnamese philosophy and on a marked tendency toward modernization in order to increase the efficiency of public services: (1) the idea of cadres of civil servants, (2) the problems of recruiting civil servants, and (3) the problem of morale-building.

The Cadre System

According to the Statute of Civil Service, all civil servants are grouped in cadres; the cadre is the combination of positions for which prospective employees are subject to the same conditions of recruiting and employment.[23] The examples given with regard to the cadres of the colonial period will serve again here. The former cadre of Indochinese *rédacteurs* became the cadre of *giam su*, or office administrators, which includes ten classes, divided in the following manner:

principal administrator, superior class	1 class
principal administrator, classes 1 to 3	3 classes
administrator, classes 1 to 3	3 classes
assistant administrator, classes 1 to 3	3 classes
	10 classes

with two seniority classes:

> principal administrator, class 1 (more than three years of
> service)
> administrator, class 1 (more than three years of service).[24]

This cadre provides all positions of director of administration
(general administration, personnel administration, accounting, legislation, and regulatory administration) in all departments and in all
provinces; this includes a large number of positions.

Civil servants from other cadres may have access to only a
limited number of positions. Thus the cadre of Water and Forest
Engineers supplies workers in planning, organizing, and directing
water and forest projects, at the national and provincial levels.[25]

The difference between the present system and that of the
colonial regime is that, in principle, there no longer exists any
grouping of cadres by categories according to the nationality of the
civil servant or according to the region in which he is to serve. For
certain cadres, however, candidates are still so rare that it is difficult
to fill the positions in accordance with the stipulations of the Statute
of Civil Service. For example, the cadre of university teachers who
have passed the examination of *agrégation* in law and medical
schools is still provisionally governed by the dispositions of the
French regulation. Distinction according to country of origin was
discontinued at the time that the *phan,* or regions, ceased to be
considered distinct administrative territorial units; even certain
dispositions concerning the civil servants in the Highlands, which
might perhaps have been justified on the basis of prerogatives
reserved for ethnic minorities, are at present only temporary.[26]

THE CATEGORIES OF CADRES

At present the cadres are grouped according to the authorities
responsible for their administration. Under this criterion, only two
groups can be distinguished: the administrative and the technical.

The administrative cadres are administered directly by the
Directorate-General of Civil Service, under the supervision of the
Secretary of State at the Office of the Prime Minister, and include:
office administrators for the bureaus, or *giam su* (this cadre has
recently been combined with the second); field administrators for the
interior, or *doc su;* senior clerks, or *tham su;* clerks, or *thu ky;*
stenographers, or *thu ky toc ky;* typists, or *thu ky danh may;* and
messengers, or *tuy phai.*

These cadres are not very numerous, but, since they serve in all
the government and in all provinces, the number of workers
belonging to these cadres is relatively high. Although statistics do not
show what percentage of the total number of civil servants are in the

administrative cadres, the ranks of qualified administrative personnel, *giam su, doc su,* and *tham su,* account for 2,705 of a total of
7,255 qualified administrative and technical civil servants, or 37 per
cent.[27] "Qualified" civil servants are those who have had a professional education at the university level (or at least at secondary
school level, with some specialization). The number of so-called
administrative civil servants must be greater in the lower cadres,
where the requirements for technical ability are less strict.

The technical cadres are administered by the technical departments: the Department of Public Works has supervision over 31
cadres (engineers of public works, technical agents of public works,
engineers of telecommunications, mechanics, pilots, meteorologists,
etc.); the Department of National Education administers the cadres
of primary school teachers, secondary school teachers first and
second cycle, teachers of technical schools, inspectors of primary
education, and so on.

The preceding classification of cadres, based in principle on
professional specialities, must be combined with classification based
on degree of professional specialization or, more precisely, on the
level of professional education required as a basis of recruiting.
According to this new criterion, both the administrative cadres and
the technical cadres are divided into three categories: Category A,
workers who have had a university education; Category B, workers
who have had a secondary school education; Category C, workers
who have had only a basic primary school education.[28]

This rather detailed description of the cadre system shows that
the Vietnamese system of classification of government workers is a
personnel rank classification system; i.e., for his specialized field,
each civil servant receives, as in the Army, a rank which corresponds
to his class and cadre.[29]

This is an impersonal system of personnel classification according to technical qualifications, and also according to the services the
government is entitled to expect from the workers admitted to the
cadres. Each cadre is divided into classes; this permits a worker of a
given cadre to advance in his career and to receive a salary increase
with each promotion. Thus, a cadre may include eight classes; the
minimum service needed to advance from one class to the next is two
years, so that, theoretically, at the end of sixteen years, the civil
servant may arrive at the highest class in his cadre. In reality,
advancement is not automatic; only the most deserving workers
advance after the minimum length of service; others may wait three
or four years or even longer in the same class.

Advancement in class provides the civil servant with an
increase in salary. He may remain in a position for years, doing
exactly the same work, yet continue to advance and earn a higher
salary. In practice, a young administrator is recruited with the rank

of *pho giam su* third class; in the course of his career, he will have the opportunity of advancing to second class, then first class, and then of becoming *giam su* third class, second class, first class, and finally *giam su thuong hang* (three classes), regardless of the functions which may be assigned to him.

COMPARISON WITH POSITION CLASSIFICATION

The Vietnamese system differs from position classification in that it presents no detailed and impersonal description of each position, but a description of each cadre, for which a number of positions are reserved.[30] In both cases, however, the descriptions are made without any consideration of the personality of the civil servant. The fact that specific statutes of several cadres do not define the nature of the positions which may be assigned to the civil servants belonging to these cadres does not mean that those employees can be assigned to any position.[31] Assignment to a definite cadre, with the degree of technical training required for admission to that cadre, is an implicit assignment to definite positions; for example, the cadre of labor and social security inspector is sufficiently explicit in itself.[32] On the other hand, many statutes define the sort of operations that the civil servants of a given cadre are expected to perform, e.g., the postal technical agent or the notary.[33] Besides, in the position classification system, the positions which are similar with respect to duties, responsibilities, and authority are grouped in classes, like the cadres; the classes are grouped into services similar to the categories of cadres. For example, in the United States, there are five services: professional and scientific; subprofessional; clerical, administrative, and fiscal; crafts, protective, and custodial; and clerical mechanical.

The idea of position classification is not completely foreign to the Vietnamese system. Although detailed position descriptions are not given, there are positions set up independently of the cadres or of the personality of the holder of the position.[34] Thus, a secretary-general, a director-general, a province chief, or a district chief receives a salary which is not determined according to the cadre of the holder of the position. Justification for the creation of these positions lies either in the fact that these functions are of a political nature or in the fact that it is difficult to find civil servants in the cadres with rank sufficiently high to perform these functions. Thus, a *giam su* first class, whose salary is comparatively low, may be appointed director-general because of his abilities. He cannot be expected to be satisfied with the salary scale of his cadre and class since his position normally entails a much higher salary.

Another variation which is a concession to the idea of position classification is the work-connected allowances. The civil servant is entitled to a salary determined according to his cadre and class;

however, if he occupies a position which requires an increase of work, or which places him under unusual responsibility, he will receive in addition a special allowance called *indemnité de fonction.* Thus, a *pho giam su* second class will receive a salary appropriate to his rank; if he occupies the position of chief of bureau, he will receive a supplemental monthly allowance corresponding to this position. Other allowances may be added to the pay attached to some positions, and may be considered as the application of the idea of position classification: representation and travel allowance, responsibility allowance, judicial responsibility allowance, hazardous duty allowance, and overtime teaching allowance, as well as other fringe benefits.[35]

COMPARISON WITH EMPLOYEE CLASSIFICATION

The cadre classification system also differs from the employee classification system in that the cadre is determined objectively, without consideration for the personality of the specific civil servant.[36] Certain authors have confused these two systems, apparently because, once admitted into a given cadre, the civil servant may change from one position to another, and still continue to enjoy all the advantages attached to his rank. It is as if the civil servant were classified once and for all, as if consideration were given to all his qualifications when he entered the civil service. In fact, the classification of the civil servants in each cadre is made according to standard objectives defined in advance. If a candidate presents the qualifications required, he may be admitted into the cadres, exactly as in the system of position classification, where a candidate fulfilling the requirements may be appointed to a given position. The only difference is that a civil servant of a given cadre may alternately hold several positions reserved to this cadre, whereas a civil servant governed by a position classification system is eligible only for a definite position.

Type of employment	Saigon Area	Field	Total
Cadre	18,600	24,400	43,000
Non-cadre	39,400	57,600	97,000
Total	58,000	82,000	140,000

A second reason for the confusion is that in addition to the so-called "cadre" civil servants (*cong chuc chinh ngach*) there are many civil servants who do not belong to the cadres. The total number of government workers in Viet-Nam is 140,000 (for a population of 14,400,000), and is divided as shown above.

Thus, only 43,000 government workers, 30 per cent of the total, belong to the cadres.[37] The reader may ask what becomes of the rest, who do not belong to a cadre.

There are three subdivisions of the non-cadre category: contractural employees (*khe uoc*), dayworkers (*cong nhat*), and laborers (*phu dong*). In principle, the difference between the cadres and the non-cadre categories is that the worker who belongs to a cadre has the right to occupy a certain position and to receive a certain salary once he is admitted to the cadre and without regard to the position to which he is assigned, whereas the worker who does not belong to a cadre is essentially temporary and can be recruited and assigned according to the needs of the service. Because of this temporary nature of his employment he enjoys fewer professional advantages (fixed pay scale, retirement, leaves, etc.), and the conditions of recruiting are less severe. Also, because of the vagueness of the recruitment criteria, salaries are determined according to the qualifications of each candidate; in this respect this system resembles the employee classification system. This is particularly true when it is a question of determining the salaries of the contractual agents who have a high degree of technical training. Mention should also be made of a special category of dayworkers called *can bo,* or provisional supervisors (*personnel d'encadrement*); these employees are essentially mobile, due to the manner in which they are recruited and dismissed and because of the many displacements required by temporary missions in places to which they may be sent to serve as supervisors in people's organizations (e.g., the campaign against malaria, etc.); they are often grouped in teams.[38] The contractual system and the system of *can bo* may rightly be compared to the system of employee classification. Assimilation is less adequate where the *cong nhat*, or dayworkers and laborers, are concerned, since a special statute regulates the conditions under which they are recruited, promoted, and licensed. In other words, although they are not in the formal cadres, they are still classed in specific categories comparable to the cadres, and to this extent the idea of employee classification is replaced by that of rank classification or statute.

CRITICISM OF THE CADRE SYSTEM

It has been stated that the cadres are objectively defined well before the recruiting of a civil servant for a specific position. This institution is universalistic, and represents a certain degree of development. However, since each cadre includes a large number of administrative positions, a certain amount of diffuseness exists, as compared to the position classification system, which is quite specific. Moreover, although the cadre system ranks the civil servants according to their type of activity, the most important criteria for differentiating between cadres are education and experience; in other words, the cadre system does not insist sufficiently on achievement, although neither does it rest on ascription.[39] This cadre system reflects properly the definition of transitional society, which immediately raises the question as to whether it is not better to advance development and frankly adopt the position classification system.

On the advice of experts, the Directorate-General of Civil Service has taken this question under study; the conclusion seems to be that the propositions are still premature. The position classification system would result in a certain rigidity in the assignment of civil servants, whereas the needs of the services in a nation still in the process of development are enormous, and require men of great versatility.[40] The cadre system may be criticized as giving rise to certain paradoxical situations; e.g., a civil servant belonging to a high cadre may occupy a modest position and still continue to receive the salary attached to his rank and class; but the same criticism can be made of the position classification system.[41] Still, by way of comparison, the cadre system is used today by very advanced countries like France (the cadre system) and England (the class system), where the benefits of the existence of an administrative class are still highly praised.[42] Besides, even when the emphasis is on the work to be performed rather than on the manner of recruiting, the position classification system cannot fail to specify the qualifications for positions. The cadre system closely resembles military rank classifications, and it is doubtful that a military government will change the current system, particularly now that military personnel and civilians are beginning to work together in the civil service.

The Recruiting of Civil Servants

The idea of achievement and universalism, on one hand, and of ascription and particularism on the other, also provides material for a discussion of the problem of recruiting.

THE TRADITIONAL METHODS OF RECRUITING

In the early history of Viet-Nam, the system of recruiting civil servants was already based on merit: in order to enter government service, a candidate was required to distinguish himself in examinations. Without going back to the period of Chinese domination, in which the examinations followed the same prescriptions as those of the T'angs,[43] under the Ly kings (1010–1225) the selection of mandarins was made according to examinations given to a small number of sons of mandarins who had studied at the *quoc tu giam,* the school for children of the state.[44] Special examinations were also organized for recruiting civil servants to work in the offices (*lai vien*), who were required to write well, to know how to perform mathematical operations, and to know penal law.[45] The principle of recruiting mandarins by competitive examinations was observed uninterruptedly from this dynasty on.

Under the Tran kings (1225–1400), the examinations took place at regular intervals, every seven years; the children of the common people were permitted to study at the *quoc tu giam*. As under the Ly kings, candidates were first examined on the three religions, Buddhism, Taoism, and Confucianism (but later only on the Chinese classics: the composition of a poem and of rhythmic prose) and on an administrative subject (the drafting of an imperial proclamation or a report to the throne). In order to permit the commoners to take part in the examinations, the candidates were divided geographically into the *kinh,* who took the examinations in the capital, and the *trai,* who took them in a southern province. The only prerequisite was a guarantee by the local mandarins as to the morals of the candidate. The Tran kings initiated the setting up of two degrees: the *tam truong,* or first degree, and the *thai hoc sinh* (later called the *tien si*), or second degree, in which the candidates who passed were given the title of doctor. Special examinations were still set up for recruiting *rédacteurs,* or *nho si,* and office workers, or *lai vien.*[46]

Examinations were given more frequently during the Le Dynasty (1427–1527)—every five years at the province level, called *huong thi,* first degree.[47] The national school was enlarged in order to prepare candidates for the central examinations, or *hoi thi,* in which doctors, or *tien si,* were recruited. It should be noted that schools were created both at the province level and at the district level. During the Le Restoration (1532–1788), the examinations were given every three years; the Nguyen princes in South Viet-Nam opened the competition to all inhabitants, without restriction as to residence or family.[48] These last conditions were later universally observed, when the Nguyens came to power as emperors (1802).

Under the Nguyens (1802–1945), at least before the French influence, the three-year examinations became really democratic. Although it was customary for the sons of scholars to follow the family tradition, it was not infrequent that sons of lower-class families succeeded in the examinations and reached the higher echelons of the mandarinate. The cases of Hoang Huu Thuong, Le Thuy, Nguyen Van Tinh, and Nguyen Van Ban [49] show that the materialistic idea that only sons of rich families could succeed in the examinations [50] is not authoritative, particularly in view of the fact that the study of the classics did not require a great deal of money. In practice, the selection of mandarins followed a pyramidal scale. The best students were selected from each locality and sent to the province seat, where the mandarin of education (*doc hoc*) twice a year gave four examinations: the *kinh nghia,* or interpretation of a passage from the five great canons; the *tu luc,* or composition of a poem; the *thi phu,* or composition of rhythmic prose; and the *van sach,* or commentary on a passage from the classics. Those who passed these were eligible for the regional examinations, given every three years, on the same four types of composition, but at a higher level. Candidates who passed the first three received the degree of *tu tai,* or bachelor, and those who passed the fourth as well were given the degree of *cu nhan,* or master.[51] Only the latter, the *cu nhan,* could take the examination given in the capital (*hoi thi*); successful candidates received the degree of *tien si,* or doctor. To give an idea of the breadth of the basic recruiting, out of 4,000 candidates presented by the provinces for the regional examination at Hue in the year 1913, 96 received the degree of bachelor and 32 the rank of master. The number of doctors was considerably smaller; during the entire Nguyen Dynasty (1802–1945) there were only 502 doctors.[52]

The question now arises whether positions could be filled by any other means—for example, in the event that the examinations did not provide enough successful candidates or in the case of positions involving a high degree of confidence.

In the first place, there were certain positions (distinct from the titles of nobility) accorded to princes of the blood, sons or descendants of the king.[53] This practice was quite common under the Trans and under the Nguyens, but the positions in question were often military. Where civil positions were concerned, these princes or sons of high mandarins were admitted automatically to the school for children of the state as *ton sinh* (students who were sons of princes or high mandarins), to prepare for examinations, which sometimes were open only to them. Similarly, the sons of ordinary mandarins were given the title of *am sinh,* which excused them from taking certain parts of the final examination, but which did not exempt them from the examinations as a means of entering the government service. These were officially recognized privileges (*the tap*); any attempt to obtain unjust promotions was severely punished; the son of a high mandarin who fraudulently obtained good marks was disqualified and his father was reduced in rank.[54]

Then there was the *tien cu,* or presentation; on occasion, the king proclaimed an edict urging the people to present virtuous men whom they considered capable of administering the regions.[55] Often, it was considered a duty of the mandarins above the third rank to present wise, honest, talented, and upright men to be appointed district chiefs, or even province chiefs.[56] Subsequently, even the provincial mandarins, the *thua chinh* and the *hien sat,* were asked to present capable men to be named district chiefs or assistant district chiefs.[57] This procedure was used either at the beginning of a dynasty or during troubled times, perhaps with a concern for the legitimation of power, and consequently should be considered exceptional.

It was also a common practice at the beginning of each dynasty for the new rulers to reward the companions of their struggles by conferring titles on them and assigning them to high positions. This practice was always of short duration; a king's successors frequently forget services rendered or resent the arrogance of the former companions of the deceased king.[58]

In addition, usually during the period of decadence of each dynasty, there was systematic venality, particularly at the lower echelons of administration. Under Le De Duy Phuong (1729–1732), Prince Trinh Giang sold the positions of *tri phu* (district chief) for 2,800 *quan*, and those of *tri huyen* (assistant district chief) for 1,800 *quan*. It should be noted that previously, during the reigns of Tran Du Ton and Le Thanh Ton, there had also been some commerce of mandarinal ranks, but only honorific ones (*nhap tu*).[59]

These practices are reported here only to emphasize the fact that they were exceptional—and quite inconceivable according to Confucian ethics. The old tradition was one of recruiting mandarins by competitive examinations.

THE COLONIAL CONTRIBUTION

The democratic system of recruiting civil servants by means of competitive examinations met with the approval of the colonial authorities, who came from a nation faithful to the revolutionary ideals of liberty, equality, and fraternity. After the inevitable vacillations at the beginning of the colonial regime—in the absence of the mandarins, who refused to co-operate, administrative positions had to be left to unscrupulous opportunists—the system of administrative examinations was restored soon after the treaty of 1862.[60]

During the colonial period, there were three distinct methods of recruiting, all based on examinations:

(1) *Recruiting by academic degrees.* This method of recruiting was a continuation of the old system of examinations, with the difference that, at the beginning, the educational institutions accorded degrees to students who had passed the final examinations, and the administration, which was a completely different institution, recruited candidates on the basis of these degrees. This is the origin of the system of grouping the cadres in three categories: the higher cadres, to which were admitted only persons holding diplomas of university level; the secondary cadres, open to holders of diplomas of secondary education, or of *enseignement primaire supérieur* (an abbreviated secondary education); and the lower cadres, open to persons without academic degrees, or who possessed only the *certificat d'études primaires* (primary school certificate).

(2) *Recruiting by academic degrees after examination.* When the holders of academic degrees were more numerous than the positions to be filled, it became necessary to develop a system of examinations in which all persons fulfilling the academic require-

ments would take a new examination, after which they would be ranked by order of merit. Starting with the candidates who performed the best on these last examinations and working down, as many candidates as there were posts to be filled were declared to have passed, and were appointed to the cadres. Another advantage of this examination was that it made it possible to require of the candidates, in addition to the general education received at school, a knowledge of certain matters necessary for the exercise of their future functions.

(3) *Recruiting after examination and training.* The candidates were obliged to hold certain academic degrees; they were given a competitive examination for a certain number of openings, determined in advance, in professional schools; only that number of candidates was considered to have passed the examination; they were admitted to these schools, where they studied a specialized course for a certain length of time (usually three years). In the course of these studies, they were given more examinations, and at the end, a final examination; the diploma awarded to the successful candidates gave them the right to be appointed to the cadres of the administration. This method of recruiting was applied particularly in the higher cadres (administration, education, public works, veterinary medicine, etc.), and the courses involved were given by the so-called University of Hanoi created in 1917, which was in reality a higher-level training establishment.[61]

In practice, all these competitive examinations were supervised by the French administrators. Consequently, a great deal depended on the integrity of these administrators; nepotism was possible if the administrator presiding at the examination could be swayed by the hidden influences of power or of money. It should be said, however, that the administration of the examination was for the most part impartial.

Although the principle of competitive examinations was widely adopted, the following practices were introduced under the colonial administration, to take into account certain specific interests: the system of reserving positions for military veterans who had participated in certain battles; and the system of discrimination based on race, which admitted the French to certain cadres which were closed to the natives; a compromise was brought about in 1935, in the system of local European cadres, to which certain Vietnamese were admitted upon examination.[62]

THE PRESENT SYSTEM OF RECRUITING

The long tradition of recruiting civil servants by means of competitive examinations is naturally upheld by the government of Viet-Nam as an integral part of the democratic principle of the equality of all citizens with respect to access to the government service, a principle solemnly proclaimed by the Constitution of 1956 (Article 19).

The Statute of Civil Service sets certain preliminary conditions for entrance into the government service (Article 22): Vietnamese citizenship, age between 18 and 30 years, good physical condition, good moral conduct (the enjoyment of full civil rights and an official certificate of good morals), and the satisfaction of technical requirements (academic degrees, professional training, required length of time in the service in the case of civil servants already in the cadres who wish to enter higher cadres).[63]

These conditions are objectively determined well in advance of the examinations. There is no reference to the social class of the applicant or to his religion. Because of the respect accorded to the civil service and because only relatively well-to-do parents can afford to give their children much education, the general impression is that civil servants are recruited from the middle class, even though there are no statistics on this subject. Similarly, since the recruiting center is in Saigon, and since most of the institutions of higher learning are also in Saigon, it is inevitable that a great many of the candidates selected will be from there, in spite of the most scrupulous application of the law of competition. Shortly after the Revolution, the government decided to recruit certain civil servants directly from the rural areas, so they would be as well adapted as possible to the regions of their employment, but a number of persons living in Saigon elected domicile in the country in order to be chosen.[64] Besides, the recruiting of candidates on the basis of their regions of origin would be a violation of the principle of equality of opportunity in entering civil service.

Academic Requirements and Examinations. Since the afore-mentioned qualifications are clearly stipulated in a general act, they are, of course, universalistic in spirit. When certain restrictions are listed in the specific statutes for each cadre, and concern especially the technical requirements, these conditions are also set down in an objective way, as soon as each cadre is created, and are not hastily devised every time a new candidate is recruited. Thus, on the whole, in order to enter Category A, all candidates must have university degrees; among the cadres of Category A, there are, for example, those of engineer of public works, for which the degree of engineer of public works is required. Similarly, and in spite of the fact that professional requirements for workers of Category B are less emphasized, the specific statute of a cadre may require a specific technical diploma; for example, to enter the cadre of *phu ta thi nghiem* (laboratory assistant), the candidate must hold the diploma of medical laboratory technical assistant; but, in general, a secondary school diploma would be sufficient.[65]

In Category A only, candidates who have the necessary diplomas are accepted automatically without examination. Although a slight excess of candidates with university degrees is beginning to appear, the Directorate-General of Civil Service is not yet in a position to change the recruiting system for this category. For the other categories, it remains the rule that candidates are selected only after a competitive examination.

The general principle is that if the number of candidates is greater than the number of positions to be filled an entrance examination is necessary.[66] All details of the administration and subject matter of this examination are determined ahead of time, and include: (1) the appointment of a jury for rating the papers, distinct from the committee which supervises the administration of the examination; the composition of this jury and of this committee is determined so that the representatives of the interested services can share the responsibility of the operations with the representatives of other services responsible for maintaining recruiting standards (usually the Directorate-General of Civil Service and the National Institute of Administration); (2) complete secrecy with reference to the choice of subjects for the examinations, which is often the responsibility of the secretaries of state; and (3) complete anonymity of the examination papers—the least indication of the identity of the candidate can lead to the annulment of the examination and possibly to the punishment of the candidate at fault.

In general, the examinations are very carefully organized, making dishonesty extremely difficult. The fairness of the examinations can be explained by a long tradition of strictness established when the Confucians were still in power, a tradition which in China was at the basis of the fifth of the five *yuan,* or powers (legislative, executive, judicial, control, and examination).[67]

But the question remains whether in point of fact all recruiting is done by means of examinations, or whether other means exist which mitigate this democratic principle. The reasons which necessarily affected the problem of civil servants during the first years of the Republic have been discussed in Chapter 2.[68]

Note should be taken of the recruiting by examination of graduates of the professional schools. The number of openings for entrance into these schools is set each year, and is based on the eventual needs of the administration. Candidates must take a very severe entrance examination for these schools; if they pass the yearly examinations and the final examination, they are sure of being appointed to the cadres. This applies at the present time to the administrators, the *doc su,* engineers of public works, and primary and secondary school teachers.[69] As a result, the examinations for direct admission into these cadres are to all intents and purposes closed; but this cannot be criticized as antidemocratic, since the entrance examinations to the professional schools are open to all comers; it is simply a question of the delay for the duration of the studies.

The only case in which there is a legal exception to the principle of recruiting for cadres on the basis of academic degrees and competitive examinations is a statute providing that the chief of state may decide on special promotions from one cadre to another "for civil servants whose achievements have been especially beneficial to the nation and the Vietnamese people." The same statute also provides that exemption from the usual requirements for a national cadre may be granted to a non-cadre employee or to a private person with such achievements to his credit.[70] This exceptional reward was intended only for very rare cases—brilliant achievements or feats of arms which would justify setting aside the general rule; it falls under the heading of building morale in the government service.

Distinction between Appointment to a Cadre and Assignment to a Position. A distinction must be made between appointment to a cadre and assignment to an administrative position. An appointment to a cadre is subject to all the rigors of the regulations, since it does not imply immediate assignment to a position. The appointment of a young man to the cadre of *doc su,* or field administrator, does not indicate that he has the right to a position as field administrator; he may be assigned temporarily, or even permanently, to an office position. As a matter of fact, the important administrative positions (province chief, director of a service) may not be assigned to cadre employees, or they may be assigned to cadre employees whose rank and class do not correspond to the conditions normally required. Of course, this is true particularly of the important administrative positions in which political considerations or personal qualities are taken into account. Indeed, during the last years of the First Republic, assignment to administrative positions tended to become more and more arbitrary, particularly as regards the positions of province chief. On the other hand, an increasing number of graduates of the National Institute of Administration are being appointed assistant province chief or provincial chief of service. One important change made by the Revolutionary Government was the systematic replacing of all assistant district chiefs—who had been recruited rather haphazardly under the First Republic from many different cadres and even from non-cadre personnel—with graduates of the National Institute of Administration. This change constitutes an important initial step toward universalism in personnel administration.[71]

Another consideration concerns recruiting employees who do not belong to the cadres. It has already been pointed out that there are many such employees (70 per cent of the total number of government workers). The casual observer might believe that the appointment of these workers is largely arbitrary.[72] However, in point of fact, statutes regarding dayworkers are becoming more and more precise. Examinations have been set up for recruiting several categories of dayworkers and standardizing the positions of certain workers recruited during times of crisis. However, since these examinations are not as strictly organized as those for recruiting cadre workers, particularistic whims may arise, especially at the province level. It is here that political pressure is brought to bear by elected officials, or by influential men in the party in power, who may recommend party members or members of their own families. However, such cases are quite infrequent and encounter strong reaction on the part of the Directorate-General of Civil Service; it might be said that patronage appointment is practically unknown at the present time, although there was some indication of it during the Bao Dai interregnum. One authority finds a certain internal contradiction in the process of political development: the spoils system is harmful to administrative efficiency, but without a spoils system there is no incentive to form an opposition party, at least during the periods of transition, when political education does not reach a high degree of objectivity.[73]

Quite a different case is another category of non-cadre civil servants: persons who have had highly specialized training, particularly abroad. In practice, these are outnumbered by the positions available to them in the government service; consequently, they are recruited according to academic degree, either as contractual workers or as technical assistants.[74] Here there can be no question of nepotism, since there are always openings for all those who fill the requirements; however, influence can be exerted in the setting of salaries, since these positions are not subject to the rigid disposition of the statutes. These appointments in the interest of added efficiency may also be regarded as a morale-building measure adopted by the government.

Problems Directly Related to the Recruiting of Civil Servants. An examination of the measures taken in the recruiting of civil servants seems to suggest that the government is trying, on the one hand, to follow the traditional democratic ideal of selecting candidates only on the basis of competitive examinations open to everyone, and, on the other, to find ways to cope with the urgent need for personnel in services in which great efficiency is required to execute government programs.

The statistics given on page 180 show that the civil servants represent a comparatively small percentage of the population. The Revolutionary Government's new all-out effort toward rural development will also require large numbers of employees. It is easy to understand that the problem of recruiting civil servants has become more than ever a major concern of the government.

Certain criticisms have appeared in the press, however, concerning the "profusion" of government workers, those budget-eaters who produce so little and consume so much money. One writer has included the 360,000 military and armed forces auxiliary personnel, and points out that there are a total of 486,000 persons on the government payroll. He explains this plethora by the following facts: that the Ngo Dinh Diem government had to absorb large numbers of government employees coming from the North after the Geneva Agreements, that there was unemployment resulting from the dismantling of the French war effort, and that the Statute of Civil Service makes it difficult to eliminate even incompetent personnel.[75]

In reality, these criticisms misrepresent the situation. In certain services there is an urgent need for personnel; "incompetent" workers can be dismissed, but it would be far more practical to take advantage of what experience they have, and increase their competence by training; in the case of an excess of employees in a given service, it would be better to transfer them to services where they are needed than to dismiss them. The major problems, then, are really the intelligent utilization of existing personnel and the training of personnel—old as well as new—for better performance of their duties. The optimum work force can be effectively evaluated only after these adjustments have been made.

On the other hand, another factor must be considered: the region of origin of the civil servants. The Ngo Dinh Diem government was often criticized for using too few workers from South Viet-Nam in the higher echelons of the government service. Technically, this criticism is inaccurate: the former President took great care to maintain balanced proportions of men from different regions in his administration,[76] although his unofficial entourage was indeed made up principally of persons from Central Viet-Nam and from North Viet-Nam. In the other echelons, however, the entrance examinations make regional favoritism impossible.

Morale Building

Humanist philosophy attaches particular importance to the problem of morale building within the bureaucracy. Morale refers to the state of mind or attitude that the members of the service entertain toward their work and the organization to which they belong.[77] In earlier times, the mere fact of belonging to the mandarinate, after the laborious examinations which automatically ranked successful candidates among the elite, constituted an encouragement to maintain high moral conduct in the accomplishment of administrative functions. This pride in belonging to the elite made the mandarin a loyal and devoted servant; but, with the progressive decline of culture as the sole criterion for social esteem, the problem of the morale of civil servants today acquires a double aspect: one which might be considered materialistic and another that is of a spiritual nature.

MATERIAL WORKING CONDITIONS

If the civil service worker is to be fired with enthusiasm and professional conscience, careful attention must be paid to the material conditions under which he works: physical conditions, such as the location of the office, lighting, working hours, lunch facilities; financial security, as provided by a salary which will permit his family to live properly and a suitable retirement plan; and moral security, as provided by opportunity for advancement in his career and a certain protection against disciplinary measures, as well as the possibility of being entrusted with an important position. According to a recent survey,[78] civil servants do not seem to pay much attention to the problems of material organization posed by physical working conditions, although the results of research done in the United States show the necessity for concern in this matter. As the study of public administration develops, this problem will certainly receive the attention it deserves.[79]

Salary and Allowances.   Contrary to popular belief, which regards the salary of a civil servant as compensation for services rendered, the Statute of Civil Service provides that he shall have a stipend which is not a salary in the economic sense, but which will enable him to maintain his social position and to devote himself entirely to his functions.[80] The fact that this salary is due only for the period during which service is rendered is the sole concession to the economic idea of salary.

Following this principle, the Statute of Civil Service sets the base salary as a function of the minimum living wage, according to a system of indexes which run from 100 to 1200. The minimum living wage (which should correspond to the index 100) was set in May, 1954, at VN $1,020 per month, and has not been increased since then, in spite of the increase of the cost of living (for example: 1959 cost of living index, 100; 1960, 105; 1961, 117; 1962, 121).[81] According to the statute, the salary is set on the basis of 120% of this minimum living wage, so that the base pay of a worker is determined by multiplying his base pay index by a "multiplier" found as follows: [82]

$$\frac{\text{VN } \$1020 \times 120}{100 \times 100} = \text{VN } \$12.24$$

If a worker has a base pay index of 400, his base pay will be:

$$VN \$12.24 \times 400 = VN \$4,896.00$$

Each cadre of the civil service has a corresponding scale of indexes. Thus, the cadre of *doc su* includes classes which have indexes running from 430 (assistant field administrator, class 3) to 1000 (principal field administrator, superior class) (see Chart VII). Since the November 1 Revolution, a salary scale equivalent to the civil service scale has been adopted for military personnel (*Décret-loi* No. 135, April 24, 1964).[83] At first glance, it might seem that a comparison of these indexes would give an idea of the spread of the salaries, that if the indexes go from 100 to 1,200, that means that the salary spread is from 1 to 12, and consequently that this system gives a distinct advantage to workers in the higher brackets and a serious disadvantage to the workers at the bottom of the scale.

In fact, the spread of base pay is equalized by a series of allowances:[84] the regional cost of living allowance, which varies according to the size of the family and according to the region in which the civil servant works; and the family allowance, based on the spouse and the number of children for whom the civil servant is responsible. Thus it can be seen that a worker with a large family may receive more take-home pay than an unmarried worker who has a higher pay index.

At the same time, in order to attract highly qualified technicians in the higher brackets, the government has been obliged to create a special cadre of technical assistants, or *tham vu chuyen mon*, for which the salary follows a normal scale of indexes, but includes a special allowance which is quite substantial.[85]

The salary is further modified by a series of work-connected allowances, among them: a representation and travel allowance, an allowance for supplementary functions, a legal responsibility allowance, and an allowance in kind (house, furnishings, etc.).

These allowances, which constitute substantial advantages for commissioners, directors, chiefs, and technical assistants are often the object of criticism,[86] but are justified by the urgent need for qualified civil servants and by the fact that many qualified candidates are being offered much more attractive salaries, particularly for executive positions, by foreign firms.

Promotions.　Another material means of improving the morale of the civil servant is a system of promotions which gives him double satisfaction—spiritual satisfaction, since his work is recognized, and material satisfaction, since he receives a higher salary.

Government employees are given a performance rating each year by their superiors on the basis of six points: health, behavior,

CHART VII
ADMINISTRATIVE CADRES: FIELD ADMINISTRATOR

Decree No. 103/CV of 9 December, 1950, as amended by Decree No. 48/NV of 1 June, 1953.

Determining the specific statute of the national cadre of Field Administrator (*Doc-su*).

1000 Principal Field Administrator, Super Class (more than 3 years)	Governor
940 Principal Field Administrator, Super Class (less than 3 years)	
890 Principal Field Administrator, Class 1	Mayor, Chief of Province, Class 1
840 Principal Field Administrator, Class 2	
790 Principal Field Administrator, Class 3	
740 Field Administrator, Class 1 (more than 3 years)	Chief of Province, Class 2
690 Field Administrator, Class 1 (less than 3 years)	
640 Field Administrator, Class 2	Chief of Province, Class 3
590 Field Administrator, Class 3	
550 Assistant Field Administrator, Class 1 (more than 3 years)	
510 Assistant Field Administrator, Class 1 (less than 3 years)	Deputy Chief of Province, Chief of District.
470 Assistant Field Administrator, Class 2	
430 Assistant Field Administrator, Class 3 (or Probationary)	

Qualification Requirements:

Assistant Field Administrator, Class 3, Probationary
non-civil servant graduate of the National Institute of Administration
holder of licence of law or equivalent diploma and direct entry examination

Assistant Field Administrator, Class 3:
civil servant graduate of the National Institute of Administration with present salary index of less than 430
Senior Clerk with salary index of less than 430 and professional entry examination

Assistant Field Administrator, Class 1, Probationary:
holder of doctorate of law or equivalent diploma and direct entry examination

Assistant Field Administrator or Field Administrator at the class immediately higher than the present salary index of:
a civil servant graduate of the National Institute of Administration
a Senior Clerk having a salary index of more than 430 and professional entry examination

political attitude, educational background, performance of duties, and ability (executive, organizational, and management). The ratings run from 1 to 20, in this manner: 1 to 5, bad; 6 to 8, poor; 9 to 11, mediocre; 12 to 14, satisfactory, 15 to 17, good; 18 to 19, excellent; and 20, exceptional.[87]

This performance rating form was modeled after forms used in the United States, England, and France, with the additional stipulation that the superior should rate not only the worker, but also the man behind the worker. Thus, under the consideration "behavior," the worker is judged according to his behavior with respect to his superiors, to his colleagues, to the public at large, in his private life, and particularly from the point of view of integrity. An additional element is the evaluation of his educational background, including in-service training courses, with an eye to encouraging the employee to improve himself constantly.[88]

With this performance-rating system, the superior must know his subordinates well. An investigation concerning a limited number of workers, however, has shown that the superior does not pay enough attention to his subordinates.[89] In addition, because of the difficulty of maintaining strict secrecy concerning the ratings given, many superiors who are not too resolute have a tendency to overestimate their subordinates on paper.

In order to compare the various ratings made by the different superiors concerning workers of the same cadre and of the same class, and also to set up as objectively as possible an order of preference among the workers of the same class and cadre who have filled the necessary requirements for being promoted (i.e., at least two years of service in a class), there is a committee on promotions for each cadre, made up of representatives of the workers of the cadre and representatives of the department concerned and of the Directorate-General of Civil Service. These committees have only advisory powers, since the final decision on promotions rests with the prime minister in the case of civil servants of Category A, and with the ministers for workers of other categories, depending on their ministries.

With a strict and regular rating system, it might be expected that annual promotions, as a recompense for the civil service workers who have performed their functions properly, would be routine. During the First Republic, promotions were not automatic, even on New Year's Day, as was the tradition during the French domination; it sometimes happened that some workers listed on the promotion table were not promoted.[90] It must be inferred that the government of the First Republic intended to make it understood that promotion was not a right of the worker, even if he had a seniority of four years in the same class, and that only those who had really distinguished themselves in performing their functions deserved to be promoted.

This point of view is contrary to the Statute of Civil Service—the whole point of the principle of legality is to avoid arbitrary actions— and contributed considerably to a feeling of dissatisfaction which existed among civil servants during the First Republic. This feeling was heightened by the cases in which workers were promoted to higher ranks in the cadre, or even to higher cadres, without having fulfilled certain requirements (length of service, or education) for admission to the new positions. As has been shown, on rare occasions these promotions were justified for civil servants whose achievements had been especially beneficial to the nation and to the Vietnamese people, but this is still arbitrary.[91] A committee set up after the November 1 Revolution to reconsider the cases of regular or civil servants who had been excessively penalized or rewarded between July, 1954, and October, 1956, has found that there were approximately 1000 of these exceptional promotions (out of a total of more than 43,000 cadre civil servants), of which some 800 involved persons who had performed no unusual achievements, but who had shown themselves devoted to the interests of the Ngo family.[92]

Discipline.   The authority which has the power of promotion also has disciplinary powers. Whenever disciplinary action is taken, the effects are felt on the entire situation of the civil service worker disciplined—at the very least in the form of a delay in promotion— since this action places him in an unfavorable light among the colleagues with whom he is competing for advancement.

The types of misconduct for which disciplinary action may be taken are theoretically countless: disobedience; irregularity in the performance of duties; behavior detrimental to the prestige of the government, either on or off duty; commercial activities for personal gain; the spouse having a lucrative business without having reported it to the authorities; etc. An ordinance dated July 6, 1955, even stipulated in addition that an employee may be considered at fault if, while carrying out his functions, he has an attitude not in keeping with the national spirit of service (e.g., passivity, shirking responsibility, counterpropaganda, conspiracy against the government, etc.). In this case, it is not merely a question of professional misconduct; the more serious of these are legal offenses. Certain offenses committed by government employees acting in their official capacities are punishable by law: violation of secrecy where national defense is involved, damaging or destroying government equipment provided for his use, abuse of authority, misappropriation of public funds, arbitrary arrests (in the case of police officials), and others.[93]

In addition to punishment directed by the court, and even in certain cases not subject to legal proceedings, the worker who is found at fault may incur disciplinary action determined according to a graduated scale. Certain punishments, to begin with, are of a moral nature: a reprimand, a recorded censure, or a transfer. More severe punishments may be: delay of promotion for one or two years, or, where pertinent, removal from the promotion list; demotion by one or two classes; temporary suspension without pay for from three to six months; indefinite suspension without pay until contrary orders are issued; dismissal without loss of pension rights; and dismissal with loss of pension rights.

The Revolutionary Government has taken special steps to discipline those civil servants who took advantage of their positions under the Ngo Dinh Diem government for purposes of extortion or misappropriation of public funds. The list of these persons is not long, but a special commission has been set up by Decree No. 17a of November 27, 1963.[94] This commission, which includes the Minister of Justice, the Secretary of State at the Office of the Prime Minister, the Inspector General for Administrative and Financial Affairs, and the Special Commissioner for Administrative Affairs, has complete freedom to propose disciplinary measures to the Prime Minister or to refer the civil servants concerned to the court.

This commission is not to be confused with the Disciplinary Council, created by the general statute, before which the worker could examine his dossier and present his defense. An ordinance dated August 1, 1954, temporarily suspended these protective measures, on the grounds that, during the period of emergency, disciplinary measures had to be taken rapidly and the interests of the state had to take precedence over the rights of the individual. Although, in practice, an investigating committee organized *ad hoc* always examined each case before proposing any punishment, the Revolutionary Government has officially re-established the Disciplinary Council, to give the civil servant the protection provided him in the general statute.[95]

Reassignment. Unlike disciplinary measures, which always constitute punishment for a misdeed, assignment to a given position can be either a reward or a punishment. For reasons of security, civil servants are always happy to be assigned to Saigon, while the provincial administrations are always complaining of the lack of qualified administrators in rural areas. From time to time, in order to remedy this situation, orders have come down from the president (or more recently from the prime minister) to set up a rotation system involving workers who have been in the cities for long periods of service and those who have been in the country.

After the November 1 Revolution, in order to increase the efficiency of the administrative machine, orders were given to the ministries to reassign 30 per cent of their Saigon-based personnel to the country. It is too soon to see to what extent these instructions will be applied, but it can already be stated that these measures tend to raise the morale of the civil servants assigned to rural positions.

WORKING CONDITIONS AND MORALE

A British author, drawing on American sources, offers the following definition: " 'High morale' would be that state of a group in which its output is above average, its members score high on job-satisfaction questionnaires and evince considerable pride in their group and cohesiveness." [96] It is up to the public and to groups representing the major interests of the population, on one hand, and to the government and the government employees themselves, on the other, to develop the spiritual aspects of this morale.

The Role of Private or Semiprivate Groups and of the Public If the public understands better the role of the administration, it will collaborate more and more voluntarily in the performance of governmental tasks. With the development of a civic spirit, the people will also learn their own rights and know what can be expected of the administration. This dual role of the public, which is expressed by the press, by the representatives of the people (for example, in the National Assembly), and by the province council, can contribute effectively toward raising the morale of government workers, who will feel better understood by the public and will realize that they are morally and professionally obligated to that public. [97]

Of course, in view of the national development toward more satisfaction of material wants, there can be no question of taking a simple step backward and of preaching a return to the principles of Confucian orthodoxy, which would serve as a basis for this moral duty. It is for this reason that, side by side with civic education, which is a slow and tedious process, organizations under the more or less apparent patronage of the government of the First Republic have been set up to raise the morale of the government workers. Among these are the Phong Trao Cach Mang Quoc Gia (National Revolutionary Movement), many of whose active members are also members of the Lien Doan Cong Chuc Cach Mang Quoc Gia (National Revolutionary Civil Servants' League); the Thanh Nien Cong Hoa (Republican Youth Group); and the Phong Trao Lien Doi Phu Nu (Women's Solidarity Movement). Of all such groups, the most important from the point of view of the government worker was the Lien Doan Cong Chuc Cach Mang Quoc Gia. It was formed in 1954 with clearly political aims: to overthrow the Bao Dai regime in order to replace it with a democratic regime, to put into effect principles which would strengthen the independence and unity of the country, to serve the people, and to create a revolutionary spirit among the government workers. All government workers could be members, provided they had the nationalist spirit. This group followed the same pyramidal organization as the administrative structure: a central administrative committee, the *Ban Chap Hanh Trung Uong*, at the head of the movement; groups in the departments and in the provinces, called *chi doan;* and other subordinate groups in the directorates or in smaller units, called *phan doan*. According to the report of the secretary-general of the League, presented in the plenary session of July 16, 1962, the movement has concentrated particularly on two objectives: (1) the improvement of the cultural and material life of the members by means of study sessions called *hoc tap*, in-service training, the publication of a monthly review, active participation in community works, a literary prize called *Giai Truoc Thuat*, the awarding of academic scholarships for children of members, the setting up of a mutual assistance fund, and the creating of consumer cooperatives; and (2) the reinforcing of the political and military struggle, through active participation in the presidential election, participation in the youth movement, the setting up of strategic hamlets, assistance to flood victims, and subscriptions for the establishment of an anti-Communist fund.[98]

In practice, the League mobilized civil servants in meetings to support the anti-Buddhist policy, and collected funds, supposedly for the struggle against communism, which were actually diverted to political use. The most common criticism concerned the loss of time and energy in interminable meetings of executive committees. Another criticism was that, instead of strengthening the bureaucracy, the League actually served the interests of antibureaucratization inasmuch as it was much more an instrument of regime control and manipulation.[99]

Theoretically, in the absence of purely spontaneous associations, in a society which has been for more than a century subjected to a foreign domination that prohibited such associations (except for religion and social security), the government may instigate the formation of groups of manageable size, which can guide the numerous interests of the nation. Even if they do not immediately bring about a full and voluntary adhesion, these movements can still inspire the civil servants with a certain revolutionary spirit, urging them to break away from the routine, negligence, and waste with which they are often reproached.

The Role of the Governmental Organizations. Among the organizations set up directly by the government, the study movement (*phong trao hoc tap*) and the in-service training movement (*lop tu nghiep*) should be mentioned.

The Study Movement. The study meetings were set up by government regulations during the First Republic. Within each separate administrative unit, discussions are held under the leadership of the head of the unit or his representative, concerning important international events, certain major decisions of the government, or technical matters coming under the special jurisdiction of the unit.[100] Special attention should be given, however, to the meetings that have as an objective the development of a spirit of stewardship among the civil servants. These meetings concern the general lines of the government policies, such as the personalist doctrine, community development, the programs of *agrovilles* and strategic hamlets, and the threefold struggle against underdevelopment, disunity, and communism. Another series of meetings concerned the means of executing intelligently the laws and instructions received from higher authority; the procedures for avoiding the more or less involuntary tendencies to fall into routine, laziness, indifference, or negligence in executing orders; and sabotage by inaction or by action. It should be noted that the study meetings were imbued with the spirit of the basic Confucian concepts regarding the characteristics of the proper civil servant: [101] *thanh,* or simplicity; *can,* or industriousness; *liem,* or honesty; and *chinh,* or rectitude; and also those regarding the cardinal social virtues: *nhan,* or humanheartedness, *tri,* or wisdom, and *dung,* or courage.

At the beginning, certain study meetings resembled the autocriticism meetings of the Communists, but later the discussions became calmer and more regular. Some civil servants complained that time was being wasted because of the many study meetings. Admitting the justness of this criticism, the government recommended that the study committees make the meetings less frequent, and choose more circumspectly the topics for discussion, so that the study sessions would be really effective. It should be noted that, in the minds of the promoters of the study movement, it was to be essentially voluntary; however, it has become linked with the National Revolutionary Civil Servants' League (Lien Doan Cong Chuc Cach Mang Quoc Gia), which has attempted to oblige its members to participate actively in the study movement.[102] There has developed a sense of obligation to participate, which has often led to an undesirable result: certain workers attended the meetings for the sake of form, and while they were present physically, in spirit they were elsewhere. Since the Revolutionary Government has given instructions for the continuation of the study meetings, an examination of the objectives will give a better idea of the practical application of the movement. These objectives can be grouped under three general headings: civic spirit, professional conscience, and technical competence.

Insofar as civic spirit is concerned, the study meetings were intended to develop national feeling, particularly among civil servants who had served the French regime and had little by little lost this feeling,[103] and among the ranks of subordinate civil servants, where the exigencies of daily life did not permit keeping up with political developments. It is interesting to compare the results obtained by this method with those obtained in the Communist autocriticism sessions. Whereas the Communists obtain the more or less voluntary adhesion of the government workers through autocriticism of the deeds and the acts of the individual worker, here the discussion sessions were concerned with more general topics, although there were occasional cases of calling an individual to task, particularly in certain provincial areas of administration. It should be noted, however, that certain study meetings, particularly in the country, tended strongly toward the personal cult of Ngo Dinh Diem and his brothers; to this extent, civic spirit became servility. The initial objective of the study meetings can be attained only if all personality cult is eliminated; i.e., if the spirit of the meetings is universalistic.

Professional conscience was to be developed through a clearer knowledge on the part of each civil servant of his role in the administrative system. In addition to the knowledge gained by participating in the in-service training classes, the study sessions often included commentaries on new dispositions concerning the service itself. In certain services, the leader succeeded in filling the workers with a real *esprit de corps,* which is very helpful for teamwork, developing in them a kind of group loyalty that is a decisive factor in the productivity of the worker. Since each session includes an oral report presented by a worker especially appointed for this purpose by the study committee, which is followed by open discussions often including workers of the upper cadres, a certain feeling of emulation was created which inspired greater attention to the preparation of the study sessions.[104] Here, however, it should be noted that it is relatively difficult to inspire in the civil servant the kind of devotion to the public interest that the employee feels for his employer, largely because of the security guaranteed the civil service worker by the Statute of Civil Service.[105]

Technical subjects were rarely placed on the agenda of the study sessions, because of the greater importance of political and moral problems, although there were instructions recommending that the directors of the services introduce technical problems which occur in the operations of the services so that each worker in the unit might benefit from the experience of his colleagues. Since in any given unit there are always many administrative workers, but usually only a small number of technical workers, the technical part of the study sessions has not received much attention. However, some discussions concerning the improvement of working methods, the elimination of red tape, and means of avoiding delays might be classified as technical.

A general evaluation of the study-meeting movement suggests that, because of a certain particularistic tendency introduced into the movement by the leaders of the First Republic, the stated objectives were not attained. Neither was the tacit objective of shaping the bureaucracy to the wishes of the dictator, as is shown by the fact that the November 1 Revolution met no resistance whatever on the part of the civil servants, many of whom were hostile to the regime, particularly during the Buddhist Affair.[106]

The Provisional Government has given instructions to the effect that the study meetings will henceforth have only two objectives (Circular 19-TTP/VP, dated December 19, 1963): (1) to study government aims in the light of the functions of each service, in order to improve its efficiency; and (2) to study measures concerning the entire structure of the government. Thus, the technical nature of the study meetings is clearly emphasized, but they must still not be confused with the in-service training sessions.

The In-Service Training Movement. Technical matters are often discussed in the in-service training sessions (*lop tu nghiep*), where workers holding similar positions in different departments meet in seminars to discuss certain common problems.

The principle of in-service training has been accepted since ancient times, when the kings required the mandarins to take examinations at regular intervals in order to make sure that they kept up with new ideas and remained in contact with daily realities. This principle was nevertheless ignored during the period of French colonization, and was practised only in the limited sphere of education: the teachers met during summer vacation to keep up with progress made in pedagogy and in their own particular fields.

Because of insufficient production on the part of new civil servants, particularly after World War II, certain units organized in-service training sessions for those of the lower cadres. The principal difficulty rests in the delicate problem of getting the administrators in the higher echelons to admit their own need for in-service training sessions wherein they could exchange accounts of their experiences with their equals and discuss theoretical contributions sometimes brought in by resource experts (usually from educational institutions). The Directorate-General of Civil Service and the National Institute of Administration have combined their efforts to intensify and institutionalize the in-service training movement, particularly through the organization of courses for training officers, who in turn will organize in-service training sessions in their respective services.[107]

In recent years, the in-service training program has been aimed particularly at the lower administrative echelons: the local civil servants. It has been observed that the workers at the commune and hamlet levels, whose recruitment is based more on the confidence shown them by the local population or on their loyalty to the republican government than on their administrative ability, are often not equal to the requirements of their work. In-service training centers have been set up in the province seats, where the commune chiefs and their assistants can participate actively in the program.

Because of its technical nature, the in-service training program was not affected by the November 1 Revolution. The National Institute of Administration, which provides advisory personnel and the use of equipment, has even proposed that the government make an official affirmation of the principle and of the need of in-service training in a circular stating that the Directorate-General of Civil Service will be in charge of the program and the National Institute of Administration will continue to give technical aid. It was also proposed that the Ministry of the Interior be responsible for co-ordinating the program in the provinces. In line with this proposal, the National Institute of Administration, in co-operation with the Ministry of the Interior, organized a great many sessions for the training of district chiefs and instructors for the cadres of pacification.

Conclusion

The in-service training movement contributes to the development of professionalization in the government service; the purpose of the study movement is to interest the civil servant more in public life, to draw him out of the narrow confines of his office and to make him aware of the general political, economic, social, and international problems. Still, in spite of the contention of the government of the First Republic that participation in the National Revolutionary Civil Servants' League or similar political groups gave the workers a closer acquaintance with the role of the public servant as educator of the people, it could, on the contrary, often lead them to neglect the public interest. With the exception of the politicization of the bureaucracy, the afore-mentioned solutions to the problem of morale building fall under the doctrine of the humanistic civil servant, in the Confucian sense of the expression. With this humanistic conception of bureaucracy, it is easier to understand the cadre system, which implies the versatility of the individual, and the promotion system based partly on performance and partly on the decision of the authority responsibile for personnel administration. It is also easier to understand the concern for the choice of good administrators through an impartial system of entrance examinations, except in certain cases where functions with a political nature are concerned.

The bureaucratic system has succeeded in becoming the "central and basic structure seeking to relate the political elite with the other components of the social system." [108] Students of political science are often apprehensive that a bureaucracy developed in this direction might have a tendency to serve its own interests and to be unwilling to submit to political control by the representatives of the people.[109] In theory, in the first Vietnamese constitutional system, since the chief executive was himself the elected representative of the people, and since the bureaucracy was brought completely in line with the general policy defined by him, the bureaucracy was subject to this political control. However, in a "strong-man government, oriental fashion, with the methodical cultivation of a single dominant personality as the exclusive national symbol, the spirit of stewardship can become servility to satisfy personal interest." [110] It would have been better simply to regard Vietnamese bureaucracy in a modern version of its traditional context, and consider the public servants as educators as well as servants of the people. On these terms, we can agree with the author who pointed out that "not all social change in modern society is bureaucratically instituted, but the deliberate introduction of a social innovation on a large scale whether it involves the production of a new weapon or the enforcement of a new law, depends on bureaucratic methods of administration." [111]

CHAPTER 6

FINANCIAL ADMINISTRATION:
FROM BOOKKEEPING TO FISCAL POLICY

> An administrative agency does not exist
> just to keep fiscal records or to observe
> financial restrictions imposed by laws. It
> exists to get some particular work done.[1]

IT HAS BEEN pointed out that public administration would never have been possible without the invention of writing and arithmetic. The first bureaucrats were scribes employed by men in power for keeping accounts either of the income from their own property or of the taxes or prestations, i.e., taxes in kind, they required from the people who lived, more or less voluntarily, under their protection.[2] This subordinate nature of the bookkeeping function remained for a long time one of the essential features of public administration in Viet-Nam, where men of high social rank preferred intellectual pursuits to these household tasks. This is why, until comparatively recent times, a number of active administrators prided themselves on being very well versed in administration, but freely admitted that they knew nothing of "finance," using the word in the limited sense of "accounting." This particular attitude of the administrator corresponds perfectly to the traditional philosophy of administration, which demanded only of the administrator that he give a good example to the people, and that he keep administrative services to a strict minimum: order and security.[3]

Historical Development

FINANCE IN THE TIME OF THE EMPERORS

From very early times, proper order in public finance has always been one of the principal concerns of the kings and their mandarins. The royal annals go back as far as the Ly Dynasty (1010–1225), at which time measures were already being taken to finance a growing administration. The measures described in these annals involved principally the levying of taxes on rice paddies and fields, and on the products of the forests and salt works. It is interesting to observe that the central organization for collecting these revenues was entrusted to princesses of the blood; this shows clearly the household nature attributed to fiscal operations in the early periods of Vietnamese history.[4] It should also be noted in passing that the mandarins directly responsible for collecting taxes were authorized to retain one-tenth of the amount collected, by way of an honorarium.[5]

Taxes were to be paid in kind; the annals make no mention of taxes payable in specie until the Tran Dynasty (1225–1400), when personal taxes could be paid in money rather than by *corvées,* although, even at this time, property taxes continued to be payable only in unhusked rice. Gold and silver money was coined during the Tran Dynasty, but a difference in monetary values between the official rate (1 *tien* for 70 *dong*) and the current rate (1 *tien* for 69 *dong*) gives evidence of the free play of supply and demand.[6]

During the Le Dynasty (1428–1788), several changes occurred in finance administration: the inauguration of a composite system of collection of property taxes (partly in money, partly in kind);[7] the establishment of a well-defined system of accounting which recorded revenues and royal disbursements;[8] and an attempt to establish an incipient budget, intended to provide for the future on the basis of revenues and disbursements of the preceding year.[9] About 1747, an attempt was made to evaluate the performance of mandarins by comparing the totals of taxes collected with those of taxes assessed.[10] The Nguyen princes, in South Viet-Nam, also set up an annual accounting system, in which the various operations of receipts and disbursements were recorded, beginning in the year 1753.[11]

In the early part of the Nguyen Dynasty (1802–1945), a number of practices of finance administration were instituted (which constituted a prelude to the introduction by the French in the second half of the nineteenth century of the application of the principles of Adam Smith): (1) a variation in the tax rate, dependent on the region (probably due to a variation in the degree of wealth in the different regions); (2) the spreading out of the payment of taxes over a period of time, and the setting of the time of tax collection in accordance with the harvest season; (3) the establishment of a personal tax register, providing for the replacement of the registry book every five years; (4) the establishment of the cadastre for keeping records of property taxes; and (5) the introduction of state monopolies for the sale of certain products (opium, salt, etc.).[12]

Although there was a certain amount of bookkeeping, it was intended only to provide records of the imperial finances; for example, on two occasions the annals report the receipts in monetary units of gold and silver, but these figures give no idea of the amounts of money involved in public finance as compared with the total national income.[13]

After the arrival of the French, the history of imperial finance is not distinguishable from that of colonial finance in Indochina, since, from the time of the Protectorate, the court of Annam lived almost exclusively from subsidies of the local budget of Annam, which was administered by the French authorities. It should be noted that at this time, although the imperial finance system was dependent on an entirely agricultural economy, in which money played only a subordinate part, there nevertheless developed within this system a summary bookkeeping of receipts and disbursements, and even a rather rudimentary sort of budget. Of course, an administrative philosophy which reduced to a minimum the intervention of the government in private affairs made further development of a financial system impossible and even unthinkable.

THE COLONIAL FINANCE SYSTEM

In view of this background, the general opinion is that it was the French who, at the time of their colonization of Indochina, introduced for the first time sound principles of public finance in Viet-Nam. This opinion is generally accepted for two reasons. First, the French had long before developed a market economy in which money played a primary role in the mechanics of determining the price of goods and services. It was the only instrument for the collection of taxes to finance state expenditures. Second, since they used money as a primary instrument, they had developed a very precise system of keeping accounts; primarily intended to record past operations, these accounts were subsequently used as the basis for determining taxes and estimating expenditures for the coming period (the budget).

When the colonial finance system is compared with the imperial system, it must indeed be recognized that although the idea of keeping accounts had existed in Viet-Nam for a long time, mathematical precision in bookkeeping matters, as well as the idea of a modern budget seem indeed to have been first introduced by the French. With the idea of a budget came also the entire judicial apparatus, which had stemmed from the mistrust with which the representatives of the French people regarded the kings of France and the executive bodies that succeeded them.[14] In the colonial regime, this apparatus was to correspond to the concern of the authorities in France for maintaining a strict control over the activities of the colonial civil servants, and included the following principles that predated considerably the codification of the colonial finance system in the Decree of December 30, 1912:[15] the annual budget, the unity of the budget, the universality of the budget, the legality of the budget, and the distinction between the *ordonnateurs* (administrative officials who decide for what purposes money may be used) of the budget and the *comptables* (treasury agents who decide whether all is legally and procedurally correct, and who make payment).

THE PROBLEM OF FINANCE TODAY

These principles of finance administration are still applied today, but the criticism is often made that they were formulated at a time when classic economists studied economic mechanisms without taking into consideration the role of the state, which was to intervene as little as possible in the mechanics of production, circulation, and the distribution and consumption of goods and services. Students of public finance nowadays are struck by the preponderant role played by the public sector in the economy of the country, basing their studies on the role of public finance in the formation of the national income, in industrialized as well as in underdeveloped countries.[16]

Thus, according to the statistics of the National Bank of Viet-Nam, in 1955, out of a gross national product estimated at VN $64,264 million, VN $14,058 million, or 22 per cent, came from government expenditures; in 1956, the figures were respectively VN $69,419 million, and VN $13,208 million, or 19 per cent.[17] Although official estimates of the national income based on precise investigation are no longer made, one economist has made estimates accurate enough to give an idea of the ratio between the national product [18] and budgetary disbursements:

RATIO BETWEEN NATIONAL PRODUCT AND BUDGETARY DISBURSEMENTS (IN MILLIONS OF PIASTERS)

Year	Estimated Gross National Product	Anticipated Budgetary Disbursements	Percentage
1960	78,000	17,548 [19]	22.4
1961	80,167	18,370 [19]	22.9
1962	82,175	26,254 [20]	31.7
1963	85,142	29,600 [20]	31.8

Although the data for the years 1962 and 1963 must be reevaluated because the estimates of the gross national product made in 1961 did not include the unexpected increase in military expenditures, the respective proportions of the state expenditures and the estimated gross national product give an adequate idea of the great importance of the problem of public finance in Vietnamese economic life and national development.

Public finance is all the more important since, when it is placed in the more general context of a society undergoing transformation, it is subject to such limitations that, according to certain authorities, finance administration cannot be conducted in an entirely rational manner. It is understood that Viet-Nam long ago cast aside two institutions characteristic of a fused society: tributes paid to the king by his vassals and prebends, or gifts, granted by the king to his mandarins without consideration of their position or of service rendered. However, the observer may well ask whether the Vietnamese fiscal system does not still correspond to the idea of tributary taxation, as long as the basis for taxation is limited, and tax avoidance and tax deviation are possible. Similarly, it might be asked if the budgetary system does not correspond to what has been described as "prebendary budgeting" to the extent that allocations of credit are not made according to the norms required in industrialized countries.[21]

These social and economic indications are presented here only for the purpose of clarifying the problems of finance administration in Viet-Nam, which might be grouped under two general headings: (1) the formulation of the fiscal policy; and (2) the implementing of that policy.

The Formulation of Fiscal Policy

The study of fiscal policy itself is beyond the scope of this work, although such a study might in fact constitute one aspect of substantive administration. The factors to be discussed regarding the formulation of fiscal policy are the predominance of expenditures for military and security operations as compared to other expenditures for economic and social development, and the preponderant role played by foreign aid in financing certain government expenditures, in particular military expenditures. These factors have had considerable influence on the roles played by different powers in the government in the formulation of fiscal policy, as well as on the old general budgetary principles, which some officials consider even today unassailable.

THE PREDOMINANCE OF MILITARY EXPENDITURES

One of the characteristic features of modern Vietnamese public finance is the great importance of expenditures for military and security operations. These expenditures decreased in proportion from 56 per cent of the total of government expenditures in 1955 to 33.6 per cent in 1960,[22] but these figures do not include direct military aid in the form of arms and munitions provided by the United States. In 1961, military expenditures increased again, and since 1962 they have been included in a special security budget, which in 1962 amounted to VN $12,105 million, 46 per cent of the VN $26,250 million total estimated expenditures, and in 1963 to 50 per cent of the VN $29,600 million total estimated expenditures.[23] The same phenomenon can be observed in a number of countries, particularly the larger industrialized countries, such as the United States.[24] But its administrative consequences are not the same in underdeveloped countries. In the first place, because of the urgency of these military expenditures in a country which is threatened by Communist subversion, it is out of the question to discuss openly the object of these expenses at the risk of aiding the enemy. Inasmuch as a large part of the budget is thus not susceptible to open debate, the various advantages of democratic budgetary procedure have not been fully enjoyed, and the democratic apprenticeship is thus delayed.[25]

From the administrative point of view, it is also difficult to link budgetary procedure with an earlier phase currently found in industrialized countries: planning.[26] Since planning is output-oriented, it presupposes that the ends are clearly defined at long range, while the "security" goal is necessarily vague, depending as it does on the play of friendly and enemy forces. To the extent that military expenditures are included in the budget, it can be only input-oriented. This explains why the first five-year plan (1957–1961) was not entirely put into execution [27] and why the second five-year plan can have only an indicative value.

Practically speaking, during the First Republic, at the time of the review of agency estimates for the establishment of the planned national budget at the level of the Presidency, the special financial advisor, who was also comptroller of military expenditures, always began by comparing the planned military expenditures with the total amount of the contribution in Vietnamese money which American aid could offer. If this aid was insufficient to cover all the prospective military expenditures, the first priority in appropriations from the national budget went to making up the difference.[28] The first time the Revolutionary Government examined the national budget in 1964, it could only continue to recognize this preponderance of military expenditures.

Of course, because of the enormous amount of military expenditures, the government still has the possibility of evaluating displacements of workers required by military needs, encouraging industries which supply military equipment, and selecting military public works which might have both strategic and commercial value. To this extent, military expenditures could be conceived of as contributing to fiscal policy.[29]

THE PREPONDERANT ROLE OF FOREIGN AID
IN PUBLIC FINANCE

Foreign aid plays a decisive part in financing military expenditures. It also makes a certain contribution toward defraying the expenses of economic and social development, as can be seen from the following table. All figures are in millions of piasters, except the fifth column, which gives figures in thousands of U.S. dollars.[30]

Year	Total Estimated Budget	American aid for military expenditures	American aid for economy	Additional American aid for economy
1962	26,250	7,275	1,857	11,946
1963	29,600	7,558	1,692	15,205

The Directorate-General of Budget and Foreign Aid gives the gross figures for the civil, military, and economic development budgets. From the civil budget, contributions for military expenditures must be deducted, which amounted respectively to VN $3,918 million in 1962, and VN $5,500 million in 1963.

To the extent that internal expenditures are financed by foreign aid, there is still a question of administrative dualism, although in this case it is of a totally different nature than that of the colonial period. There can be no question of the sincere desire on the part of the friendly countries to come to the aid of a newly independent country which firmly takes a stand on the side of the free world, but which still lives seriously threatened by subversion. Nevertheless, foreign aid has its own drawbacks. The release of funds is naturally subject to certain rigid formalities required by the finance services of the contributing countries.[31] These formalities demand, in particular, the justification of the release of funds in the form of project agreements that often necessitate long negotiations between the representatives of the two countries involved. Theoretically, these negotiations may end in decisions which differ from those that the budgetary authority would have made if it had had a free hand. Regardless of the more or less satisfactory nature of the solution adopted, it must be admitted that this solution constitutes a blow to the principle of budgetary sovereignty of an independent state.

The rigidity of these financial restrictions concerning the use of funds coming from foreign aid is often further increased by the "matching-basis" principle stipulated in a great number of projects. One of the principles of American aid is that the Vietnamese budget must support a part of the expenditures indicated in the project agreements, exactly as in the case of the grants-in-aid which the United States or federal budget accords to state and local governments.[32]

Lastly, foreign aid affects the mass of the national revenue. The countries that receive aid are often reproached with the fact that they do not make a real effort to increase internal resources, and that a large part of the government revenue is still derived from commercial aid, so that the aid produces a psychologically unhealthy multiplier effect on local powers who otherwise might become self-sufficient.[33]

Nevertheless, foreign aid has always been sincerely desired, not only to supply materials and equipment of prime necessity that could not be imported without this aid, but also because of the counterpart funds it engenders, which permit the state to finance additional public projects.[34] Although certain negotiations are necessary in order to determine the goals and the means of achieving them in certain project agreements, these negotiations often have the beneficial effect of technical assistance, inasmuch as these exchanges of points of view allow the budgetary authority to understand more clearly the often subtle details of the problems to be solved. Particularly, they permit technicians of the country receiving the aid to see how economic mechanisms well known to economists of industrialized countries must be studied in the light of new data which might change the essential nature of the problem. For instance, only the study of the economic mechanisms of the incidence and repercussions of taxes can lead to the establishing of an adequate system that will permit a better fiscal administration; it is not enough to deplore the ill will of countries that receive foreign aid to reinforce their fiscal programs; the best intentions must be supported by a scientific study of the reforms to be undertaken.

These various factors have definitely influenced the budgetary process and techniques.

BUDGETARY PROCESS: THE EXECUTIVE BUDGET

Since defense and diplomacy are domains reserved traditionally for the executive branch of the government, it is easy to understand that, in view of the importance of military expenditures and of foreign aid, the role of the president in the government of the First Republic was considered of prime importance in the budget process.[35] To assist him in filling this role, one of the first aspects of administrative reorganization was the placing of the Directorate-General of Budget and Foreign Aid under the direct control of the Presidency, as has been indicated. When the Revolutionary Government reintegrated this directorate into the Ministry of Finance, the reason was quite different: the centralization of all problems of finance in the Ministry of Finance.

Estimates and Reviews of Receipts and Expenditures.   Every year, in about April or May, the Directorate-General of Budget and Foreign Aid sends instructions to the various ministries for the preparation of the national budget. These instructions often contain dispositions concerning the proper manner of presenting estimates of receipts or expenditures, recommendations concerning areas in which economy is to be exercised, and deadlines to be observed. Regarding financial policy proper, the instructions contain passages specifying programs which require particular attention, but not limiting the expenditures of each service. Neither do the instructions refer specifically to the Five-Year Plan or to the progress of the plan; as a result, at this stage there is no clear distinction between the planning process and the budget process.

Since the colonial period, the government services have been accustomed to estimating future expenditures necessary to their operations. As a result, these evaluations were often considered an administrative routine, and were sometimes assigned to subordinate civil servants. However, during long service in executive positions, the responsible persons have learned to their sorrow that the financial organization cannot be neglected, and more and more high-ranking civil servants are beginning to think in terms of long-range programs and precise financial estimates.[36] Thus, the estimates come closer and closer to administrative reality as the public officials gain in experience and as the financial services provide adequate checks.[37] It is rather curious that the estimates in which the greatest variation occurs are those concerning public security, although in this field there are more foreign advisors than in any other. During the postwar period (1945–1954), discipline was somewhat relaxed with regard to the observing of deadlines for submitting budgetary proposals, but, in the last few years, these deadlines have been more strictly observed. From this it might be concluded that at the present time the agencies and the ministries have understood the budget as a management tool.[38]

The Role of the Directorate-General of Budget and Foreign Aid. Under the First Republic, the Directorate-General of Budget and Foreign Aid received, examined, and modified the expenditure proposals, but it was the responsibility of the Department of Finance to revise the estimates of revenues. This division of responsibility was justified by the fact that the Department of Finance was exclusively responsible for the taxes, which constitute the major source of revenue, and also for the handling of all public funds, including those coming from foreign aid (through the National Bank of Viet-Nam).

The organization of the Directorate-General of Budget and Foreign Aid also reflected the tendency to establish a rational budget, based on proposals from the departments concerned, but prepared according to the interpretation the president of the Republic intended to give to national policy during the fiscal year. The last innovation was the setting up of a corps of budget examiners, chosen from among former students of the National Institute of Administration and certain engineers of public works and of agriculture. This mixture of generalists and of technicians was intended to give more weight to the observations of the Directorate-General of Budget and Foreign Aid, and to put an end to the quarrel between administrators and technicians that occurred traditionally in the hearings on the programs proposed by the executive departments. These examiners were in constant touch with the Program Directorate of the Directorate-General of Budget and Foreign Aid, which followed the execution of programs presented by the secretaries of the state and approved for financial purposes in the annual budget. For greater detail, the examiners could consult the Directorate of Obligated Expenditures, another agency of the Directorate-General of Budget and Foreign Aid, which controlled the day-to-day utilization of credits allocated to the various units.[39] The hearings were always attended by the financial advisor to the president, who had a high reputation for acuity and integrity, and who served as a referee, generally deciding on the side of economy, whatever the sacrifice. At the present time, the same procedure is followed, as can be seen by referring to the 1964 Budget prepared by the Ministry of Finance of the Provisional Government, except that the intervention of the finance councilor is no longer possible. Since the Directorate-General of Budget and Foreign Aid no longer has to obtain the prior approval of the prime minister, it appears to have more latitude in the examination of budgetary projects.

The Role of the President.   It was very rare that the president of the Republic was obliged to intervene to settle differences between the Directorate-General of Budget and Foreign Aid and certain departments, but he had to decide to support certain new programs (for example, that of paying the youth representatives elected to the communal administrative councils, or the raising of the salaries of the civil guard and the militia in 1961). However, the role of the president of the Republic in the budget process was dominant, inasmuch as the secretaries of state received instructions from him concerning the principal activities of their departments before making their first proposals, and, at the hearing stage, the financial advisor and the director-general of Budget and Foreign Aid remained in constant communication with the secretary of state at the Presidency. It must be said that the budgetary appropriations depended on a well-defined plan of action, and not on the power of the bureaucrat at the head of each agency, although within very narrow limits, the director of a service might be able to persuade the budget examiner not to throw out certain minor provisions of his proposed budget.[40]

The role of the president of the Republic in the preparation of the proposed budget was indirectly recognized in Article 60 of the Constitution, which stipulates that the proposed annual budget must be submitted to the National Assembly before September 30 of each year. Although the Constitution did not specify the authority responsible for preparing the budget, it is obvious that the intention was to conform to the custom established both in presidential governments (e.g., the United States) and in parliamentary governments (e.g., the French Constitution of 1946), which accords this responsibility to the chief executive, since he is best able to appreciate and evaluate the operations of the various government services. In Viet-Nam, precedents regarding general budgets prepared by the governors-general and local budgets prepared by the chiefs of local administration also confirm this tradition. Thus, the budget presented to the National Assembly was indeed a presidential budget in the sense generally accepted today.[41] This document always accompanied the message read by the president at the opening session of the National Assembly, which is devoted to the examination of the budget. The message constituted a careful statement of the policy the president intended to develop.[42] In the Revolutionary Government, it is to be hoped that the role of the prime minister will still be predominant, but allowance must be made for the opinions of the minister of finance and the vice prime minister for Economy and Finance: the budget will certainly profit by the consideration of several authoritative opinions.

BUDGETARY PROCESS: THE ROLE OF THE LEGISLATIVE BODY

The observer who judges from the importance accorded to the president of the Republic may believe that the National Assembly played only a puppet's role in budgetary procedure.[43] Although in the early years of the First Republic, the Finance Commission (which was responsible for the examination of the presidential budget) and the National Assembly were feeling their way with respect to the budgetary power of the Assembly,[44] some maturity has been observed in more recent discussions.

For example, in the discussion of the 1962 budget, for which the proposal was submitted to the Assembly within the constitutional deadline, the Finance Commission spent two months and eleven days (from October 1 to December 11, 1961) examining the various proposals, first in the presence of the secretaries of state, and later in private sessions, and deciding what amendments to recommend. At the end of the deliberations, the general report of the Commission presented, in a plenary session of the Assembly (December 11, 1961): (1) an outline of the general policy adopted by the President of the Republic, which the commission had been able to verify by means of budgetary data; and (2) principal observations of the commission concerning inadequate planning of the activities of the secretaries of state responsible for liaison, insufficient control over provincial budgets, irrational distribution of personnel; and proposals of the commission concerning the spirit of economy, the granting of allowances in kind to certain public servants, and the importance to be attached to studies preparatory to certain new operations.

On the basis of this report, a discussion concerning general policy was to follow, but actually, no general discussion occurred. After certain matters of procedure, the Assembly began the discussion of receipts: there were criticisms of the injustice of the present system of income tax and of the red tape and delay in the granting of business licenses, requests for explanation of certain provisions of the fiscal law concerning the production tax, criticism of illegal taxation under the pretext of levying a security tax, and dissatisfaction with the poor financial administration of the Port of Saigon. Sometimes the criticisms were directed toward specific provisions of fiscal law (e.g., the establishment of progressive income tax brackets), sometimes toward concrete facts rather far removed from a reform proposal, and sometimes toward the procedures for the evaluation of fiscal receipts, such as that used for estimating the production tax on imported materials. Certain revenues of great importance, however, do not seem to attract the attention of the deputies: for example, customs, state monopolies, and the registration tax. In the end, the revenue proposals were adopted without modification by the Assembly.[45]

In the subsequent discussion concerning expenditures, some criticism was directed against the working methods of the Assembly itself. It was suggested that the appropriations for information were not judiciously used, that in spite of the printing of three official publications (a record of proceedings; *Noi San Quoc Hoi,* or Gazette of the Assembly; and *Cong Bao Vietnam Cong Hoa: An Ban Quoc Hoi,* or the special National Assembly edition of the Official Gazette of the Republic of Viet-Nam), the representatives were still not well informed concerning the work of the commissions to which they did not belong. Another representative proposed that 20 per cent of the salaries of the representatives be set aside as a contribution to the security budget; another criticized certain expenditures for official entertainment. There was even an extremist proposal that the National Assembly be dissolved during the period of emergency because of the law of delegation of powers; this proposal was countered with a reminder of the constitutional provisions regarding democratic principles and the republican form of government.

With regard to the various agencies attached to the Presidency, one representative asked why certain irregularities existed in the treatment of expenditures for emergency aid (to flood victims, etc.); another proposed that the Assembly increase the personnel of the Inspectorate-General of Administrative and Financial Services rather than criticize the department later because of administrative difficulties. Elements for a civil service policy were submitted, along with an appeal for the application of decisions made previously with an eye to controlling the personal wealth of the civil servants.

A cut was made by the Finance Commission in the proposed appropriations for the Department of the Interior (for police and penal services); the Commission of the Interior proposed the concentration of efforts to strengthen rural administration, but indorsed the demand for reduction of appropriations; a lengthy discussion (42 pages in *Noi-San Quoc-Hoi*) ensued, with severe criticism and some constructive proposals concerning the functioning of this department.

In the course of the discussion concerning appropriations for the Department of National Economy there occurred personal attacks against certain individuals, criticism of illegal procedures, interference of a personal nature, proposals concerning government enterprises, and requests for a detailed explanation of the policy of price stabilization. A slight cut was made by the Finance Commission in appropriations proposed for the Department of Finance, the Department of Civic Action, the Department of Foreign Affairs, and the Department of Rural Development; a more substantial cut was made in appropriations for the Department of Public Works.[46]

A careful examination of the work accomplished by the National Assembly seems to indicate that its operations were analogous to those of the legislative assemblies of industrialized countries. Some officials reacted subjectively to adverse criticism of the National Assembly made by foreign experts, without realizing that the same experts make the same criticism of similar institutions in their own countries, and that even the Congress of the United States can still be reproached by people of good faith with being "inefficient, unrepresentative and irresponsible." [47]

To the credit of the National Assembly, certain interesting measures concerning budgetary procedure should be indicated. In the course of the discussion of the 1962 budget, several representatives observed that the obliging of a committee chairman who is himself a representative to answer remarks made by other representatives is irrational; this observation gave rise to an amendment to the Constitution permitting a secretary of state to appear in person before the National Assembly in order to answer written questions put by the representatives (new Article 47, sanctioned by the amendment of July 8, 1962). Similarly, during the discussion of policy following the general report of the proposed budget, repeated appeals were made to the chief executive to heed recommendations made by the National Assembly for the initiation of reforms in policy or in procedure necessary for the effective operation of the administrative machinery. The National Assembly also discussed in detail the five-year plan of economic and social development for 1962–1966, which had already been the subject of lengthy discussion in the Economic Council and of a study by a special committee of the Assembly. This is an indication of the representatives' awareness of the close relationship between planning and budgeting.[48]

However, it must be recognized that the discussions in the National Assembly do not have the divergence of opinion that would have been introduced by a loyal opposition. Similarly, although there were appropriations cuts, they were made solely in a spirit of economy: there is no evidence of policy cuts or token cuts.[49] On the other hand, personal considerations have motivated criticism of policy in the poor performance of certain services, but this has not given rise to the practices known as "pork-barrel politics" and "logrolling," which bury the representatives of some legislative assemblies under a pile of detail, where they are in danger of losing sight of the general policy to be expressed in the budget.[50] These remarks apply only to the technical aspects of the budgetary procedure instituted by the National Assembly, and do not detract from the real value of the work of that body in the formation of a financial policy. At any rate, the acquired experience will not be lost.

GENERAL BUDGETARY PRINCIPLES

The greatest criticism made by experts of early republican budgetary practices in Viet-Nam is that they led to the establishment of a budget the details of which could be discussed, but not the programs indicated nor the policies.[51]

The principles that govern the preparation of the budget date from the colonial period, although transformations in the economic structure have brought important modifications and, at the same time, new techniques have been imported. These changes have affected the classic value of the old principles.[52]

The Old Budgetary Principles Modified by New Conditions. The first of these old principles is *budgetary unity*, which requires that all estimates of receipts and expenditures be included in a single document, so that the budgetary authority can weigh its decisions regarding each item of the proposed budget as a function of the total.

The existence of the autonomous budgets of certain agencies mentioned in Chapter 3 constitutes a first obstacle to this principle. In 1962, the total of the appropriations for autonomous budgets was only VN $1,222 million out of a total budget estimate of VN $26,254 million; a close examination of the reasons that motivated the granting of budgetary autonomy to these agencies shows that several autonomous budgets can now be reintegrated into the national budget without any disadvantage.[53]

The fact that certain expenditures financed by American aid are given only in a lump sum constitutes a second obstacle to budgetary unity. In 1962, the expenditures for social and economic development to be financed by American aid amounted to VN $1,400 million out of the total budget estimates of VN $26,254 million.[54]

In 1962, under the pressure of circumstances, the National Assembly was obliged to accept the division of the former comprehensive national budget into three distinct budgets: [55]

Budget of Revenues and Civil Expenditures	VN $12,995 million
Special Budget for Security	12,105 million
Special Budget for Economic Development	1,200 million

The National Assembly voted on the Budget of Revenues and Civil Expenditures and on the Special Budget for Economic Development, but the Special Budget for Security and the Budget of Government Enterprises and Programs Sponsored by American Aid were completely outside its jurisdiction.[56] The Revolutionary Government has maintained the division of the national budget into three distinct budgets, and has not made any changes regarding the autonomous budgets.

The second principle, a corollary of the first, is the *universality of the budget;* this requires that all proposed expenditures and all proposed revenues be introduced into the budget, without any prior cancelling out of receipts or expenditures. This principle intends to make the budget show the real revenues and expenditures, and not merely the difference given by subtracting from total revenues the expenditures incurred in collecting them, or, contrarily, the difference between certain expenditures and the revenues which the service concerned may occasionally collect as a result.

However, the cost of subsidizing autonomous budgets and provincial budgets already constitutes a deviation from this principle, since the national budget shows only the amount by which these expenditures exceed revenues from these budgets.

Since 1962, the insertion in the national budget of a fixed amount to be appropriated for the Special Budget for Security makes another substantial exception to this principle, since this figure does not constitute the total of military expenditures—indeed, this total appears nowhere in the budget—but only the difference between this total and the amount received from foreign aid.

One consequence of budgetary universality is that revenues cannot be allocated for a specific use; i.e., all revenues of the state must fall into a common fund (the treasury), from which they are withdrawn to finance all authorized expenditures. In other words, as a matter of principle, no tax money should be earmarked for financing specific activities. The major deviations from this principle are American aid, and resources reserved for autonomous agencies. These deviations seem to be justified either for political reasons or for purely practical ones, as has already been pointed out several times. This seems to confirm partly the predictions of the sala model theory that, in a society in transition, the administrative units secure for themselves a maximum of engrossed revenues, i.e., revenues earmarked or assigned for designated programs and corners (i.e., monopolistic arrangements whereby bureaucratic groups obtain an income from the sale of goods and services).[57]

The third principle is *budgetary annuality,* which means that each year the government must present to the legislative assembly for approval a proposed budget for the following year. This principle, which was formulated in order to permit the representatives of the people to control closely the financial operations of the chief executive, was imported by the French authorities in order to control the various officials working in the colonies. Since it was a common practice to prepare the budget annually, Article 60 of the Constitution of 1956 contains an implicit recognition of the principle of budgetary annuality.

In practice, however, certain appropriations allocated on the budget for one year have been carried over to the following year.[58] These carry-overs are even fairly common, with regard to programs financed by foreign aid. Similar cases have even been approved by legislative action, such as Law No. 14/62 of July 6, 1962, concerning the budget for economic development.

As a result of the traditional suspicion on the part of the representatives of the people with respect to the government, whose powers must be limited, the fourth principle imported by the French is that of *nontransferability of appropriations,* by virtue of which administrative authorities can spend only the amounts specifically appropriated in the annual budget, and can spend them only for the purposes indicated in each appropriation. In practice, the budget is presented in the final form of a law accompanied by a Table A showing the approved revenues, divided into a number of titles (*muc*), each containing several chapters (*chuong*), and a Table B showing the appropriations for expenditures divided into titles, chapters, sections, and paragraphs. Each chapter constitutes an appropriation unit, to which is applied the principle of nontransferability of appropriations.

The fact that since 1961 budgetary laws have always included clauses authorizing the chief executive to transfer appropriations from one chapter of the budget to another shows how little importance is attached to this theoretical principle. It should also be recalled that the president had special powers regarding the budget if the National Assembly did not approve it before a given deadline, or in case of national emergency (see Chapter 3). An examination of the stipulations of the budget reveals the impressive amounts appropriated in certain chapters; this gives the administrative authority great latitude of action, e.g., Title IX, Chapter 04 of the 1962 Budget, allocating VN $592,991,000 for the national police. This sum can be compared, for example, with VN $2,432,000 allocated for the Supreme Court of Appeals by Title VII, Chapter 04 of the same budget.[59] The relatively large amounts of certain appropriations in the budget, together with the authority to transfer funds from one chapter to another, recall the procedure known as prebendary budgeting, inasmuch as this is in reality the establishment of formally rational procedures for determining expense priorities, but with a flexible distribution of funds by executive authorities in accordance with personal and political considerations.[60]

New Techniques that Alter Old Traditions. The major classic budgetary principles have thus lost part of their importance. On the other hand, in reply to criticism concerning the excessive importance attached to accounting and the insufficient attention paid to the idea of programing, new principles have been adopted regarding the presentation of the budget.[61]

The present budgetary classification depends on four criteria: administrative structure, administrative function, the object of government expenditures, and the economic character of government expenditures. This classification was adopted at the suggestion of American experts, and also as the result of several ECAFE (Economic Commission for Asia and the Far East) seminars held in Bangkok, regarding budgetary classification.[62] Thus, since 1958, the national budget of Viet-Nam has been presented in the form of a set of appropriations for each department and for each directorate (classification according to administrative organization, such as appropriations for the Police Directorate, those for the Public Health Directorate, etc.). For each administrative unit, appropriations are made for specific objectives (classified according to the object of expenditures, e.g., appropriations for personnel, for matériel or equipment, etc.). The various tables group expenditures by functions (classified according to administrative function, e.g., appropriations for public security, for general administration, for economic development, for social development, etc.), and also according to the economic character (operational expenses and capital outlays).[63] An examination of the budget according to this classification by function and economic character will give a fairly precise idea of the government policy and of the contribution of the government in capital formation, particularly since a document explaining this policy always accompanies the budget.

In the national budget of Viet-Nam for the fiscal year 1958, another fundamental reform was announced: the adoption in the near future of the system of performance budgeting. This system was intended to put the accent clearly on programs, by the use of performance units and of cost accounting. These measures would have brought about a sweeping reform in accounting, not only with respect to the object of expenditures, but also with respect to the entire administrative organization. So far, however, it has been only tentatively applied to certain appropriations for the Department of Public Works, where breakdown into performance units is easier and cost accounting methods can be applied.[64]

Performance budgeting and the classification of expenditures according to their economic character mark the beginning of the integration of the annual financial budget of the state into the plan for economic development for the whole country, which is broader, in the sense that the plan includes all economic activities, even private enterprise, and longer, in the sense that the plan provides for a period of time longer than that of the budget (e.g., the five-year plan for the years 1962–1966). Financial experts in the Directorate-General of Budget and Foreign Aid calculate projections of budgetary expenditures far into the future. In the discussions of the budget in the National Assembly, mention has been made of the five-year plan, although no official document has yet established precise mathematical relationships between the budget and the provisions of the five-year plan.[65]

Set in the more general context of the national economy, the traditional principle of balancing the budget has also lost some of its value as an inalterable dogma. Until the fiscal year 1961, the presidential budget was always presented to the National Assembly in a balanced form. Thus, the proposed budget for 1961 set down both revenues and expenditures in the amount of VN $14,985,-000,000.[66] Since 1962, a deficit has been recognized,[67] as shown in the following table (all figures are in millions of piasters):

Year	Total Estimated Expenditures	Total Estimated Revenues	Deficit
1962	26,254	22,066	4,188
1963	27,000	22,500	4,500
1964	28,500	19,000	9,500

The reporter-general of the budget pointed out the urgent and exceptional financial measures to be taken by the president and expressed the hope that these measures would not bring about confusion in the economic life of the country.[68]

The traditional principles regarding the budget have been modified little by little under the pressure of political and economic circumstance and in the light of recommendations made by experts. New principles have also been introduced to cope with the need for modern budgeting. In general, the evolution of financial administration has been very rapid, in spite of several minor obstacles stemming from the old-school training of certain administrators responsible for the various budgetary operations. A careful examination of the execution of the budget, involving a greater number of civil servants at all levels, will show to what extent tradition still holds sway over this part of the financial administration.

The Execution of the Budget

In the execution of the budget, it is customary to make a distinction between the operations involving revenues and those involving expenditures, but there is also the dominant principle of separation of *ordonnateurs* and *comptables* that governs these two types of operations, and which has been the subject of heated criticism.

THE SEPARATION OF ORDONNATEURS AND COMPTABLES

Although certain principles of accounting existed in the old Vietnamese system of financial administration, the modern accounting system dates for the most part only from the period of French colonization.

The period of French colonial conquest during the French Second Empire was also a period of expansion in the colony of the French accounting system, which stems from distrust of administrators and from the necessity of setting up a system of automatic controls to prevent administrators from committing excesses, either intentionally or through ignorance, and from misappropriating funds from the public treasury. This suspicion gave rise to the principle of separating the *ordonnateurs* from the *comptables,* which was made into law in France by the Decree of May 31, 1862, and in the colonies by the Decree of December 30, 1912.[69] According to this principle, the administrator alone has the authority to pledge expenditures, and to order payment for services rendered to the state; in the performance of this function the administrator is called an *ordonnateur*. On the other hand, the administrator is not authorized to handle public money; the actual payment for operations executed on the orders of the administrator is performed by a separate officer in the administration who is called a *comptable*. In accordance with the principle of separation of *ordonnateur* and *comptable,* the latter has a certain power of control over the operations of the administrator, since he will make payments only after he has made certain that the operations are in accordance with the laws and regulations. Thus, the French legislator intended to oblige the administrators to conform strictly to the appropriations for which very precise provisions had been made, e.g., after lengthy discussion in the Chamber of Deputies and in the Senate, or, in the case of the colonial budgets, after the authorization of consultative assemblies and ratification by the higher administrative authority. This principle of separation of *ordonnateurs* and *comptables* has been retained by the Vietnamese Government.[70]

In order to be completely effective, the same principle governs the revenue operations: since the civil servant responsible for the treasury is not under the authority of the administrator, he should be empowered to perform himself the operations of receiving monies into the treasury. Indeed, if the revenues of the treasury fall directly into the hands of the administrator, he might fail to deposit them in the treasury, and might be tempted to spend them in a manner not in accordance with financial regulations.

The Responsibility of the Comptable. This principle is very ingenious, but the making sure that the *comptable* verifies carefully the operations of the administrators and looks out faithfully for the interests of the treasury, which are the interests of the state, is another problem. The Vietnamese financial system, following French tradition, specifies the *comptable's* responsibility, which falls into three categories: (1) disciplinary responsibility to his administrative superior, (2) penal responsibility for any fradulent use of public funds, and (3) civil responsibility for any unjustified authorization for payment out of public funds or any failure to collect monies due the treasury.[71]

The disciplinary responsibility resembles that of all civil servants; since the cases of failure in the performance of duty, disobedience, or negligence could be numerous where the manipulation of money is involved, the *comptable* must be much more circumspect than other civil servants in order to avoid disciplinary action.

Neither is penal responsibility essentially different from that indicated for any civil servant: if a *comptable* commits crimes or misdemeanors punishable by law (misappropriation of public funds, illegal collection of taxes, etc.), he will be prosecuted in the courts and assigned the punishment provided in the penal code (fine, imprisonment, etc.). The only difference is that the law provides for a series of crimes and misdemeanors concerning embezzlement, which thus involve *comptables* specifically.

Civil responsibility is a rather novel institution devised by the French. It presupposes that a civil servant entrusted with the handling of public monies must be extremely careful in the physical handling of all funds due the treasury and in making sure that all expenditures are made in accordance with the laws and regulations. In case of failure to administer the public funds properly, he is held accountable for any loss to the treasury. For instance, if he neglects to perform the operation of collecting any monies due, the law requires him to reimburse the treasury by the amount of these monies. As concerns disbursements, the *comptable* does not make the decision to proceed with an expenditure: for example, military expenditures are decided by some general, and expenditures for social action are decided by the director of social action, but if these disbursements are not executed in accordance with the law, it is the *comptable* who must repay to the treasury the amount of the illegal expenditure. This principle seems a priori to be unjust to the *comptable,* since he is made responsible for an act which is not imputable to him. But the law requires that he verify the regularity of the form of the disbursement before paying out of the treasury the funds to settle these expenditures: if he has not verified the file for these expenditures and has allowed payment for irregular expenditures, he is responsible. It is precisely because of this civil responsibility of the *comptable* that he may refuse to make payment for an irregular operation without being subject to disciplinary action by the administrator, since the one who is obliged to pay out of his own pocket is not the administrator who makes the decision, but the *comptable* who pays without making an objection.

The Organization of Financial Services. This principle of separating administrators from *comptables* is the foundation of the practical rules of organization of the financial services.

The functions of the treasury, which is responsible for the handling of public funds, cannot be subjected to the control of several different authorities. Consequently, it is entirely operated by the Ministry of Finance and organized according to a strict hierarchy. The relationships between the superior *comptable* and the assistants are often similar to those in civil law between the mandator and the mandatary. Thus, at the head of the treasury is the director-general, assisted by three managing directors. In the provinces, the chiefs of the provincial treasury services perform the double function of treasury correspondents (for the revenues and penditures from the national budget) and of provincial treasurers (for revenues and expenditures from the provincial budget).

All revenues are supposed to be collected by the treasury. While assessments and determination of the amounts of the taxes are made by the tax service, the collection of taxes is made by the treasury. In practice, however, it is difficult for the treasury agents to perform all the physical operations of tax collection. For example, for the indirect taxes, the tax must be collected as soon as it has been assessed and the amount due determined; the civil servant responsible for tax assessment must be able to make the collection at once, at the risk of losing the opportunity. The rule of separating the *ordonnateurs* (in this case the agents of the tax assessment service) from the *comptables* is evaded by appointing these agents "intermediate treasury agents." In reality, this measure constitutes a deviation from the principle of separation of *ordonnateurs* and *comptables.*

With regard to expenditures, since, in order to function, all government services must perform operations which incur public expenditures (payment of the salaries of the personnel, payment for equipment and public works, etc.), it would be impossible to group in one ministry all agencies which spend public funds. Consequently, all agency chiefs are designated certifying agents for expenditures, but a limited number of high-ranking officials may authorize payment (as *ordonnateurs*). Payment out of government funds is performed only by agents of the treasury, the same agents who receive money, since they are the only agents authorized to handle public funds. As in the matter of receiving monies, in reality the agents of the treasury alone would not be able to pay all expenditures, particularly as concerns paying at regular intervals the salaries of all government workers, or paying small amounts for minor expenditures. For this reason, a system involving a working capital, or petty cash fund, and pay officers was devised. These pay officers are in reality subordinates of the administrators, but are authorized to handle public funds, under strictly limited conditions.

On the other hand, in view of the fact that so many agencies are authorized to contract for goods and services at government expense, it is necessary to maintain a certain conformity in the procedure for paying out government funds. In order to correct irregularities before they reach the *comptable*, and thus to reduce to some extent his work and his responsibility, the task of seeing that this conformity is observed is assigned to a specialized agency of the Directorate-General of Budget and Foreign Aid, which is called the Directorate of Obligated Expenditures.

The preceding remarks concerning the organization of services participating in financial administration will become clearer in the light of details concerning the procedure for paying out funds and for receiving them. Only details which contribute to an understanding of problems of financial administration will be given, however.[72]

AN EXAMPLE OF THE DISBURSEMENT PROCEDURE:
A PUBLIC WORKS CONTRACT

It is customary in Viet-Nam to divide the disbursement procedure into five phases: the allotment of funds, the obligation or pledging of expenditure, the liquidation or certifying the amount of the expenditure, the authorization of payment, and the actual payment. In order to relate administrative operations to budgetary disbursements, it is important to allot the annual appropriation according to periods of time. In the course of the obligation of expenditures, for example, the administrator decides what work is to be done, and signs a contract with a contractor for the execution of the work. The liquidation of the expenditure consists of calculating precisely and according to law the amount due the contractor for the work in question. The authorization of the expenditure consists of issuing the order to pay the contractor the amount established as his due. The payment is the material operation of remitting the money to the contractor.[73]

Since 1958, the allotment system has been established on a

quarterly basis; i.e., annual appropriations for current expenditures are usually divided into four parts, each part corresponding to a given three-month period. New expenditures, however, such as those incurred in the recruiting of new personnel or by new public works, must be proposed specially, in order to be added to the regular allotment for the proper quarter. This division of the appropriation into quarters is a relatively simple operation, the only difficulty being in communication, since the proposal for special allotments must reach the Directorate-General of Budget and Foreign Aid in due time. The allotments are normally provided by chapters of the budget.

Expenditure really begins with the obligation of funds, for which a series of preparatory operations are necessary, all of which have financial implications, but are quite technical. With regard to a public works project, these operations would be, for example, finding a site for the project, studying the site from both a physical and a legal point of view, setting down general instructions regarding the work to be done, outlining the different phases of the work, calculating the requirements of the project precisely with regard to material, labor, and so forth.[74] The first act in the obligation of expenditures consists of making the decision to have the job done. This decision often takes the form of the approval by a qualified administrator of the technical file containing the results of the study. Before giving his approval, the administrator must make sure that sufficient funds are provided by the budget for this year and for this type of project. The budget does not contain precise details on the exact amounts to be used for given projects, the exact nature of the projects, or place where the project will be completed. Consequently, in this preparatory phase, which is called the budgetary imputation, the administrator actually exercises discretionary power; appropriations made on the basis of a given kind of operation can be used for any specific operation of that kind, and it is up to the administrator to choose the most urgent one. It may be that the operation finally chosen is of greater magnitude than the one originally intended, and that it is necessary to use other funds appropriated in the same chapter of the budget, or funds provided for unforeseen expenses in a special chapter. To this extent, the administrator has the power to use funds for purposes he considers important within the framework prescribed by the budget.

The decisive phase of the obligation of expenditures is in choosing the contractor. Regulations provide that this choice must be made according to a public call for bids, and that the contract must be let to the lowest bidder. At this point, there may be instances of duplex bookkeeping or discriminatory practices which favor a preferred contractor. It has been said that the existence of such practices in a society in transition is due to the fact that the mechanism of prices is not automatic, because of the limitations of the market in an underdeveloped country.[75] At any rate, it is apparently easy for administrators with dishonest intentions to conform to the various prescribed formalities of letting bids and to take many precautions not to be caught; consequently, control on paper, by whatever authority it may be exercised, is partly illusory if it is not accompanied by an on-the-spot inspection. This certainly constitutes evidence of the schism between the legalistic tendency of financial procedure and the particularistic tendency still to be found in the contractors, who fail to distinguish between the state with whom they are making a contract and the administrator with whom they are actually bargaining, as merchant with client.

After the contractor has been chosen, i.e., after the awarding of the contract has been properly approved, the actual work begins, under the supervision of technical civil servants. The principle is that the expenditures incurred by this work cannot be certified, i.e., the exact amount cannot be determined, until the job is completed. The acceptance of the completed work is also a rather important feature: How well and when was the work finished? Theoretically, the job must be completed in accordance with the provisions of the specifications set down before the bids were accepted. However, in spite of the many norms prescribed, a margin always remains with respect to the quality of the materials or the finishing off of the work. Similarly, provisions are made in the specifications for delays in finishing the work, but there is always a certain margin for setting the exact date for the formal acceptance of the completed project, i.e., when the project can be considered as really finished.[76] It is for this acceptance of the work done that the contractor must meet personally with the engineers responsible for supervising the work, who can decide to make partial acceptance of the work which will serve as a basis for making a partial payment to the contractor, or who can recommend deductions from the amount to be paid for the inevitable small imperfections in the performance of the work. At this point, there is a strong temptation to explain the phenomenon by the particularistic spirit of civil servants of countries in transition, who have to judge works according to the official norms, but who also make allowances for friendships or other relationships they may have with the contractor. One author has suggested that "the heavier the weight of bureaucratic power and the greater the range of price indeterminacy, the easier it is to conceal the practice on the part of the purchasing officer to take a kickback from the salesman." [77] It is rather suprising, however, to observe the same phenomena in industrialized countries, in which case the advocate of the theory of transitional society attempts to explain it as a remnant of transitional spirit.[78] At any rate, it still seems easy to observe the various formalities in the operation of certifying expenditures: setting up a file of documents in due form, listing the expenditures in the register, placing the stamp of approval, obligating expenditures, etc. For this reason, constant effort is being made to reduce to a minimum the time necessary for the certification of expenditures.[79]

The phase of certification of a given expenditure involves the agency which supervises the public works project. Once the rights of a creditor of the state have been established by this agency, the order must be issued to pay him. The phase of authorization of expenditures is quite distinct from the certification phase. For purposes of verification and of centralization, the authorization is the prerogative of the secretary of state, who is delegated by the chief executive to be *ordonnateur* of the budget of his department, and who can himself delegate a part of his power to the *ordonnateur secondaire,* i.e., a subordinate official whose post is in the field. The decision to pay may be delayed by the insufficiency of funds in the treasury, which is highly unlikely, as will be seen. It might also be delayed by the fact that certain formalities have not been observed. Since the creditor of the state must not suffer on this account, this phase of the disbursement procedure has been severely criticized, as has the payment phase, a discussion of which follows. As a matter of fact, the authorization of payment is almost automatic since the expenditures have been authorized, the work has been performed, and the state must acquit its obligations toward the contractor. This has been demonstrated by the fact that the Directorate-General of Budget and Foreign Aid has been assigned the function of certification of all expenditures for personnel for the entire government service, which would be impossible without the use of mechanical bookkeeping procedures.[80]

The last phase of the procedure of expenditure is the actual payment, i.e., the drawing of funds from the treasury to be remitted to the creditor of the state. At first glance, this role of banker might appear quite simple; the treasury pays upon receipt of the pay order from the *ordonnateur.* However, to establish a thorough check, the financial regulations require that the treasury, here considered the *comptable,* verify the entire file of the expenditure to be paid, in order to make sure that all formalities, from the obligation to the certification, have been observed. The least irregularity in the documents on file might cause the treasury to refuse to pay, which means new delays in settling the account. The treasury must also ascertain that the payment has not been legally attached by creditors of the creditor of the state, and finally must verify the identity of the creditor, before making payment. The responsibility of the *comptable* is really quite heavy, all the more so since the law stipulates that it is a civil responsibility. Because of the large amounts involved in public expenditures, this responsibility is sometimes out of all proportion to the personal fortune of a single individual. On the other hand, these additional checks might oblige the contractor frequently doing business with the state to develop personal relationships in order to expedite payment of his accounts.

Naturally, this complicated procedure is often the subject of criticism, both by the government services themselves and by the contractors doing business with the government, as well as by experts in the study of treasury operations.[81]

Generalizations Concerning the Disbursement Procedure. Expenditures for public works actually constitute only a small percentage of the total of public expenditures, for the good reason that at the present time the government must finance more urgent operations of public security and social development. The classification by functions of expenditures proposed in the budget for the fiscal years 1962, 1963, and 1964 will give an idea of the activities financed by the budget. All figures are given in millions of piasters.[82]

	1962	*1963*	*1964*
Administration	1,296.1	1,750.5	1,832.5
Foreign Affairs	135.7	164.3	220.0
Judiciary and Police Services	1,000.1	1,321.6	1,660.0
Social Services (health, education etc.)	2,471.8	2,208.9	2,501.0
Economic Services (including public works)	5,108.7	6,798.7	5,687.5
Service of Public Debt	90.2	109.0	96.0
Subsidies to other budgets	1,431.0	1,280.0	1,358.0
National Defense and Security	12,105.0	13,000.0	14,820.0
Miscellaneous	2,609.4	417.0	325.0
Total	26,248.0	27,050.0	28,500.0

While this table shows the administrative functions financed by the budget, it does not permit any generalization on the process of disbursement. For this purpose, another type of classification would be more suggestive. Public works fall under the general category of goods and services furnished to the state by private individuals, for which compensation must be made by the state. These goods and services constitute one object of public expenditures. Most of the goods and services furnished are certified for payment according to approximately the same procedure as public works. Another category of objects of expenditures is that which includes the services of civil servants, for example. Out of the total 1962 budget estimates of VN $26,248 million, personnel expenditures amounted to:

Civil budget	VN $ 3,733.7 million
Military budget	9,406 million
Total	VN $13,139.7 million, or one half of the total budget.

Personnel expenditures are made according to a procedure different from that used for expenditures for public works and equipment, although it can also be broken down into five phases: allotment of funds, obligation of expenditures, certification of expenditures, authorization of payment, and payment.

The allotment of funds is almost automatic, since the number of workers is known from the beginning of the year. It will vary from quarter to quarter only in the event that large numbers of workers are recruited or dismissed. As a result, the obligation of expenditures is also made at the beginning of each year, on the basis of the number of workers employed on January 1; if new workers are recruited, then new obligation must be undertaken. The liquidation of expenditures is also almost automatic; at the end of each month, each government worker receives his salary in an amount set at the time of his employment or of his most recent promotion; the family allowances are increased or reduced whenever there is a change in the composition of the family (birth, marriage, majority, or death). The same is true of the authorization of payment and of the payment itself.[83] Since this entire procedure is so nearly automatic, an important reform was introduced in 1960: all bookkeeping operations concerning the payment of salaries of civil servants were performed by business machines. The number of government workers paid by machine rose from 18,000 in 1960 to more than 30,000 in 1962, including all workers assigned to the ministries, prefectural services in Saigon, and provincial services of the departments.

It is interesting to note that this experiment in paying salaries by business machines was so successful that the government has decided to extend the use of business machines to all other expenditures (Decree of September 5, 1961), so as to reduce delays in the payment of obligations. (See Charts VIII and IX, pages 232–233.)[84]

Another innovation introduced by the Revolutionary Government will bring about even more radical changes in the disbursement procedure. According to Decree No. 203/TC, dated May 30, 1964, the ministers, as deputy *ordonnateurs*, will henceforth have the power of decision regarding all expenditures as well as all revenues. The control of obligated expenditures will still subsist, but an agent of the Obligated Expenditures Service will be assigned to each ministry, in order to eliminate certain physical movements. Expenses for pacification may be paid by a check drawn on a special fund made available to each ministry and to certain directorates, provided that the required steps of the normal disbursement procedure be subsequently performed before the fifth day of the following month. The dossier of a given expenditure will no longer have to be sent to the Obligated Expenditures Service for verification of the certification, but intermittent post-audit checks will be performed at each ministry. The Directorate-General of Budget and Foreign Aid will make only a final post-audit check of the dossiers to see that everything is in order.[85]

CHART VIII   DIAGRAM SHOWING FORMER EXPENDITURE PROCEDURE

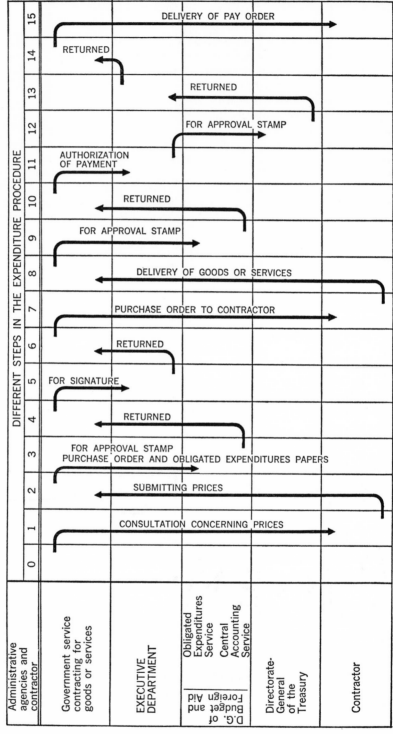

DIFFERENT STEPS IN THE EXPENDITURE PROCEDURE

| | 0 | 1 | 2 | 3 | 4 | 5 | 6 | 7 | 8 | 9 | 10 | 11 | 12 | 13 | 14 | 15 |

Administrative agencies and contractor

Government service contracting for goods or services

EXECUTIVE DEPARTMENT

D.G. of Budget and Foreign Aid — Obligated Expenditures Service — Central Accounting Service

Directorate-General of the Treasury

Contractor

1 — CONSULTATION CONCERNING PRICES
2 — SUBMITTING PRICES
3 — FOR APPROVAL STAMP / PURCHASE ORDER AND OBLIGATED EXPENDITURES PAPERS
4 — RETURNED
5 — FOR SIGNATURE
6 — RETURNED
7 — PURCHASE ORDER TO CONTRACTOR
8 — DELIVERY OF GOODS OR SERVICES
9 — FOR APPROVAL STAMP
10 — RETURNED
11 — AUTHORIZATION OF PAYMENT
12 — FOR APPROVAL STAMP
13 — RETURNED
14 — RETURNED
15 — DELIVERY OF PAY ORDER

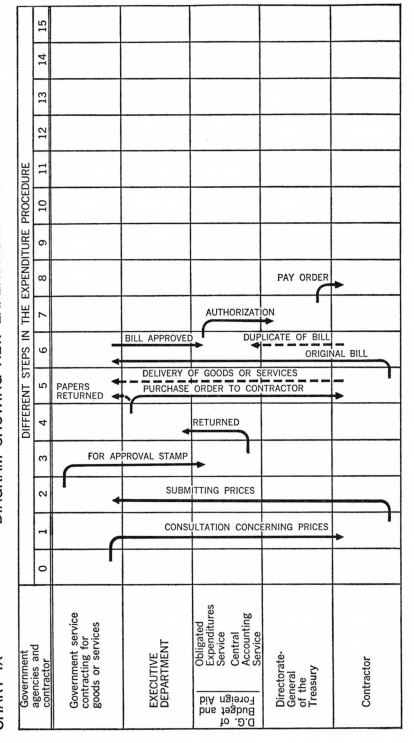

CHART IX

DIAGRAM SHOWING NEW EXPENDITURE PROCEDURE

DIFFERENT STEPS IN THE EXPENDITURE PROCEDURE

	0	1	2	3	4	5	6	7	8	9	10	11	12	13	14	15

Government agencies and contractor

Government service contracting for goods or services

EXECUTIVE DEPARTMENT

Obligated Expenditures Service / Central Accounting Service — D.G. of Budget and Foreign Aid

Directorate-General of the Treasury

Contractor

CONSULTATION CONCERNING PRICES

SUBMITTING PRICES

FOR APPROVAL STAMP

RETURNED

PAPERS RETURNED

PURCHASE ORDER TO CONTRACTOR

DELIVERY OF GOODS OR SERVICES

ORIGINAL BILL

DUPLICATE OF BILL

BILL APPROVED

AUTHORIZATION

PAY ORDER

PROCEDURE FOR THE COLLECTION OF REVENUE:
DISTINCTION BETWEEN DIRECT AND
INDIRECT TAXES

If resistance to change can be explained by the persistence of tradition, it must be pointed out that tradition in the disbursement procedure is quite recent, since it dates only from the arrival of the French, while tradition in receiving monies is, in part at least, age-old. Although, contrary to the experience of industrialized countries, in which revolutions often arose from the desire of the people to establish a control over the power of levying taxes, Viet-Nam has never known a financial revolution; still it is true that the problem of raising funds for the government is a constant preoccupation on the part of many administrators.[86]

The principal concern rests in the matter of confidence. Since the revenue of the state is absolutely necessary for the financing of governmental activities, the collection of this revenue must be placed in trustworthy hands. In the time of the emperors, the treasury was entrusted to princesses of the blood and to high-ranking mandarins. It was natural to assign to these same persons the task of collecting money for the state, but in proportion as the monarchy increased in size, the confidence based on personal relationships became no longer sufficient. It was necessary to set up an entire organization for tax collection. The royal authorities used the village as the agent of collection: it was the responsibility of the village to collect the monies due the king, either taxes on rice fields exploited by the village (property tax) or payments made by the inhabitants of the village in lieu of *corvées* (head tax in kind). At the same time, the village could be required to collect certain taxes on the production of salt, cinnamon, birds' nests, and so forth. Only those taxes requiring more powerful means of collection were at this time entrusted to specialized mandarins. Thus, the collection of taxes on importing and exporting operations was the responsibility of mandarins called *thuong bac,* who had at their command a special fleet for the prevention of smuggling.[87]

In order to solve this question of confidence, the colonial authorities preferred to adopt the system used in France: the collection of taxes in the colonies was the responsibility of a corps of treasurers, who held the same authority as the treasurers in France, and were subject to the same obligations, particularly that of posting a bond, in money or other security, high enough to cover eventual loss through maladministration of public funds.[88] To set up a rational tax-collection system, the French introduced the idea of making a clear distinction between direct and indirect taxes. The former were assessed on the basis of stable factors, such as the number of *dinh,* or taxable adults, in the villages; the areas of the rice fields cultivated;

and commercial activities. These could be recorded ahead of time in the village annual tax register. Indirect taxes (e.g., sales tax, production tax, etc.) were levied on operations which did not follow a regular pattern and which therefore could not be set down in the tax register ahead of time. The French authorities were responsible for collecting the indirect taxes and remitting them to the treasury, according to regulations patterned after those used in France. On the other hand, the Vietnamese authorities took charge of collecting the direct taxes, according to traditional methods, except that they were required to turn them over at once to the French treasury. Thus, the official responsibility of the treasury for collecting taxes was a legal fiction; in point of fact, tax collection was left to the administrative services. The government of the Republic of Viet-Nam still maintains this artificial distinction between direct and indirect taxes in the organization of the tax collection service.[89]

The Administration of Indirect Taxes. Since the indirect taxes are levied on the taxable object or operation, not through the fact of its existence, but because it is put into economic circulation, it is easy to understand that they are particularly large in urban sectors where commercial and industrial operations are concentrated, and in the field of foreign relations with the import-export trade. The first commercial firms were set up with French capital, under French management. The Vietnamese followed timidly, seeking to model their operations on those of the French concerns.[90] The techniques used were therefore developed according to approximately the same standards as those of industrialized countries. The methods of tax collection were similarly influenced by these techniques, all the more so since the government, bound by customs agreements, trade treaties, or by treaties for military and economic aid, was itself obliged to adapt its methods of tax collection to the needs of the transactions. As might be expected, because of this modernization, taxes levied on these operations are considerable; for example, during the fiscal year 1962, the indirect taxes (including customs duties) made up 89.7 per cent of the total estimated tax receipts, and 33 per cent of the total estimated revenue of the government. The following table shows pertinent figures (in millions of piasters):[91]

Fiscal Year	Estimated internal revenue (civilian)	Actual internal revenue	Estimated revenue from all taxes	Actual revenue from all taxes	Estimated revenue from indirect taxes	Actual revenue from indirect taxes
1962	12,995.0	11,767.6	9,151.7	9,987.5	8,050.5	9,025.5
1963 (until December 31)	15,000.0	10,401.5	9,377.8	9,412.3	8,190.2	8,638.5

Similarly, profound changes in the structure of the fiscal system were brought about with little confusion and in an unusually short space of time—for example, the fiscal reforms dated December 29, 1961, which eliminated the production tax on imported goods (instituted in 1957) and replaced it with a luxury tax and a surtax on exchange.[92] Although there was a certain slowing down of transactions in the early months of the application of this law, and although a certain tendentious interpretation of the law brought on some fear that the measure actually constituted a devaluation of money, it is important to point out that the civil servants concerned adapted themselves rapidly to the new measures, which completely contradicted the procedural experience acquired previously.[93]

However, some transitional effects still remain in the administration of indirect taxes. Here, particularly, there exists a certain tendency—however sporadic—to earmark certain funds. The only notable example of this was the earmarking of taxes levied on the importation of certain goods for building up the equalization fund for imported and exported goods. This fund was originally set up to standardize the prices of various imported goods to conform with those of local goods to be exported. This rule, however, has not been strictly observed, and the fund has been used for several other purposes, particularly for the construction of *agrovilles*.[94] Although this tax was eliminated in 1961, it is certain that it can be identified with the engrossed revenues of the sala model.[95] Similarly, with respect to indirect taxes, there still remains an ancient tax which puts the taxpayers to a considerable amount of trouble: the registration on contracts, legal documents, etc. Not only are there no plans for eliminating this tax, since it is still a substantial source of revenue, but recently it has been thoroughly revised with respect to the transfer of ownership of houses constructed of certain light materials, and to excessive profits gained by means of inordinate rents.[96] The durability of this tax might be explained by the existence of a strongly anchored tradition, established since the arrival of the French.

The Administration of Direct Taxes. It seems to be a general rule that the older the tradition, the greater the resistance to change. A perfect illustration is the administration of direct taxes. In the current fiscal system, there remain three direct taxes, which in the order of their introduction are: the property tax, the business license tax, and the income tax.

The property tax was the major source of revenue of the imperial treasury. It has gradually lost some of its importance because of the growing diversification of the economy since the arrival of the French (commerce and industry), but still continues to provide a stable source of revenue both for the former local budgets and for the provincial and communal budgets. The ideal would have been to assess this tax on the market value of the property, as is the case with the property tax in the United States. But the French followed the custom of the emperors in dividing the rice paddies and fields into categories, and assigning to each category an arbitrary rate which was neither proportionate nor progressive with respect to either the market value of, or the income from, the property. Moreover, although from a theoretical point of view one might establish criteria for this distinction of categories, actually, the operations of surveying the land and of evaluating the harvests were difficult to perform. Since the villages could not undertake this work, they simply made a gross estimate of the area of the rice paddies and fields in each category, in order to present to the administrative authorities the proposal of a given sum representing the tax for the whole village. Once an agreement was reached on the amount, based entirely on approximations, the leader divided the tax among the property owners according to a system called *nhat tam quy nhi*, which amounted to equalizing the rates among all the villagers. This practice continues to be followed even at present, and gives a striking example of a precise tax rate and a specific manner of assessment provided by legislation (however unscientifically), and of a customary practice of distribution which is quite different; i.e., it presents an ideal type of overlapping, in which formally differentiated structures of a refracted type coexist with undifferentiated structures of a fused type.[97]

In the cities, on the other hand, where a proper survey was possible, the property tax was assessed for each property and for each landowner. As a result, it was possible to make an initial reform in the assessment of taxes: instead of referring only to certain exterior indications (the location of the property and apparent evidence of prosperity), the new legislation provides that tax assessment will follow the market value of the property itself.[98]

A similar development has taken place regarding the business license tax, which is a tax on professional, industrial, or commercial activities. These activities have been divided into categories; in each category there are a maximum and a minimum tax rate, between which the tax office can set the assessment. It can be seen that this system permits the civil servant in charge to assess the tax rather arbitrarily, and yet, because the small merchants keep no books whatsoever, it is difficult to assess the tax otherwise, particularly in the country.[99] On the other hand, in the cities, it appears that a more scientific formula for assessment can be applied: the amount of tax can, for example, be proportionate to the total production or to the total profits of the business. This matter was the subject of a reform brought about by a *Décret-loi* dated December 29, 1961, concerning certain activities for which a business license is required (production of beer, sugar, etc.). Although the advantages of this reform are obvious, it has not been possible to impose the new legislation in all sectors of the economy.[100]

The introduction of the third tax is also indicative of the reaction to change. Before World War II, the income tax was already known in Viet-Nam, but it was applied by the colonial authorities only to French and to certain other foreigners considered on an equal footing with the French. It was not until 1952 that the income tax was applied also to Vietnamese. The income tax has always been considered in industrialized countries as socially just because it is progressive, and it brings in a great deal of revenue, since the people who owe the largest amounts are those who are solvent. However, the application of this tax has been very gradual, and the number of persons who pay income tax is still very small compared to the number of persons earning taxable incomes. Several representatives in the National Assembly have presented eloquent details regarding income tax evasion.[101] One explanation of this phenomenon is that only persons accustomed to keeping accounts can correctly declare their incomes. These are, to begin with, industrial and commercial enterprises, particularly those which are incorporated; they are generally foreign businesses which have brought with them their own bookkeeping methods; certain Vietnamese companies also keep books, because they have relations with the foreign companies or with government services. Another group includes those who receive fairly high salaries: middle and high-ranking administrative officials, and managers of businesses. There are also professional workers (particularly in the professions of independent practice), although it is difficult to ascertain precisely the income of those in this last group. Farmers, who form the largest segment of the active population, are not subject to the income tax unless their incomes are higher than a certain amount; however, it is difficult to require them to declare their incomes for the simple reason that they do not keep any books. In general, most of the persons earning taxable incomes are not prepared for the idea that they must reveal to tax agents the secrets of their fortunes and their incomes. Certain of these would certainly prefer a fixed tax, which might even be higher than the progressive tax determined according to amount of income.

A serious problem, although not a financial matter, that still creates difficulty in collecting direct taxes is the insecurity caused in the rural regions by the Viet-Minh guerrillas. Many rice fields cannot be cultivated, and since it is impossible for the government to maintain adequate inspection in these regions, the collection of property taxes is extremely difficult, particularly since certain property owners declare that they have been forced to pay taxes to the Viet-Minh. In addition, those members of the rural population who have the means take refuge in the cities, where they are often hard to find for tax assessment. These difficulties are further aggravated by lack of qualified personnel for tax assessment and collection.

In spite of these shortcomings in the administration of direct taxes, serious efforts have been made to improve enforcement of the tax laws: the organization of provincial tax services, the appointment of former students of the National Institute of Administration to direct provincial services and even those of the central government, the increasing of inspection teams, the collection at the source of income taxes of military personnel and the proportionate business license tax of contractors who do business with the government, and the setting up of a system for paying all direct taxes in installments.[102] The most important reform was the setting up in 1959 of a National Registration System, using business machines, to collect at a central point all information concerning each taxpayer, for the purpose of detecting fraud and of assessing direct taxes.[103] However, the fiscal administration encounters some resistance to change on the part of the population, and it is easy to understand that, for the present, the government must continue to count on the system of indirect taxes to make up for this delinquency in the payment of income taxes.[104]

To sum up the study of tax administration, at present the collection of indirect taxes is still much easier than that of direct taxes. From a psychological point of view, the administration considers, rightly or wrongly, that in collecting indirect taxes, it avoids intruding upon the personal affairs of the taxpayers. From a technical point of view, indirect taxes are easier to collect, because of their nature (customs duty, production tax, etc.). The people are not yet accustomed to paying a large direct tax; the payment of indirect taxes is made almost imperceptible. The principle of the separation of *ordonnateurs* and *comptables* is also partly responsible for the insufficient collection of direct taxes: in dividing the responsibility between the assessment, which falls to the administrator (Directorate of Taxes), and the collecting, which falls to the *comptable* (Directorate of Treasury), it is hard to fix responsibility and easy to shift it.[105]

Conclusion

Although certain resistance to change can be noted in the process of evaluating and executing expenditures and receipts, the general impression received from a study of financial administration in Viet-Nam is that the evolution has been rapid: e.g., the adoption of a modern budgetary system, the use of business machines, fiscal reform, and so forth.

The factors which have contributed to this rapid evolution are both exogenous and endogenous. Among the exogenous factors can be cited the effects of imitation, in areas or activities in which contacts with foreigners are frequent, and the effects of social or economic domination exerted more or less voluntarily by industrialized countries that have sent technical and financial aid to Viet-Nam. Among the endogenous factors are the pressure of circumstances, the growing cost of military activities and the establishment of strategic hamlets, and also the emergence of certain personalities among the civil servants responsible for financial administration.

However, a transitional character still remains evident in the system of public finance.[106] In the first place, there still exists some penury, i.e., the inability of the country to raise its production levels at a rate equal to that of its development; thus, the proportion of national government revenue to the gross national product is 9 per cent for Viet-Nam, as compared with an average of 12.5 per cent for twelve countries of Southeast Asia, 25 per cent for France, 32 per cent for Great Britain, and 33 per cent for the United States.[107]

This penury is often explained in theory by tax avoidance, which means net positive transfers of the power elite which seeks to shift the burden of financing governmental activities onto other classes of the population. However, it must be pointed out that the legislators have made serious efforts in the last few years to combat this tendency, by placing heavier taxes on the higher incomes, by instituting a surtax on exchange, by organizing a registration system for gathering tax information, etc. Tax avoidance in Viet-Nam seems to be more a matter of fiscal administration than of fiscal policy. The question might also be raised whether recent measures encouraging foreign investments do not also constitute a measure of tax avoidance for the power elite.[108]

Another theoretic explanation of this penury is tax deviation, defined either as protection money paid to officials by contractors who wish to avoid some obligation or as baksheesh or money paid by an individual for the enjoyment of rights unlawfully denied him.[109] From the point of view of macro-economy, this part of the revenue might have been paid into the public treasury in the form of taxes, but, instead, went into the pockets of certain officials. This poses the general problem of corruption, which may be more acute in the financial administration than elsewhere. In this domain, the services of inspection and control have been greatly developed, severe punishments have been provided by law for cases of corruption, and the study movement has been established to raise the ethical level of civil servants.

All these administrative reforms will be examined in the more general context of the decision-making process (Part IV). At any rate, the rapid evolution of financial institutions is symptomatic of the will on the part of the government to put an end to any practices of prebendary budgeting and of preferential spending which may have existed in the early years of the Republic.

PART IV

THE DYNAMICS OF ADMINISTRATION: LEGALITY AND HUMANISM

THE MEASURES adopted concerning the organization of government services, personnel administration, and the management of public finance constitute a large part of public administration. However, these measures are not ends in themselves.

The administration is organized in such a way as to achieve certain objectives; the Ministry of Rural Affairs, for example, is intended to promote agricultural programs, such as the increasing of the amount of arable land, the improvement of drainage, the selection of seeds for planting, crop rotation, and the storing of agricultural products for eventual sale. In order to accomplish these objectives, the Ministry must be organized in directorates, services, and bureaus. The personnel of the Ministry is recruited, trained, compensated, and provided with various perquisites in order to execute properly the tasks of giving information on the afore-mentioned matters, making decisions, and putting these decisions into effect. The accounting system is intended to provide these workers with the financial means for performing their daily functions. These measures, which are called procedural administration, contain certain implications which affect the substance of the social life of the country. A given agency may be restricted to activities which only a power superior to the individual could undertake; the extensive projects of agricultural hydraulics, for example. Another agency might embrace certain activities which individuals could have undertaken themselves as co-workers of the administration, such as furnishing equipment and provisions for machine agriculture. The recruiting of a large number of government workers for agricultural extension might have an influence on the labor

241

market, on employment, on the education of children, or on retirement pay. Since financial resources for carrying out these activities constitute only a part of the income which the state withdraws from private use through taxation or government bonds, these monies might have been used in a completely different way if the taxpayers had been allowed to spend them themselves. In short, through the effect of an apparently vicious circle, means are transformed into ends, to the extent that the use of the means brings about repercussions on the social life of the community. To this extent, it is important that procedural administration be carefully studied before being used by the authorities responsible.

Procedural administration is so closely related to social life that it seems to be a major concern of the government in fused societies. In the old imperial administration, the principal administrative problem was the choice of mandarins; the entire administration, which was never precisely defined, depended on the mandarin, who governed by example and administered like the good father of a family. In other words, in order to study the administration, it would suffice to study the mandarinate.

As the administration gradually developed, however, countless administrative activities were introduced which led farther away from this paternal administration of public affairs. At this point, measures of procedural administration can be distinguished from measures of substantive administration, which constitute the very essence of administration: measures concerning agricultural development as mentioned above; measures regarding public security, such as the struggle against subversive activities and checking the movements of foreigners; and measures concerning public welfare, e.g., education, public health, operations of the economic infra-structure, foreign trade, etc. Decisions concerning these problems constitute policy formulation at the upper levels of government and policy implementation at the lower levels. Current philosophy demands that the administrator must also participate in policy formulation, since he is to make decisions on problems raised by the execution of the general policy or on those not specifically foreseen in that policy. However, if "administration" were taken in this broad sense, it would be necessary to embrace in this study every detail of the operation of all government services, whether diffuse, like public security, or well defined, like public works.

In any administrative activity, several operations occur

quite regularly. Some are purely technical by nature, and vary from one service to another, such as the duty of a worker in the antimalaria service to spray DDT powder into infested houses or that of a policeman to arrest lawbreakers. Other activities are common to all administrative services, such as the employment of qualified personnel or the providing of workers with the necessary technical equipment. A third type of operation is making decisions concerning either policy formulation or simply a measure of execution. The first of these categories might be called "technical operations"; the study of them falls into the field of technology. The second group concerns "procedural administration," and has been discussed in the preceding chapters. The last category concerns "substantive administration," and will be the subject of study in the following chapters.

Substantive administration concerns particularly the decisions made by the representatives of the administration.[1] In order to study substantive administration, it is necessary first to trace the decision-making process: Why does a given problem require a decision? What form does the problem take? What means can be used to gather all information on the problem? Upon what factors will the decision depend? Of course, since the decision will always affect the whole society, certain components of the society, or certain environments, it is important to know immediately whether there are limitations to the administrator's power of decision. In the first place, to what extent is the decision adequate? Does it suit the circumstances? To what extent can it be executed in practice? This brings up the problem of the effectiveness of two-way communication between the people and the administration, which concerns mechanical limitations to the power of the administration. There are also social limitations to this power, inasmuch as processes exist by which control is exercised over the administrator's decision. Who will exercise this control? How will it be exercised? What will be the possible sanctions if the decisions made are in accord or not in accord with the public interest? To what extent do the sanctions help correct the administrator's decision?

The study of the decision-making process, as well as that of the control over administrative decisions, will bring out the importance of the human factor in substantive administration. "Clearly the improvement in our education, and in the relating of our educational institution to the recruitment process (notably at the close of secondary, college, and graduate programs) is the most important contribution to effective control over public administration in the public interest." [2] *A final general problem will quite naturally arise: How should the study of public administration be organized so as to* (1) *throw light on the work of the administrator and* (2) *fit into the normal framework of administrative activity?*

In the following three chapters these problems will be studied as functions of the major idea that Vietnamese administration must be placed within the context of development—the decision-making process (Chapter 7), *communications and control* (Chapter 8), *and the study of public administration* (Chapter 9).

CHAPTER 7

THE DECISION-MAKING PROCESS

> Power tends to corrupt, and absolute
> power corrupts absolutely.
> —Lord Acton
>
> Hanh chi nhi bat tru yen
>   Tap hi nhi bat sat yen
> Chung than do chi nhi bat tri ky dao gia
>   Chung gia.[1]
> —Manh Tu (Vietnamese for Mencius)

THE PROCESS of making administrative decisions includes a series of successive phases: the appearance of circumstances leading to the necessity for making a decision, the reporting of these circumstances to the person or body authorized to make the decision, measures taken to assure the proper execution of the decision, and the acts which bring the decision to execution.

In each phase of the decision-making process, the question arises whether the persons who are promoting the decision are not obeying certain social norms, or, more precisely, whether they are acting in accordance with a series of imperative rules forming positive law or ethical rules forming moral law, or if they are subject to multiple contingencies of social life, being simply the product of their social environment, or at best the fruit of a pyschological work of man in society. For each of these problems, there is a particular corresponding manner of studying the administrative decision: the normative approach and the behavioral approach.

The Behavioral Approach

An administrative decision may be studied either as a function of external factors, or as a function of the personality of the particular administrator making the decision.

EXTERNAL FACTORS

Practically speaking, when a civil servant chooses a course of action, there are always several other possible courses of actions which he is thrusting aside, either deliberately or subconsciously.[2]

The Goals of the Administrative Decision. Of all the factors that contribute to the choice of a course of administrative action, the most important seems to be the ultimate goal of that action. For example, one goal might be stable finances for the state; in order to provide stable finances, it is necessary to adopt an effective and rapid accounting system; at the present time, an effective and rapid accounting system requires certain mechanization; mechanization implies the purchase of certain equipment and the training of qualified personnel; this training of personnel may encounter some opposition on the part of persons trained in older methods; and so on. At each stage of the process, the purpose becomes more restricted, but still fits within the framework of the more general goal; similarly, at each stage, a certain course of action may be foreseen.[3]

The goals of the administration can be defined as the broad guiding principles of modern Vietnamese administrative philosophy, which have been treated in Chapter 2: the struggle against communism, underdevelopment, and disunity, or the pursuit of the ideals of liberty and democracy, justice and happiness, and independence and unification. It seems necessary to recall these ideals, especially for a country still in transition, like Viet-Nam, since they provide the "mass of the people with a rallying point around which they can unite in order to grapple with the imposing obstacles standing in their path." [4] It should be noted that at progressively lower levels of the administrative hierarchy, the struggle against communism seems to prevail over the two others because of the insecurity created in the provinces by the action of Communist guerrillas.[5]

Second, there are laws and regulations which, as in industrialized countries, constitute the legal basis for administrative decisions. With regard to international treaties, attention must be called to the application of bilateral agreements of economic co-operation and technical aid, since each party engaged in writing up the aid program is subject to complex internal tensions and pressures in formulating its policies, regardless of the position of the other.[6]

Aside from these impersonal bases for making decisions, allowance must be made for the fact that in practice, an elite, using extraordinary powers of insight and dominance, determines the course to be followed at a given moment in the national life. Recent sociological studies justly underline the importance of the role of the leader in developing countries: "the charismatic leader who propounds this ideology becomes a source of revolutionary change and of stability at one and the same time," because very often it is he who represents this conjunction of the past and the present and the balancing off of the conflicting strains for change and for tradition, and because he is capable of "instilling new norms in the members of the labor force." [7]

In everyday administrative life, however, it is rather the administrator himself who is constantly making a careful evaluation of the organization's mission and anticipating changes in its social and economic environment. During the First Republic, this task of the administrator was made easier by the study movement (*phong trao hoc tap*) and by special seminars (*khoa huan luyen*). In the study movement, the administrators participated with their colleagues in discussions of official documents on general policy, such as the struggle against illiteracy, the defense of human rights, or agrarian reform. The special seminars concerned developments in government policy, such as the theory of personalism applied to the administration of Viet-Nam (*lop huan luyen nhan vi*), or the policy of strategic hamlets (*khoa huan luyen ap chien luoc*).[8] These procedures helped the administrators, not only to keep the objectives of their units within the framework of the general government policy, but also to keep their organizations abreast of changing community expectations to the extent that public opinion can be expressed through the press or by means of interest groups.[9] By the same procedures, as well as by other daily contacts, the government tried to convince all civil servants that the goals of the general policy were legitimate and rational, and to inspire them with a sense of identification with the entire government, in order to provide the ethical premises for individual decisions. The Revolutionary Government has issued instructions to continue the study sessions. In other words, by means of the study sessions the administrators examine thoroughly not only the manifest goals of the organization but also the latent functions which include the organization's drive for survival, for greater programs.[10]

The Influence of Political Parties as Policy Makers.   Conformity to the general policy of the government does not imply participation in political life, taken in the sense of the conquest of power by political parties.[11] In theory, the administrator cannot legally be the leader of a political party, or even a representative of the party; he cannot belong to an illegal party, although he may belong to a legally constituted political party, provided that he does not take advantage of his official position in the interests of his party or to the detriment of other parties.[12] The government of the First Republic relied on the NRM (National Revolutionary Movement), the party in power, to carry its message to every level of Vietnamese society. Consequently, the administrators maintained a close relationship with this party: they served directly as advisors to the party; at the district level, often a chief of the information service was even elected president of the local committee of the party.[13] From this it must be supposed that the NRM could influence the decisions of the administrator, particularly in view of the fact that the government regarded the members of the party as the staunchest supporters of the government, highly dedicated to its philosophy and purpose. It is also in the light of the influence of the NRM that the intervention of individual members of the National Assembly must be viewed. A certain number of the members returned to their respective provinces or districts between sessions of the Assembly, and worked in close contact with the population. Certain of these assumed the right to give instructions to local administrators; but most frequently these relationships were held to the limits of courtesy.[14] The administrators often showed themselves to be sensitive also to the criticism of members of the National Assembly, particularly in the course of the discussion of the budget, although the National Assembly did not employ the classic practice of using appropriation cuts by way of warning. It could be inferred from this fact that the influence of the representatives is exerted rather by persuasion or by party pressure if the representative concerned is sufficiently influential in the party leadership.[15] One author has pointed out that in developing countries a natural tendency exists to use opportunities for patronage appointments and graft through public contracts to favor relatives or friends of individual politicians rather than to reward those who work for a party as an organization.[16] This remark seems to apply to Viet-Nam, if we judge by the many assertions of the press after the fall of the Ngo Dinh Diem regime.

At any rate, the NRM certainly exerted an influence in the decision-making process. Consequently it is inexact to say that this was merely an instance of showcase parties. With the historical explanation that, except on the local level, democratic institutions have not been traditionally known in Viet-Nam, it can be admitted that since these institutions are an alien importation, they must adapt themselves to the special needs of the area in order to survive.[17]

Political parties whose programs were acceptable to the government, such as Phong Trao Cach Mang Quoc Gia, Can Lao Nhan Vi, and Dang Xa Hoi, were formed with the manifest encouragement of the administrative authorities, but since everyone did not enjoy this governmental favor, certain individuals were obliged to continue to act through secret societies.[18]

At the time of the elections, particularly the presidential election of April 9, 1961, the candidates could freely and openly criticize the government policy, and, in general, theoreticians of the government spoke officially of creating an opposition party; in reality no opposition party existed during the First Republic.[19] This lack of initiative on the part of opposition groups has historical and traditional precedents. During the colonial regime, it was of course not possible to organize opposition parties, except in the form of secret societies.[20] Consequently, the opposition could make itself heard only in a roundabout way, either through a sympathetic press or by using the influence of a French party which had the same ideology, or, more frequently, by the use of violence when the opportunity presented itself. It is to be expected that the same behavior would continue to prevail for a certain period, in spite of the provisions of Article 16 of the Constitution of October 26, 1956, which provided for freedom of thought and of the press.[21] It should also be noted that some contrary opinions were expressed, particularly with the division of the National Assembly into two groups after the second session of 1959: the Khoi Cong Dong Nhan Vi, or Personalist Community Group, and the Khoi Lien Minh Xa Hoi, or Socialist Union Group. The formation of these two groups was rather artificial, however, and their difference of opinion invariably centered around minor points; when basic issues were under discussion, they showed an examplary solidarity.[22]

After the Revolution of November 1, 1963, in order to establish an interim representative body, the Provisional Government created a Council of Notables, in which were united representatives of different political views from different social and economic environments. The men chosen for this Council were either prominent men in various technical fields or men who had opposed the regime of Ngo Dinh Diem. Although these councilors had been appointed by the Provisional Government, an opposition movement developed rather rapidly. The activities of the government were examined by the Council, which did not hesitate to render severe judgment: it criticized particularly the noncommittal attitude of the Provisional Government toward General Charles de Gaulle's proposal to neutralize Southeast Asia, the delay in bringing to justice the men who had compromised the public interest by serving certain policies of the Ngo Dinh Diem regime, and the delay in initiating reform measures. Following the purge of January 30, 1964, this Council was dissolved; eventually it will be replaced by an elected Constituent Assembly.

After the fall of the First Republic, many political parties that had been functioning clandestinely came out into the open. When the Revolutionary Government was organized after the January 30 purge, a number of positions in the new administration were filled with men from these parties,[23] and the government officially declared the freedom to form political parties, except the Communist Party and the Neutralist Party (allegedly sympathetic to communism).[24] The government is at present studying the conditions required for official recognition of a party, such as the preparation of a platform or charter, a minimum initial number of members, a minimum number of members three months after organization, and so on.

Consideration of Special Interests. Although the political party may sometimes defend certain special interests, its principal goal is supposed to concern the welfare of the population in general, regarded from the particular point of view of values adopted by the party. The administrator may even be confronted with real interest groups which defend particular interests.

The administrative decision may be influenced by the region of origin of the client of the administration. During the early years of the First Republic, it was the opinion of some observers that the enthusiasm of the refugee leaders for the new regime stood in striking contrast to that of most of the Southern mandarins,[25] and, particularly, that this factor was taken into consideration in making appointments to administrative positions of confidence. Although conflicts concerning the regions of origin of the person concerned are becoming less important with the passing of time, some allowance must still be made for local peculiarities in certain decisions, such as the choice of an administrator for a position in a given province, or the distribution of positions of direction within the same agency among candidates from different regions.[26]

After the November 1 Revolution, regional discrimination again appeared in the Provisional Government, which was made up predominantly of men from the South. The formation of the Revolutionary Government constituted a reaction against this tendency and provided for an equitable distribution of positions among persons from all regions.

Officially, the matter of religion was not taken into account in making decisions, although there were rumors that conformity to the religion of the leaders of the First Republic was a favorable factor.[27] The truth is that at all levels of the government service under the Ngo Dinh Diem regime, officials of different religions were working side by side. Following the incident concerning a Buddhist procession in Hue in May, 1963, the government organized intensive study sessions regarding freedom of religion: freedom of conscience, freedom of religious practice, and freedom to spread religious beliefs. In the course of these sessions, civil servants were urged to respect this freedom.[28] Actually, in spite of these official instructions, acts of religious persecution continued to occur. For the first time the Buddhist priests and their followers began to organize; they effectively exercised a moral veto on government decision making. The failure of the government of the First Republic to respect religious freedom was declared by the promoters to be one of the principal causes of the November 1 Revolution.

Since the Revolution, religious freedom has been particularly emphasized. Government officials have visited the leaders of the Hoa Hao and Cao Dai sects, and the latter sect has been accorded the right to collect market taxes.[29] In addition, a Cao Dai general has been named province chief of Tay Ninh province, and all the common religions of the nation—Buddhist, Catholic, Cao Dai, and Hoa Hao—are represented in the present Cabinet. On May 14, 1964, a *Décret-loi* formally recognized the Unified Vietnamese Buddhist Church and abolished all restrictions imposed on Buddhism as a religion during the First Republic.[30]

In the matter of special-interest groups, mention should be

made of the interests represented by certain groups of foreigners that formerly played a very important role in political and economic affairs: the French and the Chinese, for example. Although the French have lost their political authority, their influence can still be felt through a large number of institutions that they created (legislation concerning rents, the exploitation of mines, labor organizations, homesteading, the concession of public utilities, and so forth), which have been only slowly modified, according to needs, as long as they did not run counter to republican institutions. Consideration must also be given to the fact that a great number of civil servants were trained in the French tradition and still tend to follow that tradition. The Chinese, who constitute the largest minority group in Viet-Nam, have lost a great deal of their economic influence, particularly in trade and in medium industry, since the promulgation of the *du* (ordinance) of September 6, 1956, granting Vietnamese citizenship to persons of Chinese ancestry born in Viet-Nam, and another *du* of the same date, forbidding persons not Vietnamese citizens to practice certain professions that previously had been virtually the prerogative of the Chinese.[31] However, they still try to use the traditional cultural and economic bonds between China and Viet-Nam in order to secure close relationships with the administrators who make the decisions. To this influence must be added the entrepreneurship, the know-how, and the many procedures used by the Chinese to gain the confidence of administrators in power. Generally speaking, these groups try to bring external influence to bear on the decision-making process; i.e., they attempt to have an influential person intercede in their behalf "to obviate the formidable procedural snags and thus accelerate action or at least forestall inaction," but it should be noted that "this influence very rarely modifies fundamentals of these decisions, which are ordinarily objective, but even when decisions are subjective and particularistic, they are not necessarily iniquitous." [32] In short, although the pariah entrepreneurship of the Chinese constitutes an appreciable factor in the decision-making process, it is not a determining element of the decision itself.[33]

The consideration of special interests leads to certain decisions that will have a considerable influence on the future, inasmuch as early decisions create certain vested interests which restrict future decisions. The most striking example lies in the matter of personnel: because of the disorder created by the departure of the French civil servants in 1954, a great number of subordinate civil servants were promoted to positions of command, which they were not capable of filling; a certain number of other young men were recruited to fill the gaps temporarily; the existence of these civil servants in these positions constitutes a serious obstacle to reorganization.[34] This problem of sunk cost is all the more complicated when it concerns the few inexperienced administrators who work with prejudiced or selfish motives, or without prior planning.[35]

The Influence of Organized Groups. Certain professional groups representing economic interests, such as the chambers of commerce, the association of importers, and the agricultural association, always succeed in making their wants known with respect to certain decisions. For example, after the promulgation of *Décret-loi* No. 2/63 of February 14, 1963, and of the interdepartmental *Arrête* No. 77 of April 4, 1963, concerning investment benefits, the Vietnamese, Chinese, and French chambers of commerce made various helpful proposals concerning the simplification of the procedure to be adopted and the types of economic activities which might benefit from the new measures.[36] It should also be noted that, during the First Republic, the National Economic Council was a nationwide organization composed of representatives of the various economic interests (agriculture, fishing, industry, commerce, transportation, craft, works, and co-operatives) who had extensive experience in economic matters, and, as such, constituted an important source of information as well as pressure regarding decisions of an economic nature.[37]

Similarly, groups having social aims may command attention when the interests they represent are sufficiently important: the struggle against illiteracy, the movement for restaurants for the working classes, the Veterans' Association, the workers' unions, and so on. The importance of associations in the decision-making process can be understood when it is realized that associations have been an essential part of village life in Viet-Nam for thousands of years— contrary to the observation of certain sociologists that in underdeveloped countries most of the people live and die without ever achieving membership in a community larger than the family or the tribe.[38]

As the whole social system developed on contact with Western civilization during the period of French colonization, an increase in the number of associations began to appear slowly, but soon the sphere of action of many of them extended clearly beyond the framework of the village, as the means of communication increased. This movement grew in spite of the rather stringent legislation adopted by the French concerning the rights of the associations (Decree of February 21, 1933); this legislation was made applicable to Vietnamese living under the French protectorate by parallel regulations from the Vietnamese king (Royal Decree of October 20, 1933). The authorization to form an association was given by the resident superior (administrative head of the country), or even by the governor-general (administrative head of the Indochinese Union) if the sphere of influence was to be extended to several countries. After a probationary period, a second authorization conferred a certain legal capacity on the associations which had proved their vitality. Both authorizations were discretionary; i.e., it was not necessary for the authority to give his motives for granting or refusing it. The operations of the associations were also subject to rather strict regulations: any changes in the administration, statutes, or publication of the organization had to be declared. An authorized association could be dissolved by a legal authority if it violated the regulations, or the authorization could be withdrawn if the association failed seriously in the obligations imposed on it by the decree of 1933 and subsequent decrees.[39]

Under such restrictions, it is easy to see that the associations could pursue only goals permitted by the colonial authorities, and that associations of a political nature were prohibited, so that people who wished to organize for political reasons had no other recourse than to form secret societies. The value of these associations as a means of communication between the environment and the administrative system was therefore itself limited to openly accepted goals, and of course the secret society was by definition unable to make its opinions heard directly. It should be noted that, in addition to these associations, societies organized for purely commercial reasons were still quite free; these organizations, since they pursued only industrial and commercial activities, could often express their desires openly through the press. This is particularly true of the commercial societies organized by the French, which had rather powerful publications through which they could express their opinions and so influence the decisions of the administrators, even at the highest level—the governor-general. At any rate, because of the prohibition of political activities, associations could provide only a limited means of communication between the people and the government officials, even though their activities were becoming nationwide in scope.

Under the government of the First Republic, organization of associations was regulated by Ordinance No. 10 of August 6, 1950, modified by subsequent ordinances, until the promulgation of the Constitution of October 26, 1956, which recognizes in its Article 15 the freedom of forming associations. Associations may be formed in all domains: political, religious, cultural, literary, artistic, athletic, and professional. Moreover, as soon as they are formed they possess a legal capacity restricted to the normal functioning of the association, or in some cases full legal capacity, when the association is recognized as working toward the public interest. Certain restrictions on the freedom of forming associations still existed: the association had to obtain the prior authorization of the secretary of state for the interior before it could begin to function; it could be dissolved by a legal decision, or the administrative authorization could be withdrawn if the association violated the public order or the provisions of the statutes.[40] These restrictions, however, have not prevented the number of associations from increasing.

There were 334 associations functioning in Viet-Nam in 1961; in 1962, 79 new ones were formed.[41] Social organizations, such as the Republic Youth, the Women's Solidarity Movement, and the Veterans' Association, occupied rather broad fields of action, and on certain occasions even took political action. Mention should be made also of the three labor unions (Tong Lien Doan Lao Cong Viet-Nam, Tong Lien Doan Lao Dong Viet-Nam, and Luc Luong Tho Thuyen Viet-Nam) and of the two employers' associations (Tong Lien Doan Cong Thuong Viet-Nam, and Hiep Hoi Chu Nhan Viet-Nam). The activities of these organizations were strongly felt in the many collective labor conflicts. There are also cultural associations, such as the Hoi Khong Hoc (Association for Confucian Studies), the Hoi Nghien Chu Hanh Chanh (Association for Administrative Research), the Hoi Ky Su Viet-Nam (Association of Vietnamese Engineers), and the Tong Hoi Sinh Vien (General Students' Association). The associations for cultural exchange, such as the Hoi Viet My (Vietnamese American Association), the Hoi Viet Duc (Vietnamese German Association), the Hoi Viet Phap (Vietnamese French Association), and the Hoi Viet Nhat (Vietnamese-Japanese Association) seemed to have a more restricted field of action. Religious associations, such as the Tong Hoi Phat Giao (General Association for Buddhism), were often limited to religious practice and preaching, but on certain occasions they have taken action, ostensibly to create a reaction in public opinion, concerning the freedom of religion.[42] As a result of these events concerning religion, the National Assembly set up a special committee for studying possible modifications of the rather restrictive dispositions of the ordinance of 1950.[43] The *Décret-loi* of May 14, 1964, formally recognized the Unified Vietnamese Buddhist Church.

The Ngo Dinh Diem government itself encouraged the formation of these groups with the twofold aim of permitting special interests to be heard through their representatives and of communicating government policy to the members of these groups through the leaders they had chosen themselves. Nevertheless, the assumption that political, educational, business, and labor leaders were absorbed into the propaganda network of the regime through their almost mandatory associational activities seems to be somewhat partial.[44] Although the government of the First Republic always tried to encourage the formation of a large number of associations, it did not entirely supplant private initiative in order to create artificial groups to help assure the execution of government policy.

Still, although the government tried to make use of these associations, the associations in turn made use of government support to broaden their spheres of activity. After the fall of the First Republic, many of these groups remained firmly organized, largely because of the support they had gained from the masses. This is true of the General Association for Buddhism, the General Students' Association, and the labor unions. Other groups, basically self-sustained, went through the Revolution without noticeable changes, whether they were very traditional, such as the Association for Confucian Studies, or quite modern, such as the Association for Cultural Exchange. Other government-sponsored groups constituted a good start for organizing social activities previously untouched, such as the professional group dealing with foreign trade. But many of the associations that had been artificially organized or that depended too heavily on political factors were either officially dissolved, e.g., the Women's Solidarity Movement, or simply reorganized with new executive councils, e.g., the Veterans' Association.

Conflicting Interests in Problems of Organization. Within the administration, the problem of special interest occurs in a different form. Each department and each service fills a specific function; they are often working toward similar goals but occasionally toward different ones. The distinction has already been made between overhead units and operating units in the structure of the central government. The conflicts between these two types of units, well defined by certain authors writing about the administration of industrialized countries, are slightly more accentuated in Viet-Nam, either because of the particularistic tendencies of certain chiefs of service, especially in line functions, or else because of the too strictly legal universalistic spirit of administrators in the overhead units, which prevents certain of them from taking into consideration factual elements that are extremely important in administrative decisions.[45]

But conflicts, which tend to retard decision making, or even to make decisions incoherent, are particularly aggravated by three factors: the tendency toward centralization, the overlapping of authority, and the need for co-operation with foreign counterparts.

The consensus of authors writing about public administration in Viet-Nam seems to be that the chief executive of the First Republic was "reluctant to delegate authority" to his immediate collaborators, as they, in turn, were reluctant to delegate authority to their subordinates, and so on down the hierarchical ladder.[46] This fact can be explained, first, by the tradition of centralization that has existed in Viet-Nam for thousands of years, which was reinforced by the French colonization; and, second, by the personality of the charismatic leader, who feels he is obliged, like a good father, to guide his people and to look out for everything, with the result that he does not have time to resolve conflicts. A third factor could be added: the stress upon political loyalty of subordinates and the manipulative efforts of the President's advisors.

Either because of the urgent need of solving problems of organization or in order to make allowances for certain consideration of facts or of persons, two different organizations may fill identical functions or participate in operations involving the same procedures, but so closely related that it is difficult to distinguish them. As a result, certain principles may be developed, based on unavoidable wrangling, similar to the case of conflicts between overhead units and line units. Such occasions occur particularly when new institutions are set up, as in the case of the industrial development center (*trung tam khuyech truong ky nghe*),[47] or when several agencies are regrouped within a new department.[48]

The intervention of agencies outside the administration includes particularly proposals, counterproposals, and recommendations made by experts from friendly foreign governments responsible for administering economic and financial aid to Viet-Nam. In the case of American aid, for example, the administrative relationship between the host government and the Agency for International Development mission to Viet-Nam fall into the counterpart system. This means the organization of parallel units of the AID mission and of national agencies, each unit having its own technicians working separately but exchanging information, advice, and criticism. In the upper echelons of the administration, the general policy and the programs are established separately, but ratified and amended where necessary by the other group; agreements are often reached at the technical level, but frequently political considerations intervene. These political considerations are furthermore often concealed behind details of procedure.[49] Because of differences in outlook and in methods, and particularly in the accounting procedure, it often occurs that agreements can be reached only after lengthy negotiations entailing considerable loss of time and sometimes decision changes which are prejudicial to the proper functioning of the government service.[50] This has brought one author to say that "the Vietnamese have an indisputable talent for resisting outside help," which must be interpreted to mean that the Vietnamese are cautious with respect to suggestions offered by foreigners who do not know the country and its people well, since often the acceptance of an offer of aid represents a bilateral lowest common denominator rather than the application of a theory of economic development that would be acceptable to either party.[51]

The sharpest conflicts have arisen from the paradoxical desire of private enterprise in the United States to see that government agencies dispensing aid use it to foster private entrepreneurship abroad, whereas the host country considers that in certain key sectors, in order to promote rapid economic development, it is absolutely necessary to set up government enterprises, at least in the beginning, to set industrialization in motion.[52] Practically speaking, the administrative requirements of aid sometimes induce changes in government operations as a condition of grant or of technical assistance. But the government may not possess an adequate administrative apparatus, particularly since the amount and scope of the aid is increased as a function of events outside the administration, such as fresh outbreaks of Communist subversive activity, or a threat of invasion. All these many factors make decisions more and more difficult.

As regards organizational problems, however, it should be noted that the presence of certain agencies within the administration may make the decision easier, as is the case with research and documentation services. As early as 1956, at the instigation of the National Institute of Administration, an interdepartmental committee was established for studying the means of setting up a depository of documentation (legislative acts and regulations, statistics concerning major activities, etc.) for each bureau, service, directorate, or department.[53] These archives help make decisions easier, inasmuch as they provide precedents or legal and factual data on the problems to be solved.

Delay in making decisions caused by the organization of services appears to the casual observer simply as a complicated procedure requiring the participation of many agencies to provide proposals; initials; stamps and approvals of subcommittees, interministerial committees, and commissions, etc. The guiding principle behind the creation of these commissions is that, in order to avoid unnecessarily lengthy correspondence, representatives of the agencies concerned should be brought together to exchange the various points of view, so they can rapidly reach agreements on the decision to be made. For example, in order to indicate a certain will to introduce administrative reforms, an interdepartmental committee was created in 1960 to study administrative reforms: the chiefs of the departments concerned were appointed to participate in this committee, which was headed by the Secretary of State at the Presidency.[54] It often occurs also that because major national issues are involved the problem is beyond the reach of the technical or institutional jurisdiction of the agencies participating in the commission; in this case, representatives of the interests concerned are sometimes asked to present their views directly to the commission. As a result of the incidents which occurred in the course of the demonstrations at Hue commemorating the birth of Buddha, an interdepartmental committee was organized to seek the proper means for resolving the difficulty; this committee was composed of the vice president of the Republic, the secretary of state for the interior, and the secretary of state at the Presidency (who also performed the functions of secretary of state co-ordinator for Security), as well as an equal number of representatives of the General Association for Buddhism.[55] This interdepartmental committee made decisions in an apparent effort to reconcile public order and religious interests, but representatives of the General Association for Buddhism found that administrative officials, particularly in the provinces, frequently refused to execute some of these decisions, and executed others ineffectively.[56]

THE PERSONALITY OF THE DECISION MAKER

External factors exert a definite influence on an administrative decision, since this decision is incontestably a social process, particularly when administration is developed to the point where objective considerations are of primary concern. But in that last analysis, there is always a person, an administrator who decides the course of action: an old French administrative proverb says, "Deliberation is performed by several people, but action by only one." In an administrative philosophy having humanistic tendencies, it is to be expected that the role of the ultimate decision maker will be even more important than in the legalistic administrative philosophy from which the proverb is taken.

The Influence of the Recruiting Process. One source of influence on the decision of the civil servant is the process by means of which he was recruited: the interests and demands of the social milieu from which officials are recruited will be reflected in the way they conceive their roles, the way they view problems, and the way they behave in general.[57]

The imperial bureaucracy was indeed recruited from the grass roots: although certain families or certain villages prided themselves on always producing successful candidates for the mandarinal examinations, who earned high academic degrees and became high-ranking mandarins, it was not at all rare that sons from humble families succeeded in the examinations and reached the highest echelons of the mandarinal hierarchy. Even families of the highest social rank, from which came a certain number of the mandarins, continued to live in the country, in a manner only scarcely different from that of the mass of the population. The Confucian superior man is essentially a gregarious, altruistic man who seeks integration into society.[58] The literati respected the same ideals, followed the same traditions, and had the same aspirations as the common people. In consequence, their decisions reflected indeed the character of the total cultural environment.

During the colonial regime, instructional facilities were concentrated more and more in the cities, particularly in the capitals. There, contacts with European industrial civilization began to change the values and the outlook of the Vietnamese. These changes were brought about on an even broader scale as a result of foreign teachers, particularly for children of well-to-do families who could afford to send their children abroad to school. There was a time when people in certain circles began to worry about the uprooting of young people educated abroad or by foreigners.[59] And it was these young people who became the elite that, through a favorable turn of events, was to assume the reins of power. Although they have strong ties with the rest of the people, such as the national history, a common language, and a common destiny at the most critical period in the life of the nation, these new officials cannot help having a conception of problems different than that of their compatriots. Their new culture makes it even difficult to have an insight into the common values, the current interests, and the traditional behavior of a great number of their fellow countrymen.

As regards the influence of the new recruiting process, particular attention should be given to the tendency which has developed since national independence to send the young people to schools in foreign countries other than France, particularly to the United States, which offers many scholarships. Many of the returnees, even more than their elders educated in France, are imbued with an outlook different from that of their compatriots; the confrontation of ideas and techniques imported from a country where specialization is developed to the extreme and where machines come to man's aid in his smallest daily task with the traditional conception of administration, in which moral action is still highly prized and resourcefulness must make up for the lack of material means, necessarily brings about a certain disillusionment that may have repercussions in the behavior of the new civil servant and in the decisions he is called upon to make. The old lament of the student returning from France thirty years ago might be recalled in connection with the one returning today from America:

Are we then the privileged generation which, having drunk Western knowledge at its very source, can believe itself destined to be the principal agent of the renovation and the modernization of the country? Yet I no longer feel that instinctive sympathy for my fellow countrymen, that feeling of national and ethnic solidarity which unites a man with other men of his race. I am a sort of stranger in my own country, having almost no communion of ideas and feelings with the majority of my compatriots.[60]

The conflict of generations in the early years of national independence is explained by the influx of young men with the sincere desire to serve their country coming home to work side by side with administrators trained by the colonial regime. These latter were considered old-fashioned, decrepit, and good only for the archives: "The parochial outlook is not confined to the peasantry: most of the high-ranking members of the national civil service have never been outside Vietnam, and many of the ordinary civil servants have never even been to the nation's capital." [61] The older civil servants are, of course, more strongly bound by tradition; imbued with classical literature, both Chinese and French, they are much more inclined to examine problems in a general manner, while the younger workers, trained in the American school, are more pragmatic and practical in the solution of the same problems.[62] In view of the fact that the great majority of the current civil servants follow this literary-generalist tradition, it is easy to see that the details of administrative problems are often missed.

It is a well-known fact that at each important step in the history of the republic—the mass exodus to the South in 1954, the struggle against the political religious groups, the unsuccessful *coup d'état* of November 11, 1960, the recent Buddhist conflict, and the Revolution of November 1, 1963—some civil servants, even in the highest administrative positions, consulted soothsayers, particularly astrologers, to discover either their own fates or the wisest measure to take. These men are misled by the fact that astrology, adopting a scientific disguise, pretends to keep in step with astronomy to indicate the course of human events. This spirit of superstition does not affect most of the younger civil servants.

It might be supposed that the members of the new generation, particularly those who have studied abroad, are free from this restraint of tradition. Few of them tend to follow tradition; at least they do not present traditional values as justification of their actions. On the other hand, the accusation has been made regarding most of the younger group that before becoming acquainted with Vietnamese conditions, they "voiced complaints without realizing how behavioral changes are wrought; at least, if they become resigned to the system, they adopt outwardly an attitude of passivity and acquiescence, while inwardly they are seething with bitterness and frustration." [63] It should be pointed out that, with the passing of time, these problems have become considerably less important as the government has become more stable, as the young men returning from abroad have gained more experience concerning living conditions in Viet-Nam, and as the older civil servants have had more opportunities to observe foreign techniques and to have more frequent contacts with foreign experts.

Although the number is steadily decreasing, there still remain civil servants who, because of insufficient pre-service training, are not fully prepared to perform their duties properly and whose decisions are often marked by incompetence.[64] Much consideration is still being given to pre-service and in-service training.

Lastly, attention should be drawn to a new tendency on the part of recruiting administrators. It has already been stated that during the Ngo Dinh Diem regime, because of the urgent need for security, many military officials were appointed to supervisory and executive positions, particularly as province chiefs. However, because of the concentration of power in the central government, they played only a secondary role in administration.[65] Since the November 1 Revolution, these officers have begun to accept the responsibility of their roles as leaders: the Prime Minister, a certain number of the ministers, the Prefect of Saigon and all the province chiefs are generals or high-ranking officers, and many other important administrative officials, including the Director of the Cabinet of the Prime Minister, the Director-General of National Police, and the Director of the Municipal Transport System, are high-ranking officers. This special trend in recruiting, which is recent in Viet-Nam, seems to be generalized in other developing countries, where the seizure of power by military men is explained by many factors, particularly the idea of "modernizing oligarchies." [66]

Innovation and Entrepreneurship. In a recently established government, there are countless opportunities for civil servants, young or old, to display initiative or broadmindedness. An analysis of the factors that contribute to the development of a spirit of innovation in administration reveals both extra-bureaucratic factors, such as the building of nationalism and the role of technical assistance, and intra-bureaucratic factors, such as the creation of a new service, the effect of a new decentralization measure, the appointment of a new chief of service, or the presentation of a new objective for the service. These factors have indeed a stimulating effect in a new administration like that of Viet-Nam. There are other factors, however, which inhibit this spirit of innovation, such as the inertia that exists in any organization after it has functioned for a certain time; the desire to survive on the part of the civil servant, who seeks to maintain the status quo; the administrator's fear of resistance on the part of his subordinates and of the public with regard to the introduction of new measures; and change of values in the mind of the administrator himself, who, after having introduced innovations, clings to his first ideas.

Generally speaking, a distinction might be drawn between two kinds of innovation: policy and procedural. One authority makes the following distinction: "Policy innovation may be defined as including those changes in governmental purposes or activities which embark the government upon a new course of action or accelerate sharply some present activity, or reverse some present impetus. Procedural innovations may be defined as including primarily changes in the government methods of carrying out its programs." [67]

Regarding policy innovations, certain observers have emphasized the pioneer spirit which seems to characterize the Vietnamese. "The Vietnamese display a propensity for striking out in new realms with untried methods and techniques heretofore unknown to their country. They display a high degree of flexibility and imagination." [68] Many examples of this can be found in decisions made in the setting up of the present administrative organization (see Chapters 3 and 4), decisions made on the occasion of differences of opinion between Vietnamese authorities and experts from organizations offering technical assistance, and, in general, the achievements of the Republic of Viet-Nam since 1954.[69]

However, some historians who study Confucianism seem to believe that a great conformity must rule in the bureaucracy, because "all those who finally did rise to the top by scaling the examination ladder lost whatever originality and personality they might once have possessed and became completely molded by the implacable structure of traditional scholarship, victims of a majestic brainwashing which destroyed their individual idiosyncracies but developed their social instinct to the utmost." [70] A close examination of the matter shows that this conformity, which was the subject of violent protest from generations of Chinese scholars as well as Vietnamese,[71] applied only to the rites, the external manifestations of ideal social behavior, and through these rites to the incontestable principles of social ethics: human-heartedness, righteousness, etc. Within this moral framework, nothing prevented the superior man from acting for the public good, i.e., from using his own initiative in performing his administrative duties. On the contrary, the human-heartedness, understood in the sense intended by the Master, consisted of doing good, communicating good thoughts to others, and putting good ideas into execution. Did not a remote disciple of Confucius, Wang Yang-ming (Vietnamese: Vuong Duong Minh), preach, *"Tri hanh hop nhat"* (Knowledge and action are but one)? [72] Did not Japanese educators turn this teaching to account after the Meiji Restoration to cause the great decisions to be made regarding the modernization of the country? Vietnamese history also includes important instances of initiative taken by Confucian scholars, such as the conquest of part of the delta of North Viet-Nam by the mandarin Nguyen Cong Tru, or the digging of an effective network of irrigation canals in South Viet-Nam by Nguyen Huynh Duc. The long and steady expansion toward the South was itself the work of generations of Confucian scholars who aided the kings and princes in this gigantic work. If we relate this spirit of innovation to the political setting since 1954, we may at first think that it was hampered by the authoritarian attitude of the leader. In fact, besides the reserved domain of political struggle, initiative has been shown in many spheres, such as the setting up of government enterprises, the building up of social overhead capital—sometimes against the advice of foreign experts.

Of course, to the extent that strong loyalty requirements were prerequisite for heading important public agencies, this innovative spirit has not been able to expand freely.

The conclusion might be drawn that criticism regarding the lack of spirit of innovation concerns only procedural innovation. Indeed, the author who said that the Vietnamese have an indisputable talent for resisting outside help was referring particularly to procedural innovation in the matter of taxes. On the other side, however, another observer affirms that "the Vietnamese proved to be the most successful of Southeast Asian countries in adapting to Western standards." [73] Even the most critical authors concede that "the civil service does contain progressive elements who would like to break with tradition and apply energy and imagination to pressing social economic and security problems." [74] Here also, a distinction should be made: the civil servants occupying high positions are the ones who can be expected to introduce innovations in procedure. At the present time, however, they are still too preoccupied by problems of general policy, which, in a new country, require that everything be considered and reconsidered. On the other hand, it must be recognized that civil servants at the subordinate levels are either too accustomed to the old practices to dream of changing them or too young to conceive of practical reforms—or too young to be considered capable of doing so. Gradually, with the passing of time, as more and more of the younger civil servants acquire experience through practice and through in-service training courses organized for all active workers, procedural innovations are being introduced more frequently. Although the annual bulletin of progress made by the government is necessarily concerned principally with general policy, it does reveal various procedural innovations realized in the course of the year. In 1962, for instance, the Directorate-General of Budget and Foreign Aid instituted the reform in payment procedure, and in the procedure for furnishing office supplies; the Department of the Interior set up a system of communication by telegraph and teletype between the capital, the government delegates, and the provinces; the Department of National Economy simplified the procedure for issuing importation licenses; the Department of Finance, by creating a bureau for the direct issuance to creditors of cash vouchers stamped by the Treasury, greatly simplified the procedure for paying creditors of the state.[75] Instances of procedural innovations on a scale of lesser importance are also quite numerous.[76]

Willingness to Assume Responsibility. This spirit of innovation might be regarded as an aspect of a more general attitude: the willingness of the civil servant to assume responsibility, in new as well as routine matters. Since routine constitutes an essential element of the daily conduct of administrative affairs, there might be some question as to the efficiency of a service if its administrator lacked this trait. Such a lack might stem from inexperience or from lack of professional training on the part of the administrator, particularly in a country which has just become independent and in which all posts of authority were formerly occupied by colonial civil servants. As a remedy for this, the government has organized an in-service training program, programs of foreign study, and so on.

Much more serious is the practice of fence-sitting: in the early days of the Republic a certain number of civil servants—torn between concern for personal security, which advised against committing themselves to loyalty to a given political system, and the desire to execute faithfully instructions coming from the government —preferred to wait and see "which way the wind blows." [77] The study sessions, as we have seen, were intended partly to combat this spirit, which, in fact, is diminishing as the government becomes more stable and gains prestige in the eyes of the people through its spectacular achievements.

Comparable to this egotistical practice of fence-sitting is the fear of responsibility. After many interviews with civil servants of the highest level, one author felt obliged to draw the conclusion that "most Vietnamese civil servants remain passive and uninvolved, avoiding decisions by referring them to higher levels. Following mandarin and French colonial tradition, where the administrative system is autocratic and highly disciplined, unquestioned obedience at every level is expected." [78] The unwillingness to accept responsibility is the result of insufficient "internalization of organizational goals" for a "basic motivational path toward actions." [79] In the traditional system, the spirit of loyalty toward the king, the supreme authority, was far more developed than the spirit of devotion to the public interest. When, with the intervention of the French, the actions of the mandarins ceased to be identified with the exercise of royal power, the only basic motivation remaining for the civil servant was a desire to advance in status.[80] When the country again became independent, the attempt to identify the goals of the civil servant wifh the public interest, as represented by the charismatic leader, developed, for many of the workers, into a personality cult, which did not inspire in them much willingness to accept responsibility. Other authors emphasize, more objectively, the point that the charismatic leader has such an ascendancy that even the subordinates who have received a specific delegation of power consider themselves more secure if they make oral reports and ask for instructions regarding decisions; this attitude leads irresistibly to bottlenecks at high administrative levels that are at once blamed on the leader himself.[81] Lastly, there is the fear of public opinion—that opinion which has not been rendered predictable by years of experience in democracy and which tends to judge more by personalities than by ideas, more by the civil servants than by the administrative policy in question.

This indecision or fear of responsibility is manifested in extensive correspondence asking for further explanation or supplementary details, and in interminable committee meetings, where different points of view, sometimes expressed by persons not qualified to judge, lead to contradictory conclusions which shed little light on the solution. Administrators, especially at the lower levels, often use procedure as a pretext for refusing to accept a file that is lacking in some unimportant document or a certain signature. One author, describing such an attitude among bureaucrats of some advanced countries says: "This emphasis sometimes becomes overpowering, with the result that punctilious adherence to formalized procedures is elevated into the primary objective of bureaucratic activities and displaces their original objectives in the thinking of the officials." [82]

To combat this ritualistic displacement of goals, many formal campaigns have attempted to revitalize the bureaucracy, e.g., the Week of Diligence in the Administrative Service.[83]

Comparable to this inhibitive formalism is an attitude which is totally different, but which also contributes to the slowing up of formal decisions. Faced with a difficult problem, the administrator sometimes replies with silence. This is not by omission or negligence, but a willful silence which means neither approbation nor rejection. This attitude on the part of the administrator has been explained as a combination of fear of compromising himself and a certain self-domination. In fact, this seems to be a general attitude derived from Vietnamese culture, in which the collective life has developed under a protective covering of symbols, gestures, and a vocabulary of respect, with any expression of the least original idea considered hazardous.[84] This negative form of administrative decision was conceivable in an agricultural economy in which nothing was urgent except defense against floods and piracy. With the evolution of the economic life and the parallel evolution of customs in contact with the philosophy which regards administration as a series of prestations of service, it is no longer possible to act by negation.

On the other hand, indecision may be explained by the stubbornness of narrow-minded administrators or by the limitations of the "intellectual." [85] Like his colleague in Western countries, the Vietnamese intellectual who becomes an administrator may be irresponsible (absent-minded and unpunctual), indecisive (excessively cautious or judicious in his examination of a problem), or unpersuasive (eccentric, not interested in people). Among older administrators, there sometimes occurs a tendency to follow systematically traditional practices that have proved successful, never suspecting that, in a changing world, practices must also be adapted to modern conditions. They try to justify this clinging to their preconceived ideas by using modern data interpreted in a more or less subjective manner. This helps to explain the conflict of generations mentioned above. In the light of this conflict of generations, hasty or arbitrary decisions resulting from lack of concern for responsibility are also to be feared. Inexperience leads to insufficient attention to all elements of a problem and to an insufficient control of emotions, often the result of misleading indications. This phenomenon often occurs in new agencies with newly recruited administrative leaders.[86]

Family Considerations. Sociologists writing about the social structure of Viet-Nam rarely fail to emphasize the strong family spirit which still prevails among the Vietnamese.[87] According to these writers, this spirit of family solidarity invariably influences the decision of the administrator, whenever a member of the family is concerned in an administrative affair, either to obtain a position in the government service or to sign a contract with the government.

The old proverb, *mot nguoi lam quan ca ho duoc nho* ("a mandarin can give his support to the entire family"), is often quoted to the scholar who has been appointed mandarin or to the student recently admitted to the government service, to remind him of his responsibility to give moral and material support to all persons who are more or less related to him, sometimes as many as five or even more degrees removed in paternal lineage (slightly less in maternal lineage).[88] To avoid abuses of authority in situations of this kind, the imperial administration customary forbade administrators to serve in their native districts, and also forbade brothers to sit in the same council.[89] On the other hand, the strict rule for recruiting civil servants by examination presented a serious obstacle to nepotism. In other words, the imperial administration dealt equitably with the universalistic spirit which must preside over the actions of the mandarin and which requires that he be assigned to a region where he is presumed not to have any family ties, and with the particularistic spirit which must guide the action of the cantonal and communal authorities, who are always inhabitants of the region.

From the point of view of the evolution of customs, this family spirit is mitigated proportionately by the development of urbanism, since city dwellers have less frequent opportunities to get together in family groups, and tend to develop ties based on neighborhoods or professions. This is true even in rural regions of South Viet-Nam, where the weakening of family ties can still be explained by the relatively recent colonization of this region.[90] For this reason, it is perhaps exaggerated at the present time to compare the influence of family ties on the behavior of the Vietnamese administrator with that of the administrator in pre-Communist China, where changes in social status promoted changes in family structure, so that more distant family ties were strengthened, as soon as a member of the family was admitted into the mandarinate.[91] Although the family is still a firm social unit in Viet-Nam, its dimensions are already reduced, and it is no longer true that the homogeneity of the family makes the average Vietnamese a collective being for whom the interest and the will of the family group takes precedence over the will of the individual.[92] However, in the immediate family, i.e., brothers and sisters, or fairly close cousins, some influence is still possible; but this is true even in highly industrialized societies, where, aside from political considerations, the collaborators of high administrative officials are sometimes chosen among members of the family, for reasons of confidence as well as of competence.[93] In an underdeveloped country, in which the average citizen cannot afford to send his children to the university, education is often concentrated in a small number of families, where there is an academic tradition or the financial means to support the education of the children. The nephew or grandson of an influential man, if he is given a position in the administration, is often the object of unfair criticism that does not take into consideration his qualifications or preparation for the position.

Corruption. So far this discussion has concerned only the influence of certain social or psychological factors on administrative decisions; personal interest on the part of the administrator himself has not been considered.

But the administrator himself may be directly influenced by his own interest: i.e., his decision may be swayed by corruption. Various explanations of this phenomenon have been attempted. Many authors point out that it is difficult to state with any confidence how extensive such practices as bribery, kickbacks, embezzlement, and other forms of graft are in Viet-Nam.[94] Other researchers and journalists, with more or less good intentions, consider this phenomenon as endemic and general.[95] The French insisted that corruption was a part of Vietnamese culture well before their arrival in the colonies.[96] The Vietnamese accused the colonists of having introduced or increased the occurrence of this practice.[97] A plausible explanation is that in the rare cases where corruption is proved, the press gives such exaggerated accounts as to leave the impression that the entire administrative regime is corrupt.

This is the basis for the charges of corruption made by the press, particularly since the November 1 Revolution: vehement attacks were made against the administrators of the Ngo Dinh Diem regime, generally without distinguishing political activities from clearly criminal offenses. In addition to the interministerial committee to investigate crime and the illegal acquisition of property under the First Republic (see Chapter 4), a revolutionary court was created to punish the crimes of illegal confinement, misappropriation of funds, etc. (*Décret-loi* of February 28, 1964).[98] The punishments meted out by this court are very severe, and for some offenses capital punishment is possible.[99] Government officials must declare all effects and holdings in order to enable the government to prevent graft, misuse of power, and embezzlement of funds.[100]

Although this is not the place to discuss the general problem of corruption of administrators, it is necessary to make a rather detailed analysis of this irregular element of the decision-making process. Before the arrival of the French, administration was set up so as to cost as little as possible and to keep intervention in the social life of the people to a minimum. This double principle is the result of the adoption of the idea of virtue as the basis of administrative action. In principle, the government demanded contributions from the people only to the extent that these contributions were necessary to the functioning of the administration. This contribution was first made on a voluntary basis each time a citizen had occasion to ask the services of a mandarin, but later became obligatory and uniform. Royal edicts regulated precisely the quality and quantity of gifts the communal or cantonal authorities were to make to the mandarin district chiefs on entering the administrative service, on New Year's Day, on being promoted to a higher rank, on presenting a request, etc. Similarly, gifts were presented by the mandarins themselves to their superiors, progressively up the hierarchy to the king. It should be noted that there was a certain reciprocity in this exchange of presents: on less frequent and more solemn occasions, the king himself sent gifts to the high-ranking mandarins, who did the same to their subordinates, and so on, down the ladder.[101]

Giving presents was thus a traditional part of the system of administration by rites, which is the formal expression of administration by virtue, as has been pointed out.[102] Naturally enough, there have been decadent periods of Vietnamese history, in which certain mandarins took advantage of this right to expect presents, but during the reigns of good monarchs, mandarins vied with each other in high moral conduct according to Confucian standards, and even made their families proud precisely by their honorable poverty. Quite often, the kings came to the assistance of these conscientious mandarins, by granting them the income from certain communal rice paddies, or by earmarking the taxes of a certain number of villages, by way of lifetime annuities as rewards for their devoted service.

This high moral conduct was possible in an agricultural economy, in which material needs were rather limited. When a market economy was superimposed on this traditional economy, these material needs were increased, and at the same time traditional moral values underwent a progressively deeper change. The colonial authorities, especially anxious to increase material production, were less concerned with the moral conduct of their subordinates, particularly in view of the fact that, in the colonial administrative system, the idea of the impartiality of the law excluded any consideration of morals in the functioning of the government services. It is quite possible that the colonial authorities did not intentionally encourage corruption, but the introduction of the idea of profit from a market economy into a tradition of assisting mandarins to lead a decent life by more or less voluntary presents explains the French opinion that corruption was generalized in the colony. During the Ngo Dinh Diem regime, many official statements were made in an effort to restore ancient moral values by awakening in the civil servants a new civic spirit. Although sensational discoveries have been made concerning misappropriations of funds or other abuses of power, it must be pointed out that they involved only a certain number of high officials in whom the former President of the Republic had placed his confidence. Out of 21 persons whose bank accounts have been ordered held for investigation for having collaborated in building up the personal fortune of the Ngo family, only 10 are civil servants or military officers.[103]

Two recent observers who criticize Vietnamese bureaucracy on many points feel obliged to admit that the civil servants are not often dishonest:

> Our opinion is that graft and corruption are not widespread. This view is based on discussion with former French officials and Chinese and American traders who have dealt in South Asia. They have expressed their amazement to us over the degree of incorruptibility of officials in Viet Nam and have contrasted the situation with their experience in other countries. An American trader, with 30 years of experience in the Far East, has said that with the exception of the Japanese, Vietnamese officials are the most difficult to bribe in the Orient. Several prominent businessmen have admitted privately to us that they have tried in vain to influence officials with pressure and money in order to receive a high priority for a telephone, etc.[104]

The Normative Approach

When the decision-making process is analyzed from the sociological and psychological points of view, it becomes obvious at once that the administrative decision is considerably influenced by two series of factors: (1) legal factors, which constitute the framework of the decision-making process, particularly in a country which aspires to a legal democracy; and (2) moral factors, which enter into all administrative activities based on a philosophy which favors a return to Confucian values.

The following discussion will emphasize particularly these two series of factors.

THE LEGAL APPROACH

As administrative action broadened and the ascendency of administration over private activities became greater, it became necessary to establish regulations and to institute procedures in order to make government services more efficient and to protect private interests. In other words, leadership is at present exercised within the legal framework left by the successive previous administrations. Laws and regulations applicable to administrative decisions constitute administrative law, the idea of which the French colonial authorities introduced into Viet-Nam.

With special reference to administrative decisions, administrative law helps to determine: (1) the judicial character of the administrative decision, and (2) the procedure to be followed in making the decision.

The Judicial Character of the Administrative Decision. Vietnamese administrative law identifies the administrative decision with the enforceable decision (*decision executoire*), which is considered an essential prerogative of governmental power, in accordance with French judicial doctrine. The enforceable decision creates obligations on the part of the people and on occasion grants the people rights, without the decision maker's having to be concerned about their consent.[105] For example, an *arrêté* of the minister for public works setting up a temporary administrative committee for the Port of Saigon constitutes an administrative decision as a result of which port rights are granted to people under certain conditions or obligations, such as the payment of port fees.[106] Similarly, the decision of a province chief to grant a concession of public land constitutes another administrative decision, inasmuch as the province chief does not have to obtain the consent of the interested party to minor details and adjustments of his decision.[107] In principle, administrative decision concerns acts of the administrator only when they affect legal rights and obligations (*effets de droit*), but it does not concern involuntary physical acts on the part of the administration, such as an accident caused by an official car, or voluntary physical acts, such as the emergency requisitioning of private property by the administration without completion of formalities. However, these acts, whether voluntary or involuntary, very often imply a previous decision; and to this extent they enter the domain of administrative law. For example, injury to a person involuntarily caused by a soldier in a street riot is not in itself an administrative decision; but since this occurrence was possible only because of an improper organization of the police service, which is an administrative decision, this act might be considered the responsibility of the government.[108]

Considered thus in a limited sense by administrative law, enforceable decisions fall into a hierarchical scale, similar to the administrative hierarchy itself. Under normal circumstances, at the top is the decree (*sac lenh*); at the present time, this is issued by the prime minister, and does not require any countersignatures by the ministers. Under unusual circumstances, as has already been pointed out, the prime minister may also make *décrets-lois* (*sac luat*), which have greater value than ordinary decrees. A less weighty form of the prime minister's decision is the *arrêté* (*nghi dinh*). A decision made by a minister may also be an *arrêté*. An *arrêté* made by several ministers is called an interministerial *arrêté*. At the provincial level, a decision is called *quyet dinh*. Both the decree and the *arrêté* include a preamble indicating the laws and regulations giving the authority for the decision, and the decision itself, divided into several articles.

Administrative decisions can also be made in simpler forms: circulars (*thong tu*), instructions (*chi thi*), memoranda (*diep van*), letters (*cong van*), etc. Instructions and circulars are orders of a general nature, indicating to the administrators procedures to be observed in the operation of a given part of the service. The question often arises whether these documents are simply internal orders, in which case they concern only the superior and the subordinates in the administrative hierarchy, or whether they are real enforceable decisions, creating rights and obligations on the part of the people. Jurisprudence seems to recognize in these documents the value of enforceable decisions, when the authority signing the document makes a decision that the subordinates are to execute, adding new stipulations to those resulting from the laws and regulations, and imposing new subjections or granting new guarantees to the people. Presidential Memorandum No. 5/NV of November 7, 1960, for example, provides for the election of the youth councilor in the communal council by the chiefs of the youth groups and intergroups. Another example is Circular No. 802 BTT/VP of June 28, 1956, from the Secretary of State at the Presidency, which, until May, 1963, served as a basis for the organization of the communal councils. Similarly, a circular concerning provincial budgets certainly constitutes an administrative decision to the extent that it creates for the people rights and obligations regarding provincial financial matters. It is interesting that, at the present time, there seems to be a tendency toward preferring the use of this more adaptable form of decision, particularly in matters concerning provincial administration.[109]

From a material point of view, the decision may be a regulatory act or a nonregulatory act. A regulatory act is a general and impersonal enforceable decision, for example, an *arrêté* concerning the traffic code. Among these acts, special mention should be made of decrees and *arrêtés* made in order to prescribe means of applying the law or a regulatory act made by a superior authority. A nonregulatory act may be an individual decision concerning a single person, for example, the appointment of an administrator, or a collective decision, i.e., concerning several persons individually designated, such as an *arrêté* expropriating land from several landowners for a government project. This distinction is important from the point of view of establishing judicial control over administrative activity.

From the same point of view, another distinction is quite as important, depending on the degree to which the administrator is bound by the law. In order to made a decision, the administrator must indeed combine factual considerations with legal considerations. Vietnamese administrative law, following French doctrine, makes a distinction between restricted jurisdiction (*compétence lée*) and discretionary power (*pouvoir discrétionnaire*). In the former, the administrator is obligated to decide in a certain way, without having any alternative: as soon as the citizen making the request fulfills certain conditions prescribed by law, the administrator must decide in his favor, as in the case of admitting a candidate to an examination. On the other hand, the administrator has discretionary power when the law allows him the freedom of deciding in one way or in another, as in the case of granting temporary use of public land, or of grading a candidate for public office: in these cases, the decision can be judged only from the point of view of its appropriateness, and not from the point of view of its legality. In reality, there is no administrative decision in which both restricted jurisdiction and discretionary power will not come into play simultaneously: although admitting candidates to an examination is a matter of restricted jurisdiction, there are also certain legal stipulations concerning admission procedure, such as those regarding the moral conduct of the candidate, which allow a certain latitude of decision to the administrator.[110]

The Procedure to be Followed in Making the Decision.   Procedure concerns first jurisdiction, i.e., the power of the administrator or the administrators to make the decision, and the form, i.e., the steps of the decision according to law.

In principle, the administrator can make the decision only if he has been granted the authority by the law or regulations, or by a long-established tradition. For example, the Constitution of October 26, 1956, implicitly recognizes the power of the president of the Republic to make regulations, and this tradition apparently applies equally to the prime minister. There is also a tradition that the former secretaries of state and the present ministers have this power. In principle, and also according to tradition, the director-generals do not have this power, although the special commissioner for Co-operatives and Agricultural Credit was an exception. On the other hand, the prefect of Saigon and the province chiefs have the power to make regulations.[111] At the village level, it is incontestable that the administrative council may also establish police regulations.

As regards this power to make regulations, attention should be called to a principle which is falling into disuse, since it is not stipulated in any legal act. According to French tradition, an administrator who is given certain authority by the constitution, the law, or the regulations may not delegate that authority to another, particularly in the case of authority set up in order to protect the people.[112] In practice, the ministers may delegate the power to sign regulations to certain of their subordinates, but on their own responsibility.

Normally, enforceable decisions are explicit and written. Regulatory enforceable decisions often appear in the form of decrees or *arrêtés*, and often, at the present time, in the form of instructions or circulars, or even memoranda. The administrative decision may also be simply the result of silence on the part of the administrator. For example, any legislation regarding permission to build requires the authorization of the administrative authority within a period of six months; if no official action is taken during that time, permission is considered granted. If the administrative decision is made in a written form, however, it requires a certain number of formalities, particularly official consultations and a specific amount of publicity. The laws and regulations may indeed stipulate that for certain types of decisions consultation with certain organizations is mandatory. For example, in writing up decrees and *arrêtés* (also legislative bills) regarding civil liberty, the statute of civil service, the statute of liberal professions, the administrative organization of the state and of local communities, and the floating of bonds, the advice of the council of state is obligatory, although this advice is not binding on the authority which makes the decision.[113] Certain educational institutions are provided with an administrative council that must be consulted on matters concerning administration; the same is true of agencies having autonomous budgets.[114] Particularly at the local level, the administrative authority must often seek the advice of an elected council, and this advice is binding on this authority for some particular decisions.[115]

Another formality is often necessary for local administrative units: the approval of the tutelary authority. Certain deliberations of the provincial council are subject to explicit approval by the ministers; others are not subject to approval, but are not enforceable until fifteen days after they have been received in the office of the province chief.[116]

The official announcement is the means by which enforceable decisions are brought to the knowledge of the interested parties.

There is an impersonal means of making the announcement, which consists of printing the decision in the Official Gazette of the Republic of Viet-Nam (*Cong Bao Viet Nam Cong Hoa*). As soon as the decision is published in this way, it is considered in effect one full day after publication in Saigon, or after the arrival of the *Official Gazette* at the province seat; for other regions, three full days counting from the arrival of the Gazette in the province seat.[117] Other means of making the official announcement may consist of posting the decision publicly, or of using the public crier (particularly in the villages). Finally, in cases of emergency, the announcement may be made by telegraph or by radio broadcast. For individual decisions, the announcement is made by registered letter, or by an ordinary letter for which the addressee must sign a notebook provided for that purpose.

The public announcement constitutes the starting point of the effect of the enforceable decision. Generally, these effects are perpetual, i.e., they remain in force as long as the decision has not been subject to abrogation (which terminates the effects of the decision for the future) or withdrawal (an annulment of the effects for the past as well as for the future). The administrative decision is enforceable in itself, without the consent of the interested parties; but that does not mean that the decision can be executed by force, without previous appeal to the court, except in certain cases provided by the law (such as military requisition, or cases of emergency).[118]

Observations on the Judicial Approach. The judicial approach permits the doubly useful clarification of the problem of the administrative decision. From the administrator's point of view, he knows exactly the limits of his powers and the procedure he must follow in order to make a valid decision. As for the people, they can have recourse to the court if they consider there is an abuse of authority.

However, this judicial analysis concerns only a certain number of administrative decisions. It does not include contracts made by the administration, which are certainly administrative decisions, to the extent that an administrative official must make a decision to enter a contract. There are a great many other general decisions, such as the formulation of a policy which has not been crystallized in the form of a legal act or regulation, or which will never take that form since it may concern only a line of conduct to be followed. The judicial approach also disregards other decisions of a purely technical nature: the decision to adopt a budgetary reclassification is considerably more important than the appointment of a subordinate civil servant, but it is not considered an enforceable decision, since it does not create rights or obligations for the citizen.

In short, the judicial approach does not permit the consideration of all administrative decisions, nor does it consider each decision in its entirety and in its real relations with environmental factors. It does, however, permit the delineation of an important framework.

THE ETHICAL APPROACH: THE CHARACTER OF THE IDEAL ADMINISTRATOR IN THE DECISION-MAKING PROCESS

The decision of the administrator makes him subject to considerations of another sort: the moral environment.

The Confucian Administrator. The traditional administrative philosophy, with its pragmatic nature, placed particular emphasis on the personality of the man responsible for making decisions in the administrative hierarchy. Since the legal framework of the administrative decision was not restricted by too many laws and regulations, a great latitude was left to the administrator in making decisions, although the number of occasions on which he was called to intervene with a decision were reduced to a minimum. It might be said that the decision took on a rather negative character insofar as it was usually sufficient that the administrator set a good example instead of rendering specific services to the population. As a result, instead of analyzing the decision itself, Confucian philosophy merely brought out the principal qualities the administrator should possess in both his individual character and his social action. Although this philosophy appears as a series of dogmas, the mandarins were so imbued with Confucian teachings that it does not seem an exaggeration to compare their actual behavior with the ethics professed by the Master. The many examples of suicide out of loyalty to the emperor constitute clear proof of the identification of the ethics with the action.[119] Another manifestation of this identification is the many cases in which administrators attracted the admiration and attachment of the people to the extent that they were venerated as if they were gods.[120]

According to this Confucian philosophy, the first duty of a man who wishes to become a wise administrator is to develop in himself a constant spiritual strength always ready to act, which will maintain in fine harmony (*trung dung;* Chinese, *tchong yang*) the contradictory elements contending in his heart.[121] To achieve this serenity, he must moderate his desires; since emotion is made manifest by speech and by action, he must govern his words and must act when the occasion occurs, coolly foreseeing difficulties and not calculating the praise his action will bring. He is convinced of the existence of the *menh* (Chinese, *ming*); that is, he holds a rational faith in the natural order as opposed to a blind belief in human destiny. This belief in the natural order entails resignation in the face of adversity and equanimity in success; although it does not bring the positive joys of happiness, it secures peace of mind even in misfortune. This resignation must be taken as an understanding of the fact that although the inevitable is beyond the reach of human power, the possible is within it. Man's duty toward himself and toward others falls within his possibilities, and should urge him to positive action. This duty may be regarded as a consideration of the three fundamental social virtues: *nhan,* or human-heartedness; *tri,* or wisdom; and *dung,* or courage.[122]

Human-heartedness. *Nhan* (Chinese, *jen*) is in reality a multiple virtue: it includes the greatness of soul which reaches the heart, the charity which makes it easy to lead men, the sincerity which gains confidence, the sobriety of bearing which inspires respect, and the diligence which brings about the execution of useful works.[123] According to Mencius, a disciple of Confucius, the first manifestation of our innate goodness is the sincere and tender affection we bear toward our parents; the second is the instinctive compassion a child feels for a person who is suffering. The superior man cultivates this natural disposition, which begins with filial piety and reaches its peak with a love for humanity: *tu hai giai huynh de* ("men of the four seas are all brothers"). In order to cultivate this disposition, he seeks to be master of his passions, to harmonize emotions with intelligence: the latter shapes the former, for it governs them and keeps them in their original purity. In other words, man should put forth an untiring effort to practice his duties toward others, and a continuous supervision over his conscience and his passions. When the ultimate stage of love for humanity is reached, *nhan* nullifies all hatred and all vice; it spreads over all its surroundings, inasmuch as the man of *nhan,* who stands firm himself, strengthens others; he understands the duties, and instructs others in them.

Thus the practice of *nhan* (*jen*) consists of consideration for others: the positive aspect is *trung* (Chinese, *chung*), or doing to others what you wish for yourself, and the negative aspect is *thu* (*shu*), or not doing to others what you do not wish for yourself. According to another disciple of Confucius, Trinh Hao (Ch'eng Hao), *jen* even embraces all the other cardinal virtues (discussed below): *nghia* (*yi*); *le* (*li*); *tri* (*chi*); and *tin* (*hsin*).[124]

Nghia is the formal essence of the duties and is opposed to *loi* (*li*), or profit. If duty prevails over interest, there will be peace; if not, disorder will ensue. *Nghia* applies to the five fundamental relationships in the following manner: the father should be affectionate and the son pious (*phu tu tu hieu*); the older brother should be good, the younger brother respectful (*huynh luong de de*); the husband should be equitable and the wife obedient (*phu nghia phu thinh*); old people should be benevolent, and the young people obliging (*truong hue au thuan*); and the prince should be humanitarian and his subjects faithful (*quan nhan than trung*). Moreover, *nghia* is the feeling of dignity, the feeling of personal value which causes a man to prefer death to shame.[125]

Le (*li*) are rules of conduct; although all people desire and hate the same things, men still need co-operation and mutual support. Rules of conduct are designed to avoid confusion and disorder, to restrain the conflicting desires.[126] In the earlier sense of the word, *le* refers comprehensively to the ceremonies that man performs in honor of the spirits; later it came to refer to moral and social rules. It regulates formally the five human relationships fundamentally governed by *nghia*. These rules, however, must not be confused with the *phap* (*fa*), or law; the essential difference is that *le* recommends good actions, while the law forbids bad ones.

If the *le* constitutes the external rules of conduct, in order to make life in society possible and pleasant, the *tin* (*hsin*) is an interior moral quality striving for the same goal: a man who does not have good faith resembles a wagon without a tongue; without a tongue, the wagon cannot be drawn, and without respect for his word, man cannot maintain his social relationships. Man is secure only to the extent that the men with whom he deals observe their contracts with him, and he commits the worst imprudence if he himself overthrows the barrier which protects him against the violence and disloyalty of others.[127]

Wisdom. Although *tri* (*chih*) was included by his commentators in *nhan*, Confucius originally regarded it as a separate virtue. This virtue permits man to distinguish truth from falsehood and good from evil. Man attains *tri*, first, by examining carefully the nature of things in order to determine their reason for existence, and then by studying men thoroughly, in order to know himself as well as others: "The man who knows distant things through things close at hand, who knows customs through their origins, who knows subtle things through obvious things, that man can attain virtue." [128]

The principal obstacle to understanding the truth is that man is often egotistical and egocentric; he must strive to be impersonal and impartial; he must not allow his anger toward one matter to affect his attitude toward others. On the other hand, the understanding of things embraces both *ly* (*li*), which is the first principle of the essence of things, and which exists for each thing, and *khi* (*ch'i*), which is the matter and form of things. The understanding of things implies an effort of meditation, but it must also be an effort of action inasmuch as after having acquired the knowledge of things, the wise man hastens to enlighten others.[129]

This active part of wisdom was particularly brought to light by a remote disciple of Confucius, Vuong Duong Minh (Wang Yang-ming), whose name is linked with the doctrine *tri hanh hop nhat* ("knowledge and action are but one").[130] Before Vuong Duong Minh it was customary to separate the concepts of knowledge and action, to regard them as two successive phenomena: it is important that man understand before acting. For Vuong Duong Minh, however, knowledge is the beginning of action. Without its metaphysical aspects, this doctrine contributes to making the administrator more active as soon as he receives knowledge of a fact or is aware of a situation.

Courage. Action implies a third moral virtue: courage. In reality, this virtue goes beyond action to include the domain of thought as well. Indeed, for Confucius, courage is not a brutal release of energy which leads the individual to risk death regardless of the goal to be attained. It supposes that danger is foreseen and appreciated, and that man does not confront it without a full awareness of his need. Thus, courage also implies judgment; it must serve the practicing of the other virtues, either in order to overcome man's own desires or to say or write the truth, even if it displeases others.[131]

Tuan Tu makes the distinction between three sorts of courage, in descending order: [132] (1) *Thuong dung* is superior courage, and consists of being firm in one's moral attitude, in not following blindly an imprudent leader in troubled times, nor the evil tendencies of the people. The courageous man shares the joys and sorrows of those who open their hearts to him; if others are not open with him, he will stand firm without fear. (2) *Trung dung* is intermediate courage, and consists of keeping one's word, scorning worldly goods, openly praising the wise man, and spurning the evil man. (3) *Ha dung* is the inferior courage, which consists in preferring wealth to one's own person, placing interest above duty, and in seeking to win over others at any price.

If all administrators cannot hope to achieve the qualities of *thuong dung*, at least they should have those of *trung dung*. An administrator inspired solely by *ha dung* will be a poor administrator.

The Idea of Public Interest. These three social virtues that should inspire the civil servant permit him to devote himself to the public interest. The public interest was identified with the natural order, since disruptions of the natural order were evident to the population: *Thien thi tu nga dan thi, thien thinh tu nga dan thinh* ("If the heavens see, the population also sees; if the heaven hears, the population also hears"). From this it devolves that: *dan chi so hieu hieu chi, dan chi so o o chi* ("the administrator should love what the people love, and hate what the people hate").[133]

The application of these virtues to the administration of the country must not be considered a thing of the past. In outlining the principal traits of the current administrative philosophy, it has already been shown that the Vietnamese government seeks to revive Confucian ethics in the minds of its civil servants.[134]

The Directorate-General of Civil Service has prepared a manual for civil servants, in which it is made clear that the civil service is established on a moral as well as a judicial basis, and that thus the administrator is at the same time a servant of the state and an educator of the people.[135] Similarly, at the province level the province chiefs have the opportunity of applying the Confucian principles of the superior man in their many contacts with the district chiefs, the chiefs of provincial services, and the people.[136] The district chief does not forget his ritual role in official ceremonies,[137] nor does he forget to appeal to the gentry, as did the mandarin scholars of former times.[138] But, in spite of all the political and social upheaval, it is particularly at the village level that tradition remains strong. The village council always plays a certain role, if not a pre-eminent one, in village ceremonies; it is always the indispensable agent of arbitration in the settlement of disputes, whether they concern property damage, physical conflicts, marital problems, or land disputes.[139]

To the casual observer, to speak of arbitration or to describe the role of the official in ceremonies seems a far cry from the ethical approach to the decision-making process. However, if it is kept in mind that Confucian philosophy completely assimilates virtue and rites, the leader and the head of the family, it is easy to understand that the exhortations of the government for the practice of virtue are not without sound basis or without influence on the behavior of the civil servants and on the decision-making process.

Reconciliation of the Traditional Ethics with the New Concept of the Role of the Administrator.   The importance attached to the personality and character of the leader in the decision-making process is not, moreover, simply the product of a diffuse or prismatic society. An important part of the administrative literature of industrialized countries, in which administration is specialized and compartmentalized, always recognizes that the problem of moral leadership, although it must be regarded as situational, still remains important in the decision-making process. One author has pointed out that "the administrator is not as a rule seeking power"; he performs his work often guided by an ideal. "The best administrator is the man of the most character, of independence and integrity; he is one who is principled; feeling deeply, he is often able to convey his beliefs and his enthusiasm to others." [140] It would be difficult to express better the idea of *nhan* in Oriental philosophies.

Another author has emphasized the human relations aspect of leadership, in the sense of co-ordinating and motivating individuals and groups to achieve desired ends. The leader must recognize that human motivation rests upon immediate social values rather than upon economic or individual appeal. In the most proficient units, the methods of supervision include less direct control of supervisors by their superiors and more emphasis on employee interest than on production goals. Individuals respond more fully when treated as individuals. [141] This is another aspect of *nhan;* in the relationships of the leader with his subordinates, persuasive methods are preferable to formal authority in the new democratic leadership, just as they are in Confucian teachings, practiced for thousands of years by Oriental people.

The idea of *tri* seems to be interpreted on the administrative level in the following manner: "a need of the executive for the future is for broad interests and wide imagination and understanding; therefore rigorous training in subjects of intellectual difficulty, thereby to provide himself with the tools and the mental habits for dealing with important problems." [142] "Leaders have been found to excel over the average members of their group in intelligence, scholarship, dependability, social participation, and socio-economic status." [143]

Dung, or courage in the Confucian sense, is also highly regarded by major authors who have studied the qualities demanded of the leader. "Morals are personal forces or propensities of a general and stable character in individuals which tend to inhibit, control, or modify inconsistent immediate specific desires, impulses, or interests, and to intensify those which are consistent with such propensities.[144] Another author has described more forcefully other aspects of the courage of the leader to be found in the Confucian superior man. "The need to maintain his own respect for himself was more important to him than his popularity with others. . . . His desire to win or maintain a reputation for integrity and courage was stronger than his desire to maintain his office. . . . His conscience, his personal standard of ethics, his integrity or morality were stronger than the pressures of public disapproval. . . . His faith that *his* course was the best one, and would ultimately be vindicated, outweighed his fear of public reprisal." [145]

The idea of public interest has been the object of considerable doctrinal controversy for Western political scientists. The rationalistic theories identify the public interest with the interest of the majority as expressed by the public vote; thus it is the majority political parties who determine the official public interest at any given moment. On the other hand, realistic theories preach that the supreme virtue of the democratic system is the multiplicity of points of access that it affords for the manifold conflicting interest; the public official is then a catalyst by means of which conflict among special interests is transformed into public interest. These theories contrast with the idealistic theories, which regard the public as an inadequate, incompetent source of policy, and contend that the public interest is formulated by the administrators, taking for granted a highly moral official world.[146] The idealistic theory seems to express in modern scientific terms the teachings of Confucius and of Mencius.

The conclusion arising from this ethical study of the decision-making process is that the role of the leaders remains important in this process, especially in the context of Vietnamese administration. This conclusion is confirmed, moreover, by a recent investigation undertaken by the National Institute of Administration; according to this investigation, the principal wish of administrators is, above all, to be guided by just and upright leaders, who know their personnel and who occupy a status above that of their personnel.[147]

Conclusion

The simultaneous consideration of the social factors of the administrative decision (the social environment and the legal framework) and the individual factors concerning the decision maker (his personality and his ethics) bring up the question of the extent to which decision making is an intellectual or an institutionalized process in the context of Vietnamese administration. In the first stage of the decision, the civil servant responsible for assembling the factual elements of the decision is too close to reality not to be strongly influenced by environmental factors and also too close to be able to be completely free from the influence of emotional factors which disturb the eye witness. At a higher level, in the calm of his office, the administrator will be able to examine the situation more coldly, and devise more objective solutions even though the affair has lost a certain immediate quality. Going higher up the administrative ladder, other considerations of an impersonal nature are added: a legal expert may have given his opinion from a judicial point of view, a finance official may have studied the possible financial repercussions of each alternate solution. At the final stage, the affair is brought to the knowledge of the superior chief along with other more or less complicated matters. It may reach his full attention or it may be inundated in the daily flood of matters awaiting his decision each day. With a highly hierarchical administration, it must be admitted that the leader often merely chooses among the many alternatives presented by the line and staff members, indicating with varying degrees of precision the probable consequences of each alternative. Thus, it is indeed essentially a question of an institutionalized process.

Nevertheless, at each stage, a certain number of factors of an intellectual process can be discerned. The first civil servant who gathers firsthand information may deliberately or unintentionally omit certain elements or emphasize certain factors rather than others. The same thing may occur at all other levels, where each administrator, according to his own convictions, passes on only the information he considers necessary to present to the higher authority. In the same way, the solution proposed for each problem depends partly on the temperament of the author of the proposition, even if it is only in the choice of the various alternatives presented by the staff. It is precisely because of the consideration given to the intellectualized process that Vietnamese administrative philosophy emphasizes the formation of the character of the administrator according to Confucian standards.

It must be pointed out that if the government of the First Republic was attempting to revive Confucian principles, it was because during the French domination these precepts were somewhat cast aside. The ritualism of the ancient philosophy, which existed only on certain solemn occasions in the administrative life (New Year's Day, the installation of the mandarin, etc.), had become a stereotyped formality in the daily activity. The emphasis was much more on formal authority associated with a given position regardless of the personal characteristics of the individual who might occupy the position at any given moment. For the Vietnamese, importance is always attached to the human and psychological factor in the decision-making process, even without systematic reference to tradition, and the student of administration must give special consideration to this factor in order to understand the behavior of the administrator of today.

CHAPTER 8

COMMUNICATION AND CONTROL

> Responsibility is the property of an individ-
> ual by which whatever morality exists in
> him becomes effective in conduct.[1]

THE MANY complex factors which contribute to an administrative decision give rise to two questions. The first concerns communication: considering the variety of problems and the variety of sources of information concerning these problems, how are these elements to be brought to the attention of the administrator at the proper time and place, so that the decision may be made? Even after it is made, how is the decision to be brought to the attention of the party or parties concerned, in order to assure a maximum of understanding of the decision, so that its execution may be as effective as possible? The second question involves the validity of the decision itself, since a decision concerning such complex problems runs the risk of being a poor one, even when the administrator has the best of intentions. How can effective control be organized so that administrative decisions endowed with a maximum of effectiveness with respect to public interest may be obtained?

Regarding the problems of representative government in Southeast Asia, one author made the following comment, which deserves consideration in the analysis of the problems of communication and control in developing countries:

> While recognizing that the fundamental condition for lasting and meaningful advance is the winning of the active understanding and participation of the people concerned, one should not ignore the element of danger . . . in having to submit new and complex programs to the detailed approval or control by a local electorate that cannot be assumed to have the information and experience on which to base intelligent decision.[2]

Communication

Since the ultimate goal of administration is national development, the various measures taken by the administrator must take root among the people and must be directed in the long run to the public interest. The first problem of communication, for a developing country, is to ascertain whether there are adequate means of communication to assure this two-way flow of information. Means of communication include both the infra-structure serving the various means of transportation and the various social institutions that permit the exchange or propagation of ideas. These material means of communication are distinguished from the intellectual means, which consist principally of language, the meaning of which, even within the context of a national community, often varies according to the social class, the locality, and the point of view of the speakers.

Regarded from this broad point of view, naturally the problem of communication goes beyond the framework of a simple study of public administration. Consequently, this problem will be treated here only to the extent that such treatment aids in understanding the problems of administrative communications, conceived according to the direction of the communication,[3] i.e., communications coming from or directed toward the exterior of the administrative system (communication in the input-output system) and communication within the administrative system (communication in the throughput system). In both cases, it must be pointed out that, in a developing country, a seriously inadequate system of communications (mass-media communications, in particular) combines with the underdeveloped state of social organization to make the expression of the needs of the population difficult and, at the same time, to hinder the efficient execution of government policy.[4]

COMMUNICATION FACILITIES

Channels of Communication.   The imperial administrative system was completely adapted to the available means of communication, which, reduced to their simplest expression were: poor roads, badly equipped waterways, a population largely scattered in the country, and a very small number of persons living in urban communities.[5] The kings had at their disposal neither the technical knowledge nor the financial means for making more than the slightest improvements in this system. As a result, the flow of communication between the capital and the interior of the country was necessarily at a strict minimum.

There was, however, a carefully organized postal service. Placed under the authority of the Ministry of Justice in the capital and of the provincial judges (*an sat*) in the provinces, the postal service consisted of a brigade of runners (*linh tram*), each of whom was responsible for a specific sector of the road. These runners were furnished by the villages; they carried the mail on foot. Along the mandarinal roads which went from the provinces to the capital, however, there were relay stations (*tram*) for the mounted couriers (*ma thuong*). These couriers had priority on all ferry boats. The person of the *linh tram* was protected by special laws that provided severe punishment for anyone who attempted to harm him.[6] This is probably why the postal service was placed under the authority of the Ministry of Justice.

Another means of rapid communication was the use of gongs. From prehistoric times, the ancestors of the Vietnamese have known how to use bronze gongs to announce festivals or danger. A person who has not lived in the rural areas cannot appreciate the emotion caused by the five successive series of gong beats (*trong ngu lien*) that announced approaching danger, e.g., a break in the dike or an act of piracy, or simply the regular beat of the tom tom that preceded the arrival of a mandarin, an event calling for a celebration in the village. Gong signals were transmitted from village to village according to very strict conventions.

The French developed the channels of communication by improving the system of roads so as to make them accessible to automobiles; by outfitting ports for ships and river boats; by building railroads, particularly the Indochinese railroad that connected the northern and southern borders; and even by creating an airport near the capital of each country of the Indochinese Union. All these improvements, however, affected only communication between the major cities and the capital. Communication with the villages was still difficult; it depended on roads that were not accessible to automobiles, many of which were under water during a part of the year. Of course, there was still the postal service, which served even individuals in isolated rural regions, where, in the absence of other means of transportation, the *phu tram* (postman) carried mail on foot or on bicycles. The telegraph and the telephone were still not widely used in rural communities; here the traditional gong was still used for communication.

After the country became independent, the lack of security in the rural regions and the systematic sabotaging of communications by Communists made communication more difficult in some parts of the country, particularly the marshy regions and the remote areas. Consequently, the government has made carefully organized efforts to improve the various communications channels—roads, navigable waterways, railroads, and airways—between the capital and the larger urban centers of the interior, even including a number of villages. Similarly, great improvements have been made in the postal and telecommunications services in the last few years, particularly through the installation of a radiotelephone and radiotelegraph system.[7]

This improvement in communication has permitted an intensive exchange of men and ideas among the different parts of the country, particularly within the administrative system, and has provided a means of rapid exchange of information and instructions among various administrative authorities. It has also permitted the development of mass-media communications.

Mass-Media Communication. Under the monarchy, the state of the channels of communication made it difficult to organize the propagation of ideas and news among the populace in any framework broader than that of the village community.

There did exist at that time a public opinion at the village level, made possible by personal visits, family meetings, encounters in the village market, ritual meetings in the *dinh* (hall), and religious meetings. The more important religious festivals or periodic fairs even brought together people from neighboring villages, but only at rare intervals; it was generally only on these occasions that communication went beyond the bamboo hedge which surrounded the village. On the other hand, meetings for studying commentaries on the classics occurred regularly in those villages where there was a well-known master and at the district and province seats, where mandarins always offered the official instruction. Also, the mandarinal examinations held every three years permitted students to meet periodically in the capital. It was on these occasions that a nation-wide public opinion developed—in the *thanh nghi,* or discussion meetings; however, this expression was limited to the literati.[8] The literati (*si;* Chinese, *shih*) was a class of superior men (*quan tu*) who governed or helped to govern, whereas the function of the other classes (farmers, artisans, merchants, etc.) was to produce goods or to render service. This was a division of labor according to the nature of the activity: the mental type of work, on the one hand, and the physical type, on the other. Mental labor was linked with governing, i.e., the proper ordering of people and of their activities, peace and harmony. It was expected that this group would be served and supported by the groups performing physical work. It was both a privilege and a duty of the literati to form an enlightened opinion and to spread it.[9] By means of education, this opinion was transmitted to the students, some of whom were already grown; by means of advice given to the common people who never failed to consult the scholars on important matters of personal and family life, this opinion was even transmitted to the populace, although rather haphazardly. Thus it can be seen how, in much earlier times, the Vietnamese kings succeeded in mobilizing the patriotism of the people in order to resist successfully the Chinese invasions, as, for example, at the meeting at Dien Hong (*hoi nghi Dien Hong*), when King Tran Nhan Ton convened a people's council to decide whether or not to resist the Mongols.[10]

On the arrival of the French, the literati, who did not give up their leadership, continued to mobilize public opinion through teaching and through secret meetings. From time to time, a patriotic song was written secretly and taught to strolling singers. These singers, who were often blind or otherwise handicapped and relied on their singing for their livelihood, spread the song from village to village until apprehended by a zealous administrator. The intelligentsia, on the other hand, were able to assume control of a means of mass communication introduced by the French: the press. The Vietnamese press began timidly, with translations of articles or extracts from works in Chinese or French; later it published original articles on uncontroversial aspects of social life, and, finally, it produced articles on cultural problems or criticisms of customs. Publications in French, edited by Vietnamese, even discussed the policy of assimilation or the policy of association. The awakening of public opinion began to take official form; however, the press was very strictly censored.

In Viet-Nam in 1962 there were already more than 100 newspapers and magazines. These newspapers, with an average circulation of 20,000—the largest attains a circulation of 80,000—are, for the most part, in Vietnamese (17 of the largest are in Vietnamese; 13 in other languages) and give mostly news of the day; they also often contain editorials reflecting a part of public opinion.[11] The opinion of the more advanced portion of the populace is expressed in literary or scientific periodicals. After the November 1 Revolution, the number of newspapers increased greatly: at the beginning of 1964, 40 new newspapers had been authorized, and an additional 34 requests were still under advisement.[12] It is characteristic that most of the periodicals are published in Saigon; it can be assumed that the opinion of the rural population is not sufficiently represented by the press. It is also characteristic that there are certain legal restrictions regarding the freedom of the press: the publishing of certain items is forbidden, including documents concerning criminal affairs, secrets regarding national defense, exhortations to revolt, foreign political propaganda, etc. During the First Republic, permission from administrative authorities had to be obtained before the publication of periodicals; and, although prior censorship has been annulled for newspapers in Vietnamese, this is not true for publications in foreign languages.[13] The government of the First Republic had certain means of sanction for the newspapers that violated the regulations, such as suspension of authorization to publish or control of distribution through the distributing agency, Nha Phat Hanh Thong Nhat.[14] This control was so stringently exercised during the First Republic that after the Revolution of November 1, 1963, there occurred a veritable explosion of opinions by a press freed from all restraint. Such disorganized, malicious, and destructive criticism appeared in certain newspapers that the Provisional Government was obliged to reinstate the severe sanctions provided by law regarding the press (withdrawal of authorization to publish, confiscation of malicious publications, etc.). At the request of the publishers themselves, the freedom of the press was solemnly declared in the *Décret-loi* of February 19, 1964, which also provides severe penalties for "tenden-

cious information, inaccurate news; false news intended to create
dissension among the religious groups, geographical areas, and
races; publication to harm public decency. . . .[15] A new *Décret-loi*,
No. 10/64, dated May 1, 1964, created a Press Council "to protect the
freedom of the press, to maintain a national discipline among the
members of the press, and to carry out the journalistic code to be
drawn up by the Council." [16] For example, the Press Council has
decided that no newspapers can be made available to the public
before three o'clock in the afternoon; some newspapers offered for
sale in prohibition of this regulation were confiscated. Criticism has
been raised that *Décret-loi* No. 10/64 poses too many restrictions, such
as the requirements that a bond be posted, and that the editors must
have journalism degrees before publication is authorized.[17]

Another means of mass communication is the radio broadcast.
Since the radio is a government monopoly, and all broadcasts come
from government centers, this must be considered an instrument of
information and propaganda for the government, or at least a means
of civic education of the masses. During the First Republic, however,
the law provided for strict equality among the candidates in the pre-
election utilization of the radio for campaigning. Practically speaking, the use of this means of mass communication is limited to the
communities which have electric current (the capital, the province
seats, and a few villages), although, in theory, transistor radios could
be used. The government is at present attempting to increase the
reach of radio broadcasts by equipping the villages and hamlets with
receivers given through American aid.

Other means of mass communication have less spectacular
immediate effects: the distribution of books, circulars, and tracts;
the movies; the theater; and other literary and artistic manifestations. These also appear to a far greater degree in the capital and
other urban centers than in the rural areas.

It must not be supposed that mass-media communication has
completely supplanted the traditional word-of-mouth method of
spreading opinions, especially in the rural regions. The Viet Cong
makes effective use of a variation of this method for counterpropaganda: the most unlikely rumors are whispered around, and
gain credulity largely because of their being clandestine.

It can be seen from this outline that mass-media communication is still inadequate as far as the formation of a really
enlightened and impartial nationwide opinion is concerned, although
the present communications system constitutes a substantial improvement over that which existed just before the political independence of the country. However, some consolation lies in the fact that
even in industrialized countries, defects in communication and
control persist; ". . . the extent of poor communication despite the

excellent technical media of transmission is one of the great ironies of our time." [18]

Readiness and Receptivity of Communications. Laboratory experiments show that a person who makes a communication always wishes to simplify it and to make its conveyance as pleasant and/or painless as possible for the receiver. This psychological disposition alone alters the information transmitted. Moreover, it is always assumed that words are used in only one way, and that inferences are always distinguishable from observations, but in reality these assumptions have yet to be verified.[19] The linguistic and psychological problem of communication in Viet-Nam will be treated in the light of these considerations.

Insofar as the use of written or spoken symbols is concerned, the meaning of words varies according to the circumstances, the time, or the place; according to the cultural background of the person expressing them and of the person receiving them. It is not necessary to take as examples such words as "democracy" or "liberty," which take on different meanings depending on the ideology that inspires their use. In the more restricted domain of administration, the terms "urgent" and "efficient," for example, also vary according to the public services concerned, and according to whether the action takes place in the capital or in the country. These different interpretations of a single word can lead to misunderstandings and mistakes in administrative decisions.

In order to avoid these very misunderstandings, Confucius preached the doctrine of rectification of names, urging people to designate things and ideas by their correct names, in the commonly accepted senses. Without ever using the word *communication,* Confucius made the idea of communication the basis of administrative systems.[20]

With the proliferation of new concepts, the Vietnamese language, the development of which was delayed to a certain extent during the colonial period, has taken a tremendous step forward since independence. In order to stabilize the new vocabulary and to integrate it into the national culture, the work of educating future generations is not sufficient; contemporaries must be educated as well. Much effort has been put forth to give each word a precise definition, by establishing Vietnamese dictionaries, also bilingual and trilingual dictionaries that compare Vietnamese words with English and French words. Since civil servants in administration must also possess a substantial and precise vocabulary, the study sessions (*hoc tap*) and the in-service training sessions (*tu nghiep*) are making an appreciable contribution. However, in this extreme concern for giving each word its own precise meaning, there is one danger which cannot always be avoided. Even in earlier times, certain Confucian scholars were reproached for attaching too much importance to the letter, to the neglect of the spirit, so that the studies became scholastic and the administration became formalistic. Attaching an inviolable meaning to the word freezes the thought. The concern of those administrators who have not really penetrated the spirit of the law may be reflected in the current tendency to respect excessively the letter of the laws and regulations. Similarly, the developing, in each sphere of activity, of a jargon which pretends to be technical, while it gives greater precision in the expression of ideas, makes more difficult communication between services and circles concerned with different activities.

In another respect, the meaning given to words by the superior authorities may be understood differently by their inferiors, who, because of the difference in the degree of education and in the attitude toward social life at different levels, converse with each other in a more primitive version of the vernacular. This is obvious when the central, provincial, and district administrations, where the civil servants have at least received a secondary education, are contrasted to the communal administration, where the workers have usually had only a primary education. But it is particularly striking where the mass of the population is concerned, despite the success of the anti-illiteracy campaign.

At present, the average citizen is scarcely equipped with the minimum essentials of a civic education: the skills of communication to meet the new situation; knowledge and understanding of co-operative and creative thinking, and of shared rather than individual decision making; and attitudes and outlooks necessary for the new responsibility.[21]

Mention should also be made of the problem posed by the region of origin of the civil servant: although Vietnamese is spoken throughout the nation, there are still certain regional accents, as well as certain dialectical words used only in specific localities. This difference in language was very evident when a large part of the population of the North came to settle in South Viet-Nam. Although the difference is by now considerably mitigated, due to education and to the intermingling of persons of different origins, the civil servants who must have frequent contacts with the population, particularly those who are responsible for communicating government policy to the people, are chosen when possible from candidates of the same region of origin as the people they are to serve.

Lastly, the greatest obstacle to communication in Viet-Nam seems to rest in the propaganda and the subversive activities of the Communists. By means of threats, Communist agents try to prevent people living in remote areas from expressing their ideas freely and from giving information necessary to the accomplishment of administrative goals.[22] In addition, a systematic and artful counterpropaganda tends to deform the best intentions of the administrative leaders. Illegal opposition parties, acting in secret, may exert the same pernicious influence, although on a smaller scale. The desire for safety, for being protected against reprisals, particularly in the rural regions, explains why certain information given reflects only partial reality.

These remarks partly confirm the results of studies made in an industrialized country, but the plausible reasons for this behavior are certainly different. These reasons will be examined in detail in the course of an analysis of communications between the environment and the administrative system as contrasted to communications within the administrative system.

COMMUNICATION BETWEEN THE ENVIRONMENT AND THE ADMINISTRATIVE SYSTEM

In order to assure communication between the environment and the administrative system, means of communication are set up either individually or through groups.

Communication as a Means of Input in the Administrative System. In early days, an individual might approach an administrator directly, either in his office or in the course of public visits, to present requests or to make suggestions. In order to determine the wishes of the people, some of the Tran kings traveled incognito to make inspection tours in the villages; they were even mistreated on occasion. For the same purpose, royal censors were sent across the country, leading to unpleasant surprises for dishonest mandarins.

It has been shown that under the monarchy, a certain public opinion developed, particularly within the framework of the village, on the occasion of public meetings. This opinion could even be expressed by means of associations or groups. Associations were, as a matter of fact, quite widespread in Viet-Nam under the monarchy, at least within the framework of the village.[23] Often, however, they attempted to satisfy by their own means the needs of their members, and did not generally attempt to influence the communal authorities. Influencing the communal authorities was rather the work of the village elders, as members of the village council. These elders were either retired former mandarins, holders of academic degrees who did not occupy administrative posts, rich and powerful men, or former communal authorities. In general, the elders made important decisions directly, and the communal authorities merely executed their decisions.

At the higher echelons, such as the district and the province, the expression of the public will was made, not by means of associations, but through the literati. The duty of the literati was to govern, but since within this class only those who had passed the examinations could actually govern, the others were left the duty of advising those in power. They remained in permanent contact with the population of their villages, cantons, or districts; they were the natural representatives of this population in informing the administrators of the wishes of the people.

Among the local literati were some who did not limit their activities to giving advice; they made a profession of helping the mandarin write his reports or decisions on various matters. They did not constitute an integral part of the bureaucracy, since they were not officially appointed, but, in practice, they were benevolent assistants (*nho*), paid according to a *douceur* system by individuals who had dealings with the administrator. They tended to become a class by themselves, with vested interests and considerable power over the ordinary business of the government, as is shown by the old Vietnamese proverb: *Quan xa ban nha gan* ("The mandarin is inaccessible, but the offices of the mandarin are close to the people.")[24]

The literati were more numerous in the capital of the kingdom or of the empire: young students seeking famous masters, old scholars disillusioned by successive failures in the examinations, retired mandarins, educated men of high reputation, educated foreigners seeking refuge in Viet-Nam, and so on. Because of the many relations which the court mandarins had with these literati, the opinion of the elite was transmitted more or less accurately to the prime minister or even to the king. It must be said, however, that these were only broad opinions regarding administration in general, and rarely expressed specific proposals for administrative action.

It is still possible today for the individual to express his wishes for consideration by the administration. The greater part of the time of the communal authorities is spent settling differences between individuals.[25] The offices of the district chiefs and of the province chiefs are flooded with requests. Similarly, the General Office for People's Suggestions and Complaints (like the "Mailbox Service" instituted in the Office of the Presidency during the First Republic) serves as a communication link between the individual and the highest authority of the state. However, although a given individual case might be sufficiently indicative of a general state of mind, or might present concretely a universalistic wish, in his general decisions the administrator can seldom take into consideration individual cases. This is just as true of the intelligentsia which replaced the literati. As an individual, he did not enjoy the same social position that the literati had, and could influence the administrator only to a slight extent. However, public opinion still continued to place its hope in the intelligentsia, and more than one bitter voice was heard to express its disappointment that the intelligentsia had failed to play its intended role as standard-bearer.[26]

The truth is that the role of the individual in the formation of public opinion which might influence the administration has progressively decreased with the development of mass-media communication. This has been particularly true since the November 1 Revolution. The newspapers have demanded that the overzealous collaborators of the Ngo Dinh Diem regime be punished,[27] that there be a closer collaboration between civilians and the military,[28] or that the Revolutionary Government be replaced by a government headed by a civilian.[29] However, certain individuals still make use of mass media to express personal opinions on similarly personal matters. Indeed, it was observed in the first months after the November 1 Revolution that the most virulent articles appearing in the press against the former regime were often mere outbursts of personal resentment. Even though such a declaration expresses only an individual opinion, its scope is often amplified by these means, and may create broad movements of opinion, since the masses, with insufficient civic education, sometimes follow a movement without question. This can, on occasion, cause a panic and put the administrative authorities in a difficult position; for example, the false denunciation of an official, the spreading of a rumor concerning the devaluation of the piaster, or passing the word that a certain political party intends to take over the government by force. This is also true of certain agencies of the foreign press, which strive for sensational effects, even at the expense of public security, for which they are not responsible.

Even today individuals as sources of information grow increasingly important in Viet-Nam. A great part of the information through the press stems from individuals rather than from groups. The importance of the groups, however, should not be underestimated in the matter of expressing and transmitting their interpretations of the public will to the administrative authorities, as has been shown in Chapter 7.

Associations can use mass-media communications or they may enter into direct contact with the administration in order to introduce problems of general or special interest.

The administrative questions thus brought up often fall within the jurisdiction of the Ministry of the Interior and of the province chiefs, particularly since, whenever public security is concerned, these agencies must intervene. The specialized ministries maintain a more continuous and more technical contact with corresponding associations—the Ministry of Labor with labor unions, the Ministry of Rural Affairs with the agricultural associations and the co-operatives, the Department of Education with the Association of Parents of Students and other cultural associations.

Of course, questions of general public interest can be presented to the Office of the Prime Minister, particularly through political or economic associations. Special mention should be made also of the Ministry of Information, which is responsible for making a detailed study of the daily press and of periodicals for the entire government, although each ministry also has its own press service for distilling from this information the possible elements for administrative decision. The Ministry of Information and these press services play a more important role as means of output.

Communication as a Means of Output. In addition to the regular administrative means of communication (publication in official journals, or notification through administrative channels of individual decisions), the government of the First Republic systematically organized services whose role was essentially to communicate to the people the major decisions made concerning the general policy, and to prepare the people psychologically to assist in the effective execution of these decisions. In order to co-ordinate the activities of all these communications services, the post of Secretary of State of Civic Action was created May 28, 1961, and given authority over three agencies formerly dependent directly on the Office of the President: the Commissariat of Civic Action, the Directorate-General of Information, and the Directorate-General for Youth. The principal objective of the office of the Secretary of State of Civic Action was the effective mobilization of the spirit and will of the people, beginning with the rural infra-structure, with respect to the struggle against communism and to national reconstruction.[30]

The cadres of civic action, organized into mobile teams in each province, had the mission of explaining and spreading government policy in the rural areas, which are the most remote and the most exposed to Communist counterpropaganda. They used the traditional means of communication: meetings in which the various classes of people of each village were grouped in order to discuss government programs of an economic, social, or political nature; sessions of community development work in which they participated directly or gave advice; instruction courses which were part of the struggle against illiteracy; and the distribution of tracts and brochures presenting the desired message in simple terms. They helped the people organize family groups, they campaigned for the provision of food for urban centers and explained to the people their duty to pay taxes regularly, and they assisted in the setting up of strategic hamlets.

The Directorate-General of Information worked toward the same goals as the Commissariat of Civic Action—the diffusing of information on government policies—but used different means of action. This service utilized the most modern techniques of mass-media communications: radio broadcasts, the moving electric news sign, and motion pictures. It tried to influence the press in a direction favorable to the understanding of government policies; it had at its disposition the National Printing Office for the printing of tracts, pamphlets, slogans, posters, communiqués, and daily or weekly bulletins. From the capital down to the hamlets, the Directorate-General of Information itself organized or helped in the organization of information centers in which all the afore-mentioned documents were made available to the public. This pattern, however, did not relieve the agents of the Directorate of Information from making visits to the villages, in co-operation with the agents of the Commissariat of Civic Action or with the youth associations.

Although the clientele of the Directorate-General for Youth Activities was more limited than that of the Directorate-General of Information, its activities were more far-reaching, in the sense that it encouraged and aided in the formation of youth groups which assumed the mission of guardians of the Constitution, as well as the mission of promoting the social, economic, and military revolution, of creating a new society. These youth groups were given the mission of aiding in the application of certain parts of the national policy: strategic hamlets, public security, civic formation, and physical education. The great importance of using these youth groups as means of communication is obvious in the light of the active role the chiefs of these groups played in the elections for administrative councils of the hamlets and the villages.[31]

It should be noted that in the course of the discussion concerning the 1962 budget of this department, the deputies recognized the effectiveness of the cadres of the Commissariat of Civic Action, but found that the Directorate-General of Information had not been able to realize its basic program, i.e., it was not able to organize adequate information services at the district and village levels. Similarly, some criticism was expressed regarding certain cadres of the Directorate-General for Youth Activities in the performance of their duties.[32] One author points out that poorly prepared propaganda may give the farmers the impression that they are being pushed by government agents into a repugnant program.[33]

An interesting example of inadequacy of downward communications is a survey made in 1960 among the population of a province scarcely 50 kilometers from Saigon. This survey showed that 22 per cent of the heads of families had a vague idea of the benefits of American aid in the village; 40 per cent had heard of this aid, but had not recognized any visible evidence of it at the village level; the others answered simply that they had no idea that such aid existed. All of these people regularly use a certain number of products imported as a part of American aid, but which they had to buy at the market (commercial aid); all of them enjoyed a relative security, made possible by the presence of troops armed by the United States and partly paid from counterpart funds provided by commercial aid. Some of them had borrowed money from the Agricultural Bank, part of whose working capital was provided by American aid.[34]

The grouping of these information agencies into a single department did not survive the November 1 Revolution. The Revolutionary Government attaches particular importance to the information services as such, and has grouped them in the Ministry of Information. At one time, the youth activities were given little attention because of a heavier emphasis on sports; later, with the creation of the civil defense organization, they regained importance; at any rate, the role of youth in information seems considerably reduced. The services of the Commissariat for Civic Action were for a time attached to the Commissariat-General of New Rural Life, but, when the latter became the Directorate of New Rural Life, they were simply attached to the Ministry of Information. These successive changes, which might seem to reflect some indecision, nevertheless show that the Revolutionary Government, like its predecessors, considers the problems of communication in the output system especially important.

In a more general way, the organization of the information services falls into the category of the "struggle of government services for existence." Indeed, because of the changing environment and the conflicts of interest which are common phenomena of developing countries, the government must win the support of the general public and of some specific clienteles. In order to accomplish this, the government must arouse the interest of the population in national goals, through group identification. In seeking public support, public information and propaganda must be well organized, effective publicity techniques must be used, and public statements of the administration must be carefully prepared.[35] Information is all the more important in a newly constituted nation, which must remind the people constantly of nation building as a systematic goal of public policy.[36]

Organizing the information services with the mass media, however powerful, is still not enough, particularly in a country where the actual means of communication are insufficient. This explains why the government naturally looks for intermediary groups, within the administrative organization, such as the village in the older regime, the villages and the strategic hamlets during the First Republic, and also outside of the administrative organization, such as the various groups already mentioned as factors of input communication.

Certain authors consider that in a developing country, the creation of interest groups follows bureaucratic initiative and is not a spontaneous product of citizen demands in response to felt needs. The group extends beyond the reach of the bureaucracy, providing it with transmission belts through which total mobilization can potentially be achieved.[37] This remark seems justified to the extent that certain groups were organized entirely at the instigation or because of the systematic encouragement of the government. The government even tried to use them to counterbalance the official bureaucracy, inasmuch as certain political decisions were transmitted directly to the groups instead of through official channels, leading to the observation that there was a certain tendency toward debureaucratization during the Ngo Dinh Diem regime.[38] This view seems exaggerated if we consider the many groups formed spontaneously, the administrative use of which does not seem to differ generally from the practice followed in industrialized countries.[39] These groups remained active after the fall of the First Republic, which is an indication of their vitality.

Mention should also be made of the direct relationship between the public services and the individual citizens themselves: although public relations are not directly intended to make the public understand the administrative measures, they do contribute to this end indirectly by softening the useless shocks created by measures which cause repercussions concerning private interests of individuals.[40]

COMMUNICATIONS WITHIN THE ADMINISTRATIVE SYSTEM:
THE THROUGHPUT SYSTEM

Communications between the administrative system and the exterior constitute its reason for existing. In order to exist, however, the administrative system must organize an internal communication system which permits it to transform elements of information gathered from the outside into decisions capable of influencing the behavior of the people in a way favorable to the goals of the government. In other words, administration can be considered as a communication net which consists physically of a complex of decision centers and channels which seek, receive, transmit, subdivide, classify, store, select, recall, recombine, and retransmit information.[41] Information includes policy statements, letters, memoranda, orders, instructions, directives, suggestions, requests, inquiries, reports, and so on.

It is understood that an effective communications system is almost always an important objective for public administration, whether that administration is conceived to minimize the intervention of the government, as in the old Confucian concept, or for active intervention toward national development. Only those factors of Vietnamese administration which constitute points of friction in the internal communications system will be discussed here.

The Multiplication and Specialization of Services. Since Vietnamese independence the number of agencies has increased remarkably in order to cope with problems totally unknown during the colonial period: care of refugees, agrarian reform, the democratization of institutions, public security and the struggle against Communist subversion, and, particularly since the Revolution of November 1, 1963, political harmony. With the creation of new agencies and the increasing of the responsibilities of the old agencies, it is necessary to transmit information to an ever-increasing number of responsible parties. Moreover, the multiplication of offices strengthens the tendency towards specialization, towards concentrating the attention of the persons responsible on more and more restricted problems. A narrowness of point of view necessarily results from this concentration, which is accentuated by the fact that many civil servants trained during the colonial period were really qualified for performing only the duties of minor officials. When specialization becomes a routine matter, it is not likely to facilitate communication. This disadvantage was remedied during the First Republic by the creation in the Cabinet of the posts of secretaries of state co-ordinators, and particularly by the creation of many interdepartmental committees, interservice committees, and so on. After the Revolution of November 1, 1963, the posts of the co-ordinators were reorganized in the form of offices of the vice prime ministers for Pacification, for Economy and Finance, and for Cultural and Social Affairs. These institutions facilitate verbal communications, since the representatives of the ministries or services concerned present the points of view of the agencies they represent. The question often occurs, however, whether the representatives sent to these committees are really qualified to speak for their agencies. It sometimes happens that proposals or demands made by the representatives are later denied by their ministries, or that the representatives expressing opinions specify that they are personal opinions not binding on their ministries. Under these conditions, the principal objective of the committee, which is to facilitate communications between services, is defeated.

However, the influence of specialization of services must not be exaggerated, since it is tempered by the cadre system applied to the civil service, which permits a civil servant of a given cadre to be transferred into any of several different services. Unlike the position-classification system, which keeps a civil servant in one position until he is promoted, the cadre system, permitting this transfer of personnel, allows the civil servant to develop personal relationships in several different services and to become better acquainted with administrative mechanisms used in those services. To this extent, communications between new and old services can be made more flexible.

The Administrative Hierarchy and the Formation of Classes of Civil Servants. The multiplication of services also requires an elaborate hierarchical organization, particularly because of the tendency toward centralization. The hierarchical organization itself constitutes a communication barrier: at each echelon, information is filtered and polished before being transmitted to the higher echelon; generally speaking, one echelon transmits only information which is favorable to its own interests or which conforms to its outlook. This is particularly true in the territorial administrative organization, where firsthand information is furnished by the hamlets and villages to the district chief, who communicates it to the province chief, who in turn reports to the minister of the interior and to the prime minister. Of course, all information received at the village level is not transmitted integrally to these authorities; they would be completely inundated thereby. The manner of selecting the information to be passed on varies according to the point of view of the informant, but is usually with an eye to what is favorable to himself. The following remark made concerning communications in an industrialized country applies here fully: "Information must percolate through several levels, each of which may include empire builders who consciously modify or subvert higher authority. Furthermore, individuals interpret facts differently and tend to color them in transmission." [42]

As the information works down the hierarchical ladder, there seems to develop a general law that this transmission from superior authorities to lower levels is performed with a vigor that decreases as the position of the informant decreases in importance. In the first place, the central authorities always have too much work to do; they limit themselves, then, to giving instructions, simplifying as much as possible the explanations of measures to be taken. The provincial authorities consider themselves obligated to simplify even more, and, not knowing all the elements of the decision, they tend to interpret them according to local contingency. The district chiefs, having only a limited number of assistants—and assistants who are far from having the education necessary for understanding the instructions of the central authorities—pass on only the details strictly essential for the execution of the instructions. One observer has pointed out that "at this point, the communication process breaks down as a result of channel overload. Messages transmitted to the village chief and his assistant are incomplete and contradictory; transmission becomes even physically impossible, given the communication channel or the administrative and social structure below the village level." [43] Since this same phenomenon exists in industrialized countries, attempts have been made to explain it: reasons of strategy or power; geographical dispersion increasing the difficulties of communication; indifference or unawareness on the part of the executive regarding the need for a widespread sharing of information. The "official secret" is also useful as a means of reinforcing the ego of insecure supervisors. [44]

The idea of classes tends to appear within the bureaucracy, and this tendency is also strengthened by the cadre or rank-classification system. Civil servants within the same cadre or those performing the same functions, even though they perform them in different ministries, tend to group together and to communicate to each other certain information, even when they are reluctant to communicate this same information to civil servants of different cadres or of higher or lower rank within the same service. Thus, a *doc phu su* working in the Ministry of the Interior communicates easily with another *doc phu su* working in the Ministry of National Economy, whereas he would hesitate to talk openly with an engineer working in his own department.

One attempt to counteract this tendency to form classes is the encouragement of the study sessions (*hoc tap*), in which civil servants of different categories sit side by side; this remedy is effective, however, only to the extent that the study sessions are not matters of pure form. On the other hand, the personal studies which are encouraged by the government can also remedy this class spirit effectively: Confucian teachings always encouraged the scholar to mix with the masses for the practice of human-heartedness; modern teachings of administrative science also emphasize the importance of human relations. To the extent that these teachings are followed, hierarchical communications become more flexible and more effective.

Obstacles Resulting from Procedure. One author reports that most civil servants will adhere to fixed procedures even if it means sacrificing common sense and humane principles.[45] To verify this assertion requires a detailed analysis of procedures used in administration; these fall into three categories: one which might be called customary procedures; a second, legal procedures; and a third, technical procedures.

The procedures of the first category are often expressed in the simplest possible manner. The hamlet or village affairs are most frequently handled verbally. Requests addressed to the district chief are usually made in only one copy; decisions are often simply written directly on this copy of the request (for example, various authorizations). Authors who study Vietnamese customs frequently dwell on the importance attached in Viet-Nam to the village, canton, or district seal; this seal has a ritual value and symbolizes the authority vested in the custodian of the seal, but certainly does not imply any complicated procedure.[46] It is only at the province level that procedure begins to become really complicated, because of the intervention of technical services to study administrative problems, and of the need for keeping records of administrative affairs.

At any rate, the ritualistic nature of the imperial administration is not to be confused with the procedural nature of the colonial administration. Two considerations explain this procedural nature. First, the difference of language between the rulers and the people required that all transactions be made in writing, and then translated by interpreters under oath. Second, the judicial background of the French administrators led them to the introduction of strict procedures for investigations and decisions regarding administrative affairs, particularly since these procedures were to serve also as a means of control over the various activities of the subordinate administrative authorities. One consequence of the procedural nature of the colonial administration was formalism, which means the discrepancy between the unenforced rules and the actual practice,[47] since in spite of all the regulations restricting procedures, the natives continued to follow time-honored practices. In view of the fact that, at the time of the establishing of the Republic of Viet-Nam, it was decided that all colonial legislation and regulations then in force would remain in force (except those contrary to the republican system), it must be supposed that the same formalism has continued to exist in certain domains, until such time as new regulations are made to replace the old ones.

The case is different for new institutions for which no provisions existed under colonial regulations. Partly because of the lack of experience of civil servants in the early days of the republic, partly because administration today poses technical problems requiring the assistance of trained technicians, and partly because in certain fields foreign experts introduce procedures used in their own countries, sometimes without realizing that they are not applicable, administrative procedure is becoming more and more complicated, particularly in those services which have regular contacts with foreigners: services for American aid, the foreign trade service, services of the Bank of Viet-Nam, etc. As a result, a new formalism of a technical nature is gradually being superimposed onto the old legalistic formalism.

The progression from the first to the last of these categories of procedure leads to the question whether this increasing tendency to use procedure is a traditionally Vietnamese attitude or simply a badly oriented importation of modern techniques. Indeed, the second conclusion seems more plausible. It should be noted, however, that a more or less successful tendency towards work simplification has been developed in procedure as well as in organization, as is evidenced by the setting up of a high-level commission for studying simplification of the administrative system, and asking the Michigan State University Viet-Nam Advisory Group to make reports on this subject.[48]

In one particularly interesting aspect of its application, procedure was sometimes used to produce a solution purely for appearance, to appease public opinion. It has been reported that under the

Ngo Dinh Diem regime, subordinate authorities often received, secretly or through the official political party, instructions to mitigate the enforcement of certain official decisions.[49] This caused certain critics to say that "the anti-bureaucratization interest has balanced the scales in favor of traditionalistic administration practices." [50] On the other hand, the Revolutionary Government has set out to respect the law scrupulously, to the extent that it is not contrary to the spirit of the revolution; it is to be hoped that the anti-bureaucratization interest is decreasing and that the official procedure of communication is the only one to be followed.

Informal Communication. Recent studies have shown that in addition to formal communication, a certain amount of communication not related to the organizational goal is necessary in order for the system to reach its optimum goal achievement.[51] Thus, in choosing a representative of Viet-Nam for an international conference, consideration is always made of the candidate's position, his technical qualifications, and the work he has accomplished in the field of the conference subject; this information is sent to the chief executive through official channels. However, supplementary information regarding his behavior abroad in the course of previous missions may come from other sources and influence his selection as representative.

Informal information in a throughput system can also be obtained through officials of the formal organization, without going through normal channels; an administrator might find a means of communication in a game of chess or tennis, or at the municipal swimming pool. A more direct way of obtaining informal communications consists of inviting to a party persons capable of giving such information. This, incidentally, was the traditional procedure used by the mandarins when formal communication broke down. It is still used today, and has been used considerably since the November 1 Revolution, while the formal organization is in the process of adjustment. Two striking examples of this are the working methods of the Vice Prime Minister for Pacification and the Director of the General Office for People's Suggestions and Complaints. In spite of the newness of both of these agencies, the work of the personnel is done completely informally. Lastly, information can be obtained from informal groups, whether they are antagonistic or co-operative. These groups are formed within the bureaucracy, as, for example, a group of teachers who have the same special interests, a group of officers who have all studied abroad, or a group of civil servants who regularly have coffee together. Although the informal groups formed recently seem to be of a conservative nature, information received from them can still be useful in making final decisions.[52]

Control of Public Administration

Because of communication difficulties, it is possible that an administrative decision may be made without the administrator's being in full possession of the facts; even supposing that communications were perfect, such a decision might be defective for reasons beyond the scope of the service. For this reason, a well-organized control system has always tended to limit errors or arbitrary elements in the administrative decision. This source of control already existed in imperial administration, the censorate. The censorate had a rather diffuse nature, as can be seen from the following observation, made about the Chinese censorate, but completely applicable to the former Vietnamese censorate as well: "The censorate represents an organized and systematic effort by the government to police itself. The scope of this effort was very broad, encompassing all levels of administration, all governmental personnel, and both policy-formulating and policy-implementing processes. Against the formulators of policy its weapon was remonstrance; against the implementers, impeachment." [53] In other words, the former censorate performed multiple functions, particularly through its power of remonstrance, acting as an office of external control for the administration.

At present, the distinction should be drawn between internal control, exercised by the administration itself over decisions made by the administrators, and external control resulting from sources outside the administrative system.

INTERNAL CONTROL

Internal control may be exercised either by superior authorities over subordinates or over the personnel executing decisions (hierarchical control), by tutelary authorities over the functioning of local government (administrative tutelary control), by the financial services appointed to watch over the regularity of expenditures (financial control), or by means of regular or unannounced inspections.

Hierarchical Control. The goal of hierarchical control over decisions and activities of the various administrative units is to assure conformity to the general policy lines defined by the laws and regulations and by the decisions of the prime minister. A pyramidal administrative organization is designed to facilitate hierarchical control in a centralized administrative system such as exists in Viet-Nam.

Control by the Prime Minister and the Ministers. During the First Republic, the President exercised control through several means. Although each department had its own authority, important matters had to be submitted for final decision to the President;

however, the choice of what was important was often left to the discretion of the secretary of state. References to these matters could, however, be either oral or written. Only when the laws and regulations specifically required presidential approval were matters regularly submitted in writing (for example, the appointment of a secretary-general or of a director-general, the promotion of a civil servant of Category A, or the acquisition of lands for the state). Other affairs often fell under the jurisdiction of the secretary of state, and still might require the express approval of the chief of state (for example, the appointment of a cabinet director). In order to exercise his hierarchical control, the President had data presented by the departments examined by the services of the Secretariat-General at the Presidency; sometimes the law required that documents submitted to the President for signature had to be first countersigned by the Directorate-General of Civil Service (in the case of personnel matters), by the Directorate-General of Budget and Foreign Aid (for financial matters), or by both agencies (for organizational matters).

The fact is that, although the principle of administrative hierarchy demands that all important decisions be made by the President, in reality these decisions are often of such a purely technical nature that, without the help of his overhead services, the President would not be capable of deciding on all questions submitted to him; executive approval of staff recommendations had to be based almost entirely on confidence in subordinates.[54] However, because of the autocratic nature of the President of the First Republic, many decisions were delayed precisely because the President did not have complete confidence in his staff.

At any rate, the sanction accorded by the power of control is that of bringing into play the responsibility of the secretary of state or minister: in the constitutional regime of the First Republic of Viet-Nam, the secretary of state was responsible before the President of the Republic, and before him alone. It was the President who appointed him to his post; he could recall him at any time if the responsibility of the secretary of state seemed compromised in such a way that his collaboration was no longer considered useful. In reality, no secretary of state was ever recalled: those who felt that their collaboration was no longer desired simply offered their resignations, either individually or with the entire cabinet as a group (e.g., following the promulgation of the Constitution of 1956, and on the occasion of the second election of President Ngo Dinh Diem in 1961).

The responsibility of the ministers since the Revolution of November 1, 1963, is not clearly defined either in the Provisional Constitution Act or in the decrees of appointment. It can only be supposed, following precedents and solutions adopted in other countries, that the authority which has the power to appoint also has the power to recall. According to this interpretation, the guarantee for the responsibility of the minister might be his recall by the prime minister or simply his resignation. The former Minister of the Interior, Ha Thuc Ky, who belonged to the Dai Viet party, resigned because he felt that in view of the authority held by the minister of the interior over the province chiefs, who are all military officers, the minister should be a general.[55] From this resignation it can be inferred that the old traditions are still followed at the present time, at least pending the promulgation of a constitution which will define clearly the respective responsibilities of the prime minister and of the ministers.

Each minister exercises his hierarchical power of control over the civil servants in his ministry, particularly the cabinet director, the secretary-general, and the director-generals, who are his immediate collaborators. The sanction here consists of bringing into play the responsibility of the civil servant from a disciplinary point of view. A certain parallelism is to be observed as regards this disciplinary power: the administrative authority which has the power to appoint a given civil servant also has the power to pronounce any disciplinary measure regarding that civil servant. In practice, there has not yet been a case of disciplinary recall of a high public official: when an official's responsibility is compromised, he submits his resignation, or he is transferred to another post. A great many of these resignations were tendered after the Revolution of November 1, and similarly a certain number after the purge of January 30.

As for other civil servants, there were indeed some cases of recall because of serious misconduct in the exercise of duties or even because of errors made outside of the normal line of duty. According to the Directorate-General of Civil Service, during the year 1962, out of a total of 140,000 government workers, there were 199 cases of recall.[56]

General Rules Regarding Hierarchical Control. In general, except when there is a specific regulation delegating power of decision on a certain matter to a civil servant occupying a given post, it is customary that civil servants belonging to an inferior echelon in the hierarchy make reports and proposals to the superior authorities. Since there are not many regulations delegating express authority, the system can be classified as centralized, in the sense that the power of hierarchical control is very strong, to the point that each decision must come from high authority. Moreover, even when the power of decision is expressly assigned to an inferior authority, the hierarchical power can still change the decision or cancel it, although it does not have the right to take action itself in place of the lower authority. At any rate, it should be emphasized that there are limits to the obedience required of the subordinate official: in order to avoid the charge of disobedience, the minor official must be able to prove the illegality of the order from his superior.[57]

This centralized control is so extreme that it presents a real burden for the superior official, particularly as concerns routine matters. It is true that the minister may delegate a part of his power of control to the cabinet director or to the secretary-general, who often merely confirm the proposals of the subordinate official, by signing automatically documents presented for their approval. In reality, unless there is a serious and intentional error, the theoretical responsibility of the superior in signing such documents is not compromised when there are errors or omissions in the documents themselves. The responsibility for such errors always falls on the civil servant who has prepared or approved the document to be presented to the higher official. This is why, even in a centralized system such as exists in Viet-Nam, reference can still be made to the "line of confidence" which partially replaces the formal "line of command." [58]

Special mention should be made regarding hierarchical control exercised over the province chiefs and the district chiefs. Since they are agents of the central power, and not chief executives of decentralized territories, they are subject to the hierarchical control of the central government. The laws specify that province chiefs are responsible to the prime minister; in reality, since there are regular reports between the province chief and the minister for the interior, it is the latter who often exercises this control in the name of the prime minister. Moreover, a number of the decisions of the province chief are subject to the express approval of the minister for the interior. Ordinance 59a, however, stipulates that the province chief, as representative of the central government, has the power of decision on all matters regarding laws or regulations that do not require the approval of the prime minister or of the ministers. Recently, the Revolutionary Government again officially emphasized this delegation of power to the province chief, in order to provide for the rapid management of provincial affairs. The province chief has a second title, that of chief executive in the province; this means that he is responsible for the execution of decisions made within the province by the representatives of the people.

Administrative Tutelary Control. The consideration of this second function of the province chief brings us to a second form of internal control: administrative tutelary control.

A French institution transposed to Viet-Nam, administrative tutelary control is exercised by state authorities over the activities of local territorial units, to see that the laws are observed, to avoid possible abuses of power, and to preserve the national interest with respect to local or technical interests.[59] Administrative tutelary control counterbalances the decentralization in local matters in favor of the elected representatives of the local population. It is a conditioned power: i.e., this control is not assumed, but is exercised only in the cases and in the forms stipulated in the laws and regulations. In principle, the tutelary authority may annul decisions of agencies it controls which are contrary to the laws and regulations, but it cannot, on its own initiative, add to such provisions. This constitutes the essential difference between tutelary control and hierarchical control, which is not conditioned; i.e., the hierarchical authority may give to his subordinates any orders which may seem proper to him, so long as he does not oppose the laws, and, under any circumstances, may reframe or cancel the decisions of his subordinates. Thus, administrative tutelary control has the double purpose of seeing that legality is observed, and of bringing about expertness in administration, by providing judicious advice for local administrators who lack experience or competence. As a result, it is customary to distinguish tutelary control over local authorities and tutelary control over local actions.

Tutelary Control over Local Authorities. Tutelary control over local authorities is exercised by the superior authority by means of control of the appointment or the dismissal of agents of the local administrative units. The appointment of the province chief is not considered subject to this tutelary control, because the province chief is an agent of the central government and his functions as chief executive with respect to decisions of a purely provincial nature are considered secondary. On the other hand, the temporary provisions of Decree No. 237/NV of December 8, 1961, regarding the appointment of members of the provincial council by the secretary of state for the interior are indeed an application of the idea of tutelary control enforced during the period of emergency, since the council was certainly an agent of the province, considered as a local administrative unit. Decree No. 203 b/NV, dated May 31, 1964, provides for the election of the members of the provincial council; but even though the minister of the interior no longer appoints these members, he still exerts tutelary authority over them in disciplinary matters, regarding removal from office for incompatibility, absence, or refusal to execute assignments, and even the dissolution of the council in certain cases (Article 8).[60]

As regards the administrative councils of the villages (*hoi dong xa*), tutelary control was exercised, before the Decree of May 31, 1964, by the appointment and recall of members of this council by the province chief. The Decree provides for the election of the communal council, but does not give the details of the election procedure. Under this Decree, tutelary control is exercised in the following ways: (1) the establishing of the electoral list by the district chief (Article 21) and the deciding of disputed cases in elections by a committee presided over by the province chief (Article 23); (2) the receiving of the candidacy papers by the district chief (Article 27); and (3) the verification of the regularity of the elections and of the distribution of responsibilities among the members of the communal administrative council by the district chief, and the approval of these operations by a committee presided over by the province chief, as provided in Article 23 (Article 44).

Disciplinary measures with respect to the council or to the individual members of the council, as a sanction of tutelary authority, consist of: (1) recall from office by the province chief of a member who engages in activities harmful to the security of the nation; and (2) dissolution of the council by the province chief, by delegation of the prime minister, with the agreement of the minister of the interior, for the same reasons as above.

Tutelary Control over Local Actions. In principle, the decisions of the provincial council are considered to be in force fifteen days after the council reports have been deposited in the office of the province chief, unless he disagrees. In this case, the province chief may ask the council to reconsider the matter. In the event of a disagreement after this second deliberation, the matter will be presented by the province chief or the president of the provincial council to the prime minister or to the minister concerned for a decision. Article 13 further stipulates that the decisions of the provincial council will be invalid in the following cases: (1) if they go beyond the jurisdiction provided in the decree organizing the provincial council, or (2) if they are contrary to the laws and regulations in force. In practice, when a law or regulation requires the approval of a decision by a minister, the decision is considered in effect only after this approval has been given. It should be noted that there is no stipulation that the minister may take action when the council has not performed a certain function required by the law.[61]

Although the Decree of May 31, 1964 is not explicit on the subject, it must be admitted that in principle, decisions made by the communal council are official and will be enforced, except for the limitations in Articles 6 and 7 concerning: (1) tutelary control by the minister for the interior, with the agreement of the minister concerned, over certain financial matters and over territorial modifications of the hamlet (Article 6); and (2) tutelary control by the province chief over certain financial matters of lesser importance, and over the details of public works programs (constructing and aligning roads, etc.). Regarding financial matters, the council has the power to make decisions involving VN $30,000 or less, but the approval of the province chief is required when amounts between VN $30,000 and VN $300,000 are involved, and for matters concerning more than VN $300,000, the approval of the minister of the interior, with the agreement of the minister for finance, is required. As in the case of the provincial council, tutelary control does not include taking action where the communal council has taken none.[62]

Since the administrative council of the hamlet has no power to make decisions, no tutelary control is provided over its actions.

Financial Control. Tutelary authority over actions always includes the approval of certain financial measures, i.e., of all the administrative measures, those which have financial implications are subject to the most rigorous control. This calls to mind a bitter observation made by a French jurist: "Less paradoxically than one might think, the French administration, lacking a leader through the default of the President of the Council, often found one in the Minister of Finance [as if the administration were] an enterprise directed by its cashier." [63]

Although Viet-Nam has inherited a large portion of French financial tradition, this particular observation does not seem to apply completely to Viet-Nam.

Control Exercised by the Comptable. At first glance, the degree to which the tradition of French financial control is still maintained in Viet-Nam seems quite extensive. The principle of the separation of *ordonnateurs* and *comptables* continues to govern the procedure for receipts and disbursements; we have already seen that this system is intended to maintain checks and balances between the *ordonnateurs,* who have the authority to order payments from government funds, and the *comptables,* who are responsible for actual disbursements, but only after they have made sure that all necessary formalities have been observed by the *ordonnateur*.[64] It is customary to balance the civil responsibility of the *comptable,* who is obliged to reimburse from his own pocket any irregular or unjustifiable disbursements from public funds, against the purely disciplinary responsibility of the *ordonnateur* who might have approved an expenditure which is later discovered to have been irregular or unjustifiable. Thus the *comptable,* when he finds any irregularity in an authorized expenditure, has the right to refuse to pay out funds on the basis that he would be personally responsible. In such a case, the administrator, whose own money is not at stake, may not intervene against the *comptable*. The regularity of disbursements is thus assured automatically, by the possible bringing into play of this responsibility of the *comptable*. In fact, the authority of the *comptable* is exercised by a stamp of approval, which he places on the pay order before giving it to the creditor of the state. If the *comptable* refuses this stamp, the *ordonnateur* has the alternatives of accepting the refusal of the *comptable,* or of overruling this refusal by signing a requisition for payment, in which case the civil responsibility of the *comptable* is transferred to the *ordonnateur* himself. It is understandable that, in the face of such responsibility, the administrator will hesitate to authorize irregular expenditures. At present, this system is the object of vehement criticism: because of the amounts involved in certain public expenditures, the civil responsibility of the *comptable* so far exceeds his personal fortune that the responsibility tends to become illusory; the stamp of approval of the *comptable* required on the pay order then merely constitutes one more step in the already cumbersome disbursement procedure, to the detriment of the credit of the state. For this reason, and also in order to simplify the disbursement procedure, the Revolutionary Government has abolished this control by the *comptables* in cases where pacification expenses are involved, and for these cases has instituted a new procedure of payment by check, which does not require the stamp of approval of the *comptable*. Only to the extent that the stamp of approval of the *comptable* is still required on pay orders, can it be said that the state enterprise is directed by its cashier (since the treasury is controlled by the Ministry of Finance).[65]

Control of Obligated Expenditures. The second principle of financial control is that all obligations of expenditures must have the stamp of approval of the Obligated Expenditures Service (see Charts VIII and IX, pages 232–233). The Obligated Expenditures Service maintains a record of all obligated expenditures of the state, to be compared with funds appropriated for each service and against the quarterly allotments of funds for that service. In this way, it keeps an up-to-date record of the appropriation situation, and may stop in time any effort on the part of an *ordonnateur* to authorize disbursement of funds beyond the quarterly allotment of his budget. The Obligated Expenditures Service does not limit its activities to keeping a record of credits available, but, in addition, verifies the accuracy of the budgetary imputation, the regularity of papers in each dossier, and the conformity to established procedure for each type of expenditure. Moreover, until recently it did not step in only at the beginning of each disbursement operation, i.e., at the phase properly called "obligation of expenditures," but also maintained a check after the certification of service. This second step has been abolished by Decree No. 203/TC, of May 30, 1964, but in spite of this abolition, the control of obligated expenditures still makes certain that all operations previous to the actual recognition of indebtedness of the State are correctly performed and without any irregularity. The criticism regarding the control of obligated expenditures that "the enterprise is directed by its cashier" stems from the fact that in France, as in Viet-Nam, the Obligated Expenditures Service is placed under the authority of the Ministry of Finance, which also supervises the treasury. This was not true in the case of the First Republic of Viet-Nam, since this service was transferred to the Directorate-General of Budget and Foreign Aid, which itself was attached directly to the Presidency. Control of obligated expenditures was thus intended to be a powerful means of control in the hands of the chief executive. In fact, this control remained theoretical because the chief executive could not exercise it directly; the director of the Obligated Expenditures Service, who exercised this control in his name, was much more concerned with the regularity of operations than with budgetary policy itself.

After the November 1 Revolution, the Obligated Expenditures Service was again placed under the authority of the Ministry of Finance, but in the new procedure, its stamp of approval is required only at the very beginning of the disbursement procedure. It is too soon to make any valid evaluation of this innovation.

Post-audit System. In addition to the pre-audit system described above, French colonial financial legislation provides for a post-audit system. Administrative accounts, prepared both by the *ordonnateur* and by the *comptable*, must be examined by a special tribunal called the Audit Court (Cour des Comptes). This court has to examine all accounts, whether they have been challenged or not. In the first place, accounts furnished by the administrators are compared with those furnished by the *comptables*, in order to establish a declaration of conformity; if any irregularities are found, the court informs the government by issuing an injunction or court notes, so that the proper measures may be taken; finally, the court makes a public report on financial operations, which is transmitted to the legislative assembly, where, as will be shown later, it serves as the basis for a discussion of the law which officially approves the execution of the budget of the previous year (called, in French, the *"loi des comptes"*). In the event the court discovers irregularities leading to a deficit in public funds, it must institute proceedings against the *comptable* responsible, or apparently even the certifying officer, since the recent reform of disbursement procedure.

Although theoretically this institution has not been rescinded by the Republic of Viet-Nam, and nominal appropriations are still included in the budget for the Audit Court, this court has not yet been created.[66] It is believed that the organization of the institution might be compared with that of Audit Court in France, which is an administrative jurisdiction under the supervision of the Council of State,[67] or with that of the Office of the Comptroller General in the United States, which is responsible for settling the accounts of the government disbursing offices.[68]

In fact, because of the absence of the Audit Court, the post-audit system exists only on paper. This means that for an indefinite period, the *comptables* will still be responsible for the administration of finances, because there is no final discharge which shows that their accounting is in order and that they have no further responsibility. This also means that the civil responsibility of the *comptables* is, for the time being, illusory, since, practically speaking, there is no court of justice which can hold them to it. For this reason, the *comptable* can rarely give his responsibility as a reason for refusing to approve irregular pay orders. This is another reason for the fact that, in the new pay procedure, the stamp of approval of the *comptable* is no longer required on the pay order for pacification expenses, and that provisions are made for enforcing the control of the finance inspector.

Inspection. Another means of control exercised by superior authorities consists of using a corps of inspectors who make on-the-spot observations of the operations of the various services.

The Department of Finance had a corps of financial inspectors who checked the activities of the *comptables* and of the various tax collection agents. Theoretically, these inspections were intended to provide support for the *comptables* who refused to make irregular disbursements, and thus served to strengthen the system of control derived from the principle of separating *ordonnateurs* from *comptables*. In point of fact, because of the inadequacy (in numbers) of the corps of inspection, this institution acted only intermittently. The same might be said of the corps of inspectors for military expenditures, set up by the Department of National Defense. Many technical departments also had their own corps of inspectors—rural development, agricultural credit, education, and so on—whose role was essentially technical, but who were necessarily obliged to examine the administrative aspects of technical operations, because of the intricacy of administration and techniques in all affairs conducted by public officials.

During the First Republic, inspectors of administrative affairs assisted the secretary of state for the interior in checking on the activities of province chiefs and other public officials of the interior, and thus strengthened the hierarchical authority of the secretary of state over the operations of his own services and also his tutelary power over all decentralized administrations. This corps of inspectors, created in 1961, exercised authority: (1) through inspection tours in the provinces and even in the villages, in the course of which they could stimulate the activities of provincial public officials and communal authorities; (2) through special investigation missions regarding specific matters, assigned by the secretary of state for the interior; and (3) through reports in which they could propose reform measures.[69]

Mention should also be made of the role played by government delegates for certain groups of provinces. They made frequent tours in their assigned sectors; spoke informally to the province chiefs, district chiefs, and other officials; and organized meetings of chiefs of several provinces in order to transmit orders from the government. This actually constituted a continuous and informal check, and not a formal inspection of specific affairs. Although these delegates were officially merely assistants to the chief executive and inspectors, their activities were still extremely important, and it was for this reason that, although in principle an inspector is not responsible for active administration, subsequent to the incidents which occurred at Hue on the occasion of the Buddhist holidays in 1963, the government delegate for that region was replaced.[70] After the November 1 Revolution, the functions of these delegates were assigned to the commanders of the tactical zones, who are assisted by a civil affairs service.

After the Revolution of November 1, 1963, the inspectors of administrative affairs and the financial inspectors were incorporated in the Corps of Inspectors of Administrative and Financial Affairs which constitutes the Inspectorate-General for Administrative and Financial Affairs, and is attached to the Executive Office of the Prime Minister (formerly of the President).[71] Because of this attachment, these inspectors can be sent on inspection tours to any region, either in the capital or in the provinces. Because of their functions, they can be given the most disparate missions, investigating such matters as administrative affairs, misappropriations of public funds, or activities of a government enterprise. Under the First Republic, they were not authorized to initiate such investigations: for each matter, they had to receive an order directly from the President. At present, this restriction is no longer in effect.

In the performance of their assigned duties, these inspectors have the right to enter offices or government warehouses, to consult any records, to demand the presentation of any person or any materials necessary for their work, or to demand written explanation from any official having any relationship whatsoever with the matter being investigated. The results of such an inspection are presented in the form of a report to the minister concerned, for transmission to the responsible public official, who is obliged to answer the observations of the inspector. This reply from the public official is returned, with notations by the minister, to the inspector, so that he can make his final report to the prime minister.

The inspectors are already beginning to make many inspection tours in the provinces. They have received special instructions to investigate possible abuses of power under the First Republic, but no spectacular results from these instructions have yet come to light.

EXTERNAL CONTROL

During the monarchy, it was inconceivable that the king, who ruled by a mandate from Heaven, should accept any earthly control, coming either vaguely from the people or from any other constituted body. Nevertheless, some care had to be taken that the king should conform to the natural order of things, and this doctrine of natural

order developed along the following lines. Great national catastrophes can constitute signs revealing shortcomings in the behavior
of the sovereign. In accordance with Confucian tradition, after such
events the king issued proclamation of repentance in which he called
upon his mandarins to remonstrate (see Chapter 2). Tradition also
required that the remonstrator should stand firm for his principles,
remonstrating bluntly, unflinchingly, and without compromise whatever might be the cost to him.[72]

The mandarins who performed this office of censor, often
selected from among men of high morals, sometimes stood alone and
voiced only their own opinions, in which case the remonstrance
constituted still an internal control. More frequently, however, they
took into consideration the general opinion of the scholarly class,
particularly of those members of that class with whom they were in
direct contact.

Characteristic of Confucianism is the emphasis on morals in perfect-
ing the individual, and in the organization of social relationships. This
doctrine was inculcated from the earliest years in those who aspired to
form the guiding class of the nation. Those who were imbued with this
doctrine did not all succeed in gaining power, but, even living in retirement and obscurity, they contributed to an opinion which controlled the
others, and which the latter had to take into consideration. This was
[the negative side of] *thanh nghi,* or impartial discussion [of which we
have already seen the positive side], which judged men and things
according to universally accepted principles, constituting a powerful
deterrent on the men in power, and which made and destroyed reputa-
tions.[73]

This widespread control by the most enlightened members of the
population is the logical result of the system of administration by
virtue.

Of course, there was also a judicial system organized for
imposing penalties on anyone, even mandarins, who violated the law.
But this applied rather to violations of penal law, and did not concern
administrative activities outside of political lines established by the
king.

At present, judiciary control of administration is exercised by
tribunals and is concerned with the legality of the administrative
action. If the law is considered to be the expression of the will of the
people, and of the general policy at a given moment, it might be said
that judiciary control is a technical stage of a more general control:
political control, which is established to assure the proper execution
of the policy defined by the responsible body.

Judiciary Control. The French concept of separation of powers was
introduced in Viet-Nam, although in a rather mitigated form, during

the colonial period. According to this concept, in order to assure civil liberty, governmental authority must be clearly divided into legislative, executive, and judiciary powers. Insofar as the relationships between executive power and judiciary power are concerned, this separation stems from the mistrust of the judiciary power on the part of the French people, before the Revolution of 1789, since the resistance of the judiciary corps to royal power was one of the principal obstacles to progress in administration. Several legal acts brought out the principle that "judges may not, at the risk of breach of duty, interfere in any way whatsoever with the operations of the administrative corps, nor summon administrators to appear before them on matters concerning their administrative functions." Hence, it was necessary, in order to oblige administrators to obey the law, to create a special jurisdiction, distinct from the judiciary power, to settle administrative matters in dispute: this was the Council of State, considered as a judge of common law in administrative matters. From this developed the principle of distinguishing active administration from administrative adjudication, a distinction also applied in the French colonies.[74]

In French Indochina, many administrative disputes fell to the jurisdiction of the Claims Council (Conseil du Contentieux), which settled all litigation expressly assigned to it (e.g., direct taxes, administrative responsibility, and administrative decisions regarding personnel), although the judge of common law for administrative matters for the colonies was still the French Council of State.[75]

At present, two legal acts in Viet-Nam provide for the separation of active administration and administrative adjudication. In addition, they distinguish two degrees of jurisdiction in administrative disputes, by the creation of: (1) a Claims Council (*Du* of January 5, 1950, modified by the *Du* of October 8, 1954), whose jurisdiction includes all litigation regarding the responsibility of public officials; litigation concerning the annulment of administrative acts of an individual nature; litigation regarding elections at the village, district, and province levels; and litigation concerning direct taxes and taxes assimilated to direct taxes; and (2) a Council of State (*Du* of November 9, 1954), which serves as a court of appeals for matters judged by the Claims Council, and which also has jurisdiction over demands for the annulment of administrative regulations or decisions of an individual nature made by the chief of state himself.[76]

The problem of administrative control by tribunals is very complex; here only three major aspects of this problem will be examined: general criteria for the jurisdiction of administrative tribunals, the settlement of claims for annulment (*contentieux de l'annulation*), and the settlement of claims for compensation (*contentieux de pleine juridiction*).

General Criteria for the Jurisdiction of Administrative Tribunals. Let us see how the principle of separation of administrative and judicial authorities is applied; i.e., what litigation, in accordance with this principle, is beyond the judiciary authority of common law.

It might be supposed, in the first place, that all litigation regarding the administrator, implicating the administrator, or having any relationship with his functions falls outside the jurisdiction of the common courts. Jurisprudence, in reality, more precisely defines this principle, stating that the jurisdiction of the administrative judge concerns only the activities of the government service, i.e., the activities of a public collectivity seeking to satisfy a need of general interest.

In practice, however, a certain number of acts which are included in the preceding definition are nevertheless not settled by the administrative tribunal. In the first place, actions of the chief executive and those of the government in matters of international relations must be excluded, since these relations implicate foreign powers, which do not fall under the jurisdiction of Viet-Nam. Also excluded are acts and operations of a common nature which do not involve the power of the government (French, *régime de puissance publique*): e.g., activities concerned with the administration of the property of the state or a contract in which the administration uses a private form. Finally, there exist other domains reserved either by tradition or by express legal provisions to the jurisdiction of the common courts, regardless of the functions performed by the persons concerned: the status of individuals, rights over real estate, indirect taxes, and so on.[77]

Annulment Claims. Sometimes the question arises of annulling an administrative decision because of its illegality. The claim is directed against an administrative decision, i.e., a unilateral administrative act, which excludes contracts approved by the administration, and also simple material operations. The claim is based upon the general idea of excess of power, although the *du* which creates the Council of State specifically provides four possible grounds: abuse of power, incompetence, violation of the law, and absence or misdirection of motives.

Abuse of power by an administrative authority consists of using his powers for another purpose than that for which they were conferred upon him. The crux is of a subjective nature: it is the intention of the person performing the action; for example, the case of a civil servant who has not acted in the public interest, but in his own interest; or that of an administrator who has acted in the public interest, but not the public interest he was authorized to pursue.

Violation of the law must be understood to mean violation of any rule imposed on the administrator in virtue of the principle of legality: a refusal to apply the law, or a false interpretation of it.

Misdirection of motives can also be considered as a violation of the law, although it is here a question of evaluating the facts which have served as the basis for the decision in question: when the evaluation of the facts is false, then in reality the law is not applied to the true facts.

The fourth possible grounds regards incompetence, i.e., the unfitness of a public official to accomplish an act that could be performed, but which had to be done by another official: incompetence may be *ratione materiae,* i.e., by reason of the object of the act; *ratione loci,* i.e., depending on the geographical sphere of action of the official; or *ratione temporis,* i.e., with respect to the exact time at which the act was to be accomplished.

It should be pointed out that in Vietnamese law, defective drafting of an administrative act does not constitute grounds for legal prosecution on the basis of abuse of power, contrary to French law, which inspired the organization of the Council of State.

In point of fact, although the afore-mentioned grounds for legal proceedings might have served as a deterrent to arbitrary actions in administration, such proceedings have not been very numerous.[78]

Settlement of Claims for Compensation. On the other hand, legal proceedings regarding the responsibility of the state are quite frequent; other compensation claims may concern the annulling of a contract or an election, i.e., acts which are not administrative decisions; and others tend to require a pecuniary judgment or the reduction of a tax rate.[79]

An interesting feature of these proceedings is the principle of responsibility of the state, formally expressed in the decisions of the Council of State or of the Claims Council. This principle is the result of the special nature of administrative law. The administration is not subject to common law, and is not judged by a judge of common law; since the administrative judge may establish a jurisprudence independent of civil jurisprudence, the principle established was precisely that of the responsibility of the state with respect to acts detrimental to individuals.[80]

The responsibility of the state may, indeed, be based on an official offense. The state's responsibility may even be implicated when there is no offense, whenever there is a case of imputability of the damage (because of the principle of equal distribution of public charges). A distinction must be drawn between the responsibility of the state and that of the public official who represents the state in a given matter. The responsibility of the state is brought into play when an offense is committed by an official in the proper performance of his duties. The responsibility falls to the official himself when there is no relationship between the offense and his functions. Naturally, there are cases of plurality of responsibility; i.e., when both the state and the official are responsible.

This system of responsibility of the state, which was inspired by French tradition, differs from the system which requires that administrative actions be judged by the same courts as common-law affairs. Courts of common law must necessarily apply common law; the courts stand as guarantors of legal and fair behavior by administrative agencies in regulating the conduct of the individual and in providing service to the individual. Hence, judicial supervision deals with both regulatory authority and service authority, but since, in administration there is an element of specialization (expertise), an element of preventive action, and an element of responsibility for a variety of related tasks, courts find, in particular cases, no reason to intervene. Thus, by virtue of the principle that the king (or state) can do no wrong, it has been admitted that states are free from suits for damages arising out of torts which might be committed by administrative agents, except when a local government is performing proprietary functions, or when a local government voluntarily consents to be sued for damages, especially in the field of government contracts.[81]

It can be seen from the preceding outline that judiciary control over administrative decisions seems to be strict in Viet-Nam, when it is considered that, in addition to the administrative tribunals, common courts can still be called to judge the public official in cases of criminal torts, and also to judge certain administrative actions in cases of exceptional competence of these tribunals, as has been indicated above. Nevertheless, the number of cases of breach of law discovered after the Revolution of November 1, 1963, lends credence to a rather pertinent remark made regarding the legal control in underdeveloped countries: "It may be true that evaluated in the abstract, the new law codes and courts have been uniquely successful, but judged by their political consequences, the courts would appear to have heightened bureaucratic irresponsibility rather than reduced it." [82] At any rate, since appreciation of legal and judicial matters is not yet widespread among the masses, it can be assumed that in many cases, legal rights have not been exercised against administrative decisions which might seem arbitrary.[83]

Political Control. Judicial control is exercised only over that part of administrative activity concerned with the public interest that has been institutionalized in the form of written laws and regulations. The question may still arise whether the legislative power itself can exercise a certain control over the execution of the laws that it has enacted, or even over the entire functioning of the administration. This is the problem of legislative control. A second question concerns that part of administrative action which must necessarily remain discretionary, since the laws and regulations cannot foresee the multiplicity of details of administrative life: does there exist an informal control by public opinion over public administration?

Legislative Control. The Constitution of the First Republic of Viet-Nam indeed provided for a legislative assembly, but failed to stipulate its powers and responsibilities regarding control. Nevertheless, when the operations of the legislative assembly are closely examined, it can be seen that the assembly has many opportunities to interfere in administrative matters, either to suggest certain measures that can be taken by the executive power, to support a particular point of policy developed by the chief executive, to deliberate on financial means to be placed at the disposal of administrative agencies, or to vote on a law on its own initiative or on a bill presented by the chief executive.[84]

Thus, the Assembly adopted a resolution asking the government: first, to apply as flexibly as possible the economic and financial measures adopted during the period of emergency, and to simplify the administrative procedure in order not to hinder economic activity; and, second, to organize a rational, just, and simple fiscal system adapted, not only to the ability of the people to pay, but also to their ability to understand.[85] In the discussion on this resolution, the practices adopted by certain economic services were criticized, but the resolution itself presents merely a matter of principle. It is curious to observe that this resolution contains recommendations to the executive power; that could have been enacted as law (e.g., the setting up of a taxation system). Other resolutions merely supported various points of government policy which had already been defined by the President of the Republic, as, for example, the resolutions passed regarding the policy of strategic hamlets.[86] In the course of these discussions, certain criticisms were leveled at the provincial agents responsible for applying these programs.

Without recapitulating the discussions of the annual budget, it should be emphasized that the Assembly still does not deliberate on administrative accounts, in spite of the existence of the old French principle of control over public finance, which does not seem to have been rescinded. According to this principle, the legislative body that has the power of voting the budget should also have the power of voting on administrative accounts, indicating to what extent the budget has been properly executed. It should be recalled also that it is particularly during the discussions of the budget that criticisms of the operation of certain services have been presented.

As regards voting on laws, the Assembly deliberated either on a bill presented by the government, such as the bill delegating to the President of the Republic the power of establishing a special security budget,[87] or on a proposal presented by a member of the Assembly, such as the bill regarding wards of the nation.[88]

In most democratic countries, the control of the legislative body over the administration is exercised in a considerably different way. Since there is no domain reserved for legislation, the legislator can take up a matter which has until then been left to the initiative of the executive power, and pass a law setting conditions on the exercise of the activity in question, creating or abolishing a public service, the procedure to be adopted by the service, etc. The legislative body can also set up investigation commissions to determine whether legislative provisions are properly respected by the authorities responsible for executing them, and propose proper sanctions for those authorities who are not.[89] Certain critics consider, however, that although ". . . on the surface, it appears that Congress has adequate means of controlling administration through its powers of lawmaking, appropriations, and investigations . . . for several reasons, most of which spring from the atomization of legislative time and energy, legislative control is of limited effectiveness." [90]

The Revolution of November 1, 1963, abolished the Constitution of October 26, 1956. Since the Revolutionary Military Council assumed the sovereign power, it is to be presumed that the supreme control is exercised by this Council. A Council of Notables was also established, whose function was to render opinions on important political matters for the Revolutionary Military Council and for the provisional government. This Council assumed a certain power of control, particularly as regards the attitude to be adopted in the face of the proposal of General de Gaulle, President of the French Republic, that South Viet-Nam be neutralized, but as has been stated, it was dissolved shortly after the purge of January 30.

Informal Control. The truth is that, in spite of all the mechanism of control, there inevitably still remains a discretionary domain in which the administrator is more or less obliged to act.[91] Although Vietnamese administration has inherited a well-developed judicial system, and although intensive efforts in the legislative domain have been put forth since the country became a republic, it is obvious that new needs and new conditions appear at every turn that cannot be encompassed by new legislation. The administrator, who must still act in these cases, is guided simply by his own conception of the public interest or by the ethics which govern all of his actions. Is there any control whatever over this discretionary part of administrative action?

Each society has its norms, its beliefs, and its customs as to what can be expected of the administration. It has been shown that in the older Vietnamese society, the mandarin scholar was venerated as the father and mother of the people, and he was expected to act in consequence: to render justice, to live honestly in order to serve as an example, and occasionally to give advice regarding social behavior. If he did not follow the prescribed behavior, he ran the risk of the public censure. This attitude on the part of the people persists to a certain extent in the rural regions, although, with the development of urban life and of communications between the cities and the country, face-to-face relations are slowly giving way to impersonality in the various social activities. On the other hand, with the mass media of communication, criticisms of poor administration can be intensified and can eventually constitute a deterrent to the actions of dishonest administrators.[92] This is particularly true since the Revolution of November 1, 1963, as has been indicated earlier.

Social groups also maintain a certain control over the actions of their members. Family solidarity still retains considerable influence over the individual, although less than in the past. The *esprit de corps* in certain organizations, particularly among the administrators and officers, still cannot be compared with the powerful censure of the *gioi si phu* (the literati of former times); but this spirit is already growing visibly, as the professional schools create among these public officials, not only a feeling of solidarity in the performance of their duties, but also a feeling of friendship rooted in student life. A similar *esprit de corps* exists among the technicians who also have their code of ethics to guide future members. Discipline in the political parties seems more strict and contributes, to a certain extent, to obliging those public officials who are members to follow the lines of conduct set down by the party. Details regarding these groups have already been brought out in this chapter; they are mentioned here only as one aspect of the matter of informal control.

True control rests in the conscience of the public official: it is up to him to decide his own attitude regarding the qualities of honor, conscientiousness, probity, devotion to the accomplishment of his daily tasks; in short, it is up to him to aspire to the ideal of the Confucian superior man—without becoming blindly attached to tradition—to choose between the past and certain intangible principles of moral conduct. Of course, to turn to the scarcely articulate control exercised by public opinion or to professional conscience may seem, to persons accustomed to the complicated apparatus of political responsibility, like preaching a moral lesson in the desert. But pending the effective establishment of democratic controls, the appeal to moral principles in a country where the power of tradition is still strong does not seem completely futile.

Conclusion

We have defined communication as the mobilizing and integrating of the elements of a decision, and of diffusing its content in the continual movement of administrative action. If events occurred with regularity, administration would function smoothly, and a continuous social progress would follow.

However, since there exist inevitably certain defects in the communications system—as in any other human system—the problem is to know how to detect these defects, and how to remedy them. This is precisely the problem that we have examined in the light of the idea of control, taken in the deliberately restricted sense of a system for enforcing standards of organization behavior.

The various aspects of the problem of communications, as well as the various devices used for the control of administrative activity, have been reviewed in an effort to show how the Vietnamese administration has adapted itself to new needs and how the desire to adopt new techniques in order to face the transformation of the environment has been realized. The conclusion seems to be that it would be futile to oppose administration by law to administration by men, but that it certainly must be admitted that administration is the sum total of the actions of certain men, called public servants, within a legal framework. Humanism is not opposed to legality: one idea complements the other in the Vietnamese administrative philosophy now in effect.

CHAPTER 9

THE TEACHING OF PUBLIC ADMINISTRATION IN VIET-NAM

> As a discipline, public administration is concerned with all the social sciences which provide knowledge in the areas of judgment, policy determination and organizational behaviour.[1]

IN A RECENT ARTICLE, an economist, speaking of economic development in Viet-Nam, concludes very pessimistically that, "under guerrilla warfare conditions, economic development is difficult, if not impossible."[2] Although this statement concerns only one aspect of national development, it is an important declaration, considering the predominance of the idea of economic development in current theories of national development.

A hopeful solution may be found by recourse to certain official documents. On October 7, 1963, in his last speech before the National Assembly, the former President of the Republic again declared that in spite of the conditions of guerrilla warfare, the government intended to follow the 1962–1966 Five-Year Plan, the major objective of which was to gain economic independence for the nation, and to raise the standard of living of the mass of the population.[3] Although the Revolutionary Government has not yet been able to establish a long-range program, one of its principal objectives is still national development, understood in the sense of economic development and social improvement.[4]

The difference of opinion seems to stem, on the one hand, from the rather liberal ideas of the American economist, who can judge the future only provided that the factors of development are left to private initiative, and, on the other, from the leading ideas of a new nation determined to emerge from the stage of underdevelopment in spite of difficult conditions of warfare, and to project this determination into the daily realities of governmental activity. In other words, the effective role of public administration seems to be the supreme hope of Viet-Nam, in its endeavor to promote the social and economic well-being of the nation.

Without taking sides in this theoretical debate between the partisans of the liberal school and the advocates of the *dirigiste* school on the role of the government in the national development of a developing nation, we can quote one author who has studied the Far East: "The trend of the social sciences up to that time, which

323

emphasized the determining effects of social forces on political actions, also left them unprepared to appraise correctly a situation in which the political actors deliberately and methodically sought to manipulate the social environment to achieve a preconceived purpose." [5] The question to be examined here is whether adequate teaching of public administration can contribute directly or indirectly to national development,[6] and how this teaching can, in practice, be organized to realize the proposed goals, taking as an example the teaching of public administration in Viet-Nam.[7]

The Idea of Administrative Training as Prerequisite to National Development

TRADITIONAL EDUCATION FOR THE MANDARINATE

In about 1925, the Vietnamese historian Tran Trong Kim, evaluating the economic and social situation of Viet-Nam at the beginning of French occupation, deplored the traditional education as a major cause of defeat before the invading forces of France: "In the past, the goal of the scholar was the knowledge of virtue which enables him to distinguish good from evil, and at the same time the character training which gives him the high moral traits necessary for conducting public affairs. . . . Gradually, as a result of the daily struggle for existence, these studies were aimed simply toward passing the examinations which permitted the successful candidates to become mandarins." [8]

Allusion was made to an educational system dedicated almost too exclusively to the study of classics, literature, and versification, at the expense of a more scientific education oriented toward the factors of economic progress. Tran Trong Kim did not repudiate the ancient culture. For him, the essence of Confucian teaching remains valid: human-heartedness (*nhan*), righteousness (*nghia*), proper conduct in accordance with the rituals (*le*), wisdom (*tri*), and good faith (*tin*) stand as the five basic virtues of the honest man; simplicity (*thanh*), industriousness (*can*), honesty (*liem*), and rectitude (*chinh*) are the four traits to be developed by those who aspire to govern others. Similarly, the four fundamental duties: loyalty (*trung*), filial piety (*hieu*), fraternity (*de*), and gentleness (*thu*) should govern all human relations in order to render life in society possible and pleasant.[9] What the author attacked especially was the scholastic approach that concerned itself with the letter of Confucian philosophy more than with its spirit, and sought material success rather than disinterested culture.

Tran Trong Kim, as well as his contemporaries, foresaw the importance of scientific education in national development, but could not yet clearly distinguish the ways in which scientific education might influence this development. Traditional education, inspired essentially by Confucian teaching, sought to form the "sage," the honest man well versed in general problems of human behavior, but completely unaccustomed to scientific or economic reasoning. It was from among these scholars that the mandarins or administrators were recruited; they were expected to take the lead in any reform movement in the country, if indeed there was a reform.[10] It might be supposed that this author would accompany his recommendation for reform in the teaching of public administration with similar recommendations for reform in public administration itself, but such was not the case. The proposed reforms, instead of demanding the use of scientific methods in preference to the scholastic methods, particularly recommended the teaching of scientific subjects, and essentially the teaching of engineering in preference to literary subjects, or even to studies which we now call social sciences.

The Need for a Scientific Approach to the Training of Administrators. At approximately the same period, a contemporary, Pham Quynh, after a trip to France, was particularly attracted by the grandiose products of that industrial civilization, and recommended an educational reform following a more scientific pattern. According to him, the question was not to replace humanities entirely by the natural and physical sciences, but to use scientific methods in the study of philosophy and of history, of literature and of sociology.[11] Pham Quynh also considered the teaching of humanities necessary to the formation both of the man and of the citizen, as a part of that upper layer of society which we currently call intelligentsia. This was at the time of the great colonial debate between horizontal education, which seeks to educate the mass of the population, and vertical education, which is principally concerned with the formation of the elite. The debate was broad in scope, but concerns the present study only as regards the teaching of civics in the elementary and secondary schools, and the teaching of political sciences in the institutions of higher learning.

Those in favor of horizontal education complained that there were not enough schools for primary education, and recommended that a maximum of the school budget be set aside for the construction of elementary schools and for salaries of elementary school teachers. Little was said, however, about the teaching of civics in the elementary schools, for the reason that the colonial authorities did not want to develop a civic spirit in the Vietnamese people.

The advocates of vertical education were in favor of the accelerated formation of an elite, trained to occupy, if not key positions, at least posts of medium importance in the various government services, and even in private businesses. They also felt that the colonial authorities did not permit the Vietnamese to participate sufficiently in the administration of their own affairs, although the latter had shown themselves capable of assimilating the most difficult academic subjects, by their success in the entrance examinations of the advanced French schools, or of the various universities, as soon as they had the material means for studying in France. It is among the persons anxious to develop vertical education that the various currents of opinion concerning the role of education in national development are seen most clearly. It is not the purpose of this study to retrace the various theses on the development of engineering and physical science courses designed to contribute directly to the industrialization of the country and to the mechanization of agriculture, by the formation of specialists capable of using machines or of conducting laboratory experiments.

Some currents of opinion considered that even the humanities, or more generally the social sciences, can also contribute to the economic and social development of the country. Everyone was in agreement in condemning the curriculum of the old schools for administrators, called *quoc tu giam,* in which the students worked three years on classical studies, and on the various forms of composition, including the writing of official reports, and sometimes had the opportunity of hearing lectures given by mandarin scholars. The methods used were too scholastic and the goals set were too narrowly practical; forming the spirit of the sage was neglected for the more pressing pursuit of a diploma.[12]

Measures Taken by the Colonial Government.   From the beginning of the colonial period, the colonial authorities worked hard to find an alternate system, and tried to solve the problem of education for public administration by a double formula: the French administrators were to be trained in one way, and the native administrators in another. No attempt will be made here to trace the history of the development of these two types of institutions, but only to recall the evolution of the guiding principles in the extent to which these principles contribued to the development of the colony.

This colonial organization was conceived in a very simple manner: the economic infra-structure was to be developed in such a way that the investments of French capital would show a maximum of profit with a minimum of trouble; the administration of the country was to cost as little as possible, even when this economy worked to the detriment of the public well-being.[13] The colonial administrator was then to be imbued with these principles. The classes given in 1860 at the Collège des interprètes (which became the Ecole des Stagiaires in 1873) to the naval officers who were to become later the first colonial administrators in South Viet-Nam were taught by older hands, like Luro, Silvestre, and others, who had had a great deal of experience with the country.[14] Luro had great admiration for the Vietnamese mandarins, and recommended retaining the system of mandarin authority, as well as the communal organization; his recommendations were based on a thorough study of the customs and manners of the people; as a result, the principles of administration he suggested were of an ecological nature, although this scientific word was never mentioned.[15] When the general government was established, the administrative needs became greater, because of the enlarging of the territory to be governed, as well as because of the complexity of the problems to be solved, which existed under different social conditions. In 1889, the training of administrators was transferred to schools in France, principally to the Ecole Coloniale, and later to the Ecole Nationale de la France d'Outre-Mer (National French Overseas School).[16] The training gained in scientific method what it lost in practical approach. As a matter of fact, the school easily found in law schools teachers of established authority in the domains of constitutional law, administrative law, financial legislation, and colonial legislation and economics. The school also had the collaboration of the Ecole des Langues Orientales (Oriental Language School) and of the Sorbonne (Faculty of Letters of the University of Paris) for sociological and linguistics courses concerning the colonies. But the sociological studies were presented in a theoretical form rather than with a view to applying the results to problems of administration proper. The result was that the Ecole Nationale de la France d'Outre-Mer acquired more and more the reputation of a first-rate school, at the expense of the practical formation which colonial administrators should have received. At any rate, the guiding philosophy remained that the administrator was to serve the policy of colonial development conceived in the precise sense described above.

The idea of the colonial authorities was that the gap between the work of the French administrators concerned with colonial policy and that of the Vietnamese administrators concerned with native matters was to be filled by training a core of native auxiliary administrators, who were expected to know Vietnamese manners and customs, and whose training would need to include only some of the principles of the French language, law, and administrative techniques. From this idea there developed in 1873 the Ecole des Stagiaires (School for Trainees), designed particularly to train interpreters—French as well as Vietnamese—for administrators. Despite the difficulty of the French language for people accustomed to Chinese characters, certain students of this school showed superior ability; these were to become the first Vietnamese scholars trained in a French school. Parallel to this school, the Hau Bo Truong (Trainees' School; later called Si Hoan Truong, or Mandarins' School) was set up at Hanoi in 1892; here, along with interpreters who had had some experience in administration, were admitted students who had passed the traditional three-year examinations (examinations based on the study of Chinese classics but somewhat modernized to include French, mathematics, and certain other studies). The curriculum of this school was composed largely of language study and practical work, but the level of the practical work as well as that of the study of French was not very high, because of the lack of proficiency of some students in French and of others in Chinese characters.[17] This school became a practical training center for administrative assistants, until the creation of a School of Law and Administration (Truong Phap Chinh) in the so-called University of Hanoi in 1917. The students who followed this new course of study were recruited by examination from among the students who had received the diploma of *études primaires supérieures* (an abbreviated four-year secondary-school program); they received intensive training in French, law, and administrative practices. From among these students were recruited the first Vietnamese administrators. At the time of the controversy between the doctrines of horizontal and vertical education, a concession was made in favor of the latter, by the creation, within the framework of the Indochinese University (which replaced the so-called University of Hanoi, and which later was officially renamed the University of Hanoi), of the Ecole des Hautes Etudes Indochinoises (School of Advanced Indochinese Studies), which replaced the School of Law and Administration in 1927. The curriculum of this school was very broad; the trainees were required to study Western and Oriental philosophy, law, literature, and certain administrative subjects. The courses were so varied that only the very best students were admitted to the entrance examinations, and only the best of these passed the final examinations, but to a certain extent knowledge was acquired at the expense of conscience. This generation, which grew up during the depression of 1930, was, in general, too preoccupied by the material problems of existence to acquire a thorough knowledge of the higher elements of the various Eastern and Western philosophies presented to them.[18] However, from the point of view of the colonial administration, they were efficient administrators, inasmuch as they executed quite faithfully the orders of the French authorities.

The last stage in the history of the formation of Vietnamese administrators under the French colonial regime was the complete assimilation of Indochinese education at the university level into the French university system.[19] Most of the new administrators of the period just preceding World War II were recruited from among students holding law degrees from the University of Hanoi, which was attached to the University of Paris, or from various French universities. In order to insure their understanding of Indochinese problems, a special series of examinations covering Indochinese law and economics and Far-Eastern history was established and was given each year to those holders of law degrees who were applicants for administrative positions.[20]

To summarize, training for administrative functions has always existed in Viet-Nam, in the time of the Emperors as well as in the French colonial period. Since the idea of development is a relatively new concept, it was understandably not explicitly included in this training. Still, the idea of administrative action with a view to carrying out a specific policy has always been the preoccupation of this administrative training. During the nine centuries of Vietnamese independence, from the tenth century to the end of the nineteenth century, this administrative action consisted largely of exemplary behavior on the part of the mandarins, setting an example in order to make society more orderly and human relationships more pleasant. For the eighty years of French domination, on the other hand, it was principally concerned with providing the colony with the administration and work force necessary to provide a satisfactory profit for the French capitalists. The principal idea to be retained from this historical sketch is that the teaching of public administration can contribute and has contributed to the formation of skilled administrative manpower for appreciable economic and social changes in Viet-Nam.

PUBLIC ADMINISTRATION AND NATIONAL DEVELOPMENT UNDER WARFARE CONDITIONS

National development is a social change much broader than the simple establishing of an economic infra-structure favorable to colonial investments. Aside from any possible personal disagreement with the opinion cited at the beginning of this chapter, it must be pointed out that the economist has presented an objective picture of the current economic situation in Viet-Nam. Instead of simply being pessimistic, a valuable lesson can be drawn from each affirmation for the rational planning of an educational program of public administration. It is understood that the problem of teaching public administration will always be seen from two points of view: that of the administrator responsible for the execution of governmental programs, and that of the citizen whose demands are the basis of these programs and who is supposed to benefit from the results obtained. It is also understood that the idea of public administration is meant in a broad sense, including both the substantive administration and procedural administration; in other words, it applies to "an action-oriented, goal-oriented administrative system." [21]

National Defense and Public Administration. An examination of the national budget of Viet-Nam during the last few years shows that most of the national resources of Viet-Nam must be drained for national defense. Considering the background of the officers of the armed forces, some critics do not believe them capable of directing the vast assembly of national resources towards the objectives of economic development; they feel that military expenditures have not provided a market for Vietnamese products, which would have boosted Vietnamese production greatly. It can be answered that, regardless of whether or not the national defense funds are spent on local products, the greater those funds, the more important it is that the officers of the armed forces be made aware of their responsibility, and that they seek to use these funds for a double purpose—that of advancing both military and economic ends. Moreover, the normal functions of supplying provisions to the troops require administrative training on the part of the military leaders; a more advanced study of national development could lead these officers to a clearer appreciation of the role of military consumption in the formation of the national income.[22] Purely military functions aside, because of the appointment of many military officers as province and district chiefs for the purposes of public security, it is also possible to set up special courses in public administration for this category of officers. Such a course was given experimentally in Viet-Nam in 1961 and is being given more intensively in 1964.

On the other hand, the administration of funds appropriated for military expenses does not fall exclusively to military officers. Field officers have the administration of allocations for current operations or for units stationed far from urban centers. The largest appropriations are administered by the central offices of the Ministry of Defense, and many of these offices are placed under the authority of civilian directors, aided by assistants who may also be civilians. If these civilian and military directors were given sufficient administrative education, oriented toward national development, military activities could certainly contribute to a certain extent to economic and social progress.

Capital Formation and Public Administration. The principal objection of economists to military expenditures is that they do not lead to capital formation. According to some, the rate of formation of capital over the past few years has been inadequate and would just barely have compensated for the increase of production necessary to the increased population. Regardless of the value of this argument from a purely economic point of view, there are several points here which could be effectively treated in the teaching of public administration. First, the organization of good statistics is a duty of the administration: the gathering and preparation of statistics is a matter for the technician, of course, but the spirit of the statistical method should be instilled in all administrators, since this is the major source of data, particularly in developing countries in which private sources furnish only partial, and often inadequate, information. It is only when one examines the problem with good statistical data that one can reply to other economists who ask why, with a net investment of approximately 3.4 per cent, 1.8 per cent, and 4.8 per cent, respectively, for the years 1955, 1956 and 1960, the gross national product was able to increase by 24 per cent, far above the increase of population.[23] Aside from various other reasons, there remains certainly one valid reason: statistical error that derives precisely from the lack of scientific approach to administration on the part of the responsible parties.

Since it is to be hoped, in view of the insufficiency of private capital, that a large portion of investments made to advance economic development will come from government sources, the administrators will exert a real influence if they are capable of setting up proper programs for public investments and following through with the execution of these programs, adjusting and adapting them at the proper time to progress made in other fields. Particular note should be taken here of the government enterprises that a developing country such as Viet-Nam must establish in order to give the desired impetus to key elements of economic activity, in the event private initiative falls short.[24] It is in these enterprises that the public servants with solid administrative training can show a maximum of initiative and can contribute effectively to the development of the country. Another major element of investment should be pointed out for an essentially agricultural country like Viet-Nam: the preparation of increased areas of arable land and the improvement of the existing fields. Because of the rather rudimentary knowledge of the farmer with regard to this question, the administrator is called upon to play an important advisory role, as liaison agent between agricultural extension agencies, in encouraging various forms of cooperation, and so on. In addition to agricultural information distributed by the technical services, the development of farm groups and of lines of communication falls clearly in the domain of the administrator, who must be well-prepared intellectually and technically for this role.

On the subject of farm groups, it is appropriate to mention a last factor of investment. For a developing country, the major component of capital formation is not the machine tools perfected, but its social overhead component—in this case the public works executed by the small community, i.e., the community development projects.[25] The mobilization of a work force for community development should be considered an important investment factor and should be evaluated as such in the process of capital formation. The history of Viet-Nam reveals many periods in which clever mobilization of the spirit of community development has succeeded in gaining for the country magnificent new arable lands; an example is the work of the great mandarin Nguyen Cong Tru in the provinces of Nam Dinh and Ninh Binh during the reign of Minh Mang.[26]

Human and Demographic Factors in National Development. No economic development could be brought about without this human factor; for some authors, it is one of the fundamental preconditions for the take-off which requires "the existence or quick emergence of a political, social, and institutional framework which exploits the impulses to expansion in the modern sector and the potential external economy effects of the take-off, and gives to growth an ongoing character."[27] At all levels of the administrative hierarchy, leaders must be found who are imbued with this spirit of development, and particularly, insofar as Viet-Nam is concerned, at the province and the district levels, in which the province chief and the district chief are the executive authority for all activities concerning the province.[28] In other words, the administrator should be animated with the same spirit as the "innovating entrepreneur," to use Schumpeter's term.

This expression is particularly important in studying the role played by urbanization in the process of economic growth. Although the correlation between industrialization and urbanization, on one hand, and economic and social development, on the other, has not yet been shown conclusively, the fact of the concentration of population in certain areas that economists consider as poles of growth poses for the administration the more and more complex problems of security, traffic, hygiene, lighting, drainage, and juvenile delinquency. In addition to these problems stemming directly from urbanization, the administrator in a country undergoing development must also bring his attention simultaneously to the process of adaptation and integration of farmers into urban life, and to the process of propagation of new techniques and cultural changes from the city to the country.

Besides, the teaching of administration is not concerned only with the training of administrators; in a country emerging from underdevelopment, every member of the community should be fired with the spirit of development. If every citizen can learn the rudiments of public administration, if everyone realizes the need for co-operation, for moving in a certain direction to realize the common goals, then the work of community development, as well as the government programs, will receive more readily the support of the people and will more easily inspire their participation.

National Development and Public Administration. In considering the human factor in national development, it is important to mention the cultural change that conditions all development. Using the model suggested by Talcott Parson, an economist has pinpointed the social variables which are functionally interdependent with the increase of the real per capita output. He has named five of these variables: (1) the choice between modalities of the social object (achievement versus ascription), (2) the choice between types of value orientation standards (universalism versus particularism), (3) the definition of scope of interest in the object (specificity versus diffuseness), (4) the gratification-discipline dilemma (affective neutrality versus affectivity), and (5) the private versus collectivity interest dilemma (self-orientation versus collectivity-orientation).[29]

Actually, these variables concern not only economic growth but national development in general. Thus, the increase in real per capita output may be a criterion of economic growth; but this growth is made possible by more rationality in economic activity, and it is this tendency to be rational which constitutes economic development. Similarly, an increase in effectiveness and efficiency in public administration constitutes administrative growth, but administrative development itself rests, rather, on an increase in the respect the citizens have for the law, i.e., an increase in universalism.[30]

Without going into the scientific value of the norms proposed, it is sufficient here to underline the fact that the administrator can contribute greatly to these social changes, first by revision of his own attitude toward the afore-mentioned variables, and then by the action which he exercises on the people around him and on the population he governs.[31] This is what Hoselitz calls "the degree of constraint exerted by a central political authority."

Hoselitz' statement leads to the consideration of all the problems of development in the more general context of development planning: a state which resolutely enters a period of national development should set down the general lines of this development in a document which constitutes the development plan. This plan does not at all imply the idea of a rigid document conceived in the sense of popular democracies, but one which contains at least projections for the future based on present data, and foretells the general direction that a rational development might take.[32] The establishment of this plan, as well as part of its execution, falls incontestably within the responsibilities of the administrators, seconded by technicians.

Expansion of Bureaucracy and Political Development. One current trend of thought points out the dangers of the overdevelopment of a bureaucracy at the expense of political development.[33] According to this point of view, it must not be forgotten that in a country undergoing development, a too rapid expansion of the bureaucracy when the political system remains behind might even hinder political development, for the reason that a powerful bureaucracy may refuse to submit to political control, to the detriment of the public interest.

In other words, an efficient administration can contribute largely to economic growth, but also risks retarding political development.

First, a definition of the expression "political development" must be agreed upon. If this expression is not taken in the layman's sense, i.e., the succession of political events, there still remain three possible meanings. Many authorities use it to refer to the progress of democratization, i.e., the extension of the control of the population over public affairs, or, more precisely, the control of assemblies elected by the population over the administration. This meaning seems rather narrow, since election by the population constitutes only one of several means of control. Other authorities understand political development as politicization, i.e., the participation of citizens in public affairs, either by authoritarian methods or by means of representations of the population. This again seems a subjective interpretation, because it implies value judgments. But, if political development is taken to mean the achievement and mainte-nance of self-government, with greater accountability of the elite to the whole population and more responsiveness of the elite to the needs of the people, no matter how this accountability and this responsiveness are brought about, it is difficult to understand why the development of the bureaucracy might hinder movement toward the political maturity of the country, and, particularly, how it could interfere with the firm determination of that country to move toward national development.

Furthermore, the definition of bureaucratic development is only a question of degree: in a nation in which the greater part of the population still needs a certain education in order to realize the full extent of its civic rights and duties, one well may ask who would be responsible for looking out for the public interest if there were no competent bureaucracy. On the contrary, if the administrator is regarded as being concerned with the "realization of conscious human purposes by the conscious use of human beings and materi-als," [34] a nation can only consider itself blessed in having an optimum number of persons who have had adequate administrative education. The problem of controlling this bureaucracy, although it appears to be a political problem, is in the final analysis also an administrative one, since the question is to organize the control in the most effective way, so that the bureaucrats will be obliged to account for their activities to the population and to its repre-sentatives.

The Teaching of Public Administration

The problem of teaching public administration in Viet-Nam, once it is recognized as a factor prerequisite to national development, can be considered in the light of (1) the demand for students who have completed administrative training and the number of students available, (2) the technical problems of administrative training (teaching and research), and (3) the institutions which will be responsible for administrative training.

EXPANDING NEEDS OF VIET-NAM IN THE TEACHING OF PUBLIC ADMINISTRATION

The first problem to be considered is that of supply and demand with respect to openings available for students who have completed training in public administration.

The Potential and Effective Demand for Public Administrators. In the early days of Vietnamese independence there were a great many administrative posts left vacant by the colonial authorities. Also, the partition of the country into two zones by the Geneva Agreement of July 20, 1954, caused some shuffling in the administrative organization. The need for public security as a result of the outbreak of Communist activities also created an important demand for civil servants. On the other hand, economic and financial services have been created or strengthened in order that they might be able to play their parts properly in national development. These services have branches in many regions of the country in order to increase the depth of administrative action. To be really effective, these government services must be directed by competent administrators, assisted by agents at the lower levels who have had a certain amount of administrative training. Even at the commune level, the authorities should be acquainted with the basic notions of public administration, since they have the double mission of executing instructions coming from the central authority and of themselves taking the measures necessary for the maintenance and development of local life.[35]

To be realistic, it is not enough to list Viet-Nam's needs in the matter of administrative personnel, from the time of the proclamation of the First Republic on October 26, 1955, to the present. These real needs must be expressed in terms of effective demand, i.e., they must be studied as a function of possibilities for the absorption of qualified administrative personnel. According to a recent census, Viet-Nam has a total of 140,000 civil servants, among whom 2,300 are of Category A (university graduates); and 40,700 are in Category B (graduates of secondary schools). These figures are higher than those cited in the reply to the questionnaire "Organization of the Civil Service," prepared for the Eastern Regional Organization of Public Administration (EROPA) seminar held in Bangkok, October 7–17, 1962.[36] The percentage of public servants in comparison to the population (14,400,000 inhabitants) is still very low—approximately 1.2 per cent. Although this percentage is much lower than that of the industrialized countries (United States, 5 per cent; France, 2.7 per cent), the appropriation for salaries of personnel absorb each year between 41 per cent and 55 per cent of the national budget. It would be very difficult to go beyond this percentage, particularly in view of the fact that the total national budget also constitutes a very large part of the national income.[37]

As for economic development, although this is one of the principal objectives of the Government policy, the actual rate of development is still rather far from the ideal objective, so that development itself cannot account for a substantial increase in the number of civil servants. If the staffing of these public offices is analyzed more closely, it will be seen that national defense involves already more than 70,000 civil servants and government agents (not including military personnel); general administration and security involve more than 28,000; education more than 21,000; public works nearly 20,000; with the remainder divided among other services.

According to a report from the National Institute of Administration, there are 2,400 positions that require candidates who have had training in public administration at the university level; 1,500 of these are in the offices of the central government, and 900 are in the local administrations. At present, there are only 634 workers who have had this training, leaving 1,766 to be recruited.[38] In view of the importance of this problem, the Revolutionary Government has asked the Institute of National Administration to recommend measures which might satisfy this pressing need.

When it is considered that the higher the rank of the technical civil servants the more frequently must they approach administrative problems, it becomes apparent that seminars on problems of management or of human relations can have a salutary effect on the functioning of technical government services. These technicians need administrative assistants for whom an adequate administrative education is very important. At this point, mention should be made of government enterprise: this activity of the government, undertaken to fill a need left by lack of initiative on the part of private enterprise in certain key sectors important to the economy, requires competent men inspired with a true spirit of entrepreneurship. Moreover, as has already been shown, special courses in administration have been organized for the many military officers who have been appointed to such civil posts as cabinet director, service director, province chief, and district chief.

The Potential and Effective Supply of Students. Concerning supply, it is necessary to take into consideration the tendency of the government to develop to the greatest possible extent primary and secondary education. The number of students in primary schools increased from 401,437 in the school year 1954/55, to 1,493,256 in 1962/63, while the number of secondary-school students increased from 44,200 to 264,866 over the same period. Similarly, the number of students in the various universities and advanced technical schools increased from 2,154 to 18,438. From among these students are recruited those who are to receive special training in public administration at the National Institute of Administration, whose number increased from 97 in 1955 to 283 in 1962/63. This increase is not as great as that of students in other fields, since, in order to be admitted to the National Institute of Administration, as will be seen later, the student must take a severe entrance examination. Statistics showing applicants for the entrance examination give an idea of the potential enrollment: in 1955, scarcely 100 candidates took the examination; in 1963, 1,996 candidates were examined, for 100 seats, so that only 1 out of 20 candidates could be accepted. In the examination, the students are on an absolutely equal footing: no distinction is made between boys and girls, between government and nongovernment employees, between people from the North and those from the South, or between people from rural areas and those from urban centers, as long as they were Vietnamese.[39] It is understood that those applicants who are not accepted at the Institute can still register at the School of Law (the number of students there increased from 763 in 1954/55 to 3,046 in 1962/63) or at the Faculty of Letters (the number of students there increased from 160 in 1954/55 to 4,270 in 1962/63), or in other colleges of the University.[40] In view of the great increase in the number of graduates of the School of Law and at the Faculty of Letters in 1963/64, the National Institute is considering a proposal offering advanced studies in public administration that these graduates could complete in two years instead of the usual three. Also under consideration is a one-year accelerated course which would be open to students who have received the *baccalauréat* but who did not pass the entrance examination. The adoption of these proposals would increase the number of students enrolled from 300 to 600 each year (300 for the normal three-year course, 200 for the advanced two-year course, and 100 for the accelerated one-year course).

It can be seen that there is a considerable difference between the potential supply of students of public administration and the effective supply. The colonial authorities were often reproached for limiting the number of graduates in order to obtain an "elite" completely Westernized and devoted to the interests of France. The present limitation of the supply seems a contradiction to the general tendency, prevalent since independence, to develop education as much as possible in order to obtain a large flow of well-educated men. But, examining the situation more closely, the solution adopted seems perhaps wiser, in view of the limitation of the financial possibilities. Just as production aimed solely at the satisfaction of demands for consumer goods is short-sighted compared with producing capital goods which eventually increase production, so is the production of half-educated men prepared only for subordinate positions far less desirable than the human investment of giving thorough training to produce cultured, well-educated men, particularly when resources are limited. Because of the limitations involved in recruiting for the government service in view of the "revolution of raising expectations," it is better not to create on short notice "a situation of disappointed expectations." [41]

Moreover, between the concept of equal educational facilities for the gifted children of rich and poor alike, on the one hand, and that of equal educational facilities for both the gifted and the less gifted children, on the other, the National Institute of Administration has chosen the former, and has decided to grant scholarships to all regular students of public administration who pass the difficult entrance examinations. As has been pointed out, the unsuccessful candidates can always enroll in another school and receive the benefit of a liberal university education.

Students, however, do not constitute the only source of supply in the study of public administration. Certain civil servants who fill the requirements for the entrance examination at the Institute can also take the examination; if they are accepted, they will continue to receive their entire pay for the duration of their studies. At a lower level, the civil servants can also attend the evening courses, which are specially organized for them and other persons who wish to learn the rudiments of public administration. At the end of 1962, the number of night school students who had taken the public administration course was 1,969, among whom those who had taken the political and administrative organization course numbered 1,273, students of the public accounting course 1,144, and those in the personnel management course 627. In addition, the Institute often offers in-service training seminars for civil servants of various categories, always designed to improve their knowledge of administration. At the end of 1962, a total of 18,326 government workers had participated in seminars related to functional fields where some administrative problems are involved, 3,472 had attended those concerning current administrative practices, and 1,224 had participated in seminars on questions of management and executive development. Many new in-service training courses in public administration have been organized since the November 1 Revolution, particularly for the military officers who are province and district chiefs and for those who will train mobile pacification teams.

The Appointment of Graduates to Posts. Obviously, the type of occupation of the students of the evening courses and of the participants of the in-service training seminars is known, since most of them are already employed in the various ministerial offices and in the provinces. This training has unquestionably brought about an improvement in the work of these people, particularly among the office workers, at the lower administrative levels. The success of the training is the subject of many articles written by executives or supervisors and published in the magazine *Tien Thu* (Progress), a publication of the National Institute of Administration.

Graduates of the regular course of study at the Institute are all appointed *doc su,* i.e., administrators, in the French or British sense of the word, responsible particularly for the elaboration of proposals concerning general policy, for supervising the application of the policy, and for maintaining liaison with the various technical services concerned.[42] In principle, the administrators can be divided into two groups: first, the chiefs of administrative units in the central government who are concerned principally with general policies and procedures, from section chiefs to director-generals; and, second, those more generally concerned with practical administration, such as province chiefs, district chiefs, and chiefs of various province services. By June 30, 1962, 495 students had graduated from the Institute. A study was made concerning the origin and the aspirations of the students of the National Institute of Administration.[43] Although the first assignments of these graduates may have been different from what they had hoped for, on the whole, after several years, they showed themselves quite well adapted to their posts. According to an estimate made by the Association of Former Students of Public Administration, about half of the graduates are serving in the provinces, often as chiefs of provincial services, some as district chiefs (at present these duties are mainly entrusted to military personnel), and many as deputy district chiefs (new positions, created to relieve the district chief of day-to-day administrative work). The students of the first classes are already deputy province chiefs, and one was even province chief. In the central government, the former students of the Institute are administrative bureau chiefs and service chiefs in the Ministry of the Interior (general and provincial administration), as well as in various technical ministries (Ministry of Finance, Ministry of National Economy, Ministry of Rural Affairs, Ministry of National Education, Ministry of Public Health, etc.); one is a secretary-general in the Revolutionary Government. Several graduates are on detached service in Vietnamese embassies and legations abroad.[44]

TECHNICAL PROBLEMS OF THE TEACHING
OF PUBLIC ADMINISTRATION

Because of the diversity of positions offered to students of public administration, and of the growing number of applicants for this field of study, the technical problems of organization in the teaching of administration become more acute every day. Only three of these problems will be discussed here: curriculum, the preparation of the teaching staff, and the research programs; the institutional problem will be considered separately in a final section.

The Search for an Adequate Curriculum. In planning the course of study of public administration for a country undergoing development, such as Viet-Nam, many different theories came under consideration.

The Curriculum of the Dalat School of Administration (1952). Using as a model the National School of Administration in Paris, the Vietnamese School of Administration in Dalat set up a course of study which included legal studies (particularly administrative law, financial law, and labor legislation) and an innovation (compared with the curriculum of the prewar regime): the introduction of administrative, economic, and social subjects, i.e., studies concerning the objectives of important administrative programs, such as the problems of information and propaganda, city planning, ethnic minorities, and Chinese settlements.[45] This orientation toward subjects to which we would nowadays apply the term "functional fields" presented to the student administrator daily realities which he would face in practice. But, even in the functional fields, the instructor still discussed the regulations concerning a given matter, rather than the matter itself, supporting his presentation with concrete facts. The matter presented in class was subsequently illustrated in the course of a practical training period, in which the student saw administration in action, and actually took part in organization by writing what is called a "training thesis." This curriculum represented substantial progress compared to the purely legal instruction in which the student approached reality only through law books. One of the consequences of the adoption of the functional fields was the division of the curriculum into two sections —the administrative section, in which emphasis was placed on more numerous substantive administrative subjects (immigration problems, labor problems, agrarian reform, local administration, and so on), and the economic and financial section, in which the influence of economic and financial data on administrative action was analyzed more carefully (economic development, public finance, economics, money and banking, and so on). Specialization even went so far as to divide the students into small groups; in the administrative section, there was a general administration group, a local administration group, and a social administration group, while, in the economic and financial section, there were groups for budgetary administration, tax administration, economic administration, money and banking, and so on.[46]

The Administrative Management Trend, 1955–1957. Although this policy-orientation program was of unquestionable value, experience showed that, given the present state of administration in Viet-Nam, it was more important to form administrators at the intermediate levels, familiar with modern administrative techniques and capable of introducing a maximum of efficiency in the operation of national and provincial public offices. The elaboration of the curriculum was partly influenced by the Michigan State University Group. Although the students were still divided into an administrative section and an economic and financial section, as a result of the collaboration of this group many courses in administrative techniques were introduced: introduction to the study of administration (according to the American concept), organization and methods, planning and budgeting, personnel administration, comparative administration, etc. It should be noted that courses concerning substantive administration have always been included in the curriculum; the Institute cannot be reproached as having been entirely devoted to administrative management. Moreover, the period of practical training was retained in order to allow the students to become familiar with administrative life. On the other hand, administrative techniques were also studied in many in-service training seminars in which civil servants participated actively.[47]

The Training of Generalists Since 1957. This reform in the teaching curriculum did not last very long. The need for competent administrators with a broad cultural background that would allow them to grasp the administrative problems of the day brought up again the need for training generalists instead of specialists. This led to the introduction of a certain number of general courses in 1957: comparative political science (i.e., the Orient compared with the West); the political and administrative history of Viet-Nam; sociology applied to public administration, human relations, and the study of cases in public administration. To permit the students to follow closely the important political, administrative, and economic questions of the time, high officials and other authorities are invited to give weekly lectures. In order to orient the courses toward the ultimate goals of the administration, the students are still grouped in two sections. Moreover, the practical training period (seven and one-half months) has been retained, both in the central administration and in the provinces. One change, however, involves the assembling of the students in this training period frequently in seminars where, under the direction of an experienced teacher, they discuss problems they are facing in the course of their training. The students are also required to give written accounts of their experiences, showing how the theories they have formed work in actual practice.

A point common to all the educational programs since the creation of the National Institute of Administration is the period of military training required of all students. At one time, this training was given intensively in the school for army officers at Nha Trang, where the students were taught to lead sections, but, generally, the instruction involves only giving orders in the lower military echelons, and calling on specialized units for help, since these students may in future be placed in command positions in administrative districts where military problems of security often arise.

This program, which at first glance seems quite reasonable, has nevertheless been the object of criticism.[48] The difference in orientation of the two groups, although theoretically justified, did not work out in practice when the graduate students were assigned to posts in the administrative services; the needs of the government offices did not permit the Director-General of Civil Service to take their training into account in making these assignments. Successive changes have led to confusion in the curriculum, which, in comparison with the curricula of other institutions at the same level, seemed to make too many demands on the students. The government also finds that the program seems to sacrifice the current need for dynamic administrators to the distant future need for administrative scholars. In other words, the curriculum does not seem sufficiently forceful in the sense that it does not seem to inspire in the students the pioneer spirit necessary in the Revolutionary Government. Recognizing the validity of some of these criticisms, the Institute is studying a new program which would eliminate certain courses which are too narrowly technical, abridge others which cover too broad a field, and place greater emphasis on problems of development and strategy. As has been indicated, in addition to the regular in-service training programs on office management, accounting, work simplification, in-service training techniques and typing, the Institute offers special training for military officers who have been assigned to administrative positions, and for instructors for pacification teams, whose duties will be to train local personnel in areas recently retaken from the Viet-Minh.[49] Plans are also being made for advanced courses in public administration for university graduates and accelerated courses for students who have not satisfied entrance requirements for the regular course of the Institute. In the matter of curriculum, it is useless to hope for perfection; continuous changes are an indication of the will to progress, but there is always the risk of making mistakes, if, in spite of careful planning of the curriculum on paper, there are not adequate resources to put it into practice.[50]

The Formation of the Teaching Staff. A varied teaching program that is undergoing adjustment requires a teaching staff gifted with great flexibility of mind and equipped with adequate teaching materials, constantly being brought up to date.

The Vietnamese Staff. With the government monopoly of higher education, which was characteristic of the French colonial system and which was limited both in the number of students and in the subjects taught, it was to be expected that in the beginning Viet-Nam would not have enough personnel capable of applying the new policy of the teaching of public administration. In point of fact, the first nucleus of teachers came from the Law School: because of the traditional legal concept of public administration, the first members of the faculty were recruited among the teachers of the Law School and those public servants who had had legal training. Only a few French experts were available to give advice for the short-lived National School of Administration at Dalat. Other Vietnamese teachers were recruited on a part-time basis, and had neither the time nor the training to prepare new courses.[51] In spite of their active experience in administration, administrators invited to teach courses might also either lack the general academic background so necessary to teaching, or not be capable of rising to the lasting generalities that the students need for their training.

Thus, it was necessary, from the earliest phase of the creation of a specialized institute for teaching public administration, to establish a staff of permanent teachers who could devote all their time to teaching and academic research. Since public administration had never been the subject of a special course of study in either French or Vietnamese universities, it did not seem possible to demand of the first nucleus of teachers university degrees in administrative science. A compromise was made by requiring of the first teachers that they (1) be holders of high university degrees in law or the social sciences, (2) have successful experience in an executive position in either the government or professional activities, and (3) have certain academic authority in university or administrative circles.

With these conditions as the basis for recruiting, the Institute now has 18 permanent professors for a student body of approximately 300 (exclusive of students in evening courses and in-service training courses). These requirements are becoming more severe, as gradually students receive specialized training in public administration (a Ph.D. from an American university or an equivalent degree from a foreign university). At present, the systematic program for training teachers in the United States is practically at a standstill, and has so far given the following results: between 1959 and 1961, seventeen graduate students were sent to the United States to prepare for a Ph.D. in public administration or in economic development; five of these have received the Ph.D., two of whom are now faculty members of the Institute, two are working in the Ministry of Finance, and the fifth is still in the United States; four others returned, having been able to complete only the M.A., or the comprehensive examinations for the Ph.D., but had not submitted a dissertation; these four are now faculty members of the Institute; the remaining eight are still in the United States, although the period of time allowed by the grants has lapsed for some of them. When the contract for assistance from the Michigan State University Viet-Nam Advisory Group expired, it was recommended that the program be continued under the auspices of USAID, but this has not yet been done. The criticism has been made that the possibilities of this program were not sufficiently developed, either by the Vietnamese government or by the agencies of the United States government.[52] Aside from this program, the Institute still recruits faculty members among other students who have done work toward a doctorate in France or the United States. The new teachers may, to a certain extent, lack experience in Vietnamese administration, but this has been partially overcome by choosing candidates for Ph.D. studies from among those who have already had some administrative experience in Viet-Nam. Until the number of qualified teachers can be brought up to optimum, public officials in office continue to contribute their assistance in essentially practical matters. This supplement is a valuable factor in the success of the course. Although the number of these teaching administrators will decrease in future, they will continue to form a definite link between the Institute and the administration.

The Role of Foreign Advisors. A group of American professors from Michigan State University were invited to offer their assistance. Certain of these men have exerted a valuable influence, not by relieving their Vietnamese colleagues of the burden of teaching classes, for the good reason that the language of instruction was not English, and that having just arrived in the country they would not have given adequate instruction, but by the official and unofficial contacts which arose gradually between Vietnamese and American professors. In truth, at the beginning these contacts were rather difficult because of the language and cultural barriers. These barriers were gradually overcome as the Vietnamese learned more and more about American administration and civilization in the course of study and observation trips and as the American professors became more familiar with Viet-Nam through the few materials available in English on Vietnamese history and administration and through the contacts they established with the Vietnamese outside the Institute of Administration, many of whom were more familiar with English. Through seminars, organized with great difficulty, certain ideas were exchanged; some public lectures given by American professors even reached the mass of public servants, and there were repercussions on the students. Some of the American professors expressed frustration in not being able to give the full benefit of their abilities; yet the indirect influence of the presence of the American professors on Vietnamese educational institutions should not be minimized. Their easy manner, the unofficial conferences held in private meetings, and their criticism expressed in the American press prompted their Vietnamese colleagues to examine problems that had seemed to them of minor importance but for which solutions were absolutely necessary to the advancement of administrative science and technique.[53] This kind of phenomenon has been described from another point of view: "In more general ways, one may better understand what England is like when one has seen a little of other Western countries, or understand better what Europe is like when one has looked at it from Asia." [54]

Research Activities. The American professors also played a substantial role in the field of research, either through research they undertook themselves or by their participation in developing research programs.

    Traditional Materials. Research is all the more important since the traditional conception of public administration seems not to have emphasized it. As a matter of fact, the traditional source materials of the field consist principally of important facts presented in such historical annals as the *Lich Trieu Hien Chuong Loai Chi,*[55] the imperial chronicles, such as the *Kham Dinh Viet Su Thong Giam Cuong Muc,*[56] or collections of biographies such as the *Dai Nam Chinh Bien Liet Truyen* [57] (Biographies of Great Men of Viet-Nam). These are not volumes of research, but collections of materials, sometimes systematized, intended to furnish a solid background for teaching public administration according to the Socratic method, which is somewhat different from the modern method of case studies. Upon their arrival in Viet-Nam, particularly during the last two decades of the nineteenth century, the French wrote studies of the Annamite Administration, and of the sociological data that served as a basis of this administration; examples of these French studies are Luro's "Cours d'Administration Annamite" (Course of Annamite Administration) and Pasquier's *L'Annam d'autrefois* (Annam Yesterday). Scientific research methods were introduced only in the field of administrative law (the case books of Dareste and of Penant, containing commentaries on judgments handed down in administrative matters), and in the fields of sociology, economics, and colonial law (*Revue Indochinoise Juridique et Economique,* a periodical issued since 1936).[58]

    A Progressive Research Program. Although empirical methods of investigation were not unknown, their use in the field of public administration dates from the period when the National Institute of Administration received the co-operation of the Michigan State University Group. Most of the research done by this group was concentrated in the field of local administration, although some more general publications dealt with the budget, the civil service, teaching public administration, and taxation.[59]

    The greatest difficulty lay in setting up a research program. A first attempt was made, in the form of a request that the government agencies furnish a list of subjects on which they considered systematic research would be useful. This would have been the most reasonable solution, since research would then have been made with a view to the real needs of the administration. As it happened, the government agencies, still strongly influenced by the legal approach of the French, proposed only studies of comparative legislation or asked for commentaries on proposed legislation concerning new administrative subjects. On the other hand, the Michigan State University Group considered it opportune to begin also more practical research; this would permit their members to fulfill properly their functions as consultants in problems of administrative reorganization.

A second solution consisted of setting up a rational scientific research program. A certain number of professors, who had made study trips abroad, proposed that basic research be done on the ecological data of administrative problems, such as the study of small groups, of the family in its relationships with the government, of associations, of professional activities, and of cultural changes which affect national development. These ambitious proposals were not carried out either, principally because of certain major obstacles to the elaboration of the program. Although the pioneers in the program would not need to probe too deeply into all these problems, they would have to make a summary investigation of public services. There were not enough Vietnamese workers for even this summary investigation; all efforts were being directed toward teaching a growing number of students with a small number of teachers; the members of the Michigan State University Group were also too preoccupied by the immediate problems of consultation to devote enough time to the development of a general research program. Nor were the administrators in the public offices prepared for this type of collaboration with scholars in research matters not directly concerned with their daily activities, although it would have been relatively easy to develop this rational research program, making use of the ECAFE or other study centers of UNESCO set up in Southeast Asia, of private foundations such as the Brookings Institution, or of Institutes of Public Administration.[60]

The limitations in regard to personnel, the insufficiency of financial means, and the unfavorable political climate explain why empirical research on the various aspects of public administration has not been set up systematically. However, the results obtained in a relatively short space of time have been encouraging. With the aid of the Michigan State University Group, the Institute experimented principally with three research methods: [61] (1) the pooled work of various social science specialists in a study of the village of Khanh Hau, in which political scientists, sociologists, and economists worked together; (2) the simultaneous on-the-spot investigation of a province at different administrative levels, by many workers, including American and Vietnamese professors, interpreters, and stenographers, all liberally equipped (transportation, audio-visual equipment, etc.), who interviewed and made direct observation of administrators at work (in the provinces of Vinh Long and Quang Nam); and (3) the study of specific cases of administration, at the central government level as well as at the local levels. This study required the close collaboration of administrators in office, and for this reason was possible at first only in regard to bureaus willing to co-operate with the Institute.

The Michigan State University Group has published works in the form of mimeographed brochures in English, most of which have been translated into Vietnamese. Vietnamese professors have published their works in the monthly review *Nghien-Cuu Hanh-Chanh* (Review of the Association for Administrative Studies) and in the magazine *Tien Thu*. A certain number of textbooks have also been published in Vietnamese.[62] Taking into consideration (1) the fact that a certain number of international institutions have indicated the essential directions for scientific research in the field of public administration (e.g., the International Institute of Economic and Social Development at New Delhi and the Economic and Social Council of the United Nations), (2) that a greater number of students are receiving a complete education in this field in the United States and in certain countries in Europe, and (3) that a greater atmosphere of understanding will develop gradually as high public officials have the opportunity to observe the collaboration of government offices in scientific research, it is to be hoped that in future the research program will be intensified and will be able to make a more profitable contribution, not only to teaching, but also to administration itself.[63]

THE INSTITUTIONAL SETTING

The discussion of the problem of research suggests another series of problems in the field of teaching public administration: What agency or agencies can take over the task of administrative education?[64]

The Role of the University. The traditional solution to this problem seems to be the university. It has been seen that as early as 1917, a School of Law and Administration was created within the Indochinese University at Hanoi; this school was succeeded by the *Ecole des Hautes Etudes Indochinoises* (1925), and then by the Faculty of Law (1932–1945). In the new Vietnamese universities of Hanoi and Saigon, there are faculties of Law in which students receive essentially legal and economic training, some of whose graduates take up administrative careers. Legal discipline contributes to the formation of a rigorously logical mind, all the more so since the discussions of legal theories based on social and economic data broaden considerably the views of the law student. Moreover, the study of public law (constitutional law, administrative law, and financial legislation) should be an essential part of any rational program of administrative studies. If the law student can be reproached for leaning too far toward procedure and form, it is only due to a misunderstanding of the spirit of law. It is true that the only research undertaken at the Faculty of Law is either judicial (in particular through commentaries on court decisions) or economic (statistical studies, comparative studies, and economic theory) and that special attention cannot be given to administrative problems as such. It is also true that the Faculty of Law must maintain a balanced program of private law and public law, and cannot orient its program definitely toward public administration. Moreover, university students have greater latitude in planning their school programs, and may neglect the practical work so necessary to the understanding of public administration. Lastly, the traditional academic freedom of law schools does not adapt itself well to serious collaboration with the public offices in matters of teaching.

The Role of Government Agencies. The other extreme solution would have been to assign to the public services themselves the responsibility for organizing courses in public administration, to be given to prospective public servants, or to officials already in office. Indeed, for a short time, faced with the need for filling new or vacant administrative posts, the regional administrations of North Viet-Nam and Central Viet-Nam created a training course for district chiefs. The director of the course and the teachers were recruited directly from public officials in administrative offices, although several temporary assignments were made to university professors (1950–1954). Certain technical agencies also organize special in-service training courses for the functions they perform; and a certain amount of training in public administration is included more and more as the courses are designed for officials of higher levels. Finally, at the lower levels of administrative hierarchy, there are always training and refresher courses for district officers or village officers, in which the basic ideas of public administration are reviewed. It can be seen that this sort of training cannot have a profound influence on the behavior of the administrators, since without specialized teaching staffs, the teaching can only be fundamentally practical, and cannot contribute to the formation of a spirit of development administration.[65]

The National Institute of Administration. In Viet-Nam, the teaching of public administration is assured according to a mixed formula, by a specialized institution, the National Institute of Administration

(Hoc Vien Quoc Gia Hanh Chanh). Created in 1955 to replace the former National School of Administration, which had been organized along the lines of the French school of the same name, the National Institute of Administration was assigned three important tasks: (1) the training of administrative public servants at the supervisory levels, (2) in-service training for public officials, and (3) research in administrative, economic, and financial fields. Instead of being a part of a university, as the educational level might indicate, the Institute was attached directly to the Office of the President of the Republic (now the Office of the Prime Minister). There were several reasons for this decision. Since it was a training center for future high officials, the Institute was to be placed under the direct authority of the highest official of the state. The choice of students represented the first phase in the recruiting of public servants, and this recruiting was the responsibility of the Directorate-General of Civil Service, also attached to the Office of the President. Indeed, the Institute must furnish all government offices, from the highest departments to the provincial offices, with administrators capable of handling public affairs and, at the same time, capable of contributing to the elaboration of general policy. Moreover, since a large number of public servants must improve their knowledge of administration in the special in-service training courses, it would be difficult to place a central agency for this kind of training in a specialized department, even in the Department of National Education.

Finally, a number of practical a posteriori reasons were found in favor of keeping the Institute attached directly to the Office of the President, at the time of the reform of governmental institutions on May 28, 1961, when many services formerly attached to the Office of the President were transferred to various other departments. The students of the Institute must have practical training in the various offices of the central government and of the provincial governments: although unofficial co-operation permits the Institute to organize these training programs in conjunction with the offices concerned, instructions coming directly from the President make this co-operation much stronger. In order to maintain the up-to-date character of the teaching, there are, in addition to courses in theory given by the regular teachers, lectures on current problems of the day, given by administrators who feel flattered to co-operate with an agency which is part of the Office of the President. In addition, the graduates are better assured of finding posts immediately, because of the close co-operation between the Institute and the Directorate-General of Civil Service. Finally, the Institute received technical assistance from the United States Operations Mission in Saigon, by the intermediary of the Michigan State University Group, from May 20, 1955 to June 30, 1962. Since the contract was signed for technical assistance to the Vietnamese government in very general terms, it

CHART X

PROPOSED CONTENTS FOR DISTRICT CHIEFS'
SPECIAL CIVIL ADMINISTRATION TRAINING COURSE
AT NATIONAL INSTITUTE OF ADMINISTRATION

Session		Hours of Lecture
I	Purpose and Methods	1
	need to supplement military training and experience	
	definition of course objectives	
	explanation of methods of instruction and resources	
	encouragement of active participation by all	
	assignments to ten-man discussion teams	
II	Analysis of District Chief's Responsibilities	2
	military and security	
	civil administrative	
	civil judicial	
	unofficial	
III	Structure of Local Government—Charts	2
	(each participant will prepare chart of his own province, district, canton, village, hamlet structure)	
	province, district, canton	
	villages and hamlets	
	other official and semiofficial structures	
IV	Relationships with Other Officials and Staff	2
	province chief, deputies, chiefs of service	
	deputy district chief and staff, cantons	
	village and hamlet chiefs and committees	
	others (New Rural Life, MAAG, USOM, etc. . . .)	
V	Relationships with Special Nonofficial Groups	1
	religious	
	political	
	economic	
	other informal organizational structures	
VI	District Chief's Relationship to the People	2
	responsibility for basic civil rights	
	responsibility for interpretation of policies and programs	
	responsibility for execution of programs	
	responsibility for interpretation of needs	
	responsibility for development plans	
VII	Organization of Elections	3
	establishing lists of voters and candidates	
	notices, posters, ballots, and meetings	
	selection and preparation of polling places	
	conduct and supervision of election procedures	
	determination and announcement of results	
	hearing appeals of voters and candidates	
	similarities and differences in national and local elections	

CHART X (continued)

VIII Legal and Semijudicial Responsibilities   2
  issuance of certificates and permits
  taking testimony and hearing complaints
  settling property owners' disputes
  judging minor offences

IX The Problem-solving Process   2
  techniques of problem solving
  role-playing session on settling disputes

X Civil Security and Police   2
  ID cards
  records and lists
  investigations
  controls of crowds, traffic, vehicles, firearms

XI District Office Management Responsibilities   2
  staff personnel management
  budgeting and accounting of villages
  supply and property management
  correspondence, records, files
  statistics and reports

XII The Decision-Making Process   2
  elements of decision-making process
  application of techniques to district chief's job

XIII Taxation   2
  tax rolls and lists of assessments
  collections and payments
  settlements and penalties

XIV District Economic and Social Development   6
  public works, roads, canals, bridges, wells
  agriculture and fish raising
  handicraft, small industries
  food processing and canning, rice and sugar milling
  marketing, financing
  education, schools, literacy training
  health dispensaries, first aid, maternities, clinics
  social welfare, charities
  cultural and religious activities
  youth activities and sports

XV Public Relations, Information and Propaganda   3
  bulletins, announcements, notices
  newsletters and newspapers
  radio, public address
  how to plan and conduct meetings

XVI Delegation of Authority   2
  how, when, and what to delegate, and to whom

XVII Summary and Review   3

Total hours   39

was difficult to assign this assistance to an office which was part of a particular department. In spite of the shortcomings for which this technical aid can be criticized, it helped bring to the Institute an essentially progressive spirit in its work, substantial research which can aid in the elaboration of a theory of public administration, and a plant provided with modern equipment for teaching, research, and international meetings. This aid can even be considered a model, since there was no interference on the part of the Michigan State Group in the administration of the Institute.[66]

The fact that the National Institute of Administration is still attached to the Office of the Prime Minister, even after the November 1 Revolution and the military purge of January 30, and in spite of several proposals advanced before the Cabinet that it be transferred to the Ministry of National Education,[67] contributes greatly to its prestige, as does the intrinsic value of services rendered by the Institute to the community, such as the propagation of administrative science, the technical improvement of public servants, the establishment of closer international ties through the participation of the Institute in EROPA and other international institutions.[68] Although the Institute has not completely realized the goals assigned to it, it has nevertheless been able to make a positive contribution to national development through the training of an important number of administrators, the diffusion of administrative science and techniques by means of in-service training seminars, and, particularly, through the publication of research studies made by either teachers of the Michigan State University Group or Vietnamese professors, or by the close collaboration of both.

The main argument used by those who hold the theory that the Institute should be a part of the University is indeed the freedom, considered essential to institutions of higher learning, to organize teaching, to recruit teachers and students, to design and put into practice research programs, to express scientific opinions, and so forth. However, it is important to place academic freedom in the general context of public freedom, in a country which is determined to advance toward national development, with bureaucracy as a major means.

APPENDIX
NOTES
BIBLIOGRAPHY
INDEX

APPENDIX
PRESSURE AND POWER GROUPS IN VIET-NAM

TO THE CASUAL OBSERVER the sequence of events which has taken place in South Vietnamese politics over the past two years seems bewildering.

It began with a Buddhist procession in the Central Vietnamese city of Hue on May 8, 1963, protesting a government order which forbade the display of the Buddhist flag on the anniversary of Buddha's birth. As government troops fired into the crowd, what started out to be a peaceful procession soon turned into a bloody riot. This was later followed by a popular movement against the Ngo Dinh Diem regime, culminating in the Revolution of November 1, 1963.[1]

But the military junta, headed by General Duong Van Minh, that succeeded Diem was short-lived. Barely fourteen weeks later, a so-called purge brought to power a new group of military officers, of which General Nguyen Khanh emerged as leader (January 30, 1964). By August of the same year, General Nguyen Khanh was compelled to back down, and the new military junta was forced out by a rising tide of student demonstrations in favor of civilian government.[2] A triumvirate composed of three generals was formed, with the task of convening a national convention to set up a civilian government. Instead, after elaborate consultations, a seventeen-man High National Council was formed.[3] It elected a civilian chief of state and invested a civilian government, in accordance with a Provisional Charter proclaimed beforehand (October 20, 1964).[4]

Yet, no sooner did the civilian cabinet take office than demonstrations of students, backed by various political and religious groups, occurred, which led to another intervention from the military: on December 20, 1964, the High National Council was ousted, and on January 27, 1965, the civilian government removed. General Nguyen Khanh once more appeared on the political scene as the main artisan of the bloodless coup and set about establishing a new governmental framework for the country. A provisional legislative body and a new civilian government were established, apparently in accordance with the modified Provisional Charter.[5]

However, events did not stop there. A few days later, following an abortive coup on February 19, 1965, General Nguyen Khanh himself was toppled by his fellow officers [6] and was later sent abroad as a "roving ambassador" for South Viet-Nam. After his departure, the South Vietnamese lived under a predominantly civilian government in which the military were also represented. Quite recently the military decided to withdraw from the political scene in order to devote themselves to their traditional duties, that is, to fight the enemy at the front.[7] But, only a few weeks later, they were asked to return to power (June 12, 1965).

The review of these events reminds me of a presentation entitled "Breakdowns in Modernization," made by Professor S. N. Eisenstadt at a seminar-session of the "Comparative Administration Group" at the University of Michigan in Ann Arbor in July, 1964.

In his presentation, Professor Eisenstadt pointed out the fact that in "almost all the developing countries, attempts were made to establish modern political and social frameworks and institutions, but such institutional frameworks become disorganized and unable to function, giving place to less differentiated, usually more auto-cratic or authoritarian regimes."

That phenomenon has often been described, according to the same author, as follows:

"One basic characteristic of this story is the development of continuous internal warfare and conflict between different groups within the society, without the possibility of finding any continuous and viable *modus vivendi* between them. . . . The lack of any strong acceptable leadership which could enforce legitimate author-ity and regulate these conflicts and problems, together with the growing corruption and inefficiency of the bureaucracy have often been singled out for the explanation of the downfall of the regime."

The fact is that we are witnessing a real but formless revolution in Viet-Nam. Political power is in the process of passing from a limited oligarchy, made up of some personalities in the entourage of Ngo Dinh Diem, to a number of groups who do not always act with deliberate harmony or systematic antagonism.[8]

Reviewing the events since the overthrow of Ngo Dinh Diem, we note the emergence of the following groups on the political scene: religious groups, students, political parties, and the military. We add another important group whose activities, although much less spec-tacular, have provided the continuity of action which has neutralized to some extent the impact of the repeated *coups d'etat:* the bureauc-racy.

THE BUDDHISTS

The Buddhists claim to be in the majority of the South Vietnamese population; they now total 5,700,000. Though no exact figures have ever confirmed the claim, one may say that apart from the 1,350,000 Catholics,[9] the rest of the population practice varying combinations of Buddhism, Confucianism, Taoism, and ancestor worship, and often go to Buddhist pagodas. Besides, religion is considered as an individual and family matter and requires little formal organization, though at various times, attempts have been made to form regional and national Buddhist associations. For

instance, shortly before the November 1 Revolution a General Association of Vietnamese Buddhists was organized for an exchange
of Buddhist views and to promote at the same time the idea of
religious unity among the various Buddhist sects.[10]

Only recently, as a result of the overthrow of Ngo Dinh Diem, did
Buddhist leaders become fully aware of the potential of their religion
as a political force in Viet-Nam. Those who had been mere sympa-
thizers up to the November 1 Revolution, soon after turned into
devout churchgoers. Thus, it was in an atmosphere of euphoria that
the Unified Vietnamese Buddhist Church came into being. In
contrast with the previous unorganized state of Vietnamese Buddhism, now, for the first time, a real, rational, and hierarchical
organization took form inside the Buddhist Church, with the creation
of the Institute for the Study of *Dharma* (Vien Tang Thong) and the
Institute for the Propagation of the Buddhist Faith (Vien Hoa Dao).
The sermons of the Institutes' presidents, inspired by revolutionary
political ideas as well as religious thought, have never failed to
attract a great many followers. Buddhism has developed into a
religious idea with which the majority of the Vietnamese people have
some sense of emotional identification; it has become somewhat of a
rallying symbol for nationalist aspirations, not excluding a desire to
find genuine solutions, apart from alien doctrine, to Vietnamese
political problems.

Since the November 1 Revolution the strength of the Buddhists
has been again tested on many occasions. In August, 1964, when
General Nguyen Khanh proclaimed a Provisional Charter establishing a presidential regime, the Buddhist leaders, together with the
students, organized demonstrations to call for the repeal of the
Charter which, according to them, might lead to a dictatorial
regime." [11] Then, during the months of December, 1964, and January,
1965, it was again the Buddhists who demanded a no-confidence vote
against the Tran Van Huong Government, by demonstrations, press
campaigns, sermons, and hunger strikes.[12] The importance of the
Buddhists as a political asset has been so obvious that no wise
government could afford to ignore their claim; so far, in three out of
four cabinets Buddhist interests have been well represented. Nevertheless, the bonzes themselves seem to avoid the responsibility of
political life, although they are determined to have veto power over
government policies and choice of personnel.

Buddhist pre-eminence was bound to arouse strong reactions in
other quarters, even within the Buddhist Church itself: some groups
deny the authority of the Institute for the Propagation of the
Buddhist Faith and particularly disapprove of the Institute's mixing
in politics. Under the Tran Van Huong Government (November
1964–January 1965), some of them formed the General Buddhist
Association of Viet-Nam, which claimed to practice real Buddhism

and demanded that religion be kept out of politics.[13] The same controversy still goes on between the president of the Buddhist Association of South Viet-Nam (Mai Tho Truyen) and that of the Institute for the Propagation of the Buddhist Faith (Ven Thich Tam Chau).[14]

THE CATHOLICS AND OTHER RELIGIOUS GROUPS

As for the other religious groups, it is obvious that they resent the predominant position of the Buddhists. At one time, South Viet-Nam was very close to a religious civil war, especially when the Buddhists demonstrated against the August Charter (August 17, 1964) while Catholic leaders supported it, as it was hoped it would bring a more efficient political organization for the country. Press campaigns from both sides were about to poison the relationships between followers. The office of an outspoken Catholic daily was sacked, and Buddhist and Catholic youths fought one another fiercely in the streets.[15] Fortunately, the constitution of an Inter-Faith Committee (September, 1964), combined with a timely abortive *coup d'état*, succeeded in stamping out the dawning antagonism.

Catholic political influence dates back to the period of French colonization of Viet-Nam. When Ngo Dinh Diem came to power, both the Catholics from Central Viet-Nam, where he had been born, and the militantly anti-Communist Catholic refugees from North Viet-Nam were his two major supports. The Revolution of November 1, 1963, left many Catholics frightened at their sudden loss of government protection and patronage; also, many were nervous at their new exposed position, amid a non-Catholic majority. They are today apprehensive of Buddhist leadership and fear a neutralist settlement that would throw them into Communist hands.

However, the Roman Catholic Church is well known for its efficient organization and discipline. Accepting the fact that the old order has changed, the Catholics, last April, decided to set up a "Great Unity Catholic Bloc," which aims at promoting the understanding and co-operation among individuals and among the various social, political, religious, and professional groups to form a unified anti-Communist front.[16] Only recently the Catholics twice manifested their discontent over some aspects of the government policies, particularly the planned religious legislation.[17] It was one of the causes of the present political crises, each of which nevertheless takes the form of a clash over some constitutional issue.

Two other important religious sects, the Cao Dai and the Hoa Hao, seem to play a lesser part in South Vietnamese politics, although before the Geneva Agreement, these two politico-religious sects had armies totaling 50,000 men and their authority extended over large fiefs in the Mekong delta river area. By shrewdly luring their leaders into one of his Cabinets, as a time-gaining device, Ngo

Dinh Diem had gradually broken up the sects' power. But since the November 1 Revolution, the government's official attitude toward them has been reversed. As a result of recent visits to their sanctuaries, government officials have become convinced of the importance of the two sects as potential pressure groups. Up to the present, both sects have been assured of representation in the Cabinet.

We may note in passing that, at the beginning of May, 1965, the newspapers reported an increasing activity by the Hoa Hao, who claim that they can recruit 100,000 volunteers for the Army.[18] Together with the Cao Dai and other religious groups they have formed a National Anti-Communist Bloc, whose aim is "to crush Communism, implement democracy, build social justice, protect national independence and territorial integrity." [19] It was in the name of the Bloc that the Hoa Hao, the Cao Dai, and the Catholics manifested strong opposition to the government's planned religious legislation.[20]

THE STUDENTS

It can be said that, with the Buddhists, the students were the soul of the November 1 Revolution. Indeed, just before that date, demonstrations were organized by the students to support the Buddhists' cause, despite the harsh and bloody repression from the Diem Government. (This explains why Diem's successors particularly favored the Administrative Council of the Saigon University Student Association.)

After the Revolution, the students' political strength remained in evidence. Last year, for instance, with the Revolutionary Government's tacit approval, they organized several demonstrations to protest France's proposal to neutralize South Viet-Nam.[21] At other times, they managed to maintain a real grip on the government. Once, in August, 1964, it was the students who, urged on by the Buddhist leaders, launched a campaign of vehement protest against the Charter of August 17, 1964. Their claim was so violently voiced that the Charter's principal author, General Nguyen Khanh, backed down and asked the Armed Forces Council to rescind it.[22] Another time, when the first civilian Cabinet was sworn in, in November, 1964, it was again the students who demonstrated against the composition of the Cabinet, on the ground that it did not reflect the aspirations of the people.[23] It was then that the legitimacy of the students' representation came into question. For, apart from the Administrative Council elected by the Student General Assembly, there is a committee composed of the delegates elected by the students of each college, which oftentimes did not share the view of the Administrative Council. Although in this second instance the students' action was not conclusive, nevertheless it served as a pretext for the Armed Forces Council to step in and bring the civilian government down.[24]

In weighing their aspirations we come to the fact that these students have spent their teen years in Vietnamese educational institutions mainly in making acquaintance with Vietnamese values. By and large, they seem to be potential followers in search of new native leaders who can provide Vietnamese answers to Vietnamese problems.

At present, the students number 21,300; 17,500 attend Saigon University, 3,200 Hue University, and 600 Dalat University.[25] It was chiefly Saigon and Hue university students that seemed to be the most active.

The origin of the student movement can be traced back to the Ngo Dinh Diem regime. At that time, Saigon University students and various secondary school groups were required to organize according to government instructions; the fact of belonging to a tightly disciplined body has provided them with some experience in mass-rally practices. Having become accustomed in the past to gathering in huge meetings to listen to political speeches, they have now simply moved one step forward—they meet on their own. Yet, what may be looked upon as an asset in the student movement is also a weakness, for, instead of continuous and sustained action, it is usually sporadic and spectacular and, consequently, operative only at certain moments.

THE POLITICAL PARTIES

From the above discussion, the generalization could be made that during the last two years the pressure groups have played a predominant part in the shaping of the main political decisions, but their action has seemed sporadic and not continuous. We might, therefore, think that continuity in the solving of governmental problems would result if there were well-organized parties.

Yet, under the rule of Ngo Dinh Diem, though in theory there were several political parties, actually the Personalist Labor Revolutionary Party was practically the only one. Reportedly, it commanded all the others, namely the National Revolutionary Movement, the National Revolutionary Civil Servants' League, and the Women's Solidarity Movement. Inside the National Assembly there was an attempt to form two blocs, the Community Personalism Bloc and the Socialist Coalition Bloc. Outspoken opposition was so feeble that the Ngo regime was termed the one-party regime. Genuine opposition did exist, but only in the form of secret societies operating under cover, since the least oppositionist activity was harshly repressed.[26]

Since the November 1 Revolution, a great number of political parties, apart from the Communist Party have functioned freely.[27] Some of these were former secret associations now for the first time come to light, but the popularity they had enjoyed while hidden seemed to vanish as they came into the open. The Great Viet-Nam Party (Dang Dai-Viet), for instance, was offered the majority of posts in the Nguyen Khanh Cabinet: instead of working efficiently it broke up into several factions whose political viewpoints seldom coincided; this caused General Nguyen to break with the party's leaders one by one. Nor was the Vietnamese People's Party (Viet Nam Quoc Dan Dang), whose origin goes back to the period of French domination, any more fit to organize and take the reins of government when Cabinet posts were handed to it. Other political exiles attempted to form new parties, but they have not seemed able to organize what is considered a genuine political party.

As the number of political parties tended to increase every day, the general feeling grew that some sort of regulations should be drawn up. On June 13, 1964, party leaders were asked to meet at the Dien Hong Palace for the purpose of drawing up regulations covering the organization of political parties. It was reported that some forty applications for party constitutions were filed.

The events that followed the promulgation of the August 1964 Charter have further increased the unpopularity in which political parties have found themselves. They were reported to have remained inactive while religious, professional, and student groups organized demonstrations over and over again to protest the Charter. This passive attitude in moments of crisis has not brought credit to political parties in general.[28]

THE CIVIL SERVANTS

Political parties, although they themselves are inefficient and poorly organized, have tended to look down on one category of people who, in their eyes, are ready to serve any master: the bureaucrats. From the politicians' point of view, the majority of bureaucrats are selfish, corrupt, irresponsible, with little insight into the values and interests of the vast majority of their compatriots. Though somewhat exaggerated, this opinion stresses the minimal role of the Vietnamese bureaucracy in politics.

Under the Diem regime, all civil servants were enrolled in the National Revolutionary Civil Servants' League (Lien Doan Cong Chuc Cach Mang Quoc Gia). The official objective of the league consisted of promoting solidarity and better understanding among civil servants through study sessions of governmental policies to insure a better implementation of these policies. Actually the League served as an effective arm in the hands of the Diem brothers, and was often mobilized for massive demonstrations in favor of the government.

Right after the Revolution on November 1, 1963, the military junta took steps to dissolve the League. Denied the organization which, although artificial, had served as the link among civil servants scattered all over the country, civil servants no longer stand by themselves as a coherent group. Alleged "Diemists" in the administration were marked for purging; frustration and weariness as a result of unending turmoil also have made many of the civil servants cautious to the extent that, for self-preservation, they avoid any strong commitment to any side. Moreover, lower standards of living and poor political leadership have contributed to lowering civil-servant morale. Though a number of high-ranking career officials were appointed ministers in some Revolutionary cabinets, they accomplish their functions more as professional administrators than as politicians.

In other words, the part played by civil servants in South Viet-Nam's politics has been more or less confined to the preparation of political materials, i.e., to providing Cabinet members with necessary technical information and documents, rather than to the actual making of decisions. Although their role must not be underestimated, for it helps ensure the continuity of the state's affairs even at the most chaotic moments, civil servants can hardly be considered as a group likely to affect directly the course of political action in South Viet-Nam.

THE MILITARY

The weaknesses of a bureaucracy left without political leadership, as well as the presence of barely organized political parties and other heterogeneous groups, partly account for the numerous *coups d'état* that have taken place since the November 1 Revolution. The usual alternative to the lack of a system whereby the opposition can voice its opinion, or even accede to power, is the attempt to seize power by force.

Considering themselves the champions of new causes, the military naturally were tempted to intervene in the confusing situation created by the unconcerted action of the other groups. Although, in the first days after the November Revolution, the leaders of the Military Revolutionary Council seemed to be on good terms among themselves, if only the better to hold onto the reins of government, that spirit of mutual understanding could hardly be found among the companions-in-arms once the unifying issue of Diem's dictature receded.[29]

Later, following the January 1964 purge, five generals, leaders of the Council charged with pro-neutralist intentions, were dismissed and the Council was broadened in its membership to include younger generals and high-ranking officers at the Saigon Headquarters, as well as the military heads of the four territorial tactical zones and the Saigon special zone.

Then, in August, 1964, under pressure from an important section of the population, the Council took steps to disband, though not without hot arguments among its members, revealing many dissensions, especially as concerned the choice of the leader of the Triumvirate, General Duoong van Minh or General Nguyen Khanh. In fact, the dissolution of the MRC was only formal, for the military government remained in power until November 1, 1964, as caretaker, in spite of an abortive military coup on September 13, 1964.

One month later, after the civilian government took office, the military, once more instigated by General Nguyen Khanh, formed another Council called the "Armed Forces Council," whose formal responsibility was to advise the commander in chief on major decisions involving the entire armed forces.

Actually the Armed Forces Council kept meddling in politics; on December 20, 1964, it dissolved the High National Council, and on January 27, 1965, it put an end to the first civilian government. Later (February 22, 1965) the AFC voted down its own president, General Nguyen Khanh, on the charge that he had let injustice and corruption spread and that he had sown discord among army officers, thus weakening the fighting potential of the Armed Forces.[30] On several occasions, since the departure of General Nguyen Khanh, the Council's spokesman has voiced the wishes of the Armed Forces in the following terms: "The objectives of the Revolution must focus on the renovating of the nation's forces, the establishing and maintaining of democracy and on the promoting of social justice."

It was probably in this spirit that on May 7, 1965, the AFC voted its own dissolution, trusting the present civilian government to realize the Revolution's objectives, and permitting the military to go back to strictly military duties, which are at present of first importance in the country's struggle against communism.

Though it is difficult to say of the military establishment that they constitute an important effective power group, it must be recognized, however, that the military form a thoroughly organized body, probably the best equipped to take in hand the fate of the country in critical periods. This explains why Ngo Dinh Diem was particularly concerned with not letting the Army get out of hand. Promotions to higher grades were grudgingly agreed upon, and effective command was entrusted to colonels, that is, to those who presumably would show much zeal in serving and loyalty in working for their "stars." As the commander in chief, President Diem used to reserve to himself the right to decide on the conduct of the military operations beyond a certain scale. But, in the face of deteriorating security in the countryside, he turned to the military to fill positions in the local administration, namely, those of district and province chiefs. The everyday practice in civilian functions undoubtedly helped the military in their training for higher posts in the government. Toward the end of the Ngo Dinh Diem regime there were already many officers in charge of important political functions, such as Commissioner-General for Rural Development, Commissioner-General for Intelligence Service, Director-General of Police, and Director-General of Rehabilitation Centers. On the eve of the Revolution, a general was holding the position of Saigon Military Governor.

Therefore, it was natural, given their gradual training in responsible administrative positions and their merit as the main artisans of the Revolution, that the military occupied the most important political posts in South Viet-Nam afterwards.

One might think that, with their background and the organization of the Army, together with their common experience under arms, the Military would form a coherent bloc in the vanguard of all progress. Yet, the two abortive *coups d'état* under the Diem regime had begun to shake—though for good cause—the basis of solidarity among these companions-in-arms. After the Revolution it was, reportedly, the unequal sharing of political posts of command that was the true motive behind the purge of January 30, 1964. Since then, factions have been formed within the Armed Forces, which explains the abortive coups of September 13, 1964, and February 19, 1965, against General Nguyen Khanh.[31] A group of young generals stood up and plainly stated their devotion, not to the person of any individual senior officer, but to the cause of liberty and independence for their country. In addition, they realized that public opinion tended to be severe toward those political maneuverings that aimed at furthering personal power and interests. This may be the reason P. M. Quat recently (June 10) asked the Armed Forces leaders to assume a mediating role in the present political crisis.

REGIONAL GROUPINGS

In addition to the socio-economic and group differences in Viet-Nam society, there is another social division based on regional identification.

The French policy of dividing the country of Viet-Nam into three regions with different political set-ups—the South as a colony, the North and the Center as protectorates—together with the poor communications network have made the peoples of each region tend to keep away from the others. The Geneva Agreements reduced the province of action by the Nationalist government to that area below the 17th parallel, with its 65,700 square miles of land and a population of 15,300,000, consisting of nearly 10 million Southerners and including Vietnamese of Chinese descent, 4 million Central Vietnamese and including some 250,000 hill tribes, and nearly 1 million Northern refugees.

The bulk of the refugees were Catholics, and both as Catholics and refugees fleeing from the North, their loyalties naturally gravitated toward Ngo Dinh Diem, a Catholic. That is why, under the First

Republic, the refugees and the Catholics were the two main groups that the Ngo Dinh Diem government relied on, though not all the refugees were Catholics nor were all Catholics refugees. Despite President Diem's efforts to balance the composition of his Cabinet by fairly equal regional representation and an equitable distribution of administrative favors, the truth nevertheless is that real power was wielded by those who had Ngo Dinh Diem's confidence. Thus Diem's policy of reliance on personal loyalty and preferential treatment tended to widen somewhat the gap existing between various groupings rather than to promote national unity, as one might have thought it would among the people of South Viet-Nam who have developed many economic and social bonds, thanks to more than ten years of common living.

The Revolutionary governments, in the light of Diem's experience, tried to take a reverse course of action by appointing representatives from various groups to governmental posts. The First Revolutionary Government, for instance, included a large majority of Buddhist civil servants (November 1963–January 1964). General Nguyen Khanh, in his government (February 1964–October 1964) did better in choosing his cabinet members among the Buddhist group as well as from political parties. The first civilian government, headed by Tran Van Huong (November 1964–January 1965), met with fierce hostility on the part of the main groups (Buddhists, students, political parties) because he allegedly overlooked political considerations in forming his Cabinet. The government under the leadership of Dr. Phan Huy Quat was a coalition of various groups [32] and seemed to pay some attention to the factor of regional identification in a last reshuffle.[33]

As pointed out earlier, the above groups seem to have developed common symbols—nationalism and anti-Communism—as the leitmotiv of their activities, although the strength of the symbols varies from group to group. Another symbol seems also to appeal to the majority of the groups: the formula of a popularly elected government. All groups have appeared on the political scene, at the same time, much less as a result of deliberate intent than as a response to the Ngo Dinh Diem regime. There still remains, therefore, a high degree of social and cultural closeness and self-centeredness in each group and subgroup, however great their dependence on other groups and subgroups might have become. Pushed into the revolutionary framework, they still perpetuate traditional relationships and are reluctant to take new responsibilities in the new setting. In other words, even though they have been drawn into a new common framework, they have not yet created a new viable institutional structure. Moreover, what makes South Vietnamese politics extremely complicated is that, however strong these groups may be, most of them tend to be built around dominant personalities rather than around any program of ideology. Although the tendency to rely on charismatic leadership has declined with President Ngo Dinh Diem's downfall, it still lingers under the lesser form of popular tacit approval of the choice of the chief of state and civilian premiers. Examples of this tendency were seen in the demonstrations against some members of the Tran Van Huong Cabinet on the grounds of their political and administrative past records and not by reason of their performance. The tradition of government by personality, together with the importance of face-saving, gives rise to many cases of conflict between groups.

If one understands by political development "the broadening of the base of participation" (L. Pye), then in the last two years there has been political development in South Viet-Nam. But, if one understands by this term "the acquisition by a political system of new performance capabilities" (G. Almond), then recent events do not justify a claim to political development.

NOTES

PART I

1. Jean Rivero, *Droit Administratif* (Paris: Dalloz, 1960), pp. 1–32.
2. See T. J. Davy, "Public Administration as a Field of Study in the United States," *International Review of Administrative Science,* XXVIII, No. 1 (1962), 63–78.
3. See F. W. Riggs, *The Ecology of Public Administration* (New York: Asia Publishing House, 1961).
4. F. W. Riggs, "Agraria and Industria: Toward a Typology of Comparative Administration," in W. J. Siffin, ed., *Toward the Comparative Study of Public Administration* (Bloomington, Indiana: Indiana University Press, 1959), pp. 23–29.
5. E. Weidner, "Development Administration: A New Focus for Research," in F. Heady and S. L. Stokes, eds., *Papers in Comparative Administration* (Ann Arbor, Michigan: Institute of Public Administration, 1962), pp. 97–115.
6. M. E. Dimock, *A Philosophy of Administration* (New York: Harper & Brothers, 1958), pp. 1–2.

CHAPTER I

1. G. Myrdal, *Development and Underdevelopment* (Cairo: National Bank of Egypt, 1956).
2. O. Janse, *Archeological Research in Indochina,* Vol. I (Cambridge: Harvard Yenching Institute, 1949), pp. xvi-xl.
3. L. Aurousseau, "La Première Conquête chinoise des pays annamites," *Bulletin de l'Ecole française d'Extrême-Orient* (Hanoi), XXIII, 137.
4. Le Thanh Khoi, *Le Viet-Nam: Histoire et Civilisation* (Paris: Editions de Minuit, 1955), pp. 98–99.
5. Hisayuki Miyakawa, "The Confucianization of South China," in Arthur Wright, ed., *The Confucian Persuasion* (Stanford: Stanford University Press, 1960), pp. 21–46.
6. Course given by E. Gaspardone at the Collège de France, Paris, in 1950–1953, entitled, "Les Pays du Sud et la Chine des derniers Hans et des Trois Royaumes."
7. H. Maspero, "La Dynastie des Ly antérieurs," *Bulletin de l'Ecole française d'Extrême-Orient,"* XVI, 1–26.
8. Miyakawa, *op. cit.,* p. 41.
9. For further details see Le Thanh Khoi, *op. cit.,* pp. 135–242.
10. *Kham Dinh Viet Su Thong Giam Cuong Muc* (Imperial Annals of Former Dynasties) (Hue: Imperial Archives), the years 1009, 1195.
11. *Ibid.,* during the reign of Tran Minh Ton.
12. Le Thanh Khoi, *op. cit.,* pp. 243–273.
13. Phan Huy Chu, *Lich Trieu Hien Chuong Loai Chi* (transcribed into romanized Vietnamese) (Saigon: School of Law, 1957), p. 99.
14. For instance, the *xa.* See L. W. Woodruff, *The Study of a Vietnamese Rural Community: Administrative Activity* (Saigon: Michigan State

University Viet-Nam Advisory Group [hereafter M.S.U.G.], 1960), Vol. II, pp. 21–24, 26.

15. G. Coedes, *Histoire ancienne des états hindouisés d'Extrême-Orient* (Hanoi: Imprimerie d'Extrême-Orient, 1944), pp. 84–85.

16. G. Maspero, *Le Royaume du Champa* (Paris: Editions Van Oest, 1929), pp. 9–29.

17. P. Pelliot, "Le Fou Nam," *Bulletin de l'Ecole française d'Extrême-Orient,* III (1903), 248–303.

18. F. W. Riggs, "Economic Development and Local Administration: A Study in Circular Causation," in *Philippine Journal of Public Administration,* III, No. 1 (January, 1959), 86–146, esp. 99–101.

19. *Ibid.*

20. G. Maspero, *op. cit.,* p. 13.

21. Le Thanh Khoi, *op cit.,* pp. 264–266.

22. P. Boudet, "La Conquête de la Cochinchine par les Nguyen et le rôle des émigrés chinois," *Bulletin de l'Ecole française d'Extrême-Orient,* XLII (1942), 115–132.

23. Quoted by G. Taboulet in *La Geste française en Indochine* (Paris: Maisonneuve, 1955), p. 542.

24. *Ibid.,* p. 507.

25. J. Chesneaux, *Contribution à l'histoire de la nation vietnamienne* (Paris: Editions Sociales, 1955), p. 115.

26. R. F. Betts, *Assimilation and Association in French Colonial Policy* (New York: Columbia University Press, 1961).

27. R. Maunier, *The Sociology of Colonies,* E. O. Lorimer, trans. (London: Routledge and Kegan Paul, 1949), pp. 297–309, Chap. 28, "Hierarchic Partnership."

28. J. Chesneaux, *op. cit.,* p. 158.

29. J. Chesneaux, *op. cit.,* p. 223.

30. V. Thompson, *French Indochina* (New York: The Macmillan Company, 1937), pp. 96–97.

31. R. Jumper and Nguyen Thi Hue, *Notes on the Political and Administrative History of Vietnam, 1902–1962* (Saigon: M.S.U.G., 1962). Available through the National Institute of Administration, Saigon.

32. J. Decoux, *A la Barre de l'Indochine: Histoire de mon gouvernement général* (Paris: Plon, 1949).

33. P. Devillers, *Histoire du Vietnam de 1945 à 1952* (Paris: Editions du Seuil, 1952), pp. 106–111.

34. H. J. Van Mook, *The Stakes of Democracy in South East Asia* (New York: Norton & Company, 1950), p. 77.

35. Paul Bernard, *Le Problème économique indochinois* (Paris: Nouvelles Editions Latines, 1934), pp. 16, 18–21, 24.

36. For the use of models of public administration, see F. W. Riggs, "Agraria and Industria," in W. J. Siffin, ed., *Toward the Comparative Study of Public Administration,* pp. 23–116.

37. J. Buttinger, *The Smaller Dragon* (New York: Frederick Praeger, 1958), pp. 106–110.

38. Dao Duy Anh, *Viet-Nam Van Hoa Su Cuong* (Saigon: reprinted by Xuat Ban Bon Phuong, 1951), p. 23.

39. Tran Trong Kim, *Viet Nam Su Luoc* (Saigon: Tan Viet, 1958), p. 540.

40. *Su Quoc Trieu Chanh Bien Toat Yeu* (Imperial Annals of Current Dynasties; transcribed into romanized Vietnamese) (Saigon: Vien Khao Co., 1962), the year 1823.
41. *Message of President Ngo Dinh Diem*, September 28, 1962 (Saigon: Directorate-General of Information, 1962).
42. *Chinh-Luan*, No. 9 (April 25, 1964).
43. J. Buttinger, *op. cit.*, p. 172. For general considerations, see R. Maunier, *op. cit.*, pp. 118–128.
44. J. M. Kitagawa, "Buddhism and Asian Politics," *Asian Survey*, II, No. 5 (July, 1962), 1–11.
45. William Theodore de Bary *et al.*, *Sources of Indian Tradition* (New York: Columbia University Press, 1958), pp. 216–257.

CHAPTER 2

1. Victor Hugo, *Les Châtiments*. Those who live are those who struggle;/ whose souls and brows are crowned with a firm purpose;/ who with a high destiny scale the rugged heights;/who walk thoughtfully, inspired by a sublime goal.
2. Le Thanh Khoi, *Le Viet-Nam: Histoire et Civilisation*, pp. 468–475. For details, see Donald Lancaster, *The Emancipation of French Indochina* (London and New York: Oxford University Press, 1961).
3. W. R. Fishel, "Problems of Democratic Growth of Free Vietnam," in W. R. Fishel, ed., *Problems of Freedom: South Vietnam Since Independence* (New York: The Free Press of Glencoe, Inc., 1961), pp. 9–28.
4. Vu Quoc Thong, "Cong Cuoc Thanh Lap Che Do Cong Hoa Nhan Vi Tai Viet-Nam Tu Do" (The Establishment of a Republican Personalist Regime in Free Vietnam), *Nghien-Cuu Hanh-Chanh*, IV, No. 10 (October, 1960); also R. Scigliano, *South Vietnam: Nation Under Stress* (Boston: Houghton Mifflin Co., 1964), pp. 26–46.
5. J. Dorsey, Jr., "Stresses and Strains in a Developing Administrative System," in Fishel, ed., *Problems of Freedom*, pp. 139–152. See also Nguyen Thai, *Is South Viet-Nam Viable?* (Manila: Carmelo and Bauermann, Inc., 1962), pp. 44–46.
6. *Cong-Bao Viet-Nam Cong-Hoa* (Official Gazette of the Republic of Viet-Nam), October 27, 1962; also Law No. 20/63, October 22, 1963.
7. Nguyen Thai, *op. cit.*, pp. 175–222.
8. *Chinh-Luan*, Nos. 41–46 (May 21–27, 1964); also *Viet-Nam Thong-Tan-Xa*, Nos. 4833, 4834 (June 2, June 3, 1964).
9. See the Proclamation of the Military Revolutionary Council of November 1, 1963, and the Proclamation of the Provisional Government of November 4, 1963, *Cong-Bao Viet-Nam Cong-Hoa*, New Series, No. 1 (November 9, 1963); also "Program of Activities of the Government of the Republic of Viet Nam," *Viet-Nam Press*, No. 2980 (special edition, March 5, 1964).
10. *Viet-Nam Press, Tai Lieu Quan Trong Ve Cuoc Cach Mang Ngay 1 Thang 11 1963* (special edition of *Viet-Nam Thong-Tan-Xa*), II (1963), 24–26; also *Viet-Nam Thong-Tan-Xa*, No. 4743 (February 20, 1964); also *Ngay Nay*, No. 56 (February 28, 1964).
11. W. W. Rostow, *The Stages of Economic Growth* (Cambridge: Cambridge University Press, 1961), pp. 4–11.
12. United States Operations Mission to Viet-Nam (hereafter USOM),

Annual Statistical Bulletin #5: Data through 1962 (Saigon: USOM Finance Office, 1963), p. 6.

13. Republic of Viet-Nam, *Bilan des Réalisations Gouvernementales, 1954–1962* (Saigon: Directorate-General of Information, 1962), pp. 375–389.

14. J. B. Hendry, "Some Social and Economic Characteristics of the Work Force of Saigon," in Fishel, ed., *Problems of Freedom*, pp. 191–205.

15. J. W. Kendrick, *Productivity Trends in the United States* (Princeton: Princeton University Press, 1961), p. 89.

16. F. Child, "Essays on Economic Growth, Capital Formation and Public Policy in Vietnam," in his *Toward a Policy for Economic Growth in Viet Nam* (East Lansing: M.S.U.G., 1962), p. 5.

17. *Viet-Nam Press, Tai Lieu Quan Trong Ve Cuoc Cach Mang Ngay 1 Thang 11 1963*, I, pp. 36–37.

18. USOM, *Annual Statistical Bulletin #5*, pp. 14, 19, 25.

19. See R. Braibanti and J. J. Spengler, eds., *Tradition, Values and Socio-Economic Development* (Durham, N. C.: Duke University Press, 1961), pp. 6–9.

20. Republic of Viet-Nam, *Thanh Tich Chin Nam Hoat Dong Cua Chinh Phu* (Saigon: Directorate-General of Information, 1963), pp. 36–40; also *Saigon Post*, March 9, 1964, "Program of Action of the V.N. Government."

21. Paul Mus, *Viet-Nam chez lui* (Paris: Centre d'Etudes de politique étrangère, 1946).

22. W. I. Ladejinsky, "Agrarian Reform in the Republic of Vietnam," in Fishel, ed., *Problems of Freedom*, pp. 153–176.

23. Republic of Viet-Nam, *Bilan des Réalisations Gouvernementales, 1954–1962*, pp. 560–563.

24. For more detail, see the official publications on government achievements; also Sirdar Ikbal Ali Shah, *Viet Nam* (London: The Octagon Press, 1960); also *Saigon Post*, March 9, 1964, "Program of Action of the V.N. Government."

25. B. F. Hoselitz, "Tradition and Economic Growth," in Braibanti and Spengler, eds., *Tradition, Values and Socio-Economic Development*, pp. 86–87.

26. M. E. Dimock, *A Philosophy of Administration*, pp. 2–4.

27. Ch'ien Tuan-Sheng, *The Government and Politics of China* (Cambridge: Harvard University Press, 1961), pp. 24–25. Also see Tran Trong Kim, *Nho Giao* (reprint; Saigon: Tan Viet, n.d.), Vol. II, pp. 26–45.

28. P. Huard and M. Durand, *Connaissance du Viet Nam* (Paris: Imprimerie Nationale, 1954), p. 48.

29. A. de Riencourt, *The Soul of China* (New York: Coward McCann, 1958), pp. 11–18; also Huard and Durand, *op. cit.*, pp. 64–73.

30. *Kham Dinh Viet Su Thong Giam Cuong Muc* (Imperial Annals of Former Dynasties), the years 1129 and 1449; also *Su Quoc Trieu Chanh Bien* (Imperial Annals of the Present Dynasty), the year 1844.

31. S. N. Eisenstadt, "Religion and Politics in Centralized Empires," *The Journal of Asian Studies*, XXI, No. 3 (May, 1962), 275–288.

32. Fung Yu-lan, *A Short History of Chinese Philosophy* (New York: Macmillan, 1961), pp. 181–182; also Tran Trong Kim, *Nho Giao,* Vol. I, p. 125.

33. *Su Quoc Trieu Chanh Bien* (Imperial Annals of the Present Dynasty), the year 1860.

34. Nguyen Dong Chi, *Viet Nam Co Van Hoc Su* (History of the Ancient Literature of Vietnam) (Hanoi: Han Thuyen Xuat Ban Cuc, 1942), pp. 258–259. See also A. de Riencourt, *op. cit.,* p. 43; and Fung Yu-lan, *op. cit.,* p. 74.

35. Quoted (in French) in A. Schreiner, *Les Institutions annamites en Basse Cochinchine avant la conquête française* (Saigon: Claude et Cie, 1900), p. 229.

36. Tran Van Minh, "La Théorie Vietnamienne des droits de l'homme" (unpublished Doctoral thesis defended at the Faculté de Droit [Law College], Paris, 1958), pp. 256–272. Also see Vu Quoc Thuc, *L'economie communaliste du Vietnam* (Hanoi: Presses Universitaires du Vietnam, 1951), pp. 8–41.

37. Dao Duy Anh, *Viet-Nam Van Hoa Su Cuong,* p. 131. It should be noted that in this work, the basic Vietnamese administrative unit will be referred to as the "commune" (Vietnamese, *xa*), which virtually the same community, regarded from a sociological point of view will be called the "village" (Vietnamese, *lang*).

38. *Ibid.,* p. 23; also *Su Quoc Trieu Chanh Bien* (Imperial Annals of the Present Dynasty), the years 1859 and 1871; also Tran Trong Kim, *Nho Giao,* Vol. I, pp. 170–171.

39. Fung Yu-lan, *op. cit.,* pp. 196–197, 214; also Huard and Durand, *op. cit.,* pp. 85–86.

40. Tran Trong Kim, *Nho Giao,* Vol. I, pp. 145–155.

41. Fung Yu-lan, *op. cit.,* p. 215.

42. R. Deloustal, "La Justice dans l'ancien Annam," *Bulletin de l'Ecole française d'Extrême-Orient* (Hanoi), 1908, 1922.

43. H. Miyakawa, "The Confucianization of South China," in Arthur Wright, ed., *The Confucian Persuasion,* p. 30.

44. M. Kaltenmark, "Le Taoisme," *Aspects de la Chine* (Paris: Publications du Musée Guimet, 1959), Vol. LXIII (1959), pp. 146, 159; also Fung Yu-lan, *op. cit.,* p. 213.

45. Dao Duy Anh, *op. cit.,* pp. 139–160. For a comparative study, see P. M. Linebarger, *The China of Chiang K'ai-Shek* (Boston: World Peace Foundation, 1941), pp. 3 ff.

46. Karl Wittfogel, *Oriental Despotism* (New Haven: Yale University Press, 1957), pp. 3, 22.

47. J. de Galembert, *Les Administrations et les Services Publics Indochinois* (Hanoi: Imprimerie Mac Dinh Tu, 1931), pp. 121–126.

48. V. Thompson, *French Indochina,* p. 36.

49. Max Weber, *Essays in Sociology,* translated and edited by H. H. Gerth and C. W. Mills (New York: Oxford University Press, 1946), pp. 196, 331–340.

50. L. Rolland, P. Lampue, *et al., Legislation et finances coloniales* (Paris: Librairie du Recueil Sirey, 1930), pp. 44–49.

51. Le Thanh Khoi, *op. cit.,* p. 406.

52. R. Maunier, *The Sociology of Colonies*, pp. 487–499, 509–544.
53. J. Chesneaux, *Contributions à l'histoire de la nation vietnamienne*, pp. 206–233.
54. Rolland, Lampue, *et al.*, *op. cit.*, pp. 28–30.
55. Nguyen Van Luong, *Thuc Thi Dan Chu Phap Tri Tai Ap Chien Luoc.* Lecture delivered at the Central Commission for Official Studies (Saigon: Uy Ban Lanh Dao Hoc Tap Trung Uong, 1962).
56. *Cach Mang Quoc Gia* (Saigon), September 28, 1962.
57. Tran Van Minh, "La Théorie Vietnamienne des droits de l'homme" Chap. 2, sec. 2.
58. J. C. Donnell, "Personalism in Vietnam," in Fishel, ed., *Problems of Freedom*, p. 63.
59. See, for instance, Erich Wulff, "The Buddhist Revolts," *New Republic*, CXLIX, No. 9 (August, 1963), 11–14.
60. *Viet-Nam Press, Tai Lieu Quan Trong Ve Cuoc Cach Mang Ngay 1 Thang 11, 1963*, I, 3.
61. *Saigon Post*, March 9, 1964.
62. Francis J. Corley, "The President in the Constitution of the Republic of Vietnam," *Pacific Affairs*, XXXIV, No. 2 (Summer, 1961), 166.
63. J. C. Donnell, "Personalism in Vietnam," in Fishel, ed., *Problems of Freedom*, pp. 29–68.
64. Nguyen Thai, *op. cit.*, pp. 100–109.
65. Address given by President Ngo Dinh Diem at a meeting of public servants at the Palace of Independence, August 8, 1955, *Con Duong Chinh Nghia* (Saigon: Directorate-General of Information), II, 71–77; cf. New Year's Day Address, 1963: *Viet-Nam Thong-Tan-Xa*, No. 4342 (January 27, 1963).
66. See the treatment of Confucianism by Tse-Tsung Chow, "Anti-Confucianism in Early Republican China," in Wright, ed., *The Confucian Persuasion*, pp. 292–304.
67. M. E. Dimock, *op. cit.*, pp. 52–61, 71–78.
68. Circulars No. 19 TTP/VP (December 19, 1963) and No. 457 BPTT (February 20, 1964).
69. J. T. Dorsey, Jr., "The Bureaucracy and Political Development in Viet Nam," in Joseph G. La Palombara, ed., *Bureaucracy and Political Development* (Princeton: Princeton University Press, 1963), pp. 318–359.
70. J. M. Pfiffner, *Public Administration* (New York: The Ronald Press, 1953), pp. 9–11.
71. F. Riggs, "Political Interference: Theory and Practice," *Philippine Journal of Public Administration*, IV, No. 4 (October, 1960).
72. Walter Van Dyke Bingham, *Administrative Ability: Its Discovery and Development*, quoted by H. Lepawsky, in *Administration: The Art and Science of Organization and Management* (New York: Alfred A. Knopf, 1960), p. 61.
73. L. Gulick, "Politics, Administration, and the New Deal," *Annals of the American Academy of Political and Social Sciences*, September, 1933.
74. J. M. Pfiffner and R. Presthus, *Public Administration* (4th ed.; New York: The Ronald Press, 1960), pp. 154–175.

75. Lepawsky, *Administration: The Art and Science of Organization and Management*, pp. 62–66.
76. Jean Rivero, *Droit Administratif*, p. 54.
77. An American author also points out, justifiably, that administrators often complain that they must bear the weight of an inert mass of employees (M. E. Dimock, *op. cit.*, p. 9).
78. See R. Braibanti, *Transnational Inducement of Administrative Reforms: A Survey of Scope and Critique of Issues.* Occasional Paper (Bloomington, Indiana: Comparative Administration Group, 1963), pp. 124–126.
79. E. J. Hammer, "South Vietnam: The Limits of Political Action," *Pacific Affairs*, XXV, No. 1 (Spring, 1962).
80. Van Phong Uy Ban Lanh Dao Hoc Tap, *Ke Hoach Kien Thiet Quoc Gia Trong Khuon Kho Cong Dong Dong Tien* (Planning for the Reconstruction of the Country in the Context of Community Development and Community Problems) (Saigon: Bo Cong Dan Vu, 1962).
81. Tong Nha Thong Tin, *Tu Ap Chien Luoc Den Xa Tu Ve* (Saigon: Bo Cong Dan Vu, 1962).
82. For greater detail, see Chap. 4 of the present work, on local administrations.
83. Republic of Viet-Nam, *Bilan des Réalisations Gouvernementales, 1954–1962*, p. 240.
84. *Viet-Nam Press*, No. 3067 (June 3, 1964).
85. *Décret-loi*, April 4, 1964, modified May 6, 1964, *Cong-Bao Viet-Nam Cong-Hoa*, No. 19 (April 6, 1964), 1210, and No. 24 *bis* (May 9, 1964).
86. See, for example, the "Resolution on the Five-Year Plan," *Noi-San Quoc-Hoi*, Nos. 68, 69, and 70; or the "Resolution on Strategic Hamlets," *ibid.*, No. 67.
87. *Saigon Daily News*, No. 121 (April 13, 1964).
88. *Cong-Bao Viet-Nam Cong-Hoa*, No. 24 (May 9, 1964), 1578–1580.
89. *Viet-Nam Press*, No. 2980 (March 8, 1964).
90. G. J. Pauker, "Political Doctrines and Practical Politics in Southeast Asia," *Pacific Affairs*, XXXV, No. 1 (Spring, 1962).
91. Riggs, "Bureaucrats and Political Development: A Paradoxical View," in La Palombara, ed., *Bureaucracy and Political Development*, pp. 139–142.
92. M.S.U.G., *Final Report Covering Activities of the Michigan State University Vietnam Advisory Group (May 20, 1955, to June 30, 1962)* (Saigon: National Institute of Administration, 1962).
93. Vu Van Thai, "Le Programmation linéaire et l'établissement du budget," Talk given at the National Institute of Administration, March, 1959.
94. Le Van Kim, *Report on the Mechanization of Administration* (Wiesbaden, Germany: Conference of the International Institute of Administrative Sciences, 1959).
95. H. Lasswell and A. Kaplan, *Power and Society: A Framework for Political Inquiry* (New Haven: Yale University Press, 1950), p. 51.
96. See also Braibanti, *Transnational Inducement of Administrative Reform: A Survey of Scope and Critique of Issues*, pp. 69–80.

97. B. F. Hoselitz, "Tradition and Economic Growth," in Braibanti and Spengler, eds., *Tradition, Values and Socio-Economic Development,* pp. 86–87.

PART II

1. See Pfiffner and Presthus, *Public Administration,* pp. 215–234, "Contemporary Organizational Theory."
2. See F. Riggs, "Industria and Agraria," in Siffin, ed., *Toward the Comparative Study of Public Administration,* pp. 27–30.
3. R. Braibanti, "The Relevance of Political Science to the Study of Underdeveloped Areas," in Braibanti and Spengler, eds., *Tradition, Values, and Socio-Economic Development,* pp. 139–180.
4. See M. P. Sharma, *Public Administration in Theory and Practice* (Allahabad: Kitab Mahal Private, Ltd., 1962), pp. 80–138.

CHAPTER 3

1. M. E. Dimock, *A Philosophy of Administration.*
2. See Vu Quoc Thong, "Cong Cuoc Thanh Lap Che Do Cong Hoa Nhan Vi Tai Vietnam Tu Do"; also J. A. C. Grant, "The Viet Nam Constitution 1956," *American Political Science Review,* LII, No. 2 (June, 1958), 437–462.
3. *Cong-Bao Viet-Nam Cong-Hoa,* New Series, No. 1 (November 9, 1963), 4; No. 9 (February 17, 1964), 478.
4. Francis J. Corley, "The President in the Constitution of the Republic of Vietnam," pp. 165–174; also R. Scigliano *South Vietnam: Nation Under Stress,* pp. 26–46.
5. *Quoc Hoi Tap San* (Bulletin of the National Assembly), No. 67 (July, 1962), 15–22, concerning *Décret-loi* 11/61, of August 18, 1961, on the medical, dental, and pharmaceutical professions.
6. *Quoc Hoi Tap San,* Nos. 62, 63 (February, March, 1962), 82–95; No. 68 (August, 1962), 84–86, concerning *Décret-loi* 15/61, of November 28, 1961, delegating authority for a two-year period, for the president to set up a special budget for public security and take the necessary measures for balancing the budget.
7. See for instance the account of the returning to the Assembly for new deliberation of a law on the improvement of public morals, *Quoc Hoi Tap San,* No. 68 (August, 1962), 4–26.
8. Jean Rivero, *Droit Administratif,* pp. 48–59, 282–283.
9. Tong Thong Phu, *Quy Phap Vung Tap* (Collection of Regulations) (Saigon: Toa Tong Thu Ky, 1962), Vol. IV, pp. 68, 168, 466, 733.
10. P. Durand, "La Décadence de la loi dans la Constitution de la Cinquième République," *Jurisclasseur Périodique* (Paris), I, No. 1470 (1959).
11. *Tai Hio,* quoted by M. Granet, in *La Pensée Chinoise* (Paris: Albin Michel, 1934), p. 574.
12. Ch'ien Tuan-Sheng, *The Government and Politics of China,* pp. 133–149, 156–160.
13. F. M. Marx, *Elements of Public Administration* (Englewood Cliffs, N. J.: Prentice-Hall, Inc., 1959), pp. 147–155.

14. Cf. J. M. Burns and J. W. Peltason, *Government by the People* (Englewood Cliffs, N. J.: Prentice-Hall, Inc., 1957), pp. 431 ff.

15. Nguyen Thai, *Is South Viet-Nam Viable?*, pp. 13–19.

16. See A. de Riencourt, *The Soul of China*, pp. 61–62.

17. *Cong-Bao Viet-Nam Cong-Hoa*, New Series, No. 1 (November 9, 1963), 4; No. 9 (February 17, 1964), 478.

18. For instance, *Chinh-Luan*, No. 54 (June 5, 1964); *Tu-Do*, No. 2075 (June 6, 1964); and *Dan-Chu*, Nos. 1005, 1006 (June 5, 6, 1964).

19. An old custom was to place a large drum at the gate of the Imperial Palace, to permit anyone who considered himself unjustly treated to appeal to the supreme power for justice. *Kham Dinh Viet Su Thong Giam Cuong Muc*, the years 1052 and 1746.

20. See Bui Quang Khanh, *To Chuc Chanh Tri Va Hanh Chanh Viet Nam* (Saigon: Viet Lien, 1963), p. 129.

21. *Cach-Mang Quoc-Gia*, No. 1312 (November 9, 1962).

22. H. Zink, H. R. Penniman, and G. B. Hathorn, *American Government and Politics* (New York: D. Van Nostrand Co., Inc., 1958), p. 150.

23. Phan Huy Chu, *Lich Trieu Hien Chuong Loai Chi*, pp. 54, 55, 67.

24. L. Gulick, "Notes on the Theory of Organization," in *Papers of the Science of Administration* (New York: Institute of Public Administration, 1937).

25. J. T. Dorsey, Jr., *Report and Recommendations on the Reorganization of the Presidency* (Saigon: M.S.U.G., 1955).

26. Nha Tong Giam Doc Ke Hoach, "Ke Hoach Ngu Nien" (The Five-Year Plan), in *Tam Nam Hoat Dong Cua Chanh Phu* (Saigon: Tong Nha Thong Tin, 1962), pp. 37–45; also *De Nhi Ke Hoach Ngu Nien 1962–1966* (Saigon: Tong Nha Ke Hoach, 1962).

27. Cf. F. M. Marx, *op. cit.*, pp. 112–122.

28. Rivero, *op cit.*, p. 386.

29. Burns and Peltason, *op. cit.*, p. 504.

30. For a discussion of the role of this agency in the central government, see Chap. 5 of the present work.

31. See Chap. 9 of the present work.

32. M.S.U.G., *Final Report Covering Activities of the Michigan State University Vietnam Advisory Group (May 20, 1955, to June 30, 1962)*.

33. For discussion of the concepts of organization, see F. M. Marx, *op. cit.*, pp. 129–146.

34. For discussion of the role of the Directorate-General of Budget, see Chap. 6 of the present work.

35. D. Waldo, *The Study of Public Administration* (New York: Random House, 1955), p. 47.

36. Le Tan Nam, "Thanh Tra Hanh Chanh Va Tai Chanh," *Nghien-Cuu Hanh-Chanh*, V, No. 5 (March, 1961), 53–83.

37. Phan Huy Chu, *op. cit.*, pp. 107, 131.

38. Viet Nam Cong Hoa, *Noi-San Quoc-Hoi: So Dac Biet Ve Ngan Sach Quoc Gia Tai Khoa 1962* (Saigon: So Thong Tin Quoc Hoi, 1962).

39. *Cong-Bao Viet-Nam Cong-Hoa*, New Series, No. 24 (May 9, 1964), 1581.

40. *Ibid.*, No. 5 (November 30, 1963), 57; No. 7 (December 14, 1963), 133.

41. *Viet-Nam Press*, No. 3018 (April 15, 1964).

42. These reasons are approximately the same as those presented by H. A. Simon, D. W. Smithburg, and V. A. Thompson in *Public Administration* (New York: Alfred Knopf, 1950), pp. 150–179.

43. *Cong-Bao Viet-Nam Cong-Hoa,* New Series, No. 5 (November 30, 1963), 55.

44. *Viet-Nam Press,* No. 2014 (April 14, 1964).

45. *Saigon Post,* No. 128 (May 26, 1964); also *Cong-Bao Viet-Nam Cong-Hoa,* No. 29 (May 30, 1964), 1864.

46. *Cong-Bao Viet-Nam Cong-Hoa,* No. 12 (March 7, 1964), 721.

47. *Arrêté* No. 112 PBD/ND, May 14, 1964.

48. *Tu-Do,* No. 1729 (December 18, 1962).

49. *Viet-Nam Press,* No. 2922 (January 10, 1964).

50. See, for instance, R. Scigliano, "Vietnam: A Country at War," *Asian Survey,* III, No. 1 (January, 1963); also W. R. Fishel, ed., *Problems of Freedom.*

51. *Cong-Bao Viet-Nam Cong-Hoa,* New Series, No. 1 (November 9, 1963), 5.

52. *Ibid.,* No. 9 (February 17, 1964), 482; No. 12 (March 17, 1964), 722.

53. Bui Quang Khanh, *op. cit.,* pp. 54–55; 131–135. Cf. Burns and Peltason, *op. cit.,* pp. 436–440.

54. Le Van An, *To Chuc Hanh Chanh Viet Nam* (Saigon: Hoc Vien Quoc Gia Hanh Chanh, 1962), pp. 200–205.

55. *Sac Lenh* 5-TTP, January 12, 1956, in Tong Thong Phu, *Quy Phap Vung Tap,* Vol. I, 434.

56. *Sac Lenh* 74-D T/CCDD, April 4, 1957, *ibid.,* p. 487.

57. *Sac Lenh* 244-TTP, July 11, 1957, *ibid.,* p. 493.

58. *Cong-Bao Viet-Nam Cong-Hoa,* No. 14 (March 21, 1964), 924–925.

59. *Ibid.,* No. 16 (March 28, 1964), 1029.

60. *Ibid.,* No. 23 (May 2, 1964), 1488.

61. *Ibid.,* p. 1489.

62. *Du* (Presidential Ordinance) No. 17, dated December 24, 1955, in Tong Thong Phu, *Quy Phap Vung Tap,* Vol. I, pp. 60–61. Also M.S.U.G. Field Staff, *Recommendations Concerning the Department of the Interior, the Regions, and the Provinces* (Saigon: M.S.U.G., 1956). Now available from the National Institute of Administration, Saigon.

63. *Cong-Bao Viet-Nam Cong-Hoa,* No. 18 (April 4, 1964), 1129–1132.

64. Viet Nam Cong Hoa, *Noi-San Quoc-Hoi: Ngan Sach Quoc Gia Tai Khoa 1962, Phan Chi* (Saigon: So Thong Tin Quoc Hoi, 1962), 68–110.

65. Simon, Smithburg, and Thompson, *op. cit.,* pp. 280–295.

66. Bui Quang Khanh, *op. cit.,* pp. 138–142.

67. Republic of Viet-Nam, *Report on Government Progress, Published on the Occasion of the Seventh Anniversary of the Vietnamese Republic* (Saigon: Directorate-General of Information, 1962), pp. 252–253.

68. Gulick, "Notes on the Theory of Organization," in *op. cit.,* p. 15.

69. Five-man team of M.S.U.G. and the Department of Agriculture, *Report of the Comparative Study of Agricultural Administration in Japan, Taiwan and Viet-Nam* (Saigon: M.S.U.G., 1956).

70. Republic of Viet-Nam, *Seven Years of the Ngo Dinh Diem Administration, 1954–1961.* Published on the sixth anniversary of the Republic of

Viet-Nam, October 26, 1961 (Saigon: Directorate-General of Information, 1961), pp. 319 ff.

71. Le Van An, *op. cit.*, pp. 216–224. Cf. Lepawsky, *Administration: The Art and Science of Organization and Management*, pp. 386–416, "The Process of Reorganization."

72. M.S.U.G., *Final Report*, pp. 73–74.

73. *Sac Lenh* 230 TTP, October 25, 1961, in Tong Thong Phu, *Quy Phap Vung Tap*, Vol. IV, pp. 685–686.

74. *Cong-Bao Viet-Nam Cong-Hoa*, New Series, No. 6 (December 7, 1963), 85; No. 17 (March 31, 1964), 1116/5.

75. Cf. Sharma, *Public Administration in Theory and Practice*, pp. 172–211, "The Department"; Lepawsky, *Administration: The Art and Science of Organization and Management*, pp. 322–340, "The Organization in Practice."

76. Tong Thong Phu, *Quy Phap Vung Tap*, Vol. I, p. 14.

77. *Ibid.*, p. 407.

78. Claude A. Buss, *The Arc of Crisis* (New York: Doubleday & Co., Inc., 1961), pp. 340–365, Chap. 14, "Democracy in Asia."

79. Cf. C. H. Sisson, *The Spirit of British Administration* (New York: Frederick A. Praeger, Inc., 1959), pp. 13–24, "What Administration Is"; also F. M. Marx, *op. cit.*, pp. 183–187, "The Secretary's Business."

80. Viet Nam Cong Hoa, *Thanh Tich Tam Nam Hoat Dong Cua Chinh Phu* (Saigon: Tong Nha Thong Tin, 1962).

81. For discussion of this amendment, see *Noi-San Quoc-Hoi*, No. 66 (June, 1962).

82. See National Institute of Administration, *Nien Giam Hanh Chanh* (Government Organization Manual) (Saigon: National Institute of Administration, 1963).

83. For instance, the organization of the General Office for People's Suggestions and Complaints; see also *Cong-Bao Viet-Nam Cong-Hoa*, No. 24 (May 9, 1964), 1582–1583.

84. Viet Nam Cong Hoa, *Noi-San Quoc-Hoi: So Dac Biet Ve Ngan Sach Quoc Gia Tai Khoa 1962*, Vol. II, 436, 442.

85. Bui Quang Khanh, *op. cit.*, pp. 173–185.

86. For a discussion of these agencies, see Nghiem Dang, *Tai Chinh Hoc Dai Cuong* (Saigon: Hoc Vien Quoc Gia Hanh Chanh, 1960), Vol. II, pp. 214, 215, 251; also W. Snyder, *Autonomous State Organizations: Government Enterprises and Public Corporations of Vietnam* (Saigon: M.S.U.G., 1957); also, cf. Marx, *op. cit.*, pp. 219–245. "Government Corporations"; and Lloyd Musolf, "Public Enterprise and Development Perspectives in Viet Nam," *Asian Survey*, III, No. 8 (August, 1963), 357–371.

87. See Republic of Viet-Nam, *Viet-Nam Government Organizational Manual 1957–1958*, pp. 206–230 and also *Supplement to Government Organizational Manual 1957–1958*, pp. 161, 169 (Saigon: National Institute of Administration); for discussion, see Simon, Smithburg, and Thompson, *op. cit.*, pp. 296–311.

88. See F. W. Riggs, *The Ecology of Public Administration*, pp. 142–143.

89. Cf. Simon, Smithburg, and Thompson, *op. cit.*, pp. 150–179, 296–311.

90. L. W. Pye, "The Politics of Southeast Asia," in G. A. Almond and J. S.

Coleman, eds., *The Politics of the Developing Areas* (Princeton: Princeton University Press, 1960), pp. 94–96.

CHAPTER 4

1. "Imperial orders give way to village customs."
2. Dao Duy Anh, *Viet-Nam Van Hoa Su Cuong*, p. 127; P. Pasquier, *L'Annam d'autrefois* (Paris: Challamel, 1907), pp. 45–50; Luther A. Allen and Pham Ngoc An, *A Vietnamese District Chief in Action* (Saigon: National Institute of Administration, 1961), p. 36; G. C. Hickey, *The Study of a Vietnamese Rural Community: Sociology* (Saigon: M.S.U.G., 1960), p. 52.
3. Nguyen Huu Khang, *La Commune annamite: Etudes historiques, juridiques et economiques* (Paris: Librairie du Recueil Sirey, 1946); John D. Donoghue, *My Thuan, A Mekong Delta Village in South Viet Nam* (Saigon: M.S.U.G., 1961). Available in printed form from U.S.A.I.D., Washington 25, D. C.
4. Republic of Viet-Nam, *Bilan des Réalisations Gouvernementales, 1954–1962*, pp. 237–258.
5. Lloyd W. Woodruff, *Local Administration in Viet Nam: The Number of Local Units* (Saigon: M.S.U.G., 1960), p. 2.
6. Le Van An, *To Chuc Hanh Chanh Viet Nam*, pp. 326–329.
7. Dao Van Hoi, *Lich Trinh Hanh Chanh Nam Phan* (Saigon: Imprimerie Van Khoa, 1961), pp. 38, 68.
8. See H. A. Simon, *Administrative Behavior* (New York: Macmillan, 1961), pp. 79–109.
9. Nghiem Dang, *Tai Chinh Hoc Dai Cuong*, Vol. III, *Tai Nguyen Quoc Gia*, pp. 445–446.
10. Woodruff, *Local Administration in Viet Nam*, p. 11.
11. *Ibid.*, p. 21.
12. For discussion, see Tran Van Dinh and Jason L. Finkle, *Provincial Administration in Vietnam: A Study of Vinh Long Province* (Saigon: National Institute of Administration, 1961), pp. 9–22.
13. Nguyen Thanh Cung, "Cong Cuoc Cai To Hanh Chanh Tai Vietnam Cong Hoa, Vai Khia Canh Cua Viec Cai Thien Hanh Chanh Dia Phuong Tu Nam 1949" (Administrative Reform in Viet-Nam: Some Aspects of the Evolution of Regional Administration Since 1949), *Nghien-Cuu Hanh-Chanh*, II, No. 2 (April, 1958), 9–36.
14. M.S.U.G. Field Staff, *Recommendations Concerning the Department of the Interior, the Regions, and the Provinces*.
15. Vu Quoc Thong, "Van De Tap Quyen Hanh Chanh Tai Viet Nam Cong Hoa," *Nghien-Cuu Hanh-Chanh*, IV, No. 8 (August, 1960), 1–12.
16. F. Riggs, "Economic Development and Local Administration: A Study in Circular Causation," *The Philippine Journal of Public Administration*, III, No. 1 (January, 1959), 86–146.
17. Vu Quoc Thong, "Van De Tap Quyen Hanh Chanh Tai Viet Nam Cong Hoa," Section II; L. W. Woodruff, *Local Administration in Viet Nam*, pp. 1–44; 309–314.
18. See M.S.U.G. Field Staff, *Recommendations Concerning the Department of the Interior, etc.;* for a more general point of view, see U.N. Technical Assistance Program, *Decentralization for National and*

Local Development (New York: United Nations, 1962) (St/Tao/M/19).

19. Tong Thong Phu, *Quy Phap Vung Tap*, Vol. I (1959), pp. 179–183; Vol. IV (1962), pp. 768–773.

20. Cf. J. B. Burns and J. W. Peltason, *Government by the People*, pp. 762–811; also see M. P. Sharma, *Public Administration in Theory and Practice*, pp. 273–277, "Governmental and Administrative Areas."

21. G. Vedel, *Droit Administratif* (Paris: Presses Universitaires de France, 1960), pp. 461–462.

22. *Su Quoc Trieu Chanh Bien Toat Yeu* (hereafter *Su Quoc Trieu*), pp. 297, 298, 300.

23. J. de Galembert, *Les Administrations et les Services Publics Indochinois*, pp. 228–238.

24. Woodruff, *Local Administration in Viet Nam*, p. 6; R. Jumper, "Mandarin Bureaucracy and Politics in South Vietnam," *Pacific Affairs*, XXX, No. 1 (March, 1957), 57. See also *Cong-Bao Viet-Nam Cong-Hoa* for 1960, 1961, 1962, 1963, sections entitled "Personnel." Cf. Ch'ien Tuan-Sheng, *The Government and Politics of China*, pp. 175–190.

25. P. Pasquier, *L'Annam d'autrefois*, pp. 94–98.

26. This was the case of Nguyen Tri Phuong, Hoang Dieu, and Hoang Ke Viem, well known for their resistance against the French. See Nguyen Huyen Anh, *Viet Nam Danh Nhan Tu Dien* (Saigon: Van Hoa An Quan, 1961), pp. 71–73, 75–77, 228–230.

27. Phan Ke Binh, *Viet-Nam Phong Tuc* (Manners and Customs of Viet-Nam) (mimeographed; Saigon: Institute of Historical Studies, 1962), pp. 167–169.

28. *Su Quoc Trieu*, pp. 339, 361.

29. The case of Nguyen Dang Giai, mentioned in *Su Quoc Trieu*, p. 300.

30. Cf. Vedel, *Droit Administratif*, pp. 475–483, 492. Also, cf. Sisson, *The Spirit of British Administration*, pp. 71–82, "The Administrator as Governor."

31. For details of the terms *"ordonnateur principal"* and *"ordonnateur secondaire,"* see Chap. 6 of this work.

32. The Directorate-General of Civil Service, *The Provincial Administration in Vietnam* (mimeographed; Saigon, 1958).

33. F. Riggs, "Bureaucrats and Political Development: a Paradoxical View," in La Palombara, ed., *Bureaucracy and Political Development*.

34. Woodruff, *The Study of a Vietnamese Rural Community*, Vol. I, pp. 271–272.

35. For a theoretical comparative discussion, see Tran Van Dinh and Finkle, *Provincial Administration in Vietnam;* also Simon, Smithburg, and Thompson, *Public Administration*, pp. 296–311, section on Intergroup Relations; and N. Luykx, "Local Government in Viet Nam." Doctoral thesis, Cornell University, 1962.

36. Bui Quang Khanh, *To Chuc Chanh Tri Va Hanh Chanh Viet Nam*, pp. 215–224; and Nguyen Thanh Cung, "Cong Cuoc Cai To Hanh Chanh Tai Vietnam Cong Hoa, Vai Khia Canh Cua Viec Cai Thien Hanh Chanh Dia Phuong Tu Nam 1949."

37. See *Cong-Bao Viet-Nam Cong-Hoa*, No. 11 (February 29, 1964), 574,

and No. 24 (May 9, 1964), 1581. The nation is currently divided into five tactical zones, in addition to the zone of Saigon. The boundaries of these zones vary slightly from those of the territories of the government delegates of the First Republic.

38. Nghiem Dang, *Tai Chinh Hoc Dai Cuong,* Vol. II, pp. 423–501, section concerning budgets; see also Luykx, "Local Government in Viet Nam," pp. 606–645.

39. D. C. Cole and Nguyen Bich Mac, *Provincial and Local Revenues in Viet Nam* (Saigon: National Institute of Administration, 1957).

40. Nghiem Dang, *Tai Chinh Hoc Dai Cuong,* Vol. III, pp. 382–472; also Woodruff, *Local Administration: Its Future Development,* pp. 108–125; 315–337.

41. Bui Quang Khanh, "Cach Xu The Cua Cac Vi Chi Huy Hanh Chanh Dia Phuong," in *Nghien-Cuu Hanh-Chanh,* VI, Nos. 5, 6 (May, June, 1962), 107 ff.; cf. J. T. C. Liu, "An Administrative Cycle in Chinese History," *Journal of Asian Studies,* XXI, No. 2 (February, 1962), 141.

42. G. Vedel, *Droit Administratif,* pp. 475–492.

43. J. de Galembert, *Les Administrations et les Services Publics Indochinois,* pp. 228–238; also Vu Quoc Thong, "Van de Thiet Lap Cac Hoi Dong Hang Tinh Duoi Thoi Phap Thuoc," *Nghien-Cuu Hanh-Chanh,* III, No. 10.

44. G. Vedel, *Droit Administratif,* pp. 485–493.

45. Burns and Peltason, *Government by the People,* pp. 773–777.

46. *Saigon Post,* No. 136 (June 4, 1946).

47. See *Noi-San Quoc-Hoi, So Dac Biet Ve Ngan Sach Quoc Gia,* 1962, p. 73.

48. See Bui Quang Khanh, *To Chuc Chanh Tri Va Hanh Chanh Viet Nam,* pp. 232–238.

49. *Viet-Nam Press,* March 19, 1963.

50. Tran Van Dinh and Finkle, *op. cit.,* pp. 10–20.

51. Tran Van Dinh and Finkle, *op. cit.,* pp. 24–54; also, Luykx, *op. cit.,* pp. 679–702.

52. *Décret-loi* No. 116 SL/CT, April 4, 1964.

53. Bui Quang Khanh, *To Chuc Chanh Tri Va Hanh Chanh Viet Nam,* p. 232.

54. See the theoretical discussions in Simon, Smithburg, and Thompson, *op. cit.,* pp. 296–311, section on Intergroup Relations; and in Tran Van Dinh and Finkle, *op. cit.,* section on Provincial Government Bureaus, pp. 38–54.

55. Phan Cong Tam, "Su Lien Lac Giua Ong Tinh Truong Va Cac Co Quan Chuyen Mon," *Nghien-Cuu Hanh-Chanh,* II, Nos. 3, 4 (March, April, 1962), 159–192; also Tran Van Dinh and Finkle, *op. cit.,* pp. 23–25.

56. Cf. F. M. Marx, *Elements of Public Administration,* pp. 246–273, section on Field Organization.

57. See Pfiffner and Presthus, *Public Administration,* pp. 252–262.

58. Burns and Peltason, *op. cit.,* pp. 789–795.

59. Bui Quang Khanh, *To Chuc Chanh Tri Va Hanh Chanh Viet Nam,* pp. 255–262.

60. H. G. Creel, "The Beginnings of Bureaucracy in China: The Origins of the Hsien." Paper delivered at the 15th annual meeting of the

Association for Asian Studies, Philadelphia, March 25–27, 1963; also Kung-Chuan Hsiao, *Rural China: Imperial Control in the 19th Century* (Seattle: University of Washington Press, 1960), pp. 4–10.

61. Nguyen Sy Giac, *Le Trieu Chieu Linh Thien Chinh* (transliterated from Chinese characters) (Saigon: Binh Minh Imprimerie, 1951), p. 45; also A. Schreiner, *Les Institutions annamites en Basse Cochinchine avant la conquête française*, pp. 109–111, 314–315; also Bui Quang Khanh, *To Chuc Chanh Tri Va Hanh Chanh Viet Nam*, pp. 256–262.

62. Nguyen Khac Nhan and J. J. Zasloff, *A Study of Administration in the Binh Minh District* (mimeographed; Saigon: National Institute of Administration, 1961); also Luther A. Allen and Pham Ngoc An, *A Vietnamese District Chief in Action*.

63. Woodruff, *Local Administration in Viet Nam: The Number of Local Units*, p. 17. Regarding the cadres of *doc su* and *tham su*, see also Chap. 5 of the present work.

64. M.S.U.G. Field Staff, *Recommendations Concerning the Department of the Interior, etc.*, pp. 22–23.

65. *Kham Dinh Viet Su Thong Giam Cuong Muc*, the years 1430, 1707, and 1741.

66. Department of the Interior, "Power and Duties of the District Chief," in M.S.U.G., ed., *Area Administration in Viet-Nam* (Saigon: M.S.U.G., 1961), pp. 231–252.

67. Allen and An, *op. cit.*, pp. 64–65.

68. Allen and An, *op. cit.*, p. 121.

69. The Prime Minister must present his respects to the district chief (i.e., when he returns to his own native village).

70. Noi-San Quoc-Hoi, *So Dac Biet Ve Ngan Sach Quoc Gia Tai Khoa 1962*, Vol. I, p. 71.

71. Woodruff, *Local Administration in Viet Nam: The Number of Local Units*, pp. 23–24.

72. Nhan and Zasloff, *op. cit.*, pp. 33–34.

73. Bui Quang Khanh, *To Chuc Chanh Tri Va Hanh Chanh Viet Nam*, pp. 266–268.

74. Do Chau Ngoc *et al.*, "The Role of the Canton Chief in South Vietnam," in M.S.U.G., ed., *Area Administration in Vietnam*, pp. 220–232.

75. For the prefecture of Saigon, see Tran Van Dinh, *Hanh Chanh Do Thanh Saigon* (Saigon: National Institute of Administration, 1959); also C. A. Joiner, *Public Administration in the Saigon Metropolitan Area* (Saigon: National Institute of Administration, 1962). For the other municipalities, see L. W. Woodruff, *Local Administration in Viet Nam: The Number of Local Units*, pp. 12–16.

76. Quach Tong Duc, "Van De Dia Phuong Phan Quyen Trong To Chuc Hanh Chanh Cac Do Thi Tai Viet Nam," *Nghien-Cuu Hanh-Chanh*, IV, No. 7, 1–36.

77. Nguyen Sieu, *Phuong Dinh Dia Du Chi*, Ngo Manh Nghinh, trans. (Saigon: Tu Do, 1960), pp. 19, 24.

78. Kung-Chuan Hsiao, *Rural China: Imperial Control in the 19th Century*, pp. 26, 27.

79. *Ibid.*, pp. 27, 569.

80. *Ibid.,* pp. 36–39.
81. *Ibid.,* pp. 27, 37.
82. Phan Huy Chu, *Lich Trieu Hien Chuong Loai Chi,* p. 7.
83. Tran Trong Kim, *Viet Nam Su Luoc,* pp. 71, 122.
84. Kung-Chuan Hsiao, *op. cit.,* pp. 33, 36–39. Also Vu Quoc Thong, *La Centralization Administrative au Vietnam,* p. 20.
85. Phan Huy Chu, *Lich Trieu Hien Chuong Loai Chi,* p. 991.
86. P. Gourou, *Le Tonkin* (Paris: Exposition Coloniale Internationale, 1931), pp. 98–109.
87. Vu Quoc Thuc, *L'economie communaliste du Vietnam,* pp. 21–38.
88. Hsiao, *op. cit.,* pp. 20, 264–275.
89. Dao Duy Anh, *op. cit.,* pp. 125–132.
90. See Simon, Smithburg, and Thompson, *op. cit.,* pp. 188–200.
91. Vu Quoc Thong, "Che Do Xa Thon Tu Tri Tai Viet-Nam Truoc Hoi Phap Thuoc," *Nghien-Cuu Hanh-Chanh,* VI, Nos. 5, 6 (May, June, 1962), 1–32; cf. Hsiao, *op. cit.,* pp. 264–275.
92. Phan Ke Binh, *Viet-Nam Phong Tuc,* pp. 104–116.
93. Nguyen Huu Khang, *La Commune annamite,* p. 64.
94. See Vu Quoc Thong, "Che Do Xa Thon Duoi Thoi Phap Thuoc," in *Nghien-Cuu Hanh-Chanh,* IV, Nos. 7, 8, 9, 10 (July, August, September, October, 1962); also Woodruff, *The Study of a Vietnamese Rural Community: Administrative Activity,* Vol. I, pp. 33–54. Cf. Kung-Chuan Hsiao, *op. cit.,* pp. 371–500, on rural reactions to control.
95. Nguyen Xuan Dao, "Village Government in Viet-Nam: A Survey of Historical Development," in L. W. Woodruff, *The Study of a Vietnamese Rural Community: Administrative Activity,* Vol. I, pp. 26–33.
96. Dao Van Hoi, *Lich Trinh Hanh Chanh Nam Phan,* pp. 46–49.
97. Do Van Ro, "The Village Budget," in M.S.U.G., ed., *Area Administration in Vietnam,* pp. 132–140.
98. B. Fall, *The Viet Minh, 1940–1960* (Paris: Librairie Armand Colin, 1960), p. 75.
99. Woodruff, *The Study of a Vietnamese Rural Community: Administrative Activity,* Vol. I, pp. 130–132.
100. Nguyen Sieu, *op. cit.,* pp. 221, 224; also Quoc Su Quan, *Dai Nam Nhat Thong Chi Tinh Thanh Hoa* (Saigon: Bo Quoc Gia Ciao Duc, 1960), p. 9.
101. Woodruff, *Local Administration in Viet-Nam: The Number of Local Units,* pp. 21, 31, 33. See also J. D. Donoghue, *Cam An: A Fishing Village in Central Vietnam* (Saigon: M.S.U.G.–N.I.A., 1962), p. 6; and G. C. Hickey, *The Study of a Vietnamese Rural Community: Sociology,* p. 3.
102. Dao Duy Anh, *op. cit.,* pp. 136–137.
103. Truong Nhoc Giau and L. W. Woodruff, *My Thuan: Administrative and Financial Aspects of a Village in South Vietnam* (Saigon: National Institute of Administration, 1961), pp. 6–13; also Woodruff, *The Study of a Vietnamese Rural Community: Administrative Activity,* Vol. I, p. 5.
104. Woodruff, *Local Administration in Viet Nam: The Number of Local Units,* pp. 41, 44.

105. J. B. Hendry, *The Study of a Vietnamese Rural Community: Economic Activity* (Saigon: M.S.U.G., 1959), pp. 332–364, on the functioning of a village economy.
106. For details, see Luykx, *op. cit.*, pp. 789–793.
107. Nguyen Van Nhan, "The Village Administrative Agency," in M.S.U.G., ed., *Area Administration in Vietnam*, pp. 1–45; also Woodruff, *The Study of a Vietnamese Rural Community: Administrative Activity*, Vol. I., p. 62.
108. Woodruff, *The Study of a Vietnamese Rural Community: Administrative Activity*, Vol. II, p. 282.
109. Lam Le Trinh, "Some Remarks on the Necessity for the Consolidation of Village Councils," in M.S.U.G., ed., *Area Administration in Vietnam*, pp. 111–131.
110. Woodruff, *Local Finance in South Vietnam* (Saigon: M.S.U.G., 1961); also Nghiem Dang, *Tai Chinh Hoc Dai Cuong*, Vol. II, pp. 480–601.
111. J. D. Donoghue, *My Thuan, a Mekong Delta Village in South Viet Nam*, pp. 21–39; also Woodruff, *The Study of a Vietnamese Rural Community: Administrative Activity*, Vol. II, p. 275; also Luykx, *op. cit.*, pp. 798–833.
112. J. D. Donoghue, *Cam An: A Fishing Village in Central Vietnam*, p. 9.
113. Republic of Viet-Nam, *Tu Ap Chien Luoc Den Xa Tu Ve* (Saigon: Directorate-General of Information, 1962), pp. 68–69.
114. Viet Nam Cong Hoa, *Noi-San Quoc-Hoi: So Dac Biet Ve Ngan Sach Quoc Gia Tai Khoa, 1962*, I, 80, 85.
115. Truong Ngoc Giau and Woodruff, *op. cit.*, pp. 78, 79; also R. Scigliano, *South Vietnam: Nation Under Stress*, p. 33.
116. Donoghue, *My Thuan, a Mekong Delta Village in South Viet Nam*, p. 16.
117. *Ibid.*, p. 56.
118. Nguyen Thai, *Is South Viet-Nam Viable?* p. 70.
119. *Saigon Post*, No. 136 (June 4, 1964).
120. *Hanh-Dong*, No. 66 (March 29, 1964).
121. Quach Tong Duc, "Khu Tru Mat," *Nghien-Cuu Hanh-Chanh*, III, No. 10 (October, 1959), 1–32.
122. Republic of Viet-Nam, *Tam Nam Thanh Tich Cua Chanh Phu 1954–1962* (Saigon: Directorate-General of Information, 1962), pp. 112–113, 693.
123. J. J. Zasloff, "Rural Resettlement in South Vietnam: The Agroville Program," *Pacific Affairs*, XXXV, No. 4 (Winter, 1962–1963), 327–340.
124. B. F. Hoselitz, *Sociological Aspects of Economic Growth* (New York: Free Press of Glencoe, 1962), p. 162.
125. Republic of Viet-Nam, *Viet Nam's Strategic Hamlets* (Saigon: Directorate-General of Information, 1963); also *Viet-Nam Press, Ky Niem De Nhat Chu Nien Quoc Sach Ap Chien Luoc* (First Anniversary of the National Strategic Hamlet Policy), special edition, April 17, 1963; also *Viet-Nam Press*, No. 4596 (October 7, 1963).

126. Source made available to the author by an expert working with the Ministry of the Interior.
127. Woodruff, *The Study of a Vietnamese Rural Community: Administrative Activity*, Vol. I, pp. 68–70.
128. Luykx, *op. cit.*, pp. 797–798.
129. Government of Viet-Nam, *Tu Ap Chien Luoc Den Xa Tu Ve*, pp. 68–69.
130. Nha Tong Giam Doc Thong Tin, *Than The Va Su Nghiep Tong Thong Ngo Dinh Diem* (Saigon: Directorate-General of Information, 1962), pp. 18–30.
131. *Du-Luan*, New Series, No. 10 (December 5, 1963); also *Saigon Post*, March 9, 1964.
132. See Chapter 3, p. 78, of the present work.
133. G. Schubert, *The Public Interest* (New York: The Free Press of Glencoe, Inc., 1961), pp. 1–6.
134. Michael S. Olmstead, *The Small Group* (New York: Random House, 1959), pp. 19, 46–64.
135. *Ibid.*, p. 19.
136. U.N. Technical Assistance Program, *Decentralization for National and Local Development*, p. 9.
137. *Ibid.*, p. 10.
138. F. Riggs, "Economic Development and Local Administration: A Study in Circular Causation," pp. 86–146.

PART III

1. For an account of the evolution of the idea of efficiency and economy, see D. Waldo, *The Study of Public Administration* (New York: Random House, 1955), pp. 5, 41–45.
2. F. Riggs, *Administration in Developing Countries: The Theory of Prismatic Society* (Boston: Houghton Mifflin Company, 1964), pp. 3–42.

CHAPTER 5

1. If the people are kept in system by administration and all are treated as equals in the matter of punishment, they may succeed in doing no wrong, but they will also feel no sense of shame. If they are kept in system by excellence and are treated as equals before the rites, they will reform themselves through a sense of shame. (Confucius, translated by J. R. Ware; the Vietnamese version above is taken from Tran Trong Kim, *Nho Giao*, Vol. I, p. 171.
2. From Max Weber, *Essays in Sociology*, pp. 196–198.
3. Pfiffner and Presthus, *Public Administration*, pp. 47–61.
4. A. de Riencourt, *The Soul of China*, pp. 69–70.
5. Dao Duy Anh, *Viet-Nam Van Hoa Su Cuong*, p. 149.
6. Phan Ke Binh, *Viet-Nam Phong Tuc*, pp. 167–169.
7. Nigel Walker, *Morale in the Civil Service: A Study of the Desk Worker* (Edinburgh: University Press, 1961).
8. Phan Huy Chu, *Lich Trieu Hien Chuong Loai Chi.*
9. Cf. R. Des Rotours, *Le Traite des examens (traduit de la nouvelle histoire des T'ang)* (Paris: Librairie Ernest Leroux, 1932), pp. 3–10. 22–25.

10. Tran Trong Kim, *Viet Nam Su Luoc*, pp. 124–125, 241–243. It should be noted that for fear of the re-establishment of the power of the *chua* (see Chap. 1, present volume, p. 24) the positions of *te tuong* were not filled under the Nguyen emperors, pp. 411–412.

11. Phan Huy Chu, *op. cit.*, pp. 107–109.

12. C. K. Yang, "Chinese Bureaucratic Behavior," in D. S. Nivison and A. F. Wright, eds., *Confucianism in Action* (Stanford: Stanford University Press, 1959), p. 139.

13. Tran Trong Kim, *Viet Nam Su Luoc*, pp. 433–434.

14. Phan Huy Chu, *op. cit.*, p. 193.

15. J. de Galembert, *Les Administrations et les Services Publics Indochinois*, p. 294.

16. Nha Tong Giam Doc Cong Vu, *Quy Che Cong Vu Gian Yeu* (Summary of the Statute of Civil Service) (mimeographed; Saigon: the Directorate-General, 1960), pp. 13–14; also R. Jumper and Nguyen Thi Hue, *Notes on the Political and Administrative History of Vietnam, 1902–1962*, pp. 88–101.

17. Nguyen Dinh, *Recueil des textes concernant le personnel indigene des Services Generaux et Locaux de l'Indochine* (Collection of Acts Regarding the Native Personnel of the General and Local Services of Indochina) (Hanoi: Thuc Nghiep, 1925).

18. J. Le Prevost and H. Meyrat, "L'Admission des Indochinois dans les cadres des administrations et services publics francais de l'Indochine," *Revue Indochinoise Juridique et Economique* (Hanoi), No. 18 (1942), 218–243.

19. Gouvernement General de l'Indochine, Residence Superieure au Tonkin, *Statut du personnel de l'administration indigene du Tonkin* (Status of Personnel in the Native Administration of Tonkin) (Hanoi: IDEO, 1917); also R. Jumper, "Mandarin Bureaucracy and Politics in South Vietnam," pp. 47–58.

20. Vedel, *Droit Administratif*, pp. 535–563. For greater detail, see C. Senegas, *Les Droits et obligations des fonctionnaires* (Paris: Charles Lavauzelle et Cie, 1955).

21. Translated from Article I of Ordinance No. 9, July 14, 1950, in Dale Rose, with the assistance of Vu Van Hoc, *The Vietnamese Civil Service System* (Saigon: M.S.U.G., 1961), p. 10.

22. See Nha Tong Giam Doc Cong Vu, *Quy Che Cong Vu Gian Yeu;* also Rose, *The Vietnamese Civil Service System.*

23. G. Vedel, *Droit Administratif*, p. 534.

24. Rose, *The Vietnamese Civil Service System*, pp. 141–142.

25. *Ibid.*, p. 197.

26. Nguyen Thanh Cung, "Cong Cuoc Cai To Hanh Chanh Tai Vietnam," *Nghien-Cuu Hanh-Chanh*, 9–39.

27. Nha Tong Giam Do Cong Vu, *Quy Che Cong Vu Gian Yeu*, p. 108.

28. *Ibid.*, pp. 16–18.

29. D. C. Rowat, ed., *Basic Issues in Public Administration* (New York: The Macmillan Company, 1961), pp. 246–248.

30. *Ibid.*, pp. 225–234.

31. For a contrary opinion, see Rose, *The Vietnamese Civil Service System*, p. 20.

32. *Ibid.*, p. 302.
33. *Ibid.*, pp. 372, 390.
34. *Ibid.*, pp. 61–62.
35. *Ibid.*, pp. 43–56.
36. See Rowat, ed., *Basic Issues in Public Administration,* pp. 225–234; for a contrary opinion, see Rose, *The Vietnamese Civil Service System,* pp. 3–5.
37. National Institute of Administration, *Answers to the Questionnaire on the Organization of the Civil Service* (mimeographed for the EROPA Seminar in Bangkok, October 7–17, 1962; Saigon: National Institute of Administration, 1962); also statistics made available to the author by the Directorate-General of Civil Service in April, 1964.
38. Doan Them, "Mot Khuynh Huong Moi Trong To Chuc Hanh Chanh Tai Cac Nuoc Dong Nam A" (A New Tendency in Administrative Organization in the Countries of Southeast Asia), *Nghien-Cuu Hanh-Chanh,* II, No. 2 (April, 1958), 167–174.
39. Nguyen Thai, *Is South Viet-Nam Viable?,* p. 52.
40. Republic of Viet-Nam, *Bilan des Réalisations Gouvernementales,* 1954–1962, p. 32.
41. See Simon, Smithburg, and Thompson, *Public Administration,* pp. 172–173 (the case of the influential but undesirable executive who is "kicked upstairs"), and pp. 333–352 (general discussion on careers in government).
42. C. H. Sisson, *The Spirit of British Administration,* pp. 13–24, "What Administration Is."
43. R. Des Rotours, *Le Traite des examens,* pp. 26–55.
44. Le Thanh Khoi, *Le Viet-Nam: Histoire et Civilisation,* p. 149.
45. *Kham Dinh Viet Su Thong Giam Cuong Muc,* the year 1077.
46. *Ibid.*, the years 1256, 1314, and 1363.
47. Le Thanh Khoi, *op. cit.,* pp. 227–228.
48. *Ibid.*, p. 264.
49. Cao Xuan Duc, *Quoc Trieu Dang Khoa Luc* (Saigon: Bo Quoc Gia Ciao Duc, 1962), pp. 185, 237.
50. Jumper, "Mandarin Bureaucracy and Politics in South Vietnam," 47–58.
51. Phan Ke Binh, *Viet-Nam Phong Tuc.*
52. R. Jumper and Nguyen Thi Hue, *Notes on the Political and Administrative History of Viet-Nam, 1802–1962,* pp. 41–49.
53. Nha Tong Giam Doc Cong Vu, *Quy Che Cong Vu Gian Yeu,* p. 9.
54. The case of Le Quy Don and his son. See *Kham Dinh Viet Su Thong Giam Cuong Muc,* the year 1765.
55. *Ibid.*, the reign of Le Nhan Ton, year 1449.
56. *Ibid.*, the reign of Le Thai To.
57. *Ibid.*, the year 1707.
58. Tran Trong Kim, *Viet-Nam Su Luoc,* pp. 448–457.
59. *Ibid.*, pp. 308–309.
60. Jumper and Nguyen Thi Hue, *op. cit.,* pp. 88–90.
61. J. de Galembert, *op. cit.,* p. 308.
62. J. Prevost and H. Meyrat, *op. cit.,* 218–243.

63. Nha Tong Giam Doc Cong Vu, *Quy Che Cong Vu Gian Yeu,* pp. 18–25.
64. Personal experience of the author during the period of organization of the cadres for pacification.
65. Rose, *op. cit.,* pp. 332, 324.
66. Nha Tong Giam Doc Cong Vu, *Quy Che Cong Vu Gian Yeu,* p. 37.
67. Ch'ien Tuan-Sheng, *The Government and Politics of China,* pp. 152, 233–246.
68. See also J. Dorsey, "Stresses and Strains in a Developing Administrative System," in Fishel, ed., *Problems of Freedom,* pp. 139–152.
69. Republic of Viet-Nam, *Bilan des Réalisations Gouvernementales 1954–1962,* pp. 111–128, 409–411.
70. Rose, *op. cit.,* translation of Ordinance No. 56, of October 13, 1956, p. 86.
71. Out of 495 graduates of the National Institute of Administration, more than 200 are assigned to executive or supervisory positions. (Author's note, based on an interview with the president of the Association of Alumni of the National Institute of Administration.)
72. J. D. Montgomery and the NIA Case Seminar, *Cases in Vietnamese Administration* (Saigon: National Institute of Administration, 1959), pp. 204–215, "The Commissioner and the Law."
73. F. Riggs, "Bureaucrats and Political Development: A Paradoxical View," in La Palombara, ed., *Bureaucracy and Political Development,* pp. 120–167.
74. Nha Tong Giam Doc Cong Vu, *Quy Che Cong Vu Gian Yeu,* pp. 38, 93.
75. R. Scigliano, *South Vietnam: Nation Under Stress,* pp. 47–68.
76. *Ibid.,* pp. 51–52.
77. M. P. Sharma, *Public Administration in Theory and Practice,* pp. 460–462.
78. Vu Uyen Van, "Nghien Cuu Ve Giao Te Nhan Su Trong Hanh Chanh," *Nghien-Cuu Hanh-Chanh,* VII, No. 1 (January, 1963), 73–74.
79. Michael S. Olmstead, *The Small Group,* pp. 25–29.
80. Nha Tong Giam Doc Cong Vu, *Quy Che Cong Vu Gian Yeu,* p. 86.
81. United States Operations Mission to Vietnam, *Annual Statistical Bulletin #6; Data through 1962,* p. 19.
82. Rose, *op. cit.,* pp. 31–43.
83. *Cong-Bao Viet-Nam Cong-Hoa,* No. 27 (May 23, 1964), 1793–1795.
84. Rose, *op. cit.,* pp. 59, 60. The same tendency has been observed in the United States for other reasons; see Simon, Smithburg, and Thompson, *Public Administration,* pp. 360–364, "Compensation."
85. Nha Tong Giam Doc Cong Vu, *Quy Che Cong Vu Gian Yeu,* p. 93.
86. Rose, *op. cit.,* pp. 49–53.
87. Rose, *op. cit.,* pp. 80–88, 446–452.
88. Nha Tong Giam Doc Cong Vu, *Quy Che Cong Vu Gian Yeu,* p. 84; also Scigliano, *South Vietnam: Nation Under Stress,* p. 51.
89. L. Woodruff, "Y Kien Cua 67 Vien Chuc Ve Nhung Vi Chi Huy Cua Ho Trong Cac Co Quan Chinh Phy Vietnam" (The Opinions of 67 Government Employees regarding their Superiors in Government

Organizations of Vietnam), *Nghien-Cuu Hanh-Chanh,* III, No. 11 (November, 1959), 147–154; and IV, No. 1 (January, 1960), 95–118.
90. Rose, *op. cit.,* p. 85.
91. Rose, *op. cit.,* pp. 86–87.
92. *Dan-Chu,* No. 951 (March 18, 1964).
93. Nha Tong Giam Doc Cong Vu, *Quy Che Cong Vu Gian Yeu,* pp. 59–76.
94. *Cong-Bao Viet-Nam Cong-Hoa,* New Series, No. 7 (December 14, 1963), 29.
95. *Saigon Post,* No. 84 (April 3, 1964); also *Cong-Bao Viet-Nam Cong-Hoa,* No. 17 (May 31, 1964), 1115/3.
96. Walker, *Morale in the Civil Service,* p. 61.
97. W. R. Fishel, "Problems of Democratic Growth," in Fishel, ed., *Problems of Freedom,* pp. 23–24.
98. Report of the Secretary-General of the National Revolutionary Civil Servants' League before the Seventh Annual Plenary Session, Saigon, March 16, 1962.
99. *Viet-Nam Press,* No. 2922 (January 10, 1964); also C. A. Joiner and R. Jumper, "Organizing Bureaucrats: South Viet-Nam's National Revolutionary Civil Servants' League," *Asian Survey,* II, No. 4 (June, 1962), 214 ff.; and G. H. Fox and C. A. Joiner, "Perceptions of the Vietnamese Public Administration System," *Administrative Science Quarterly,* VIII, No. 4 (March, 1964), 443–481.
100. Luykx, "Local Government in Viet Nam," pp. 600–605; Also Ton That Trach, "Phat Trien Viec Hoc Tap Cua Cong Chuc," *Hanh-Chanh Khao-Luan,* II (1958), 5–9.
101. These characteristics can be compared with those expected of civil servants in the Republic of China: *hsu* (Vietnamese, *hua*), or impartiality; *kung* (*cong*), or openness; *hsiang* (*tuong*), or thoroughness; and *shen* (*than*), or carefulness. See C. K. Yang, "Chinese Bureaucratic Behavior," in *op. cit.*
102. Joiner and Jumper, "Organizing Bureaucrats: South Viet-Nam's National Revolutionary Civil Servants' League"; also Scigliano, *South Vietnam: Nation Under Stress,* pp. 50–51.
103. Jumper, "Mandarin Bureaucracy and Politics in South Vietnam," 50.
104. Report of the Secretary-General of the NRCSL (see footnote 98).
105. This appears to be a general phenomenon. See Pfiffner and Presthus, *Public Administration,* pp. 268–270.
106. See Chapter 7 of the present work, regarding the decision-making process.
107. *Hoi Thao Lien Bo Ve Tu Nghiep 1959* (Saigon: Chi Vu Tu Nghiep Hoc Vien Quoc Gia Hanh Chanh, 1959).
108. J. Dorsey, Jr., "The Bureaucracy and Political Development in Viet Nam," in La Palombara, ed., *Bureaucracy and Political Development,* pp. 318–359.
109. F. Riggs, "Bureaucrats and Political Development," in *op. cit.*
110. F. M. Marx, "Control and Responsibility in Administration: Comparative Aspects," in F. Heady and L. Stokes, eds., *Papers in Comparative Public Administration,* pp. 159–161.

111. Peter M. Blau, *Bureaucracy in Modern Society* (New York: Random House, 1962), p. 92.

CHAPTER 6

1. J. Millet, *Management in Public Service* (New York: McGraw-Hill Book Co., Inc., 1954), p. 280.
2. T. F. Tout, "The Emergence of Bureaucracy," in R. K. Merton *et al.*, eds., *Reader in Bureaucracy* (New York: The Free Press of Glencoe, 1960), p. 70.
3. It should be noted that students of public administration have an aversion to studying public finance, even in industrialized countries. See Pfiffner and Presthus, *Public Administration*, pp. 377 ff.
4. Tran Trong Kim, *Viet Nam Su Luoc*, p. 98.
5. *Kham Dinh Viet Su Thong Giam Cuong Muc*, the year 1019.
6. Tran Trong Kim, *Viet Nam Su Luoc*, p. 123.
7. *Kham Dinh Viet Su Thong Giam Cuong Muc*, the year 1728.
8. Phan Huy Chu, *Lich Trieu Hien Chuong Loai Chi*, pp. 161, 171.
9. *Ibid.*, 507.
10. *Kham Dinh Viet Su Thong Giam Cuong Muc*, the year 1747.
11. Tran Trong Kim, *Viet Nam Su Luoc*, pp. 326–327.
12. *Ibid.*, pp. 413–416, 437, 477.
13. *Ibid.*, pp. 252–253, 327. Cf. Ch'ien Tuan-Sheng, *The Government and Politics of China*, pp. 205–206.
14. M. Duverger, *Institutions financieres* (Paris: Presses Universitaires de France, 1961).
15. C. M. Merly and B. Sol, *Le regime financier des territoires d'Outre-Mer* (Paris: Larose, 1952); also Nghiem Dang, *Tai Chinh Hoc Dai Cuong*, Vol. I, *Ngan Sach*, pp. 30 ff.
16. Nghiem Dang, "Co Cau Kinh Te Va Tai Chanh Cong Quyen Tai Cac Nuoc Cham Tien," *Nghien-Cuu Hanh-Chanh*, V. Nos. 3 and 4 (March and April, 1962), 19–64.
17. National Bank of Vietnam, *Estimations du Revenu National, 1955, 1956* (Saigon: Banque Nationale du Viet-Nam, 1956).
18. F. Child, *Toward a Policy for Economic Growth in Viet Nam*, pp. 22–23.
19. Estimates made by the author, based on information gathered regarding the budget and American aid (Nghiem Dang, *Tai Chinh Doc Dai Cuong*, Vol. III, *Tai Nguyen Quoc Gia*, pp. 380–381) and on expenditures proposed by the Directorate-General of Budget and Foreign Aid in 1962.
20. Annual publication of the Directorate-General of Budget and Foreign Aid, *Ngan Sach Quoc Gia Tai Khoa 1963* (Saigon: Nha Tong Giam Doc Ngan Sach, 1963).
21. F. Riggs, "Prismatic Society and Financial Administration: A Bazaar Canteen Model," *Administrative Science Quarterly*, June, 1960, 1–46. Also F. Riggs, "Sala Finance: Tributary, Prebendary, Donative," in *Administration in Developing Countries: The Theory of Prismatic Society*, pp. 286–312.
22. Nghiem Dang, *Tai Chinh Hoc Dai Cuong*, Vol. II, *Cong Phi*, p. 93.
23. Annual publication of the Directorate-General of Budget and Foreign

Aid, *Ngan Sach Tong Quat 1962*, pp. 11, 17; also for the following year under the new title, *Ngan Sach Quoc Gia Tai Khoa 1963*, p. A2.

24. Pfiffner and Presthus, *Public Administration*, pp. 390–400, "Congressional Review of Military Policy."

25. See the account of the intervention of a deputy in Noi-San Quoc-Hoi, *Ngan Sach Quoc Gia Tai Khoa 1963* (Saigon: So Thong Tin Quoc Hoi), Vol. II, pp. 435, 450 ff.

26. Lepawsky, *Administration: The Art and Science of Organization and Management*, pp. 497–536.

27. Vu Quoc Thuc, "Van De Ke Hoach Quoc Gia," in *Luat-Hoc Kinh-Te Tap-Chi*, Nos. 1 and 2 (1960), 5–11; also by the same author, "Dieu Kien An Ninh Trong Cong Cuoc Ke Hoach Hoa," *ibid.*, Nos. 2 and 4, 5–12.

28. R. G. Scigliano and W. W. Snyder, "The Budget Process in South Viet Nam," *Pacific Affairs*, XXXIII, No. 1 (March, 1960), 51.

29. Nghiem Dang, *Tai Chinh Hoc Dai Cuong*, Vol. II, *Cong Phi*, pp. 93–101.

30. *Thong Ke Ngan Sach Thang 12 Nam 1963* (Saigon: Directorate-General of Budget and Foreign Aid, 1964); see also Scigliano, *South Vietnam: Nation Under Stress*, pp. 111–113, 124–129.

31. See for instance the USOM *Annual Statistical Bulletin #4: Data through 1962* (Saigon: USOM, 1962), pp. 117–119.

32. For discussion, see J. D. Montgomery, "Political Dimensions of Foreign Aid," in Braibanti and Spengler, eds., *Tradition, Values and Socio-Economic Development*, pp. 243–275.

33. See Milton C. Taylor, "South Vietnam: Lavish Aid, Limited Progress," *Pacific Affairs*, XXXIV, No. 3 (Fall, 1961), 242–286.

34. C. Goodrich, *Perspectives on Economic Development in Viet Nam* (New York: United Nations, 1956), pp. 471–476.

35. Scigliano and Snyder, "The Budget Process in South Viet Nam," 48–60.

36. Cf. Jesse Burkhead, *Government Budgeting* (New York: John Wiley and Sons, 1956), p. 246.

37. Viet Nam Cong Hoa, *Noi-San Quoc-Hoi: So Dac Biet Ve Ngan Sach Quoc Gia Tai Khoa 1962*, I, 8.

38. Lepawsky, *op. cit.*, pp. 462–466.

39. Nghiem Dang, *Tai Chinh Hoc Dai Cuong*, Vol. I, *Ngan Sach*, pp. 71–75, "Nha Tong Giam Doc Ngan Sach Va Ngoai Vien"; also Pfiffner and Presthus, *Public Administration*, pp. 403–411, "The Bureau of the Budget."

40. Cf. Riggs. "Prismatic Society and Financial Administration."

41. See Arthur Smithies, *The Budgetary Process in the United States* (New York: McGraw-Hill, 1955), pp. 129 ff.

42. See, for instance, President Ngo Dinh Diem, *Message to the National Assembly, October 1, 1962* (Saigon: Directorate-General of Information, 1962).

43. Viet Nam Cong Hoa, *Noi-San Quoc-Hoi: So Dac Biet Ve Ngan Sach Quoc Gia Tai Khoa 1962*, II, 468.

44. Scigliano and Snyder, "The Budget Process in South Viet Nam."

45. Viet Nam Cong Hoa, *Noi-San Quoc-Hoi: So Dac Biet Ve Ngan Sach Quoc Gia Tai Khoa 1962*, I, 64.
46. *Ibid.,* II, 471.
47. Burns and Peltason, *Government by the People,* pp. 425–430.
48. *Noi-San Quoc-Hoi,* No. 69 (September, 1962), 8, 35–77; also No. 70 (October, 1962), 3–74; No. 71 (November, 1962), 3–55.
49. See Ch. P. Bhambhri, *Public Administration: Theory and Practice* (Meerut City: Jai Prakash Nath, 1960), Part III, pp. 46–47; also Pfiffner and Presthus, *Public Administration,* p. 422.
50. Burns and Peltason, *op. cit.,* pp. 740–741.
51. Michigan State University Staff, *Budgetary Administration in Vietnam: A Report to the Presidency and to the Cabinet of the Republic of Vietnam* (Saigon: M.S.U.G., 1957). Now available through the National Institute of Administration, Saigon.
52. Nghiem Dang, "Su Doi Lap Giua Dinh Che Ngan Sach Thuoc Dia Va Dinh Che Ngan Sach Doc Lap" (A Comparison of Colonial Budgetary Institutions with those of the Republic of Vietnam), *Que Huong,* No. 32 (February, 1962), 191–214.
53. M. H. Murphy and W. W. Snyder, *An Analysis of Revenues and Expenditures of Vietnamese Agencies Having Budget Autonomy, Fiscal Year 1956* (Saigon: M.S.U.G., 1957); also L. D. Musolf, "Public Enterprise and Development Perspectives in South Viet Nam," *Asian Survey,* III, No. 8 (August, 1963), 357–371; and L. D. Musolf "Public Enterprise and 'Developed' Organizational Forms: South Viet Nam," *International Review of Administrative Science,* XXIX (1963). See also F. Riggs, "Prismatic Society and Financial Administration."
54. See annual publications of the Directorate-General of Budget and Foreign Aid, *Ngan Sach Tong Quat,* for 1960, 1961, 1962, and USOM, *Annual Statistical Bulletin* for 1960, 1961, 1962, etc.
55. *Ngan Sach Tong Quat 1962.*
56. *Noi-San Quoc-Hoi: Ngan Sach Tai Khoa 1962* (Saigon: So Thong Tin Quoc Hoi, 1962), Vol. II, p. 436.
57. Riggs, "Sala Finance: Tributary, Prebendary, Donative."
58. Nghiem Dang, *Tai Chinh Hoc Dai Cuong,* Vol. I, *Ngan Sach,* pp. 158, 159.
59. *Noi-San Quoc-Hoi: So Dac Biet Ve Ngan Sach Tai Khoa 1962* (Phan Chi), pp. 473–481.
60. Riggs, "Sala Finance," in *op. cit.;* also Scigliano, *South Vietnam: Nation Under Stress,* p. 41.
61. Nghiem Dang, "Su Bien Cai Ky Thuat Tai Chinh Thuoc Dia Thanh Tai Chinh Doc Lap" (The Transformation of Colonial Budgetary Technique to Fit the Republican System), *Que Huong,* No. 33 (March, 1962), 156–175.
62. ECAFE, *Report on the Workshop on Problems of Budget Reclassification and Management,* First Workshop, 1956; Second, 1957; Third, 1961 (Bangkok: ECAFE).
63. Tong Nha Ngan Sach, *Ngan Sach Quoc Gia Viet-Nam Tai Khoa 1958: Tuong Trinh Ve Cai To Ngan Sach* (National Budget of Vietnam: Fiscal Year 1958: Report on Budgetary Reforms); also A. Murphy,

"Overcoming Resistance to Major Change: Viet-Nam Budget Reform," *Public Administration Review,* XX, No. 3 (Summer, 1960), 148–151.

64. *Report of the Vietnamese Delegate to the Third ECAFE Workshop at Bangkok, 1961;* also Ali Eghtedari *et al.,* "Symposium. Performance Budgeting: Has the Theory Worked?" *Public Administration Review,* XX, No. 2 (Spring, 1960), 63–85.

65. *Noi-San Quoc-Hoi,* Nos. 69, 70, 71 (September, October, November, 1962).

66. Viet Nam Cong Hoa, *Noi-San Quoc-Hoi: So Dac Biet Ve Ngan Sach Quoc Gia Tai Khoa 1961* (Saigon: So Thong Tin Quoc Hoi, 1961), I, 11–12.

67. *Ngan Sach Tong Quat 1962;* also, *Ngan Sach Quoc Gia Tai Khoa 1963.*

68. *Noi-San Quoc-Hoi: So Dac Biet Ve Ngan Sach Quoc Gia Tai Khoa 1962,* I, 13.

69. A posteriori, many other reasons have been presented to justify the separation: technical qualities, procedure, rational division of labor, etc. See Merly and Sol, *Le regime financier des territoires d'Outre-Mer.*

70. Nghiem Dang, *Tai Chinh Hoc Dai Cuong,* Vol. II, *Cong Phi,* pp. 229–238.

71. *Ibid.,* pp. 391–422.

72. For further detail, see Nha Tong Giam Doc Ngan Sach, *Thu Tuc Thi Hanh Ngan Sach Quoc Gia: Thong Tu So 183 Ngay 11–12–1957* (mimeographed; Saigon, 1957); also M. H. Murphy, *Budgetary Administration* (Saigon: M.S.U.G., 1957).

73. Nghiem Dang, *Tai Chinh Hoc Dai Cuong,* Vol. II, *Cong Phi,* pp. 253–286; also J. R. Adamson, *A Proposed Budgetary Accounting Procedures Manual for the Republic of Viet Nam* (Saigon: M.S.U.G., 1957).

74. See J. D. Montgomery *et al., Cases in Vietnamese Administration,* pp. 247–270, "Planning the Municipal Market at Dalat."

75. Riggs, "Sala Finance: Tributary, Prebendary, Donative," in *op. cit.;* cf. William J. Schultz and C. Lowell Harriss, *American Public Finance* (New York: Prentice-Hall, Inc., 1949), pp. 103–127, "Economy and Control in Governmental Expenditures."

76. G. Lupi, "La Regle du service fait et ses interpretations recentes," *Revue de Science Financiere* (Paris), II (1956), 682.

77. Riggs, "Sala Finance: Tributary, Prebendary, Donative."

78. "The Affair of the High-speed Subway in Philadelphia," *New York Times,* May 28, 1961.

79. Viet Nam Cong Hoa, *Thanh Tich Tam Nam Hoat Dong Cua Chinh Phu* (Saigon: Tong Nha Thong Tin, 1962), p. 10.

80. Nghiem Dang, *Tai Chinh Hoc Dai Cuong,* Vol. II, *Cong Phi,* pp. 283–286.

81. M.S.U.G., *Report of the Operations of the Treasury* (Saigon: M.S.U.G., 1959); also, the Director-General of Treasury, *Comments of M.S.U.G. on the Remarks of the Treasury on the Study by M.S.U.G. at the General-Directorate of Treasury* (confidential letter to the Secretary of State for Finance, Saigon, May 27, 1960); and Adamson, *A Proposed*

Budgetary Accounting Procedures Manual for the Republic of Viet Nam.

82. *Ngan Sach Tong Quat 1962*, p. 11.
83. Nghiem Dang, *Tai Chinh Hoc Dai Cuong*, Vol. II, *Cong Phi*, pp. 283–286.
84. Republic of Viet-Nam, *Bilan des Réalisations Gouvernementales 1954–1962*, p. 17.
85. *Cong-Bao Viet-Nam Cong-Hoa*, No. 31 (June 13, 1964), 2007.
86. Phan Huy Chu, *Lich Trieu Hien Chuong Loai Chi*, "Quoc Dung Chi."
87. Tran Trong Kim, *Viet-Nam Su Luoc*, pp. 413–415.
88. De Galembert, *Les Administrations et les Services Publics Indochinois*, pp. 381–414. Also Merly and Sol, *Le regime financier des territoires d'Outre-Mer*, pp. 165–179.
89. Nghiem Dang, *Tai Chinh Hoc Dai Cuong*, Vol. III, *Tai Nguyen Quoc Gia*, pp. 289–296.
90. Paul Bernard, *Les Problèmes posés par le développement industriel de l'Indochine* (Paris: A. Toulon, 1938).
91. *Thong Ke Ngan Sach Thang 12 Nam 1963.*
92. Tong Nha Thong Tin, *Thanh Tich Tam Nam Hoat Dong Cua Chanh Phu* (Saigon: Directorate-General of Information, 1962), pp. 582–587; also Nghiem Dang, "Chanh Sach Tai Chanh" (Fiscal Policy), in *Que Huong*, No. 39 (December, 1962).
93. *Noi-San Quoc-Hoi*, No. 68 (August, 1962), 30–86.
94. Nghiem Dang, *Tai Chinh Hoc Dai Cuong*, Vol. III, *Tai Nguyen Quoc Gia*, pp. 27–44.
95. Riggs, "Prismatic Society and Financial Administration."
96. Viet Nam Cong Hoa, *Seven Years of the Ngo Dinh Diem Administration*, p. 270; also Republic of Viet-Nam, *Bilan des Réalisations Gouvernementales, 1954–1962*, p. 339.
97. For greater detail see M. C. Taylor, *The Taxation of Real Property in Viet Nam* (Saigon: M.S.U.G., 1959), and F. Riggs, *An Ecological Approach: The Sala Model*, etc., *op. cit.*, p. 22.
98. *Décret-loi* No. 13/62 of July 3, 1962, in *Phap Ly Tap San*, No. 3 (1962), 191–192.
99. M. C. Taylor, *The Patente (Business License Tax) in Viet Nam* (Saigon: M.S.U.G., 1959).
100. Nghiem Dang, "Tu Tai Chinh Thuoc Dia Den Tai Chinh Doc Lap" (From Colonial Finances to the Finances of an Independent State), *Que Huong*, No. 36 (June, 1962), 229.
101. *Noi-San Quoc-Hoi: So Dac Biet Ngan Sach Quoc Gia Tai Khoa 1963* (Saigon: So Thong Tin Quoc Hoi, 1963), Vol. I: *Phan Thau*, p. 51; see also Riggs, "Prismatic Society and Financial Administration."
102. Republic of Viet-Nam, *Bilan des Réalisations Gouvernementales 1954–1962*, pp. 336–340.
103. Nghiem Dang, *Tai Chinh Hoc Dai Cuong*, Vol. II, *Cong Phi*, pp. 370–371.
104. M. C. Taylor, *The Taxation of Income in Viet Nam* (Saigon: M.S.U.G., 1959).
105. R. Lindholm, *Analysis of Viet Nam's Tax System* (Saigon: USOM,

1956—confidential); also Nha Tong Giam Doc Ngan Sach Va Ngoai Vien, *A Preliminary Report of the Brookings Institution (Ford Foundation) Economic Specialists Group* (Saigon: Directorate-General of Budget and Foreign Aid, 1961).

106. Riggs, "Prismatic Society and Financial Administration."

107. Nha Tong Giam Doc Ngan Sach và Ngoai Vien, *A Preliminary Report by the Brookings Institution (Ford Foundation) Economic Specialists Group*, p. 8; also *United States Statistical Yearbook, 1956.*

108. *Times of Viet Nam*, VII, Nos. 117, 132 (May 4, 19, 1963).

109. Riggs, "Sala Finance."

PART IV

1. H. A. Simon, *Administrative Behavior*, pp. 1–11.

2. J. M. Gaus, *Reflections on Public Administration* (Birmingham, Alabama: University of Alabama Press, 1958), p. 119.

CHAPTER 7

1. "To act without knowing why; to do a thing habitually without examining the reasons; to pursue an activity all life long without understanding inherent process—this is to be one of the crowd," *The Sayings of Mencius*, James R. Ware, trans. (New York: Mentor Books, 1960), p. 149. The Vietnamese translation is from Tran Trong Kim, *Nho Giao*, Vol. I, p. 236.

2. H. A. Simon, *Administrative Behavior*, p. 3.

3. J. D. Montgomery and the NIA Case Development Seminar, *Cases in Vietnamese Administration*, pp. 20–32, "The Decision to Introduce Mechanical Accounting to the National Budget."

4. G. Sjoberg, "Political Structure, Ideology and Economic Development." Paper presented at the Carnegie faculty seminar on political and administrative development, Indiana University, 1963.

5. Tran Van Dinh and Jason L. Finkle, *Provincial Administration in Vietnam: A Study of Vinh Long Province*, pp. 55–64.

6. J. D. Montgomery, "Political Dimensions of Foreign Aid," in Braibanti and Spengler, eds., *Tradition, Values and Socio-Economic Development*, pp. 243–275; also F. Riggs, "Bureaucrats and Political Development: A Paradoxical View," in *op. cit.*

7. G. Sjoberg, "Political Structure, Ideology and Economic Development."

8. *Viet-Nam Thong-Tan-Xa, So Dac Biet Quoc Sach Ap Chien Luoc*, April 17, 1963.

9. See, for instance, "Intervention of a District Chief: The Construction of Dap So Dam," in Montgomery *et al.*, *Cases in Vietnamese Administration*, pp. 2–19.

10. See Pfiffner and Presthus, *Public Administration*, pp. 120–121.

11. For a study of political parties, see R. G. Scigliano, "Political Parties in South Viet Nam Under the Republic," *Pacific Affairs*, XXXIII, No. 4 (December, 1960), 327–346; also Scigliano, *South Vietnam: Nation Under Stress*, pp. 69–74.

12. Nha Tong Giam Doc Cong Vu, *Quy Che Cong Vu Gian Yeu*.

13. Tran Van Dinh and Finkle, *op. cit.*, pp. 6–8; also Nguyen Khac Nhan

and J. J. Zasloff, *A Study of Administration in the Binh Minh District,* p. 26; and Luther A. Allen and Pham Ngoc An, *A Vietnamese District Chief in Action,* p. 51.

14. Allen and An, *op. cit.,* pp. 50–51; also Tran Van Dinh and Finkle, *op. cit.,* p. 7.

15. Nguyen Thai, *Is South Viet-Nam Viable?* pp. 230–244; also Scigliano, *South Vietnam: Nation Under Stress,* pp. 75–80.

16. Riggs, "Bureaucrats and Political Development," in *op. cit.*

17. R. Emerson, "Problems of Representative Government in Southeast Asia," *Pacific Affairs,* XXVI, No. 4 (December, 1953), 291–302.

18. R. Scigliano, "Political Parties in Viet Nam Under the Republic," *Pacific Affairs,* XXXIII, No. 4 (December, 1960), 327–346; also *Times of Viet Nam,* VII, No. 185 (July 11, 1963), 1, the case of Phan Quang Dan.

19. Scigliano, *South Vietnam: Nation Under Stress,* pp. 80–91.

20. W. R. Fishel, "Problems of Democratic Growth of Free Vietnam," in Fishel, ed., *Problems of Freedom,* p. 15.

21. Tran Van Dinh, "Luoc Khao Ve Nhung Quyen Tu Do Cong Cong," *Nghien-Cuu Hanh-Chanh,* V, No. 5, pp. 114–122.

22. Scigliano, *South Vietnam: Nation Under Stress,* p. 43.

23. *Saigon Post,* No. 113 (May 8, 1964).

24. *Dan-Chu,* No. 960 (April 14, 1964); also *Viet-Nam Press,* No. 2983 (March 11, 1964).

25. R. Jumper, "Mandarin Bureaucracy and Politics in South Vietnam," p. 56.

26. G. Fox and C. A. Joiner, "Perceptions of the Vietnamese Public Administration System," pp. 465–466.

27. *Ibid.,* pp. 459, 467; also Scigliano, *South Vietnam: Nation Under Stress,* pp. 52–53.

28. *Viet-Nam Thong-Tan-Xa* (*Viet-Nam Press* in Vietnamese), No. 4465 (May 29, 1964), morning ed., p. 3; No. 4467 (May 31, 1963), morning ed., p. 4 and evening ed., p. 5; and No. 4469 (June 1, 1963), morning ed., p. 1.

29. *Than-Dan,* No. 19 (February 21, 1964), and No. 25 (February 28, 1964).

30. *Saigon Post,* No. 119 (May 15, 1964).

31. Father R. J. de Jaeger, "The Chinese in Viet-Nam," with commentary by B. B. Fall, in R. W. Lindholm, ed., *Viet Nam: The First Five Years* (Lansing: Michigan State University Press, 1959), p. 107; also Scigliano, *South Vietnam: Nation Under Stress,* pp. 4–5.

32. Fox and Joiner, *op. cit.,* p. 475.

33. Cf. F. W. Riggs, *The Ecology of Public Administration,* pp. 123, 124.

34. Montgomery *et al., Cases in Vietnamese Administration,* pp. 204–215, "The Commissar and the Law: Deviation from Civil Service Regulations."

35. See Pfiffner and Presthus, *Public Administration,* p. 118.

36. *Times of Viet-Nam,* VII, No. 117 (May 4, 1963); VII, No. 132 (May 19, 1963).

37. For details concerning the role and the operation of the National Economic Council, see Law No. 5/61 of March 15, 1962, in Tong

Thong Phu, *Quy Phap Vung Tap* (Saigon: Toa Tong Thu Ky, 1962), Vol. IV, pp. 30 ff.

38. E. C. Banfield, *The Moral Basis of a Backward Society* (New York: The Free Press of Glencoe, 1958), p. 7. Speaking of the French colonial period, Pierre Gourou says, "The inhabitants group themselves into associations of members of neighborhoods, writers, military mandarins, older persons, wrestling enthusiasts, doctors, musicians, merchants, cock-fight fans, songbird fanciers, students of the same teacher, or even persons born in the same year," quoted by Paul Mus in *Viet Nam: Sociologie d'une guerre* (Paris: Editions du Seuil, 1952), p. 334.

39. R. Pinto, *Aspects de l'évolution gouvernementale de l'Indochine française* (Paris: Librarie du Recueil Sirey, 1946), pp. 83–91.

40. Tran Van Dinh, "Luoc Khao Ve Nhung Quyen Tu Do Cong Cong," *Nghien-Cuu Hanh-Chanh,* V, No. 5, 114–122.

41. Republic of Viet-Nam, *Bilan des Réalisations Gouvernementales 1954–1962,* p. 243; also *Seven Years of the Ngo Dinh Diem Administration, 1954–1961,* p. 182.

42. Cf. the incidents at Hue regarding a Buddhist procession in commemoration of the birth of Buddha, May 19, 1963. *Times of Viet-Nam,* VII, Nos. 123, 131, 135, 143, 149, 156, 157, and 160.

43. *Viet-Nam Press,* No. 4480 (June 13, 1963), morning ed., pp. 4–5.

44. Joiner and Jumper, "Organizing Bureaucrats: South Viet Nam's National Revolutionary Civil Servants' League," p. 214.

45. Cf. Simon, Smithburg, and Thompson, *Public Administration,* p. 150, "Dividing the Work: Specialization among Organizational Units," and pp. 280–311, "Large Scale Organization: The Consequence of Centralization."

46. Scigliano, *South Vietnam: Nation Under Stress,* p. 56.

47. M. N. Trued, "South Vietnam's Industrial Development Center," *Pacific Affairs,* XXXIII, No. 3 (September, 1960), 250–267.

48. See Chapter 3 of the present work, on Ministry of Rural Affairs, pp. 99–103.

49. Cf. the classrooms controversy in Montgomery *et al., Cases in Vietnamese Administration,* pp. 270, 294; also Scigliano, *South Vietnam: Nation Under Stress,* pp. 196–216.

50. Montgomery *et al., Cases in Vietnamese Administration,* pp. 270, 294.

51. Taylor, "South Vietnam: Lavish Aid, Limited Progress," p. 255.

52. Montgomery, "Political Dimensions of Foreign Aid," in *op. cit.,* pp. 249, 255; also Scigliano, *South Vietnam: Nation Under Stress,* pp. 196–216.

53. Nghiem Dang and G. Fox, "The National Institute of Administration," in R. W. Lindholm, ed., *Viet-Nam: The First Five Years,* p. 164.

54. Tong Thong Phu, *Quy Phap Vung Tap.*

55. *Times of Viet-Nam,* VII, No. 149 (June 5, 1963).

56. *Ngay Nay,* No. 14 (January 4, 1964); No. 15 (January 6, 1964); also *Dong Nai,* January 25, 1964.

57. J. Dorsey, "Stresses and Strains in a Developing Administrative System," in Fishel, ed., *Problems of Freedom,* p. 143.

58. Cf. A. de Riencourt, *The Soul of China*, p. 29; also Chung Li Chang, *The Chinese Gentry: Studies on their Role in 19th Century Chinese History* (Seattle: University of Washington Press, 1955).

59. Paul Mus, *Viet Nam: Sociologie d'une guerre*, pp. 138 f., "L'Elite Vietnamienne"; also Scigliano, *South Vietnam: Nation Under Stress*, pp. 48–49.

60. Pham Quynh, *Essais franco-annamites (1929–1937)* (Hue: Editions Bui Huy Tin, 1937), pp. 303–304.

61. Fishel, "Problems of Democratic Growth of Free Viet-Nam," in Fishel, ed., *Problems of Freedom*, p. 12.

62. Nguyen Thai, *Is South Viet-Nam Viable?*, pp. 40–44.

63. Fox and Joiner, "Perceptions of the Vietnamese Public Administration System," p. 451.

64. *Ibid.*, p. 471.

65. *Ibid.*, p. 459.

66. See E. Shills, "The Military in the Political Development of the New States," in John J. Johnson, ed., *The Role of the Military in Underdeveloped Countries* (Princeton: Princeton University Press, 1962), pp. 7–68.

67. W. S. Sayre, "Some Problems of Public Administration in a Developing Economy," *Indian Journal of Public Administration*, VIII, No. 2 April-June, 1962), p. 143.

68. M. Mansfield, Introduction to W. R. Fishel, ed., *Problems of Freedom: South Vietnam Since Independence*, p. xi.

69. Republic of Viet-Nam, *Bilan des Réalisations Gouvernementales 1954–1962.*

70. A. de Riencourt, *op. cit.*, p. 68.

71. Tse-Tsung Chow, "The Anti-Confucian Movement in Early Republican China," in A. Wright, ed., *The Confucian Persuasion*, pp. 288–311; also Tran Trong Kim, *Nho Giao* (reprint; Saigon: Tan Viet, n.d.), Vol. II, p. 385.

72. Dao Trinh Nhat, *Vuong Duong Minh* (Saigon: Tan Viet, n.d.), pp. 151–171.

73. L. W. Pye, "The Politics of Southeast Asia," in G. A. Almond and J. S. Coleman, eds., *The Politics of Developing Areas*, pp. 94–96.

74. Fox and Joiner, *op. cit.*, p. 451; also Scigliano, *South Vietnam: Nation Under Stress*, pp. 38–39.

75. Republic of Viet-Nam, *Bilan des Réalisations Gouvernementales, 1954–1962*, pp. 17, 240, 293, 324.

76. See, for instance, "Reorganizing the Fishing Cooperative on Phu Quoc Island," in Montgomery *et al.*, *op. cit.*, pp. 78–93.

77. Jumper, "Mandarin Bureaucracy and Politics in South Viet-Nam," p. 52.

78. Fox and Joiner, *op. cit.*, pp. 450–451; also Nguyen Thai, *op. cit.*, pp. 55–57.

79. Fox and Joiner, *op. cit.*, pp. 450–451.

80. Nguyen Thai, *op. cit.*, p. 53.

81. E. J. Hammer, "South Viet-Nam: The Limits of Political Action," *Pacific Affairs*, XXXV, No. 1 (Spring, 1962), 25.

82. Peter M. Blau, *Bureaucracy in Modern Society*, p. 89.

83. J. C. Donnell, "National Renovation Campaign in Viet Nam," *Pacific Affairs*, XXXII, No. 1 (March, 1959), 75. Cf. R. Braibanti, "Reflections on Bureaucratic Corruption," in *Public Administration* (London) (Winter, 1962).

84. Huard and Durand, *Connaissance du Viet Nam*, p. 105.

85. C. I. Barnard, *Organization and Management: Selected Papers* (Cambridge: Harvard University Press, 1948), p. 98.

86. Cf. the case "New Leadership at the Viet Nam Press," in Montgomery *et al.*, *Cases in Vietnamese Administration*, pp. 50–77.

87. Huard and Durand, *Connaissance du Viet Nam*, p. 91; also G. Hickey, *The Study of a Vietnamese Rural Community: Sociology*, p. 134.

88. Pham Huu Khanh and Nguyen Tran Nguyen, *Tuc Ngu Luoc Giai* (Saigon: Nha Xuat Ban Mai Quang, 1956), p. 131.

89. Dao Duy Anh, *Viet-Nam Van Hoa Su Cuong*, p. 150.

90. Hickey: *The Study of a Vietnamese Rural Community*, pp. 134, 263–264.

91. See M. Freedman, "The Family in China, Past and Present," *Pacific Affairs*, XXXIV, No. 4 (Winter, 1961–1962), 323.

92. Huard and Durand, *Connaissance du Viet Nam*, p. 99. Also Jumper, "Mandarin Bureaucracy and Politics in South Viet-Nam," p. 51.

93. For instance, the cabinet of President John F. Kennedy included Attorney General Robert Kennedy, the President's brother; also the brother of Governor John A. Burns of Hawaii is State Commissioner for Internal Revenue.

94. J. Dorsey, "Stresses and Strains in a Developing Administrative System," in Fishel, ed., *Problems of Freedom*, p. 147.

95. Fishel, "Problems of Democratic Growth of Free Viet-Nam," in Fishel, ed., *Problems of Freedom*, p. 24; also Jumper, "Mandarin Bureaucracy and Politics in South Viet-Nam," pp. 51, 58.

96. E. Luro, *Le Pays d'Annam* (Paris: Leroux, 1878), p. 101.

97. See R. Braibanti, "Reflections on Bureaucratic Corruption," *op. cit.;* also Tran Thuc Linh, "Nan Tham Nhung," *Bach-Khoa*, No. 174 (April 1, 1964).

98. *Viet-Nam Press*, No. 2972 (February 29, 1964).

99. *Viet-Nam Press*, No. 3000 (March 18, 1964).

100. *Saigon Post*, No. 85 (April 4, 1964).

101. *Le Trieu Chieu Linh Thien Chinh* (Collection of Regulations of the Le Dynasty) (Saigon: Nha In Binh Minh, 1961), pp. 115–119, 407; see also Phan Huy Chu, *Lich Trieu Hien Chuong Loai Chi*, pp. 245–263, 269–281.

102. Huard and Durand, *op. cit.*, p. 89.

103. *Thoi Luan*, No. 484 (March 1, 1964).

104. Fox and Joiner, *op. cit.*, p. 474; for a contrary opinion, see Nguyen Thai, *op. cit.*, pp. 77–82.

105. G. Vedel, *Droit Administratif*, pp. 140 ff.

106. The case of Durand and associates vs. the president of the Provisional Administrative Council of the Port of Saigon, *Luat-Hoc Kinh-Te Tap-Chi*, II, No. 2 (1957), 57 ff.

107. The case of Tang Thi Mau vs. the Province of Tay Ninh, *Luat-Hoc Kinh-Te Tap-Chi*, IV, Nos. 3 and 4 (1959), 71 ff.

108. The case of the Department of National Defense vs. Tran Duy Hong, *Luat-Hoc Kinh-Te Tap-Chi,* IV, Nos. 3 and 4 (1959), 81 ff.

109. Tran Van Dinh and Finkle, *op. cit.,* pp. 21, 29, 35.

110. See the case of Durand and associates in *Luat-Hoc Kinh-Te Tap-Chi, loc. cit.;* also, for a discussion, see Vedel, *op cit.,* pp. 176–223.

111. Bui Quang Khanh, *To Chuc Chanh Tri Va Hanh Chanh Viet Nam,* pp. 123, 228.

112. Vedel, *op. cit.,* p. 152.

113. *Viet Nam Cong Hoa, Ban Van To Chuc Tu Phap Viet Nam* (Saigon: Bo Tu Phap, 1962), p. 248.

114. Bui Quang Khanh, *To Chuc Chanh Tri Va Hanh Chanh Viet Nam,* pp. 192–193.

115. *Ibid.,* pp. 235–236.

116. Le Van An, *To Chuc Hanh Chanh Viet Nam,* p. 347.

117. Tong Thong Phu, *Quy Phap Vung Tap* (Saigon: Toa Tong Thu Ky Phu Tong Thong), Quyen I, pp. 397–398.

118. Vedel, *op. cit.,* pp. 140–163.

119. The case of Hoang Dieu and of Phan Thanh Giang, reported in Nguyen Huyen Anh, *Viet Nam Danh Nhan Tu Dien,* pp. 71–73; 282–287.

120. Ly Te Xuyen, *Viet Dien U Linh Tap,* Le Huu Muc, trans. (Saigon: Nha Sach Khai Tri, 1961), pp. 65–67, "Ly Hoang."

121. Chaucer Yuan, *La Philosophie morale et politique de Mencius* (Paris: Librairie Orientaliste, 1927), pp. 117, 118, 122, 134, 142.

122. Chaucer Yuan, *op. cit.,* p. 147, quoting Confucius, *Lwen Yu,* Vol. VII and Vol. XIV, paragraph 30; also p. 217, quoting Mencius, *Tchong Yong,* paragraph 20.

123. Chaucer Yuan, *op. cit.,* pp. 147–170.

124. Fung Yu-lan, *A Short History of Chinese Philosophy,* p. 282; also Tran Trong Kim, *Nho Giao,* Vol. I, pp. 80–82, 132–133.

125. Tran Trong Kim, *Nho Giao,* Vol. I, p. 313; also Fung Yu-lan, *op. cit.,* p. 42; and Chaucer Yuan, *op. cit.,* pp. 171–184.

126. Fung Yu-lan, *op. cit.,* p. 146; also Tran Trong Kim, *Nho Giao,* Vol. I, p. 145; and Chaucer Yuan, *op. cit.,* pp. 185–200.

127. Tran Trong Kim, *Nho Giao,* Vol. I, p. 115; also Fung Yu-lan, *op. cit.,* pp. 281, 287.

128. Chaucer Yuan, *op. cit.,* quoting Mencius, *Tchong Yong.*

129. Fung Yu-lan, *op. cit.,* pp. 294–318; also Chaucer Yuan, *op. cit.,* pp. 207–210; and Tran Trong Kim, *Nho Giao,* Vol. I, pp. 72, 96, 119.

130. Dao Trinh Nhat, *Vuong Duong Minh,* pp. 151–171.

131. Chaucer Yuan, *op. cit.,* quoting Confucius, *Lwen Yu,* Vol. IX; Vol. XVII, paragraph 22.

132. Tran Trong Kim, *Nho Giao,* Vol. I, p. 312.

133. *Ibid.,* pp. 167–168, "Thien Y Dan Tam."

134. Joiner and Jumper, *op. cit.,* p. 211.

135. Nha Tong Giam Doc Cong Vu, *Quy Che Cong Vu Gian Yeu,* pp. 113–119.

136. Tran Van Dinh and Finkle, *op. cit.,* pp. 55–76.

137. Nhan and Zasloff, *op. cit.,* p. 37.

138. Allen and An, *op. cit.,* pp. 91–93.

139. Woodruff, *The Study of a Vietnamese Community: Administrative Activity* (Saigon: M.S.U.G., 1960), pp. 175–191, 192–215.
140. Dimock, *A Philosophy of Administration*, p. 54.
141. Pfiffner and Presthus, *op. cit.*, pp. 92, 96.
142. C. I. Barnard, "Education for the Executives," in Robert Dubin, ed. *Human Relations in Administration* (Englewood Cliffs, N. J.: Prentice-Hall, Inc., 1961), pp. 17, 18.
143. Pfiffner and Presthus, *op. cit.*, pp. 97, 98.
144. C. I. Barnard, *The Functions of the Executive* (Cambridge: Harvard University Press, 1938), p. 261.
145. John F. Kennedy, *Profiles in Courage* (New York: Pocket Books, 1956), p. 203.
146. Glendon Schubert, *The Public Interest* (New York: The Free Press of Glencoe, 1961), pp. 35, 38, 79, 80, 136, 137.
147. Vu Uyen Van, "Nghien Cuu Ve Giao Te Nhan Su Trong Hanh Chanh," *Nghien-Cuu Hanh-Chanh*, II, No. 1 (January, 1963), 33–87.

CHAPTER 8

1. Chester Barnard, *The Functions of the Executive*, p. 267.
2. R. Emerson, "Problems of Representative Government in South East Asia," p. 297.
3. H. Simon, *Administrative Behavior*, pp. 154–171.
4. See J. Dorsey, "An Information-Energy Model," in F. Heady and S. L. Stokes, eds., *Papers in Comparative Public Administration*, pp. 37–58.
5. Huard and Durand, *Connaissance du Viet Nam*, pp. 223–234, "Techniques des Transports et des Communications."
6. P. Pasquier, *L'Annam d'autrefois*, pp. 115–116.
7. Republic of Viet-Nam, *Bilan des Réalisations Gouvernementales, 1954–1962*, pp. 381–398.
8. F. Riggs makes a distinction between three types of enlightened men: the "literati," who are characteristically self-taught, whose learning is the total corpus of knowledge (history, philosophy, sacred texts, myths and rituals—the tradition given by the past); the "intellectuals," who are the product of extensive schooling, who concentrate attention on a part of life, examining it ever more intently and more intensively; and the "intelligentsia," who are painfully both; that is, much-schooled, but their schooling clashes with the education provided by life experiences. Whereas the literati look to the past and the intellectuals to the future, the intelligentsia are simultaneously pulled in both directions. F. Riggs, "Higher Education in a Developing Society: Conference Summary and Comments," in R. L. Crabbs, ed., *Report of the Midwest Fullbright Conference on Higher Education in the United States, June 7–10, 1960* (Bloomington, Indiana: Indiana University, 1960), pp. 67–77.
9. Cf. T'ung-Tsu Ch'u, "Chinese Class Structure and Its Ideology," in J. F. Fairbank, ed., *Chinese Thoughts and Institutions* (Chicago: University of Chicago Press, 1957), pp. 235–250.
10. Tran Trong Kim, *Viet Nam Su Luoc*, pp. 483–484.

11. Republic of Viet-Nam, *Bilan des Réalisations Gouvernementales,* 1954–1962, pp. 479–483.
12. *Journal d'Extrême-Orient,* No. 4553 (January 17, 1964).
13. Tran Van Dinh, "Luoc Khao Ve Nhung Quyen Tu Do Cong Cong," *Nghien-Cuu Hanh-Chanh,* V, No. 5.
14. Fishel, "Problems of Democratic Growth of Free Vietnam," in Fishel, ed., *Problems of Freedom,* pp. 23–24; also Scigliano, *South Vietnam: Nation Under Stress,* pp. 174–177.
15. *Viet-Nam Press,* No. 2971 (February 28, 1964).
16. *Saigon Post,* No. 112 (May 7, 1964).
17. *Chinh-Luan,* No. 29 (May 7, 1964).
18. Pfiffner and Presthus, *Public Administration,* p. 134.
19. W. V. Haney, "Serial Communication of Information in Organizations," in Sidney Mailick and E. H. Van Ness, eds., *Concepts and Issues in Administrative Behavior* (Englewood Cliffs, N. J.: Prentice-Hall, 1962), pp. 150–165.
20. Tran Trong Kim, *Nho Giao,* Vol. II, pp. 164–165.
21. S. C. Dutta, "The Problems of Urban Areas," in *Asian Conference on Adult Education, April 16–24, 1962* (Saigon: Vietnam National Commission for UNESCO, 1962), p. 34.
22. J. J. Zasloff, "Rural Resettlement in South Vietnam: The Agroville Program," *Pacific Affairs,* XXXV, No. 4 (Winter, 1962–1963), 330. Also H. J. Hammer, "South Vietnam: The Limits of Political Action," *Pacific Affairs,* XXXV, No. 1 (Spring, 1962), 29, 32.
23. Pierre Gourou, quoted by Paul Mus in *Viet Nam: Sociologie d'une guerre,* p. 334.
24. Phan Ke Binh, *Viet-Nam Phong Tuc,* pp. 167–169. See also W. T. de Bary, "Chinese Despotism and the Confucian Ideal: A Seventeenth Century View," in J. F. Fairbank, ed., *Chinese Thoughts and Institutions,* pp. 184–186, "Petty Bureaucracy."
25. L. W. Woodruff, *The Study of a Vietnamese Rural Community: Administrative Activity,* Vol. I, pp. 175–193.
26. *Hanh-Dong,* No. 105 (May 15, 1964).
27. The case of Dang Sy, told in *Hanh-Dong,* No. 122 (June 4, 1964); and the case of certain secretaries of state, told in *Hanh-Dong,* No. 117 (May 29, 1964).
28. *Dan-Chung,* No. 47 (June 8, 1964).
29. *Dan-Ta,* No. 25 (June 10, 1964).
30. *Bilan des Réalisations Gouvernementales,* 1954–1962, p. 433; also Scigliano, *South Vietnam: Nation Under Stress,* p. 159.
31. *Bilan des Réalisations Gouvernementales,* 1954–1962, pp. 431–516.
32. Viet Nam Cong Hoa, *Noi-San Quoc-Hoi: So Dac Biet Ve Ngan Sach Quoc Gia Tai Khoa 1962,* I, 197–233.
33. J. J. Zasloff, "Rural Resettlement in South Vietnam," p. 330.
34. J. Hendry, "American Aid in Viet Nam: The View from the Village," *Pacific Affairs,* XXXIII, No. 4 (December, 1960), 387–391.
35. Simon, Smithburg, and Thompson, *Public Administration,* pp. 381–401, "The Struggle for Existence: Organizational Equilibrium"; and pp. 402–422, "The Tactics of Survival."

36. Lucian W. Pye, *Communications and Political Development* (Princeton: Princeton University Press, 1963), p. 12.
37. F. Riggs, "Bureaucrats and Political Development: A Paradoxical View," in Joseph G. La Palombara, ed., *op. cit.*, pp. 120–167.
38. Fox and Joiner, *op. cit.*
39. F. W. Riggs, *The Ecology of Public Administration*, pp. 20–23.
40. Cao Huu Dong, *Giao Tiep Voi Quan Chung* (Saigon: Thu Lam An Quan, 1950), pp. 7–22; 37–48.
41. J. Dorsey, Jr., "A Communication Model for Administration," *Administrative Science Quarterly*, II, No. 3 (December, 1957), 307–324; also J. Dorsey, Jr., "The Bureaucracy and Political Development in Viet Nam," in *op. cit.*, pp. 318–359.
42. Pfiffner and Presthus, *Public Administration*, pp. 142–143. Cf. the case of Tan Luoc and Caisan, cited by Zasloff, *op. cit.*
43. John D. Donoghue, *My Thuan, a Mekong Delta Village in South Viet Nam*, p. 58.
44. Pfiffner and Presthus, *Public Administration*, p. 143.
45. G. Fox and C. A. Joiner, "Perceptions of the Vietnamese Public Administration System," p. 457.
46. Pasquier, *L'Annam d'autrefois*, pp. 155–157, 160–161.
47. Riggs, *The Ecology of Public Administration*, pp. 99–117.
48. M.S.U.G., *Final Report*.
49. *Ngay Nay*, No. 14 (January 4, 1964), and No. 15 (January 6, 1964); also *Dong Nai* for January 25, 1964.
50. Fox and Joiner, *op. cit.*, p. 481; see also Scigliano, *South Vietnam: Nation Under Stress*, *op. cit.*, pp. 186–187.
51. Dorsey, "A Communication Model for Administration," in Heady and Stokes, *op. cit.*, p. 321.
52. L. R. Sayles distinguished the types of informal groups thus: the apathetic (few grievances, internal disunity), the erratic (behavior inconsistent), the strategic (continuous pressure, high degree of internal unity), and the conservative (restrained pressure for highly specific objectives, moderate internal unity and self-assurance). See "Informal Work Groups and the Formal Organization," in Robert Dubin, ed., *Human Relations in Administration* (Englewood Cliffs, N. J., Prentice-Hall, 1961), pp. 90–96.
53. Charles O. Hucker, "Confucianism and the Censorial System," in Nivison and Wright, eds., *Confucianism in Action*, p. 186.
54. See Simon, Smithburg, and Thompson, *op. cit.*, pp. 532–539, "Hierarchical Control."
55. *Dan-Chu*, No. 954 (April 7, 1964).
56. Statistics drawn by the Directorate-General of Civil Service to August 31, 1962, *Annual Report* (Saigon, 1962).
57. G. Vedel, *Droit Administratif*, pp. 199, 548; cf. the Dang Sy case, *Viet-Nam Press*, No. 4833 (June 2, 1964).
58. See Simon, Smithburg, and Thompson, *op. cit.*, pp. 533, 534.
59. Vedel, *Droit Administratif*, pp. 462–466.
60. Bui Quang Khanh, *Hanh Chanh Dia Phuong* (Saigon: Nha In Thai Hung, 1963), pp. 42–48.
61. *Ibid.*, pp. 45–46; also Vedel, *op. cit.*, p. 466.

62. Bui Quang Khanh, *Hanh Chanh Dia Phuong*, pp. 84–86.
63. Vedel, *op. cit.*, p. 472.
64. See Chap. 6 of the present work, p. 205.
65. Nghiem Dang, *Tai Chinh Hoc Dai Cuong*, Vol. II, *Cong Phi.*
66. *Ibid.*, Vol. I, *Ngan Sach*, pp. 368–377.
67. A. P. de Mirimonde, *La Cour des Comptes* (Paris: Librairie du Recueil Sirey, 1947), pp. 72–111.
68. J. D. Millett, *Government and Public Administration: The Quest for Responsible Performance* (New York: McGraw-Hill, 1959), pp. 176–191.
69. *Bilan des Réalisations Gouvernementales, 1954–1962*, p. 239.
70. *Viet-Nam Thong-Tan-Xa* (*Viet-Nam Press*), evening edn., No. 4462 (June 1, 1963), p. H1.
71. Le Tan Nam, "Thanh Tra Hanh Chanh Va Tai Chanh," *Nghien-Cuu Hanh-Chanh*, V, No. 5 (March, 1961), 53–83.
72. *Ibid.*, also the case of Phan Thanh Gian, cited by Taboulet in *La Geste française en Indochine*, p. 507.
73. Pham Quynh, *Essais Franco-annamites*, pp. 319–328, "L'Ecole dirigeante."
74. Vedel, *op. cit.*, pp. 57–67; also Rolland and Lampue, *op. cit. Legislation et finances coloniales.*
75. R. Pinto, *Aspects de l'évolution gouvernementale de l'Indochine française*, pp. 171–179.
76. *Viet Nam Cong Hoa, Ban Van to Chuc Tu Phap Viet Nam* (Saigon: Bo Tu Phap, 1962), pp. 217–254.
77. Vedel, *op. cit.*, pp. 67–114; also Vu Quoc Thong, "Van De Phan Biet Khe Uoc Hanh Chanh Voi Khe Uoc Dan Su," *Nghien-Cuu Hanh-Chanh*, V, Nos., 2, 6, 7, 8 (1961); Le Van Dinh, "Tuong Quan Phap Ly Giua Toa An Hanh Chanh Va Tu Phap," *Phap-Ly Tap-San*, Nos. 1 and 2 (1960), 125–134; 114–118.
78. See, for instance, the case of H. Q. C. before the Council of State, December 30, 1961, in *Phap-Ly Tap-San*, No. 1 (1962); and that of P. N. K. before the Council of State, May 24, 1961, in *Phap-Ly Tap-San*, No. 3 (1962), 103–114.
79. See the case of Cong Ty Bao Hiem Phat Ba before the Administrative Tribunal, in *Phap-Ly Tap-San*, No. 3 (1962), 120–128; the case of Nguyen Thi Phu before the Council of State, in *Phap-Ly Tap-San*, No. 2 (1961), 114–119.
80. Vedel, *op. cit.*, pp. 224–280, "La Responsibilité de l'administration et de ses agents"; also Tran Tac Lam, "Co Quan Tai Phan Hanh Chanh," in *Ban Van To Chuc Tu Phap Viet Nam*, edited by the Department of Justice (Saigon: Bo Tu Phap, 1962), pp. 59–84.
81. Cf. Millett, *Government and Public Administration: The Quest for Responsible Performance*, pp. 397–403, 421–426.
82. F. Riggs, "Bureaucrats and Political Development: A Paradoxical View."
83. See Simon, Smithburg, and Thompson, *op. cit.*, pp. 514–522, "Judicial Controls."
84. Scigliano, *South Vietnam: Nation Under Stress*, pp. 43–46.
85. *Noi-San Quoc-Hoi*, No. 68 (August, 1962), 29–86.
86. *Noi-San Quoc-Hoi*, No. 67 (July, 1962), 28–51.

87. *Noi-San Quoc-Hoi,* Nos. 61, 62 (January and February, 1962), 81–95.
88. *Noi-San Quoc-Hoi,* No. 64 (April, 1962), 3–27.
89. For details, see Millett, *op. cit.,* pp. 63–282, especially 193–212, "The Legislature as Administrative Overseer."
90. Pfiffner and Presthus, *op. cit.,* p. 535.
91. See Simon, Smithburg, and Thompson, *op. cit.,* pp. 541–561, "Administrative Responsibility: Informal Controls."
92. *Hanh-Dong,* No. 70 (April 3, 1964); also No. 75 (April 9, 1964); also *Dan-Chu,* No. 951 (March 18, 1964).

CHAPTER 9

1. Pfiffner and Presthus, *Public Administration,* p. 6.
2. James B. Hendry, "Economic Development under Conditions of Guerrilla Warfare: the Case of Viet Nam," *Asian Survey,* II, No. 6 (June, 1962), 1–12.
3. *Thanh Tich Chin Nam Hoat Dong Cua Chinh Phu 1954–1963* (Nine Years of Government Achievement 1954–1963) (Saigon: Directorate-General of Information, 1963), "Message of the President," no pagination.
4. *Viet-Nam Press,* No. 2980 (March 8, 1964).
5. Tang Tsou, *America's Failure in China* (Chicago: University of Chicago Press, 1963).
6. See E. Weidner, "Improving the Resource Base in the United States for Technical Assistance Overseas in Development Administration and Law." Paper presented at a meeting sponsored by the Ford Foundation, New York City, October 26–27, 1962.
7. See *Report of Achievements of the National Institute of Administration in Eight Years of the Vietnamese Administration* (Saigon: Directorate-General of Information, 1962).
8. Tran Trong Kim, *Viet Nam Su Luoc,* p. 484.
9. *Ibid.,* pp. 75–77; also Dao Duy Anh, *Viet-Nam Van Hoa Su Cuong* (reprint; Saigon: Thu Lam An Quan, 1938), pp. 240–243.
10. See F. Riggs, "Higher Education in a Developing Society: Conference Summary and Comments," pp. 67–77.
11. Pham Quynh, *Thuong Chi Van Tap* (re-edited; Saigon: Department of Education, 1962), Vol. III, pp. 41–70; Vol. IV, pp. 185–198; also Pham Quynh, *Nouveaux essais franco-annamites* (Hue Editions Bui Huy Tin, 1938), pp. 71–110.
12. E. Luro, *Etude sur l'organisation politique et sociale des Annamites* (Paris: Leroux, 1897), pp. 150–151.
13. Chesneaux, *Contribution a l'histoire de la nation vietnamienne,* pp. 173–182.
14. R. Cultru, *Histoire de la Cochinchine française des origines à 1883* (Paris: Challamel, 1910), p. 207.
15. Luro, *op. cit.*
16. J. Guignard, *Une Grande Administration Indochinoise: Les Services Civils de l'Indochine* (Paris: Larose, 1931), p. 65; also De Galembert, *Les Administrations et les Services Publics Indochinois,* pp. 374–379.
17. Louis Cury, *La Societé annamite: les lettrés, les mandarins, les peuples* (Paris: Jouve, 1910), pp. 25–55.

18. Pham Quynh, *Nouveaux essais franco-annamites*, pp. 111–138.
19. See Carl S. Friedrich, "The Continental Tradition of Training Administrators in Law and Jurisprudence," *Journal of Modern History*, II (June, 1939).
20. J. Decoux, *A la Barre de l'Indochine: Histoire de mon gouvernement général*, p. 397; also Scigliano, *South Vietnam: Nation Under Stress*, pp. 48–49.
21. E. W. Weidner, "Development Administration: A New Focus for Research," in F. Heady and S. L. Stokes, eds., *Papers in Comparative Administration*, p. 98.
22. Nghiem Dang, *Tai Chanh Hoc Dai Cuong*, Vol. II, pp. 93–101.
23. F. C. Child, "Essays in Economic Growth, Capital Formation, and Public Policy in Vietnam," in *op. cit.*, pp. 6–8.
24. Vu Van Thai, "Vietnam's Concept of Development," in W. Fishel, ed., *Problems of Freedom*, pp. 69–74.
25. B. Higgins, *Economic Development: Problems, Principles, and Policies* (New York: W. W. Norton, 1959), pp. 678–686.
26. Le Thanh Khoi, *Le Viet Nam: Histoire et Civilisation*, pp. 358–359.
27. W. W. Rostow, *The Stages of Economic Growth*, p. 39.
28. Tran Van Dinh and J. Finkle, *Provincial Administration in Viet Nam: A Study of Vinh Long Province*, p. 23.
29. B. F. Hoselitz, *Sociological Aspects of Economic Growth*, pp. 30, 35.
30. F. Riggs, "Reflections on Development." Paper presented at a seminar at the East-West Center, Honolulu, January, 1963; mimeographed.
31. See J. J. Spengler, "Bureaucracy and Economic Development," in La Palombara, ed., *Bureaucracy and Political Development*, pp. 199–232.
32. Nguyen Cao Hach, "Phuong Phap Hoach Dinh Co Trai Voi Tinh Than Dan Chu Khong?" (Is Economic Planning Contrary to the Democratic Ideal?), *Luat-Hoc Kinh-Te Tap-Chi* (Saigon), Nos. 3 and 4 (1960), 31–50.
33. Riggs, "Bureaucrats and Political Development: A Paradoxical View."
34. C. A. Beard, "Philosophy, Science, and Art of Public Administration," quoted in A. Lepawsky, *Administration: The Art and Science of Organization and Management*, p. 661.
35. Nha Tong Giam Doc Cong Vu, *Quy Che Cong Vu Gian Yeu* (mimeographed; Saigon, 1960), pp. 108–112.
36. Answers to the questionnaire "Organization of the Civil Service," prepared by the National Institute of Administration, Saigon, 1962.
37. Nghiem Dang, "Co Cau Kinh Te Va Tai Chinh Cong Quyen Tai Cac Nuoc Cham Tien" (Economic Structure and Public Finances in Underdeveloped Countries), *Nghien-Cuu Hanh-Chanh*, V, Nos. 3 and 4 (1962)', 19–63.
38. *Report of the National Institute of Administration to the Administrative Council, Session of April 2, 1964.*
39. National Institute of Administration, *Report of Achievement in Viet-Nam after 8 Years* (Saigon: Directorate-General of Information, 1962). The examinations are graded under rigorous conditions of justice and anonymity: the administrative personnel of the Institute have nothing to do with the examination, except that the director formally accepts the candidates judged admissible by a special jury

appointed each year and composed of both teachers and high officials.

40. *Thanh Tich Chin Nam Hoat Dong Cua Chinh Phu.*

41. Hla Myint, "The Universities of Southeast Asia and Economic Development," *Pacific Affairs*, XXXV, No. 2 (Summer, 1962), 116–127.

42. C. H. Sisson, *The Spirit of British Administration and Some European Comparisons*, pp. 13–24.

43. J. L. Finkle, *A Profile of N.I.A. Students* (Saigon: M.S.U.G., 1961), "Despite the varied educational preference pattern found in the preceding set of questions, four out of five NIA students would voluntarily enter government service even if they were not required to do so upon graduation. This is not an unusually high figure when consideration is given to the fact that government service in Viet-Nam, as in most developing nations, offers many advantages: job security, status, perquisites, career advancement, and an above-average salary."

44. Hoi Cuu Sinh Vien Hanh Chanh, *Dac San Nam 1961* (Saigon: Hoi Cuu Sinh Vien Hanh Chanh, 1961).

45. Henri Bourdeau de Fontenay, *La Fonction Publique: recrutement et formation du fonctionnaire* (Paris: Armand Colin, 1959).

46. "Hoc Vien Quoc Gia Hanh Chanh," *To Trinh Nien De Ve Hoat Dong Nam Thu Nhat* (First Annual Report of the National Institute of Administration, July 7, 1955 to July 7, 1956.

47. Nghiem Dang and G. Fox, "The National Institute of Administration" in *Viet-Nam: The First Five Years*, R. W. Lindholm, ed. (East Lansing: Michigan State University Press, 1959).

48. See Vu Quoc Thong, "Van De Dao Tao Can Bo Hanh Chanh Tai Viet Nam Cong Hoa Va Cac Nuoc Ngoai" (The Problem of Training Administrative Officials in the Republic of Viet Nam and other Countries), *Que Huong*, December, 1959, and January, 1960; also W. S. Sayre, "Some Problems of Public Administration in Developing Countries," *Indian Journal of Public Administration*, VIII, No. 2 (April-June, 1962), 137–153.

49. *Saigon Daily News*, Vol. I, No. 96 (March 14, 1964).

50. Hoc Vien Quoc Gia Hanh Chanh, *Bien Ban Uy Ban Hoc Vu* (Records of the Meeting of the Academic Committee) (Saigon: National Institute of Administration, 1962).

51. Hla Myint called these early faculty members "flying professors," both figuratively and literally. See Hla Myint, *op. cit.*: also E. W. Weidner, *The World Role of Universities* (New York: McGraw-Hill, 1962), pp. 32–38.

52. Scigliano, *South Vietnam: Nation Under Stress*, p. 65.

53. M.S.U.G., *Final Report.*

54. C. H. Sisson, *The Spirit of British Administration and Some European Comparisons*, p. 11.

55. Phan Huy Chu, *Lich Trieu Hien Chuong Loai Chi.*

56. Bo Quoc Gia Giao Duc, *Kham Dinh Viet Su Thong Giam Cuong Muc* (Saigon: Tu Sach Vien Khao Co., 1960).

57. "Dai Nam Chinh Bien Liet Truyen," reprinted by the Institute of Linguistic Studies of Keio University (Tokyo: Institute of Linguistic Studies, 1962).

58. E. Luro, "Cours d'Administration Annamite," manuscript, Hanoi Ecole française d'Extrême-Orient, n.d. For greater detail see Roy Jumper, *Bibliography on the Political and Administrative History of Vietnam (1502–1962)* (Saigon: M.S.U.G., 1962).
59. M.S.U.G., *Final Report.*
60. Riggs, "Agraria and Industria: Toward a Typology of Comparative Administration," in W. Siffin, ed., *Toward the Comparative Study of Public Administration;* also R. E. Asher *et al., Development of the Emerging Countries: An Agenda for Research* (Washington, D. C.: The Brookings Institution, 1962); also Weidner, "Development Administration," in *op. cit.*
61. For reference to methodology, see Siffin, ed., *Toward the Comparative Study of Public Administration,* pp. 12–16.
62. Jumper, "Mandarin Bureaucracy and Politics in South Vietnam."
63. Concerning the role of technical assistance in this field, see E. W. Weidner, *The World Role of Universities,* pp. 120–133, 258–261, 281–287.
64. For a comparative study of this problem, see A. Molitor, *Les Sciences sociales dans l'enseignement superieur: Administration publique* (Paris: UNESCO, 1958).
65. Hoc Vien Quoc Gia Hanh Chanh, "Hoi Thao Lien Bo Ve Tu Nghiep," (Interdepartmental Seminar on In-Service Training) (Saigon: National Institute of Administration, 1959).
66. Nghiem Dang and G. Fox, *The National Institute of Administration in Viet-Nam: the First Five Years;* also John T. Dorsey, "Viet-Nam's National Institute of Administration," *Philippine Journal of Public Administration,* II, No. 2 (April, 1958).
67. The author has been informed that this measure was again considered in June, 1964.
68. Hoc Vien Gia Hanh Chanh, "Hoat Dong Tu 7–7–1962 Den 7–7–1963," *Chin Nam Hoat Dong Cua Chanh Phu* (Saigon: Directorate-General of Information, 1963).

APPENDIX

1. *Newsweek,* May 27, 1963, p. 30.
2. *Newsweek,* September 7, 1964.
3. *Saigon Post,* September 25, 1964.
4. *Newsweek,* November 2, 1964.
5. *Saigon Post,* February 16 to February 18, 1965.
6. *Time* (Asia ed.), February 26, 1965.
7. *Saigon Daily News,* May 7, 1965.
8. J. A. Carver, Jr., "The Real Revolution in South Viet Nam," *Foreign Affairs,* XLIII, No. 3 (April, 1965), 387–405.
9. *Saigon Post,* May 15, 1965.
10. "Exploding Power of the Buddhists," *Life,* LVII, December, 1964, 34–41.
11. *Newsweek,* September 7, 1964.
12. *Newsweek,* December 7, p. 34; February 1, 1965; *Time* (Asia ed.), December 4, 1964.
13. *Saigon Daily News,* December 14, 1964.

14. *Tu-Do,* April 27, 1965.
15. *Time* (Asia ed.), September 4, 1964, p. 27.
16. *Saigon Daily News,* April 22, 1965.
17. *Saigon Daily News,* May 14, 1965; *Saigon Post* (No. 435), May 28, 1965.
18. *Chinh-Luan,* May 6, 1965.
19. *Saigon Daily News,* April 26, 1965.
20. "Communique of the Interfaith Liaison Committee," *Saigon Daily News,* May 14, 1965.
21. *Newsweek,* December 30, 1963; January 27, 1964.
22. *Newsweek,* September 7, 1964.
23. *Time* (Asia ed.), December 4, 1964.
24. *Saigon Daily News,* January 28, 1965.
25. *Viet-Nam Combat et Edifie No. 5,* December, 1964.
26. R. Scigliano, *South Viet-Nam: Nation Under Stress.*
27. *Saigon Post,* May 8, 1964.
28. *Bach-Khoa* (Nos. 193–194) January 15, 1965, p. 186.
29. *Newsweek,* October 5, 1964; *Time* (Asia ed.), October 9, 1964; *Newsweek,* December 28, 1964.
30. *Time* (Asia ed.), February 26, 1965.
31. *Newsweek,* September 28, 1964.
32. *Saigon Post,* February 16, 1965.
33. *Saigon Post,* May 26, 1965.

BIBLIOGRAPHY

Adamson, J. R. *A Proposed Budgetary Accounting Procedures Manual for the Republic of Viet Nam.* Saigon: Michigan State University Viet-Nam Advisory Group (hereafter M.S.U.G.), 1960.

Allen, Luther A., and Pham Ngoc An. *A Vietnamese District Chief in Action.* Saigon: National Institute of Administration, 1961.

Almond, G. A., and J. S. Coleman, eds. *The Politics of the Developing Areas.* Princeton: Princeton University Press, 1960.

Asher, R. E., ed. *Development of the Emerging Countries: An Agenda for Research.* Washington, D. C.: The Brookings Institution, 1962.

Aurousseau, L. "La Première Conquête chinoise des pays annamites," *Bulletin de l'Ecole française d'Extrême-Orient* (Hanoi), XXIII (1923).

Banfield, E. C. *The Moral Basis of a Backward Society.* New York: The Free Press of Glencoe, 1958.

Barnard, C. I. *The Functions of the Executive.* Cambridge, Mass.: Harvard University Press, 1938.

———. *Organization and Management: Selected Papers.* Cambridge, Mass.: Harvard University Press, 1948.

Bernard, Paul. *Le Problème économique indochinois.* Paris: Nouvelles Editions Latines, 1934.

Betts, R. F. *Assimilation and Association in French Colonial Policy.* New York: Columbia University Press, 1961.

Bhambhri, Ch. P. *Public Administration: Theory and Practice.* Meerut City: Jai Prakash Nath, 1960.

Blau, Peter M. *Bureaucracy in Modern Society.* New York: Random House, 1962.

Boudet, P. "La Conquête de la Cochinchine par les Nguyen et le rôle des émigrés chinois," *Bulletin de l'Ecole française d'Extrême-Orient* (Hanoi), XLII (1942).

Bourdeau de Fontenay, H. *La Fonction Publique: recrutement et formation du fonctionnaire.* Paris: Armand Colin, 1959.

Braibanti, R. *Transnational Inducement of Administrative Reforms: A Survey of Scope and Critique of Issues.* Occasional Paper. Bloomington, Ind.: Comparative Administration Group, 1963.

———. "Reflections on Bureaucratic Corruption," in *Public Administration* (London), Winter, 1962.

——— and J. J. Spengler, eds. *Tradition, Values and Socio-Economic Development.* Durham, N. C.: Duke University Press, 1961.

Bui Quang Khanh. *Hanh Chanh Dia Phuong.* Saigon: Nha In Thai Hung, 1963.

———. *To Chuc Chanh Tri Va Hanh Chanh Viet Nam.* Saigon: Viet Lien, 1963.

———. "Cach Xu The Cua Cac Vi Chi Huy Hanh Chanh Dia Phuong,"

Nghien-Cuu Hanh-Chanh, VI, Nos. 5, 6 (May, June, 1962).

Burkhead, Jesse. *Government Budgeting.* New York: John Wiley and Sons, 1956.

Burns, J. M., and J. W. Peltason. *Government by the People.* Englewood Cliffs, N. J.: Prentice-Hall, Inc., 1957.

Buss, Claude A. *The Arc of Crisis.* New York: Doubleday & Co., Inc., 1961.

Buttinger, J. *The Smaller Dragon.* New York: Frederick Praeger, 1958.

Cao Huu Dong. *Giao Tiep voi Quan Chung.* Saigon: Thu Lam An Quan, 1950.

Cao Xuan Duc. *Quoc Trieu Dang Khoa Luc.* Saigon: Bo Quoc Gia Giao Duc, 1962.

Carver, J. A., Jr. "The Real Revolution in South Viet Nam," *Foreign Affairs,* April, 1965.

Chesneaux, J. *Contribution à l'histoire de la nation vietnamienne.* Paris: Editions Sociales, 1955.

Ch'ien Tuan-Sheng. *The Government and Politics of China.* Cambridge, Mass.: Harvard University Press, 1961.

Child, F. *Toward a Policy for Economic Growth in Viet Nam.* East Lansing: M.S.U.G., 1962.

Chung Li Chang. *The Chinese Gentry: Studies on their Role in 19th Century Chinese History.* Seattle: University of Washington Press, 1955.

Coedes, G. *Histoire ancienne des états hindouisés d'Extrême-Orient.* Hanoi: Imprimerie d'Extrême-Orient, 1944.

Cole, D. C., and Nguyen Bich Mac. *Provincial and Local Revenues in Viet Nam.* Saigon: National Institute of Administration, 1957.

Corley, Francis J. "The President in the Constitution of the Republic of Vietnam," *Pacific Affairs* XXXIV, No. 2 (Summer, 1961).

Crabbs, R. F., ed. *Report of the Midwest Fulbright Conference on Higher Education in the United States, June 7–10, 1960.* Bloomington, Ind.: Indiana University, 1960.

Creel, H. G. "The Beginnings of Bureaucracy in China: The Origins of the Hsien." Paper delivered at the 15th annual meeting of the Association for Asian Studies, Philadelphia, March 25–27, 1963.

Cultru, R. *Histoire de la Cochinchine française des origines à 1883.* Paris: Challamel, 1910.

Cury, Louis. *La Société annamite: les lettrés, les mandarins, les peuples.* Paris: Jouve, 1910.

Dao Duy Anh. *Viet-Nam Van Hoa Su Cuong.* Saigon: reprinted by Xuat Ban Bon Phuong, 1951.

Dao Trinh Nhat. *Vuong Duong Minh.* Saigon: Tan Viet, n.d.

Dao Van Hoi. *Lich Trinh Hanh Chanh Nam Phan.* Saigon: Imprimerie Van Khoa, 1961.

Davy, T. J. "Public Administration as a Field of Study in the United States," *International Review of Administrative Science,* XXVIII, No. 1 (1962).

De Bary, William Theodore, et al. *Sources of Indian Tradition.* New York: Columbia University Press, 1958.

De Galembert, J. *Les Administrations et les Services Publics Indochinois* (Summary of the Statute of Civil Service). Hanoi: Imprimerie Mac Dinh Tu, 1931.

De Jaeger, (Father) R. J. "The Chinese in Viet-Nam," with commentary by B. B. Fall, in R. W. Lindholm, ed., *Viet Nam: The First Five Years.* Lansing: Michigan State University Press, 1959.

De Mirimonde, A. P. *La Cour des Comptes.* Paris: Librarie du Recueil Sirey, 1947.

De Riencourt, A. *The Soul of China.* New York: Coward-McCann 1958.

Decoux, J. *A la Barre de l'Indochine.* Paris: Plon, 1949.

Deloustal, R. "La Justice dans l'ancien Annam," *Bulletin de l'Ecole française d'Extrême-Orient* (Hanoi), 1908, 1922.

Des Rotours, R. *Le Traite des examens (traduit de la nouvelle histoire des T'ang).* Paris: Librairie Ernest Leroux, 1932.

Devillers, P. *Histoire du Vietnam de 1945 à 1952.* Paris: Editions du Seuil, 1952.

Dimock, M. E. *A Philosophy of Administration.* New York: Harper & Brothers, 1958.

Doan Them. "Mot Khuynh Huong Moi Trong To Chuc Hanh Chanh Tai Cac Nuoc Dong Nam A" (A New Tendency in Administrative Organization in the Countries of Southeast Asia), *Nghien-Cuu Hanh-Chanh,* II, No. 2 (April, 1958).

Donnell, J. C. "National Renovation Campaign in Viet Nam," *Pacific Affairs,* XXXII, No. 1 (March, 1959).

Donoghue, John D. *Cam An: A Fishing Village in Central Viet-Nam.* Saigon: M.S.U.G.-N.I.A., 1962.

——— and Vo-Hong-Phuc. *My Thuan, A Mekong Delta Village in South Viet-Nam.* Saigon: M.S.U.G., 1961.

Dorsey, J. T., Jr. *Report and Recommendations on the Reorganization of the Presidency.* Saigon: M.S.U.G., 1955.

———. "A Communication Model for Administration," *Administrative Science Quarterly,* December, 1957.

———. "Viet-Nam's National Institute of Administration," *Philippine Journal of Public Administration,* April, 1958.

Dubin, Robert, ed. *Human Relations in Administration.* Englewood Cliffs, N. J.: Prentice-Hall, Inc., 1961.

Durand, P. "La Décadence de la loi dans la Constitution de la Cinquième République," *Jurisclasseur Périodique* (Paris), I, No. 1470 (1959).

Dutta, S. C. "The Problems of Urban Areas," in *Asian Conference on Adult Education, April 16–24.* Saigon: Viet-Nam National Commission for UNESCO, 1962.

Duverger, Maurice. *Institutions financières.* Paris: Presses Universitaires de France, 1961.

ECAFE. *Report on the Workshop on Problems of Budget Reclassification and Management.* First Workshop, 1956; Second, 1957; Third, 1961. Bangkok: ECAFE.

Eisenstadt, S. N. "Religion and Politics in Centralized Empires," *The Journal of Asian Studies,* XXI, No. 3 (May, 1962).

Emerson, R. "Problems of Representative Government in Southeast Asia," *Pacific Affairs*, XXVI, No. 4 (December, 1953).

Fairbank, J. F., ed. *Chinese Thoughts and Institutions*. Chicago: University of Chicago Press, 1957.

Fall, Bernard. *The Viet Minh, 1940–1960*. Paris: Librairie Armand Colin, 1960.

Finkle, J. L. *A Profile of N.I.A. Students*. Saigon: M.S.U.G., 1961.

Fishel, W. R., ed. *Problems of Freedom: South Vietnam Since Independence*. New York: The Free Press of Glencoe, Inc., 1961.

Fox, G. H., and C. A. Joiner. "Perceptions of the Vietnamese Public Administration System," *Administrative Science Quarterly*, VIII, No. 4 (March, 1964).

Freedman, M. "The Family in China, Past and Present," *Pacific Affairs*, XXXIV, No. 4 (Winter, 1961–1962).

Friedrich, Carl S. "The Continental Tradition of Training Administrators in Law and Jurisprudence," *Journal of Modern History*, II (June, 1939).

Fung Yu-lan. *A Short History of Chinese Philosophy*. New York: Macmillan, 1961.

Gaspardone, E. Course given at the Collège de France, Paris, in 1950–1953: "Les Pays du Sud et la Chine des derniers Hans et des Trois Royaumes."

Gaus, J. M. *Reflections on Public Administration*. Birmingham, Alabama: University of Alabama Press, 1958.

Goodrich, C. *Perspectives on Economic Development in Viet Nam*. New York: United Nations, 1956.

Gourou, P. *Le Tonkin*. Paris: Exposition Coloniale Internationale, 1931.

Granet, M., *La Pensée Chinoise*. Paris: Albin Michel, 1934.

Grant, J. A. C. "The Viet Nam Constitution 1956," *American Political Science Review*, LII, No. 2 (June, 1958).

Guignard, J. *Une Grande Administration Indochinoise: Les Services Civils de l'Indochine*. Paris: Larose, 1931.

Gulick, L. "Notes on the Theory of Organization," in *Papers of the Science of Administration*. New York: Institute of Public Administration, 1937.

Hammer, E. J. "South Viet-Nam: The Limits of Political Action," *Pacific Affairs*, XXV, No. 1 (Spring, 1962).

Heady, F., and S. L. Stokes, eds. *Papers in Comparative Administration*. Ann Arbor, Michigan: Institute of Public Administration, 1962.

Hendry, J. B. *The Study of a Vietnamese Rural Community: Economic Activity*. Saigon: M.S.U.G., 1959.

———. "American Aid in Viet Nam: The View from the Village," *Pacific Affairs*, December, 1960.

———. "Economic Development under Conditions of Guerilla Warfare: The Case of Viet Nam," *Asian Survey*, June, 1962.

Hickey, G. C. *The Study of a Vietnamese Rural Community: Sociology*. Saigon: M.S.U.G., 1960.

Higgins, B. *Economic Development: Problems, Principles, and Policies*. New York: W. W. Norton, 1959.

Hoselitz, B. F. *Sociological Aspects of Economic Growth.* New York: Free Press of Glencoe, 1962.

Huard, P., and M. Durand. *Connaissance du Viet Nam.* Paris: Imprimerie National, 1954.

Janse, O. *Archeological Research in Indochina.* Cambridge, Mass.: Harvard Yenching Institute, 1949.

Johnson, John J., ed. *The Role of the Military in Underdeveloped Countries.* Princeton: Princeton University Press, 1962.

Joiner, C. A. *Public Administration in the Saigon Metropolitan Area.* Saigon: National Institute of Administration, 1962.

Joiner, C. A., and R. Jumper. "Organizing Bureaucrats: South Viet-Nam's National Revolutionary Civil Servants' League," *Asian Survey,* II, No. 4 (June, 1962).

Jumper, R. "Mandarin Bureaucracy and Politics in South Viet-Nam," *Pacific Affairs,* XXX, No. 1 (March, 1957).

Jumper, R., and Nguyen Thi Hue. *Notes on the Political and Administrative History of Vietnam, 1902–1962.* Saigon: M.S.U.G., 1962.

Kaltenmark, M. "Le Taoisme," in *Aspects de la Chine.* Paris: Publications du Musée Guimet, 1959.

Kendrick, J. W. *Productivity Trends in the United States.* Princeton: Princeton University Press, 1961.

Kennedy, John F. *Profiles in Courage.* New York: Pocket Books, 1956.

Kham Dinh Viet Su Thong Giam Cuong Muc (Imperial Annals of Former Dynasties). Hue: Imperial Archives.

Kitagawa, J. M. "Buddhism and Asian Politics," *Asian Survey,* II, No. 5 (July, 1962).

Kung-Chuan Hsiao. *Rural China: Imperial Control in the 19th Century.* Seattle: University of Washington Press, 1960.

Lancaster, Donald. *The Emancipation of French Indochina.* London and New York: Oxford University Press, 1961.

La Palombara, Joseph G., ed. *Bureaucracy and Political Development.* Princeton: Princeton University Press, 1963.

Lasswell, H., and A. Kaplan. *Power and Society: A Framework for Political Inquiry.* New Haven: Yale University Press, 1950.

Lepawsky, H. *Administration: The Art and Science of Organization and Management.* New York: Alfred A. Knopf, 1960.

Le Prevost, J., and H. Meyrat. "L'Admission des Indochinois dans les cadres des administrations et services publics français de l'Indochine," *Revue Indochinoise Juridique et Economique* (Hanoi), No. 18 (1942).

Le Tan Nam. "Thanh Tra Hanh Chanh Va Tai Chanh," *Nghien-Cuu Hanh-Chanh* V, No. 5 (March, 1961).

Le Thanh Khoi. *Le Viet-Nam: Histoire et Civilisation.* Paris: Editions de Minuit, 1955.

Le Van An. *To Chuc Hanh Chanh Viet Nam.* Saigon: Hoc Vien Quoc Gia Hanh Chanh, 1962.

Le Van Dinh. "Tuong Quan Phap Ly Giua Toa An Hanh Chanh Va Tu Phap," *Phap-Ly Tap-San,* 1960.

Le Van Kim. *Report on the Mechanization of Administration.* Wiesbaden, Germany: Conference of the International Institute of the International Institute of Administrative Sciences, 1959.

Lindholm, R. W. *Analysis of Viet Nam's Tax System.* Saigon: United States Operations Mission (hereafter USOM), 1956.

Lindholm, R. W., ed. *Viet Nam: The First Five Years.* Lansing: Michigan State University Press, 1959.

Linebarger, P. M. *The China of Chiang K'ai-Shek.* Boston: World Peace Foundation, 1941.

Liu, J. T. C. "An Administrative Cycle in Chinese History," *Journal of Asian Studies* XXI, No. 2 (February, 1962).

Lupi, G. "La Regle du service fait et ses interpretations recentes," *Revue de Science Financiere* (Paris), Vol. II (1956).

Luro, E. *Le Pays d'Annam.* Paris: Leroux, 1878.

―――. *Etude sur l'organisation politique et sociale des Annamites.* Paris: Leroux, 1897.

Luykx, N. "Local Government in Viet Nam." Doctoral thesis, Cornell University, 1962.

Ly Te Xuyen, *Viet Dien U Linh Tap.* Le Hu Muc, trans. Saigon: Nha Sach Khai Tri, 1961.

Mailick, Sidney, and E. H. Van Ness, eds. *Concepts and Issues in Administrative Behavior.* Englewood Cliffs, N. J.: Prentice-Hall, 1962.

Marx, F. M. *Elements of Public Administration.* Englewood Cliffs, N. J.: Prentice-Hall, Inc., 1959.

Maspero, G. *Le Royaume du Champa.* Paris: Editions Van Oest, 1929.

Maspero, H. "La Dynastie des Ly antérieurs," *Bulletin de l'Ecole française d'Extrême-Orient,* XVI (1916).

Maunier, R. *The Sociology of Colonies.* E. O. Lorimer, trans. London: Routledge and Kegan Paul, 1949.

Merly, C. M., and B. Sol. *Le regime financier des territoires d'Outre-Mer.* Paris: Larose, 1952.

Merton, R. K., ed. *Reader in Bureaucracy.* New York: The Free Press of Glencoe, 1960.

M.S.U.G. *Budgetary Administration in Vietnam: A Report to the Presidency and to the Cabinet of the Republic of Vietnam.* Saigon: M.S.U.G., 1957.

―――. *Final Report Covering Activities of the Michigan State University Viet-Nam Advisory Group. May 20, 1955, to June 30, 1962.* Saigon: National Institute of Administration, 1962.

―――. *Report of the Comparative Study of Agricultural Administration in Japan, Taiwan and Viet-Nam.* Saigon: M.S.U.G., 1956.

―――, ed. *Area Administration in Viet-Nam.* Saigon: M.S.U.G., 1961.

―――. Field Staff, *Recommendations Concerning the Department of the Interior, the Regions, and the Provinces.* Saigon: M.S.U.G., 1956.

Millet, J. D. *Management in Public Service.* New York: McGraw-Hill Book Co., Inc., 1954.

―――. *Government and Public Administration: The Quest for Responsible Performance.* New York: McGraw-Hill, 1959.

Molitor, A. *Les Sciences sociales dans l'enseignement superieur: Administration publique.* Paris: UNESCO, 1958.

Montgomery, J. D., and the NIA Case Seminar. *Cases in Vietnamese Administration.* Saigon: National Institute of Administration, 1959.

Murphy, A. "Overcoming Resistance to Major Change: Viet-Nam Budget Reform," *Public Administration Review,* XX, No. 3 (Summer, 1960).

Murphy, M. H., and W. W. Snyder. *An Analysis of Revenues and Expenditures of Vietnamese Agencies Having Budget Autonomy, Fiscal Year 1956.* Saigon: M.S.U.G., 1957.

Mus, Paul. *Vietnam chez lui.* Paris: Centre d'Etudes de politique étrangère, 1946.

———. *Viet Nam: Sociologie d'une guerre.* Paris: Editions du Seuil, 1952.

Musolf, Lloyd. "Public Enterprise and Development Perspectives in Viet Nam," *Asian Survey,* III, No. 8 (August, 1963).

———. "Public Enterprise and 'Developed' Organizational Forms: South Viet Nam," *International Review of Administrative Science,* XXIX (1963).

Myint, Hla. "The Universities of Southeast Asia and Economic Development," *Pacific Affairs,* Summer, 1962.

Myrdal, G. *Development and Underdevelopment.* Cairo: National Bank of Egypt, 1956.

National Bank of Viet-Nam. *Estimations du Revenu National, 1955, 1956.* Saigon: Banque Nationale du Viet-Nam, 1956.

National Institute of Administration. *Nien Giam Hanh Chanh* (Government Organization Manual). Saigon: National Institute of Administration, 1963.

———. *Republic of Viet-Nam Government Organizational Manual 1957–1958.*

———. Answers to the Questionnaire on the Organization of the Civil Service. Mimeographed for the EROPA Seminar in Bangkok, October 7–17, 1962; Saigon: National Institute of Administration, 1962.

Nghiem Dang. *Tai Chinh Hoc Dai Cuong.* 3 vols. Saigon: Hoc Vien Quoc Gia Hanh Chanh, 1960.

———. "Co Cau Kinh Te Va Tai Chanh Cong Quyen Tai Cac Nuoc Cham Tien," *Nghien-Cuu Hanh-Chanh,* V, Nos. 3 and 4 (March and April, 1962).

———. "Su Bien Cai Ky Thuat Tai Chinh Thuoc Dia Thanh Tai Chinh Doc Lap" (The Transformation of Colonial Budgetary Technique to Fit the Independent Financial System), *Que Huong,* March, 1962.

———. "Tu Tai Chinh Thuoc Dia Den Tai Chinh Doc Lap" (From Colonial Finances to the Finances of an Independent State), *Que Huong,* No. 36 (June, 1962).

——— and J. Fox. "The National Institute of Administration," in R. W. Lindholm, ed., *Viet-Nam: The First Five Years.* East Lansing: Michigan State University Press, 1959.

Ngo Dinh Diem. *Message to the National Assembly, October 1, 1962.* Saigon: Directorate-General of Information, 1962.

Nguyen Cao Hach. "Phuong-Phap Hoach Dinh Co Trai Voi Tinh Than Dan Chu Khong?" (Is Economic Planning Contrary to the Democratic Ideal?), *Luat-Hoc Kinh-Te Tap-Chi* (Saigon), 1960.

Nguyen Dinh. *Recueil des textes concernant le personnel indigene des Services Generaux et Locaux de l'Indochine* (Collection of Acts Regarding the Native Personnel of the General and Local Services of Indochina). Hanoi: Thuc Nghiep, 1925.

Nguyen Dong Chi. *Viet Nam Co Van Hoc Su* (History of the Ancient Literature of Viet-Nam). Hanoi: Han Thuyen Xuat Ban Cuc, 1942.

Nguyen Huu Khang. *La Commune annamite: Etudes historiques, juridiques et economiques.* Paris: Librairie du Recueil Sirey, 1946.

Nguyen Huyen Anh. *Viet Nam Danh Nhan Tu Dien.* Saigon: Van Hoa An Quan, 1961.

Nguyen Khac Nhan and J. J. Zasloff. *A Study of Administration in the Binh Minh District.* Mimeographed; Saigon: National Institute of Administration, 1961.

Nguyen Sieu. *Phuong Dinh Dia Du Chi.* Ngo Manh Nghinh, trans. Saigon: Tu-Do, 1960.

Nguyen Sy Giac. *Le Trieu Chieu Linh Thien Chinh* (transliterated from Chinese characters). Saigon: Binh Minh Imprimerie, 1951.

Nguyen Thai. *Is South Viet-Nam Viable?* Manila: Carmelo and Bauermann, Inc., 1962.

Nguyen Thanh Cung. "Cong Cuoc Cai To Hanh Chanh Tai Viet-Nam Cong Hoa, Vai Khia Canh Cua Viec Cai Thien Hanh Chanh Dia Phuong Tu Nam 1949," (Administrative Reform in Viet-Nam: Some Aspects of the Evolution of Regional Administration Since 1949), *Nghien-Cuu Hanh-Chanh,* II, No. 2 (April, 1958).

Nha Tong Giam Doc Ngan Sach. *A Preliminary Report of the Brookings Institution (Ford Foundation). Economic Specialists Group.* Saigon: Directorate-General of Budget and Foreign Aid, 1961.

———. *Thu Tuc Thi Hanh Ngan Sach Quoc Gia: Thong Tu So 183 Ngay 11–12–1957.* Mimeographed: Saigon, 1957.

Nha Tong Giam Doc Thong Tin. *Than The Va Su Nghiep Tong Thong Ngo Dinh Diem.* Saigon: Directorate-General of Information, 1962.

Nivison, D. S., and A. F. Wright, eds. *Confucianism in Action.* Stanford: Stanford University Press, 1959.

Olmstead, Michael S. *The Small Group.* New York: Random House, 1959.

Pasquier, P. *L'Annam d'autrefois.* Paris: Challamel, 1907.

Pauker, G. J. "Political Doctrines and Practical Politics in Southeast Asia," *Pacific Affairs,* XXXV, No. 1 (Spring, 1962).

Pelliot, P. "Le Fou Nam." *Bulletin de l'Ecole française d'Extrême-Orient,* III (1903).

Pfiffner, J. M. *Public Administration.* New York: The Ronald Press, 1953.

——— and R. Presthus. *Public Administration.* 4th ed.; New York: The Ronald Press, 1960.

Pham Huu Khanh and Nguyen Tran Nguyen. *Tuc Ngu Luoc Giai.* Saigon: Nha Xuat Ban Mai Quang, 1956.

Pham Quynh. *Essais franco-annamites* (*1929–1937*). Hue: Editions Bui Huy Tin, 1937.
————. *Thuong Chi Van Tap.* Re-edited; Saigon: Department of Education, 1962.
Phan Cong Tam. "Su Lien Lac Giua Ong Tinh Truong Va Cac Co Quan Chuyen Mon," *Nghien-Cuu Hanh-Chanh,* II, Nos. 3, 4 (March, April, 1962).
Phan Huy Chu. *Lich Trieu Hien Chuong Loai Chi* (transcribed into romanized Vietnamese). Saigon: School of Law, 1957.
Phan Ke Binh. *Viet-Nam Phong Tuc* (Manners and Customs of Viet-Nam). Mimeographed; Saigon: Institute of Historical Studies, 1962.
Pinto, R. *Aspects de l'évolution gouvernementale de l'Indochine française.* Paris: Librarie du Receuil Sirey, 1946.
Prevost, J., and H. Meyrat. "L'Admission des Indochinois dans les cadres des administrations et services publics français de l'Indochine," *Revue Indochinoise Juridique et Economique* (Hanoi), No. 18 (1942).
Pye, Lucian W. *Communications and Political Development.* Princeton: Princeton University Press, 1963.
Quach Tong Duc. "Khu Tru Mat," *Nghien-Cuu Hanh-Chanh,* III, No. 10 (October, 1959).
————. "Van De Dia Phuong Phan Quyen Trong To Chuc Hanh Chanh Cac Do Thi Tai Viet Nam," *Nghien-Cuu Hanh-Chanh,* IV, No. 7.
Quoc Su Quan. *Dai Nam Nhat Thong Chi Tinh Thanh Hoa.* Saigon: Bo Quoc Gia Giao Duc, 1960.
Republic of Viet-Nam. *Bilan des Réalisations Gouvernementales, 1954–1962.* Saigon: Directorate-General of Information, 1962.
————. *Report on Government Progress.* Published on the Occasion of the Eighth Anniversary of the Vietnamese Republic. Saigon: Directorate-General of Information, 1962.
————. *Seven Years of the Ngo Dinh Diem Administration, 1954–1961.* Published on the sixth anniversary of the Republic of Viet-Nam, October 26, 1961. Saigon: Directorate-General of Information, 1961.
————. *Thanh Tich Chin Nam Hoat Dong Cua Chinh Phu.* Saigon: Directorate-General of Information, 1963.
Riggs, F. W. *Administration in Developing Countries: The Theory of Prismatic Society.* Boston: Houghton Mifflin Co., 1964.
————. *The Ecology of Public Administration.* New York: Asia Publishing House, 1961.
————. "Economic Development and Local Administration: A Study in Circular Causation," *The Philippine Journal of Public Administration,* III, No. 1 (January, 1959).
————. "Political Interference: Theory and Practice," *The Philippine Journal of Public Administration,* IV, No. 4 (October, 1960).
————. "Prismatic Society and Financial Administration: A Bazaar Canteen Model," *Administrative Science Quarterly,* June, 1960.
Rivero, Jean. *Droit Administratif.* Paris: Dalloz, 1960.

Rolland, L., P. Lampue, *et al. Legislation et finances coloniales.* Paris: Librairie du Recueil Sirey, 1930.

Rose, Dale, with the assistance of Vu Van Hoc. *The Vietnamese Civil Service System.* Saigon: M.S.U.G., 1961.

Rostow, W. W. *The Stages of Economic Growth.* Cambridge, England: Cambridge University Press, 1961.

Rowat, D. C., ed. *Basic Issues in Public Administration.* New York: The Macmillan Company, 1961.

Sayre, W. S. "Some Problems of Public Administration in a Developing Economy," *Indian Journal of Public Administration,* VIII, No. 2 (April–June, 1962).

Schubert, G. *The Public Interest.* New York: The Free Press of Glencoe, Inc., 1961.

Scigliano, R. *South Vietnam: Nation Under Stress.* Boston: Houghton Mifflin Co., 1964.

———. "Vietnam: A Country at War," *Asian Survey,* III, No. 1 (January, 1963).

———. "Political Parties in South Viet Nam Under the Republic," *Pacific Affairs,* XXXIII, No. 4 (December, 1960).

——— and W. W. Snyder. "The Budget Process in South Viet Nam," *Pacific Affairs,* XXXIII, No. 1 (March, 1960).

Schreiner, A. *Les Institutions annamites en Basse Cochinchine avant la conquête française.* Saigon; Claude et Cie, 1900.

Schultz, William J., and C. Lowell Harriss. *American Public Finance.* New York: Prentice-Hall, Inc., 1949.

Senegas, C. *Les Droits et obligations des fonctionnaires.* Paris: Charles Lavauzelle et Cie, 1955.

Sharma, M. P. *Public Administration in Theory and Practice.* Allahabad: Kitab Mahal Private, Ltd., 1962.

Siffin, W. J., ed. *Toward the Comparative Study of Public Administration.* Bloomington, Indiana: Indiana University Press, 1959.

Simon, H. A. *Administrative Behavior.* New York: Macmillan, 1961.

———, D. W. Smithburg, and V. A. Thompson. *Public Administration.* New York: Alfred Knopf, 1950.

Sirdar Ikbal Ali Shah. *Viet Nam.* London: The Octagon Press, 1960.

Sisson, C. H. *The Spirit of British Administration.* New York: Frederick A. Praeger, Inc., 1959.

Sjoberg, G. "Political Structure, Ideology and Economic Development." Paper presented at the Carnegie faculty seminar on political and administrative development, Indiana University, 1963.

Smithies, Arthur. *The Budgetary Process in the United States.* New York: McGraw-Hill, 1955.

Snyder, W. *Autonomous State Organizations: Government Enterprises and Public Corporations of Vietnam.* Saigon: M.S.U.G., 1957.

Su Quoc Trieu Chanh Bien Toat Yeu (Imperial Annals of Current Dynasties; transcribed into romanized Vietnamese). Saigon: Vien Khao Co., 1962.

Taboulet, G. *La Geste française en Indochine.* Paris: Maisonneuve, 1955.

Tang Tsou. *America's Failure in China.* Chicago: University of Chicago Press, 1963.

Taylor, Milton C. "South Vietnam: Lavish Aid, Limited Progress" *Pacific Affairs,* XXXIV, No. 3 (Fall, 1961).

———. *The Patente (Business License Tax) in Viet Nam.* Saigon: M.S.U.G., 1959.

———. *The Taxation of Real Property in Viet Nam.* Saigon: M.S.U.G., 1959.

Thompson, V. *French Indochina.* New York: The Macmillan Company, 1937.

Ton That Trach. "Phat Trien Viec Hoc Tap Cua Cong Chuc," *Hanh-Chanh Khao-Luan,* II (1958).

Tong Nha Thong Tin. *Tu Ap Chien Luoc Den Xa Tu Ve.* Saigon: Bo Cong Dan Vu, 1962.

Tran Tac Lam. "Co Quan Tai Phan Hanh Chanh," in *Ban Van To Chuc Tu Phap Viet Nam,* edited by the Department of Justice. Saigon: Bo Tu Phap, 1962.

Tran Thuc Linh. "Nan Tham Nhung," *Bach-Khoa,* No. 174 (April 1, 1964).

Tran Trong Kim. *Nho Giao.* Reprint; Saigon: Tan Viet, n.d.

———. *Viet Nam Su Luoc.* Saigon: Tan Viet, 1958.

Tran Van Dinh. *Hanh Chanh Do Thanh Saigon.* Saigon: National Institute of Administration, 1959.

———. "Luoc Khao Ve Nhung Quyen Tu Do Cong Cong," *Nghien-Cuu Hanh-Chanh,* V, No. 5.

——— and Jason L. Finkle. *Provincial Administration in Vietnam: A Study of Vinh Long Province.* Saigon: National Institute of Administration, 1961.

Tran Van Minh. "La Théorie Vietnamienne des droits de l'homme." Unpublished Doctoral thesis, Faculté de Droit (Law College), Paris, 1958.

Trong Ngoc Giau and L. W. Woodruff. *My Thuan: Administrative and Financial Aspects of A Village in South Vietnam.* Saigon: National Institute of Administration, 1961.

Trued, M. N. "South Vietnam's Industrial Development Center," *Pacific Affairs,* September, 1960.

U. N. Technical Assistance Program. *Decentralization for National and Local Development.* New York: United Nations, 1962.

United States Operations Mission. *Annual Statistical Bulletin,* for 1960, 1961, 1962, etc. Saigon: USOM Finance Office.

Van Mook, H. J. *The Stakes of Democracy in South East Asia.* New York: Norton & Company, 1950.

Vedel, G. *Droit Administratif.* Paris: Presses Universitaires de France, 1960.

Vu Quoc Thong. "Cong Cuoc Thanh Lap Che Do Cong Hoa Nhan Vi Tai Viet-Nam Tu Do" (The Establishment of a Republican Personalist Regime in Free Viet-Nam), *Nghien-Cuu Hanh-Chanh,* IV, No. 10 (October, 1960).

———. "Van De Tap Quyen Hanh Chanh Tai Viet Nam Cong Hoa," *Nghien-Cuu Hanh-Chanh,* IV, No. 8 (August, 1960).

————. "Van De Thiet Lap Cac Hoi Dong Hang Tinh Duoi Thoi Phap Thuoc," *Nghien-Cuu Hanh-Chanh*, III, No. 10.

————. *La de Centralization Administrative au Vietnam.* Hanoi: Presses Universitaires du Vietnam, 1952.

————. "Che Do Xa Thon Tu Tri Tai Viet-Nam Truoc Hoi Phap Thuoc," *Nghien-Cuu Hanh-Chanh,* VI, Nos. 5, 6 (May, June, 1962).

————. "Che Do Xa Thon Duoi Thoi Phap Thuoc," *Nghien-Cuu Hanh-Chanh,* VI, Nos. 7, 8, 9, 10 (July, August, September, October, 1962).

————. "Van De Phan Biet Khe Uoc Hanh Chanh Voi Khe Uoc Dan Su," *Nghien Cuu Hanh Chanh,* 1961.

Vu Quoc Thuc. *L'économie communaliste du Vietnam.* Hanoi: Presses Universitaires du Vietnam, 1951.

————. "Van De Ke Hoach Quoc Gia," in *Luat-Hoc Kinh-Te Tap-Chi,* No. 1, 2 (1960).

————. "Dieu Kien An Ninh Trong Cong Cuoc Ke Hoach Hoa,"

Vu Uyen Van. "Nghien Cuu Ve Giao Te Nhan Su Trong Hanh Chanh," *Nghien-Cuu Hanh-Chanh,* VII, No. 1 (January, 1963).

————. "Nghien Cuu Ve Giao Te Nhan Su Trong Hanh Chanh," *Nghien-Cuu Hanh-Chanh,* January, 1963.

Waldo, D. *The Study of Public Administration.* New York: Random House, 1955.

Walker, Nigel. *Morale in the Civil Service: A Study of the Desk Worker.* Edinburgh: University Press, 1961.

Ware, James R. *The Sayings of Mencius.* New York: Mentor Books, 1960.

Weber, Max. *Essays in Sociology.* Translated and edited by H. H. Gerth and C. W. Mills. New York: Oxford University Press, 1946.

Weidner, E. "Improving the Resource Base in the United States for Technical Assistance Overseas in Development Administration and Law." Paper presented at a meeting sponsored by the Ford Foundation, New York City, October 26–27, 1962.

————. *The World Role of Universities.* New York: McGraw-Hill, 1962.

Wittfogel, Karl. *Oriental Despotism.* New Haven: Yale University Press, 1957.

Woodruff, L. W. *Local Administration in Viet-Nam: The Number of Local Units.* Saigon: M.S.U.G., 1960.

————. *Local Finance in South Viet-Nam.* Saigon: M.S.U.G., 1961.

————. *The Study of a Vietnamese Rural Community: Administrative Activity.* Saigon: M.S.U.G., 1960.

Wright, Arthur, ed. *The Confucian Persuasion.* Stanford: Stanford University Press, 1960.

Wulff, Erich. "The Buddhist Revolts," *New Republic,* CXLIX, No. 9 (August, 1963).

Yuan, Chaucer. *La Philosophie morale et politique de Mencius.* Paris: Librairie Orientaliste, 1927.

Zasloff, J. J. "Rural Resettlement in South Vietnam: The Agroville Program," *Pacific Affairs,* XXXV, No. 4 (Winter, 1962–1963).

Zink, H., H. R. Penniman, and G. B. Hathorn. *American Government and Politics.* New York: D. Van Nostrand Co., Inc., 1958.

INDEX